Cognitive
Neuropsychology

Cognitive Neuropsychology
A Clinical Introduction

Rosaleen A. McCarthy
Department of Experimental Psychology
University of Cambridge
Cambridge, CB2 3EB, England

Elizabeth K. Warrington
The National Hospital for Neurology
   and Neurosurgery
London, WC1N 3BG, England

ACADEMIC PRESS
A Division of Harcourt Brace & Company
San Diego   New York   Boston
London   Sydney   Tokyo   Toronto

This book is printed on acid-free paper. ∞

ACADEMIC PRESS
525 B Street, Suite 1900
San Diego, California 92101-4495

United Kingdom Edition published by
Academic Press Limited
24–28 Oval Road, London NW1 7DX

Library of Congress Cataloging-in-Publication Data

McCarthy, Rosaleen A.
    Cognitive neuropsychology : a clinical introduction / Rosaleen A. McCarthy, Elizabeth K. Warrington.
        p.   cm.
    ISBN 0-12-481845-5 (alk. paper). -- ISBN 0-12-481846-3 (pbk. : alk. paper)
    1. Brain damage. 2. Cognition disorders. 3. Cognition.
4. Clinical neuropsychology. I. Warrington, Elizabeth K.
II. Title.
    [DNLM: 1. Brain Diseases--complications. 2. Cognition.
3. Cognition Disorders--etiology. 4. Neuropsychology. WL 103
M478c]
RC387.5.M39   1990
153--dc20
DNLM/DLC
for Library of Congress   89-18030
                                                                    CIP

PRINTED IN THE UNITED STATES OF AMERICA
    97 QW 9 8 7 6

Contents

17. Conclusion

Preface

The aim of this book is to provide a broad introduction to the core subject matter of clinical cognitive neuropsychology. It is intended both for those coming to this topic for the first time and also for those already in the field interested in an overview of areas which are outside their own specialty. The development of this book had its beginnings in both authors' attempts to communicate "cognitive neuropsychology" to clinical and academic colleagues as well as to students. In this interdisciplinary area of investigation concepts of cognitive psychology are often unfamiliar to those approaching brain–behaviour relationships from the perspective of neurology and physiology. Equally, neurological issues may present difficulties for those with a background in experimental cognitive psychology. We hope that this book will open lines of communication in both directions making the domain of neuropsychology accessible to these audiences and to the wider community of cognitive and neuroscientists.

In order to make the material as widely accessible as possible we have attempted to explain issues in a way that assumes only a limited degree of prior psychological or neurological knowledge. We hope that we have been able to give a reasonably comprehensive overview of this large and complex area of investigation despite our strenuous attempts to avoid the use of undefined specialist jargon and abstruse theoretical discussion. This does not mean that we have avoided "difficult" areas or discussion of controversial theoretical issues. Our primary aim has been to give an overview of areas of debate and to avoid the minutiae of academic arguments and counterarguments.

After a general introduction to the subject matter, the book is divided into chapters, each of which deals with a specific cognitive ability and the analysis of its breakdown in patients with cerebral lesions. Both the choice of topics and their treatment is, of course, necessarily influenced by our research and clinical activities and those of our colleagues, past and present, of the Clinical Psychology Department of the National Hospitals in London. The clinical influence is perhaps most clearly shown in the organisation of the chapters which directly mirrors the way in which much research has been conducted in direct response to a patient's problems.

First, we give a general introduction to the historical background, followed by a more detailed consideration of the relevant empirical findings. These basic facts are essential for any further analysis of an individual patient's difficulties and provide a necessary starting point for any research. This is followed by a discussion of the neuro-anatomical correlates and the issues and debates which these have raised. The third section of each chapter is concerned with theoretical analyses of the relevant complex skills and abilities, drawing both upon the empirical evidence and on the relevant data from neuro-anatomy.

We have confined our account entirely to cognitive disorders in neurological patients. The vast literature on animal lesion studies has not been considered; neither has the evidence from studies of neurologically intact subjects. This is not because we consider such work irrelevant for neuropsychology, but rather because any adequate and balanced treatment of this material would have resulted in a volume of encyclopaedic proportions. Whilst clearly realising the limitations of this perspective, it is our belief that a consideration of the evidence from clinical cases provides the central core for an introduction to cognitive neuropsychology.

The writing of this book would not have been possible were it not for the tolerance and good will of our colleagues and students who put up with closed doors and absent supervisors for nearly two years. To them we extend our gratitude. Our thanks are also due to Dr. Marianne Jackson, who provided us with translations of many German texts; to our institutions, the National Hospitals in London and the University of Cambridge, which have supported our research; and to Academic Press for seeing this project through to its fruition. Finally, we are most indebted to the many patient individuals who, despite the personal tragedy of brain damage, have nevertheless cheerfully helped in our research efforts.

1

Introduction to Cognitive Neuropsychology

Introduction

Damage to the brain often has tragic consequences for the individual. It can affect those basic skills and abilities which are so necessary for normal everyday life and which are largely taken for granted. The rather hybrid term *cognitive neuropsychology* is applied to the analysis of those handicaps in human cognitive function which result from brain injury. Cognitive neuropsychology is essentially interdisciplinary, drawing both on neurology and on cognitive psychology for insights into the cerebral organisation of cognitive skills and abilities. By cognitive function is meant the ability to use and integrate basic capacities such as perception, language, actions, memory, and thought. The focus of clinical cognitive neuropsychology is on the many different types of highly selective impairments of cognitive function that are observed in individual patients following brain damage. The functional analysis of patients with selective deficits provides a very clear window through which one can observe the organisation and procedures of normal cognition. No account of "how the brain works" would even approach completeness without this level of analysis.

Consideration of cognitive impairments in people with brain damage has a long tradition in clinical medicine. However, as a coherent domain of investigation it has a relatively short history. The description and discussion of cognitive deficits following brain injury dates back to the earliest written records. For example, there is mention of specific language loss in the Edwin Smith papyrus of 3500 B.C., and selective impairments in face recognition and letter recognition were noted by Roman physicians. Few advances were made over the following 2000 years. Despite discovering the orbits of the planets, the circulation of the blood, and the laws of mechanics, the "seat of the mind" had only moved from the liver to the pineal gland.

By the beginning of the nineteenth century a number of patterns of deficit had been described and were accepted as being due to disease of the brain itself. In the early nineteenth century there were significant advances in medicine, anatomy, and physiology which provided the basis for a more adequate analysis of the sequelae of brain injury. In their first investigations the nineteenth-century researchers placed considerable emphasis on the localisation of damage which gave rise to impaired function. This approach led to a number of insights and arguably led to the development of clinical neurology as an independent specialty. Subsequently the quest for localisation led to a realisation of the complexities of cognitive function. It was recognised that abilities such as language were composed of a number of distinct processing components, each of which could break down independently of the others. This analytic approach to patterns of breakdown forms the basis of much contemporary cognitive neuropsychology. The background to both of these issues and their contemporary relevance will be considered in the following two sections. First, the evidence for localisation and lateralisation of function in the human brain will be considered. Second, the evidence for dissociation of function and the basic methodological approaches of contemporary neuropsychology will be introduced.

Localisation and Lateralisation of Function

Historical Background

In the early years of the nineteenth century the phrenologists Gall & Spurzheim (1809) speculated that the convoluted surface of the brain reflected the juxtaposition of a large number of discrete cerebral organs. Each organ was thought to subserve a particular psychological faculty (or in more contemporary terms, function). Individual differences in endowment for a specific faculty would result in different degrees of development of particular convolutions of the brain. By analogy with muscular development, they suggested that endowment with mental muscles would result in an increase in the size of cerebral organs. They further speculated that this endowment would be reflected in bulges on the skull. In support of their hypothesis they produced evidence from anthropological studies of races with supposed differences in intellectual endowment, and clinical post-mortem evidence from brain-injured individuals. One of their speculations, that the language faculty might be located in the anterior sectors of the brain, was tentatively supported by post-mortem evidence. This was corroborated in independent clinical studies conducted by the eminent French physician Bouillaud (cited by Benton, 1984). However other workers reported conflicting evidence of patients whose language abilities were preserved despite damage to this part of the brain (e.g., Andral, 1834, cited by Benton, 1964).

In 1861, the anthropologist and physician Paul Broca reported the case of a patient who had lost the ability to utter a single word, but who had retained his ability to understand what was said to him. The patient, a Monsieur LeBorgne, was a long-term resident in an institution who had been nicknamed "Tan" by the staff because this was the only sound he ever uttered. Despite having no meaningful speech, "Tan" (although reportedly a difficult patient) was able to cooperate with staff and to assist in the care of other inmates. Broca argued that the patient's disorder was not one which affected the muscles which were necessary for speech, because he was able to eat and drink. The patient appeared to have a specific impairment of language. Broca suggested that the patient's disease had damaged a specific centre in the brain which was responsible for mediating articulate language, a deficit he termed "aphemie." In fact, the area of tissue loss or lesion in Tan was quite extensive, spreading from the frontal to the temporal lobes of the brain. Such large areas of damage would appear to pose considerable, if not intractable, problems for precise localisation. However, Broca drew on his clinical knowledge to infer the likely sequence of events which had led to the loss of language. On the basis of the progression of Tan's difficulties, Broca argued that the onset of language disturbance was attributable to damage in a critical and restricted area, namely the third frontal convolution of the left hemisphere. This part of the brain is still termed "Broca's area" in recognition of his pioneering attempts to localise and lateralise the site of damage responsible for disrupting speech (see Fig. 1.1).

Karl Wernicke (1874) described patients with the opposite pattern of

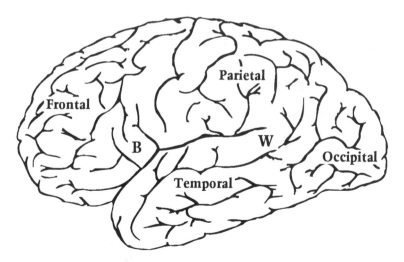

Figure 1.1 Lateral surface of the left hemisphere showing the four major lobes. B, Broca's area; W, Wernicke's area.

speech difficulty to Broca's cases—they could speak fluently, but they were unable to understand what was said to them. The patients' speech, though fluent, was by no means normal, indeed it was virtually unintelligible. They used words inappropriately and made errors in pronunciation which reflected the wrong choice of word sounds. These errors often resulted in words which were not part of the language, an error termed a *neologism* (literally, a "new word"). One patient died, and when her brain was studied at post-mortem she was found to have a lesion in the left temporal lobe, near to primary auditory cortex. However, the damage was not in the primary auditory cortex itself, but slightly more posterior, extending from the first temporal convolution into the parietal lobe (see Fig. 1.1).

Broca had also noted that damage to the *left* hemisphere appeared to be critical for language impairment. His observations were confirmed by other researchers and appeared to be valid even when the pattern of language deficit was not identical to that described in the original cases. The idea that the left hemisphere might play a special role in language function became widely accepted. This hypothesis has stood the test of time. Post-mortem studies of the brains of patients who had shown language disturbances in life indicated that damage to the left hemisphere was usually critical. This gave rise to the view that the left hemisphere was the "dominant" or leading side of the brain in most people. It is now universally accepted that the human brain has an asymmetric organisation of function. Language abilities are compromised by damage to the left hemisphere in the vast majority of people and appear to be unaffected by damage to the right side.

A strong emphasis on the lateralisation of language, rather than on the organisation of other cognitive skills, has been characteristic of many neurological and neuropsychological studies of patients. It is easy to understand why this has happened. Language deficits are obvious and a cause of considerable concern, making them somewhat easier to detect and investigate than other types of disorder. This should not blind one to the fact that damage to the right hemisphere of the brain may also have considerable effects on other types of cognitive function. The first to recognise that the right hemisphere might have specialised functions of its own was the English neurologist Hughlings Jackson (1876). On the basis of his clinical observations of a single patient he argued that whilst the left hemisphere might be important in language, the right hemisphere was critical in "visuoperceptual" abilities. The idea that the right hemisphere might be "dominant" for some types of ability was not followed up in any great detail at the time. The prevailing viewpoint was that the cerebral hemispheres existed in a "dominance" relationship with the left hemisphere being "in charge" in most people. It is only since the 1940s that systematic investigations of perceptual and spatial abilities have been conducted in patients with unilateral lesions. The results of these investigations have supported Jackson's original observations. It is now universally recognised that the two cerebral hemispheres have complementary, but very different, specialisations. The term *cerebral dominance* still continues in modern usage, however, it now has a much more restricted meaning, namely "dominance for language."

Individual Differences?

Broca's view that the left hemisphere was necessarily dominant for language in all individuals was challenged by other neurologists. They argued that the cerebral organisation of speech would be directly related to hand preference (e.g., Wernicke, 1874). It was suggested that writing was intimately linked with spoken language and could even be considered as "parasitic" upon it and making use of the same brain centres. It would therefore be eminently reasonable if language and writing were organised in close proximity in the brain. Since control over motor function is primarily organised in a contralateral manner (with the left hemisphere controlling the movement of the right hand and the right hemisphere controlling the left hand), then the dominant hand would be contralateral to the dominant (language) hemisphere. Individuals with right-hand preference for writing would show left-hemisphere dominance for language, whereas left-handed people would show the opposite pattern and have dominant right hemispheres.

The view that language laterality and hand preference would be invariably linked became widely accepted and persisted for many decades. For the vast majority of right-handed people this "rule" does apply. However, since the majority of the population is right handed this could easily reflect a general population bias toward being "left brained" rather than a link between language laterality and hand dominance (Annett, 1985). Left-handed individuals provide the crucial test. Examples of language disorders following lesions to the left hemisphere in left-handed patients were sporadically reported in the literature up until the 1950s as examples of "crossed dominance." However, when systematic surveys of left-handed patients with unilateral lesions and language impairment were carried out this received wisdom was questioned (Zangwill, 1960). The occurrence of "crossed dominance" was by no means as rare as had been assumed (see Table 1.1).

There are two ways of interpreting these findings. The first, and the one which has been most frequently expressed in the literature, is that left-handed people have a bilateral organisation of language. This, it is argued, accounts for the similar numbers of left-handed patients with language difficulties following either right- or left-sided lesions. The inference that left handers have a bilateral organisation of language function is based on the assumption that all the individuals making up the clinical group of left handers can be considered to have the same fundamental organisation of function. This assumption is perhaps most clearly expressed by Hécaen & Sauget (1971): "If the bilaterality of cerebral dominance is the rule in left handed subjects . . . the

Table 1.1 Left-Handedness and Laterality[a]

Investigation	Lesion location	
	Right (N)	Left (N)
Conrad (1949)	7	10
Goodglass and Quadfasel (1954)	5	5
Hécaen and Ajuriaguerra (1963)	7	13

[a]Laterality of lesion site in left-handed patients with language disorders.

frequency of language difficulties should be about the same in both hemispheric (lesion) groups." There is, of course, a second way of interpreting this data: exactly the same pattern would be expected were some of these patients right brained and others left brained with respect to the organisation of language.

Another source of evidence for "bilateral" organisation of language function in left handers has been derived from estimates of the overall *risk* of language impairment following damage to the right or to the left hemisphere in this group. If language is bilaterally organised, then there should be either an increased or a decreased incidence of language disorders regardless of the location of the lesion. Thus if language was bilaterally organised then patients might be placed at greater risk of showing a disturbance following damage to either hemisphere. Alternatively, they might be "protected" from the effects of unilateral damage because function is duplicated in both sides of the brain. It has been suggested that bilateral organisation of language should result in a very different distribution of impairment than should unilateral organisation. At first sight the data in Table 1.2 appear to support this hypothesis, showing an increased incidence of language disorders in left-handed patients with unilateral lesions.

Overall, the left-handed patients have a higher incidence of language impairment, suggesting that there is an increased risk for left-handed people. However, the increased risk is not equivalent between the two hemispheres as would be expected on the bilateral hypotheses. The increased risk in left handers is entirely due to the comparatively large number of cases with language disorders following right-hemisphere

Table 1.2 Incidence of Aphasia in Left- and Right-Handed Patients[a]

Lesion site	Left handers		Right handers	
	Left	Right	Left	Right
Aphasia (N)	56	26	625	16
No aphasia (N)	46	63	422	879
% Aphasic	43		33	

[a]Data collated from 5 studies. Adapted from Zangwill (1967).

lesions. This pattern would also be consistent with there being a heterogeneity in the lateral organisation of language in left handers. Some might have right-hemisphere dominance and some might have left-hemisphere dominance, and there could possibly also be a small subgroup with bilateral language.

Surveys of patients with unilateral lesions are not really suitable for answering questions about bilateral organisation. Once damage has been done to the brain it is impossible to conclude whether remaining capacities are attributable to residual activity of the damaged side, to activity of the undamaged side, or to a contribution from both cerebral hemispheres. What is needed is a technique for temporarily "blocking" the activity of one side of the brain which can subsequently be applied to the other side. This would enable a direct comparison to be made between the language capacities of the two sides of the brain functioning in isolation.

Two such procedures have been reported. Milner and her colleagues (Milner, Branch, & Rasmussen, 1964; Milner, 1975) have used Wada's intracarotid sodium amytal test (Wada & Rasmussen, 1960), and Warrington & Pratt (1973) have used unilateral electroconvulsive shock. In the carotid amytal study patients with epilepsy who were about to undergo surgery were tested. In this procedure the barbiturate sodium amytal is introduced into the brain via the left or right internal carotid artery during the course of a standard preoperative radiological examination (angiography). This temporarily sedates one hemisphere and allows testing of the other side of the brain in relative isolation. In the Warrington & Pratt study, patients undergoing electroconvulsive therapy (ECT) as a treatment for depression were given unilateral shocks on alternate sides of the head on two different days. ECT has the effect of temporarily disrupting normal activity in the brain. When the shock is administered unilaterally (i.e., with the electrodes placed on one side of the head), then this disruption is largely confined to one cerebral hemisphere.

The results which have been obtained using these two techniques are in very good agreement (see Table 1.3). This is all the more impressive considering the differences in population and the relatively small numbers which are involved. The evidence appears consistent with the "mixed group" hypothesis, namely that left handers are a heterogeneous population with respect to their language laterality. The majority of left handers have unilateral representation of language, and a small proportion have bilateral organisation. If one considers the ratio of left-brained language organisation to right-brained and bilateral cases, both of these studies are also remarkably consistent with the surveys of unilateral lesion cases which were discussed above. It is therefore safe to conclude that for the vast majority of the population the left hemisphere is specialised for language processing. In left handers, the incidence of right-hemisphere and bilateral language organisation is increased.

Table 1.3 Language Lateralization[a]

	Handedness	N	Left[a] (Percentage)	Bilateral[a] (Percentage)	Right[a] (Percentage)
Amytal	Right	140	96	0	4
	Left	122	70	15	15
ECT	Right	53	98	0	2
	Left	30	70	6	23

[a]Patients without history of early brain lesions as established using reversible procedures.

These considerations are far from being purely "scientific." When surgery is being considered on one side of the brain it is often necessary to consider whether this will pose a risk to language function. Loss of the ability to speak or to understand language is both personally distressing and socially isolating. The relative incidence of left-hemisphere and right-hemisphere language in different handedness groups can therefore provide a guide as to whether further investigations (such as sodium amytal or ECT) are likely to be indicated in the individual case.

Plasticity of Cerebral Organisation?

To what extent can these patterns of lateralisation be modified in the face of brain damage? If the organisation of function were relatively flexible, this would offer some hope of restitution of function following brain damage. Unfortunately, the weight of the evidence suggests that when damage occurs after infancy or childhood, then little or no "re-lateralisation" of function is possible. Two sources of clinical evidence are relevant to this issue, namely sodium amytal studies and investigations of patients who have had one hemisphere removed (hemispherectomy).

Sodium Amytal Studies   In the preceding section the transient sedation of one hemisphere by the use of the barbiturate sodium amytal was discussed. It appears to provide a good technique for assessing lateralisation of language function and for estimating the incidence of bilateral language representation. The technique was pioneered by Milner and her colleagues as a preoperative assessment for patients who were about to have surgery to remove tissue which was thought to be the source of their epileptic fits. In the course of these investigations, Milner (1975) assessed a number of patients who had sustained brain damage early in life. The pattern of their language organisation appeared very different from people whose damage was sustained in late childhood or adulthood. Table 1.4 shows the results of sodium amytal testing in patients who had evidence of early left-hemisphere damage. If these figures are compared with those in Table 1.3, it is clear

Table 1.4 Early Brain Damage: Lateralization of Language[a]

Handedness	N	Language lateralization		
		Left (Percentage)	Bilateral (Percentage)	Right (Percentage)
Right	31	81	6	13
Left (or mixed)	78	30	19	51

[a]Language laterality in patients who had sustained *left* hemisphere damage early in life (Adapted from Milner, 1975.)

that there is an increase in the incidence of bilateral and right-hemisphere language in both "handedness" groups. There is also a vast increase in the proportion of people designated as left handers. This latter increase is possibly attributable to a shift in hand preference as a result of residual motor impairment in the right hand following left-hemisphere damage. Overall, these findings indicate that following early damage to the left hemisphere of the brain there is considerable potential for reorganisation of function. It is clear that the lateralisation of function in patients who have suffered early brain damage is very different from that which is observed in patients whose damage has occurred later in life.

Hemispherectomy   This is a radical operation typically involving removal of the cortical structures of one hemisphere (subcortical structures are usually not removed). It has been carried out in adults in an attempt to restrict the spread of tumours or to relieve very severe epilepsy arising in the context of extensive damage to one side of the brain. The operation has also been used with children and infants who have extensive unilateral damage resulting in severe epilepsy and hemiplegia. The results of these operations have differed according to the laterality of the lesion and the age of the patient at the time of brain damage. With adults, language ability is not usually affected by right hemispherectomy, but left hemispherectomy appears to result in a profound and global loss of language abilities with only very limited recovery of function (Smith, 1966). By contrast, left hemispherectomy in young children appears to have far less drastic consequences. Indeed, normal levels of language development have been shown by at least *some* patients. More than one case is on record with average levels of language and intellectual abilities following left hemispherectomy during infancy (McFie, 1961; Smith & Sugar, 1975).

Although some patients with removal of the left hemisphere in childhood appear to show normal levels of language development, this may be at the expense of functions normally subserved by the right hemisphere, namely perceptual and spatial skills (Dennis and Whitaker, 1977; Woods, 1980). Thus, although there is evidence consistent with there being some plasticity in the lateralisation of function in the immature brain, there appear to be limitations on any reorganisation which may take place (McFie, 1961). However, individuals with intact function following hemispherectomy are probably exceptional. McFie's study of a consecutive series of 28 hemispherectomy cases showed that their average IQ levels were in the defective range. For most people (if not all!) two hemispheres are better than one.

Lateral Asymmetry of Function: Relative or Absolute?

The evidence which has been reviewed so far appears to indicate that language function, at least, is unilaterally represented in the brain of most adult humans. However, this view has been challenged by studies of patients with surgical separation of the two cerebral hemispheres, the commissurotomy or "split-brain" operation.

Commissurotomy In the 1940s Akelaitis reported on a series of patients whose chronic and generalised epilepsy had been treated surgically by cutting the major fibre links between the two cerebral hemispheres (e.g., Akelaitis, 1944). Using a number of comparatively unsophisticated tests he was unable to demonstrate any lasting consequences of the operation. Subsequently Sperry, Bogen, and their colleagues studied a new series of patients following a similar operation: the corpus callosum, anterior commissure, and hippocampal commissure were cut, resulting in a "split brain" (Bogen & Vogel, 1962). In most situations these patients appeared to behave much as they had preoperatively (following an initial period of recovery). However more systematic investigation has shown a range of deficits (e.g, Sperry, Gazzaniga, & Bogen, 1969; Bogen, 1985).

The patients were tested on a variety of tasks which were designed to limit input to one side of the brain. With somatosensory input this is comparatively straightforward: sensation on one half of the body is initially dealt with by the contralateral cerebral hemisphere. Thus asking a split-brain patient to identify objects by touch could be informative about the resources of one hemisphere for naming or object recognition. In the case of vision one hemisphere receives input from the contralateral side of space necessitating the presentation of material to either the left or the right visual field for durations less than those required to perform reflex (saccadic) eye movements ($\approx$ 100 ms). Other investigations have restricted visual input by the use of specialised contact lenses. The assumption is that if sensory input is confined to one hemisensory channel then processing is carried out by the contralateral hemisphere in the split-brain patient (Gazzaniga, 1970; Zaidel, 1976).

The results of the split-brain investigations have been complex (e.g., Gazzaniga, 1983; Zaidel, 1983a; Bogen, 1985). In general they have indicated a major division of function between the hemispheres and, as such, are consistent with studies of patients with unilateral lesions.

However, there are also some important discrepancies: the right hemisphere of the split-brain patient is credited with a considerable degree of language ability. However, patients may have severe chronic and global language loss following unilateral damage to the left hemisphere despite an intact right hemisphere. This would not be expected if the right hemisphere were able to support some functional language abilities or even some rudimentary language skills. Similarly it has been shown that commissurotomy patients can comprehend the written word with their right hemispheres (albeit that they are unable to pronounce the word aloud). Yet there are patients with unilateral lesions of the left hemisphere whose comprehension of the written word is all but obliterated (e.g., Goodglass & Kaplan, 1972).

One possibility is that this conflict of evidence can be attributed to differences in the populations which have been investigated. Many of the patients who show evidence of language processing in the right hemisphere sustained brain damage in early childhood. In a review of the 10 split-brain cases who have been the focus of research, Whitaker & Ojemann (1977) noted that 7 (including 2 of the right-hemisphere language cases) appear to have sustained their lesions in infancy or childhood. Of the others 1 was injured at 15 (and remains aphasic) and another at 30. All of the patients had structural damage to their brains before the operation—and 8 appeared to have developed further neurological complications after the operation. Broadly based generalisations about the bilateral organisation of language-processing systems or about the language "competence" of the right hemisphere are based on a subset of a population, most of whom sustained early brain damage—an incidence of bilateral language organisation which is comparable to that observed in sodium amytal studies of patients with childhood lesions (see Table 1.4). In view of the evidence for plasticity in the developing nervous system, the patterns of cerebral lateralisation which have been demonstrated in the commissurotomy patients cannot easily be generalised to the developmentally normal adult brain. However, they may be very telling with regard to the potential and limitations of the right hemisphere in the development of certain types of language ability (e.g., Zaidel, 1983b).

Specialisation of Function

In Broca's original observations he emphasised that his patients had lost the "faculty of articulate language," that is, the ability to produce speech. He contended that they were not impaired in language understanding. Wernicke's subsequent observation of the complementary pattern of disorder, namely failure to comprehend language with preservation of the ability to produce speech, indicated that there were at least two "subcomponents" of the language processing system: one concerned with production, the other with comprehension. Wernicke's

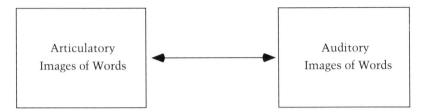

Figure 1.2 Schematic representation of Wernicke's model.

contribution went beyond the simple description of a different type of language disturbance associated with a lesion to a different part of the brain. He developed a theoretical framework which formed the basis of much subsequent work and which continues to have influence today. He drew on two traditions in the development of his theory. First, there was the influential psychological theory of associationism, which suggested that learning involved the establishment of links or associations between different sets of "images." Secondly, there was neuroanatomical and neurophysiological evidence for fibre tracts linking different regions of the nervous system which were involved in reflexes. Wernicke suggested that language could be thought of as a complex type of reflex in which the "auditory images" of words and the "motor images" of words were associated by fibre tracts. Acquisition of language was dependent on this linkage. Wernicke considered that in learning to talk it was necessary for the child to link the sounds of words which had been heard with articulatory images. This resulted in a "reflex" association between two cortical centres which was mediated by a specific neural pathway (see Fig. 1.2).

Damage to either the articulatory or the auditory centres would result in different patterns of language disturbance. Loss of the articulatory images would give rise to impoverished spontaneous speech, but normal comprehension. Damage to the auditory centres would result in poor language comprehension. Because speech and hearing were closely linked, such a lesion would also have a disruptive effect on the patients' ability to produce the correct word sounds in their spontaneous speech. With some refinement (see below) this profile of language disturbance is still termed "Wernicke's" or "sensory" aphasia.

Wernicke's model predicted that a third type of aphasic deficit should be observed when damage affected the links between the auditory and the motor "centres" for words. Such damage should result in a specific impairment in the repetition of the spoken word, together with errors in the selection of word sounds in spontaneous speech. These deficits would be expected because the auditory and the motor centres were no longer able to communicate with each other (there would be a deficit in conducting information between them). The disconnection of two centres would therefore have qualitative differences from damage to the centres themselves. The disconnection syndrome

termed "conduction aphasia" was subsequently documented as an isolated deficit some years later (Lichtheim, 1885).

Diagram Making

Wernicke's tripartite division of the aphasias into motor, auditory, and
conduction subtypes was refined by Lichtheim (1885), who added another critical element to Wernicke's model. He postulated that in addition to "auditory word images" and "articulatory images" there were
also "concept centres" which were required for comprehending word
meaning (see Fig. 1.3). In support of his argument he described cases
with relative preservation of repetition: for repetition to be spared the
auditory and articulatory images and the links between them must be
intact. He described two "transcortical" aphasias (termed transcortical
because they were thought to involve a disconnection of transcortical
fibre tracts). In the case of transcortical motor aphasia, the impairment
of language had all the characteristics of a Broca's/motor type of a-
phasia except for the preservation of repetition. In transcortical sensory
aphasia the impairment of language had all the characteristics of a
Wernicke's/sensory aphasia except for the preservation of repetition.
The transcortical aphasias were viewed as a consequence of disruption
of communication between concept centres and the centre for the
auditory images of words (transcortical sensory aphasia) or between

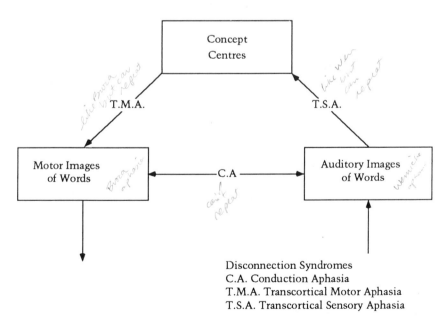

Figure 1.3 Schematic representation of Lichtheim's model showing hypothetical disconnection syndromes.

conceptual processing and the centre for the motor images of words (see Fig. 1.3).

The approach pioneered by Wernicke and Lichtheim, which analysed disorders of language either in terms of damage to specific centres in which memory images were retained or to damage to the pathways which connected different types of image, became the dominant framework in nineteenth-century aphasiology. Individual patients were studied in detail and their patterns of impairment were documented. Subsequently, post-mortem investigations were carried out in order to establish the location of the lesion which had given rise to the deficit. Elaborate diagrams were constructed which postulated a number of centres, each of which was thought to be located in a specific area of the brain. Communication between these centres was thought to be mediated by fibre tracts. This approach resulted in a number of detailed accounts of the organisation of the language system and its links to other domains of information processing such as reading, writing, and object recognition. The emphasis which these investigators placed on devising graphic schemes led to the label of "diagram making" being applied to their endeavours by those who were sceptical about the usefulness of this analytic approach to language disturbances. They were almost entirely based on clinical impressionistic accounts rather than on controlled observation and quantification of phenomena.

However with the benefit of hindsight many of these diagrams appear not only plausible, but very similar in their organisation to many of the more modern flow diagram models of "information-processing" psychology. A classical example of such a flow diagram is Morton's (1969, 1970) scheme of the processing involved in word recognition shown in Fig. 1.4. However, the diagram makers' approach, unlike that of the information-processing model makers, was inextricably linked to the enterprise of precise cerebral localisation of function. When the

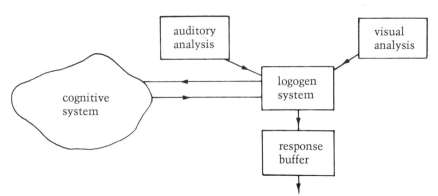

Figure 1.4 Morton's 1969 logogen model showing stages in processing verbal information (Morton, 1980) [Logogen system ≃ 'images' of words and cognitive system ≃ concept centres.]

evidence for localisation was called into question in the early years of the twentieth century, the clinical evidence for a principled distinction between the subcomponents of complex abilities was rejected as well.

Globalist Accounts

There were a number of critiques of the multicomponent view of language disorders which was put forward by the "diagram makers." These critiques, perhaps epitomised by the work of Marie (1906a,b), Head (1926), and Goldstein (1948), emphasised similarities between various patterns of language disorder rather than differences. They also challenged the view that particular patterns of deficit could be attributed to loss of particular cortical centres. For Marie and for Head, language disorders were viewed as failure of intellectual function. In a similar vein, Goldstein viewed the majority of aphasias (as well as virtually any cognitive deficit) as resulting from a failure to adopt an abstract attitude. These cognitive deficits varied in their severity and might or might not be associated with a primary motor disorder. Marie (1906a,b) contended that there was only one type of aphasia, Wernicke's aphasia. Broca's aphasia was held to be the result of a superimposed "anarthria" or motor deficit. This emphasis on a single common factor involved in language disturbances has been termed the "globalist" perspective.

The globalist critique of earlier work was useful, if somewhat overstated. These writers drew attention to the fact that clinical patterns of language disorder rarely conformed to the precise patterns of deficit predicted by models postulating centres which were selectively spared or impaired. Head (1926) also emphasised the variability in performance seen in patients who would appear to be unable to perform a task on one occasion but would perform normally when conditions were slightly changed. At the very least, this indicated that language processing was a more complex ability than that envisaged by the simple models of the nineteenth-century diagram makers. Rather than attempt to elaborate these models, however, the globalists insisted on a reduction of language disorders to a single, loosely defined common causative factor. Thus, terms such as "intellect" and "abstract attitude" could be, and were, applied indiscriminately to reasoning abilities in addition to highly specific language deficits such as errors in the use of word sounds.

Globalist critiques of narrow localisationist theories of language were paralleled by the development of "mass-action" theories of other aspects of cerebral function. Mass-action analyses proposed that there was no differentiation in the cortex for specific cognitive functions; rather, it was equipotential with respect to cognitive abilities. Instead of examining patterns of selective disruption to component processes of complex abilities such as talking, writing, remembering, or route-finding, theoreticians simply pointed out that these abilities could be impaired by a variety of cerebral lesions and that they tended to be more disrupted by more extensive brain damage (Lashley, 1929). The intellectual rejection of the nineteenth century viewpoint arose partly because of evidence that there was not necessarily a one-to-one mapping between the structural damage observed post mortem and cognitive dysfunction. It was also due to a shift in emphasis on the types of behavioural task considered theoretically appropriate to evaluate functional specialisation.

Whereas the nineteenth-century pioneers of neuropsychology had focused on an analysis of the subcomponents of complex abilities, the globalists had emphasised their fundamental unity. Whilst it is true that more widespread brain damage will typically result in more severe impairments, it does not necessarily follow that a single core factor is involved. The view that there may be multiple contributions from different component processes in performing complex tasks regained its respectability in psychology toward the middle of the 1940s. By the 1950s it was clear that by using the appropriate assessment procedures highly specific patterns of deficit could be identified in patients with cerebral lesions. Failure on more complex tasks could be attributed to impairments in one or more of the component processes which were required to perform the task adequately. More widespread brain damage could be viewed as compromising a larger number of these components, thereby resulting in a more severe impairment. The global perspective was gradually abandoned as being untenable in the face of the evidence for more specific patterns of deficit.

Information Processing

In the intervening decades, the psychological investigation of normal cognitive function has increasingly emphasised an analysis of the subcomponents of complex cognitive abilities. This approach, termed "information processing," has focussed on the way that information (e.g., sensory input) is transformed and translated in order to achieve a particular endpoint. On this approach, the human processing system is viewed as being analogous to a computer, with a large number of specialised subsystems. Routine information processing appears to require the use and interaction of a number of these different systems. These might include systems responsible for analysing the physical properties of the input, categorising it perceptually, extracting meaning, and the production of an appropriate response. The way in which these systems are organised is often characterised in terms of computer-programming conventions using flow diagrams which attempt to specify the way in which different components are brought together to perform a specific task.

The broad similarity between the flow diagrams of the information-processing approach to the analysis of cognitive skills and the diagrams of the nineteenth-century neurologists has already been discussed (see Figs. 1.3 and 1.4). However, the growth of experimental psychology and the development of explicit theories of the way systems are organised in the normal information-processing system has given a more secure grounding for these types of analysis. Furthermore, these models are no longer tied to an anatomical substrate but are schematic, or formalised, characteristics of normal human cognitive processing.

This information-processing approach can be harnessed to the analysis of patients who have sustained cognitive deficits due to brain damage. By focusing on the selective impairment and selective preservation of particular aspects of information processing it has been possible to analyse the subcomponents of complex skills.

Dissociations of Function

The major successes of this approach, which is often termed "cognitive neuropsychology," have been in demonstrating the independence of specific types of information processing. This is based on evidence for dissociation and double dissociation of function (Teuber, 1955; Weiskrantz, 1968; Shallice, 1979, 1988). In principle, dissociation of function means that two types of information processing can be distinguished. When Broca described patients who were unable to talk but who could understand language, he had demonstrated a *dissociation* between speech production systems and speech comprehension systems. Wernicke's observations of the reciprocal pattern (impaired comprehension with preservation of speech production) provides what is now known as a *double dissociation*.

The concepts of dissociation and double dissociation of function are central theoretical concepts in neuropsychology. A dissociation occurs when a patient is impaired in one aspect of function but another is relatively preserved. Whilst (as in the case of Broca's patients), this *may* indicate that there are distinct processing systems involved, there are other more prosaic explanations. If both of the tasks were dependent on a single processing system but one task was more difficult than another, then failure might represent some general limitation on performance which was due to brain damage. The same pattern might be found in normal people in an extreme state of fatigue, or it might be observed in young children or in the elderly. If, however, another patient is observed who shows the reciprocal pattern, failing the tasks which the other case passed and vice versa, then it is no longer plausible to think in terms of general limitations on performance or a "task-difficulty" effect. This reciprocal pattern, a double dissociation, can

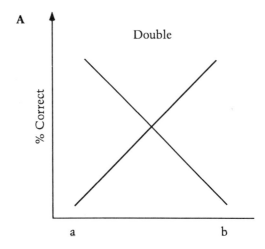

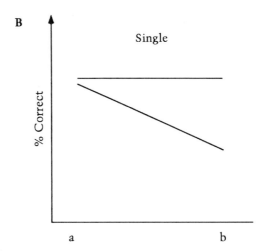

Figure 1.5 (A) Diagram showing the crossover pattern of a double dissociation. (B) Diagram showing the V-shaped pattern of a single dissociation.

~~provide critical evidence for a degree of independence between compo-~~
~~nents of information processing.~~

For the mathematically minded, a double dissociation can be likened to a "crossover interaction" in an analysis of variance (see Fig. 1.5A). This X-shaped pattern cannot be eliminated by any single mathematical transformation. By contrast, the V-shaped pattern of a single dissociation (see Fig. 1.5B) could be eliminated by changing or transforming the scale of measurement. If one adopts the X pattern as defining a double dissociation, then there is one further interesting conclusion: it is not strictly necessary that the patients should be entirely normal on the "preserved" tasks in order to demonstrate a double dissociation. What is critical is the pattern of relative preservation and relative impairment of function. Although a double dissociation often provides the strongest evidence for independence or separability of function, there are caveats. Most critically, the patients in question must be matched on potentially confounding variables. For example, failure on a test of word retrieval would lose its significance in the case of a patient with impairment of speech production. Nevertheless, double dissociation provides an invaluable methodological tool for establishing the subcomponents of complex skills (Shallice, 1988).

If evidence is available to show that the doubly dissociated deficits in question are the product of damage, or lesions in different sectors of the brain, then it is possible to infer that these areas differ in their processing. More specifically we can conclude that the neurological correlates of particular types of impairment are different. However, it should be noted that even in the absence of precise anatomical or localising information a double dissociation of function still stands in its own right. The question of "what is impaired" is quite distinct from the question of "what are the anatomical correlates."

Unlike the nineteenth-century researchers, cognitive neuropsychologists have often tended to avoid questions of precise localisation, realising that there are numerous pitfalls in assigning function to specific cerebral centres. This is particularly the case when single patients with highly specific patterns of deficit are considered: brain damage is typically quite gross in its effects and may upset biological function in relatively large sectors of the brain. In depth studies of single cases are useful in determining the component-processing systems involved in more complex tasks. In order to achieve more precise information with regard to the anatomical correlates of impairment it is often necessary to carry out more extensive surveys of groups of patients, selected according to the site of their lesions (rather than because of their deficits). In other situations (particularly when a deficit is rare), it may be necessary to combine pathological evidence from a number of single cases in order to establish a tentative correlation between structure and function.

Clinical cognitive neuropsychology has been successful in demonstrating a large number of dissociations between the subcomponents of cognitive skills. This enables one to conclude that such components are dependent on distinct neural systems (even when their location is not precisely known!). Independence is always easier to establish than a necessary interrelationship between components such as when a damaged system has effects later in the information-processing sequence (an *association* of function). This is because it is virtually impossible to establish that impairments on two tasks are attributable to a single functional deficit. There are common co-occurring patterns of deficit in patients with cerebral lesions. Such patterns, or syndromes, are not infrequently interpreted as being due to a single core deficit (e.g., the cluster of deficits, acalculia, dysgraphia, left–right disorientation and finger agnosia, termed the Gerstmann syndrome: Gerstmann, 1927). However this interpretation of syndromes is seriously undermined by the observation of patients who fail to show the full pattern, and more critically by evidence of double dissociations between the co-occurring components of the syndrome (Benton, 1961). In such cases the occurrence of syndromes, or associated deficits, can equally easily be accounted for in terms of the proximity of their anatomical substrates. For these reasons, neuropsychologists have tended to place far greater weight on the evidence for dissociation rather than on the evidence of association.

Contributions of Cognitive Neuropsychology

As a result of this emphasis (some would say overemphasis) on dissociations and double dissociations, cognitive neuropsychology might even be characterised as an exercise in "carving cognition at its seams." Nevertheless, as a field of endeavour it has provided valuable insights into the way in which different components of the human information-processing system are organised. "Cognitive difficulties experienced by neurological patients are to be understood to a first approximation in the terms of the normal information processing system with certain isolable subsystems or transmission routes operating in an impaired fashion" (Shallice, 1988, p. 24). Thus, it has been possible to establish that there are distinct processing stages implicated in skills such as reading, writing, and object recognition.

It has also been possible to use neuropsychological evidence to infer how these components are organised and relate to each other. This is no mean achievement, however, the techniques of cognitive neuropsychology are capable of more than this. Once a selective and seemingly "pure" deficit has been delineated there are still further possibilities. In-depth analysis of the characteristics of the patients' impairment may yield valuable (even critical) insights into the processing or procedures within the damaged system itself. Patients with a selective type of reading difficulty have allowed inferences to be drawn about the procedures of turning print into sound. Other patients, with difficulties in understanding the spoken word, have provided valuable information with regard to the cerebral representation of meaning. Still others have been studied with a view toward understanding the complex procedures involved in perceiving objects.

Neuropsychology has come a long way since the pioneering work of the nineteenth-century neurologists. There have been a number of false starts and to the "outsider" what would seem to be a continual rejection of one set of ideas, followed at 40-year intervals by a return to the earlier framework. The last 20 years have seen a continuing and highly productive interaction between the clinical neurological tradition and the functionalist information-processing approach of contemporary cognitive psychology. Whether the next 20 years will bring back mass action and globalism remains to be seen.

2

Object Recognition

Introduction

Visual object recognition is experienced as an automatic and effortless process. One can look out of the window and see a complex scene consisting of multiple objects at different distances which overlap and even move. The starting point of this skill is merely the different patterning of light and darkness on the retina. The ability to recognise objects is quite remarkable: visual experiences are rarely, if ever, repeated exactly—levels of illumination change, shadows are cast on objects, they are viewed from different perspectives, and objects with similar functions come in a wide range of shapes and sizes. Despite the continually changing nature of visual information it is nevertheless possible to recognise each of the objects in a scene easily. Not only is it possible to achieve what is apparently immediate recognition, but one can also interpret what has just happened and what may be about to happen.

Analysis of neuropsychological disorders of object recognition began in the latter half of the nineteenth century, and the classification of these impairments has continued to make use of the terminology introduced by writers such as Lissauer (1890) and Freud (1891). Lissauer (1890) drew a major distinction between those deficits which might affect the individual's ability to consciously perceive and discriminate stimuli and those which affected the patient's ability to interpret what was seen. He termed these two subtypes of deficit *apperceptive* "mindblindness" (seelenblindheit) and *associative* "mindblindness." Lissauer's concept of apperceptive mindblindness was very general, and it was proposed on theoretical grounds rather than on the basis of empirical observation. He used the term to encompass a wide range of disorders including the ability to discriminate colours and to detect differences between shapes and in novel patterns, in addition to impairments specific to object perception. Lissauer described a patient

(Gottlieb L.) who misidentified many common objects. For example, he became muddled when attempting to use cutlery and he had difficulty in choosing the appropriate pieces of clothing when dressing. At the same time the patient was capable of copying drawings and did not appear to be confused or otherwise intellectually impaired. This pattern of deficit was, for Lissauer, an associative mindblindness. Lissauer defined apperceptive disorders somewhat idiosyncratically, not in terms of a specific pattern of deficit, but rather in terms of what Gottleib L. *could* do. He speculated that apperceptive deficits could exist, and were likely to give rise to other types of object recognition impairment.

One year after the publication of Lissauer's paper, Freud (1891) introduced the term *agnosia* (from the Greek, *without knowledge*) as a refinement of the concept of mindblindness. He contended that agnosic deficits were not simply disorders of sensory processing, but rather that they reflected impairments affecting previously established knowledge.

Taken together, the concepts introduced by Lissauer and Freud offer a useful starting point for analysing disorders of object recognition. Lissauer postulated a discontinuity between apperceptive and associative disorders; Freud, between disorders of sensation on the one hand and disorders of "gnosis" on the other. A tripartite distinction can be constructed from these early accounts of disorders of object recognition: (1) deficits affecting sensory processing, (2) deficits affecting the perceptual analysis of known objects (apperceptive agnosia), and (3) disorders in deriving the meanings of objects (associative agnosia).

Empirical Characteristics

Disorders of Sensory Discrimination

The normal individual is able to detect and discriminate differences along a number of visual dimensions. The ability to make these discriminations does not depend on the structure, familiarity or even the category of the stimuli which are being viewed. One can make discriminations of "sameness" or "difference" not only between familiar objects and faces but also between novel shapes and surfaces (even when they have no constant or distinct form). The capacity for discriminating differences between stimuli which vary along sensory dimensions is a fundamental prerequisite of normal object recognition.

Acuity   Many cerebral disorders of visual processing are qualitatively similar to those which can result from damage to the eye or optic nerve. These include the capacity to determine the presence or absence of light, to detect a single target varying in size (target resolution) whether one or more stimuli are present in the visual field (two-point discrimination), and to detect different types of change in contrast (spatial frequency and contrast sensitivity). These disorders are broadly subsumed under the single label of "acuity." It hardly needs to be stated that the loss of one or more of these capacities will have profound implications for object recognition.

More counterintuitive is the observation that a patient may be more impaired in resolving large contours than in processing fine details. Abadi, Kulikowski, & Meudell (1981) described a patient (R.C.) who had very grave difficulty in recognising any common object encountered in daily life. By contrast, he was able to locate objects and comment on their texture and colour. On quantitative investigation it was found that on certain acuity measures (i.e., low spatial frequency resolution) he was markedly impaired. His object recognition difficulties were reasonably attributed to this basic deficit in his visual sensory acuity. This same patient was investigated by Campion & Latto (1985). He was asked to rate the brightness of lights which were briefly presented in all sectors of his visual field. He showed considerable variability, which they interpreted as evidence of a "peppering" of areas of blindness across the whole visual field. Campion & Latto considered that these multiple blind areas were more than sufficient to account for this patient's failure to recognise common objects.

Shape Discrimination   The normal visual system is capable of very fine discriminations between similar shapes: one side of a square needs only to be very slightly elongated for it to be perceived as a rectangle rather than a square, and only a slight amount of curvature needs to be made for a line to lose its "straight" appearance.

The ability to discriminate shapes can be selectively impaired in patients with cerebral disease. The first systematic documentation of this class of disorder was reported by Efron (1968). He reported a patient (Mr. S.), whose recognition of objects and faces in the real world was grossly defective. Efron was able to demonstrate that the patient had normal or near normal levels of acuity when this was tested by his ability to detect the presence or absence of a single small target. The patient was also able to discriminate subtle changes in the brightness of stimuli and had no difficulties on a stringent test of colour discrimination. On tests of spatial processing (see Chapter 4) it was determined that the patient was near normal in pointing to stimuli located at different visual angles and at different depths.

However, the patient was found to be very impaired on tests requiring him to discriminate between shapes. For example, he could make use of his preserved colour vision and acuity in order to trace the outline of a shape if it was presented against a uniform background. However, he had grave difficulties when the same stimulus was presented against a patterned or multicoloured background. In order to document the patient's shape-discrimination impairment quantitatively, Efron devised a test in which the patient was simply asked to

Figure 2.1   Efron Squares Test: square matched for total flux with a series of oblongs. (Adapted from Warrington, 1986.)

judge whether two stimuli were the same or different. The stimuli were squares and rectangles which were matched for their surface area equated for total flux (see Fig. 2.1). This was necessary so that the discrimination could not be performed on the basis of information about size or brightness. The patient was gravely impaired on this task and indeed was only above chance when the "rectangle" had the appearance of a line! Very reasonably, the patient's severe disorder of object recognition was traced back to this fundamental loss of shape discrimination.

The observation of impaired shape discrimination with normal acuity has since been replicated and extended. Warrington (1986) described two cases (J.A.F. and R.B.C.) with entirely normal visual acuity on conventional testing who nevertheless showed severe difficulties with object and face recognition in everyday life. One of these patients (J.A.F.) described her visual world as being "very indistinct and distorted" and when pressed to explain what things looked like she said "just like blobs."

These patients' performance on an adaptation of the Efron shape discrimination test was markedly impaired (see Fig. 2.2). It was shown that their performance was a function of the degree of similarity between stimuli. When the ratio between the height and width of the stimulus was small their performance was very weak, but increasing the ratio resulted in substantial improvements. In one case (J.A.F.) it was possible to establish that there was no effect of the absolute size of

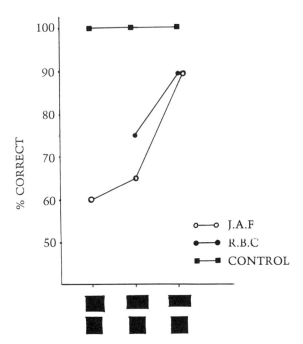

Figure 2.2 Percentage correct for three levels of discrimination difficulty on the Efron Squares Test (control, J.A.F., and R.B.C.). (Adapted from Warrington, 1986.)

stimuli. Almost identical discriminability functions were found over a range of different stimulus sizes (Warrington, unpublished). These findings showed that the patients (like the case described by Efron) had impaired shape discrimination. Once again this deficit was considered to be sufficient to account for their difficulties with object recognition in everyday life.

It was established that other aspects of shape discrimination were impaired in one of these cases (J.A.F.). She was unable to discriminate whether a triangle had straight or curved sides until the triangle was almost circular. She could not tell which was the larger of two circles or which was the longer of two lines until they differed by approximately 50% (see Fig. 2.3). Despite these impairments, the patient was able to make discriminations between stimuli in which there were clear differences in contour, such as between a square and a cross. This preserved skill was in fact sufficient for her to be able to read small print at a normal speed!

Warrington & Taylor (1973) devised a test of shape detection in which the subject's task was to detect the presence or absence of a shape (O or X) when this was signalled by a change in texture density (see Fig. 2.4). In two cases with normal acuity (the same two patients with a shape-discrimination impairment who were discussed above, R.B.C. and J.A.F.) performance on this task was markedly impaired. However, there is preliminary evidence that these two aspects of shape

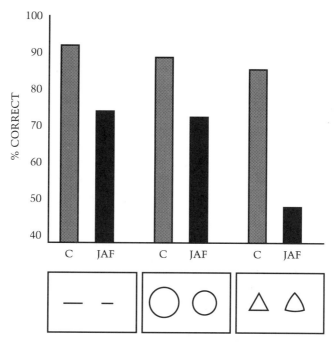

Figure 2.3 Performance by controls and J.A.F. on shape-discrimination tests (lines, circles, triangles) Warrington, unpublished.

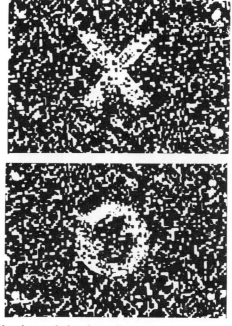

Figure 2.4 Example of stimuli for shape detection test (Warrington & Taylor, 1973).

perception, shape discrimination, and shape detection may be dissociable (Vaina, 1987).

Humphreys & Riddoch (e.g., 1984, 1987a; Riddoch & Humphreys, 1987a) have also described a case (H.J.A.) with gravely impaired shape discrimination abilities but preserved acuity on conventional tests. The patient was unable to discriminate the size or shape of stimuli, but could often report information about details (or features) of objects. Recognition of objects was gravely impaired in everyday life. When attempting to recognise drawings he would name the details which he could discriminate. For example, when given the drawing of a carrot he responded, "I have not even the glimmerings of an idea. The bottom point seems solid and the other bits are feathery. It does not seem to be logical unless it is some kind of a brush" (Humphreys & Riddoch, 1987a). Humphreys & Riddoch have argued that the patient was unable to integrate the information about the details he could see into a "global" form or shape.

Colour Disproportionate impairment of colour perception, termed *achromatopsia*, can occur as a selective deficit in patients with cerebral lesions. The patient typically describes the visual world as being "drained of colour" and in the extreme case may describe it as being black, white, and shades of grey "like a black and white movie." Unlike disorders of shape discrimination, achromatopsia may have relatively little effect on object recognition in everyday life. For example, a case described by Pallis (1955) could recognise most common objects but complained that he had difficulty in discriminating between bronze and silver coins or between a jar of pickles and a jar of jam.

Impairments on tests of colour vision are relatively common in cerebral disease: indeed some loss of the ability to discriminate colours (particularly in the "blue" sector of the spectrum) may occur with lesions at any point in the post-retinal visual system (Meadows, 1974a). For these reasons neurologists often assess a patient's visual function with coloured stimuli (red pins) as well as with simple monochromatic targets. However, the global impairment of colour vision is considerably less common. The relative rarity of achromatopsia has meant that its existence as a selective deficit has sometimes been doubted. Holmes (1918) conducted an extensive survey of visual impairments following gunshot wounds and never observed a case of achromatopsia, leading him to suggest that the disorder was attributable to more global disorders of visual function.

Meadows (1974a) summarised 14 cases of achromatopsia from the published literature and described a further case whom he had investigated himself. His analysis demonstrated that a virtually total achromatopsia could occur in patients whose visual acuity was normal. The patient's colour discrimination was tested by asking him to arrange colour patches into an orderly progression so that they represented a continuum along the colour spectrum (Farnsworth–Munsell 100-Hue

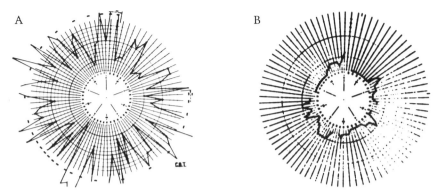

Figure 2.5   Performance of (A) an achromatopsic patient (C.O.T.) (Warrington, 1986) and (B) a normal subject on the Farnsworth–Munsell 100-Hue Test. (The magnitude of displacement indicates severity of impairment.)

Test: Farnsworth, 1957). Normal subjects can perform this task with a minimal error rate, and people with congenital (retinal) colourblindness are only impaired on certain sectors of the spectrum. However, in the severely achromatopsic patient performance is impaired in *all* sectors of the spectrum. Figure 2.5 shows a patient with a normal pattern of performance on the Farnsworth–Munsell test together with a patient with a very severe achromatopsic impairment.

There is evidence that distant hue contrasts may be discriminated by some achromatopsic patients. Thus, their performance may approach normal limits on tasks which are used for testing retinal colourblindness such as the Ishihara (1983) plates, which measure the discrimination between red and green and blue and yellow (Meadows, 1974a; Mollon, Newcombe, Polden, & Ratcliff, 1980). Heywood, Wilson, & Cowey (1987) have shown that failure on the Farnsworth–Munsell test cannot be attributed to a more general impairment of discriminating subtle visual attributes of stimuli. They demonstrated that a patient with severe achromatopsia was nevertheless capable of processing differences between achromatic stimuli varying along the "grey" scale. Mollon *et al.* (1980) have gone somewhat further and demonstrated psychophysically that an achromatopsic patient (M.S.) had normal thresholds for detecting the presence of changes in colour. This sensitivity corresponded to the information derived from the three cone (retinal) processing systems.

Disorders of Object Perception (Apperceptive Agnosia)

For efficient perception, differences in many sensory dimensions must be ignored. In this context, it would be highly uneconomical for each instance of an object to be processed "from scratch." An object such as a bucket can be perceived regardless of the angle of view, or lighting conditions. The observer achieves a structured percept of the bucket so that its size, volume, and angle of view are obvious: information that goes well beyond that provided by visual sensory analysis. This level of processing or representation requires access to stored information about the structure of objects which have been experienced in the past.

Investigation of impairments in this level of processing, here termed *apperceptive agnosia,* have primarily used a group study methodology. In an early quantitative study, Milner (1958) demonstrated a deficit in the McGill Anomalies Test, which requires patients to identify an anomaly in a sketchily drawn scene. A deficit was also documented on a task requiring patients to identify incomplete silhouette drawings of objects using the Street (1931) completion test (De Renzi & Spinnler, 1966; Kerschensteiner, Hartje, Orgass, & Poeck, 1972; Wasserstein, Zappulla, Rosen, Gerstman, & Rock, 1987). De Renzi, Scotti, & Spinnler (1969) demonstrated an impairment on Ghent's overlapping figures task, a test that was originally devised for assessing perceptual development in children. This test requires the subject to identify items from overlapping line drawings. In their investigation De Renzi *et al.* (1969) eliminated any confounding effect of impaired language by asking their patients to point to an item in an array which matched one of the overlapping figures (see Fig. 2.6). De Renzi *et al.* found that some patients were only able to recognise and match one or two objects in the overlapping figures. By contrast, these same patients were able to identify the individual (nonoverlapping) line drawings with a normal degree of accuracy. Kerschensteiner *et al.* (1972) found that some patients were unable to state how many objects were represented in a drawing of overlapping figures (Poppelreuter's, 1917, procedure).

Warrington & James (1967a) also used a test originally devised for children. This consists of a graded series of incomplete line drawings of

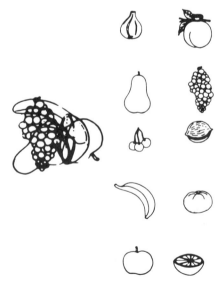

Figure 2.6   Example from Ghent's overlapping figures test (De Renzi *et al.,* 1969).

Figure 2.7   Example from Gollin's (1960) incomplete drawing test.

common objects (Gollin, 1960). A very fragmented version of the drawing is presented initially, and the subject is asked to identify it. If the subject fails, then it is followed by increasingly complete versions of the drawing until the object is identified (see Fig. 2.7). Patients may require a more "complete" picture than controls. These findings were subsequently replicated by Warrington & Taylor (1973).

What these tasks appear to have in common is that complex or degraded pictorial representations of common objects are more difficult than simple clear pictures. Visual "difficulty" is manipulated more naturalistically by lighting conditions and angle of viewpoint. Some patients have greater difficulty recognising objects that are unevenly lit, causing misleading shadow contours, as compared with evenly illuminated objects (Warrington, 1982a; see Fig. 2.8). The role of angle of viewpoint was investigated by Warrington & Taylor (1973). The "Unusual Views" task consists of black and white photographs of common objects pictured from an unusual or unconventional angle (see Fig. 2.9). Although the view of the object was one which would be relatively familiar in everyday life, it was considered to be unusual as a photographic representation of the stimulus. Patients were selectively impaired in identifying the "unusual-view" objects as compared with the same items pictured from a conventional viewpoint.

Informally it has been noted that there are particularly high error rates for the four unusual views shown in Fig. 2.9. For example, the iron might be called "a cap on its side," the bucket "a fried egg," the basket

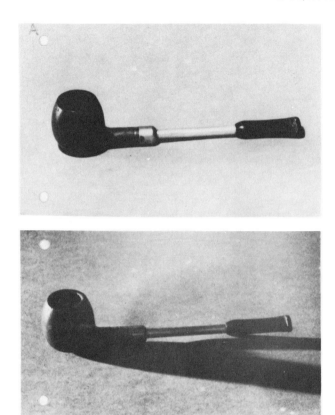

Figure 2.8   Example from an uneven lighting test (Warrington, 1982).

"a table mat," and goggles "a belt." The patients' errors appear to reflect the visual properties of the stimulus, either overemphasising some detail in the stimulus or ignoring a major detail. Errors which were related to the target in terms of functional similarity (semantic errors) were very rare.

Humphreys & Riddoch (1984) and Riddoch & Humphreys (1986) also found that in four patients the ability to recognise photographs of foreshortened objects was impaired. In a further extension of the unusual-views manipulation Warrington & James (1988) demonstrated a comparable impairment with foreshortened silhouette drawings of objects (see Fig. 2.10).

The impairment in perceiving stimuli which are degraded or incomplete is not confined to objects. Patients may also be impaired in identifying degraded letters. Faglioni, Scotti, & Spinnler (1967) investigated patients' ability to match letters which differed in their "case," in the complexity of their typeface, or which were degraded by superimposing a number of random lines (see Fig. 2.11B). Some patients were unable to recognise letters in the degraded condition but were able to

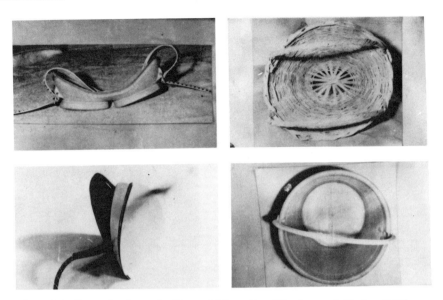

Figure 2.9 Examples from the Unusual Views Test (Warrington & Taylor, 1973).

match upper and lower case letters and letters from complex type-scripts. Warrington & James (1967a) manipulated a different dimension of perceptual complexity in a letter-recognition task. The stimuli were degraded by the addition of visual "noise" (see Fig. 2.11A). The patient's task was to name or trace the stimulus. This is a particularly easy test for normal subjects. However, patients with an impairment in perceiving fragmented letters commonly perceive the stimuli as randomly scattered black marks. Their inability to trace the letter appears to confirm that they have failed to achieve an appropriately structured percept.

Figure 2.10 Examples from the Foreshortened Silhouettes test (Warrington & James, 1988).

A   B

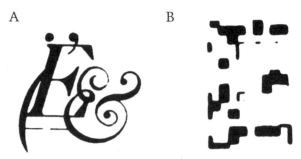

Figure 2.11 Examples of degraded letters (A, Faglioni *et al.*, 1969; B, Warrington & James, 1967a).

Disorders of Object "Meaning" (Associative Agnosia)

Objects are more than coherent structured percepts: they have significance and meaning for the viewer. The normal individual has no difficulty in recognising a hollow object 6 inches in height with a cylindrical cross section and loop-shaped protuberance on one side as a vessel which is used for hot drinks (conventionally called a mug). This level of semantic processing entails the assignment of "meaning" to a percept whose structure is fully specified.

Patients with intact visual sensory functioning and adequate object perception skills may nevertheless be impaired in recognising objects. They fail to assign meaning to visually presented objects. It should be emphasised that patients' impairment is more profound than that of a failure at the level of finding the right name. It can be shown that the patient has achieved an adequate and fully structured percept, but it is a percept which has lost much of its meaning. For these patients, termed *visual associative agnosics*, common objects may be perceived in the same way that the normal person would be able to perceive a novel object such as an unfamiliar piece of machinery. One could examine it thoroughly and attain a full specification of its perceptual properties and dimensions, yet still fail to recognise it as being similar to or different in function from other pieces of machinery.

Convincing cases with a selective impairment in assigning meaning to visually presented objects have been relatively rare, and in fact the existence of the syndrome has sometimes been disputed (Bay, 1950; Teuber, 1965). However, there is now sufficient evidence, both from group studies and from investigations of single cases, to indicate that although the deficit (like all pure cognitive deficits) is uncommon in a highly selective form, it nevertheless does occur. Hécaen & Angelergues (1963) detected 4 cases in a retrospective survey of 415 patients, and De Renzi & Spinnler (1966) reported a similar low incidence (1 in 122 patients).

An early quantitative study of a case of visual associative agnosia was reported by Rubens & Benson (1971). They described a patient (a physician) with superior verbal intellectual skills who was impaired in identifying and demonstrating the use of visually presented objects. He could identify these objects immediately when he touched them. For example, when shown a stethoscope he responded "a long cord with a round thing at the end" and asked if it could be a watch. When asked to demonstrate the use of objects which he misnamed, his gestures corresponded to the spoken name and not to the actual object. At the same time his ability to perceive and remember complex nonrepresentational pattern material was at a normal level and his drawing skills were excellent. He was able to copy complex pictures, even those which he misidentified. For example, he copied the picture of a train (see Fig. 2.12) but commented "a wagon or a car of some kind. The larger vehicle is being pulled by the smaller one."

The integrity of visual perceptual abilities was also very clear in a case (F.L.) studied by Taylor & Warrington (1971). The patient was very profoundly impaired in recognising common everyday objects. For example, when he was given a cup of tea which he stirred and tasted he said "needs more sugar." He failed to recognise the sugar bowl, and when it was pointed out to him he put some sugar in his mouth and again tasted the tea and was still dissatisfied. When told to put the sugar into his cup he queried whether this was all right. Like Rubens & Benson's case, this patient was also able to copy detailed drawings which he failed to recognise. When asked to match a "usual" and an "unusual" view of the same object he was able to score 16/20 despite only recognising four of the objects in the photographs. Although his detailed knowledge of all but the most common objects appeared to be gravely compromised it was noted that he retained some crude information about the broad class to which an object belonged. For example,

Figure 2.12 Copy of line drawing by a patient with visual associative agnosia. (Adapted from Rubens & Benson, 1971.)

he could state whether an object was a container or not, but not which type of container it was (e.g., cup vs. jug).

Other studies have used techniques which minimise the verbal components of object recognition. De Renzi *et al.* (1969) were the first to develop a visual–visual matching task in which physically dissimilar items with the same name or function must be judged as being the same. They paired a real object with a photograph of a similar but not identical object. Subsequent adaptations of this technique have used pairs of real objects (Warrington & McCarthy, 1983), pairs of photographs of objects (Warrington & Taylor, 1978), or line drawings (McCarthy & Warrington, 1986a: see Fig. 2.13). Such tests have established that patients may have an impairment in their precise knowledge of objects.

Partial Knowledge Visual associative agnosia is rarely absolute. Patients may retain some broad or partial information which is too crude to permit the fine differentiation of similar objects. The relative preservation of knowledge of the broad category to which an object belongs was explored in three cases (Warrington, 1975). It was found that the patients could typically assign a visually presented stimulus to a superordinate class (e.g., selecting the picture of a mammal, insect, or bird from a choice of three different animals). However, their knowledge of

Figure 2.13 Examples from a Visual–Visual Matching task (McCarthy & Warrington, 1986).

more specific attributes and associations of these stimuli appeared to be even more impaired. (For example, in the case of animals, information about the attributes of size and colour were probed. Associative information was probed by asking which of three animals was foreign, or dangerous.) This early evidence of the relative preservation of superordinate information and the relative vulnerability of subordinate information (attribute and association) has been extended and replicated in other studies (e.g., McCarthy & Warrington, 1986a; Sartori & Job, 1988; Bub, Black, Hampson, and Kertesz, 1988). These findings indicate that there are degrees of impairment in assigning meaning to visually presented stimuli which may follow a regular pattern in some cases.

Category Specificity. Patients may not necessarily have equivalent impairment in recognising all categories of visual "objects" (the special case of faces will be considered in Chapter 3). Anecdotal evidence of seemingly very bizarre dissociations was described by Nielsen (1937, 1946). For example, he claimed to have observed patients whose recognition deficits were confined to living things, their knowledge of objects being relatively well preserved. McCrae & Trolle (1956) described a single case with severe impairment in his ability to recognise animals. For example, the patient confused pictures of a squirrel and a cat, stating that they must both be cats because of the whiskers. At the same time, he was described as having no difficulties in recognising trees, flowers, or common objects. The converse pattern of deficit was documented by Hécaen & Ajuriaguerra (1956). They described a patient in whom the recognition of inanimate objects was more impaired than the recognition of animate things.

Quantitative evidence to support such dissociations has since been obtained by using picture description tasks . Two patients (S.B.Y. and J.B.R.) studied by Warrington & Shallice (1984) were impaired in recognising animals, foods, and plants as compared with inanimate objects (see Table 2.1). The patients were virtually unable to recognise any items from the animal and plant stimuli as compared with their significantly superior ability to give definitions of pictures of inanimate objects (i.e., living things 0 and 6% correct and inanimate objects 75 and 90% correct). These same two patients also had enormous difficulty in identifying foods as compared with inanimate objects. In one case (J.B.R.) it was possible to test this knowledge nonverbally by using "pantomime" gestures appropriate to eating a food or to using an object. He scored 20% and 65% correct, respectively. These findings of a dissociation between animate and inanimate categories have been extensively replicated (e.g., Sartori & Job, 1988; Silveri & Gainotti, 1988; Farah, Hammond, Mehta, & Ratcliff, 1989). The complementary dissociation has been documented in a single case (Y.O.T.) on a visual–visual matching task (see Fig. 2.13). The patient was very impaired in matching objects (e.g., two types of glass, two types of vase) but within normal limits on the animals version of the task (e.g., matching two types of dog, two types of cow) (Warrinton & McCarthy, 1987).

Table 2.1 Examples of Picture Naming or Description Given by Two Patients (S.B.Y. and J.B.R.) with Category-Specific Semantic Impairments

		S.B.Y.	
Giraffe	bird, not sure what it is used for	*Umbrella*	a tube used to provide protection against rain
Frog	bird with no arms	*Scales*	measuring weight of things
Poppy	plant/tree of some sort	*Mittens*	device for keeping hands warm
Rhinoceros	animal can be used for eating	*Wallet*	for carrying things to buy things with
		J.B.R.	
Bear	dog	*Calculator*	electronic calculator
Sheep	dog pet	*Binoculars*	binoculars
Rabbit	animal	*Drums*	musical instrument called drums
Holly	fruit, not apple	*Shovel*	metal made tool for digging holes in earth

The dissociation between visual knowledge and animate and inanimate things by no means exhausts the category-specific effects which are documented in patients with impaired visual object recognition. Selective preservation of knowledge of the abstract connotations of a scene is on record (C.A.V. in Warrington, 1981a), as is the selective preservation of the ability to recognise visually presented actions (F.R.A. in McCarthy & Warrington, 1986a). Both of these patients were gravely impaired in recognising common objects but were nevertheless able to comprehend scenes in which these same objects were a central component. Thus one patient (C.A.V.) could not recognise a carrot, but could recognise Fig. 2.14A as depicting "enticement." The other case (F.R.A.) could not recognise a cup, but was able to recognise (and name) Fig. 2.14B as "drinking."

Colour Agnosia   The object attribute of "colour" has sometimes been singled out for special consideration as a potential visual category, to the point that for some commentators colour agnosia has the status of a definable independent syndrome (Sittig, 1921; Hécaen & Albert, 1978). Agnosia for colours implies a loss of colour knowledge in patients with intact colour discrimination and adequate language skills. The latter consideration is important since the retrieval and/or comprehension of spoken colour names may be specifically impaired in some patients (see Chapters 6 and 7).

There are three main methods for the assessment of knowledge by colours independently of their names. The first test, colour sorting, was originally devised by Sittig (1921), who described patients who were unable to sort colour patches into coherent groups so that the ones that were alike were together (e.g., all shades of red, all shades of green). This has the disadvantage of being a conceptually abstract task demanding concept formation which is also sensitive to impairments of problem solving (see Chapter 16).

Stengel (1948) introduced another nonverbal task which required patients to judge whether pictures of objects which have a very specific

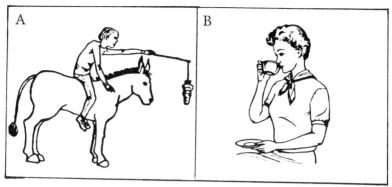

Figure 2.14   (A) Example from Shallice's Abstract Word–Picture Matching test. (B) Example from Action Naming test (McCarthy & Warrington, 1986).

colour had been correctly coloured or not (e.g., a red banana). This appears to be a relatively easy task, and there is no case on record with intact colour discrimination and intact object recognition who has failed this task (see Beauvois & Saillant, 1985).

The third type of task is that of colouring black and white line drawings. Very obvious mistakes in colouring have been documented both in single case studies and in larger-scale group studies of patients. One patient (W.K.) was impaired on a wide range of tasks involving colours and colour names (with the exception of identifying wrongly coloured objects). He was described as colouring drawings by a process of trial and error. He was unable to choose the appropriate crayon, but having coloured a drawing he was capable of saying whether it was appropriate or not (Kinsbourne & Warrington, 1964a). De Renzi & Spinnler (1967) and Tzavaras, Hécaen, & LeBras (1971) used this task in group studies. Both investigations found that a high proportion of patients obtained scores below that of the worst control. The problem with this procedure is that any misrecognition of the object may confound results.

Anatomical Considerations

Sensory Discrimination

Unilateral occipital lobe lesions give rise to impairment in processing visual sensory information in the visual field which is contralateral to the site of the lesion. Damage to either the right or the left occipital lobe gives rise to comparable patterns of visual sensory impairment (see Fig. 2.15). Such deficits are said to be "retinotopic" because they maintain the topography, or spatial coordinates, of the retina. Loss of visual acuity can be severe following bilateral lesions of visual cortex, however, it can and often does occur with lesions anywhere from the eye to the brain.

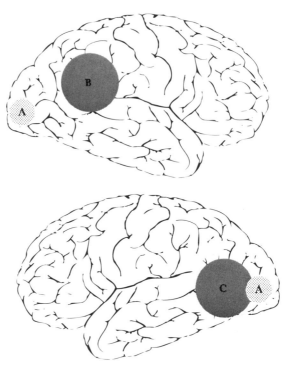

Figure 2.15 Diagram showing approximate locus of visual sensory impairment (A), locus of apperceptive agnosia (B), and locus of visual associative agnosia (C).

Shape Discrimination In all of the patients in whom there has been preservation of acuity but loss of visual shape discrimination, bilateral posterior cerebral lesions have been observed. Visual field defects as measured on conventional tests of acuity do not appear to be a necessary correlate of this deficit (Efron, 1968; Benson & Greenberg, 1969). Deficits in visual shape discrimination may be confined to one visual half-field and are therefore retinotopic. In a preliminary account, Weiskrantz (1980) reported that there was evidence of a disproportionate level of impairment in shape discrimination in the visual field contralateral to a cerebral lesion.

Colour The cases of cerebral achromatopsia reviewed by Meadows (1974a) all had bilateral occipital lobe lesions. He inferred on the basis of a high incidence of superior altitudinal defects that bilateral damage to the region of the fusiform and lingual gyri of the occipital lobes was implicated in this syndrome. Lesions in these gyri were present in all three cases of cerebral achromatopsia for whom autopsy evidence was available.

As was the case for shape discrimination, achromatopsia can be confined to the half-field contralateral to the lesion site. In such cases, the impairment in colour processing is not necessarily apparent in free vision and the patient may be unaware of the deficit. Specialised testing using stimuli presented to one side of fixation is necessary in order to elicit the deficit. Thus colour processing provides another example of a retinotopic visual sensory skill. Indeed the first description of impaired hue discrimination was of a deficit confined to the right visual half-field (Verrey, 1888). Autopsy evidence in this patient demonstrated a lesion which was in the region of the left lingual and fusiform gyri. Albert, Reches, & Silverberg (1975a) and Damasio, Yamada, Damasio, Corbett, & McKee (1980) have replicated the observation that a colour-discrimination deficit can be confined to one half-field. There is no evidence that the laterality of lesion is in any way critical for this pattern of impairment and, it appears that unilateral impairments of colour perception are equally common following right- or left-hemisphere lesions.

Disorders of Object Perception: Apperceptive Agnosia

There is overwhelming evidence of a syndrome of impaired object perception associated with lesions of the right hemisphere (see Fig. 2.15). These are nonretinotopic deficits insofar as a unilateral lesion may give rise to impairment anywhere in free vision, including the intact visual field. In her study of the McGill Anomalies test (see above), Milner (1958) investigated a group of patients with surgical ablations of the right or left temporal lobe for the relief of epilepsy. In this sample the right-temporal-lobe lesion group showed the greatest impairment. Subsequently De Renzi and his colleagues (1966, 1969) tested a series of patients with unilateral lesions arising (primarily) as a consequence of cerebrovascular disease. Patients with damage to the right hemisphere (as established on clinical neurological criteria) were more impaired than were left-hemisphere cases on matching of overlapping figures. Furthermore it was those patients with more posterior lesions (as inferred on the basis of the presence of a hemianopia) who were more impaired.

The original patient populations studied by Warrington and her colleagues (between 1967 and 1978) were primarily cases in whom space occupying lesions had been demonstrated radiologically. For this reason lesions in all sectors of the cortex were represented. This allowed for a more detailed analysis of the anatomical correlates of impairment. On the Gollin Pictures test the highest incidence of deficit was in patients with involvement of the right parietal lobe (Warrington & James, 1967a). Moreover, as a group their performance was significantly worse than that of right-hemisphere cases whose lesions spared the right parietal lobe. A very similar result was obtained with the Unusual Views Test (Warrington & Taylor, 1973, Layman & Greene, 1988). A statistical "map" of the locus of the lesions was constructed by summing the locus of the lesions of those patients whose scores were in the lower third of the group. A fairly restricted area in the right inferior parietal lobe was found to be implicated in the unconventional-views deficit. Those patients who have been the subject of detailed single case studies because of the relative selectivity and severity of their impairment in object perception have all had lesions involving these regions (Landis, Regard, Bliestle, & Kleihues, 1988; Warrington & James, 1988).

Disorders of Object Meaning: Associative Agnosia

In the majority of single cases with impairment in deriving the meaning of visually presented objects (despite normal sensory and perceptual abilities) there has been evidence of bilateral brain damage. Such cases are neutral with respect to the issue of the critical or minimal lesion site in the aetiology of this syndrome. The brain of the original case reported by Lissauer (1890) was studied at post mortem. The lesion was in the left hemisphere and located at the junction of the occipital and temporal lobes. This localisation has since been confirmed in other well-documented single cases (see Fig. 2.15). Two patients studied by Hécaen and his colleagues (Hécaen & Ajuriaguerra, 1956; Hécaen, Goldblum, Masure, & Ramier, 1974) were reported to have relatively large space occupying lesions of left occipital lobe. A similar locus was implicated in a case studied by Ferro & Santos (1984). Magnetic resonance image (MRI) localisation was available in one patient (F.R.A.); he was found to have a left occipitotemporal lesion which in his case spared the splenium of the corpus callosum (McCarthy & Warrington, 1986a).

The findings from single cases selected on the basis of a clinically obvious syndrome are complemented by those of group studies devised to study the localising significance of the syndrome in a milder form. De Renzi et al. (1969) investigated a series of patients with unilateral cerebral lesions, most of which had arisen on a vascular basis. They found that an impairment on the visual–visual matching task (e.g., matching a real object with a visually dissimilar photograph of a similar object such as two types of doll) was associated with lesions to the posterior sectors of the left hemisphere (as inferred on the basis of the presence of a right-sided hemianopic defect). With a somewhat different patient population consisting mostly of patients with space occupying lesions, Warrington & Taylor (1973) obtained similar results: patients with damage to the posterior sectors of the left hemisphere had a disproportionate impairment on their visual–visual matching test. Thus, unilateral lesions give rise to a deficit in object recognition which affects material presented to the intact visual field. Object recognition appears to be another example of a nonretinotopic visual skill.

In the case of the attribute of colour, the neurological syndrome of colour agnosia has been associated with posterior lesions of the left hemisphere. However, in such cases it is typically seen in the context of marked language deficits (De Renzi & Spinnler, 1967; De Renzi, Faglioni, & Scotti, 1972a,b).

In summary the three major types of disordered object recognition, visual sensory impairments, apperceptive agnosia, and associative agnosia, each have distinctive clinicopathological correlates. In the case of impaired visual sensory discrimination, bilateral posterior cerebral lesions are necessary for the disorder to affect both visual fields. Unilateral lesions give rise to deficits restricted to the contralateral visual field; they are retinotopic deficits. In the case of disordered object perception or apperceptive agnosia the minimal lesion is in the right parietal lobe. In the case of impairments of object meaning or associative agnosia, damage to the occipitotemporal regions of the left hemisphere is critical.

Theoretical Considerations

Three major subtypes of impaired object recognition have been discussed in the preceding empirical and anatomical sections. First there are disorders in which the failure appears to be at the level of discrimination of certain visual sensory attributes. Second there are disorders in which recognition may be impaired when perceptual dimensions of a task are manipulated. This occurs despite the patient having adequate sensory-discrimination capacities. The third type of disorder implicates a deficit at the level of assigning meaning to an adequately structured percept.

A basic theoretical framework is necessarily embodied in these distinctions. On this perspective, these disorders are viewed as affecting qualitatively distinct aspects of the complex skill of object recognition. The evidence for these distinctions rests not only on the characteristics of the patient's deficits, but also on the anatomical correlates, which differ in the three types of disorder (see Fig. 2.16).

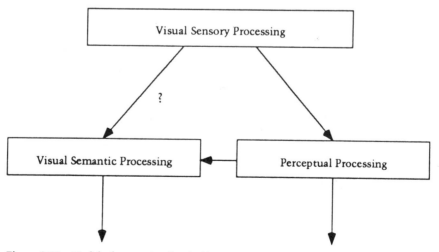

Figure 2.16 Model of stages in visual object recognition.

Visual Sensory Discrimination

The evidence from patients with impairments of visual sensory processing has direct implications for our understanding of the organisation of these abilities in the normal individual. To anticipate, the evidence from patients with visual sensory deficits has shown that these disorders are not on any simple continuum of task difficulty. As such they have direct implications for our knowledge of the normal organisation of visual sensory processing.

Shape Discrimination In the empirical section the impairment of shape discrimination was described in patients in whom acuity was within normal limits. It was also noted that this type of discrimination is one for which normal subjects have exceptionally fine levels of resolution. Indeed, performance on the shape-discrimination task can be entirely normal in control subjects wearing lenses which substantially decrease their resolution of single contours (Warrington, unpublished data). The question remains as to whether the ability to discriminate differences in shape is necessarily dependent on a prior analysis of the constituent contours or edges of the shapes concerned. If this were the case, then shape-discrimination tasks would be simply more difficult for patients with lesions of the visual system than are conventional measures of acuity. The evidence indicates that this is not the case, shape discrimination may be preserved despite a severe impairment of acuity.

One patient (C.O.T.) described by Warrington (1986) had severely impaired visual acuity. His functional vision was so poor that he was unable to perform any conventional test of acuity and could not even state whether the examiner was showing him one or more fingers. Nevertheless his performance on the most difficult square/rectangle discrimination was error free and he also obtained near perfect scores on a task of shape detection (see Figs. 2.1 and 2.4).

Colour Whereas by definition achromatopsia is the impairment of colour perception in patients with normal acuity, again, this cannot in some sense be attributed to any general or special vulnerability of colour discrimination. The converse pattern, namely the preservation of colour discrimination in patients with very marked loss of visual acuity, has also been documented. Wechsler (1931) briefly described a patient in whom (it was claimed) there was selective preservation of colour discrimination, with other visual abilities being very severely impaired. Hyvarinen & Rovamo (1981) described a patient whose acuity was measured using both achromatic (black and white or grey) and coloured stimuli. The patient had normal sensitivity to contrast for the coloured material but was grossly impaired on the achromatic stimuli. Remarkably, Hyvarinen and Rovamo found that the patient who was unable to read normal black and white print was helped to read by giving her glasses with coloured lenses.

Two further cases (B.R.A. and T.H.R.) with a selective preservation of colour discrimination were described by Warrington (1986). The patients were gravely impaired on tests of acuity and shape discrimination and in addition had severe impairments on simple tests of spatial localisation (see Chapter 4). Despite these deficits they were nevertheless capable of fine hue-discrimination judgments. The demands of the Farnsworth–Munsell test were too stringent for these two patients (because of additional spatial deficits) and they were tested using strands of coloured wool which they were able to name using a wide colour name vocabulary (e.g., "turquoise blue," "sandy yellow," "lime green"). Although they had no useful vision for monochromatic stimuli and were unable to discriminate between squares and elongated oblongs they were able to report the shade of a single strand of wool with a low saturation hue with great accuracy.

Perhaps the most fundamental theoretical insight which this evidence offers is that the various sensory abilities are not organised in any simple hierarchical manner, with some processes being necessarily "prior" to others. The apparent rarity of disorders such as pure achromatopsia reflects physiological "risk" rather than functional organisation. Shape discrimination reciprocally dissociates both from acuity and from colour discrimination. Colour discrimination and acuity also dissociate from each other (see Table 2.2).

Object Perception (Apperceptive Agnosia)

In introducing the problems of analysing object recognition it was argued that deficits affecting established representations could and should be distinguished from disorders of sensory discrimination. In this section the relationship between sensory discrimination and failure on tests of object perception will be considered first. This will be followed by a more detailed consideration of the theoretical frameworks which have been advanced to interpret perceptual disorders.

Table 2.2 Reciprocal Dissociation of Visual Sensory Function[a]

Impaired	Preserved		
	Acuity	Shape	Colour
Acuity		C.O.T.	B.R.A. T.H.R.
Shape	J.A.F. R.B.C.		B.R.A. T.H.R.
Colour	J.A.F. R.B.C.	C.O.T.	

[a]Dissociation of preserved and impaired visual sensory processing in five patients (C.O.T., J.A.F., R.B.C., B.R.A., T.H.R.) with partial cortical blindness (Warrington, 1985).

Relationship to Sensory Processing Prior to invoking the concept of a selective *perceptual* deficit it is essential to demonstrate adequate visual sensory abilities. First, the deficits in object perception shown by these cases cannot be interpreted as the trivial consequence of a visual field defect: those studies which have contrasted patients with lesions of the left or right hemisphere have included both right-sided visual field loss as well as left. Nevertheless, they have consistently demonstrated a deficit in the right posterior lesioned group. Secondly, these disorders cannot be explained by impaired sensory efficiency in the intact visual field. In fact all patients with brain lesions tend to have elevated thresholds for detecting a briefly presented stimulus. However, patients with right posterior lesions are not specifically worse as a group on such tasks (Ettlinger, 1956; Warrington & James, 1967b).

In group studies it has been shown that patients with right posterior lesions may perform within the normal range on tests of form discrimination. These tests have included discrimination between lines of different lengths, circles of different sizes, and triangles with straight or curved sides (see Fig. 2.17). At the same time these same patients were markedly impaired on tests of the perception of unconventional views and incomplete pictures (Warrington & Taylor, 1973). This evidence is supported by studies of single cases with markedly impaired performance on tests of object perception. Two cases studied by Humphreys & Riddoch (1984) with severe impairments in recognising objects photographed from an unusual angle were within the normal range on tests of discriminating whether two lines were parallel and in judgments of relative lengths of lines and size of circles. Three further cases studied by Warrington & James (1988) had no difficulty in discriminating between a square and an oblong matched for total flux (the Efron Squares Test, see Fig. 2.1). Warrington & James also showed that these patients were normal in detecting the presence of a degraded "X" presented against a "noise" background despite impairments on the superficially similar task of identifying a single degraded letter (see Figs. 2.4 2.11B). The preservation of stimulus detection in patients with right posterior lesions has been replicated by De Renzi, Bonacini and Faglioni (1989). Further evidence for normal detection and impaired figure identification has been reported in the context of tests of stereopsis (Benton & Hécaen, 1970). These findings considered as a whole indicate that impairments of perceptual analysis are distinguishable from the stage of sensory processing at which shapes are perceived as coherent bounded wholes. There is thus a major discontinuity between visual sensory processing and the processes which are involved in perceiving objects.

Perceptual Processing Warrington and her colleagues have argued that an impairment in recognising unusual-view photographs was attributable to a failure in a postsensory stage of object perception. This stage was considered to be one in which two or more instantiations of a stimulus were categorised as identical. The most direct evidence for

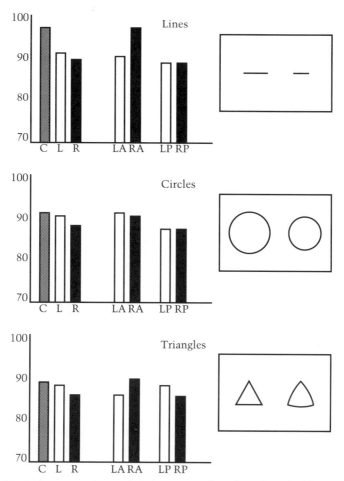

Figure 2.17 Performance of controls (C) patient with unilateral cerebral lesions (L, left; R, right; A, anterior; P, posterior) on three shape-discrimination tests. (Adapted from Taylor & Warrington, 1973.)

this interpretation was derived from a task requiring subjects to match stimuli according to their structural identity (see Fig. 2.18). An unusual view photograph of an object was paired either with a conventional view of the same item or with a visually similar photograph of a different object. The subjects were asked to judge whether the pairs of photographs were of the identical object. Right posterior lesions resulted in a deficit on this simplified structural matching task. These findings ruled out the possibility that the patients' deficit could be attributed to a failure in verbal mediation: they were able to recognise and to name the objects when they saw them from a conventional viewpoint but not when shown from an unconventional one. A similar failure in structural matching has been observed in tasks using buildings and landscapes (Whiteley, cited by Warrington, 1982a).

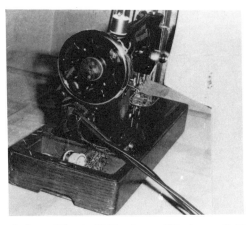

Figure 2.18   Example from "Physical" Match test (Warrington & Taylor, 1978).

Warrington & Taylor (1978) argued that the whole range of deficits in object perception shown by right parietal patients could be encompassed by the concept of impaired perceptual categorisation. Their deficits were thought to implicate an independent stage of processing; namely stored structural knowledge of objects ("structural descriptions," Sutherland, 1973). If this stored knowledge of object structures were damaged, then the perception of objects would be faulty despite adequate processing of sensory information.

In his influential development of this theoretical framework, Marr (1982) termed this level of processing the "3-D Model." He considered it to be based on stored information about the geometry and volume of the object being perceived. How is the 3-D Model derived from the sensory information available to the viewer? Marr emphasised the importance of deriving the major and minor axes of an object. So for example, in recognising the structure of a tennis racket photographed from the side one might use information about the major axis (length) to retrieve information about the geometry and volume of the object such as the width of the handle and head. Marr interpreted the "unusual views" findings in these terms and argued that they were difficult because a major axis had been foreshortened or obscured. The patients were unable to retrieve the necessary information to access a stored "catalogue" of object structures. Humphreys & Riddoch (e.g., 1984, 1987b) concurred. They considered the unusual views deficit observed in their four patients to be a primary deficit in axis transformation, or a "transformational agnosia." A similar argument was made by Layman and Greene (1988) who noted that there was a close relationship between failure on the unusual views task and impairment on a test of mental rotation.

An alternative to the "axes" position has been advanced by Warrington & James (1986). They noted that some unusual views which patients found difficult to perceive did not foreshorten a major axis (e.g., Fig. 2.9). The basic limitation on unusual view photographs is that only two arbitrarily selected viewpoints are sampled, and these may or may not foreshorten a major axis. Warrington & James attempted to specify the properties of an "unusual" view empirically by exploring the function relating an "unusual" to a "usual" viewpoint. They rotated three-dimensional shadow images in a series of steps with a starting point which was 90° to the longest axis of the object. The subjects' task was to identify the object, and thresholds were measured in terms of the angle of rotation which was required for successful recognition. For normal subjects, each of the objects in each of the rotation conditions had its own "fingerprint" or recognition threshold function (see Fig. 2.19). Patients with damage to the posterior right hemisphere had reliably elevated recognition thresholds for all objects, but these followed the same pattern as those observed in the control group: there were no discontinuities between the performance of the controls and the critical lesion group as would be predicted on the "axis transformation" position.

Warrington & James suggested that their data could be explained by a distinctive-features model of object recognition. According to this account, features are mapped onto stored volumetric descriptions of objects, a fully specified percept being achieved when sufficient features have been processed to specify the stimulus and differentiate it from other perceptually similar stimuli. They suggested that "features" can be conceptualised as relatively unique clusters of visual contours (e.g., curvature and angle) and the relative positions of such clusters independent of their absolute orientation in space. Thus sets of distinctive features can directly specify an object's structural identity. At the same time the relative retinal positions of features can be used to specify an object's orientation. In the context of the shadow-rotation experiment the threshold for any single object would depend on the number of critical distinguishing features which became available as the shadow was rotated through a specific angle. Thus each object would have not so much a "usual" view, but rather a "minimal" view.

The evidence of merely quantitative inefficiency in the right-hemisphere group was interpreted in terms of there being a degradation of their "visual vocabulary" such that more distinctive features needed to be in view in order for the object to be recognised. This interpretation

Lateral rotation   Base rotation

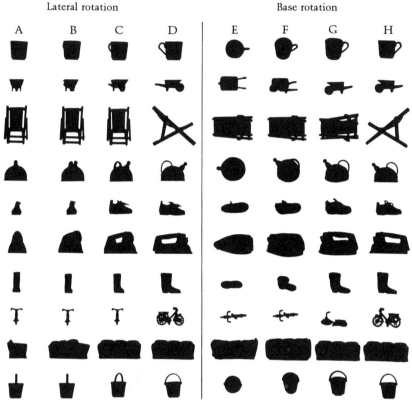

Figure 2.19   Rotated three-dimensional shadow images: projected image of each object (drawn to scale). A & E, initial image; B & F, image of object recognised by 50% of control group; C & G, image of object correctly recognised by 100% of controls; D & H, image of object rotated through 90° (Warrington & James, 1986).

has the advantage of being able to account for the evidence that object-perception deficits can be "triggered" by a number of visual stimuli in which the distinctive features are obscured (overlapping figures, Fig. 2.6), degraded (Gollin figures, Fig. 2.7), or distorted (unusual lighting, Fig. 2.8).

Some Complications   Although the distinctive-feature model can encompass all the postsensory object-perception deficits which are associated with right-hemisphere lesions there is now some tentative evidence that these deficits do not form an entirely homogeneous class. There is some suggestion of dissociations between broad classes of familiar visual stimuli. Whiteley (cited by Warrington, 1982a) assessed 50 consecutive cases with unilateral lesions of the right hemisphere on tests of perceptual categorisation using buildings, objects, landscapes, and letters. He found an unexpectedly high incidence of dissociations in performance between these tasks. It remains to be established whether all of these dissociations can be accounted for in terms of the intrinsic properties of the stimulus (e.g., a two-dimensional letter vs. a solid object) or whether there are dissociable procedures for achieving a structural description depending on the class of object.

In this section a postsensory categorical stage of object perception has been discussed. It has been argued that the product of this stage is a fully specified structural, volumetric description of an object. Is this stage an obligatory one or is it an optional resource that is invoked under those conditions where structure cannot be derived directly from the products of visual sensory analysis? Following Warrington & James (1988), Rudge and Warrington (1990) have argued for the optional resource position. They described a series of patients with lesions of the splenium that all showed deficits on the Unusual Views task but were normal in recognising pictures which were not "perceptually difficult." The splenial disconnection had not caused a visual agnosia, as would be expected in the original serial model proposed by Warrington and Taylor (1978). Their framework was therefore modified to allow for parallel processing routes (see Fig. 2.16). (A related perspective has been put forward by Humphreys, Riddoch, & Quinlan, 1988.) This implies that there are at least two routes to object meaning. One, may proceed directly on the basis of evidence from visual sensory information processing. The second, involving the right hemisphere and splenium, may only be required when the analysis of object structures results in ambiguity or contextual implausibility.

Disorders of Object Meaning (Associative Agnosia)

Knowledge of an object cannot be said to be fully established unless its meaning or functional significance can be computed. In the previous section one discontinuity in the process of object recognition was discussed, namely the distinction between visual sensory processing and perceptual processing in which objects are recognised in terms of their structural and volumetric properties. Failure to assign meaning to an adequately structured percept implicates a second major discontinuity in object recognition. In this section the evidence for this distinction will be discussed together with a consideration of its anatomical basis. This will be followed by a consideration of the properties of this level of analysis and its relationship to other systems.

Relationship to Sensory and Perceptual Processing Ever since Lissauer's classical account of the syndrome of associative agnosia a major criterion for the diagnosis of impairment at this stage of processing has been that the patient should show intact visual sensory abilities. Failure on tasks dependent on visual semantic processing also dissociates from failure in visual perceptual processing. De Renzi and his colleagues (De Renzi *et al.*, 1969) found that there was a double dissociation between failure on a test requiring visually presented objects to be matched in terms of their function and failure on a test of perceptual processing (overlapping figures, Fig. 2.6). Patients with lesions in the left hemisphere were impaired on the former but not the latter. Patients with right-hemisphere lesions showed the converse pattern of deficit. These findings were corroborated in a group study by Warrington & Taylor (1978). In studies of single cases there has also been evidence of a dissociation between these stages of processing. Patients with impaired knowledge of object meaning may show equivalent levels of performance with real objects as with visually complex scenes, and they may be capable of performing perceptual matching tasks or overlapping figures tasks (e.g., Rubens & Benson, 1971; Hécaen, et al., 1974; Warrington, 1975; McCarthy & Warrington, 1986a). Remarkably, face recognition may also be relatively preserved in patients with visual associative agnosia (Hécaen et al., 1974; Albert, Reches, & Silverberg, 1975b; Ferro and Santos, 1984; McCarthy and Warrington, 1986a; see Chapter 3.)

The evidence both from group studies and from the investigation of single cases therefore indicates that visual associative agnosia may implicate impairment at a distinct and dissociable stage in the process of visual *object* recognition. The patients' impairments cannot be reduced to a more or less severe deficit in sensory or perceptual processing since these abilities may be disproportionately well preserved. Rather, it appears to implicate a system which permits the derivation of object meaning.

The findings that there is a clear cerebral asymmetry in the systems which are implicated in impairments of object meaning are in direct conflict with the commonly expressed view that the cerebral hemispheres are equipotential with regard to their capacity for processing visual material. This is perhaps most clearly expressed in the context of discussion of patients with section of the cerebral commissures, the so-called "split-brain" patients (see Chapter 1). The object and picture recognition abilities of the two cerebral hemispheres in these patients have been investigated using lateralised presentation: because the major cerebral commissures (corpus callosum, splenium, anterior commissure) have been divided there is no corticocortical route for cerebral communication in these patients. The assumption that input/processing is therefore restricted to one hemisphere has been questioned (e.g. Sergent, 1987; Rudge & Warrington, 1990). In a series of investigations using lateralised tachistoscopic presentation to either the right or the left visual field, Sperry and his co-workers found no differences between the patients' right or left hemispheres in terms of their capacity to recognise objects (e.g., Sperry, Gazzaniga, & Bogen, 1969). The fundamental difference appeared to be in the left hemisphere's capacity to express the visual knowledge in verbal form. However, these patients are by no means directly comparable neurologically with unilaterally lesioned cases. They have all had long-standing epileptic disorders, often on the basis of early brain damage, and thus the functional organisation of a brain which has been damaged in early childhood is not comparable to that of the majority of the population (Rasmussen &

Milner, 1977; see also Chapter 1, Table 1.4). The conflict of evidence is therefore more apparent than real; whilst some of the split-brain patients may have bilateral representation of visual object recognition systems this parallels the high incidence of bilateral language representation in individuals with early brain damage. As with language, the evidence from patients with lesions acquired in adulthood indicates that there is a fundamental cerebral asymmetry in object recognition.

Disconnection Hypothesis   The classical neurological account of the syndrome of visual associative agnosia was quite explicit. The disconnection position took as its starting point the asymmetry between the cerebral hemispheres in verbal function. Failure to recognise visually presented objects was viewed as an impairment of communication between visual processing systems in the right hemisphere and verbal processing systems in the left. Many patients with impaired object recognition do have damage which involves a transmission tract which links the visual areas of the two cerebral hemispheres: the splenium of the corpus callosum. If visual input is confined to the right hemisphere and can not be sent to the left hemisphere, then the patient should manifest a failure of object recognition (see page 53).

This interpretation may be appropriate in some cases. Albert *et al.* (1975b) investigated their patient's ability to recognise objects presented either to the intact left visual field or to the intact quadrant of the right visual field. They found that, although the patient was impaired in free vision, he was significantly worse with presentation of stimuli to the left visual field/right hemisphere. They concluded that the visual-field asymmetry could be accounted for in terms of a classical disconnection syndrome. However, in addition, they argued that the patient must have had a second deficit within the left hemisphere since he had significant difficulties when stimuli were presented so that he could make use of the "intact" areas of his right visual field.

Although the disconnection interpretation is probably adequate for some patterns of deficit, it is by no means a complete account of disorders of object meaning. First, this theory is dependent on the patient showing a primary visual deficit which is sufficient to prevent any information from being received directly by the left hemisphere—a homonymous hemianopia. Whilst many cases do show hemianopic deficits these are not necessarily complete and may be confined to one quadrant of the visual field (Albert *et al.*, 1975b). In other cases with a disproportionate impairment of visual object recognition (albeit in the context of some language deficits) the visual fields may actually be full (Taylor & Warrington, 1971; Warrington, 1975). Second, damage to the splenium is not necessary for the deficit to occur (McCarthy & Warrington, 1986a).

Modality-Specific Meaning Systems?   There are two main theoretical positions. The most widely held is the shared-system account, which proposes that there is a single all-purpose meaning system (common to objects, words, and other meaningful stimuli). The alternative is that there is a separate meaning system which is specialised for visual object recognition.

The shared-system account is broadly similar to the disconnection model, although it makes no reference to anatomical substrates. Specifically it is held that associative agnosia is a failure in linking the output of the perceptual analysis stage of object recognition with a more general-purpose knowledge base. One such model suggests that this involves damage to a transmission route which connects the perceptual & semantic knowledge domains (Riddoch, Humphreys, Coltheart and Funnell, 1988). Somewhat more elaborate accounts incorporate "interfaces" or "object recognition units" within this transmission route (Ratcliffe & Newcombe, 1982; Ellis & Young, 1988). Disorders which disproportionately affect one class of material, leaving others intact, would not be anticipated on this framework. Indeed, this evidence is also highly problematic for the anatomical variant of the disconnection hypothesis. As was discussed in the empirical section (p. 37), there is evidence of multiple and reciprocal category-specific dissociations in the domain of visual object recognition. The behavioural disconnection or single-meaning-system account needs to make numerous ad hoc assumptions to incorporate such evidence (e.g., Humphreys, Riddoch, & Quinlan, 1988; Riddoch & Humphreys, 1987b).

The independent-system account considers visual object recognition as being relatively self-contained. It is held to consist of a body of knowledge which differs from that which is needed for verbal comprehension. Thus the ability to recognise a visually presented glass may use a different knowledge base from that which is used in understanding the meaning of the spoken word "glass."

Whilst at first sight it may seem implausible to postulate a separate knowledge base for the two modalities, there are a number of examples which can be drawn from everyday life which make the development of such independent systems a plausible way for the brain to be organised. Children recognise and use objects long before they know their names, and adults show considerable skill in dealing with objects, and components of objects, even when the verbal label would be meaningless (e.g., the "squirting thing" on top of an aerosol can). Many tasks involve the simultaneous processing of visual and verbal information but are relatively effortless. Were a common system implicated these "dual tasks" of everyday life would almost certainly interfere with each other. However, when one is driving a car, a conversation with the passenger is not peppered with involuntary intrusion errors based on the visual obstacles in the scene.

The neuropsychological evidence for independent (or at least partially independent) meaning systems is as follows. First, impairment in visual knowledge is not necessarily paralleled by comparable impairments in the verbal domain. Conversely, severe impairments of verbal knowledge may occur without similar impairments in deriving the meaning from visually presented material (Warrington, 1975; McCarthy

& Warrington, 1988, see also Chapter 6). Performance can be entirely normal in one modality but severely defective in the other. Since this is a double dissociation it is difficult to argue that either of the domains of visual knowledge or auditory comprehension is parasitic upon the other.

Second, patients with impairments within the visual domain may show partial knowledge of objects they "fail" to recognise. One (unpublished) case (S.T.U.), when being asked to recognise a cup, vehemently stated, "No, not another —— household object, I don't recognise those!" More formal documentation has shown that such patients have sensitivity to broad-class semantic information (i.e., animal/ object, bird/insect). At the same time they may be unable to discriminate more specific attributes of the stimuli (English/foreign; dangerous/tame). (see page 37) In this regard it is worth noting that the attribute of colour often appears to be the most vulnerable—a deficit which has sometimes been equated with colour agnosia (Lhermitte, Chain, Aron, Le Blanc, & Soaty, 1969). The phenomena of partial knowledge have been interpreted in terms of an impairment within the meaning system itself rather than in transmission to it. When such deficits are confined to the visual domain they provide evidence which is at the very least consistent with the multiple-systems view.

Third, and potentially the strongest evidence for multiple systems, is the observation that disorders can be modality specific, show partial knowledge effects, *and* be specific to a particular semantic category. For example, impairments may affect the ability to recognise common real objects but spare recognition of more complex pictorial material (such as visual representations of abstract concepts, actions, or occupations and faces). Taken as a whole, the evidence is more adequately encompassed within a framework which postulates an independent, or at least partially independent, knowledge base which is specialised for visual object recognition: visual semantics. (These issues are discussed in more detail in the context of verbal semantic knowledge in Chapter 6.)

Conclusion

The understanding of visual object recognition has clearly progressed considerably from the vaguely stated hypotheses of Lissauer and Freud. It is now clear that at least three distinct processing stages are required for recognising objects (see Fig. 2.16). Objects have to be analysed for their visual sensory properties. There is no lateralisation of function at this level of processing, rather, information is represented retinotopically. The next stage of object recognition which is likely to be optional, lateralised to the right hemisphere, derives a fully specified structural description of the object. The third stage, lateralised to the left hemisphere, assigns meaning to a percept. Whether *all* forms of object recognition require the participation of all three stages remains a viable empirical question.

3

Face Recognition

Introduction

The ability to process the visual information conveyed by the human face is an important skill in many of our normal social interactions. Although the nonverbal cues provided by voice, posture, gait, and dress are useful, those conveyed by faces are uniquely important. For example, by looking at a face we can immediately determine the identity or "familiarity" of an individual; moreover, by attending to changes in facial expression and the lip movements used in speech one is provided with information which goes beyond mere "recognition."

There were only sporadic accounts of patients who were impaired in processing the information conveyed by faces in the early neurological literature (e.g., Charcot, 1883; Willbrand, 1887). These patients were described as having lost the ability to recognise faces (including their own). However, their difficulties with faces occurred in the context of other more pervasive visual impairments, including gross deficits in object recognition. For these reasons, their impairment in facial recognition was simply considered to be a manifestation of a severe visual agnosia (see Chapter 2). However, Bodamer (1947) reported on a small series of patients who had a disproportionate impairment in recognising faces, with relative preservation of the ability to recognise objects. He coined the term *prosopagnosia* (meaning "loss of knowledge of faces") in order to designate their deficit. He considered it to be a distinct neurological syndrome characterised by an inability to appreciate the "visual category, the most profound and genetically the most primitive in our perception", namely faces.

Empirical Characteristics

In a clinically extreme form, prosopagnosia can be very dramatic. Hécaen & Angelergues (1962) reported clinical descriptions of the remarkably large number of 22 cases of prosopagnosia. One patient describing his difficulties stated, "I can tell the difference between a man and a woman from across the street, but I failed to recognise the face of an old friend and I mistook my mother for my wife." Another patient commented when shown his wedding picture, "Two people . . . one of them could be my wife because of the silhouette . . . if it is my wife, the other person could be me." Patients with a clinically severe prosopagnosia may fail to recognise even the most salient and familiar faces (even their own). Their identification of other people may be dependent on cues from their dress or from the characteristics of the speaker's voice.

As with many neurological and neuropsychological syndrome groupings, prosopagnosia does not appear to be a unitary deficit. At least three broad subtypes can be identified: impaired visual analysis of faces, impaired perception of faces, and impaired recognition of individual faces. In the first two types of disorder, the deficit affects the patient's ability to derive adequate information from the visual stimulus, a face. In the third, the ability to recognise a face as being familiar, or of a specific individual, is compromised. These disorders have been studied both in individual cases with clinically pronounced prosopagnosia and in series of patients with known brain lesions.

Visual Analysis of Faces

It is almost a truism to state that faces are extremely complex three-dimensional visual stimuli. For example, in perceiving similarities and differences between faces it is often insufficient to rely on "simple" differences in features (e.g., size of nose, fullness of mouth) unless the faces concerned are very dissimilar. In addition, the relative positions of features (height of forehead, closeness of eyes) and their position within the overall three-dimensional configuration of the face may need to be taken into account.

Impairment in the visual analysis of faces can be very severe. In patients with visual sensory impairments, such as impaired shape discrimination (see Chapter 2), face perception may be all but impossible even though the patient's visual acuity may be normal (Efron, 1968; Warrington, 1986). The most detailed popular description of one such case was provided by Sacks (1985) in his description of Dr. P., "The Man Who Mistook His Wife for a Hat." Another case (J.A.F., described in more detail in Chapter 2) complained specifically of difficulties with recognising faces (Warrington, 1986). Her acuity was sufficient for her to read small print, however, she could not recognise herself in a mirror and commented that her reflection did not look like a face. On testing she was found to have a marked impairment in visual shape discrimination (see Fig. 2.2). Her difficulty in the visual analysis of faces could therefore be attributed to a more fundamental disorder of visual sensory discrimination. In cases like this with a primary visual sensory loss, face-processing abilities may appear to be disproportionately bad because of the "difficulty" of this visual task. In such cases, it is a debatable point as to whether their deficit should be considered as a primary prosopagnosia. It seems more reasonable to consider the deficit as a secondary effect of impaired visual sensory processing.

In some cases impaired visual analysis of faces takes the form of the patient's experiencing both familiar and unfamiliar faces as being warped, or distorted. The precise characteristics of the distortion appear to vary somewhat from case to case. A patient from Bodamer's series (case 1) described faces as appearing "strangely flat, white with dark eyes as if in one plane, like white oval plates." One of Hécaen & Angelergues' (1962) patients stated, "faces don't look normal anymore, they are quite distorted and contorted like some sketches of Picasso." Another patient (W.G.), reported by Whiteley & Warrington (1977), described faces as appearing "like fish heads." Metamorphopsias may be entirely restricted to faces; comparable distortions are not necessarily experienced with other complex visual stimuli such as objects or pictures. Metamorphopsias may also be confined to real faces, with photographs of faces being unaffected. A patient of Hécaen, Angelergues, Bernhard, & Chiarelli (1957) had no difficulty with photographs "because of the immobility of the features." Remarkably, in some cases of facial metamorphopsia, the ability to recognise familiar faces may be relatively preserved despite the visual distortion experienced by the patient (Bodamer, 1947; Hécaen & Angelergues, 1962).

Perceptual Analysis of Faces

Group studies of patients with known cerebral lesions have used a variety of tests requiring the perceptual analysis of faces. These tasks have typically used photographs of people who are unknown to the patient in order to emphasise the visuoperceptual aspects of the task. De Renzi, Faglioni, & Spinnler (1968) and De Renzi, Scotti, & Spinnler (1969) identified a comparatively high incidence of impaired perceptual analysis of faces in a same–different matching task (see Fig. 3.1).

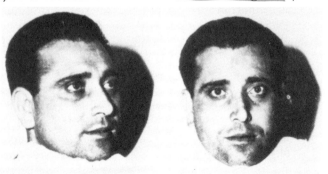

Figure 3.1 Example of stimuli from same–different matching test (De Renzi *et al.*, 1969).

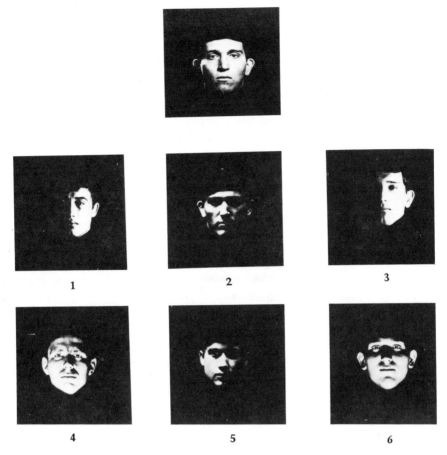

Figure 3.2 Example of stimuli from Benton's face-matching test (Benton & Van Allen, 1968).

Their stimuli consisted of pairs of photographs which showed either two different views of the same person or photographs of two different (but similar looking) people. The subject's task was to determine whether the photographs were of the same individual. So that the subject would focus on face information, the stimuli showed clean-shaven people without glasses and with their neckline covered with a concealing white cloth. Comparable same-different matching tasks have been widely used (e.g., Tzavaras, Hécaen, & Le Bras, 1970; Whiteley & Warrington, 1977; Warrington, 1982a). In a development of this technique, Benton & Van Allen (1968) developed a test which required subjects to match a front view of a stimulus face with an array of six faces. The targets in the array showed (1) three-quarter views of the same face, (2) the same face under different lighting conditions, and (3) an identical photograph (see Fig. 3.2). De Renzi, Bonacini, & Faglioni (1989) have developed another stringent and highly sensitive test of face perception in which the subject has to rank quadruplets of faces according to their age. De Renzi (1986a) reported that a single case with a marked prosopagnosia was also impaired on this test.

Studies of face matching have shown that difficulties in the perceptual analysis of faces are relatively common in patients with cerebral lesions. Some patients with a clinically severe prosopagnosia have difficulty with this type of task. Indeed the same-different matching of faces has almost become the definitive test for a deficit in face perception (e.g., Whiteley & Warrington, 1977; Malone, Morris, Kay, & Levin, 1982; Newcombe, Young, & De Haan, 1989; De Renzi, 1986b). As an aside, it should be noted that in the absence of time constraints even severely impaired patients may "clamber through" matching tests of face perception by using a feature-by-feature strategy (matching hairlines, eyebrows, etc.).

Another task requiring the perceptual analysis of faces was developed by Newcombe (1969). She asked subjects to judge the orientation of the profile and the sex of a schematically drawn face and found a comparatively high incidence of impairment on this task in patients with cerebral lesions. Two patients with a clinically pronounced prosopagnosia were also impaired on this test.

Facial Features   Bodamer suggested that mild cases of prosopagnosia might show sparing of their perceptual analysis of the region around the eyes, an area he termed the "occula." Gloning & Quatember (1966) used a face-fragment matching task to explore this possibility. They asked two patients with clinically pronounced prosopagnosia to match fragments of faces containing the eye region or the mouth region to whole-face pictures of unfamiliar people. They found that their patients were relatively *more* impaired on the "eye" matching task, findings which appear to contradict Bodamer's hypothesis. De Renzi, Faglioni, & Spinnler (1968) used a comparable task and compared eye, mouth, and half-face conditions both in a group study of patients with cerebral lesions and in a single case of prosopagnosia. They found no difference between eye and mouth fragments and the half-face condition was relatively more difficult for patients. The prosopagnosic case was impaired on all three tasks. There is therefore no support for Bodamer's hypothesis that specific facial regions are differentially affected in prosopagnosia.

Facial Expressions   Facial expressions are an important visual cue in normal communication. There are some pointers to suggest that the ability to interpret expressions may be relatively selectively impaired. Bornstein (1963) reported two cases who had made a partial recovery from prosopagnosia. These patients however, complained of a persisting difficulty in recognising the expressions on faces. One patient complained, "It is clear that I have lost the ability to read a person's facial expression. This is apparent in situations such as seeing a film in which everyone can easily understand what is taking place from the facial expression."

De Kosky, Heilman, Bowers, & Valenstein (1980) conducted a group study in which the ability to match faces with a neutral expression was compared with matching of faces with emotional expressions. Although three subjects were impaired on both tasks, three further cases were most impaired on matching faces for their emotional expressions. Etkoff (1984) reported a double dissociation between patients' ability to discriminate facial identity and facial emotion. The patients were required to classify pictures into those which showed the same person or the same emotion (see Fig. 3.3). Two patients were selectively impaired on facial identity, and two on facial emotions. Etkoff commented that patients with difficulty in discriminating emotions adopted a feature-searching strategy when attempting to perform the task (e.g., whether the teeth were showing or whether a dimple was present).

The ability to interpret lip movements in a lip-reading task may dissociate from the interpretation of facial expressions. Campbell, Landis, & Regard (1986) studied one patient (D.) who was unable to identify the emotional expressions conveyed by faces. Remarkably,

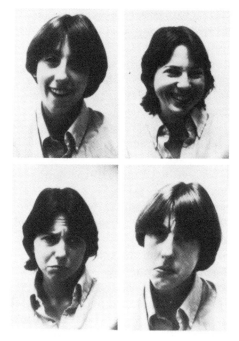

Figure 3.3 Example of stimuli for matching by expression and by identity (Etkoff, 1984).

Campbell *et al.* were able to establish that she retained the ability to lip-read. For normal people, the information provided by lip movements provides information which can disambiguate the sounds of language. McGurk & MacDonald (1976) have shown that if normal subjects are shown the lip movements appropriate to the sound "ba" and are presented with the sound "ga," they are strongly influenced by the visual information and have the illusion of hearing "da." The prosopagnosic patient studied by Campbell *et al.* showed the normal illusion on this task, indicating that her lip reading was intact. She could also perform at a normal level in lip reading the sound being made on a silent film.

Visual Recognition of Faces

Patients may be impaired in recognising familiar faces despite normal performance on tests of facial perception. In a group study, Warrington & James (1967c) showed that patients had difficulty in recognising photographs of well-known people. The test consisted of portraits of 10 of the most famous figures of the time (1963–64) and included people such as Marilyn Monroe, General DeGaulle, John F. Kennedy, and Winston Churchill. Apart from errors of naming (common in aphasic subjects) some patients totally failed to recognise the individuals or misidentified them.

The selective impairment of familiar face recognition with normal levels of performance on tests of face matching has also been documented in a number of single cases (e.g., Rondot & Tzavaras, 1969; Tzavaras, Hécaen & Le Bras, 1970; Benton & Van Allen, 1972). De Renzi (1986a,b) described the case of a 73-year-old public notary who had a profound impairment in recognising the most familiar faces: "If his wife, daughter, or secretaries approached him without speaking, he gave no evidence of recognition. He spent many hours with his doctor and with a psychologist (both females), but never succeeded in recognising them, or in pointing to them when they were shown to him along with other female doctors or medical students" (De Renzi, 1986a, p. 385). Even after 12 months the deficit was still pronounced. Once he asked his wife, "Are you . . . ? I guess you are my wife because there are no other women at home, but I want to be reassured." Despite these profound impairments in face recognition, the patient was considered to have normal or near normal performance on stringent tests of face perception.

One aspect of visual memory for faces which has received considerable attention is the relative sparing of "implicit" knowledge of faces. The patient (W.) described by Bruyer, Laterre, Seron, Feyereisen, Strypstein, Pierrard, & Rectem (1983) was impaired on recognising all but the most familiar faces. Despite this deficit, he was able to learn to associate names with faces that he initially failed to recognise. When he was given a "false" name to learn to associate with a face, he was much slower in learning the association. Bruyer *et al.* interpreted these findings in terms of implicit or unconscious knowledge of faces that the patient was unable to recognise overtly. Comparable findings have been reported by De Haan, Young, & Newcombe (1987a,b).

The phenomenon of covert or implicit recognition of faces in prosopagnosia has also been demonstrated using electrodermal responses. Bauer (1984) used the "guilty knowledge" test (based on changes in skin conductance) in order to evaluate covert recognition of faces. The patient (P.K.) was unable to overtly recognise any familiar face and scored at chance when matching a spoken name to a face. He was presented with a picture of a face, together with a list of spoken names. Bauer found that the patient showed an increase in skin conductance to over half of the "correct" face/name pairings. Similar findings have been reported by Tranel & Damasio (1985).

Delayed Matching   Delayed matching of unknown faces was initially introduced as a potentially sensitive measure of face perception (De Renzi & Spinnler, 1966). In this task the subject is presented with a photograph of an unknown face to study for a few seconds and almost immediately afterward is asked to find an identical photograph of the face in an array of photographs of faces. De Renzi & Spinnler found that some patients were clearly impaired on this task, a finding which was replicated by Warrington & James (1967c). An alternative technique has been to present the subject with an array of faces to be memorised for a few seconds. The target faces must then be selected from a larger array (Milner, 1968). Whilst these delayed matching tasks detect impairments in a substantial number of patients, it is unclear whether failure in the individual case is due to poor retention of faces or to poor perceptual analysis. Bruyer *et al.* (1983) described a case who scored normally on tests of the perceptual analysis of faces but who was impaired on tests of face memory and on a variant of the Milner delayed-matching task. The patient (Mr. W.) was only able to score at chance, regardless of whether the faces were of people he knew or of strangers.

Tests of the acquisition and retention of new (i.e., previously unknown) faces have been extensively employed in studies of material-specific memory disorders and will be discussed in Chapter 15.

Anatomical Considerations

Hécaen and his colleagues emphasised the importance of right-hemisphere lesions in giving rise to prosopagnosia (e.g., Hécaen & Angelergues, 1962). They noted that there was a positive association between impairment on face recognition and other symptoms of right-hemisphere disease. There was no correlation between impairment of face recognition and those disorders of language, calculation, and voluntary action (apraxia) which were associated with left-hemisphere damage. In reviewing these findings Hécaen & Albert (1978) concluded that "disorders of visual recognition of human faces constitute a specific neuropsychological deficit linked to right hemispheric lesions."

Whilst there is no controversy that damage to the posterior right hemisphere is *necessary* for these deficits to occur, the question remains as to whether they are *sufficient*. Damasio, Damasio, & Van Hoesen (1982) have argued that there is evidence of bilateral cerebral damage in all eleven of those cases of clinically severe prosopagnosia who have come to autopsy. On the basis of this evidence they have concluded that a unilateral lesion of the right hemisphere is, by itself, insufficient for prosopagnosia. This position was reiterated by Damasio and Damasio (1986) in a review including one further case.

There are a number of questions which remain with regard to this issue. First, although the patients reviewed by Damasio and his colleagues have shown bilateral brain damage, it is not necessarily symmetrical. Although a posterior right-hemisphere lesion is common to all cases, associated damage to the left hemisphere is not consistently located (Benton, 1985). Second, although all of the 12 autopsy cases reviewed by Damasio *et al.*, had bilateral damage, patients whose lesions have been verified surgically or radiologically suggest a very different account. According to De Renzi (1986b) there are six cases of prosopagnosia with surgical evidence of a unilateral lesion (Hécaen & Angelergues, 1962; Assal, 1969; Meadows, 1974; Lhermitte & Pillon, 1975; Whiteley & Warrington, 1978). Computerised tomography (CT) scan evidence has also indicated that a unilateral right-hemisphere lesion may be sufficient for a clinically significant prosopagnosia. Whiteley & Warrington (1977) described one case and De Renzi (1982) described two more, each with damage to the posterior regions of the right hemisphere. Subsequently Landis, Cummings, Christen, Bogen & Imhof (1986) described no less than six patients with persistent prosopagnosia arising from unilateral right-hemisphere lesions; Torii & Tamai (1985) describe three and Tiberghen & Le Clerc (1986) another single case. Third, group studies investigating perception and/or memory of faces have been highly consistent in showing a deficit in patients with unilateral lesions of the posterior right hemisphere (e.g., De Renzi & Spinnler, 1966; Benton & Van Allen, 1968; Warrington & James, 1967c; Newcombe, 1969; Tzavaras *et al.*, 1970). Those studies focusing on the perception and recognition of facial expressions have also shown marked deficits in patients with unilateral lesions of the right hemisphere (e.g., De Kosky *et al.*, 1980; Bowers, Bauer, Coslett, & Heilman, 1985).

Although bilateral lesions have been present in the limited number of cases who have come to autopsy, there are good grounds for concluding that the minimal sufficient lesion may be unilateral. As Nielsen (1937) stated when considering the anatomical locus of visual recognition deficits: "It is clear that if in any case a unilateral lesion produced (the syndrome), there can be no point in citing cases of bilateral lesions."

Localisation within the Right Hemisphere

Meadows (1974b) reviewed all cases of prosopagnosia for whom clinical or anatomical evidence was available and added a single case study of his own. He noted that there was a very high incidence (33 of 34 cases) of visual-field defects affecting the left upper quadrant. Since this type of visual-field deficit usually results from damage at the occipitotemporal boundary of the right hemisphere, Meadows inferred that lesions in the region of the parahippocampal gyrus and lingual and fusiform gyri were critical. Similar loci have been identified by De Renzi (1986a & b), however both he and Benton (1985) have suggested that damage to the splenium may also be necessary (see Fig. 3.4).

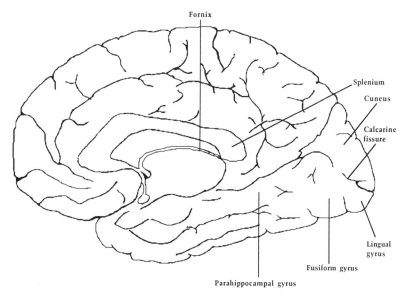

Figure 3.4 Schematic diagram showing critical structures implicated in prosopagnosia.

The majority of single case studies of the anatomical correlates of prosopagnosia have tended to consider the syndrome as a unitary deficit. In those cases of visual sensory loss in whom the visual analysis of faces appears to be particularly impaired, bilateral occipital lobe lesions have been identified (Efron, 1968; Warrington, 1986). In single cases with impaired perceptual analysis or impaired memory for faces, the anatomical correlates have yet to be differentiated. In discussing the CT evidence from one case with a primary impairment in face memory, De Renzi (1986a) stated that the patient's lesion involved "the entire territory of the distribution of the cortical branches of the right posterior cerebral artery. It encompassed the para-hippocampal gyrus, the lingual and fusiform gyri, both lips of the calcarine fissure, the cuneus. The splenium of the corpus callosum was also involved" (p. 386). A patient with a profound impairment in face perception had an infarct "which almost exactly replicated" this lesion. Evidence from one group study indicated that there was a high incidence of misrecognition for familiar faces following damage to the right temporal lobe. Impairment on the delayed-matching test for faces was associated with lesions in more posterior (parietal and occipital) regions (Warrington & James, 1967c). (For further discussion of memory for faces see Chapter 15.)

Theoretical Considerations

Two major theoretical issues will be considered in this section. First, whether prosopagnosia should be considered as a specific disorder: are faces really special? Second, the implications of disorders of face recognition for models of normal face processing will be discussed.

Specificity of Face-Processing Disorders

In defining the syndrome of prosopagnosia Bodamer (1947) postulated that this was a specific type of recognition disorder in which a specific (innate) mechanism concerned with faces was disrupted. The evidence for and against the specificity of the perceptual analysis of faces and visual face recognition will be considered separately.

Perceptual Analysis of Faces Faust (1955) argued that the core disorder in prosopagnosia was not specific to faces. Rather, it affected those classes of visual stimuli for which fine-grain discriminations had to be made in order to differentiate individual items. He worked with a patient who, in addition to a severe prosopagnosia, showed a deficit in discriminating between different types of chairs. De Renzi and Spinnler (1966) explored this hypothesis in a group study. They found that right-hemisphere-lesioned subjects were generally impaired on a test

of face discrimination and on a test of nonsense figure discrimination. They concluded that faces were not special, but rather that the patients' deficits on these tasks reflected a more general deficit in "processing of complex sense data."

The problem of the selectivity of impaired perceptual analysis of faces has also been explored in single case studies. Patients have been described with impairments in discriminating between items within other "visually similar" categories (and therefore "matched" for difficulty). These have included buildings (Cole & Perez-Cruet, 1964), chairs (De Renzi & Spinnler, 1966), flowers, and makes of car (Newcombe, 1979). These additional deficits have often been considered as evidence for there being an intrinsic continuum of task difficulty. This interpretation denies any special status for faces.

These examples of associated deficits lose some of their force in the context of evidence for fractionation. Whiteley & Warrington (1977) showed that there was no relationship between scores on stringent tests of visual perception and performance on tests of face perception in two cases with a marked prosopagnosia (see above). There is also evidence from group studies which argue for the selectivity of disorders of face perception. Tzavaras et al. (1970) investigated subjects' ability to match photographs of faces shown from different angles and with false beards, caps, and glasses. Performance on this task was contrasted with pictures of cups, cathedrals, and meaningless line drawings. They found no correlation between performance on the faces test and scores on the other perceptually "confusable" tasks.

The overall evidence is broadly consistent with the hypothesis that the perceptual analysis of faces may, at some level, dissociate from the perceptual analysis of other "confusable" stimuli. However, it is fair to say that this dissociation has yet to be conclusively established.

Visual Recognition of Faces   Visual recognition of known people is differentiated from impairments in the perceptual analysis of face stimuli (whether known or unknown premorbidly). Patients are on record for whom the deficit in recognising even the most familiar faces can be attributed to a failure in face recognition rather than to difficulties with face perception. How selective are deficits in face recognition? That is, are there patients who have a selective deficit in the recognition of faces with recognition of other classes of visual stimuli being normal? The evidence for the selectivity of this impairment is largely based on single case studies of patients with pronounced prosopagnosia or object agnosia.

Damasio et al. (1982) placed considerable emphasis on associations between impairments in face recognition and impaired recognition of other visually confusable stimuli. In support of their argument they cited the patients reported by Bornstein, Sroka, & Munitz (1969). One patient was a bird watcher who lost the ability to recognise different species of birds as well as failing to recognise faces. The second case was a farmer who had lost the ability to recognise his cows as well as his friends and members of his family. Although patients with impaired face recognition can often recognise common objects, Damasio *et al.* (1982) pointed out that the task of recognising a face as "belonging" to a specific individual was very different from that of recognising, for example, a vehicle as a "car" or an item of clothing as "shoes." In the first instance it would be necessary to recognise a specific face and differentiate it from other faces which were relatively similar (roughly oval shape, similar eyes, nose, mouth, etc.). In the case of object recognition, the comparable task would require the subject to be able to recognise a specific car (such as their own) or a specific item of personal clothing rather than the stimulus class per se.

Damasio *et al.* (1982) studied three cases who showed deficits in recognising, or identifying different species of cats, visually similar symbols ($, &), and articles of clothing. They contended that "the notion that prosopagnosia is limited to agnosia for human faces proved easily falsifiable" (p. 338). Rather the deficit should be thought of as "the result of a defective contextual evocation for stimuli belonging to a visually 'ambiguous' category" (p. 338).

However, there is growing evidence of dissociations between face recognition and the ability to recognise specific individual items drawn from other categories of ambiguous or confusable stimuli. Assal, Faure, & Anderes (1984), for example, reported a farmer (M.X.) who lost the ability to recognise his cows ("zooagnosie") but recovered the ability to recognise members of his family and the faces of celebrities. (The selective sparing of cows with impairment of face recognition was reported by Bruyer *et al.*, 1983). Further evidence for a clear dissociation between recognition of faces and other confusable stimuli was provided by De Renzi (1986b). He described a prosopagnosic patient (case 4) who was unable to recognise even highly familiar people including members of his family. Nevertheless, it was established quantitatively that he had no difficulty in recognising his own car or in recognising his own clothing and personal possessions when they were placed with other similar items of the same type.

It seems most unlikely that these dissociations can be simply discounted in terms of the relative vulnerability of faces, with object recognition being spared in mildly affected cases. Hécaen, Goldblum, Masure, & Ramier (1974) described a patient with grave impairment of object recognition but preserved recognition of faces. A similar dissociation was reported by Ferro & Santos (1984) and by McCarthy & Warrington (1986a).

Recognition of familiar faces can be either selectively spared or selectively impaired. At this level of processing, the evidence is clearly in favour of the position that "faces are special." Whilst some cases may show complex associated deficits, these are most plausibly interpreted as the consequence of more extensive cerebral dysfunction. Why are faces special? Bodamer suggested that the human brain is genetically predisposed for processing this class of material. However, Meadows (1974b) suggested that "we might acquire the same perceptual skill in relation to the configuration of one tree relative to the next, if tree configuration were as major a determinant of behaviour as faces." The evidence of "zooagnosie" provided by Assal *et al.* (1984) would appear consistent with this position.

Models of Face Processing

Bruce & Young (1986) developed an "information-processing" model of face recognition which incorporates much of the evidence from neuro-psychological and normal studies of face processing (see Fig. 3.5). Their model distinguishes several different components in the complex skill of facial processing. Following the visual analysis of a face (structural encoding) several subprocesses can be conducted in parallel. Matching of faces for sameness or difference across viewpoints (directed visual processing) is distinguished from facial speech analysis (lip reading), and expression analysis. These procedures are distinguished from face recognition ("face recognition units"). The parallel organisation of this

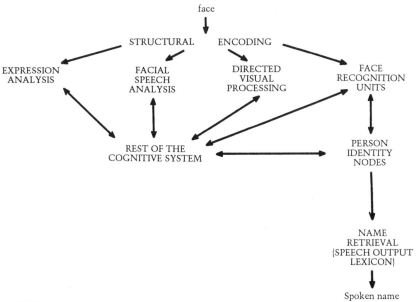

Figure 3.5 Bruce & Young's (1986) information-processing model of face recognition (From Ellis & Young, 1987.)

model is necessary in order to encompass the range of dissociations in face-processing skills which are seen in patients.

Bruce and Young (1986) suggested that there were established "template" representations of familiar faces. These are linked with specialised memory systems which allow precise identification of a person (person identity nodes). Bruce & Young summarised their model thus: "Recognition of familiar faces involves a match between the products of structural encoding and previously stored structural codes describing the appearance of familiar faces held in face recognition units. Identity specific semantic codes are then accessed from person identity codes" (Bruce & Young, 1986, p. 305).

A major aspect of the Bruce & Young model is that the relationship between performance on tests requiring subjects to perceive and analyse unfamiliar faces and to recognise familiar faces depends on different parallel processing systems. This somewhat counterintuitive analysis is supported by neuropsychological data. In a group study of patients with cerebral lesions Warrington & James (1967c) showed that there was only a very weak relationship between patients' performance on a delayed-matching test using unfamiliar faces and the ability to recognise the faces of famous personalities. Not only could delayed matching of unfamiliar faces be spared in patients with impaired recognition of famous faces, but a number of those patients who *failed* the matching task could recognise familiar faces. This double dissociation has since been replicated and extended in two single cases studied by Malone *et al.* (1982). They found that a patient who was impaired on the perceptual matching task developed by Benton & Van Allen (1968; see Fig. 3.2) was able to recognise 14 of 17 pictures of famous statesmen. More critically, the patient scored at a comparable level in identifying degraded photocopies of the same individuals. Another patient showed the more widely documented deficit of impaired facial recognition, with preservation of performance on the matching task.

Different Types of Face-Recognition Deficit? Impairment in recognising familiar faces is a defining feature of prosopagnosia. Such patients may be quite unable to overtly discriminate well-known or familiar faces from those of strangers (although some limited discrimination may be possible on implicit measures). Failure to recognise familiar faces also occurs in the global amnesic syndrome, however, in these cases the ability to judge overtly whether a face is familiar or not may be preserved (Warrington & McCarthy, 1988; see Chapter 14). One patient (R.F.R.) failed to recognise famous people and pictures of his close family, but when asked to "select the famous person" from a choice of three faces (one famous and two visually similar distractor faces; see Fig. 3.6) his score was within the range of controls.

In discussing their findings in the amnesic patient, Warrington & McCarthy suggested that the faces of well-known personalities might have a double representation. One would be in a dynamic and updatable memory system which was inoperative in the amnesic, thereby preventing him from identifying precisely whose face he was viewing. The other representation would be in a more passive vocabulary of faces which could be used for familiarity judgments—"face recognition units" in Bruce & Young's terminology. Damage to either system might result in a failure of face recognition in everyday life, in one case due to a primary failure of material-specific memory (see Chapter 15) and in the other due to an impairment of an established vocabulary of faces. Perhaps it is this latter disorder which is responsible for the profound impairments of face recognition and face familiarity which occur in prosopagnosia.

Conclusion

The descriptive model proposed by Bruce & Young (see Fig. 3.5) has some points of similarity with models of object recognition and reading (see Chapters 2 and 10). The processing involved in visual analysis of faces is separated on the one hand from perceptual processing of unfamiliar faces and on the other from a stage in which the faces of familiar people are represented. It is uncertain whether the critical distinction to be made here is like that in reading, between "known"

Figure 3.6 Example of face triplet from the familiarity judgment test.

and "unknown" faces (analogous to known words and nonwords), or whether it should be one in terms of process, as in the case of object recognition (analogous to structural descriptions and semantic representations).

4

Spatial Perception

Introduction

Our environment does not simply consist of multiple objects, but multiple objects which exist in definable spatial interrelationships. The ease with which the normal individual can cope with the spatial world in routine tasks such as walking, driving, or eating a meal belies the considerable complexity of the processing which is involved. At any moment in time it is necessary to know the locations of single objects with respect to oneself, to know how objects are located with respect to others, and to be able to appreciate and anticipate the relative locations of moving objects. The ability to perceive spatial relationships between objects in the environment does not appear as open to introspection as many other skills. It is only when relatively precise spatial information is being used that we are even aware of thinking "spatially," for example, when we are playing certain games (such as space invaders or perhaps tennis), hanging a picture, or organising furniture.

Empirical Characteristics

Investigations of spatial processing in patients with cerebral lesions have largely been concerned with visual material. Two main aspects of spatial processing have been studied: first, impairments in locating single objects in space (single point localisation), and second, disorders of spatial processing in more complex tasks (spatial analysis). These will be considered in turn.

Single Point Localisation

Impairments in the ability to perceive the location of single points in space have been extensively (and almost exclusively) documented in the visual domain. The impairment of visual localisation, termed

73

visual disorientation, is a gravely disabling disorder. Patients with this deficit may appear to grope their way across a room as if they were blind. They frequently bump into large pieces of furniture, may fail to locate the doorway, and have grave difficulties in "finding" the door handle. The mechanics of eating a meal may present a major hurdle to these patients because they have difficulty in locating a plate or finding food on it. Although when handed a cup they may drink from it normally, they have great difficulty in placing it back on a table, let alone in its saucer.

The classical account of visual disorientation was given by Holmes (1918). He described patients who were unable to localise the position or distance of objects in space by sight alone. The patients were unable to reach for objects and were unable to judge the relative size of objects in their field of view. For example, one patient (Private M.) made errors when asked to say which of two objects was the nearer to him; even when they were separated by 10 to 15 centimetres, at a distance of half a metre from his eyes, he made many mistakes. He commented, "When I look at one it seems to go further away. When I try to see which is the nearer they seem to change in position every now and then; that one at which I look directly seems to move away". When his finger was moved from one object to the other by the examiner he had no difficulty in discriminating which of the two objects was the closer to him; thus the deficit appeared to be confined to vision. The patients described by Holmes also had difficulty in fixating on single objects, their eyes did not converge to an approaching object, and they were unable to visually track (pursue) the movement of objects. The patient reported that "sometimes I can see it quite well but sometimes I cannot see what I want to look at." When asked to look at the examiner's face, he stared open-eyed in the wrong direction and then moved his eyes about in an irregular manner. When the examiner brought his hand rapidly toward the patient's face, as if he was about to strike him, the patient did not show the normal automatic "blink" response to a threatening stimulus Holmes 1918, p. 450–454.

Holmes noted that for his patients the ability to judge the distance of objects (i.e., how close or far they were in depth) was more impaired than the ability to judge their location in the coronal plane (i.e., to the right and left of the body position). The converse pattern of deficit has been informally noted: A patient (Mrs. A.) would move her hand to the appropriate depth. However she would then sweep her hand across in the coronal plane in order to reach the object. (Warrington, clinical observation) There are also some suggestions that the ability to locate stimuli may differ according to whether they are within "reaching distance" or are further away. Holmes (1918) reported one case who had a subjective impression of greater difficulty with near objects (case 3), he stated, "When I got near them I did not know how near they were." Brain (1941) drew a similar distinction between reaching space and more distant space, again on the basis of clinical observation.

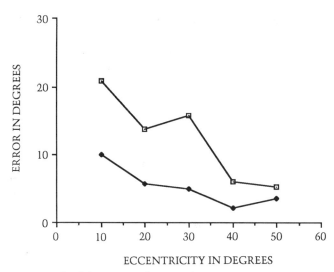

Figure 4.1   Magnitude of the error on the Aimark Perimeter for two patients (♦, T.H.R.; □, B.R.A.) with impairment in single point localisation.

Despite having marked difficulty in locating visual points in external space, Holmes' patients were able to locate sound sources at a normal level and locate points on their own body in response to tactile stimulation. These preserved abilities effectively rule out a motor component of the disorder. Holmes and his colleagues were also able to demonstrate intact visual acuity and colour perception in the context of a severe visual disorientation syndrome. A comparable pattern of preserved and impaired functions was formally documented by Godwin-Austin (1965). He reported one patient (S.G.) who was capable of identifying complex stimuli if they were placed at the point of fixation. For example, material such as faces, letters, or even overlapping drawings could be recognised or identified. These preserved abilities can be functionally useless in everyday life. Indeed, Holmes described the patient's condition as being "worse than blind."

Quantitative investigations of this syndrome have mostly used the technique of pointing to a light stimulus presented in various positions in the visual field. With a piece of apparatus, the Aimark Perimeter, it is possible to record the magnitude of a patient's error in reaching to stimuli varying in their position in the coronal plane (e.g., Ross-Russell & Bharucha, 1984). For example, using this technique two patients (B.R.A. and T.H.R.) made errors which averaged 12 inches (and could be as much as 20 inches) when reaching for a single target (Warrington, 1986; see Fig. 4.1).

Unilateral Impairment   Disorders of visual localisation can be confined to one visual half-field. Visual disorientation confined to homonymous half-fields was first documented by Riddoch (1935). His observations were replicated and extended by Cole, Schutta, & Warrington (1962). Errors of point localisation were also documented in a single quadrant of the visual field (Ross-Russell & Bharucha, 1984). In cases with hemianopic, or quadratic, failures of single point localisation the patient may be able to compensate for the deficit by using the intact sectors of the visual field. In order to detect these more restricted deficits, systematic perimetric testing is necessary.

Visuomotor Coordination   Failure on tests of visual localisation can occur in patients without a primary visual disorientation syndrome. The ability to integrate information about the location of a stimulus and somatosensory information about hand/arm position may be selectively impaired. The deficit has been termed *optic ataxia* (e.g., Perenin & Vighetto, 1983, 1988). The patients whom Perenin & Vighetto described were able to fixate on visual stimuli (thereby ruling out a primary deficit of visual localisation) and were able to point appropriately to tactile and auditory stimuli. However, the patients were impaired in reaching for objects under visual guidance. Their movements were inaccurate, poorly formed, clumsy, and slower than normal. As in visual disorientation, the deficit in optic ataxia may be confined to one half of visual space, however, it may also be confined to one arm within the affected side of space. This indicates that the disorder is neither purely visual nor exclusively motor, but rather is a failure in coordination between the two domains.

Spatial Analysis

In everyday life the demands on spatial skills go beyond those tapped by single point localisation. The normal individual can carry out tasks which require complex sequential and parallel analyses of spatial information. Early descriptions of patients with spatial impairments did not differentiate between disorders affecting the ability to locate single objects and disorders of spatial analysis in more complex tasks. The first study specifically concerned with an impairment in spatial analysis was that of Paterson & Zangwill (1944). They gave a thorough and detailed description of two patients who were quite unable to perform even comparatively simple spatial tasks, making gross errors of alignment when copying simple figures (for example by displacing the horizontal and vertical axes). In more complex drawings there was "faulty articulation of the constituent parts," resulting in piecemeal reproductions (see e.g., Fig. 5.5).

The patients were both very severely impaired on one task which required them to count the number of constituent blocks in a solid $3 \times 3 \times 3$ cube. In one case: "It was found that he counted correctly the 9 blocks in the front elevation to which he added 6 from the top surface.

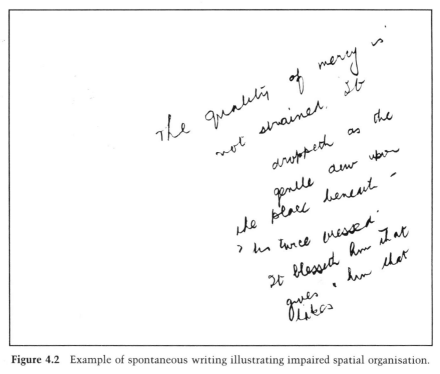

Figure 4.2   Example of spontaneous writing illustrating impaired spatial organisation.

He then repeated this procedure for the remaining three sides in each case adding the top 6 blocks. He thus arrived at the grand total of 60 blocks" (Paterson & Zangwill, 1944). The other patient persisted with the response that there were only 9 blocks. Despite these gross impairments on tasks of spatial analysis the patients were able to recognise complex and sketchily drawn pictures, scoring within the normal range on the McGill Anomalies Test (see Chapter 2) and on the pictorial subtests of the Stanford–Binet test of intelligence.

This syndrome of spatial impairment was convincingly established in a number of later studies of selected patients in whom it appeared as a particularly pronounced and isolated clinical sign. McFie, Piercy, & Zangwill (1950) described five cases who were impaired on the seemingly simple task of counting scattered objects. This deficit occurred despite the complete preservation of the patients' ability to locate single objects. The patients were also unable to draw or copy, to construct simple patterns using matchsticks, or to mark places on maps. McFie *et al.* (1950) termed this syndrome of faulty analysis of relative spatial information *visuospatial agnosia*. A further analysis of ten cases was reported by Ettlinger, Warrington, & Zangwill (1957).

On clinical testing a number of types of errors are observed on tasks with a spatial component. Patients may misalign words on a page,

On his way out of the town he//had to pass the
prison, and as he looked in at the//windows, whom
should he see but William himself peeping out of the
bars, and looking very sad indeed. //"Good morning,
brother," said Tom, "have you any//message for the
King of the Golden River?" William//ground his
teeth with rage, and shook the bars//with all his
strength; but Tom only laughed at him//and advising
him to make himself comfortable till//he came back
again, shouldered his basket, shook the//bottle of holy

Figure 4.3 Failure to read words on the left of the page: the patient (V.S.N.) read only
those words to the right of the parallel bars (Kartsounis & Warrington, 1989).

either failing to keep their writing on a line or confining their words to
one side of a page (see Fig. 4.2). When presented with normal text or
words in columns, patients may only report the words from one end of
a line (see Fig. 4.3). They may also make errors in reading individual
words ("neglect dyslexia," see Chapter 10). Spatial deficits may also
result in difficulties with written calculation because the patient fails
to keep numbers aligned in columns or completely misses numbers on
one side (spatial dyscalculia, Cohn, 1961a, see chapter 12). Copying
and drawing tasks may be virtually impossible for patients with spatial
impairments. (This type of deficit is discussed in more detail in Chapter 5: see Figs. 5.5 and 5.6.). In addition to errors involving faulty
articulation of component parts of a drawing, the patient may show
errors of spatial bias or neglect, failing to copy figures on one side of a
multielement drawing (see Fig. 4.4) and/or producing only one side of a
figure (Gainotti, Messerli, & Tissot, 1972; Ogden, 1987; see Fig. 4.5).
   There are two main types of test that have been specifically devised
to provide quantitative measures of disorders of spatial analysis, name-

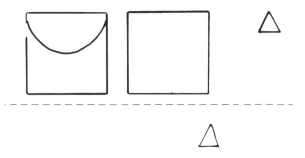

Figure 4.4 Example of omission of left-sided elements in a copying task. (Adapted from
Kartsounis & Warrington, 1989.)

Figure 4.5   Copy of stimulus array illustrating neglect within each part of the figure.

ly, tasks of spatial discrimination and tasks of spatial search. The more complex tests involving memory for spatial information will be discussed in Chapters 13 and 15.

Spatial Discrimination: Line Bisection   One of the easiest and long-established tasks of spatial discrimination is that of line bisection. The patient is presented with a line or a series of lines and asked to indicate the central point. The commonest error on such tasks is to systematically displace the central point to one side (e.g., Colombo, De Renzi, & Faglioni, 1976; Bisiach, Capitani, Colombo, & Spinnler, 1976; Schenkenberg, Bradford, & Ajax, 1980). Riddoch & Humphreys (1983) reported that patients' performance improved by asking them to name a letter at the end of the "neglected" side of the line. Similar facilitatory effects were reported by Halligan & Marshall (1989) who varied the starting position (extreme left or extreme right). However, cues may not be effective in overcoming spatial neglect in all patients (Heilman & Valenstein, 1979a). This spatially determined error has been termed *unilateral spatial neglect*. Patients may be affected by the location of

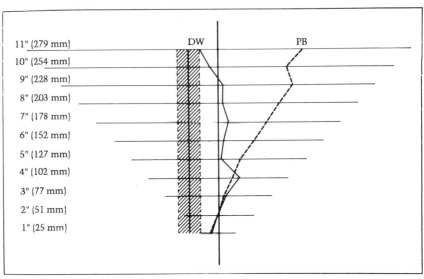

Figure 4.6 Example of line-length effect by patient (P.B.) on a line-bisection task (Halligan & Marshall, 1988).

lines on a page, those appearing on the "neglected" side of space being more affected than those on the other side (e.g., Heilman & Valenstein, 1979a).

The properties of the stimulus may also affect the magnitude and direction of neglect. Halligan & Marshall (1988) studied one case with a pronounced spatial bias on a wide range of tasks. They found that his line-bisection errors were most pronounced for lines longer than 2 inches (on which the patient displaced the midpoint of the line toward the right). The error in bisection was systematically greater for longer lines (11 inches). With lines of 1 inch, however, the patient reliably misplaced the midpoint toward the left (see Fig. 4.6).

Position Discrimination A number of simple two-dimensional stimulus arrays have been used to assess the discrimination of relative spatial positions. For example, Warrington & Rabin (1970) developed a series of same–different matching tests using "nonrepresentational" stimuli. These included a test in which subjects had to determine whether gaps in a contour were the same or different and a position-discrimination task in which the location of a dot in a square had to be compared with a dot in a second square. In a further investigation of the dot matching task it was found that there was a systematic relationship between the difficulty of the spatial discrimination task and the accuracy of performance (Taylor & Warrington, 1973). Similar findings were reported by Hannay, Varney, & Benton (1976), who presented patients with brief exposures of single or double dot stimuli. Following

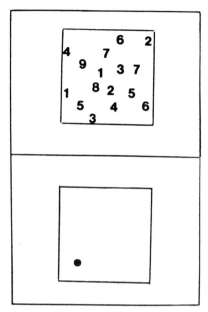

Figure 4.7   Example of stimuli from a DOT-POSITION task (Warrington & James, 1988).

presentation the patient was asked to recall the position of the dot or dots by referring to a card on which numbers were displayed including the positions in which the dot or dots appeared. They found a comparatively high incidence of deficit on this task. These findings have been replicated using a similar task with untimed presentation (Warrington & James, 1988; see Fig. 4.7).

Orientation.   Warrington & Rabin (1970) reported that the ability to match two lines as having the same or different slant could be impaired in patients. Benton, Hannay, & Varney (1975) and Bisiach, Nichelli, & Spinnler (1976) reported similar findings. Testing discrimination of line orientation has been developed by Benton and his colleagues into a formal test of spatial discrimination (Benton, Varney, & Hamsher, 1978). They extended and developed the line-orientation matching task by incorporating different levels of task difficulty. They used stimuli of different orientations which had to be matched to the identical slope in a "sun ray" of lines. In the easiest version of the task, the test stimulus is identical in length to one of the "rays" in the matching stimulus (see Fig. 4.8). Difficulty was manipulated either by requiring the subject to match two lines or by using a very short portion of the target stimulus.

De Renzi and his colleagues have developed a three-dimensional test of spatial orientation: rod orientation. De Renzi, Faglioni, & Scotti (1971) presented their patients with two pairs of rods. Each pair was made up of a vertical rod which could rotate 360° around its axis and a second rod which was fixed to the first by a hinged joint so that it could

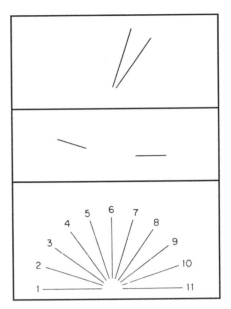

Figure 4.8   Example from Benton's line-orientation task (Benton *et al.*, 1978).

be moved up and down in the sagittal plane (see Fig. 4.9). The rods could either be presented for matching (i.e., same–different discrimination), or the patient could be asked to manipulate the apparatus so that the two pairs of rods were in the same alignment. Both visual and tactile versions of the task were used and the patients found them

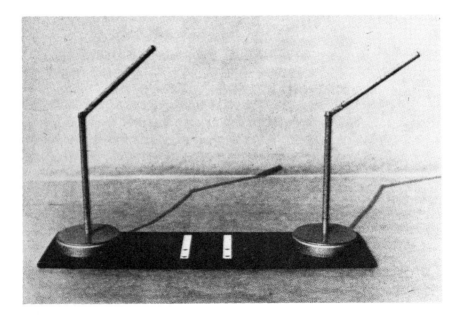

Figure 4.9   Rod-orientation apparatus (De Renzi *et al.*, 1971).

equally difficult. In a related task Layman & Greene (1988) observed a high incidence of deficit in a task requiring subjects to match nonsense objects photographed from different angles. They found rotation in depth (3D) was more difficult than rotation in the picture plane (2D) but significant impairments were noted in both conditions.

Spatial Search: Cancellation Albert (1973) developed a test in which the subject is required to cancel each item in an array of 40 differently oriented scattered lines. This task has the advantage of minimising the requirement for verbal responses. Cancellation tasks are considered to be especially sensitive to unilateral spatial biases or spatial neglect. Indeed, they are often used as a criterion for diagnosis of the syndrome. Typically, failure on this task consists of the patient's omitting to cancel lines on one side of the page. In the extreme case a patient may be observed to cancel only those lines bordering one edge of the array (see Fig. 4.10). In some cases, errors of omission also occur in other sectors and may appear to be "random."

Detection Search tasks do not necessarily require the subject to respond to every item in an array. Looking for a single target amongst a background of distractor items may also be a sensitive test. Poppelreuter (1923) first developed a test of search for a single target

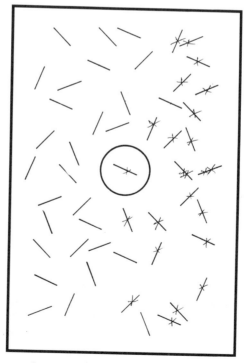

Figure 4.10   Performance by a patient (V.S.N.) on an adaptation of Albert's (1973) line-cancellation task (Kartsounis & Warrington, 1989).

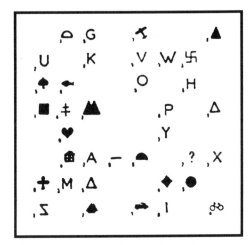

Figure 4.11   Example of stimulus array for visual-search task (Chedru *et al.*, 1973).

amongst scattered stimuli as a means of evaluating deficits in visual
exploration. In an attempt to quantify the magnitude and direction of
spatial bias De Renzi, Faglioni, & Scotti (1970) investigated the speed of
visual search for target digits in a spatially complex array of numbers.
The patient was told which target to search for, and the speed of search
for targets located on the right or left side of the array was measured.
De Renzi *et al.* (1970) found that for some patients search latencies
were considerably greater for one side of the array than for others.
Patients had a spatial preference for searching one side of the array and
tended to neglect the other. Chedru, Leblanc, & Lhermitte (1973) extended and replicated these findings. They required subjects to search
for a symbol (e.g., a letter, a silhouette of a house, a square) (see Fig.
4.11). Chedru *et al.* recorded their subjects' eye movements, measuring
both their direction and their duration. They found that spatial biases
in searching using as a measure the time taken to reach a target. Chain,
Leblanc, Chedru, & Lhermitte (1979) used the somewhat more naturalistic task of picture inspection. They found that some patients were
systematically biased to searching one side of a picture and at the same
time were slower to look toward the other. Tasks in which the target
can be easily discriminated from the background are less likely to give
rise to errors than those in which the discrimination is more demanding (Riddoch & Humphreys, 1987a; Rapcsak, Verfaellé, Fleet, &
Heilman, 1989).

Detection tasks have also lent themselves to the investigation of
modalities other than vision. De Renzi, Gentilini, & Barbieri (1989)
documented unilateral spatial biases in a task requiring subjects to
detect interruptions in binaurally presented sounds. This deficit appeared to dissociate from tasks of visual detection. De Renzi *et al.*
(1970) developed a tactile search task. Patients were required to search
for a marble hidden in one arm of a symmetrical six-arm maze. They

documented biases in search with patients consistently commencing their exploration of the maze on one side.

It is perhaps unsurprising that clinical tests which require the subject to choose stimuli from a spatial array may also elicit a spatial biases. Campbell & Oxbury (1976) used Warrington & James' (1967a) test of immediate visual memory, in which the subject is presented with a stimulus of five black squares randomly positioned within a 4 × 4 matrix. Recognition was tested by asking the patient to choose the target item from a 2 × 2 array. Campbell & Oxbury found that patients with impaired spatial analysis and clinically significant neglect (on drawing tasks) were systematically biased in their choices, tending to ignore alternatives on one side of the array. Patients may also be spatially biased in their choice of targets on Raven's Coloured Progressive Matrices (e.g., Costa, Vaughan, Horwitz, & Ritter, 1969; Colombo *et al.*, 1976).

Stimulus Enumeration   Kimura (1963) asked patients to report the number of dots in arrays which were presented briefly (using a tachistoscope) and found a significant incidence of errors. A similar task was used by Warrington & James (1967b). They noted that patients sometimes made gross errors of both under- and over-estimation. Comparable errors were noted in a second task, in which stimuli were presented for counting in free vision. It was often clinically apparent from the pointing responses made by the patients on this latter task that in some cases the array was scanned in a haphazard fashion, the same dot being counted more than once (giving rise to overestimations). In other cases only the stimuli appearing on one or the other side of the array were missed or neglected (giving rise to underestimations). A somewhat more complex spatial counting task is the test of

Figure 4.12   Example from Binet's cube analysis test.

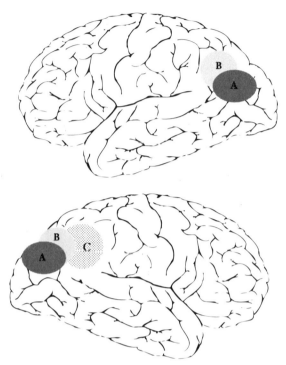

Figure 4.13   **Diagram showing approximate locus of lesion of visual disorientation (A), optic ataxia (B), and visuospatial agnosia (C).**

cube analysis (see Fig. 4.12). In this test the subject is asked to report how many cubes would be needed to make up the model. A high proportion of patients with cerebral lesions fail on this demanding task (Warrington & Rabin, 1970; Oxbury, Campbell, & Oxbury, 1974).

Anatomical Considerations

Single Point Localisation

The original cases of visual disorientation described by Holmes had difficulty in locating objects placed anywhere in the visual field. Holmes and his colleagues noted a high incidence of bilateral inferior hemianopic field defects in these cases and inferred from the known organisation of the visual system that the critical lesion site must be bilateral and at the junction of the occipitoparietal boundary (see Fig. 4.13). This lesion location has been confirmed for all of the more recent cases for whom data are available (Warrington, 1986; Ross-Russell & Bharucha, 1978, 1984).

Difficulties with visual location may be confined to one half or even to one quadrant of the visual field. Such difficulties in visual location are invariably contralateral to the lesion site and have been observed in both right- and left-hemisphere cases (Riddoch, 1935; Cole *et al.*, 1962;

Ratcliffe & Davies-Jones, 1972). Thus it appears that the systems which subserve the visual localisation are bilaterally represented and are "crossed" like other primary visual capacities with one hemisphere subserving the processing of material in the contralateral side of the visual world (see Chapter 2). These clinical visual-field defects mirror the mapping of visual sensory input onto the receptive fields of cortex. Impairments of visual localisation therefore maintain the spatial organisation which occurs at the level of the retina: they are said to be topographically or "retinotopically" organised.

The disorder of optic ataxia is associated with posterior parietal lesions of either hemisphere, possibly implicating the interparietal sulcus and zones medial and superior to it (Perenin & Vighetto, 1988) see Fig. 4.14. This deficit is both retinotopic and somatotopic since it is not only confined to the visual field contralateral to the lesion (retinotopic) but it may also be confined to the contralateral limb (somatotopic). Thus, a right-hemisphere lesion may give rise to misreaching in the left visual field with the left hand with relative preservation of performance in other field/limb combinations.

Spatial Analysis

The investigation of the cerebral correlates of impairments of spatial analysis has focussed on two issues, first, on the localising significance of tasks requiring spatial analysis and, second, on the incidence and characteristics of spatial-neglect errors in patients with right- and left-hemisphere lesions.

One of the main goals of early studies of spatial processing was to establish a syndrome of cognitive impairment which was lateralised to the right hemisphere. To this end patients were selected for investigation who had right-hemisphere lesions *and* an impairment of their spatial skills (e.g., McFie *et al.*, 1950; Ettlinger *et al.*, 1957). There was no attempt in these studies to assess whether spatial disorders would occur as frequently, or with comparable severity, in patients with left-hemisphere lesions. McFie & Zangwill (1960) conducted a further study of 8 patients with left-hemisphere lesions and "visuo-constrictive" difficulties (constructional apraxia; see Chapter 5). These patients' performance on tests of spatial analysis was compared retrospectively with the cases reported by McFie *et al.* (1950) and Ettlinger *et al.* (1957). Unlike the right-hemisphere cases, the left-hemisphere patients were considered to have relative preservation of their spatial analysis skills.

Quantitative estimates of the incidence and severity of spatial discrimination impairments is derived from group studies. Impairments in judging line orientation in two and three dimensions and in discriminating gaps in a contour are associated with right-hemisphere lesions (Warrington & Rabin, 1970; De Renzi, *et al.* 1971; Benton, *et al.*, 1975; Layman & Greene, 1988). In those studies of line-orientation judgment where it has been possible to compare sectors within the right hemisphere, performance by patients with right posterior lesions has been the worst. On the dot-position discrimination test, it was again the patients with posterior lesions of the right hemisphere whose performance was significantly worse than either the right-anterior or left-hemisphere groups (Warrington & Rabin, 1970; Taylor & Warrington, 1973). Comparable findings were reported by Hannay *et al.* (1976) for their stringent test of position recall.

Kimura (1963) reported that patients with right temporal lobe lesions were worse than patients with left temporal lesions on a task of reporting the number of briefly presented dots. However, in their similar tachistoscopic task Warrington & James (1967b) found a greater deficit in patients with right parietal lesions than in cases with right temporal lobe damage. The deficit for the right temporal lobe group was only significantly different from controls when stimuli were presented in the left visual field. When scattered stimuli were presented for counting in free vision, they found no evidence of cerebral asymmetry. On such tasks both patients with left-hemisphere lesions and patients with right-hemisphere lesions were worse than controls, but the lesion groups did not differ from each other. Findings have been similar for the more complex task of cube analysis (Fig. 4.12): both right- and left-hemisphere lesions may give rise to impairment on this task. It has been suggested that failure in the two groups is likely to have a different basis: spatial in the right-hemisphere group and aphasic in the left (Warrington & Rabin, 1970).

Spatial Neglect   In a retrospective study in which clinical records of 413 cases were examined, Hécaen & Angelergues (1963) reported that in 59 of these patients unilateral spatial neglect had been documented on a mixed range of clinical tasks such as writing, copying, and spontaneous drawing. They found that 51 of these cases had right-hemisphere lesions, 4 had damage to the left hemisphere, and the remainder had bilateral lesions. This marked asymmetry in the incidence of neglect on a range of clinical tests has been replicated in a large number of studies. Thus Gloning, Gloning, & Hoff (1968) found an incidence of 31% of right-hemisphere-lesioned cases and only 2% of left-hemisphere cases. Weinstein & Cole (1963) found a ratio of 22:3, and Cohn (1961b) found an incidence of 3:1, and Zarit & Kahn (1974) found an incidence of 2:1. However, the reliability of these studies has been questioned by Ogden (1987), who has argued that they confound the absolute *incidence* of neglect with the *severity* of the deficit. In her series of 101 cases, she classified any omissions in drawing or cancellation on the side contralateral to a patient's lesion as a "neglect error." On these criteria 50% of left-hemisphere cases and 44% of right-hemisphere cases were classified as showing signs of neglect. On a composite score of performance on the drawing and cancellation tests, patients with right posterior lesions were identified as being more severely affected. She concluded that if larger batteries of tests and stricter criteria were used then a significant proportion of left-hemisphere cases would be diagnosed as showing signs of neglect.

On the very simple and basic test of spatial discrimination line bisection (see Fig. 4.6), errors of spatial bias occur most frequently in patients with lesions of the posterior right hemisphere. Bisiach *et al.* (1976a) found that both patients and controls tended to bisect lines somewhat inaccurately. Patients with left-hemisphere lesions bisected the line to the left. Only those patients with posterior lesions of the right hemisphere (as inferred on the basis of visual-field deficits) were significantly different from controls in bisecting the line to the right. Colombo *et al.* (1976) reported that whereas posterior lesions of the right hemisphere gave rise to larger errors of displacement, there was also a trend for patients with posterior lesions of the left hemisphere to be worse than controls.

Albert (1973) reported that lesions of either the right or the left hemisphere could result in errors on the test of line cancellation (see Fig. 4.10). A total of 37% of patients with right-hemisphere lesions and 30% of cases with left-hemisphere lesions missed one or more lines. However, even though there was no difference in the incidence of errors, the overall severity of neglect or spatial bias was greater for patients with right-hemisphere lesions. There was also a difference in the distribution of omissions: right-hemisphere cases missed more target stimuli on the left, whereas left-hemisphere cases made more "random" errors, not only failing to cancel stimuli on the left and centre of the page but also missing stimuli on the right.

Spatial biases in detecting a single target amongst randomly scattered stimuli have been documented in patients with either right- or left-hemisphere lesions. In a task of visual search De Renzi *et al.* (1970) found that both controls and patients with left-hemisphere lesions showed a bias in detecting stimuli. Targets on the right of the page took longer to find. This spatial bias was very pronounced in patients with posterior left-hemisphere lesions. Patients with posterior lesions of the right hemisphere were slower to detect stimuli on the left. Chedru *et al.* (1973) obtained substantially similar findings in their study in which eye movements were directly recorded. They found that, although left-hemisphere-lesioned cases were slow to find targets on the right, they nevertheless scanned into their right fields. Patients with right-hemisphere lesions often failed to scan into the left field.

Other investigations have systematically examined the role of task demands in eliciting neglect following right- or left-sided lesions. Gainotti, D'Erme, Monteleone, & Silveri (1986) carried out an investigation in which an array of animal pictures had to be examined in order to detect the presence or absence of a visually presented target. They found a comparable incidence of neglect in right- and left-sided lesions. In a perceptually more complex task (searching for a target in an overlapping figure, see Fig. 2.6), the right-sided lesion group was selectively impaired missing stimuli on the left side of the composite. They considered that patients with right-hemisphere lesions (and left-sided neglect) showed the disorder with those stimuli which could be "viewed in a single fixation." Left-hemisphere lesions gave rise to neglect in more open-ended tasks requiring active search.

Another possibility is that the specific types of cognitive processing which are required by different material may be critical in eliciting neglect phenomena. Leicester, Sidman, Stoddard, & Mohr (1969) investigated the effects of different types of verbal material in giving rise to spatial biases in a search task. Their experiment focussed on patients with left-hemisphere lesions. Leicester *et al.* used a matching task in which the subject was required to match a target stimulus (presented either visually, auditorially, or by touch) to a set of choice stimuli presented as an array (in a 3×3 matrix). They found that patients were more prone to make errors of spatial bias or neglect when searching for material that was already difficult for them. Thus, a patient with problems in number processing would be more likely to show a spatial bias away from the right side of space when numbers were the targets. Similarly, for patients with impaired reading, requiring them to choose a word in a spatial array to match a spoken target elicited more spatial biases.

Overall, the evidence indicates that whilst both right and left lesions may give rise to neglect errors, the severity of neglect is greater for right-parietal cases than for patients with lesions elsewhere in the brain. Milder neglect, and possibly different neglect phenomena, may be associated with lesions of the left hemisphere. It is also possible that the tasks on which left-hemisphere neglect has been identified are those in which a stricter scoring criterion has been used, that is, they are simply more sensitive to neglect errors.

Theoretical Considerations

Single Point Localisation

Visual disorientation, or the failure of stimulus localisation, appears to be a retinotopic impairment which can be restricted to stimuli presented to the visual field contralateral to the lesion. There is no evidence for any cerebral asymmetry and the disorder is as likely to occur in the right as the left visual fields. In these respects it is comparable to the other visual sensory processes of acuity, form, and colour (see Chapter 2).

Holmes characterised this pattern of disorder as a failure to utilise "local retinal cues" for object position. Since our eyes are constantly moving, the distribution of points of stimulation at the level of the retina is by itself insufficient to provide a "map" of objects in space. These cues have to be processed further so that the locations of objects retain their stability regardless of momentary changes in the site of retinal stimulation. Such processing requires information from points of stimulation at the level of the retina to be coordinated with other sources of information about eye, head, and body position. Patients with an impairment in locating single visual targets in space can be thought of as being reduced to the use of retinal information for object position. They are therefore unable to construct a stable representation of the locations of objects in the visual world on the basis of these cues alone. As an aside it should be noted that the ability to locate points in space dissociates from the ability to detect the presence of stimuli or their *motion* of points. There are a number of cases on record who are able to locate stimuli remarkably accurately in their blind field (Weiskrantz, Warrington, Sanders & Marshall, 1974; Perenin & Jeannerod, 1978). Holmes' cases could detect movement, and even report on its direction (Holmes & Horrax, 1919). By contrast, a case described by Zihl, Von Cramon & Mai (1983) could not detect movement, but could locate stationary points and was not visually disorientated.

Patients with a visual disorientation can, under certain circumstances, accurately identify complex meaningful visual stimuli such as a face or photographs or objects. However, just as intact shape discrimination appears to be a prerequisite for object recognition, it also seems as though intact single point localisation is a prerequisite for space perception. Those tasks of space perception which go beyond simple stimulus localisation appear to be gravely impaired. Thus, such patients' performance is impaired on a wide range of tasks that demand more complex spatial analysis (e.g., Godwin-Austin, 1965).

Visuomotor Coordination   The ability to utilise local retinal cues appears to be insufficient by itself for eye/hand coordination. Perenin & Vighetto (1983, 1988) have argued that the fundamental disorder in optic ataxia (misreaching in the absence of a primary failure of visual stimulus localisation) is one of coordinating visual information about target position and somatosensory information about limb position. They found that their patients' deficit was particularly severe when they could see the target but not their arms. It was argued that in these circumstances the patient had to rely on somatosensory cues about arm position and had to link this with visual information about target location. Allowing the patient to see his hand before he commenced the movement reduced errors.

Spatial Analysis

Theoretical accounts of impairment on more complex spatial tasks have mostly focussed on errors of spatial bias or unilateral spatial neglect. The more general problem of the nature of the central representations which are required for spatial perception has been largely unexplored outside of this restricted context. In this regard it is worth emphasising that many of the more complex tasks which have been used in an attempt to measure primary deficits of spatial processing have had multiple components and may therefore be failed for a number of reasons (other than a primary impairment of spatial processing). For example, failure on drawing tasks has been extensively investigated (see Chapter 5) and it is clear that, although deficits may arise because of a primary spatial disorder, other factors (e.g., control of voluntary movement) may also be important. Even the apparently elementary tasks of dot counting or cube analysis may be failed by left-hemisphere cases with dyscalculia or more general aphasic difficulties.

There are, however, some pointers to dissociations between performance on tests of spatial analysis and other perceptual tasks which would appear to have a spatial component. As was the case of single point localisation, performance on tests of spatial analysis dissociates from tests of picture perception. Early examples of this dissociation were the cases of Paterson & Zangwill (1944). The patients were able to recognise the complex and sketchily drawn pictures of the McGill Anomalies Test despite having marked deficits on tests of spatial analysis. The converse dissociation was documented by Warrington & James (1988). They reported a patient who was severely impaired in recognising objects photographed from unusual angles, but whose performance on a stringent test of spatial analysis (cube analysis, see Fig. 4.12) was within the normal range. Newcombe (1969) reported a similar dissociation in a group study of patients who had sustained gunshot wounds: there was only a minor degree of overlap in the individuals who failed a test of face perception (see Chapter 3) and those who failed a test of maze learning (see Chapter 15). Warrington & Rabin (1970) found no correlation between performance on the Gollin Test of fragmented picture identification (see Fig. 2.7) and scores on a test of dot-position discrimination. Overall, the right posterior lesion group was impaired on both the object-perception test and the spatial task, however there was no relationship between them. There appears to be convincing evidence that the cerebral systems subserving the higher-order perceptual skills of "where" a visual stimulus is and "what" a visual stimulus is, are functionally and anatomically distinct.

What then, is the nature of the deficit underlying disorders of spatial analysis? Since Paterson & Zangwill's (1944) seminal work on this topic it has been usual to invoke concepts of disordered central representations of space. Following Koffka (1935), Paterson & Zangwill suggested that a central spatial representation, or framework, was necessary so that objects could be perceived as having stable position with respect to other objects in the environment despite repeated shifts in the position of the observer. However, the concept of a "central spatial representation" appears to require elaboration, to include the possibility that there are multiple frames of reference, and possibly multiple spatial representations. The evidence for this is drawn from studies of the phenomena of spatial bias or neglect. First it appears as though it may be necessary to postulate modality-specific representations of space. Barbieri and De Renzi (1989) documented all possible patterns of dissociation between neglect tasks presented to the auditory, visual, and tactile modalities. There was no necessary relationship between any of the tasks.

Within the domain of visual tasks it has been established that spatial bias may be both "egocentric" and "environment" centred. Ladavas (1987) studied five patients with left-sided neglect documented on cancellation tasks. The subjects were required to respond as rapidly as possible to a light stimulus. In one condition, the subject was seated with his/her head in an upright position. The coordinate frames of egocentric space (right–left) and environmental space (i.e., east–west) were therefore congruent. In a second condition, the subject tilted the head either to the right or to the left bringing the environmental and the egocentric frameworks out of alignment. Ladavas found that in the conventional test (head upright) patients were slower to respond to stimuli on the left. However, when the patient's head was tilted, stimuli on the left of the environment were responded to more slowly than stimuli on the right. In this condition the environmental "left" stimuli could either be in the subjects' right or left visual field. Ladavas interpreted her findings in terms of a distinction between retinal and "gravitational" coordinate frames. A similar effect of absolute environmental location was reported by Calvanio, Petrone, & Levine (1987) in the context of a search task. Their interpretation was very similar and they argued that there were both environment-centred and body-centred spatial coordinates. Overall, it appears that the complex phenomena of attentional biases had considerable potential for informing more general theoretical speculations about the organisation of central representations of space.

Theories of Spatial Neglect

Two main theoretical approaches have been developed which broadly attempt to provide a coherent theory of spatial bias in a wide range of tasks. On one account, the core deficit is viewed as the result of a failure in attentional processing. The other position suggests that there may be a more fundamental disorder in a central representation of space.

Attentional Theories.   The starting point for the attentional theories is the clinical observation that spatial neglect is more severe, if not more common, in patients with lesions of the right hemisphere. It is then suggested that the right hemisphere is normally dominant for attention in all sectors of the spatial environment. The left hemisphere is thought to be restricted to processing information in the right side of space (e.g., De Renzi *et al.*, 1970). Heilman and his colleagues have taken this account further and view attention as being directly related to physiological "arousal" or "activation" (e.g., Heilman & Valenstein, 1979a,b; 1985). If the right hemisphere has systems which are important in the control and modulation of arousal, then an underactivated right hemisphere might affect attentional processing on both sides of space. However, the left hemisphere may have some capacity for "local attention" to the right side. Thus the patient with a damaged right hemisphere could demonstrate unilateral neglect of the left, whereas the patient with a left-hemisphere lesion should be able to utilise the normally functioning spatial attention systems subserved by structures in the right hemisphere.

Kinsbourne (e.g., 1977) has postulated an activation model of neglect which does not assume right hemisphere dominance. He has suggested that the two cerebral hemispheres normally operate in competition for attention to the contralateral side of space. They are normally balanced in terms of a gradient of attention covering the entire spatial field. In the context of damage, this finely balanced gradient would be disrupted with the intact hemisphere "dominating" the damaged one. This would result in a bias in the spatial gradient of attention. Thus in the case of damage to the right hemisphere there would be a general bias towards right-sided stimuli and away from left-sided stimuli, even within the "intact" right side of space. In support of this position a number of investigators have noted a gradient of attentional bias affecting stimuli presented to the left of an array not only in the left-, but also in the right-visual field (e.g., Ladavas, 1987; De Renzi, Gentilini, Faglioni, & Barbieri, 1989). However this phenomenon may not be observed in all individual cases of neglect (Marshall & Halligan, 1989).

Posner and his colleagues have suggested that neglect may affect one component of the visual attentional system (e.g., Posner, Cohen, & Rafal, 1982; Posner, Walker, Friedrich, & Rafal, 1984). In an account which bears some similarity to Kinsbourne's, they have suggested that the patient's impairment is not so much one of moving attention *toward* the impaired side of space as in moving attention *away* from the normal side of space. Posner and his colleagues conducted a series of experiments in which subjects were required to respond to the onset of a single stimulus presented in the right or left visual field. For example, a light might be presented to one side of fixation and the subject required to press a button as rapidly as possible in order to indicate that the stimulus had been detected. Posner and his colleagues induced a bias in attention to different locations in the visual field by providing subjects with a cue as to the likely location of the stimulus. In these conditions both normal subjects and patients with a tendency to ignore or neglect one side of visual space detected the target stimulus more rapidly with a cue. However, on "catch" trials in which the cue misled the patient to expect the target to occur on the normal side (but instead it was presented on the neglected side of space), they were disproportionately impaired. Indeed one case missed the majority of catch trials in this condition. Posner and his colleagues have argued that the effect of a misleading cue was due to a difficulty in voluntarily shifting an attentional "spotlight" *away* from the normal to the affected side of space. By cuing the patient to shift this spotlight to the affected side the deficit could be overcome.

A related interpretation was put forward by Kartsounis & Warrington (1989). They described a patient (V.S.N.) whose neglect was determined by the configuration of the stimulus materials. When he was presented with arrays of geometric shapes he showed florid neglect of the left (see Fig. 4.4). In describing pictures, he did not make neglect errors when the stimuli were interactive (eg 2 women having a conversation) but continued to make these errors when noninteractive pictures were shown (eg 2 inanimate objects) . This effect occurred even when the elements of the picture were spatially separated. Kartsounis & Warrington considered that the patient was guided toward the left side of space by "attention-directing" stimuli in the unaffected side of space.

Representational Theory   On the representational account of neglect it is proposed that the individual constructs a central map of space which is a direct analogue of sensory experience. The phenomenon of neglect reflects a distortion of the central map of spatial information (De Renzi *et al.*, 1970). Bisiach and his colleagues have demonstrated neglect using visual imagery tasks. Bisiach, Luzzati, & Perani (1979) presented subjects with random cloudlike shapes which were only visible when moving past a small slit in a display (see Fig. 4.14). The subjects' task was to say whether two sequentially presented stimuli were the same or different. In order to make this judgment it is necessary for the observer to construct a mental image of the stimulus since

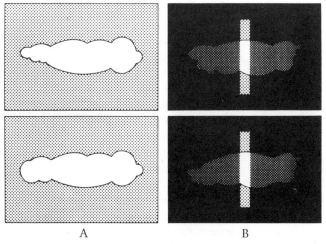

A	B

Figure 4.14   Examples of random cloudlike shapes used by Bisiach *et al.* (1979).

only partial information is available to central vision at any one time. Patients with a florid left neglect syndrome (as identified on tasks such as line bisection and drawing) made a significantly higher proportion of errors by saying that stimuli were the same when they differed on the left side. These findings have been extended by Ogden (1985a), who found that neglect errors were also obtained in left-hemisphere cases with a milder neglect syndrome.

In another experiment Bisiach & Luzzati (1978) asked their Milanese patients to describe the view (shops, landmarks, etc.) from the Piazza del Duomo (a central square in Milan dominated by a Gothic cathedral). In one condition the subjects were asked to imagine they were viewing the Piazza when looking toward the cathedral. In the other condition they were to imagine they were standing on the cathedral steps and looking in the opposite direction. They found that the items which were omitted in their subjects' descriptions depended on their imagined viewpoint. The landmarks which were on their imagined left side were omitted on both occasions. Bisiach & Luzzati further suggested that in forming a mental image or mental representation the same anatomical structures are involved as those which are used in normal visual perception. This, they argue, can account for similarities between neglect of the external spatial world and neglect of an internally generated spatial image.

Dissociations Both the attentional and the representational theories of spatial bias can account for many of the empirical phenomena. However, the phenomena of neglect are complex, and it seems highly unlikely that any single unitary theory will prove satisfactory. Quite apart from modality-specific effects (see above), the dissociation of neglect in external space and neglect of imagined space was recorded by Brain (1941). He described patients who, in walking around the environment, consistently turned to the right and not to the left. Nevertheless, they were reportedly capable of describing the spatial layout of their homes and describing routes from memory. Further dissociations are also on record. Costello & Warrington (1987) described a patient (JOH) who showed a marked *right*-sided neglect in copying, drawing, and line-bisection tasks. He also made errors of neglect in reading single words, however, this neglect was for the *left* side of words (see Chapter 10).

Gainotti *et al.* (1986) pointed out that impairments on visual-search tasks could arise for (at least) two different reasons. Patients might "neglect" part of a stimulus in central vision, or they might show bias in the search operations themselves. It is of interest to note that only the former condition gave rise to the classical right-hemisphere deficit. Gainotti's hypothesis is to some extent borne out by the observation that in a large number of tasks requiring active search and spatial analysis there is a less pronounced "right-hemisphere effect" than in tests of spatial discrimination in which stimuli are available to central vision.

A further complication is the distinction between explicit and implicit knowledge of neglected stimuli. Marshall & Halligan (1988) described a patient who failed to detect flames drawn on the left side of a house. When given a choice of houses, she "preferred" the house which was not on fire.

Conclusion

Spatial processing is clearly a highly complex activity which has yet to be integrated into any coherent model of cognitive function. Any adequate theoretical account will need to incorporate not only the bizarre and compelling phenomena of "neglect" but also to address wider issues such as the content of spatial representations and their interrelationships. For example, how is the retinotopic representation of single point localisation "mapped" onto more central spatial schemas which represent relative spatial relationships? These questions in turn have to be related to even more complex issues of how "where" a stimulus is is integrated with "what" a stimulus is.

5

Voluntary Action

Introduction

Impaired motor function is a common correlate of cerebral disease. The deficits shown by patients include paralysis caused by lesions in the primary motor areas or the descending motor tracts, complex patterns of involuntary movement such as the resting tremor of Parkinson's disease, the inability to reach or aim accurately seen in cerebellar ataxia, and the bizarre, writhing, involuntary movements which are observed in syndromes such as Huntington's Chorea. Such disturbances have a degree of consistency about them, they can be elicited comparatively reliably, and the muscle groups which are affected remain constant across a wide range of triggering conditions.

There are certain types of movement disorder which are not characterised by this consistency and reliability of dysfunction: these are the complex disorders of voluntary action. These disorders are often defined, in somewhat negative terms, as a pattern of impairment in voluntary action which cannot be accounted for in terms of a primary motor weakness, paralysis, or sensory loss. The fundamental integrity of primary motor function is evident in the patient's ability to use a specific set of muscles or produce a particular gesture under one set of conditions but not under others. It is this latter class of impairments which will form the focus of this chapter.

Steinthal (1871) coined the term *apraxia* to designate a deficit distinct from paralysis which affected the patient's ability to produce voluntary actions related to object use. However, in his account he did not clearly differentiate between disorders occurring at the level of object recognition (visual agnosia: see Chapter 2) and those specifically affecting actions. This distinction was made explicit by Meynert in 1890 (cited by Hécaen & Albert, 1978), who contrasted "sensory asymbolia," an impairment of object recognition, and "motor asymbolia," which affected the memory images of movement. Subsequently de Buck in 1899 (cited by Hécaen, 1972) suggested that the memory images of movement might be subdivided into the concepts of an action and the kinetic (movement-related) images of the action.

The first convincing single case report of an apraxic patient was presented by Liepmann (1900). He described the case of an "ambidextrous syphilitic" imperial councillor (M.T.) who was initially considered to be very demented. The patient was unable to imitate simple hand positions (such as placing his thumb on his little finger) or perform pantomimes (e.g., gesturing the use of an object) with his right hand. However, he was considerably less impaired with his left hand (although reportedly imperfect) (Liepmann, 1905). This marked difference in the patient's performance when he used his right or his left hand led Liepmann to infer that the disorder could not be attributed to poor comprehension or dementia (which should have affected both hands equally). Rather, the patient had a specific difficulty in performing skilled motor actions with his right hand.

Subsequently, Liepmann performed a number of further systematic investigations of impairments of voluntary action (including the first group study of patients with cerebral lesions: Liepmann, 1905) which firmly established the validity of the syndrome of apraxia as a clinical entity in its own right. He documented both unilateral and bilateral forms of the syndrome in patients with cerebral disease. Not only did Liepmann show that impairments of voluntary action could be differentiated from language disorders and paralysis, but he also argued that apraxia was not a simple unitary disorder. The disorder could arise at a number of stages in the complex processes involved in organising a voluntary action.

Empirical Characteristics

The terminology for discussing disorders of voluntary action has been particularly inconsistent if not confusing. There is still no agreed classificatory scheme. For these reasons, a strictly empirical, task-oriented framework will be adopted in this section, rather than one which is based on particular theoretical perspectives. The main types of task which have been considered are (1) single repetitive movements, (2) unfamiliar actions and action sequences, (3) familiar gestures, (4) object use, (5) body-part-specific actions, and (6) constructional tasks.

Single Repetitive Movements

Unimanual Movements   Wyke (1967) asked patients to tap alternately on two sides of a line using a hand-held stylus. The number of taps produced in three 15-second intervals was counted. She found that patients could show a bilateral slowing of tapping rate which could not simply be explained in terms of hemiparesis or sensory loss. Carmon (1971) attempted to control tapping rate by asking subjects to keep

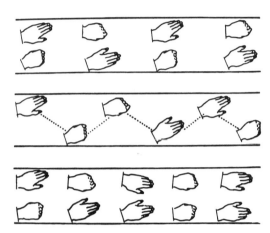

Figure 5.1 Luria's bimanual coordination test: Row 1 illustrates normal performance; Row 2 illustrates patient alternating rather than coordinating hand shift; Row 3 illustrates patient making the same action with both hands.

pace with an auditory signal. He found that whilst some subjects made errors regardless of the rate of stimulus presentation, others were surprisingly worse when the slow rate was used. Heilman (1975) found that patients who were diagnosed as having a disorder of voluntary action on the basis of their performance on tasks such as flipping a coin on command were also poor on a test of rapid tapping. Once again this deficit was independent of primary motor and sensory loss. However, it is unclear whether such tasks should be conceptualised in terms of disorders of "voluntary action" rather than tests of alertness or sustained attention.

Bimanual Coordination of Repetitive Movements It is commonly necessary to coordinate the timing and movement of two limbs simultaneously (e.g., Todor & Smiley, 1985). This ability can be impaired in patients with cerebral lesions. Luria (1966) described one such coordination task. The patient is asked to place both hands on the desk, making a fist with one hand and placing the other hand palm down. He is then required to alternate "fist" and "flat" positions simultaneously (see Fig. 5.1). Patients may have specific difficulty in the simultaneous coordination of these movements, tending to alternate them or to perform the same action with both hands (Laplane, Talairach, Meninger, Bancaud, & Orgogozo, 1977).

Unfamiliar Actions and Action Sequences

Copying Single Hand Positions Pieczuro & Vignolo (1967) formalised a clinical neurological test of movement imitation. Patients were asked to reproduce a single hand position [e.g., thumb to ring

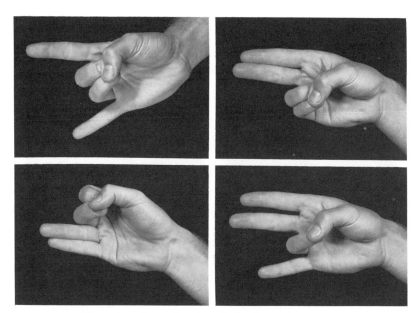

Figure 5.2   Examples of single hand positions.

finger other fingers extended (see Fig. 5.2)]. They used 10 items of this type, and the patient's performance was judged on a 3-point scale (correct, partially correct, and totally incorrect). A comparable task has since been used by Kimura & Archibald (1974) and Kimura (1982) and has been developed and extended by De Renzi, Motti, & Nichelli (1980). These investigations have shown that copying single meaningless hand positions may be surprisingly difficult for some patients with cerebral lesions.

Action Sequences   Luria (1966) devised a task in which patients were required to copy a series of three novel hand postures and reproduce them in their correct order (see Fig. 5.3). Subsequently Kimura & Archibald (1974) used six sequences of meaningless hand movements (e.g., fingertips and thumb tip together in a ring, all touching forehead, hand moves out from forehead rotating and opening wide as it moves). They found that the test of sequence copying was more difficult for patients than was the test of copying single movements.

Kimura (1977) introduced a piece of apparatus which enabled the subject to perform three easily distinguishable but constrained movements (see Fig. 5.4). In this new test the patient was required to press a button with the index finger, to pull a handle, and finally to depress a lever with the thumb. Measures of learning time and the time taken to produce a sequence were recorded in addition to errors in the action

Figure 5.3 Example of sequence of three hand movements. (Based on Luria, 1966.)

sequence. Some patients were slow in learning the sequence, were slow in executing it, and made mistakes. Kimura analysed the patient's errors using five different categories (perseverations, unrelated movements, errors of sequencing, incomplete movements, and delays in making a transition onto the next movement in sequence). The commonest error type was a perseveration, in which the patient produced "movements or postures which resembled the movement executed (and correct) at the immediately preceding position on the box" (Kimura, 1977).

Both Kolb & Milner (1981) and Lehmkuhl, Poeck, & Willmes (1983) used a battery of unconstrained arm and hand movements in an attempt to detect disorders of voluntary action. In the Lehmkuhl *et al.* study, 40 meaningless movements were used (e.g., place hand on opposite shoulder, place palm of hand on neck). In the course of a detailed analysis of errors they noted that perseverations were extremely common. These errors did not necessarily take the form of a simple reproduction of the preceding movement, but sometimes included elements of actions which had been produced up to 13 trials before.

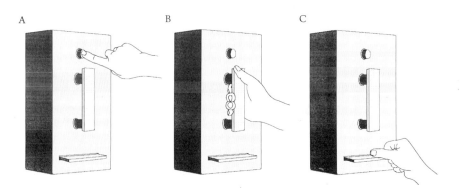

Figure 5.4 (A–C) Kimura's (1977) box. Example of series of three actions.

Motor Skill Learning   Heilman, Schwartz, & Geschwind (1975) found that patients who were diagnosed as apraxic (on the basis of a screening test using novel and familiar movements) were significantly impaired on a test of motor skill acquisition (pursuit rotor). Whilst nonapraxic patients and control subjects showed learning of the task over a series of trials, no improvement was noted in the apraxic patients.

The Relationship between Single and Multiple Movements   De Renzi *et al.* (1980) and De Renzi, Faglioni, Lodesani, & Vecchi (1983) have systematically compared large groups of patients on single vs. sequences of hand postures: in the movement-sequence task the patients were presented with pictorial "reminders" of the different hand positions which were required. Under these conditions there was no evidence of a disproportionate impairment in the performance of the sequential task. Indeed, fewer patients showed difficulty with multiple movements. Overall these findings indicate that sequential movements may achieve their greatest sensitivity in the context of tasks requiring the retrieval of a pattern of movements from memory rather than in conditions in which step-by-step imitation is required (see also Jason, 1983).

Familiar Gestures

Hécaen and his co-workers have investigated patients' ability to perform a range of different types of familiar gesture (Hécaen, 1978; Hécaen & Rondot, 1985). In their investigation, gestures were subdivided into those which were primarily symbolic, such as the "thumbs up" sign to indicate that things were fine, and those which were expressive, such as shaking of the fist to indicate threat. Although a significant proportion of patients were impaired on these tests, no difference was found between the different types of gesture, despite their somewhat different communicative functions. De Renzi and his colleagues analysed patients' ability to imitate a number of familiar but non-object-related gestures (e.g., salute, wave goodbye, threaten somebody). They found that a significant proportion of their patients (43%) had difficulty with this task (De Renzi et al., 1980).

A number of investigations have contrasted patients' ability to imitate unfamiliar hand postures with their ability to perform meaningful gestures. Pieczuro & Vignolo (1967) found that imitation of a meaningless movement was generally more difficult than the test of familiar gesture imitation. They found that when patients were required to imitate either type of hand posture, there was a relatively high incidence of perseveration: patients might produce the same posture on successive trials despite being presented with two different postures.

The meaningless & gestural types of movement-copying task did not appear to dissociate. Pieczuro & Vignolo argued that these tests differed on a task-difficulty dimension rather than in terms of a qualitative difference between test demands. Subsequently Lehmkuhl et al. (1983) obtained similar results on an extensive (200-item!) test battery. De Renzi et al. (1980), however, noted that a small proportion of patients found a test of symbolic gesture production more difficult than a test in which novel hand positions had to be copied. This finding was not subsequently replicated (De Renzi et al., 1983). It therefore seems likely that any dissociation between symbolic and nonsymbolic gestures may be rare.

Object Use

Real Objects   Pick (1905) noted that some patients might have particular difficulty in producing actions appropriate to objects. He observed patients trying to light a candle with matches and noted errors such as attempting to strike the match on the candle or failing to blow out the match once it was alight. De Renzi, Pieczuro, & Vignolo (1968) investigated patients' ability to demonstrate the use of single real objects. They found a comparatively high incidence of errors in their patient sample (22%). They commented that the deficits shown by the patients on the formal test of object use were not "obvious" in natural contexts. For example, a patient who failed to demonstrate the use of a toothbrush in the testing session was subsequently observed to use one quite normally in the bathroom! It appeared as though the artificial demands of the testing situation elicited mild deficits.

Few other investigators have used real objects in systematic investigations. Poeck & Lehmkuhl (1980) examined patients' abilities to utilise several objects in a frequently used sequence (e.g., opening a tin of soup with a can opener). Patients made errors such as beating the side of the can with the can opener rather than using it appropriately. They commented that tests requiring the sequential utilisation of objects might be more sensitive to impairment than tests of single object use. In analysing the types of error made on such tasks, Poeck and Lehmkuhl noted that the actions were usually well formed but were inappropriate to the specific objects being used. These "parapraxic" errors could consist of gross mistakes (such as that cited above); in other cases the patient might make "spatial errors" (such as using the wrong end of the can opener or writing with the wrong end of a pencil). De Renzi & Lucchelli (1988) also studied patients' ability to demonstrate the use of multiple objects. In addition to the error types noted by Poeck & Lehmkuhl (1980), they noted a high incidence of errors of omission in which a patient might miss a critical step in performing an action. For example, in lighting a candle the patient might fail to ignite the match, or in attempting to pour water from a sealed bottle the patient might fail to remove the lid.

Pantomimed Use of Objects   Other investigators have investigated patients' ability to "pantomime" the use of single (or multiple) objects in an attempt to achieve an appropriate level of test sensitivity. Goodglass & Kaplan (1963) investigated patients' ability to mime the use of objects which were shown visually. They found a significant degree of deficit amongst a group of patients with language impairments. In their analysis of errors made by the patients, Goodglass & Kaplan found that a significant proportion made an error which was designated "body part as object." For example, when asked to show how one would use a comb or how to brush one's teeth the patient would run fingers through his hair or rub his index finger across his teeth. The "body-part-as-object" error was not, however, limited to patients. Goodglass & Kaplan noted that less able control subjects and children might make the same type of mistake. Other types of error which they identified included facial or gestural enhancement of the action. For example, the mime for stirring a cup of tea might be elaborated to include pouring cream and drinking the tea. Subsequently Hécaen (1978) reviewed a large series of patients who had been clinically assessed for their ability to produce pantomimes. He found that failure on the pantomime task was correlated with difficulties in demonstrating the use of real objects. Hécaen & Rondot (1985) concluded that the distinction between tests of pantomime and tests of real object use was one of task difficulty: there was a strong relationship between failure on one task and failure on the other.

Heilman (1973) described three patients who were specifically impaired in miming the use of objects when given the spoken name of an object (such as "show me how you would use a cup"). They were reportedly quite capable of producing the appropriate action when the object was seen or touched. When the patients were asked to imitate the movements made by the examiner, their performance was entirely normal. This contrasts with early case reports of patients in whom the ability to mime the use of common objects was better when the name of the object was spoken (Strohmeyer, 1903, cited in Hécaen & Albert, 1978).

The effects of verbal or visual presentation of object stimuli have since been investigated systematically by De Renzi and his colleagues (De Renzi, Faglioni, & Sorgato, 1982). They found that there was a double dissociation between patients' ability to pantomime when given the spoken name of an object and their ability to mime when shown the object (i.e., out of reach). Some patients were able to perform the pantomime when presented with the spoken word but not when they saw the object. Others showed the converse pattern of performance. Although tactile presentation of the actual object (with the patient being blindfolded) was commonly the easiest condition, two patients were disproportionately impaired on this task.

Body-Part-Specific Actions

It is axiomatic that there are different neural systems implicated in the control of different limbs and different types of body movements; hence the possibility that this has direct consequences for disorders of voluntary action has been explored by a number of workers. In their large-scale study Lehmkuhl et al. (1983) contrasted patients' ability to perform single and multiple, meaningful and meaningless movements using either their upper or their lower limbs. No significant differences emerged. Furthermore they found no evidence for there being any difference between tasks which required the use of fine (differentiated) finger movements and those which required movement of a whole limb—both types of task could elicit deficits.

Geschwind (1975) reported that there was a dissociation between measures of limb-apraxic impairment and patients' ability to produce axial body movements, such as generation of a particular body posture (stand like a boxer, stand like a golfer). The best-documented example of this class of deficit is apraxia of gait (difficulty in walking). Patients with a marked degree of apraxia of gait may be very severely handicapped, and even wheelchair-bound. Their deficit may extend to encompass any voluntary movement with the feet or legs (e.g., moving the foot in a circle, kicking a ball). (e.g., Meyer & Barron, 1960).

Oral Apraxia There is a clear dissociation between impairments of voluntary movement affecting the limbs and those affecting the mouth and tongue. In the syndrome which has been labelled *oral apraxia* the patient may have difficulty in producing various oral and thoracic movements on command. Indeed the first clinical description of an impairment of voluntary action (Jackson, 1870) identified just this pattern of deficit. The patient was unable to cough, protrude her tongue, or open her mouth on command, although all of these gestures were quite possible in "naturalistic" circumstances (e.g., when eating a meal). Jackson pointed out that such a pattern of deficit could give the impression of a dementia or failure of cooperation in standard physical examinations. A number of quantitative investigations of oral apraxia have since been conducted. These have required patients to produce a fixed set of different oral gestures (e.g., Goodglass & Kaplan, 1963; Matteer & Kimura, 1977; Kolb & Milner, 1981). These studies have shown that oral apraxia may occur as a highly selective deficit.

Lateralised Disorders Impairment in producing voluntary actions may be confined to one side of the body; indeed, this was the type of deficit observed in Liepmann's original case. The patient may be able to demonstrate the use of objects or perform actions to verbal command with one hand but be incapable of doing so with the other. In most patients, the nondominant arm or hand is more affected than the dominant limb, and the deficit may therefore simply be dismissed as "longstanding clumsiness." One of the most detailed investigations of a unilateral apraxia was reported by Geschwind & Kaplan (1962). The patient was unable to perform actions on verbal command with his left hand, however the same movements were possible using the right hand. By contrast, there was no asymmetry between the limbs in demonstrating the use of visually presented objects.

Constructional Tasks

Kleist (1912) described an impairment in the organisation of complex actions in space, a deficit which has been termed *constructional apraxia*.

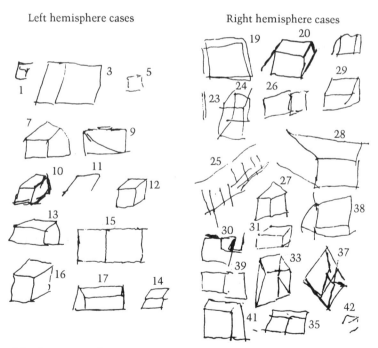

Figure 5.5   Copying a cube. Examples from patients with and left- and right-hemisphere lesions (Piercy *et al.*, 1960).

Kleist argued that this was a disorder affecting movements under visual control in which the spatial components of the task were particularly vulnerable. Tests of copying and drawing have been widely used in order to evaluate the characteristics and incidence of constructional apraxia. Drawing abilities, both when copying a model and when drawing from memory, appear to be particularly vulnerable in patients with cerebral lesions. Simple geometric shapes, such as a diamond, or more complex figures, such as a star and cube, may prove impossible for patients to copy accurately. Piercy, Hécaen, & Ajuriaguerra (1960) found that both spontaneous drawing and copying could be quite impaired (see Fig. 5.5). Copying of stick patterns and constructing stick patterns from memory were investigated by McFie & Zangwill (1960). They found that this somewhat less demanding task was also sensitive to constructional difficulties (see Fig. 5.6).

There are a number of difficulties in deriving precise quantitative measures of "accuracy" and "error" in such tasks since there are con-

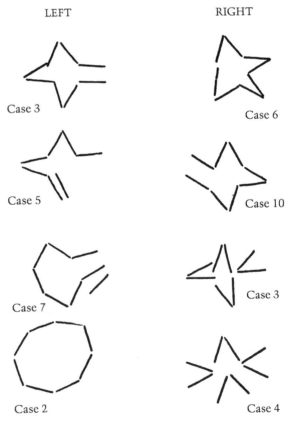

Figure 5.6 Copying a star with matchsticks. Examples from and left- and right-hemisphere lesions (McFie & Zangwill, 1960).

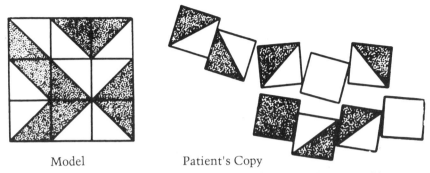

Model   Patient's Copy

Figure 5.7 Example of constructional failure on Koh's Blocks. (From Critchley, 1953.)

siderable individual differences in the development of constructional skills in the normal population. In the case of drawing tasks, various scoring procedures have been put forward in an attempt to achieve an objective measurement. Benton (1962) required patients to copy stimuli from his Visual Retention Test. This test consists of arrays of geometrical figures and patterns (see Fig. 4.4). Benton scored as errors those reproductions in which part or all of a figure was omitted or grossly distorted. Only those patients whose reproductions contained more errors than those of the poorest control were considered to have failed the task. Arrigoni & De Renzi (1964) also used a simple copying test and measured both patients' and control subjects' performance on a 3-point scale. As in the Benton (1962) investigation, failure was defined as performance which was poorer than that of any control subject. Arrigoni & De Renzi also used the Koh's Blocks Test as a measure of constructional abilities (see Fig. 5.7). Although this is a complex test, it has the advantage of being easy to score objectively, and in addition there are extensive norms available.

Warrington, James, & Kinsbourne (1966) used a somewhat different approach to the detection of impairment and error classification. They asked an independent judge to rate drawings and copies on a 4-point scale (ranging from satisfactory to very impaired). In addition to the use of a rating scale they attempted to quantify specific attributes of the drawings, such as orientation on the page, number of right angles, and number of extraneous or additional lines (and errors of spatial bias, see Chapter 4). This more detailed analytic approach has been quite widely used (e.g., Gainotti & Tiacci, 1970; DuCarne & Pillon, 1974; Collingnon & Rondeaux, 1974).

Anatomical Considerations

The evidence which has been reviewed in the empirical section has been concerned with those disorders of voluntary action associated with cortical lesions. The complex and controversial disorders of movement arising as a consequence of lesions to the basal ganglia and related structures have not been considered (see Wing, 1984; Hardie & Lees, 1985).

Single Repetitive Movements

Unimanual Movements   Wyke (1967) found that patients with left-hemisphere lesions were bilaterally slow on her test of stylus tapping. In a paced tapping test Carmon (1971) found that, whereas left-hemisphere lesions gave rise to impairment at all rates, right-hemisphere cases were disproportionately impaired when the rate of tapping was slow. In the somewhat different task of finger flexion, no hemisphere asymmetries have been reported.

Bimanual Coordination   Patients with lesions in the supplementary motor region or in the frontal lobes may show highly specific impairments in the coordination of bimanual hand movements (see Fig. 5.1). This type of disorder is rarely observed in patients with more posterior lesions (Laplane *et al.*, 1977).

Unfamiliar Actions and Action Sequences

Single Hand Positions   Pieczuro & Vignolo (1967) found that patients with left-hemisphere lesions were worse at copying single hand movements than were those with right-hemisphere lesions (see Fig. 5.2). Using a small sample, Kimura & Archibald (1974) were unable to find any asymmetry, but in a larger patient group Kimura (1982) noted that patients with damage to the left parietal lobe were significantly impaired. De Renzi *et al.* (1983) also found that left parietal lesions gave rise to a deficit on this task.

Unfamiliar Sequences   Kimura & Archibald (1974) reported that left-hemisphere lesions differentially affected performance on the "box" test of motor learning (see Fig. 5.4). In a later report, including a larger number of patients, Kimura (1982) was able to be more specific about the critical locus of lesion. She found that lesions of both the left frontal and the left parietal lobe resulted in impairment. Other studies using "unconstrained" sequences of free-arm and hand movements have indicated that the left parietal deficit in sequencing tasks is more common and more severe than that observed after frontal-lobe lesions.

Thus, although both right and left frontal cases scored slightly worse than controls in a study by Kolb & Milner (1981), only the left parietal group was significantly impaired. De Renzi et al. (1980, 1983) have also emphasised the disproportionate severity of the left parietal lobe deficit in their sequencing tasks.

Familiar Gestures

Patients who are impaired in producing meaningful gestures on command have consistently shown a left parietal locus of lesion. This is comparable to that documented in patients with disorders in producing single hand positions (e.g., Hécaen, & Angelergues, 1963; Hécaen, 1972; De Renzi et al., 1980; Hécaen & Rondot, 1985).

Object Use

Impairments in demonstrating the use of objects were initially thought to reflect widespread and nonspecific brain damage (Pick, 1905; Dejerine, 1914; Denny-Brown, 1958). However, other writers have challenged this view and contended that the critical lesion site is in the left hemisphere (Foix, 1916; Liepmann, 1920; Morlaas, 1928; Ajuriaguerra, Hécaen, & Angelergues, 1960). In a quantitative study of patients with unilateral lesions, De Renzi et al. (1968) found that impairment in object use could be demonstrated in 28% of left-hemisphere cases. Patients with right-hemisphere lesions scored at the level of controls. Within the left hemisphere, it has been suggested that regions around the parietal and temporal junction may be implicated, although the evidence is not conclusive (e.g., Ajuriaguerra et al., 1960; De Renzi & Lucchelli, 1988).

Body-Part-Specific Impairments

There is no conclusive evidence for the anatomical correlate of impairments in producing specific postures (Geschwind, 1975). However in the case of "apraxia of gait" bilateral frontal lesions have been demonstrated (Meyer & Barron, 1960).

Oral Apraxia   Impairments in the acquisition of a sequence of oral movements have been documented systematically in group studies of patients with unilateral lesions. The disorder is most pronounced in patients with damage to the anterior sectors of the left hemisphere

(Matteer & Kimura, 1977; Tognola & Vignolo, 1980). Kolb & Milner (1981) suggested that damage to the right frontal lobe could occasionally give rise to a deficit on a difficult test of oral movements. However, the disorder was more than three times as frequent in patients with left frontal lesions. On the basis of CT scan evidence from patients who had sustained cerebrovascular accidents, Tognola & Vignolo (1980) suggested that highly specific lesion sites are implicated in oral apraxia, namely the left central operculum and insula.

Unilateral Impairments   Unilateral impairments of voluntary action may arise as a consequence of a lesion in the truncus of the corpus callosum. The nondominant hand is typically affected, consistent with the view that lesions to the corpus callosum result in a disconnection between the processing systems in the right and left hemispheres. If the left hemisphere is critically involved in the organisation of action, then a lesion to the corpus callosum would disconnect the systems for action organisation in the left hemisphere from the right hemisphere systems responsible for left hand action implementation. The best documented cases of unilateral deficit have shown a significantly greater impairment in performing actions to verbal command than in imitating an action or using an object (Geschwind & Kaplan, 1962; Watson & Heilman, 1983). The absence of a "total" unilateral deficit in these cases is possibly accounted for by preservation of some connections between the right and left hemispheres. In this regard it is relevant that both of the relevant cases had sparing of the major interhemispheric visual pathway: the splenium.

Constructional Tasks

Early analyses of failure on constructional tasks were primarily focused on quantitative estimates of the incidence of impairment in

Table 5.1   Incidence of Constructional Apraxia[a]

	Right hemisphere (%)	Left hemisphere (%)
Piercy *et al.* (1960)	38	17
Benton (1962)	23	14
Benton & Fogel (1962)	32	14
Arrigoni & De Renzi (1964)	38	18
De Renzi & Faglioni (1967)	38	27
Gainotti (1972)	47	30
Colombo, De Renzi, & Faglioni (1976)	36	31
Arena & Gainotti (1978)	37	37
Mack & Levine (1981)	95	36

[a]In patients with unilateral lesions reported in 10 separate group studies.

patients with right- and left-hemisphere lesions. The outcome of this endeavour was that constructional apraxia was considered to be more common and more severe in patients with lesions of the right hemisphere than in those with lesions of the left. A number of these studies are summarised in Table 5.1.

However, such an analysis ignores the qualitative differences in failure shown by patients with right- and left-sided lesions. Quantitative studies of the qualitative errors made by patients on drawing tasks have indicated that the types of mistakes differ according to the laterality of the lesion (e.g., Arrigoni & De Renzi, 1964; Warrington *et al.*, 1966). Arrigoni & De Renzi reported a difference in incidence of two types of error in right- and left-hemisphere cases. Left-sided cases more frequently oversimplified in copying a cube, indeed five of them copied it as a simple square, while none of the right-sided cases did this. Right-hemisphere cases were observed to make gross alterations in the spatial arrangements between the parts. Warrington *et al.* (1966) reported that patients with right-hemisphere lesions showed failure in spatial organisation of their drawings, failing to articulate the constituent parts, an error termed *the exploded diagram*. Patients with left-hemisphere lesions tended to oversimplify their drawings and showed a high incidence of right angles in their copies of cubes. However, they maintained the basic spatial organisation of the target. This feature was also present in the patients reported by Gainotti & Tiacci, 1970 (see Fig. 5.8).

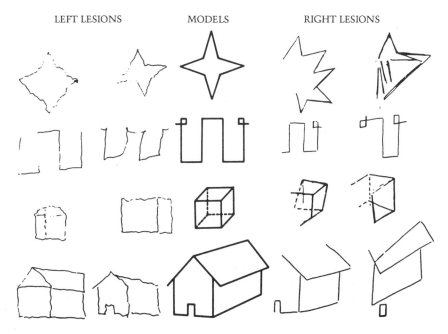

LEFT LESIONS   MODELS   RIGHT LESIONS

Figure 5.8 Examples of patients' errors in copying tasks (Gainotti & Tiacci, 1970).

Such observations led to the hypothesis that the syndrome of constructional apraxia might have (at least) two dissociable components. Failure by the right-hemisphere group was dependent on a primary impairment in the processing of spatial relationships; failure in the left-hemisphere group was due to a deficit in the organisation of those actions necessary for performing the drawing task. This analysis is supported by the documentation of specific deficits in the analysis of relative spatial information by patients with posterior right-hemisphere lesions. Damage in the right parietal lobe, the classical locus for right-hemisphere constructional apraxia, can result in failure of spatial analysis on tasks for which there is no explicit motor component (see Chapter 4). Conversely, patients with left parietal damage (the classical locus for left-hemisphere constructional apraxia) may show impairment on tasks requiring the organisation of actions which cannot be attributed to a primary spatial disorder.

Theoretical Considerations

In this section the following points will be considered: first, the relationship between disorders of voluntary action and disorders of language, and second, the evidence for dissociations between different aspects of voluntary action. Finally, the implications of these dissociations will be considered from the perspective of cognitive models of the organisation of action.

Relationship to Language

Ever since Liepmann's original case, the frequent co-occurrence of language disorders and impairments on tests of voluntary action has motivated interpretations that have adopted a "single common factor" approach. For example, Goldstein (1948) attributed impairments on tests of voluntary action and impairments in speech to a single core disorder of "symbolisation."

The relationship between language and performance on tests requiring the learning and production of unfamiliar movements and movement sequences was investigated by Kimura in a major series of experiments (reviewed in Kimura, 1982). On the basis of her results, Kimura argued strongly for there being a common set of processes implicated in disorders of action and in disorders of language. The common attribute was held to be the ability to organise behaviour serially with respect to time. In the case of language, words are spoken in a particular order to express concepts, and the sounds within words are also strictly constrained in their temporal order. In the case of actions (and perhaps more critically, in the case of action sequences), a temporal dimension is also critical. Kimura conceptualised disorders of language as implicating impairment within a complex system of motor control with oral-motor, auditory-motor, and manual-motor components.

Whilst this account is parsimonious, there are a number of problems. First, as acknowledged by Kimura (1982), there is by no means a direct relationship between disorders of voluntary action and disorders of language. Although these symptoms are associated in as many as 80% of unselected cases with left-hemisphere lesions (De Renzi, 1985), there appears to be a double dissociation between these abilities in individual cases. For example, Kertesz, Ferro, & Shewan (1984) studied 177 cases with left-hemisphere strokes (most of whom were referred because of language difficulties) on systematic tests of language and voluntary movement. They found 4 cases with very severe (receptive and expressive) language disorders whose scores on tests of voluntary movement were within the range of normal controls. De Renzi *et al.* (1980) reported the converse pattern, namely impaired voluntary action with preserved language function in 5% of a series of left-hemisphere-lesioned cases. Selnes, Rubens, Risse, & Levy (1982) reported a case of a patient who had a language disorder which recovered quite rapidly. However, she remained profoundly impaired on tests of voluntary action. Perhaps more critically, there is evidence suggesting dissociations between language abilities and performance on tests of voluntary action when the same "effector" systems are being used in the two situations. For example, two deaf patients with left-hemisphere lesions who became impaired in communication using manual sign language were reportedly normal on tests of learning and producing unfamiliar hand movements (Poizner, Klima, & Bellugi, 1987). The body-part-specific deficit "oral apraxia" also dissociates from impairments in articulating the sounds of the language and other aspects of impaired language function (e.g., Kolb & Milner, 1981). The frequent co-occurrence of aphasia and apraxia is therefore likely to reflect the anatomical proximity of processing systems rather than a single common factor.

Dissociations within Different Aspects of Voluntary Action

There are two types of dissociation within these disorders. First there are the body-part–specific deficits, which are by definition distinct from other types of voluntary action and need not be considered further in this context. More problematic is the association or dissociation that may arise between different classes of manual actions. There appears to be evidence both for continuity and for discontinuity within these broad classes.

Continuities The ability to perform single hand movements and to perform sequences of unfamiliar movements appear to lie on a continuum of task difficulty rather than depending on qualitatively distinct processes. The reproduction and imitation of meaningful gestures may possibly dissociate from these skills, however, the evidence is far from conclusive (De Renzi, 1986c). There also appears to be a basic continuity between tasks requiring the use of a single object and tests of multiple object use. A high correlation has been found between performance on tests of single and multiple object-use tasks in a group of 11 patients (De Renzi & Lucchelli, 1988). It was argued that these two procedures differed only on the task-difficulty dimension.

Discontinuities There appears to be a major discontinuity between tests of unfamiliar gesture production and tests of object use. This discontinuity is embodied in a neurological typology. In the first subtype, termed *ideomotor apraxia*, the patient is differentially impaired when required to imitate an unfamiliar action or series of actions. In the other major subtype, termed *ideational apraxia*, the patient is specifically impaired in the ability to recall previously well-established actions, such as those involved in object use. This typology has sometimes been challenged (e.g., Sittig, 1931). Thus, it has been argued that failure to demonstrate the use of objects is simply a more severe form of the disorder which affects the production of unfamiliar actions or action sequences.

In a review of the literature, De Renzi (1985) pointed out that there were at least four cases on record for whom novel actions were easier than object-related actions. The more usual observation is that familiar object-related actions are somewhat easier for patients. De Renzi, therefore, argued for a principled distinction to be drawn between actions specific to objects and other types of action (e.g., novel action sequences). This contention was substantiated in a systematic group study of 20 patients with left-hemisphere lesions (De Renzi & Lucchelli, 1988). They found a nonsignificant correlation between performance on tests of object use and tasks requiring subjects to imitate novel movements. In three cases there was a clear dissociation between impaired ability to demonstrate the use of several real objects and normal performance on tests of single and multiple (meaningless and gestural) movements. One of the patients who could imitate unfamiliar movements, was even gravely impaired in demonstrating the use of a single real object. Another patient showed the converse dissociation, with near perfect performance on demonstrating the use of multiple objects but severe impairment in imitating unfamiliar actions with his hands and arms.

The other major discontinuity which has been postulated in the neurological literature is that between constructional disorders, or *constructional apraxia*, and other deficits in voluntary movement.

Kleist (1912) originally identified constructional apraxia as a specific disconnection syndrome. The patients' impairment was neither purely one of spatial analysis nor one of voluntary action, but a loss of the ability to transmit information between these two domains. Many, if not the majority, of patients who have been designated as "constructional apraxics" appear to have primary impairments either within the domain of spatial processing or in voluntary movement. However, the question remains as to whether the pattern of disorder hypothesised by Kleist occurs as a dissociable deficit. Given our knowledge of the organisation of intermodal and cross-domain processing by the brain, such a deficit seems an almost certain possibility, but after 50 years it has yet to be documented convincingly.

Models of Apraxia

Liepmann (1905) considered that disorders of voluntary movement could be explained in terms of deficits in conceptualisation or in linking concepts with sensory motor associations. The formal organisation of his model is closely related to the Wernicke's-Lichtheim account of language disorders (see Chapter 1). Liepmann postulated three distinguishable "stages" in the production of voluntary actions which corresponded to different types of deficit observed in patients with cerebral lesions. First, the patient had to formulate an "idea" of the movement, that is, to conceptualise the necessary actions and action sequences. A disorder at this level, termed *ideational apraxia* ("ideatorische apraxie"), might be most pronounced when the patient was given verbal instructions to perform a task.

If the conceptual level of processing was disconnected from output systems, then the patient might know what to do but be unable to carry out the movement. Impairment at this level might be most pronounced with unfamiliar actions. Object-related actions might be relatively easy because of the constraints which objects made on the range of possible movements. Liepmann termed this disorder *ideokinetic apraxia* ("ideo-kinectische apraxie"), implying that the links between the idea and the movement were lost. Liepmann's third form of apraxia, kinetic apraxia (kinetisch-apraxie) was thought to implicate disorders in the melody of movements especially for those under proprioceptive control. Geschwind (1975) adopted and extended Liepmann's model. He was somewhat more specific about the anatomical substrata of the disorder and suggested that the linkage of verbal–conceptual processing and motor output systems was mediated by the arcuate fasciculus.

Whilst both of these models are useful, they require extra assumptions to explain the higher incidence of disorders in patients with left-hemisphere lesions. On Geschwind's interpretation, this fundamental asymmetry could be viewed as the result of a disconnection between

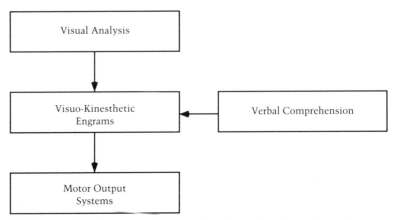

Figure 5.9   Flow diagram to illustrate the relationship of visuokinesthetic engrams to other forms of processing.

language systems and motor production. However, patients also show deficits with visually presented objects and in copying visually presented unfamiliar actions. Unless it is assumed that such visual tasks require verbal mediation then these deficits cannot simply be explained by Geschwind's disconnection account.

The fundamental facts of cerebral asymmetry and unilateral apraxia lead one to entertain the possibility that there might be a specialised left-hemisphere system in which established action patterns are stored. Both Heilman & Rothi (1985) and De Renzi & Lucchelli (1988) have postulated that there is a specialised store of movement programmes. In Heilman's terminology, these are called "visuo-kinesthetic motor engrams." Damage to this store should give rise not only to a failure in producing familiar actions, but also to a failure to recognise the correct action as performed by the examiner (see Fig. 5.9). Heilman, Rothi, & Valenstein (1982) have shown that for some patients with disorders of voluntary action, impairment in action recognition can be relatively severe (e.g., failure to discriminate the appropriate pantomime action for tossing a coin from the gesture for brushing one's teeth). They interpreted these findings in terms of damage to the store of visuo-kinesthetic engrams or of their disconnection from visual and or motor processing systems. Patients who can neither recognise an action nor produce it spontaneously are thought to show damage to the store itself. In those cases in which the appropriate action can be recognised but cannot be generated spontaneously, the deficit may be a disconnection from the motor output systems rather than a loss of the postulated memory store. Disorders in which patients show disproportionate impairments in producing actions appropriate to stimuli presented to a visual, verbal, or tactile stimulus are also viewed as disconnection syndromes. For example, a failure to show the appropriate gesture to the spoken word "cup" with normal performance when the object is seen would be attributed to a disconnection of verbal knowledge from the store of visuokinesthetic engrams.

This model, as it stands, does not allow for a possible discontinuity between the ability to *recall* a movement appropriate to a specific object and the ability to *copy* novel or familiar movements made by the examiner (Zangwill, 1960b; De Renzi, 1985). It therefore needs to be elaborated to include the possibility that there is a specialised memory representation for the knowledge of object-use, a concept originally introduced by Morlaas (1928). Patients lose the ability to recognise the uses of objects but are nevertheless able to retrieve the appropriate visuokinesthetic motor information when asked to copy the examiner.

In terms of an information-processing account, failure to recall the uses of objects might be interpreted as a failure to link knowledge of object use with a central representation of overlearned routines or action programmes (sometimes termed *schemas*; see also Chapter 16). Such overlearned routines can be performed without having to use much in the way of feedback from muscles, proprioception, or vision. These programmes or schemas are thought to be organised hierarchically, so that they can call up the components of complex actions. The component actions in an established motor programme can be run off relatively automatically, without "thinking" about the action. Thus when drinking from a cup, or turning a key, one rarely has to attend minutely to the exact coordination and timing of movements. The action is "run off" as a sequence. One recognises the use of the object, then accesses the appropriate central motor programme which is then implemented.

The psychological concept of a central programme or schema for established actions is consistent with the neurological formulation of visuokinesthetic engrams (Heilman, 1979). In the individual case of "ideational apraxia" the deficit might be attributable to a disorder at the level of access to knowledge about the uses of objects, failure to reach or access a central motor programme, or damage to the central programme itself (see Heilman & Rothi, 1985, for discussion).

There is no reason to suppose that failure to acquire or produce unfamiliar actions should be directly related to impairments in access to, or processing within a "store" of well-established skilled actions. The two types of deficit show a double dissociation. The movements on which patients described as ideo-motor apraxics fail are "unfamiliar" in that they are not normally produced in isolation or comprise sequences of movement which are not dependent on overlearned action patterns. The actions which are to be produced are actually novel combinations of familiar movements, however these actions have to be "reassembled" and "reproduced" in an unfamiliar form. In cognitive psychology this type of action is thought to be very different from those familiar, well-established routines which are dependent on the implementation of central motor programmes or schemas. In the normal individual the establishment of a new action pattern progresses through stages in which movement is closely and actively monitored. For example, in the early stages of learning how to drive a car, individual arm and leg movements have to be carefully and slowly produced with attention being given to each individual action and its consequences. Each action has to be selected, and sequences of action have to be assembled and maintained in memory so that they are produced in the correct order and at the correct time. With practice, however, skill improves and integrated patterns of action (starting up, changing gear) can be produced on the basis of an established motor programme (paying attention to individual arm and leg movements at this stage of skill acquisition can actually prove highly disruptive). In information-processing terms, selective impairment in learning or producing unfamiliar actions can be conceptualised as affecting a stage in which the programmes for action must be selected, assembled, and/or maintained prior to their implementation (e.g., Jeannerod, 1988).

Deficits affecting the selection of actions, their assembly, or their maintenance in memory prior to implementation might have some consequences for the performance of familiar actions (such as the imitation of symbolic gestures in an unfamiliar context). However, they would be most pronounced when the individual was asked to learn or produce a sequence of unfamiliar movements.

Whether there are different subtypes of ideomotor apraxia is unknown. Heilman, for example, has stressed the general "clumsiness" of action, however other analyses have stressed the high incidence of perseveration in action sequences rather than the malformation of individual movements (Poeck & Lehmkuhl, 1980; Kimura, 1982). It is more than likely that there are a number of dissociable disorders subsumed by the label "ideomotor apraxia," just as there may be within the "ideational" category.

Conclusion

Whereas the concept of disorders affecting central motor programmes or schemas appears to offer a plausible framework for analysing the apraxic disorders, such an account is far from being a "complete" theory of disorders of voluntary action. Take, for example, the task of picking up a glass in order to drink from it. Whilst a central motor schema may be able to specify the sequences of action which are required for carrying out the movement, there is no reason to suppose that the situation-specific aspects of the task would be represented in such a programme. The same action is rarely if ever repeated exactly in everyday life. One needs to coordinate visual knowledge (e.g., the location and shape of the glass) with somatosensory and proprioceptive information (e.g., position of limbs, trajectory of movement, weight of glass) and use this information to produce a fluent action which is initiated and terminated appropriately. There are pointers from the neurophysiological literature to suggest that these aspects of voluntary action may be mediated via a different, and parallel, processing system (Goldberg, 1985). It remains an open question as to whether this multiple motor route hypothesis will be equally applicable to the disorders of voluntary action which are observed in patients with neurological disease.

6

Auditory Word Comprehension

Introduction

When one listens to a spoken word it is necessary to process an exceptionally complex set of sound waves, to make crucial distinctions between similar patterns of sounds, and to extract meaning from the utterance. This process normally requires a degree of concentration and focused attention and does (not infrequently) fail. Thus when listening to speech against a noisy or echoing background (such as when a phone line or radio is faulty) it may be difficult to "pick out" the words and hear them clearly. In the extreme case it may not be possible to hear "words" at all. The problem arises because the background noise or distortion interferes with one's ability to perform an adequate acoustic analysis of the speech wave-form.

Words spoken in isolation may also easily be confused with other similar-sounding words. For example, the names of some letters are very similar to each other (e.g., "B" and "D"). Since listeners can get these letter names confused when they are heard in isolation, a specialised "alphabet" has been devised for professionals who have to be totally accurate in discriminating these sounds (e.g., police, airline pilots). Rather than the words "B" (bee) or "D" (dee) the letter name is replaced by a very distinctive-sounding word ("Bravo" and "Delta" in these instances).

Having achieved an adequate perceptual analysis of the sound pattern it is necessary to process the meaning of the spoken word. This can sometimes be problematic when listening to speech referring to words which are at the "edges" of one's vocabulary. It is possible to have a "rough" idea of what a particular word means but be unable to pin down its meaning precisely. For example, most people could give an approximate definition for the words *schooner, alpacca,* or *cistus* but be hard pressed to give dictionary definitions.

These aspects of processing spoken words, namely, analysis of the sound pattern of words and processing for meaning, can break down selectively in patients with cerebral lesions. This breakdown is, of course, only relevant in the present analysis for patients who would not clinically be considered to have a primary impairment of hearing.

Karl Wernicke (1874) is generally credited with producing the first description of patients with a primary disorder of comprehension (see Chapter 1). He described patients who could speak fluently but were unable to understand what was said to them. The patients' speech, though fluent, was by no means normal; indeed it was virtually unintelligible. They used words inappropriately and made errors in pronunciation which reflected the wrong choice of word sounds. These errors often resulted in "words" which were not part of the language, an error termed a *neologism* (literally, a "new word"). The disorder was interpreted in terms of damage to a centre for the images of word sounds. Wernicke's model was elaborated by Lichtheim (1885), who proposed that in addition to a centre for "word sounds" there were additional "concept centres" which were required for processing word meaning (see Chapter 1). Lichtheim suggested that these centres were associated with each other by means of transcortical fibre pathways. This led him to postulate three different types of comprehension disorder. First, the patient might be deaf for the sounds of words (word deaf). Lichtheim described one patient who was reportedly unable to comprehend or repeat words and appeared deaf to the sounds of language. Second, a patient might have a lesion affecting the transcortical pathways and so could not transmit information about word sounds to concept centres (transcortical sensory aphasia). Lichtheim gave an anecdotal account of one such case; that of a man whose wife stated that he had been able to repeat what was said to him and speak sensibly at a time when he was unable to understand speech. The preservation of repetition showed that the patient had intact word-sound perception but was unable to transmit this information to the intact concept centres. Third, the patient might have damage to the concept centres themselves. In such a case the patient, although able to repeat, would neither be able to comprehend words nor to use them spontaneously. This distinction was also made explicit by Liepmann (1898), who proposed that there was a major subdivision to be drawn between patients who were deaf for word sounds and those who were deaf for word meanings. These analyses are still valid, although they have been refined in the intervening years.

Empirical Characteristics

In this section disorders affecting the analysis of word sound characteristics will be considered first. This will be followed by a more detailed consideration of the impairments in the comprehension of individual word meanings (or verbal semantic knowledge). The more complex issues of sentence comprehension will be discussed in Chapter 8.

Word-Sound Processing

Acoustic Analysis of Word Sounds   Originally, patients with a differential impairment in processing spoken words were globally designated as "word deaf." By 1908 Quensel (cited by Hécaen & Albert, 1978) reported that some 200 cases of word deafness had been published in the literature. Many of the early cases of word deafness were initially considered to be "aphasic" because of their poor ability to comprehend the spoken word. Further investigation showed that they were able to read, write, and speak normally, thereby bringing into question the diagnosis of a primary disorder of language. These patients were also able to recognise and identify sounds in the environment, giving the impression that they were purely deaf for the sounds of words.

Patients with this type of deficit may describe their auditory experience of language as "distorted" or "foreign." For example, "It's like a great noise all the time . . . when people speak loudly or quickly the words just run together" (Klein & Harper, 1956). "Language sounds like a wind in the trees, a murmuring of a foreign language" (Zeigler, 1952), and "Like the rustling of leaves on a tree" (Luria, 1966). "Words come too quickly or sound like a foreign language" (Albert & Bear, 1974). These same patients may react normally to environmental sounds, orienting to the sound of breaking glass or to a telephone ringing.

Experimental analysis of patients with this profile of impairment has suggested that the severe form of word deafness may be attributable to a more fundamental deficit in acoustic processing rather than to a specific deafness for words. Albert and Bear (1974) described a case whose primary impairment appeared to be in the processing of acoustic stimuli which changed rapidly in time. He had an increased threshold for discriminating whether one or two clicks had been presented, requiring a longer gap between them than normal subjects. In contrast to this, the patient was able to discriminate acoustic changes which were not dependent on fine temporal resolution. Thus he was normal in the perception of pitch and had a normal threshold for sound volume. Albert & Bear also commented that he had difficulties in determining the order of auditory sequences. The patient's deficit was less severe if single words were presented at a very slow rate. His deficit in word perception was therefore attributed to difficulties in temporal acuity. In this sense, his deficit is analogous to a patient with reduced visual acuity who might have no difficulties in recognising colour or large shapes, but be unable to read small print. In the perception of speech (especially consonants) it is essential that very fine discriminations are made with regard to rapid changes in the auditory wave-form over time. Such changes are less important in discriminating between the sounds of, say, running water and breaking glass: in these cases pitch and volume information may be more salient.

Auerbach, Allard, Naeser, Alexander, & Albert (1982) investigated the role of temporal acuity in a patient with "pure word deafness." They found that the patient was markedly impaired in detecting gaps between stimuli or in determining when two stimuli were simultaneous. So, for example, if two successive clicks were presented, then like Albert & Bear's case, a longer gap was necessary for him to detect that two stimuli had been presented. The patient was also impaired in counting a sequence of rapid clicks and needed a far slower rate than normal subjects. Subsequent cases with a clinically profound "word deafness" syndrome have all been shown to have a similar severe impairment in auditory temporal acuity (e.g., Tanaka, Yamadori, & Mori, 1987; Yaqub, Gascon, Al-Nosha, & Whitaker, 1988). Other deficits may also be present, such as difficulties in pitch discrimination, loudness discrimination, and the ability to discriminate between the durations of tones. These additional deficits may result in less adequate perception of nonverbal sounds (Tanaka *et al.*, 1987).

Phonemic Processing The ability to distinguish between similar sounding words such as *bat* and *pat* or *pit* and *kit* is quite commonly impaired in patients who do not appear to have a clinically profound word deafness syndrome. This type of discrimination depends on the subject being able to perceive the critical sounds of words in the language. These critical sounds, termed *phonemes*, are like the letters of written language: they are few in number but can be combined and recombined to make up the thousands of words which are in the average individual's vocabulary. Take, for example, the words *bat* and *pat*. Each word is made up of three phonemes, but only the initial consonant sound "b" or "p" is different. The distinction between "b" and "p" is dependent on a relatively subtle change in the acoustic wave-form or, more accurately, in subtle differences between sets of acoustic patterns. Such distinctions between phonemes are maintained over considerable variation in the actual sounds which are heard. The actual physical characteristics of the acoustic wave-form differ according to the speaker, the rate of speech, and the context in which a phoneme occurs: thus the "p" of *pat, spill,* and *hope* is very different, but is heard as "the same" by skilled listeners. It is perceived as a member of the category of "p" sounds. In English, we distinguish and recognise approximately 38 different phonemes. (As an aside, it should be noted that the way a word is written is no reliable guide to its constituent phonemes; see Chapters 10 & 11.)

The ability to discriminate phonemes has been tested using tasks in which the subject is required to judge whether two similar sounds such as *bear* or *pear* are the same or different (Blumstein, Baker, & Goodglass, 1977a). Subjects can also be asked to identify a single sound. For

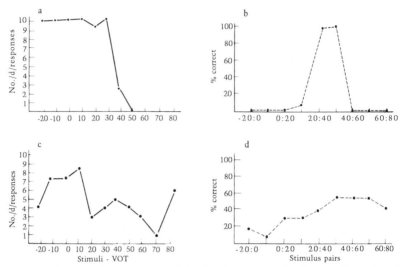

Figure 6.1 Phoneme discrimination: (a) & (b) shows normal subject making clear discriminations between stimuli varying along a single acoustic dimension. (c) & (d) shows chance level of performance in an aphasic patient. (Adapted from Blumstein *et al.*, 1977b.)

example, they may be asked to say if they have heard "ba" or "pa." Presenting sounds which are distorted along an acoustic continuum (so there is a gradual transition between, e.g., "d" and "t") shows that patients may show a breakdown in the strict boundaries between similar sounds which are perceived by normal subjects. Thus whilst normal subjects can distinguish between a distorted "d" and a distorted "t" (analogous to hearing these sounds in different contexts), patients may fail to make a clear discrimination (see Fig. 6.1). Rather than hearing a clear difference between sounds, patients may only discriminate or identify very clear instances of a sound (e.g., Blumstein, Baker, & Goodglass, 1977b). Although this pattern of deficit has been most extensively investigated using consonant perception, there is evidence that the ability to discriminate vowels (e.g., *pat* vs. *pot*) may be impaired in a similar manner (Lund, Spliid, Andersen, & Møller, 1986).

There also appears to be a clear "task difficulty" effect: more distinct contrasts (e.g., between the words *pot* and *got*) are more likely to be discriminated than stimuli which sound more alike (e.g., *tot* and *dot*). Furthermore, within the class of "similar" sounds some discriminations are easier than others. For example, "d" (as in *dot*) vs. "t" (as in *tot*) is an easier discrimination to make than "t" (as in *tot*) vs. "p" (as in *pot*) (Blumstein *et al.*, 1977a,b; Blumstein, Tarter, Nigro, & Statlender, 1984; Miceli, Caltagirone, Gainotti, & Payer-Rigo, 1978). These impairments in discriminating the sounds of words do not appear to be secondary to more general deficits in discriminating complex sounds. Sitdis & Volpe (1988) found that patients with impaired phoneme discrimination were not necessarily impaired on a task requiring them to discriminate acoustically complex tones.

Word Meaning

Difficulties in comprehending the single word can and do occur in the absence of any significant impairment in the auditory perception of words. Patients may have no problem in repeating words which they can no longer comprehend. This indicates that at the very least their speech perception is sufficient for mediating spoken word comprehension (Weisenburg & McBride, 1935). Patients may spontaneously repeat words which they are asked to define, looking puzzled and failing to comprehend them. For example, when asked to define the word *bed* one patient (K.T.) responded, "Bed, bed?, I've no idea what that is." Another (T.O.B.), when asked what the word *swan* meant, replied, "Swan, that sounds familiar, I'm sure I once knew it." When asked to define the proverb "too many cooks spoil the broth" a patient (A.B.) replied, "If I knew what broth was I expect I could explain it." (These cases are discussed in more detail below.)

Two main types of task have been used to assess word-comprehension capacities formally. Spoken word definition tasks can provide a direct measure of auditory word comprehension in those few patients who have satisfactory expressive language skills. Spoken word-to-picture matching tasks are a flexible technique for assessing a range of language comprehension variables in other cases who are unable to express themselves. In this technique the subject is presented with an array of stimuli and simply asked to point to a specific item. Such tasks can be varied in difficulty in systematic ways. For example, a patient might be asked to point to the picture of a telephone or point to the picture of "communication" (see Fig. 6.2).

Schuell, Jenkins, & Landis (1961) tested a group of patients with diverse language disorders on a spoken word–picture matching task and found that there was a direct relationship between a word's frequency in the language and the patient's ability to comprehend it (see Fig. 6.3). Poeck and his colleagues have replicated these findings in a number of careful investigations (Poeck, Hartje, & Kerschensteiner, 1973; Poeck & Stachowiak, 1975). Using word-definition tasks massive word-frequency effects have been demonstrated in selected single cases (e.g., Warrington, 1975; Warrington & Shallice, 1984; McCarthy & Warrington, 1987a). Poeck and his colleagues have contended that word frequency is the most important (if not the only) factor in determining comprehension failure in aphasic patients (Poeck *et al.*, 1973; Poeck & Stachowiak, 1975).

Whilst the importance of word frequency cannot be underestimated in clinical assessment, it is clear that it is far from being the sole determinant of single-word comprehension failure in aphasia.

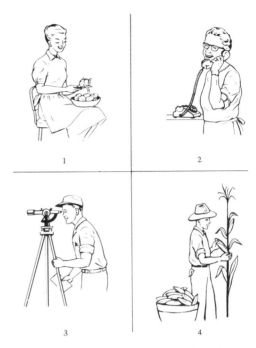

Figure 6.2 Example of stimulus for word–picture matching from Peabody Picture Vocabulary test (Dunn, 1965).

Neurologists have long recognised that some patients may have disproportionate impairments in the comprehension of certain categories of verbal information. In the case of the names of colours and body parts these deficits have been given the status of syndromes (labeled *colour agnosia* and *autotopagnosia*).

Colour Names Willbrand (1887) first identified a specific impairment in colour identification which appeared to be limited to the language domain. He termed this deficit *amnestic colour blindness*. Sittig (1921) described two types of impairment involving colours. In three cases, the patients could neither retrieve the name of a colour nor point to a named colour. At the same time they were able to sort colours into categories (e.g., shades of red, shades of green) and were so distinguished from patients with a primary agnosia for the visual attribute of colour (see Chapter 2). Since then there have been a number of single case reports in which the focus has been on colour name comprehension impairments (e.g., Stengel, 1948; Oxbury, Oxbury, & Humphrey, 1969; Mohr, Leicester, Stoddard, & Siman, 1971). Kleist (1934) described a patient who showed impairment in pointing to named colours, however the names "black" and "white" were spared. Kinsbourne

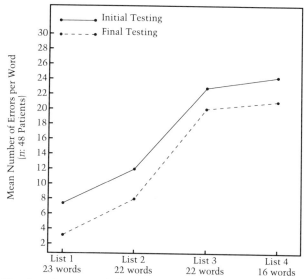

Figure 6.3 Number of errors made by aphasic patients on word–picture matching tests at four levels of word frequency (List 1, high frequency; List 4, low frequency).

& Warrington (1964a) described a patient with a similar pattern of impairment.

Body-Part Names Impairment in the comprehension and localisation of body-part names was first singled out as a specific neurological syndrome by Pick (1908, 1922). The syndrome of "autopagnosia" probably has multiple components. However, for some patients at least, the disorder may be confined to comprehending the spoken names of body parts. This is tested by asking the patients to point to parts of their own body (e.g., show me your nose). Hécaen (1972) described a patient who was able to point to garments that he was wearing but not to parts of his body. Dennis (1976) reported a further case (D.L.A.) who had no difficulty in comprehending the terms *right* and *left* but who failed to point to the appropriate part of her body on verbal command. A further case (J.P.B.) with an impairment in comprehending the names of parts of the body was described by Ogden (1985b). In contrast to his deficit in pointing to named body parts, the patient was quick and efficient in pointing to named animals, fruit, and even to parts of objects. For example, when shown a toy truck he had no difficulty in pointing to driver's seat, front wheels, headlights, engine, passenger seat, door to the driver's seat, etc. A further demonstration that autopagnosia is not merely difficulty in comprehending "part names" was that the patient could point, on a real vase of flowers, to petals, leaf, stem, vase, and water.

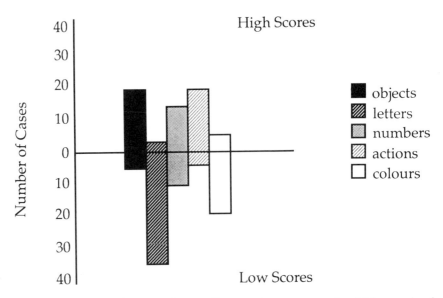

Figure 6.4 Number of patients showing disproportionate preservation (high scores) and impairment (low scores) for words in five semantic categories. (Adapted from Goodglass *et al.*, 1966.)

Category Specificity Goodglass, Klein, Carey, & Jones (1966) were the first to investigate the incidence of category-specific disorders in a group study of patients with a mixed range of language impairments. They selected five categories for specific attention, namely, colours, concrete nouns, action words, letters, and numbers. They noted that patients could have selective difficulties in comprehending any of these categories. Other cases showed islands of preserved knowledge. Overall there was evidence of multiple reciprocal dissociations in comprehension (see Fig. 6.4). On the basis of this data Goodglass et al. (1966) concluded that category-specific comprehension disorders might be the rule rather than the exception. Subsequent investigations have brought to light many other category-specific effects.

The distinction between a "concrete" and an "abstract" vocabulary has been widely explored and is known to be a significant variable in many aspects of verbal processing in normal subjects (e.g., Paivio, 1971). A number of studies have obtained ratings of concreteness and abstractness for large word pools (Brown & Ure, 1969; Paivio, 1971). Concrete words are defined as those which have a direct sensory referent. Words such as house, potato, and rose have high concreteness ratings, whilst words such as luck, idea, and hope are rated low. This dimension has also been found to be a significant determinant of comprehension in aphasic patients. Difficulties in comprehending abstract words are relatively common (Goldstein, 1948), which is perhaps un-

Table 6.1 Examples of Definitions of Words with High and Low Concrete Ratings

Target	Response	Target	Response
		A.B.	
Corn	Vegetation	Advantage	The gain you get
Poster	Don't know	Supplication	Making a serious request for help
Alligator	Forgotten	Hint	Leaking what will occur
Star	Little insect	Know	Making oneself mentally familiar with a subject
		S.B.Y.	
Barber	Concerned with mean	Opinion	A viewpoint of any person held by person or number of persons
Garment	A piece of property	Accent	The way in which different people talk
Column	An area where you keep things	Expensive	To cost a lot of money
Cork	Corky, a wooden thing	Purpose	The reason why some action is done

surprising in that these words are acquired later in childhood and are in some sense more difficult to comprehend. Less common, but also observed, are specific difficulties in comprehending the concrete-word vocabulary. There are two well-documented cases with this syndrome (case A.B., Warrington, 1975; case S.B.Y., Warrington & Shallice, 1984). Their ability to define words with high concrete ratings was significantly worse than their ability to define abstract words which were matched for frequency (i.e., abstract words 90% and 93% correct and concrete words 50% and 63% correct; see Table 6.1).

The broad category of concrete words subsumes an enormous vocabulary including such disparate groupings as foods, animals, flowers, occupations, actions, and various types of man-made objects. There is increasing evidence for fractionations of knowledge of words within the broad concrete-word vocabulary.

S.B.Y. (who was described above) was investigated together with another case (J.B.R.) (Warrington & Shallice, 1984). They found that these patients were particularly impaired in their knowledge of foods and living things (i.e., 52% and 79% for man-made objects and 10% and 8% for living things; see Table 6.2). Two severely aphasic patients (K.B. and I.N.G.) were tested using word–picture matching tests (see above). The stimuli were arrays of coloured pictures of animals, foods, and objects. The patients showed a selective impairment in comprehending the categories of foods and living things (see Table 6.3). This dissociation has been replicated in a number of patients with diverse language backgrounds (e.g., Sartori & Job, 1988; McCarthy & Warrington, 1988; Silveri & Gainotti, 1988; Basso, Capitani, & Laiacona, 1988).

Table 6.2 Examples of Definitions of Foods, Living Things, and Objects

Target	Response	Target	Response
		J.B.R.	
Camel	Don't know	Torch	Device for showing way in dark
Wasp	Bird that flies	Thermometer	Device for registering temperature
Buttercup	Cup full of butter	Helicopter	Flying, for vertical take-off
Swan	Forgotten	Binoculars	A system for seeing things far away
		S.B.Y.	
Frog	Animal, not tamed	Hammer	Device used to hit things
Cheese	You eat one of your foods	Taxi	Machine that takes you around, a vehicle of transportation
Mutton	Some sort of rubbish	Camera	Device for taking photos
Butterfly	A thing that flies through the air, a bird that flies	Pamphlet	Written piece of work describing something

The converse pattern of dissociation has also been documented (Warrington & McCarthy, 1983, 1987). This evidence for a double dissociation within the concrete-word vocabulary rules out any simple explanation in terms of task difficulty. Two patients (V.E.R. and Y.O.T.) had such severe global aphasic impairments that they were unable to comprehend the most rudimentary verbal instructions or utter a single word. Although they totally failed all standard clinical tests of verbal comprehension they were discovered to have remarkable islands of preservation (although their response to gesture was good). Despite being gravely impaired in their ability to point to named objects, they were significantly better in pointing to named foods and animals (see Table 6.3). Perhaps even more remarkable was the observation that their ability to point to named flowers was at least as good as their ability to point to named animals (86 and 96% correct, respectively). Frequently (and for good practical reasons) the assessment of object-name comprehension in severely aphasic patients has relied on the use of small manipulable stimuli. A clinical case report by Yamadori &

Table 6.3 Word–Picture Matching[a]

Case	Foods	Animals	Objects
J.B.R.	60	67	98
K.B.	55	45	85
I.N.G.	85	80	97
V.E.R.	88	86	58
Y.O.T.	93	85	63

[a]Percentage of correct for each patient on each category.

Albert (1973) suggested that there may be a dissociation between knowledge of large outdoor objects and other artifacts. The patient was able to recognise the names of objects in the street, such as cars and other forms of transport, but was impaired in recognising the names of room objects. For example, when asked to point to a chair, "the patient stood up looked around the room, then sat down, spelling to himself, c-h-a-i-r; c-h-a-i-r. Crossing his arms on his chest he finally said 'I have to double check that word later, I don't know.' " This subdivision between "indoor" and "outdoor" objects was explored and refined in a further single case study (Warrington & McCarthy, 1987). The patient (Y.O.T.) was tested for her knowledge of small manipulable objects and large man-made artifacts (e.g., cup, plate, vs. bus, train). In a series of experiments it was demonstrated that her comprehension of the large man-made objects was invariably better than her comprehension of small manipulable objects (78% and 58% correct, respectively).

Proper Names The individuals' vocabulary for living things and artifacts by no means exhausts those words which have high concrete imageable ratings. Another large class of words is that of proper nouns. In the investigation of the globally aphasic patient referred to above (Y.O.T.), the status of her knowledge of proper nouns was investigated in addition to the categories of foods, living things, and objects. She had no difficulty in pointing to named maps of countries or pictures of famous buildings or of famous people. Indeed these were the only categories sampled in the entire series of experiments on which her performance was almost error free.

The converse dissociation, namely the failure to comprehend the names of people, has since been observed. A patient (T.O.B., described in McCarthy & Warrington, 1988) was severely impaired in comprehending the names of famous people. Thus when asked, "Who was Shakespeare?" he stated that he didn't know. When asked, "Who was Henry the Eighth?" he responded, "Since it's a King, he might be the father of the present Queen." His impairment in comprehending the names of historical figures which he must have known all his life was even more striking considering his ability to recall the names of people in his present environment. The name Christopher Columbus meant absolutely nothing to him, but the name Christopher Pugh (a young doctor) was instantly recognised. Furthermore, he had no difficulty in defining the names of man-made objects such as telephone, microcomputer, or stethoscope.

Action Names A further subcomponent of the concrete/imageable-word vocabulary is that of the names of actions: a category singled out by Goodglass et al. (1966) as one which could be selectively impaired in aphasia. This observation has been replicated and extended in a single case (R.O.X.) by McCarthy & Warrington (1985). The patient was unable to comprehend the names of actions. Thus, when asked to

A

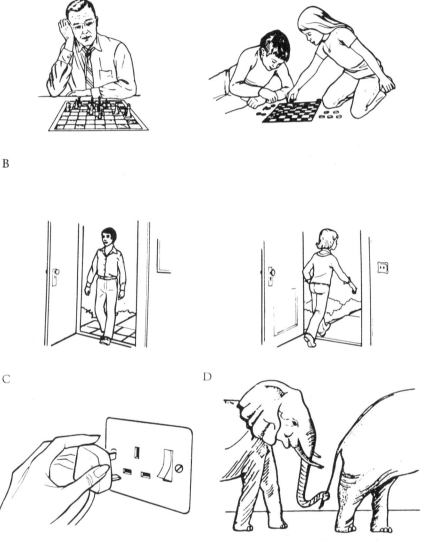

B

C

D

Figure 6.5 (A–D) Examples of stimuli from a word–picture matching test that compares nouns and action names (McCarthy & Warrington, 1985).

demonstrate "sitting" he stood to attention, and when asked to demonstrate "opening" he closed an open drawer. His difficulty was not in performing actions, since he could both imitate and spontaneously produce entirely appropriate actions. On tests of single word comprehension with noun targets his performance was comfortably within the normal range. Word–picture matching tasks were designed to compare his comprehension of related nouns and related action names (e.g., chess vs. draughts; coming vs. going; see Fig. 6.5). The patient was selectively impaired on the related action names (74% correct vs. 99%). He had particular difficulties in comprehending verbs which were appropriate to one actor in an interactive scene (see Fig. 6.5). The patient was quite unable to point to the appropriate part of the picture for "leading" or "following" and scored at a chance level (59%). His comprehension of nouns referring to the components of an interactive scene (e.g., "plug" vs. "socket") was significantly better (89%).

Partial Comprehension Clinical examination of patients with impaired comprehension may suggest that there is a clear dividing line between those words which are "preserved" and those which are "forgotten." Such an impression is often misleading. In many cases there is a very large "grey area" in between these two extremes in which partial knowledge can be demonstrated. The pattern is that of a continuum between a full and intact specification of the verbal concept, through to words for which there is a loss of the fine detail, on to the extreme of the continuum in which only crude information is available.

A variety of techniques have been used to investigate the characteristics of this grey area of knowledge in patients with verbal comprehension impairments. [These overlap to some extent with the techniques which have been used to probe knowledge about visual concepts (see Chapter 2).] Residual verbal knowledge can be probed by questions about the properties of the concept to which a spoken word refers. These questions can range from the superordinate level (Is it an animal or an object?) through to more detailed probes about attributes (Is it yellow or grey?) or associations (Is it more likely to be owned by a man or a woman?) (Warrington, 1975; Sartori & Job, 1988; Bub, Black, Hampson, & Kertesz, 1987).

Using these techniques it has been shown that general, superordinate knowledge is less vulnerable than is more specific knowledge about the target. For example, the patient might be able to state that a canary was a living thing rather than an object but score at chance if asked to decide if it was yellow or grey. It has also been noted that some of the words which appear to be "known" to the patient may nevertheless have lost some of the precision in their reference. Words which the patient may seem to have "forgotten" may still be explicitly categorised according to their superordinate properties (e.g., animal/ object). The data from a patient (E.M.) on superordinate and fine detailed knowledge for "known" and "unknown" words is shown in Fig. 6.6.

Word–picture matching tasks can be adapted so that information may be obtained with regard to the "precision" with which the spoken word refers to a concept. This is achieved by the simple expedient of varying the items in an array so that they are sampled in "semantically close" groups (e.g., arrays of types of clothing, kitchen utensils, or

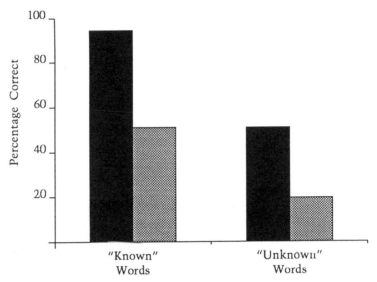

Figure 6.6 Performance of one patient (E.M.) on probe test for superordinate knowledge of "known" and "unknown" words. Solid black bar represents superordinate category; shaded grey bar represents subordinate attributes (Warrington, 1975).

different types of furniture or office objects). The subject's ability to perform this task can be contrasted with that when arrays are constructed from more disparate items. Spoken word–picture matching has typically shown marked effects of "semantic distance" in aphasic patients (e.g., Lesser, 1978; Butterworth, Howard, & McLoughlin, 1984).

Not only is there evidence for partial knowledge but, in addition, there is evidence that such partial loss of information may be confined to particular semantic categories. For example, patients may be able to give a full and adequate account of the meanings of objects, but at the same time their knowledge of living things may be reduced to superordinate information alone (e.g., cases J.B.R., and S.B.Y.).

Comparable effects have been documented in word–picture matching tests. Category-specific semantic distance effects may be obtained even when broad superordinate category information would be insufficient to mediate performance. Arrays can be constructed in which the semantic distance of the target is varied systematically. In one case (Y.O.T.) it was shown that word–picture matching tests using arrays of semantically "close" items such as clothing or kitchen utensils were harder than arrays of common objects which crossed these narrow category boundaries (e.g., one item of clothing, one kitchen utensil, etc.). No such distance effects were noted within the patient's preserved categories, on which she scored at ceiling levels regardless of the difficulty of the discrimination (Warrington & McCarthy, 1987).

Consistency of Impairment A distinction can be drawn between those patients who appear to have a consistent and reliable impairment of their comprehension of individual words and those whose comprehension of individual words is variable. In the first class of patients, the same items will have been forgotten and the same items retained when they are tested over weeks or months. (e.g., Coughlan & Warrington, 1981). This consistent pattern of responding can be specific to a particular semantic category (McCarthy & Warrington, 1988). In other patients however, there may be considerable variability in the items that are available from one minute to the next: this type of response can also be category specific.

An inconsistent but category-specific impairment has been documented in two cases (V.E.R. and Y O T.). Both of these patients scored at a generally lower level on one category than another. However, their ability to comprehend individual items within the affected category was variable. For example, the word *knife* might be comprehended on one occasion but not on another. This was tested by asking the patients to match a spoken word to an array of pictures, however, each item in the array was sampled four or five times within a testing block. Typically their first few responses were correct but declined to chance levels as testing continued.

With both of these cases it was possible to establish that this was not simply attributable to arbitrary random noise in the system. Not only were they affected by the serial position of the test stimulus; they were also sensitive to the temporal relationships between their last response and presentation of the next stimulus. If they were given a few seconds of silence *after* each trial (30 seconds in the case of V.E.R.), then their performance improved. Under normal testing conditions their comprehension seemed to "jam up": they would be accurate on the first few trials on an array from one of their impaired categories and then become chaotic in their responding. In one patient (Y.O.T.) the effect of presentation rate was shown to be specific to the affected category (see Table 6.4 from Warrington & McCarthy, 1987).

Table 6.4 Category Specificity and Rate[a,b]

Response stimulus interval	Foods	Animals	Objects
2 seconds	93	85	63
5 seconds	93	93	90

[a] Figures reflect percentage correct on spoken word–picture matching test for each category and at each Response Stimulus Interval (RSI).
[b] $n = 60$; chance = 20%.

Anatomical Considerations

Word-Sound Impairments

Acoustic Analysis In those patients with an impairment in the temporal resolution of acoustic signals for whom anatomical correlates are available, the evidence points toward bilateral lesions of the temporal lobes (Auerbach *et al.*, 1982; Brick, Frost, Schochett, Gutman, & Crosby, 1985; Yaqub *et al.*, 1988). The patient's lesions may occur independently in time and, in these cases, the impairment is only manifest after the second lesion. Such observations suggest that a bilateral lesion is a necessary requirement for the full syndrome to occur. Patients with this disorder should probably be considered as showing a partial cortical deafness, that is, an acoustic deficit rather than a primary impairment in the perception of word sounds. There is evidence for a double dissociation between the ability to match meaningless auditory patterns of spectrally complex sounds (like the random noises heard on an out-of-tune radio) and the ability to recognise familiar environmental sounds. Faglioni, Spinnler, & Vignolo (1969) have shown that patients with damage to the right hemisphere were impaired on the meaningless-sounds task, but damage to the left hemisphere resulted in impairment of meaningful sound recognition. These findings were replicated and extended by Vignolo and his colleagues (Faglioni, Spinnler, & Vignolo, 1969; Vignolo, 1982). They found not only that there was a laterality effect, but also that patients with bihemispheric lesions showed a double deficit.

In a study directly contrasting discrimination of speech sounds with discrimination of complex tones, Sitdis & Volpe (1988) also found a double dissociation. Patients with left-hemisphere lesions were impaired in discriminating word sounds but not necessarily in discriminating tones. The converse pattern was observed in right-hemisphere cases.

Phonemic Impairments Impairment of consonant and vowel sound discrimination is well documented in patients with unilateral lesions of the left hemisphere. These deficits have been documented in patients with lesions over a wide area of the left hemisphere and with a variety of different language impairments. However, the highest incidence of deficit and the most severe impairments are observed in patients with left temporal lobe lesions (Luria, 1976; see Fig. 6.7). In a detailed group study of vowel perception in patients with focal unilateral lesions Lund *et al.* (1986) found that patients with damage in Wernicke's area of the left temporal lobe were markedly impaired (see Fig. 1.1). Patients with lesions outside this region of the left hemisphere or with right-hemisphere lesions in the homologue of Wernicke's area were able to score at the level of controls (speech therapists).

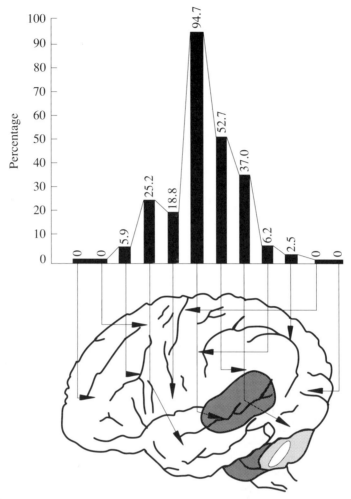

Figure 6.7 Incidence of impairment on phoneme-matching task by patients with left-hemisphere lesions. (From Luria, 1976.)

Word Meaning   There is only limited evidence from group studies on the localising significance of word-comprehension impairments. Coughlan & Warrington (1978) used a two-choice auditory vocabulary test in which the subject was required to decide which of two words was closest in meaning to a target word (e.g., *flag: banner, pole*). The left temporal lesion group was significantly impaired compared with patients with left-hemisphere lesions sparing the temporal lobe (i.e., frontal and parietal). The incidence of cases scoring below the fifth percentile is shown in Fig. 6.8. This group study result has been corroborated in a number of clinico-anatomical investigations based on single cases (e.g., Damasio, 1981; Benson & Geschwind, 1985; Alexander, Hiltbrunner, & Fischer, 1989).

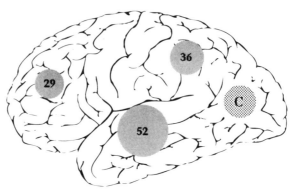

Figure 6.8 Percentage of patients with lesions involving the frontal, temporal, and parieto-occipital lobes, scoring below a 5% cut-off. C marks the approximate locus of colour-name comprehension deficits. (Adapted from Coughlan & Warrington, 1978.)

A number of the most fully documented single case studies of verbal comprehension impairment have been conducted in patients in whom the pathology was bilateral and/or poorly localised. These deficits have been documented in progressive degenerative conditions and in herpes simplex encephalitis. In other cases, although the damage has been confined to the left hemisphere, extensive lesions have been present. One case (T.O.B.) with a selective impairment in animal-name comprehension was found to have a very restricted metabolic abnormality in the left temporal lobe maximal in the superior temporal gyrus (Tyrrell, Warrington, Frackowiak, & Rossor, 1990). In cases with a selective impairment in the comprehension of colour names more posterior left-hemisphere lesions have been identified. In vascular cases, the lesion appears to implicate the territory of the posterior cerebral artery (Sittig, 1921; Kleist, 1934; Mohr *et al.*, 1971). Hécaen & Angelergues (1963) reported eight cases with colour-name comprehension impairments whose lesions were largely restricted to the left occipital lobe.

Theoretical Considerations

In the empirical section a broad distinction was made between those impairments which affect the processing of word sounds and those which affect the analysis of word meanings. In this discussion, the evidence for possible discontinuities within word-sound analysis will be considered first. This will be followed by a discussion of the different subtypes of impairment in processing word meaning and their implications for theories of the organisation of "knowledge."

Word-Sound Analysis

In order to process the sounds of spoken words, it is necessary to perform a complex analysis of the acoustic pattern. Changes in the pattern over time or changes in the various components of the pattern must be adequately processed in order for word perception to proceed. Furthermore, this pattern must be categorised as being an instance of a particular word sound, regardless of context, speaking voice, or speech rate (see above).

Auerbach *et al.* (1982) have argued that patients with bilateral temporal lobe lesions giving rise to impaired temporal acuity may be considered as showing an acoustic (prephonemic) disorder of word perception. That is, their impairment in perceiving the spoken word is secondary to a more elementary sound-processing deficit. The patient's reduced ability to resolve changes in the sound wave which occur rapidly in time would result in difficulties in dealing with certain types of acoustic signal. This would particularly affect the resolution of speech in which rapid changes in the acoustic pattern are critical for adequate perception. In support of their argument, Auerbach *et al.* demonstrated that their patient was more impaired on time-dependent discriminations than on those which were not so strictly constrained by time (e.g., pitch and volume).

Auerbach *et al.* argued that patients with a prephonemic acoustic disorder of temporal acuity should be contrasted with those with a deficit at a *phonemic* level. Impairments resulting from left-hemisphere lesions affect processing at a level which is subsequent to sensory analysis of the wave-form. It is a level of auditory perception in which sounds with different acoustic characteristics are categorised as being instances of a single phoneme. This is a stage of categorical perception in which sound patterns which fall on a physical continuum are "parsed" or "categorised" into psychologically distinct percepts: the phonemes of the language. Blumstein *et al.* (1977b) gave patients the task of identifying or discriminating the sounds "da" and "ta" but systematically distorted them so that the "d" and "t" sounds fell on an acoustic continuum. Whereas normal subjects showed a clear boundary at a point along the continuum when the distorted signal was classified as an example of a "d" rather than "t," patients with left-hemisphere lesions had much "fuzzier" boundaries between the phonemes (see Fig. 6.1). Only the clearest examples of the sounds were heard as being "ba" or "pa." This was interpreted in terms of a breakdown in the categorical perception of these sounds.

Saffran, Marin, & Yeni-Komshian (1976) described one case in whom the deficit in phoneme discrimination was severe enough to render him virtually "word deaf." In an analysis of the patient's ability to judge whether two consecutively presented words were the same or different, Saffran and her colleagues showed that the patient was highly sensitive to the context in which a phoneme occurred. The patient was able to make use of some acoustic information but this was insufficient for him to categorise sounds as instances of a particular phoneme when there was a minor degree of distortion.

Whilst the analysis offered by Auerbach *et al.* in terms of a distinction between prephonemic disorders of acoustic processing and disorders of categorical phoneme perception is astute, and *a priori* entirely reasonable, the empirical evidence is as yet only preliminary. Most critically, more information is needed on the acoustic processing abilities of patients whose deficit appears to be confined to the categorical perception of phonemes.

Relationship to Comprehension In his original description of patients with impaired comprehension of the spoken word, Wernicke (1874) placed emphasis on the patient's difficulty with processing the "auditory images of words." That is, their deficits were considered to result from a failure in word-sound perception. Luria (1976) argued that auditory perceptual impairments were at the core of those comprehension deficits which were observed following left temporal lobe lesions: "With the general inconstancy of phonemes and phonemic sequences the part of the word which conveys its basic meaning becomes distorted so that it loses its significance altogether." Unsurprisingly, severe impairments of word-sound discrimination arising as a consequence of left temporal lobe damage may result in a degree of word deafness (Saffran *et al.*, 1976). However, the corollary of Luria's hypothesis, namely that failure of comprehension is necessarily due to impaired sound discrimination, is not tenable. For example, it has been noted that failure on tests of sound discrimination, common in all patients with language disorders, is by no means specific to those cases with impaired comprehension (Goodglass & Blumstein, 1973). Most critically, patients with impaired comprehension do not necessarily have any difficulties with phoneme discrimination tasks (e.g., Gainotti, Caltagirone, & Ibba, 1975; Coughlan & Warrington, 1978).

Since patients may have very poor comprehension despite normal word-sound processing, the evidence is in favour of there being a major discontinuity between these two components of spoken word comprehension. The apparent paradox that patients with impaired word-sound discrimination may nevertheless show normal levels of comprehension is most likely the consequence of the differing demands of the tasks which are used. For example, it is rarely necessary to make fine discriminations between similar-sounding words in normal conversational speech. In addition, nonverbal information (e.g., lip reading, gesture) is of importance in facilitating a particular interpretation of an ambiguous sound. Both of these sources of information may help patients in compensating for their deficit on sound-discrimination tasks despite some loss of the precision in their perception of word sounds. This appears to hold true even for severely impaired patients:

the case studied by Saffran *et al.* (1976) was significantly helped by placing a word in a sentence context. Such additional information and redundancy in language may, however, be of little or no benefit to patients with an acoustic disorder.

Word Comprehension

It has been established that disorders of language comprehension can occur independently of impairments in other aspects of language processing. Despite an inability to comprehend low frequency words or words from specific semantic categories, patients may be able to perceive language normally and have no difficulties with producing speech fluently within the limitations imposed by their restricted vocabulary. The preservation of fluent speech may be particularly clear in those patients with specific impairments of the concrete/imageable vocabulary who are capable of producing normal, complex, linguistically well-formed utterances and are even able to write fluently and coherently (albeit with a paucity of concrete words). For example, one patient (A.B.) was asked to write a brief account of the Common Market issue. This was done effortlessly using a fairly wide vocabulary and range of sentence structures (see Fig. 6.9).

Two types of explanation have been proposed to account for impairments of word comprehension. First, they have been viewed as arising from the isolation or disconnection of a verbal comprehension system from other components of the language-processing system. Damage to the pathways which permit information to be transmitted from auditory perceptual analyses to the comprehension system would result in failure to understand words, even if the comprehension system itself were intact. Second, impaired comprehension of words has been viewed as the product of a disorder within a specialised verbal semantic processing system. These hypotheses are by no means mutually exclusive and indeed can be seen as broadly complementary and applicable to different patterns of deficit (cf. Lichtheim, 1885). These two possibilities are illustrated schematically in Fig. 6.10.

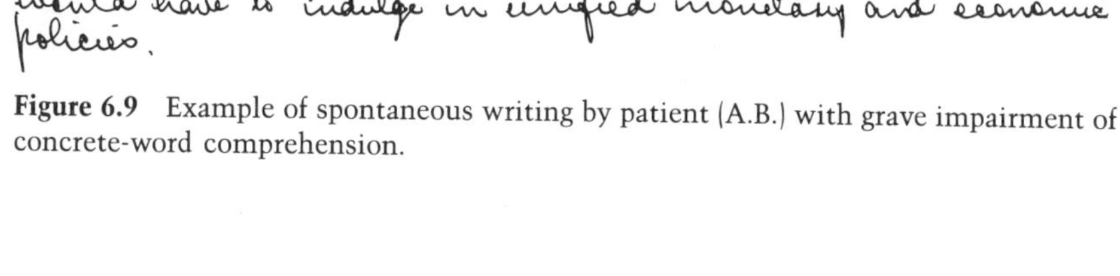
the Common Market that it behaved internationally rather than almost exclusively domestically. Another important element is the question of currency policy. It is already a problem for the six countries who have agreed that they would like to achieve a European Currency Unit. But they already understand that to make sense of that they would have to indulge in unified monetary and economic policies.

Figure 6.9 Example of spontaneous writing by patient (A.B.) with grave impairment of concrete-word comprehension.

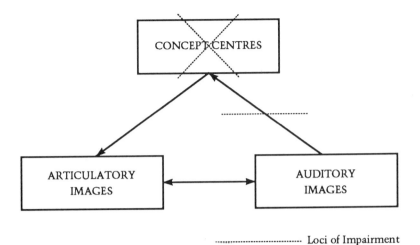

Figure 6.10 Model derived from Lichtheim (1885) illustrating two possible loci for comprehension deficits.

Disconnection Hypothesis There are a number of patients whose deficits have been interpreted within a disconnection framework. Geschwind, Quadfasel, & Segarra (1968) described a case who was able to repeat but was neither able to speak nor understand (the classical syndrome of transcortical sensory aphasia; see Chapter 1). The patient's repetition was not merely an echo of what was said to her; she was also able to complete stereotyped phrases. Thus when given "ask me no questions" she responded "tell me no lies." Whitaker (1976) described another similar case, who was not only able to complete phrases but was also able to "correct" anomalous sentences in her repetition. In these cases the verbal comprehension systems were considered to be disconnected from other areas of language processing. The patient was unable to transcode, or translate word sounds into word meanings. In essence, a double disconnection was postulated implicating the loss of links between the conceptual knowledge of words and other components of the language system. A single "disconnection" clearly cannot fully account for such cases, who, in addition to comprehension difficulties, were unable to generate any meaningful spontaneous speech.

Heilman, Tucker, & Valenstein (1976) described a case who was able to name objects but at the same time was unable to comprehend spoken language. When testing of comprehension was attempted using word–picture matching tests the patient simply named the stimuli. He was quite unable to follow simple spoken commands or match a spoken name to an object. Language perception was considered to be intact because the patient could repeat what was said to him. This dissociation between naming, repetition, and comprehension was interpreted as being due to a disconnection between the auditory analysis of words and the meanings of words. Because of the severity of the patient's deficit Heilman and his colleagues were unable to test the status of the patient's verbal knowledge directly. This makes the disconnection hypothesis a highly plausible explanation rather than an established phenomenon. Without evidence (other than naming) for the integrity of semantic knowledge, it remains an open question as to whether this information could not be reached (disconnected) or was actually damaged.

Other examples of the ability to retrieve the names of objects whose spoken name could not be comprehended are also on record, however it is uncertain whether these patients should be thought of as showing a classical disconnection syndrome (e.g., Kremin, 1986). In some cases the contrast of impaired spoken word comprehension and intact word naming can be specific to a particular semantic category. This pattern has been documented in two cases with impairment in comprehending the names of body parts (De Renzi & Scotti, 1970; Ogden, 1985b). Goodglass, Wingfield, Hyde, & Theurkauf (1986) obtained similar findings in a group study. These findings seem secure and will need to be accounted for in any adequate theoretical formulation (see also Chapter 7).

Semantic-Processing Hypothesis   There are two major signs which argue for an interpretation in terms of a disorder within the semantic system itself: these are the effects of category specificity and partial knowledge. First, in the case of category-specific deficits a disorder of semantic processing itself appears to be the most plausible interpretation. For category-specific effects to arise in the first place, the word must have been "semantically categorised." There is nothing "special" about the perceptual attributes of the names of, say, animals or foods that would allow such a specific dissociation to arise. The evidence of category specificity, perhaps most especially in the spoken word domain, virtually compels an interpretation in terms of a semantic processing deficit.

Secondly, disorders within the semantic system can be identified when patients are able to demonstrate that some aspects of a word's meaning have been processed but not others. In the empirical section it was noted that in some cases there is evidence that words are not simply "lost" from the patient's vocabulary. Rather, they may show partial knowledge (such as the category to which a stimulus belongs) but have lost the more precise information which differentiates it from other similar things (see Fig. 6.6). Evidence that words have been processed to the level of superordinate category membership indicates that something has gone wrong in deriving the full meaning of a particular word rather than in transcoding between sound and meaning.

Access vs. Degradation   The evidence that patients may retain partial information and show category specificity indicates that for such cases the deficit is one which affects the semantic processing system itself. This conclusion is further supported by a consideration of the two subtypes of verbal knowledge loss which have been identified. In one, the patient shows a consistent pattern of impairment, with partial knowledge of the same individual words being demonstrated reliably. These patients have been described as having *degradation* of their verbal knowledge base. Degradation deficits can be specific to particular categories (see Table 6.3: case J.B.R.) and are clearly compatible with a disorder affecting semantic knowledge (Warrington & Shallice, 1984).

The other type of disorder, in which patients show variability in their comprehension, has been termed an *access* deficit. By this is meant that the patients have a specific impairment in the procedures required for processing the target word. Since these disorders can be category specific (see Table 6.4), it seems plausible to suggest that the impairment lies within the procedures of semantic processing themselves rather than being the consequence of a "disconnection" between an earlier stage of processing and the derivation of meaning. Patients with an access deficit may be very sensitive to the timing of test presentation (see above). They appear to need longer than normal to "recover" from the task of single word comprehension. It has been argued that these effects can be interpreted in terms of a buildup of "refractoriness" in the procedures required for computing an adequate semantic representation. The suggestion is that the reactivity of the semantic processing system is altered so that it is necessary to allow a longer than normal period of time for recovery following stimulation. Attempts to access a target may therefore be ineffective during the refractory period.

Access cases may show worse performance on word–picture matching tests using arrays from a single semantic category (e.g., knife, fork, spoon, cup, saucer), than when the semantic distance is greater (e.g., knife, desk, hat, book, spade). There are two possible, but not mutually exclusive, interpretations for the interaction between refractoriness and semantic distance. The ability to discriminate items drawn from several semantic categories could be interpreted in terms of the relative preservation of superordinate broad category information despite refractoriness. Alternatively, the refractoriness of a particular target item might affect its near neighbours in categorically organised semantic space.

Organisation of Semantic Knowledge   It has been argued that selective impairments in the knowledge of certain categories of verbal information provide evidence for the way in which the meanings of words are organised. The theoretical analysis of these category-specific effects has focused on the dissociations which have been documented within the concrete word vocabulary. An early formulation based on anecdotal accounts described the observations in terms of a dissociation between "animate" and "inanimate" concepts (Nielsen, 1946). Whilst this distinction is a rough approximation to the types of disorder which have been documented, it fails to account for other clusterings of preserved and impaired comprehension. For example, impairment in the comprehension of colour words or food words does not fall easily into either of these categories.

An alternative hypothesis put forward by Warrington (1981b) was that the division should be recast in terms of those "facts" which were known in terms of their *sensory* properties (incorporating, e.g., foods, animals, and flowers) and those that were known in terms of their *functional* properties (artifacts). This formulation allowed the incorporation of apparent anomalies in the broad animate/inanimate distinction, in particular, the co-occurrence of impairments in food- and animal-name comprehension (Warrington & Shallice, 1984). In addition to an impairment in these categories, one case (J.B.R.) was also unable to comprehend certain inanimate categories. He could not explain the meaning of such high frequency words as *gold* or *silver*. By contrast, parts of the body (surely an animate category) were well preserved.

It was argued that these categories differed in their reliance on sensory and functional properties. Thus distinguishing between a carrot and a parsnip, a lion and a tiger, or gold and silver requires one to utilise sensory properties (e.g., flavour, colour, pattern, and shape), whereas distinguishing between a screwdriver and a chisel or an arm and a leg requires the use of functional information (how and where and what they are used for). Clearly this account can also be applied to the opposite pattern of dissociations, namely, the relative preservation of comprehension of things known by their sensory properties as compared with things known by their function (Warrington & McCarthy, 1983).

More detailed consideration of the patterns of category specificity in patients with cerebral lesions suggests that the sensory/functional distinction is also an oversimplification. Further dissociations within the broad class of things known by their function and within the class of things known by their sensory properties have been observed. Thus, within the class of things known by their function there may be selective impairment of small manipulable objects and relative preservation of large man-made objects (case Y.O.T., see above). Within the broad category of things known by their sensory properties the names of living things can be impaired and the names and colours can be preserved (Warrington & Shallice, 1984).

A development of the sensory/functional account was therefore put forward (Warrington & McCarthy, 1987). This analysis drew on the theoretical frameworks of the nineteenth-century neurologists, whose ideas were in turn derived from associationist philosophy and psychology. It was argued that conceptual information was stored in "association cortex," (i.e., regions of the brain which in turn received their input from the primary sensory analysis systems). The associations which were required for word meaning were build up on the basis of linkages between different sources of sensory information. For example, Lissauer gave the example of recognising a violin:

> With the violin's image there are connected a number of recollections which concern its name, its sound, its image. The sound of the instrument, the sensations and tactile experience which go with its handling. In addition there may be the optical image of a violinist in his characteristic pose. It is only when these associations between the percept of the instrument and the above-mentioned recollections occur promptly in consciousness that one is enabled to interpret the object as a musical instrument and differentiate it from other instruments and generally to categorise it. If, however, this association is delayed or disrupted through some pathological process then even if the image of the violin is perceived, however precisely, there are no associations with prior experiences and recognition is therefore not possible. (Lissauer, 1890; p.182).

In this example, it is clear that Lissauer wished to emphasise the relevant contribution of various modalities of experience toward the acquisition of meaning. The idea of knowledge being based on the linkages of different types of sensory information offers an attractive starting point for formulating a biologically plausible model of the organisation of meaning. Indeed this type of framework has been of considerable influence in cognitive psychology (e.g., Allport, 1985).

In acquisition of a concept, the relative salience of various sources of sensory-motor information is very different, not only for the major semantic categories but also for subdivisions within them. In acquisition it is necessary to learn how to differentiate between closely related exemplars, and such differentiation is dependent upon the relative salience or weighting (Hinton & Sejnowski, 1986) of different sources of evidence from sensory, motor, and functional channels. The knowledge base required for word comprehension is "fed" by very different sensory sources of evidence. These differing types of information become associated in the course of learning. It was argued that such polymodal information confers meaning and can be thought of as constituting a central semantic representation of a concept (Warrington & McCarthy, 1987).

All types of information are clearly not equal in particular concepts. It has been suggested that this differential salience of particular types of information may be at the basis of the phenomena of category-specific deficits. Consider first the dissociation which has been documented in patients' ability to comprehend the abstract- and concrete-word vocabularies. The acquisition of a concrete concept can be thought of as evolving through a finer and finer differentiation of the physical world in which we live. All of the major sense modalities will make an integral contribution to this knowledge base, but for any particular concrete concept the salience of visual, tactile, auditory, or taste information will differ. By contrast, the acquisition of abstract concepts is likely to be very different and perhaps dependent on actions, emotions, and contextual cues as well as verbal information. If the central representation of concepts is based upon information derived from anatomically distinct input channels, then it seems likely that the semantic knowledge base is itself differentiated either topographically or physiologically. Given a lesion to a specific part of this system, then a category-specific impairment of abstract or of concrete knowledge might be observed.

This formulation can be elaborated to account for the finer-grain dissociations which have been observed. Take, for example, the distinction between animals and objects, perhaps the most widely reported of the category-specific dissociations. Differentiation between different species of animals depends almost entirely on vision, and within the separate visual channels visual shape is often more critical than colour. So, in learning the difference between a cat and a dog, colour is irrelevant: they tend to be found in the same types of place and kept as pets. Visual shape is likely to be an important differentiating cue. By contrast, a scarf and a belt do not have any characteristic or defining shape, colour, or size. They are clearly associated with different parts of the body and different contexts of use. These sensory/functional distinctions can clearly be subsumed within the "associationist" framework discussed above.

More critically, this account can subsume the finer-grain dissociations which have been observed within the "functional" class, namely the distinction between large man-made objects and small manipulable objects. In acquiring the concepts of small manipulable objects such as a knife and a fork it is important to coordinate information gained from proprioception and vision in addition to contextual (e.g., used in eating) and functional (e.g., for cutting vs. for picking up food) information. By contrast, in learning the distinction between large man-made objects such as a bus and a train proprioceptive information is less salient although visual and functional knowledge is important. It is not unreasonable to suppose that the convergence of information from sensory and motor systems which is critical for small manipulable objects would be topographically or physiologically differentiated from the information required for comprehending large man-made objects (Warrington & McCarthy, 1987).

The other two commonly observed fine-grain category-specific deficits are the selective impairment of the comprehension of colour names and impairment in the comprehension of body-part names. These disorders can clearly be accommodated within the same associationist theoretical framework. Thus, in acquiring the concept of *red* the highest priority of weighting must be given to colour information (excluding information from shape, texture, and motion). This almost exclusive weighting on the colour "channel" is perhaps reflected in the distinct anatomical correlates of impaired colour-name comprehension. The unique combination of weightings on sensory, functional, and motor sources of evidence for body parts would easily account for their selective impairment and preservation (Goodglass & Budin, 1988).

Modality-Specific Impairments In this discussion so far, reference has been made to impairments of word comprehension without any attempt to specify whether these disorders implicate a specific verbal knowledge base or whether there is a common "encyclopedic" type of knowledge base which is shared by all sense modalities. It has been commonly assumed that a unitary semantic system is shared between the various sense modalities. That is, the processing of information conveyed by a drawing of a tiger and the information conveyed by the spoken name *tiger* (i.e., a large, dangerous, foreign member of the cat family) is subserved by the same neural structures.

In the discussion of visual object recognition (Chapter 2) some pointers to partially independent verbal and visual semantic systems were discussed. Patients with impaired object recognition who are unable to assign meaning to visual stimuli (visual associative agnosics) may have no problem in comprehending their spoken names. The view that there may be at least partially independent systems for comprehending the spoken word and visual objects is rendered more secure by evidence from a single case. The patient (T.O.B.) had a category-specific impairment of verbal knowledge, in that his comprehension of the names of animals and living things was inferior to his comprehension of man-made objects. For example, on one test he scored 33 and 89% correct, respectively. Thus he was able to define *lighthouse* as "round the coast, built up, tall building, lights revolve to warn ships," but when asked to define a pig he was only able to respond "animal." (McCarthy & Warrington, 1988).

Not only was his deficit category specific, it was also modality specific in that his ability to define the names of animals was inferior to his comprehension of pictures (see Table 6.5). Presented with the spoken word *rhinoceros* he was only able to say, "animal, can't give you any functions." However, when shown a picture of a rhinoceros he responded, "Enormous, weighs over one ton, lives in Africa." Indeed, his performance on the living things category improved to 94% under these conditions. The patient's deficit was highly consistent over test-

Table 6.5 Examples of Word Definitions and Picture Descriptions by Patient (T.O.B.) with a Category-Specific Word-Comprehension Deficit

Word definitions		Picture descriptions
Target	Response	Response
Kangaroo	Common name	Famous animal from Australia, jumps
Dolphin	Animal or bird	Some in Brighton, sea-animal trained to swim around
Rhino	Totally new word	Enormous animal, lives in Africa, weighs a ton
Swan	Another animal	Common for this country, on the Thames and canals

ing sessions; indeed his vocabulary remained static for months. This evidence for a consistent, category-specific, modality-specific impairment of semantic knowledge cannot easily be accommodated within a theory which postulates a "single semantic system."

Conclusion

The evidence from patients with impairments of single word comprehension provides an excellent example of the usefulness of an information-processing approach to cognitive skills. The analysis of speech requires fine auditory temporal resolution, categorical perception of phonemes, and, most critically, derivation of meaning. These are separable stages of the processing system, each with unique characteristics. The ramifications of the study of impairments in word comprehension are considerable and provide the beginnings of an answer to the thorny philosophical problem of the meaning of meaning.

7

Word Retrieval

Introduction

A potentially vast stock of words is available to the average adult speaker, most of which can be retrieved fluently in the course of spontaneous speech. Occasional word finding difficulties may be noticed by anyone. Uncommon or infrequently used words may give rise to the need to pause and search one's "mental dictionary" in order to retrieve the appropriate target. Problems with automatic retrieval may sometimes result in the experience of a "tip-of-the-tongue" state, in which a considerable amount of information about the required word may be available (such as its meaning, and the broad outline of its sound structure) (Brown & McNeil, 1966).

Observations that certain patients may have particular difficulty in the retrieval of words dates back to the prehistory of neurology (Benton & Joynt, 1960). The identification of a specific impairment in retrieving words was a comparatively late development. Pitres (1898) first differentiated word-finding difficulties as a specific aphasic deficit which he termed *amnestic aphasia*. The core symptom of this syndrome was the simple "forgetting" of words. He considered that nouns were the most vulnerable part of speech to be affected, although he did note that one case was on record for whom the ability to retrieve the names of actions was more impaired than the ability to retrieve nouns (Heilbronner: cited in Pitres, 1898). This asymmetry in the vulnerability of different parts of speech to word-finding impairments became reified in the label of "nominal" (i.e., name) aphasia. In clinical practice, when word-retrieval difficulties occur as a relatively selective deficit, in the context of normal sentence formation the deficit is termed *anomic*, *amnestic*, or *nominal* aphasia. These terms tend to be used interchangeably in the literature, without any strong theoretical implications.

The very existence of such impairments as a distinct type of aphasia was somewhat controversial. For example, the possibility of a selective impairment in word retrieval was rejected by writers such as Marie (1906a,b). These deficits were viewed as a "mild" form of more generalised language disorders. For example, Head (1926) thought of word-retrieval deficits as a phase in the recovery from a loss of word comprehension.

Empirical Characteristics

The impairment of word retrieval has usually been studied in the context of "confrontation naming tasks" in which the patient is simply required to name single stimuli (usually pictures or objects). Whilst these procedures have proven clinically useful, they have their limitations. A major limitation is that they do not sample word-retrieval difficulties in response to the more natural circumstances of spontaneous speech. A second limitation is that, with the possible exception of colours, these tasks have mainly focused on patients' abilities to retrieve nouns. Word retrieval in the context of active conversation may well pose a different set of problems for the aphasic than those which are assessed by the naming of visually presented objects. This chapter will focus on impairments of single word retrieval; discussion of the relationship between single-word retrieval difficulties and impairments in spontaneous speech will be discussed in Chapter 8.

Classification of Errors Impairments in the retrieval of words are commonly seen in patients with acquired language disorders. In spontaneous speech, the patient may make frequent pauses whilst searching for the appropriate word, and various types of error can occur. The target word may be replaced with a generic term such as "thing" or by an approximate definition or explanation of the target. For example, the word *pen* might be substituted with the circumlocutory phrase "what you write with," or the word *clock* by "the thing you use to tell the time." Patients may also produce a similar sound to the target (pen → sen) or produce a word with related meaning (pen → pencil). Despite these errors patients may be able to talk fluently, but they are unable to say very much; indeed their speech gives the impression of "emptiness."

In several studies there have been formal counts of the different types of errors produced by patients on naming tasks. The most commonly occurring errors identified in these counts are neologisms (e.g., orange → astkoss), phonemic paraphasias (single-sound errors, e.g., lemon → demmun), semantic errors (boots → shoes), and circumlocutions. Three such counts are summarised in Table 7.1.

Word Frequency In naming tasks word frequency is an important variable. The measure of word frequency is based on "counts" of words occurring in popular written material or samples of conversation. For

Table 7.1 Types of Error in Naming Tasks[a]

Study	Circumlocutions	Literal paraphasias	Neologisms	Semantic	Random	Other
Coughlan & Warrington (1978)	24%	1%	3%	12%	8%	23%
Butterworth *et al.* (1984)	13.8%	9%	19%	53%	5.7%	
Howard & Orchard-Lisle (1984)		3.3%	3%	45.7%[b]	41.8%	

[a] Summary of the incidence of different types of errors in three independent studies.
[b] Includes circumlocutions.

normal people low-frequency words take longer to retrieve (Oldfield & Wingfield, 1965) and give rise to more retrieval failures or partial failures (e.g., the tip-of-the-tongue phenomenon; Brown & McNeil, 1966). Weisenburg & McBride (1935) first noted that word frequency was an important determinant of success or failure in word retrieval by aphasics. On confrontation naming tasks low-frequency words were more likely to elicit word-retrieval difficulties than were high-frequency, common words. This finding was replicated and made more secure by a number of investigations of picture naming carried out in the 1960s (Schuell, Jenkins, & Jimenez-Pabon, 1964; Newcombe, Oldfield, & Wingfield, 1965; Rochford & Williams, 1965: see Fig. 7.1).

The parameter of word frequency can be thought of as an estimate of the "average" probability of individual words being produced by members of a language group. It takes no account of individual variability in vocabulary size or language ability. In Fig. 7.1 Newcombe *et al.*'s (1965) data show that highly educated "university subjects" have a much less marked word-frequency effect than "hospital controls." This does not mean that they do not show a word-frequency effect, but rather that the target words were relatively easy for them (Oldfield, 1966). Since word-retrieval difficulties are more marked for the lower-frequency words of the normal individual's vocabulary, then it is important to make allowances for individual differences in the clinical assessment of aphasic patients. The task has to be "tailored" to the patient so that normal variability in the size of vocabulary can be taken into account. To give an example: whilst failure to retrieve the word *stethoscope* would not have much clinical significance in the case of a poorly educated individual with a relatively small vocabulary, failure in the case of a consultant physician would suggest an acquired impairment. Naming tests have been constructed which cover a wide range of word frequencies, thereby allowing this aspect of task difficulty to be taken into account (Newcombe *et al.*, 1965; McKenna & Warrington, 1980, 1983). Examples of stimuli from one such task, the Graded Naming Test, are shown in Fig. 7.2. In this task, the kangaroo was known by every subject in the normal sample, whereas the mitre was known only by a small minority.

The importance of achieving an appropriate level of task difficulty, particularly in individuals with a large "premorbid" vocabulary, can be

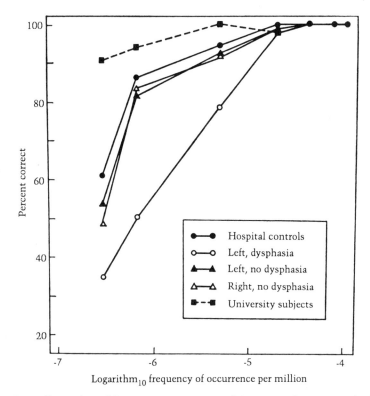

Figure 7.1 Effects of word frequency on accuracy of naming in five groups of subjects (Newcombe *et al.*, 1965).

illustrated by the following case (Tyrrell, Warrington, Frackowiak, & Rossor, 1990). The patient was a highly able professional man who complained of "difficulties with memory." When tested he achieved excellent scores on all tests, even on the "Vocabulary" subtest of the Wechsler Adult Intelligent Scale (WAIS), on which he was above the ninety-fifth percentile. He had no difficulty in naming common objects. However, he only succeeded in naming 2 out of 30 items from the Graded Difficulty Naming Test—a score well below the fifth percentile (McKenna & Warrington, 1980). Figure 7.3 shows the performance of controls and patients with language difficulties on this graded difficulty test.

Cuing Group studies have shown that many patients with word-retrieval difficulties are able to benefit from presentation of an auditory prompt, or cue. Rochford & Williams (1962, 1963) gave rhyme cues. For example the target word *watch* would be cued by the phrase "It's not a scotch but a ?" Myers & Goodglass (1978) used rhyme cues and cuing with the initial syllable of the word (such as "la" for ladder). Both studies found that for some cases presentation of cues could facilitate word retrieval. Other sound-mediated cuing tasks such as completion

Figure 7.2 Examples of stimuli from the Graded Difficulty Naming Test (McKenna & Warrington, 1983).

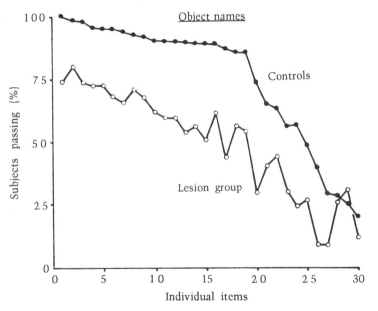

Figure 7.3 Performance of controls and patients with left-hemisphere lesions on the Graded Difficulty Naming Test (McKenna & Warrington, 1980).

of stereotyped phrases ("knife and ?") or cliches have also been found to facilitate retrieval. Providing additional verbal information about the meanings of the target (such as reading a definition or providing the name of the category to which an object belongs) has yet to be found to be of benefit (e.g., Rochford & Williams, 1965) and indeed may even be deleterious.

Podroza & Darley (1977) used a technique which they termed *prestimulation*. Prior to being shown a picture for naming, patients were presented with a phonemic cue, an incomplete sentence, or a list of words which were related to the target in terms of meaning (e.g., for the target word *bee* the list was *sting, honey, hive*). They found that patients were actually hampered in their word retrieval if presentation of the picture was preceded by such lists of semantically related names.

Categories In the earliest discussions of word-finding difficulty, it was apparent that certain categories of words might be differentially impaired or differentially preserved. It is clear that some dissociations occur which can in no way be accounted for in terms of word frequency or familiarity in usage. In some instances, category-specific naming difficulties have been accorded the status of syndromes in their own right (see Chapter 6). Thus specific impairment in colour matching (colour anomia), letter naming (letter anomia), or body-part naming (autotopagnosia) have been sufficiently striking in the individual case to be considered as a particular class of deficit. The first systematic investigation was conducted by Goodglass, Klein, Carey, & Jones (1966). They tested patients' ability to retrieve (and to comprehend; see chapter 6) names from a number of categories which had been identi-fied as being of potential clinical significance (viz. colours, shapes, letters, numbers, objects, actions). They found a high incidence of cate-gory-specific impairment and preservation of word retrieval in their large group of aphasic patients (n = 135) (see Fig. 7.4).

The dissociation between action naming and object naming observed in the early study by Goodglass *et al.* (1966) was replicated and ex-tended by Miceli and his colleagues (Miceli, Silveri, Villa, & Car-amazza, 1984). They reported that some patients showed a differential impairment in their ability to name actions as compared with their retrieval of object names. Other patients found the action-naming task easier than object naming. This latter pattern of deficit has been docu-mented in some detail by Zingeser & Berndt (1988). In their case (H.Y.), the preservation of action naming as compared with noun-naming was observed using test material in the two categories which was carefully matched for word frequency.

Further patterns of selective deficit have been documented showing fractionation within the broad class of nouns. Gardner (1973) reported that three patients were more impaired in naming items which are nor-mally known through vision ("figurative" stimuli, e.g., cloud, ceiling)

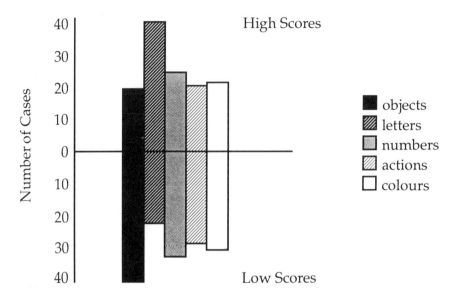

Figure 7.4 Number of patients showing disproportionate preservation (high scores) and impairment (low scores) for words in five categories. (Adapted from Goodglass *et al.*, 1966.)

rather than through touch ("operative" stimuli, e.g., rock, vase). An even more specific pattern of impairment was reported by Hart, Berndt, & Caramazza (1985). They described a patient (M.D.) who was particularly impaired in retrieving the names of common fruit and vegetables. The patient's ability to retrieve the names of objects was within the normal range. Thus he failed to name a peach and an orange but successfully named an abacus and a sphynx!

A quite different class of nouns are those termed *proper names,* words which have a single unique referent. Semenza & Zettin (1988) have reported two cases with particularly striking category-specific impairments in their retrieval of proper names. For example one patient (P.C.) could remember his own name and had only managed to relearn the names of his wife and son over the course of a year. However, he was unable to retrieve the names of any other people. Country names and town names were also gravely impaired. Given a blank map he could not retrieve a single name correctly. This was contrasted with his perfect performance in naming numerous objects from other categories (see Table 7.2) including body parts, means of transport, and even types of pasta!

Patients may show selective preservation or impairment of particular types of word within the broad class of proper names. The relative preservation of the names of countries is on record in a single case

Table 7.2 Category Naming[a],[b]

Common names	No. correct	Proper names	No. correct
Vegetables	15/15	Relatives	2/8
Fruits	15/15	Famous people	0/15
Body parts	18/18	Cities	0/15
Means of transportation	15/15	Mountains	0/5
Pasta types	6/6	Countries	0/10

[a] Number of words correctly named in each category by one patient (P.C.)
[b] Adapted from Semenza & Zettin (1989)

(F.C.). This patient was gravely anomic on formal testing, however it was noted that in his attempts to name famous people he would typically give their nationality (e.g., Gandhi, "India"). He was tested on five different categories, namely, countries, body parts, animals, objects, and colours. His scores in the countries category were significantly better than those in other categories (McKenna & Warrington, 1978; see Table 7.3). In another case (G.B.L.), the ability to retrieve the names of people was selectively impaired. At the same time, when she was given a map she could name both towns and countries (McKenna & Warrington, 1980).

Modality-Specific Impairments

For some patients, naming difficulties may be specific to one of the sense modalities. Modality-specific disturbances were first documented for visual presentation (Freund, 1889). The patient was able to name things when they were presented by touch but failed to name them when they were presented visually. This type of deficit, termed *optic aphasia*, has been studied in some detail by Beauvois and her colleagues (Lhermitte & Beauvois, 1973; Beauvois, 1982; Beauvois & Saillant 1985). The patient (J.F.) was impaired in naming a wide range of visually presented stimuli including objects, colours, and faces. At the same time he was able to define the spoken names of objects and name them from tactile presentation. His deficit did not appear to be attributable to a primary impairment of visual recognition since he was able to pantomime the use of the objects. Similar cases have been described by Gil, Pluchon, Toullat, Micheneau, Rogez & Lefevre (1985) and by Coslett & Saffran (1989a).

The selective impairment of naming to tactile presentation has also been documented (Raymond & Egger, 1906). A detailed study of a single case (R.G.) was described by Beauvois, Saillant, Meninger, & Lhermitte (1978). One patient had no difficulty in naming visually presented objects. However, when blindfolded and given the objects to explore by touch he had a very significant error rate. Under these conditions he

Table 7.3 Category Naming[a,b]

	Countries	Colours	Objects	Body Parts	Animals
Naming to confrontation	13	0	2	10	1
Naming from auditory description	15	0	2	0	1

[a]One patient's (F.C.) attempt to name to confrontation and to name from auditory description stimuli from five categories.
[b]Adapted from McKenna & Warrington (1978).

was unable to name such common objects as a cup and a pair of scissors. His deficit could not be attributed to an impairment in tactile sensation since he had no difficulty in miming the use of the same objects.

There is evidence to suggest that modality-specific impairments of naming may be a relatively frequent clinical phenomenon. Spreen, Benton, & Van Allen (1966) documented a significant dissociation between visual and tactile naming in 5 of 21 cases, and Goodglass, Barton, & Kaplan (1968) found a double dissociation between olfactory and auditory naming in two single cases from 25 consecutively studied patients. In the case of touch and vision, there is also evidence that in certain cases the deficit may be confined to one hand or one side of vision: patients may fail to respond to stimuli presented to one visual field or to one hand (e.g., Geschwind & Kaplan, 1962).

Naming pictures and naming from spoken definition have been contrasted directly in a number of group studies. Barton, Marwjewski, & Urrea (1969) found that naming from auditory description was generally the most difficult condition. Other workers have obtained similar results (e.g., Goodglass & Stuss, 1979). As an aside it should be noted that effects of manipulating perceptual dimensions of pictorial material in naming tasks have been inconclusive. Bisiach (1966) and Benton, Smith, & Lang (1972) found that degradation of visual stimuli led to increased difficulties in word retrieval for aphasic patients. However, other studies have failed to find any significant effects (Corlew & Nation, 1975; Hatfield, Barber, Jones, & Morton, 1977).

The modality of stimulus presentation is not the only consideration: the modality of "output" may also be important. Hier & Mohr (1977) described a patient with a very dramatic deficit affecting spoken but not written word retrieval. The patient (A.F.) could speak fluently (if somewhat inaccurately), characterised by circumlocutions. For example, in answer to questions about the onset of his illness he replied, "I couldn't say it that I didn't feel good and the one I'm married to took me down there and they couldn't find nothing to me." On testing he was only able to name 1 of 25 pictures of common objects (e.g., cat, dog, car, train) but could correctly write the names of 13 (making only minor spelling errors on most of the remainder). The patient's deficit was not simply one of word production since he could repeat the target accurately.

Rather his difficulty appeared to be in retrieval of words for speech; to quote the patient, "I can't say it but I can stick it down." Another similar case has been described by Bub & Kertesz (1982a).

Anatomical Considerations

Failure on clinical tests of word retrieval, which for the most part have used confrontation naming of pictures or objects, is commonplace in patients with language disorders. This has led some investigators to suggest that impaired word retrieval has no localising significance. For example, Kertesz, Lesk, & McCabe (1977) and Kertesz, Harlock, & Coates (1979) found that impairments on confrontation naming tasks were associated with damage over a wide range of areas of the left hemisphere. They regarded word-finding difficulties as a sign of mild aphasia or of a partially recovered aphasic deficit in chronic vascular cases. Benson (1985) has also contended that naming difficulties have no precise localising significance. However, there are other group studies that appear to point to a more specific localisation.

Hécaen & Angelergues (1964) studied 214 cases with unilateral lesions of the left hemisphere. Although naming difficulties were present following lesions to any sector of the left hemisphere, the incidence of impairment was greatest if there was temporal lobe involvement (see Fig. 7.5). In a group study of 57 cases, Coughlan & Warrington (1978) found that patients with left temporal lobe involvement

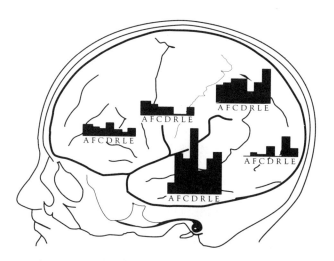

Figure 7.5 Schematic histograms showing incidence of different aphasic impairments in relation to locus of lesion indicating maximum naming difficulties in the temporal lobe. (From Hécaen & Angelergues, 1964.) A, articulatory disturbance; F, difficulties in the fluency of speech; C, disturbances of verbal comprehension; D, disturbances of naming; R, disturbances of repetition; L, disturbances in reading; and E, disturbances of writing.

were significantly worse on naming tasks than were patients with left-hemisphere lesions sparing the temporal lobe. This finding was replicated in a further study of naming in patients with unilateral lesions (McKenna & Warrington, 1980). These group studies of word-retrieval impairments have for the most part used visual object-naming tasks. It is therefore implicitly assumed that the naming deficits would be comparable to other modalities (e.g., naming to description, by touch, or by smell).

The study of category-specific deficits has focused on single cases, most of whom have had widespread or poorly localised lesions. It is fair to say that in all cases the left temporal lobe has been involved, but it has not proven possible to identify more specific structures or regions in such cases. A possible exception to this generalisation is the selective impairment of colour naming, for which a relatively precise localisation in the occipitotemporal region extending to the splenium has been claimed (Geschwind & Fusillo, 1966).

In the case of modality-specific word-retrieval impairments there are indications that the critical lesion may involve more posterior sectors of the temporal lobes or lesions of the corpus callosum. In the case of impairment of naming objects presented visually (with preservation of the ability to name them by touch), patients have been shown to have lesions in the posterior temporal/occipital areas (Beauvois, 1982). In the case of a patient with an impairment in naming objects presented by touch, a parietotemporal locus was implicated. In those cases in which the modality-specific deficit is confined to one visual field or to one hand, there is evidence of a corpus callosum lesion. The best known examples are patients with surgical section of the corpus callosum ("split brain", see Chapter 1). These patients can name objects by touch when they are placed in their right hand (i.e., in the hand contralateral to their language hemisphere) but fail to name objects placed in their left hand. Similarly, they can name objects shown to the right visual field but cannot name those presented to the left (e.g., Bogen, 1985).

Theoretical Considerations

The common clinical observation that patients may fail to name a common object has given rise to a considerable amount of theoretical speculation. Two main classes of theory have been put forward. First it has been suggested that impairments in naming tasks are merely a manifestation of a more pervasive intellectual or language impairment (Single Common Factor Theories). The second, broad class of framework has taken as its starting point the naming task itself, and attempted to characterise the different sources of failure on clinical tests (Multi-Component Theories).

Single-Common-Factor Theories

Hughlings Jackson (1880) suggested that word-retrieval difficulties reflected a deficit in "propositionising," that is, in the derivation of an adequate verbal–conceptual structure. Patients with aphasia were considered to show this fundamental intellectual deficit due to loss of the higher levels of language organisation. Patients might fail to name an object in a confrontation naming task, but might use the same word in a cliché or platitude. The higher, essentially human, forms of intellectual organisation were disrupted by cerebral lesions. The aphasic patient was reduced to the vocabulary of overlearned and stereotyped utterances which Jackson considered to be characteristic of more primitive forms of speech.

The "intellectual deficit" account of word-finding difficulties was made fully explicit by Goldstein (1948). He argued that patients with word-retrieval difficulties had a deficit in abstraction—they lacked the abstract attitude that was a prerequisite for the formulation of thought. Such impairments would necessarily lead to a difficulty in naming. In support of his argument he cited cases with prominent difficulties in word-retrieval who also showed impairment on tests of abstract reasoning and categorisation. Head (1926) remained sympathetic to the intellectual-deficit account of aphasia but attempted to redefine it as a specific verbal intellectual deficit. His viewpoint is perhaps transitional between the early single-common-factor accounts and those which regarded word-retrieval difficulties as a more circumscribed disorder.

Whilst general intellectual difficulties may be associated with naming impairments they are by no means a necessary feature. Deficits in intellectual abilities should probably be viewed as giving rise to a "secondary" impairment rather than a primary deficit (nonaphasic misnamings: Geschwind, 1967). A large number of cases have now been described where ability to perform abstract reasoning tasks is intact, despite profound difficulties in ability to retrieve words (e.g., Kinsbourne and Warrington, 1963a; Zangwill, 1964; Warrington, 1975). As a source of word-retrieval impairment, failure due to intellectual dysfunction can be considered as comparable to other secondary causes of difficulty such as fatigue or impaired attention (Hécaen and Albert, 1978).

Multicomponent Theories

There are a number of frameworks that take account of the complexities of the naming task, and recognise that failure on word-retrieval can be attributable to a variety of disparate sources (e.g., Benson, 1979a,b; Ellis, 1985; Gainotti, Silveri, Villa, & Miceli, 1986). These theoretical accounts have to a large extent focused on the naming task, and specified different sources of failure. Consider the task of naming a cup. This could fail for a number of reasons. First because of some impairment in deriving adequate semantic information (about the target word), second, because of failure in retrieving the appropriate word despite a full and adequate semantic specification; or third, because of inability to specify the exact pronunciation of the target word.

Derivation of Adequate Semantic Information

Quite apart from any primary deficit in visual object recognition (see Chapter 2), two sources of impairment in deriving semantic information adequate for naming have been identified. First, in the case of the modality-specific naming impairments (e.g., optic aphasia, tactile aphasia), it has been suggested that there may be some form of disconnection between processing in the affected modality and verbal knowledge. Second, in those deficits which do not appear to be confined to a single modality, it has been argued that naming difficulties may be a direct consequence of impaired verbal knowledge.

Modality-Specific Naming Impairments   The modality-specific subtypes of naming disturbance have classically been considered as disconnection syndromes. Specifically, they are considered to result from a failure of communication between sensory information about the target and verbal knowledge (e.g., Geschwind, 1967). Geschwind noted that the naming responses of patients with modality-specific disorders bore little formal relationship to the target, either in terms of word sound or word meaning. A patient described by Geschwind and Kaplan (1962) who had a naming deficit confined to the tactile modality misnamed a ring as "an eraser," a watch as "a balloon," and a screwdriver as "a piece of paper." The patient had a deficit confined to one hand (the left) and the impairment was considered to result from a disconnection between tactile information in the right hemisphere and verbal information in the left. This interpretation was supported by the observation of a corpus callosum lesion. Similarly, a patient described by Coslett and Saffran (1989a) with a deficit confined to the visual modality was also thought to manifest a disconnection syndrome. He misnamed a pair of scissors as a "clock" and a volcano as a "pillar." Coslett and Saffran argued that his lesion, and concomitant dense-right hemianopia restricted the processing of visual information to his right hemisphere. However, not all modality-specific impairments of naming result in bizarre or inappropriate responses. In the case of an optic aphasic (J.F.) Lhermitte and Beauvois noted that the majority of errors were either semantic or perseverative in nature. The incidence of semantic errors increased as a function of task difficulty and visual complexity of the stimuli. In the tactile aphasic (R.G.) studied by Beauvois, Saillant, Meininger, & Lhermitte (1978) 66% of naming errors were semantically related to the target. Such mistakes could clearly arise as a consequence of faulty processing of stimuli within the affected modality. Beauvois and her colleagues used miming tasks as a means of assessing this possibility. The subject was presented with an object in the affected modality and asked to produce the appropriate gesture (e.g., making a cutting action when shown scissors). If the subject was able to produce an appropriate gesture, then this would indicate that some degree of recognition was possible within the affected modality. The patients performed well on these tasks. In discussing the optic aphasic case, Beauvois (1982) noted that the patient performed worse on these critical miming tasks if he was allowed to verbalise at the same time. This verbalisation was "discouraged" by the simple expedient of placing an adhesive plaster over the patient's mouth and in these conditions his pantomime performance improved!

Beauvois (1982) has interpreted modality-specific aphasias as a disconnection between modality-specific semantic systems (see Chapter 6). Beauvois postulated that there were meaning systems associated with touch and vision that were independent of the knowledge base used in verbal comprehension. Patients with a modality-specific anomia could be thought of as having "disconnected" their verbal knowledge base from the semantic knowledge base of the affected modality. Thus, in the case of optic aphasia, the patient would show normal visual recognition (mediated by visual semantic knowledge) and normal verbal comprehension (mediated by verbal knowledge). However, these two systems had become disconnected resulting in a failure on the cross-modal task of verbally naming a visual object. The account given by Beauvois (1982) has much in common with the classical "disconnection" position expressed by Geschwind (1967). However, Beauvois and her colleagues consider that the patient's deficits are attributable to an intra-hemispheric disconnection, rather than a failure of communication between right and left hemispheres. In the case of the tactile aphasic the deficit was bilateral, and not confined to one side [as in Geschwind and Kaplan's (1962) patient]. Furthermore, the errors made by the optic- and tactile-aphasic patients were often semantically related to the target, rather than the "bizarre" responses given by callosal disconnection cases.

Riddoch & Humphreys (1987b) and Riddoch, Humphreys, Coltheart, & Funnell (1988) have argued that these findings do not compel an interpretation in terms of modality-specific meaning systems. Rather, they suggest that many of the characteristics of visual modality-specific impairments (optic aphasia) can be thought of in terms analogous to that of the classical "disconnection syndrome" account. Specifically, they argued that the integrity of visual knowledge (visual semantics) could not be adequately established by the use of miming and gesture. For example, the semantic distinction between a brush and a comb could not be unequivocally demonstrated by gesture. They therefore preferred to interpret the modality-specific phenomena in terms of a failure to transmit information from perceptual systems to semantic knowledge (see also Chapter 2). In support of their argument, Riddoch and Humphreys described a patient who made errors which were both visually and semantically related to the targets. This type of "mixed error" might be accounted for in terms of a faulty transmission of information from perceptual processing to meaning systems. A partial-disconnection account of this type might be appropriate in some cases. However, it is clearly insufficient for those patients in whom the integrity of knowledge within the affected modality has been established using more demanding tests such as visual–visual matching (e.g., Fig. 2.13; Coslett and Saffran, 1989a). Furthermore, it cannot easily account for cases of category specific optic aphasia. Cases are on record with selective impairment in naming colours and facial expressions (Geschwind & Fusillo, 1966; Rapcsak, Kaszniak, & Rubens, 1989). At the very least, a disconnection account requires modification to postulate category-specific transmission routes.

Target Word Comprehension   Studies of patients with impaired naming skills have often noted that such deficits may be underpinned by a deficit in comprehending the spoken word (e.g., Luria, 1976; Goodglass, Gleason, & Hyde, 1970; Gainotti, Caltagirone, & Ibba, 1975; Coughlan & Warrington, 1978; Gainotti, Miceli, Caltagirone, Silveri, & Masullo, 1981; Allport and Funnell, 1981; Butterworth, Howard, & McLoughlin, 1984). It is argued that if the verbal knowledge-base itself is degraded, this will have direct consequences for word-retrieval. For example, if the patient's comprehension of the words *fork* and *spoon* is degraded than there may be significant impairments in correctly retrieving the words *fork* and *spoon* in the context of a naming task (Goodglass, Gleason, & Hyde, 1970). However, it is also clear that impaired word-retrieval can occur in patients in whom intact word knowledge can be demonstrated on the most stringent tasks. In such cases, a "pure anomia" or "word-selection anomia" is identified (cf, Benson, 1979a).

   Gainotti, Silveri, Villa, & Miceli (1986) described two types of patient with word-retrieval difficulties. One subtype was characterised by impaired ability to discriminate between the meanings of closely related spoken words, whilst the other group had marked naming difficulties despite intact comprehension. Gainotti, Miceli, Caltagirone, Silveri, & Masullo (1981) found that those patients who produced words which were semantically related to the target on a confrontation naming task were also likely to have impaired word comprehension. Thus when shown a picture of an orange, they would produce the word *apple* and not attempt to correct their error, probably because they did not realise that they had made one. The other type of patient could specify the initial sound of the target words (cf. also Goodglass, Kaplan, Weintraub, & Akerman, 1976) and sometimes benefited from cuing with the first one or two syllables of the target. The patients occasionally made "semantic errors" (e.g., calling an apple an orange), however they tended to prefix their utterance with "it's not a . . .".

Knowledge of the sound pattern or the pronunciation characteristics of words which cannot be retrieved is also observed in normal subjects when they attempt to produce low frequency words (the "tip-of-the-tongue" effect). Gainotti *et al.* (1986) investigated the extent to which the two classes of patient could give information about words which they were unable to retrieve. Patients with impaired comprehension were unable to estimate the number of syllables in the target word, and did not appear to have any more specific information. By contrast, patients with intact comprehension were able to give information about the words for which they were searching and could therefore be thought of as being similar to normal subjects in a tip-of-the-tongue state. Patients with impaired comprehension were unable to get as far as being in a tip-of-the-tongue state because of inadequate or imprecise information at the level of word meaning.

In a complementary single case study Howard & Orchard-Lisle (1984) investigated the word-retrieval difficulties of a patient (J.C.U.) with a disorder of single word comprehension. She was only able to produce a small number of high-frequency words in standard confrontation naming tasks, however, she was helped by provision of the initial sound of a word (e.g., "t," tiger). However, presentation of a cue which was misleading and appropriate to a semantically related target induced the patient to make semantic naming errors. For example, if shown a picture of a lion and given the cue "t," the patient was likely to produce the semantically related misnaming response "tiger." Howard & Orchard-Lisle argued that the presentation of cues triggered one of the possible naming responses to poorly differentiated semantic information. They interpreted the patient's difficulties in uncued naming tasks as being a consequence of her semantic impairment: she had insufficient unambiguous information in her semantic knowledge base to produce the object's name.

Somewhat counterintuitively, impairments in comprehending spoken words need not necessarily result in a failure in naming the same items (Goodglass, Wingfield, Hyde, & Theurkauf, 1986). Perhaps the best documented cases of this phenomenon are those patients with a specific impairment in the comprehension of the names of body parts (autotopagnosia: see Chapter 6). Such patients may actually be able to name parts of their body even though they fail on such elementary tasks as "point to your hand" (e.g., Ogden, 1985). The preservation of naming in the context of impaired comprehension has been interpreted as evidence that there is a direct link between perception and speech production which bypasses the verbal meaning system (Kremin, 1986).

Impaired Selection of Target Words

Impaired word retrieval can arise in patients whose ability to comprehend the spoken word is intact (Luria, 1964; Benson, 1979a). For at least some patients, the disorder can be thought of as a failure to *retrieve* the target word, rather than a secondary consequence of

impaired semantic knowledge, or impaired speech production. Zingeser & Berndt (1988) documented a patient with a very clear deficit in
this aspect of word retrieval. The patient had intact comprehension but
showed a category-specific pattern of impairment in word retrieval,
with nouns being more affected than verbs. Whilst the patient was poor
on standard confrontation naming tests, he was nevertheless able to
retrieve target words when asked to complete a sentence frame (e.g.,
the dog chased the cat up a . . .".). Zingeser & Berndt interpreted the
patient's deficit in terms of a failure at a stage of processing which was
intermediate between word meaning and speech production. They suggested that, at this level, information was organised in terms of grammatical class. The facilitation of word retrieval in the context of an
incomplete sentence was viewed as evidence in favour of there being
multiple influences on this stage of processing, including syntax.

Whilst grammatical class may be one organising principle for this
stage of processing, there is evidence that semantic category may also
be important. As has been discussed in the empirical section, deficits
in word selection can be specific to particular semantic categories, the
best documented examples being in the retrieval of proper names. The
patient (P.C.) described by Semenza & Zettin (1988) had an almost
absolute loss of the ability to retrieve proper names. However, he was
able to achieve some limited success in retrieving these names when
they had alternative "meanings." Thus when asked, "What is the name
of the composer of Aida and Traviata? His name reminds us of a colour." the patient responded "A colour? . . . Let's see . . . red . . . no, yellow . . . no, green . . . yes, greens". (verde . . . si, verdi) (p. 717). The
word was clearly available to him, however he was unable to retrieve it
as a proper name.

The organisation of the intermediate stage of word selection, or word
search appears to have some similarities in its characteristics to that of
the verbal semantic knowledge-base in that semantic category and
grammatical class are relevant variables (see Chapter 6). However, the
procedures of word retrieval are likely to prove very different from
those which are required for word comprehension.

Impaired Word Production

The relationship between word search and the procedures for producing the word has given rise to some debate. For some writers no clear
discontinuity is postulated between the stages of search and production (Kay & Ellis, 1987). Kay & Ellis suggested that following the derivation of the appropriate semantic information, the sound pattern of
words is directly accessed in a stored "lexicon" for production. They
reported a patient (E.S.T.) whose naming errors were often phonemic
paraphasic distortions of the target word. The patient had preservation
of semantic comprehension and a considerable degree of tacit knowledge of the sound or pronunciation of the target. Kay & Ellis argued

that anomia, in patients with intact comprehension, could be viewed as a partial disconnection of the semantic processing of word meaning from the speech-production systems.

Gainotti and his colleagues (1986) offered a somewhat different account. They described patients with marked word-finding difficulties who did *not* make phonemic errors on naming or in their spontaneous speech. These cases had intact comprehension and furthermore they demonstrated a considerable degree of tacit knowledge about words which they were unable to retrieve. Gainotti *et al.* argued that the patients' deficit lay "near the stage in which the selected lexical item is specified into the appropriate phonological form."

Both of these accounts imply a two-stage model of the word-retrieval process, although the stages which have been identified differ. Perhaps there are three stages implicated by these data—word meaning, word selection, and target realisation (see Fig. 7.6). Perhaps the best evidence that there is a genuine discontinuity between the stages of target word selection and word production is the evidence for dissociation between the ability to retrieve words for writing and speaking. The ability to retrieve the written form of a word may be spared even though the patient may be unable to retrieve it for speech, with other aspects of speech production being relatively well preserved (e.g., Hier & Mohr, 1977; Bub & Kertesz, 1982a). This dissociation suggests that there may be a separation between the stages of target selection and word production.

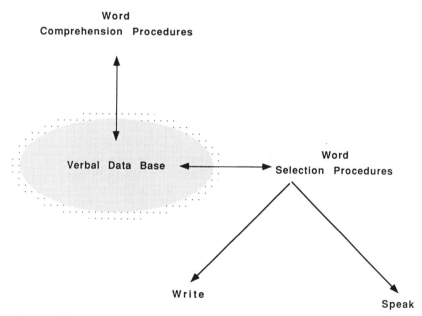

Figure 7.6 Descriptive model of word-retrieval processes.

Conclusion

The analysis of impairments in word retrieval which has been discussed in this section is of necessity only a very limited outline, painted with a very broad brush. Failures on a confrontation-naming task can arise for disparate reasons, and patients with word-retrieval difficulties are far from being a homogeneous group (Howard, Patterson, Franklin, Morton, & Orchard-Lisle, 1984). In this light, it is perhaps unsurprising that there has been controversy with regard to its precise anatomical correlates. Theoretical accounts have tended to be extremely broad, and as a consequence of their focus on specific tasks, have extended to encompass a variety of skills other than word retrieval itself. Patients may fail because they have difficulties in comprehension of the target, or in making the necessary links between different modalities of sensory or semantic information. They may also be impaired in the procedures of word search, or in specifying the appropriate phonological form of the target on the basis of search procedures.

Perhaps surprisingly, the core skills of word search or word-retrieval have received less theoretical attention than have the minutiae of the artificial task of naming pictures or objects. It is becoming clear, however, that there is no simple continuum between the ability to comprehend the spoken word, and the ability to retrieve it. As a working assumption, both comprehension and retrieval processes can be considered to utilise a common database. In the case of comprehension, the task is to access an appropriate target. In the case of word selection, the task is to retrieve the appropriate target. Whilst these seem to be symmetrical operations, there is no reason to assume that they have similar dynamic properties, or common search procedures. The possibly puzzling examples of patients whose naming is superior to their comprehension of particular classes of word may well be accounted for within a dual-process framework of this type.

8

Sentence Processing

Introduction

Language is often thought of as consisting of individual words which are organised according to the rules of the language into phrases, sentences, and longer stretches of conversation. The individual words of the language might be considered to have the status of building blocks, which can be combined and reordered into a vast, near-infinite number of different sentences. The way in which words are put together to form sentences is highly constrained in all human languages. It is not only necessary that words with the appropriate and complementary meanings are selected and used in order to convey a specific message; it is also necessary that they should be ordered and organised according to the syntax of the language. Thus a statement such as "John hit Mary" informs us about the agent of the action (John) and the recipient of the act (Mary): simply changing the order of the words in the sentence so that it reads "Mary hit John" conveys a totally different meaning.

The rules of grammar are not simply confined to the ordering of individual words, but reflect the ways in which whole phrases can take on different meanings as a function of their context within a sentence. For example, whilst the sentence "The cat ate the mouse" forms a perfectly meaningful "unit" when considered in isolation, in other contexts the same words do not constitute a self-contained phrase (e.g., "The dog that chased the cat ate the mouse").

Furthermore, words often have to be modified in very specific ways in the context of a sentence. In English, there are a relatively restricted set of conventions for word modification. For example, plural nouns are usually indicated by the addition of an "s" (e.g., boy vs. boys), and the verb inflection has to be modified according to number (boy walks vs. boys walk) and tense (boy walks/boy walked). These "rules" for changing words in the context of a sentence (which are technically termed *morphological rules)* vary in their complexity in different languages. Thus whilst English has only a restricted set of changes, languages such as French, Spanish, and Italian are slightly more complex, with rules including changes in adjectives so that they are congruent with the masculine/feminine status of nouns. German and Russian are even more complicated, with additional rules for word modification.

Empirical Characteristics

Impairments in the patient's ability to comprehend and produce sentences are extremely common in aphasia. The question arises as to whether disorders of sentence processing arise which are over and above those which can be explained at a single word level. Disorders of sentence comprehension will be considered first, followed by a discussion of impaired sentence production.

Sentence Comprehension

When understanding sentences in the context of conversational speech there are numerous verbal and nonverbal cues which help in interpretation. For example, when listening to speech in a language which one has only partially mastered, it is possible to work out the "gist" of what someone is saying without full comprehension of many of the words and with only a rudimentary knowledge of syntax. For many aphasic patients, any primary difficulty in sentence comprehension would be overcome by making use of additional "clues" to the meaning of an utterance. Why bother with analysing sentence-comprehension impairments if they usually only have very limited functional significance? There are two concerns which have motivated this type of investigation. One has been the need to develop tests which are sensitive to mild degrees of language impairment and so provide more adequate diagnostic tools for the clinician. The second has focused on theoretical analyses of the actual processes involved in comprehending sentences.

The first attempt to evaluate sentence comprehension systematically was reported by Salomon (1914). He provided a very exhaustive study of a single case (A.St) whose first language was German. Over the course of several months of daily sessions, the patient's difficulty with sentences was documented both in spontaneous speech and in comprehension. Salomon's investigation of the patient's difficulties in comprehending spoken and written sentences appears remarkably modern; in addition to tests of single word processing (including the classification of words into parts of speech) he included judgments of syntactic acceptability, comprehension of active and passive sentences (e.g., "John hit Mary" vs. "Mary was hit by John"), and the patient's reactions to "agrammatic" utterances produced by the examiner.

Although many of the early clinicians and researchers included tests which were regarded as measures of sentence comprehension, they were inadequate in many cases. In some tests (such as those introduced by Marie & Foix, 1917 and Head, 1926), there were considerable intellectual demands in addition to those required for processing words and sentences. Pierre Marie's "Three Paper Test" consisted of a series of unrelated commands to be performed with three pieces of paper, vis: "Here are three papers, a big one, a middle-sized one and a little one. Take the biggest and crumple it up and throw it on the ground. Give me the middle-sized one. Put the smallest in your pocket." In Head's "Coin-and-Bowl" test the subject was presented with an array of coins and bowls and asked to perform instructions such as "first coin into third bowl." In the "Hand–Eye–Ear" test the subject was asked to act on instructions such as "right hand touches left eye." These tests "worked" in that they were sensitive to acquired language difficulties. However failure could also occur with normal subjects of restricted intellectual capacity (Head, 1926). Weisenburg & McBride (1935) also used tests of sentence comprehension, but following in the tradition of Head's work their tasks were relatively nonspecific and could be failed for a number of reasons. The patient might fail to comprehend the constituent words of the sentence, have difficulty in processing sentences, or be unable to cope with the intellectual demands of the test.

De Renzi & Vignolo (1962) were first to acknowledge that the established clinical tests of sentence processing were inadequate. They developed a test, the Token Test (Fig. 8.1), which was designed to control for or eliminate the confounding variable of word knowledge. Furthermore, the task was designed so that patients were unable to obtain any cues from the environment as to how a sentence might be interpreted. The test consists of a graded series of instructions in which the patient is asked to "touch" or move coloured shapes (rectangles and circles) which are either large or small. The first sections of the test are essentially a screening procedure for assessing the patient's ability to comprehend the names given to the tokens (e.g., "pick up the yellow rectangle" and "pick up the large blue circle"). The last section of the test evaluates the processing of more complex sentence constructions (e.g., "touch the blue circle with the red triangle").

Despite the very limited intellectual demands of this test, De Renzi & Vignolo found that it was sensitive to a wide variety of aphasic disturbances. Even those patients whose ability to comprehend speech was clinically normal, and whose language disturbances were therefore very mild, failed on this task. De Renzi & Vignolo realised that failure on the Token Test could arise for a number of different reasons, including failure to comprehend "grammatical words" rather than sentence structure or the abstract names given to the tokens. The Token Test has continued to be very popular for the assessment of language disturbances since it is capable of detecting mild degrees of impairment. Shortened versions of the test have also been developed which allow for

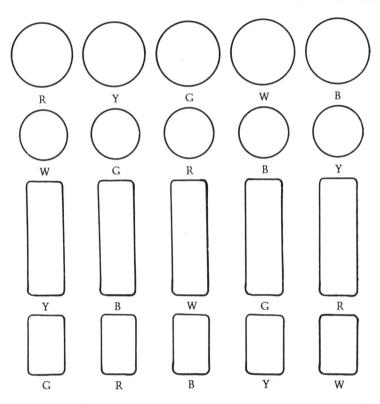

Figure 8.1 Standard presentation array for the Token Test (De Renzi and Vignolo, 1962).
R, red; B, blue; G, green; Y, yellow; W, white.

a very rapid screening of aphasic patients (e.g., Spellacy & Spreen,
1969; De Renzi & Faglioni, 1978; Coughlan & Warrington, 1978). However, the Token Test was not designed to formally manipulate different
types of sentence construction and does not include a wide range of
parts of speech. This means that, whilst the Token Test is an effective
clinical and diagnostic instrument, it has limitations for analysing the
different ways in which sentence comprehension can break down.

Syntax Parisi & Pizzamiglio (1970) attempted to examine a range of
different sentence types in a specific test of "syntactic comprehension." The test requires the patient to match a spoken sentence to one
of two pictures in which the target and distractor could be easily confused (Fig. 8.2). For example, when matching a sentence such as "The
boy is chasing the dog," the distractor picture would show a dog chasing a boy. In addition to "order-dependent" constructions (actives, pas-
sives, prepositions, and subordinate phrases), the test samples a number of other sentence constructions including verb tense, genders, and
plurality (see Table 8.1).

Parisi & Pizzamiglio found that the test was sensitive to a wide range
of aphasic disturbances and that there were no significant differences

Figure 8.2 Example of picture choices from Parisi and Pizzamiglio's (1970) syntax-comprehension test.

Table 8.1 Syntax Test: Contrasts Clustered into Types

Word order
A. Reversible active: The boy is chasing the dog/The dog is chasing the boy.
B. Direct/indirect object: The boy brings the cat to the mouse/. . . the mouse to the cat.
F. From object and to object: The dog is going from the tree to the house/. . . from the house to the tree.
O. Reversible passive: The bicycle is being followed by the car/The car is being followed by the bicycle.
S. Subordinate phrase: The guard who has the rifle stops the robber/The guard stops the robber who has the rifle.

Verb tense
L. Present/past: The boy is bathing/. . . has been bathing.
M. Present/future: The boy is drawing/. . . will draw.

Singular–plural
P. Possessive pronoun: This is his mother/This is their mother.
Q. Noun (± verb): It's the chair/It's the chairs: The man is walking/The men are walking.

Negative–affirmative
J. The boy is pulling the train/. . . isn't pulling the train.

Reflexive–nonreflexive
C. The man is shaving him/The man is shaving himself.

Gender
K. The grandmother is telling a story/The grandfather is telling a story.

"Difficult" locative prepositions
I. to/from: The bird is flying to the tree/. . . from the tree.
N. behind/beside: The house is behind the tree/. . . beside the tree.
T. beside/between: The lamp is beside the table and chair/. . . between the table and chair.

"Easy" locative prepositions
D. behind/in front of: The cat is behind the tree/. . . in front of the tree.
E. on(in)/under: The dog is on the chair/. . . under the chair.
G. near/away from: The dog is near the fire/. . . away from the fire.
H. in/out of (outside): The flowers are in the vase/. . . outside the vase.
R. up/down: She is looking up/She is looking down.

between patients who were diagnosed as showing disturbances of comprehension, and those who were considered to be "unimpaired." Similar findings were reported by Lesser (1974) for an English version of the test. Overall, the test appeared to be as useful as the Token Test for screening aphasic patients insofar as a comparable incidence of impairment was detected. Parisi and his colleagues further suggested that it might be a clinically useful technique for eliciting deficits specific to particular types of sentence. Lesser's investigation of English-speaking aphasics broadly replicated their findings. Aphasic subjects had a significant error rate on this test as compared with nonaphasic subjects.

Other investigators have studied groups of patients classified into the classical aphasic categories of "Broca's" "Wernicke's" and "Conduction" subtypes (Goodglass and Kaplan, 1972; see Chapter 1). The aim of these investigations has been to establish whether there are specific impairments of sentence comprehension associated with different aphasia subtypes. In this regard "Broca's" aphasics with normal, or near normal comprehension of single substantive words, but impaired sentence production have been the major focus of interest.

Caramazza & Zurif (1976) used a sentence–picture matching test which required the interpretation of two types of sentence, termed *semantically constrained* and *reversible*. The semantically constrained sentences were of the type "the dress that the woman is washing is torn." Such sentences are constrained in that the adjective *torn* can only apply to the dress, rather than to the woman. In the reversible condition the adjective could apply to either of the two nouns in the sentence (e.g., "The horse that the bear is kicking is brown"). They found that Broca's aphasics whose single-word comprehension was relatively intact were able to take advantage of semantic constraints in sentence interpretation. However they scored at chance on the reversible condition, which was designed to place greater demands on syntactic and sentence-level processing. Adverse effects of sentence reversibility (hinging on the location of the words *the* or *a*) were also documented by Heilman & Scholes (1976). They used sentences of the form "She showed her the baby pictures" vs. "She showed her baby the pictures." Impairment was noted in all groups of patients, including those whose comprehension of the single word was thought to be intact (*viz.* Broca's and Conduction aphasics).

Subsequent studies have demonstrated that simple order-dependent sentences using active and passive constructions are vulnerable in a number of Broca's aphasics whose ability to comprehend single substantive words is relatively well preserved (e.g., Schwartz, Saffran, & Marin, 1980a). They found that patients were impaired in matching the appropriate picture to a spoken sentence such as "The dancer is applauded by the clown" when the distractor picture depicted the dancer applauding the clown (see Fig. 8.3).

Prosody Variation in emphasis, pitch, and timing together constitute what is known as melody of speech or *prosody*. Changes in prosody

Figure 8.3 Example of picture choice from Schwartz *et al.*'s (1980a) sentence-comprehension test. "The clown applauds the dancer."

provide cues to the listener as to the beginning and end of sentences or phrases and indicate what is important. They are also a useful "para-linguistic" cue for the listener as to the emotional state of the speaker. The ability to comprehend the emotional prosodic aspects of speech may be relatively selectively impaired in patients with normal comprehension. The ability to comprehend affective sentence prosody has been tested by presenting subjects with sentences (e.g., "I'm going to the movies") which are spoken with a particular affective tone (e.g., angry, happy, sad, indifferent). Judgment of the affective tone of voice is given by pointing to one of a set of schematic faces showing the appropriate expressions (e.g., Heilman, Scholes, & Watson, 1975; Bowers, Coslett, Bauer, Speedie, & Heilman, 1987). When the affective tone is congruent with the verbal content of the sentence (e.g., "The couple beamed at their new grandson" said in a happy voice), the task may be somewhat easier than when the affective tone is incongruent (e.g., "I'm feeling awful today" said in a happy voice).

Sentence Construction

Turning now to the ability that normal people have for talking in sentences. By the age of four or five the ability to produce a wide range of novel sentence constructions is achieved by the vast majority of children. Adequate sentence formation is also possible even for people of restricted verbal capacities; their speech consists of grammatically correct sentences. In considering the production of sentences in language disorders, two issues are important. First, the variety of ways in which sentence formation can break down, and second, the relationship between failure in retrieving single words and failure in retrieving sentences.

Although writers such as Wernicke and Lichtheim tended to give emphasis to an analysis of disorders arising at the level of the single word, other nineteenth-century commentators drew attention to the diverse patterns of abnormal sentence formation which patients showed in their spontaneous speech. The most extensive of the early studies of patients whose deficits encompassed sentence processing were conducted by German investigators. Since the grammatical rules of the German language are far more complex than those of English or French, patients' difficulties were perhaps more apparent.

Syntax   The ability to produce sentence constructions may be impaired in a variety of complex ways in patients with language disorders. These deficits have been commented on and analysed ever since the beginnings of the study of aphasia. Kussmaul (1877) suggested that sentence formulation could be specifically impaired in aphasia and distinguished between failures to produce words in their correct order and failure to produce word endings appropriate to the sentence context. He proposed that the term *agrammatism* should be used for the deficit in which word order was impaired and *aktaphasie* for the deficit in which word endings were absent or anomalous. The distinction which Kussmaul drew between impairments in the ordering of words and the absence or misuse of word endings was maintained in the early French literature (Pitres, 1898; Dejerine, 1892).

Heilbronner (1906) provided the first detailed case report and experimental analysis of a patient with a specific difficulty in sentence formation. His patient was able to retrieve uncommon words on naming tasks and was also able to comprehend complex questions, nevertheless his spontaneous speech and writing showed marked anomalies in sentence formation. The following translated example gives an approximate "flavour" of the patient's speech (cited by De Bleser, 1987): "First morning, drink coffee, and sweep and go field, afternoon such a pill, one and go field . . . "

Kleist (1934) and Goldstein (1948) drew attention to the differences between patients in the "facility" or ease with which erroneous sentences were produced as well as maintaining a distinction in the type of errors that were made. In one type of patient, termed the *paragrammatic*, mistakes were uttered in the course of well-articulated fluent speech. The patients' mistakes consisted of substitutions of words and word endings. In the other subtype, termed the *agrammatic*, speech was laboured and word endings and words were omitted rather than erroneously produced. Kleist viewed these patterns of deficit as reflecting two distinct types of disorder affecting the retrieval of sentences.

However, other authors contended that the errors of omission made by agrammatic patients might simply reflect a difficulty with articulation which resulted in the patient relying on the most informative words of the language (in order to save effort). Impaired articulation may result in very limited conversational speech. However, dysarthric patients or those with a kinetic deficit in speech production are not necessarily agrammatic (see Chapter 9).

Tissot, Mounin, & Lhermitte (1973) investigated five patients with impaired speech production. They spoke slowly, with multiple hesitations, and had very limited prosody (see below), but their sentence construction was normal. Tissot *et al.* found that this group was clearly differentiated from agrammatic patients. Despite the sparse nature of their speech these patients used appropriate word inflections, function words, and verbs. It has also been demonstrated that patients with normally fluent speech may nevertheless show agrammatic sentence constructions (Kolk, Van Grunsven, & Kuper, 1985). Taken together, these findings indicate a double dissociation between fluency and the production of grammatical speech.

Pictures depicting complex interactive scenes have frequently been used in the assessment of aphasics (an example of such a picture is shown in Fig. 8.4). Although picture-description tasks introduce a degree of artificiality into the "spontaneous" nature of speech they have been found to be of considerable practical use and appear to be sensitive to many of the difficulties in sentence formulation which are

Figure 8.4 Example of complex interactive scene for eliciting conversational speech. (From the Queen Square Screening Test for Cognitive Deficits, 1989.)

observed in free conversation (Goodglass & Kaplan, 1972). Interpretation of picture-description tasks is unfortunately often confounded with impairments in the ability to retrieve the specific vocabulary necessary to describe a picture. Furthermore, picture-description allows the patient a number of options with regard to the specific types of sentence which can be produced. Such tasks therefore run the risk of being more sensitive to the individuals' ability to compensate for their deficit, rather than their impairment per se.

One of the most useful tests for eliciting a variety of grammatical constructions, with a controlled vocabulary, is the Reporter's Test described by De Renzi & Ferrari (1978). This task is essentially a "production" version of the Token Test (see above). The patient is asked to describe a variety of actions involving the use of coloured rectangular and circular tokens. The task ranges in complexity from requiring a simple sentence construction to describe an action involving a single token (e.g., the examiner picks up the green circle) to requiring a more complex sentence describing a sequence of actions (e.g., when the examiner places a blue circle on a red rectangle).

Fluency   Quantitative studies of the "free" spontaneous speech of aphasic patients (which perhaps introduce complications over and above that of the level of the sentence) were introduced in the 1950s and 1960s. These were concerned first with quantifying the incidence of different parts of speech in spontaneous utterances and second with the fluency of utterances. Wepman, Bock, Jones, & Van Pelt (1956) conducted the first detailed statistical analysis of the spontaneous speech of aphasics. They found a pronounced effect of word frequency in a corpus of the "free" conversational speech (14,486 words) produced by one female patient. There was a shift toward usage of a high-frequency vocabulary which was most pronounced for nouns and somewhat less marked for verbs and "descriptive modifiers" (adjectives and adverbs). An example of the patient's spontaneous speech was given by Wepman *et al.*: "She's a good one, I like her. And then I had another one and she comes different on her time. Each one, and they're very good. They're wonderful; I love them and they're always anxious to face what they're doing if they have something to do or anything. And . . . I'd like to tell what they say. . . . Why don't want say that one? I know what she feels. Like she wants to, she wants me to know. . . ." It was as if the patient's vocabulary for lower-frequency words had been affected and she was relying on a reduced stock of "favourite" words. More detailed analysis suggested that she also tended to use a large number of common well-established language "formulae" or habitual conversational routines. Wepman *et al.* commented that this was not the only pattern of language breakdown to be observed in aphasia. They cited the case of another patient who showed preservation of substantive words and word order but an almost complete lack of function words.

Howes & Geschwind (1964) analysed large samples of conversational speech produced by aphasic patients (5000 words). Two main subtypes of patient were represented in their corpus. One subtype (termed *standard aphasics*) was characterised by sparse output, whereas the other category of patient had fluent, but nevertheless aphasic, speech. The standard aphasics produced content words but few grammatical words (function words and word endings, e.g., *but, if, the, a*, and endings such as *girl's walked*). The converse pattern was noted in the fluent cases with a dearth of content words but abundant function words. In both types of patient the profile was one of a bias toward use or avoidance of a particular component of the vocabulary rather than absolute loss or preservation. These findings have been substantiated in further studies of spontaneous speech and also in a number of more constrained tasks. For some patients, function words are more common than substantive words, and the converse pattern is shown by others (Jones & Wepman, 1965; Goodglass, Hyde, & Blumstein, 1969).

Goodglass, Quadfasel, & Timberlake (1964) added an important dimension to the analysis of aphasic speech which avoids the circularity involved in simply redescribing clinical phenomena in a more rigorous form. They found that the length of *phrases* (defined as word groupings delivered without pause or hesitation) was bimodally distributed. All of their sample who were clinically diagnosed as "Broca's aphasics" produced very short runs of speech, whereas with only one exception, Wernicke's aphasics and nominal aphasics produced utterances which were near normal or normal in length. Phrase length has become widely used as a defining characteristic for the classification of aphasic disorders. Indeed for some clinicians it supplanted previous classifications which gave more weight to what was said rather than to how fluently it was produced (e.g., Benson, 1967).

Lecours & Lhermitte (1979) have added one qualification to the distinction between fluent and nonfluent aphasic speakers. They pointed out that in a significant number of cases who speak "fluently" there may actually be multiple hesitations. In some cases, the number of words occurring before a "significant pause" is actually considerably below normal (although to the clinician the speech of these "loggorheic" patients may appear "pressured"). They tend to keep on talking in response to minimal stimulation, or even in the absence of stimulation. They can't keep quiet, and were described by Alajouanine (1968) as "indefatigable chatterboxes."

Jargon Aphasia   This pattern is taken to its extreme in jargon aphasia in which the patient may produce a copious flow of unintelligible speech (Alajouanine, Sabouraud, & Ribacourt, 1952). They suggested that jargon-aphasic speech should be further subdivided according to the types of errors which occurred. In *semantic jargon* the patient mostly produces real words, however they are put together in such a way that the meaning of the utterance is quite unintelligible. For example, one case (E.F.) produced, "Tape recording and automatic winding voice and the very very recording the typewriting and memorandum and tensioning and dialing to winding and balancing very very good" (Kinsbourne & Warrington, 1963). In *phonemic jargon* patients produce some real words, but also introduce multiple neologisms in their running speech. For example, "Yes, well I don't know what we'd particularly missed kerdiz or hekitz but we had the burrest. They were invernted kassterz wiss kisstek an niches ik hampess for nekstes an terress and so on" (adapted from Buckingham, 1981). In some cases a rudimentary sentence structure is also detectable through the meaningless speech. A patient (K.C.) described by Butterworth (1979) replied to the question, "What is your favourite food?" with "I'm not very happy doctor. I've not norter with the verker, because I don't enough. I just have er, krossy stuff. I don't have nood just the ordery heavy grass."

In another, extreme type of impaired spontaneous speech, the patient may be reduced to producing undifferentiated jargon or "recurrent utterances." These consist of the same word or neologism being said repeatedly, and in some cases even fluently produced. Strings of recurrent sounds, "ka, ka, ka" or "yes yes yes, yes yes" may be uttered with varying emphasis and pitch, suggesting that the patient is actively trying to communicate (e.g., Alajouanine *et al.*, 1952; Poeck, De Bleser, & Von Kanenlingk, 1984).

Dynamic Aphasia   In one variant of nonfluent aphasia, the patient may appear to be almost mute in conversational speech. Typically, there is an almost total failure to initiate speech, and sparse responses are given with exceptionally long latencies. By contrast, the patient may show a dramatic preservation of the ability to name objects, and to read, and repeat sentences. Indeed, patients may be able to produce perfectly adequate sentences "spontaneously" under limited task constraints. For example, the patient might be unable to frame an answer to a simple question such as "What is your job?" but nevertheless be capable of responding to the question, "Isn't it a nice day?" with "Yes it is a nice day" (e.g., Luria, 1970; Von Stockert, 1974; Rubens, 1976). Luria has termed this disorder *dynamic aphasia*. One patient (R.O.H.) with virtually no spontaneous speech was studied by Costello & Warrington (1989). The patient had above average scores and normal latencies on a stringent naming test. However, when asked simple questions such as "Tell me about your time in the RAF" he simply responded with "er." Although he was efficient in completing a sentence with a single word (e.g., "the boat passed easily under the . . .") he had great difficulty in completing a sentence with a phrase (e.g., "the black cat . . ."). Most strikingly, even though he was completely unable to converse, he was able to describe pictorial material well. Thus he described Fig. 8.5 in the following terms: "The little girl and the little boy are listening intently to a story by the Grandma."

Prosody   Patients may show a deficit in producing the appropriate melody of speech, termed *expressive dysprosody*. In the absence of

Figure 8.5 Picture used to elicit speech in a dynamic aphasic (R.O.H.) (Costello and Warrington, 1989).

variation in pitch or timing, the patient's speech may give the listener the impression of being "computer generated." In other cases timing, pitch, and volume abnormalities may combine together to sound as if the patient is speaking with a "foreign accent (see also Chapter 9)." This syndrome was first convincingly described in a single case (Astrid L.) by Monrad-Krohn (1947). Her speech was characterised by a "broken foreign accent" and a "completely changed melody of accent." Monrad-Krohn commented that the change in her accent was difficult to describe: "Her melody of language could not be said to be constant; it varied somewhat from time to time. But she never had the natural Norwegian accent when she had to link several words together into a sentence. . . . In short sentences like 'jeg sa det' (I said it) she pronounced the final pronoun slightly over emphasised and with a raised pitch of voice rather than a lowered one (p. 411)." Interestingly enough he noted that her musical abilities were normal. Her sense of rhythm was good, and when the examiner hummed she joined in and could continue correctly both as to time and tune. She was never heard to sing a false note or hum out of tune. Indeed it was because of her intact musical abilities that Monrad-Krohn coined the term *dysprosody.* Similar cases, albeit with impairments at the single word level also, have been described in a number of studies (e.g., Graff-Radford, Cooper, Colsher, & Damasio, 1986; Gurd, Bessel, Bladon, & Bamford, 1988; Blumstein, Alexander, Ryalls, Katz, & Dworetzky, 1987). Group studies have used a variety of techniques to assess prosodic impairments including impressionistic descriptions of spontaneous speech (Gorelick & Ross, 1987) as well as more detailed acoustic analyses of pitch and timing (Cooper, Soares, Michelow, & Goloskie, 1984;

Shapiro & Danley, 1985; Behrens, 1988, 1989). These studies have shown an unexpectedly high incidence of deficits in patients with cerebral lesions.

Anatomical Considerations

Sentence Comprehension

The precise anatomical correlates of impaired sentence comprehension are poorly defined. Coughlan & Warrington (1978) found that performance on a shortened version of the Token Test was impaired by lesions virtually anywhere in the left hemisphere; in no sector (i.e., frontal, temporal, or parietal) was there a selective deficit. However, in a larger-scale study Basso, Lecours, Moraschini, & Vanier (1985) found a significantly higher incidence of impairment in the classical posterior sectors of the left hemisphere (see Fig. 8.6). They also noted that a small proportion of patients with more anterior lesions were impaired.

Studies of the comprehension of prosodic aspects of sentences have produced somewhat counterintuitive results. Heilman et al. (1975) contrasted patients with posterior lesions of the right or left hemispheres. They found that the right-posterior group was more impaired on the prosodic task. These findings were replicated by Bowers et al. (1987). They also demonstrated that patients with posterior right-hemisphere lesions were significantly more impaired when the verbal content of the sentences was in conflict with the emotional information conveyed by prosody. Overall these findings point to a role for the posterior sectors of the right hemisphere in processing at least the affective information conveyed by speech prosody.

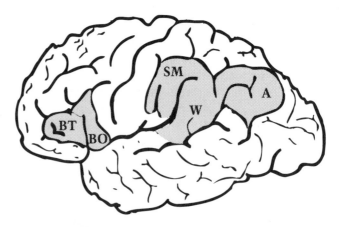

Figure 8.6 Figure showing classical anterior and posterior language areas from Basso *et al.* (1986). BT, Broca's area, pars triangularis of the third frontal convolution; BO, Broca's area, pars opercularis of the third frontal convolution; W, Wernicke's area, caudal half of the first-temporal convolution; SM, supramarginal gyrus; A, angular gyrus.

Sentence Construction

There have been a number of investigations of the anatomical correlates of impaired sentence construction (Benson, 1985; Kertesz, Lesk,
& McCabe, 1977; and Kertesz, 1979). These have largely been consistent in showing that patients with more anterior lesions of the left
hemisphere (see Fig. 8.6) are likely to show nonfluent and even agrammatic speech. However it is also clear that the syndrome complex of
laboured, agrammatic speech, with poor sentence structure (Broca's
aphasia), is often associated with relatively widespread lesions affecting both anterior language areas (frontal lobe), deeper structures (insula), as well as anterior temporal lobe damage (Mohr, 1976; Kertesz,
1979).

Abnormal sentence structures occurring in the context of fluent
speech are more likely to be associated with temporal lobe and parietal
lobe damage. In the case of jargon aphasia, Kertesz & Benson (1970)
noted that the common site of damage in 9 patients with neologistic
errors involved posterior temporal lobe, inferior parietal lobe, and the
arcuate fasciculus. In a subsequent study of 10 cases Kertesz & Shephard (1981) replicated these findings and concluded "the parieto-tem-
poral junction and parietal operculum is the crucial cortical area and
the underlying white matter, the arcuate fasciculus is always involved." In one case who came to autopsy, involvement of the temporal
lobe was limited to the posterior surface of the first temporal convolution. In the case of semantic jargon, the majority of cases have had
bilateral or poorly localised left-hemisphere lesions.

Goldstein (1948) considered that the critical lesion site in dynamic
aphasia was in structures between the anterior frontal lobe and the
motor speech area. Kleist (1934) observed this pattern of deficit in
patients with anterior lesions sparing Broca's area. Luria (1970) also
considered the critical lesion site to be anterior in the left hemisphere,
sparing Broca's area. He suggested that inferior frontal lesions might be
critical. This localisation was confirmed in a series studied by Rubens
(1976).

In the case of prosodic deficits there has been some controversy with
regard to the laterality of the critical sites of damage. Some investigations have shown that patients with right-hemisphere lesions may
have abnormalities in their production of prosody (e.g., Tucker, Watson, & Heilman, 1977; Gorelick & Ross, 1987). However the deficit
may not be as severe as in patients with left-hemisphere lesions (e.g.,
Shapiro & Danley, 1985). Two single cases with "foreign accent syndrome" in whom a prosodic disorder was prominent with well-circum-
scribed lesions both had anterior lesions of the left hemisphere, which
included the underlying white matter and left basal ganglia (Graff-
Radford et al., 1986; Gurd et al., 1988). Whether the dysprosodic difficulties documented in right-hemisphere cases have the same basis or
are of the same type as those documented in left-hemisphere cases
remains an open question.

Theoretical Considerations

The theoretical issues relevant to the comprehension and production of sentences (over and above those which are relevant at the single-word level) have focused on two main issues: first, on the evidence for integrative semantic processing spanning units larger than the single word, and second, on whether there is any evidence for specific disorders of syntax. In each of these issues the question as to whether comprehension, production, or both are involved has received attention. However, it is fair to say that the "semantic" level of processing has received most attention in the context of sentence-construction deficits and has only rarely been considered in the context of comprehension impairments. Deficits in the comprehension and production of prosody have yet to receive comparable analysis in theoretical neuropsychology.

The history of this debate starts with Hughlings Jackson (1879, 1880), who drew a firm distinction between automatic speech (such as the expression of clichés and swear words) and propositional speech, in which there was a voluntary act of propositioning. This distinction has been gradually refined (Head, 1926; Pick, 1931). By the time of Kleist (1934), a distinction was drawn between "nominalising" speech and "propositionising" speech. This distinction contrasted the act of naming with the act of producing a sentence. Following Kleist, the linguist Jacobson (1971) drew a distinction between "paradigmatic" speech, as required in naming, and "syntagmatic speech," in which words were modified in the context of others. This same distinction was maintained by Luria (1970), who investigated this dichotomy in aphasic patients.

It is now recognised that there are two partially overlapping issues involved in considering the "propositional" level of speech. In order to communicate or to understand multiword utterances it is necessary both to appreciate the changes in meaning which occur when words are juxtaposed (e.g., going out, passing out) or when they vary in order (e.g., blue sky, sky blue). When words form part of a sentence, additional levels of complexity are involved, so that meaning may be entirely changed according to the position of "grammatical words" (e.g., "The bird flew from the tree to the house" vs. "The bird flew to the tree from the house"). Sentences, in terms of either their semantics or their syntax, are more than just the sum of their words.

Sentence Comprehension

Under the heading of semantic aphasia Head (1926) considered that certain patients had specific difficulties in extracting the meaning from multiple word units. Luria (1970) adopted Head's terminology and cited cases of patients who had difficulty in comprehending constructions such as "brother's father" or "triangle over circle." Whilst failure on tasks such as these could be attributed to a failure to extract meaning from multiword units, the tasks are also critically dependent on an appreciation of syntactic rules and word order. Analysis of word order was tested directly in a series of experiments with "agrammatic" patients (Schwartz *et al.*, 1980a). The patients were asked to point to pictures in order to match a spoken sentence. These included pictures of "realistic" interactions (Fig. 8.3) together with specially devised "abstract" subject–object constructions such as "The circle phones the square." The actors in these sentences were stick figures (see Fig. 8.7). These rather unusual test materials were chosen so that there would not be any intrinsic bias toward interpreting a certain dominant word order (e.g., "The elephant trod on the mouse" vs. "The mouse trod on the elephant"). They found that their patients were very impaired on this task, scoring at chance levels. Schwartz and her colleagues considered that the patients' deficit was attributable to a difficulty in using word-order information in order to extract meanings from the relationships between words.

An alternative explanation of these results is that the patients were impaired in processing the actual syntax of the sentence (e.g., Caplan,

Figure 8.7   Example of "circles and squares" sentence-comprehension test (Schwartz *et al.*, 1980a).

1985). This could arise because of difficulty in dealing with the grammatical words of the sentence. If patients have difficulty in dealing with words such as *and, the, by,* etc., then they will have difficulty in distinguishing sentences of the type "The boy was hit by the girl" from "The girl hit the boy." Linebarger, Schwartz, & Saffran (1983) showed that there was a major discontinuity in agrammatic patients' ability to recognise grammatical anomalies and their ability to comprehend information conveyed by word order. The patients scored at chance in picture-pointing tests when word order was critical (e.g., "The circle is phoned by the square"). However, these same patients were capable of detecting badly structured sentences and the misplacement of function words (e.g., "The man is enjoying the view" vs. "The man is enjoyed the view"; "How many birds did you see?" vs. "How many did you see birds?"). Indeed, the patients' performance was almost perfect on many of these conditions (over 90%). This indicates that there may be a dissociation between the ability to "perceive" syntax and the ability to comprehend syntax. These findings have since been replicated (Wulfeck, 1988).

The ability to comprehend syntax is unlikely to be dependent on a single unitary "faculty" or process. Some patients may have little or no difficulty in comprehending order-dependent constructions under some conditions but fail under others. Two patients (R.A.N. and N.H.A.) were able to demonstrate comprehension of phrases such as "black above white" in baseline conditions when either of the tokens could be moved and when the white token was "fixed" and the black token could be moved.   However, their scores were only at chance when the black token was fixed and they had to move the white token below the black one (McCarthy & Warrington, 1987b; see Fig. 13.6). It was argued that the more difficult sentences could not be understood immediately "on line" as they were spoken, but rather needed restructuring for adequate understanding.

A somewhat different aspect of syntactic processing might affect the ability to determine which words "belong together" or modify each other. Luria (1970) described patients who made systematic errors in comprehending sentences such as "The circle is above the square and below the triangle." The patients appeared to "break" the sentences down inappropriately, putting the triangle at the bottom of the array. Luria considered this to reflect a failure in parsing the spoken utterance, "and below the triangle" being misinterpreted as "and below [everything] the triangle." Parsing is clearly a complex linguistic skill, and there are pointers to suggest that it may break down highly specifically in patients with cerebral lesions (e.g., Caplan, 1987; Caplan & Hildebrandt, 1988).

Sentence Construction

In considering the construction of multiword units, a distinction can be drawn between impairments affecting the ability to express the semantic content of an utterance and those which affect the production of word order and grammatical rules or syntax.

Semantic Propositional Level   There does not appear to be any simple relationship between the ability to retrieve words in isolation and the ability to retrieve them in the context of a sentence. A number of the classical authors, including Lichtheim (1885), Kleist (1916), Goldstein (1915, 1948), and Pick (1931), commented that there could be dissociations between these two skills. In an attempt to bridge the gap between the conditions of word retrieval in spontaneous speech and the more artificial object-naming task, Williams & Canter (1982) directly contrasted naming of items in scenes with naming of the same objects presented in isolation (see Fig. 8.8). Overall they found that patients classified as Broca's and Wernicke's were differentially affected by the demands of the task. Whereas the Broca's aphasic patients performed better on confrontation naming, patients with Wernicke's aphasia performed better with scene description. In a subsequent study, Williams & Canter (1987) used pictured actions in the same two types of picture (see Fig. 8.9). Although performance on these tests was not systematically related to aphasia type, once again there was evidence of a double dissociation between individual patient's performance on the two tasks.

Agrammatism   Saffran, Schwartz, & Marin (1980a) and Schwartz *et al.* (1980a) have argued that a disorder in deriving sentence-level verbal semantic relationships (thematic roles) or in translating such relationships into ordered sentences is a root cause of agrammatic speech. They found that patients had particular difficulty in producing sentences when a normally low-salience or inanimate item had to be produced in the "subject" position. Thus, shown a picture of a boy being hit on the head with a ball, the agrammatic patients produced sentences such as "The boy hits the ball" and "The teenager hits the ball on the head" (Schwartz, Linebarger, & Saffran, 1985). The patients were capable of producing simple ordered sentences (as the above examples show). However, Saffran and her colleagues (1980) argued that the patients were unable to code the relationships in the picture into a verbal propositional form.

Semantic Jargon Aphasia   Failure to express semantic propositions is almost a defining characteristic of the syndrome of semantic jargon aphasia. Kinsbourne & Warrington (1963a) described two remarkable cases of semantic jargon aphasia whose spontaneous speech was an unintelligible mixture of real words. For example, when asked to define the words *Safety First* one case (E.F.) responded, "To look and see and the Richmond Road particularly and look traffic and hesitation right and strolling, very good cause maybe, zebras maybe these, motor car and the traffic light." At the same time, the comprehension of complex spoken sentences (Marie's test) was intact in one case and only mildly impaired in the other. Both cases were able to pick synonyms when

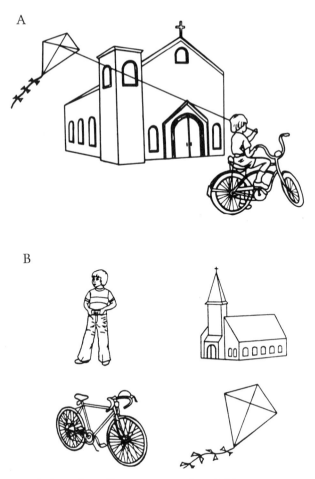

Figure 8.8   Example from the Williams & Canter (1982) object-naming test. (A) objects in scenes; (B) isolated objects.

presented with spoken words. One case was even able to repeat 10-word sentences verbatim (e.g., "Last year fifteen new houses were built on the street"). Both patients were able to read single words and text aloud at a good normal level and were above average on nonverbal tests of intellectual function.

These patients clearly had large vocabularies at their disposal, as was shown in a number of their responses. Thus, when asked "Who is the Prime Minister?" one patient (E.F.) responded, "Oh yes Mr. McMillan, and well, yes, Chris Chattaway maybe at any rate, Hugh Gaitskell, Nye Maybe, Aneurin Bevin, Edith Kummerskill. Well, then, schoolmasterly, deliberation promise shopping ginger group maybe and agitation, I don't know the speaker, resignment, no, I don't think much Paris maybe, finish." Despite these large vocabularies the patients were unable to use them in order to express propositions and semantic relationships.

A

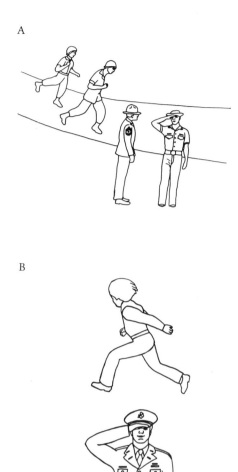

B

Figure 8.9 Example from the Williams & Canter (1987) action-naming test. (A) interactive scene; (B) individual actions.

Dynamic Aphasia A strikingly different impairment of sentence production is that of the dynamic aphasic. In spite of an adequate vocabulary and adequate grammatical and syntactic skills, the patient's ability for propositional speech may be negligible. Kleist (1934) suggested that patients might have intact verbal propositional thought and intact "sentence schemas" but that these were disconnected. Kleist's concept of a "sentence schema" referred to a stored set of grammatical frameworks which could be retrieved in much the same way as single words were retrieved. If the sentence schemas and verbal thought became disconnected, the patient would be impaired in translating between thought and sentence schemas.

Luria & Tsetskova (1978) and Luria (1970) attributed such impairments to faulty "inner speech." This inner speech was considered to be a crucial stage in developing the "final extended scheme of sentence." Luria suggested that unlike the agrammatic, the adynamic patient could overcome his problems with inner speech if external cues were provided for the "linear scheme of the sentence." In one clinical description he suggested that a patient's failure to retrieve the linear sentence scheme in picture description could be overcome by the use of simple environmental cues, such as the examiner pointing to three sheets of paper placed on the desk in order to indicate the first, second, and third of the ideas which were to be communicated.

However, there is evidence that this pattern of disorder can be modality specific. Costello & Warrington (1989) have therefore called into question any analysis in terms of a general failure to activate a linear scheme of the sentence. They studied a patient (R.O.H.) in whom there was a dramatic contrast in ability to generate sentences in response to verbal or visual input. His difficulty in the verbal domain appeared to be confined to tasks in which several words had to be put together in order to express a proposition. He was also unable to re-arrange 3 or 5 written words into a meaningful phrase (e.g., *head, hurts, my; car, move, we, the, must*). This was contrasted with his average score on a test requiring him to organise pictures into a meaningful sequence (WAIS picture arrangement). The patient also had no difficulty in producing well-formed sentences to describe complex visual material. For example, he described one set of scenes as follows: "Two boys fighting over a comic. One gent comes along and sees them and says 'what have you here.' He makes them shake hands. He makes them wander off, and then he wanders off himself reading the comic." His impairment was considered to reflect a failure of verbally mediated thought or planning, that is, at a stage prior to the generation of a sentence scheme. Since his deficit was confined to the verbal domain, it was not planning per se that was affected, rather he had a specific failure of verbal planning. Since this is a prerequisite for sentence production, his almost total inability to converse could be accounted for in these terms.

Syntactic Production   With regard to the syntactic aspects of sentence production there is evidence of multiple dissociations. Tissot *et al.* (1973) differentiated two forms of agrammatic impairment on the basis of their analysis of patients' spontaneous speech. One subtype, termed *morphological agrammatism*, was characterised by specific difficulties in using function words and the appropriate grammatical word endings. The patients' spontaneous speech maintained the word-order conventions of the language, but their "sentences" were tele-graphic in style. (See also Miceli, Mazzucchi, Menn, & Goodglass, 1983.) In the other subtype, termed *syntactic agrammatism*, the pa-tient was able to produce function words and word endings, but made errors with choice of verbs and in word order. To give an (idealised) example, when attempting to say, "The girl was giving flowers to the teacher" the morphological agrammatic might produce "girl give flower teacher," whereas the syntactic agrammatic might say, "The girl is flowering the teacher."

A particularly clear case of morphological agrammatism was re-ported by Nespoulos, Dordain, Perron, Ska, Bub, Caplan, Mehler, & Lecours, (1988). The patient (Mr. Clermont) made errors of omission and substitution of function words in spontaneous speech and in read-ing. However his deficit appeared to be confined to the production of sentences. They commented that individual words could be produced accurately (e.g., the patient read single function words rapidly and ac-curately, and he could supply function words to complete a spoken sentence), but he could not produce sentences spontaneously. The in-vestigators attempted to help the patient to read by asking him to produce sentences written in columns. They commented that he start-ed one column appropriately, then commented, "Oh it's a sentence!", and then made multiple errors. Nespoulos and his co-workers in-terpreted the patient's impairment in terms of a failure to select the appropriate function words with which to fill a sentence framework.

Within the class of patients with morphological agrammatism there may be even more subtle dissociations! Miceli and his colleagues (1989) have noted that some types of grammatical word ending were more vulnerable than others. Their (Italian) patient could produce end-ings such as the "er" in *dancer* but omitted other types of ending such as the "s" of *sings*. Their conclusion was that these two types of word ending are processed differently, the first being an intrinsic component of a word the other being added onto a word according to the rules of syntax and sentence context. Another dissociation between function words and word endings has also been reported (Berndt, 1987; Parisi, 1987). Two patients produced function words but omitted word end-ings; another case showed the opposite pattern of impairment.

Conclusion

The working assumption which has been adopted in this survey of impairments in sentence comprehension and sentence production has been that the patient's deficit cannot be accounted for in terms of deficits at the level of the single word (either in comprehension or in retrieval). In many cases, this possibility has not been considered, the empirical evidence being limited to an evaluation of the production and comprehension of propositional speech. A broad distinction has also been made between disorders at a "semantic" level and those which reflect impairments in word order or grammar. Whilst this provides a scheme for organising the data, it should not be taken as a rigid distinction; the two putative levels of processing are clearly closely interrelated.

9

Speech Production

Introduction

In order to communicate using the spoken word, we need to make skilled use of our ability to pronounce the "sounds" of the language. Each language contains a finite set of distinctive sounds or phonemes. These phonemes are a basic set of "building blocks" which are combined and recombined to make up all of the words in the language (see also Chapter 6). Although the exact pronunciation of an individual phoneme may vary slightly according to the context in which it is produced (see below) each phoneme has certain unique characteristics that distinguish it from others. Altering even one of these features can change the meaning of a word. Thus *bat* and *pat* are identical except for one critical feature in the initial sound. Although there are only a limited number of phonemes in any of the world's languages, each language has its own unique set, a fact which is immediately obvious to anyone who has attempted to learn a foreign language (e.g., the "u" sounds in the French *plus* and the pronunciation given to "c" in the Spanish *Barcelona* are not identical to any English phoneme). This is one reason why it is difficult to acquire the correct "accent" when learning a foreign language.

Phonemes are more than linguistic abstractions—they appear to reflect a specific level of processing which we all use in producing speech. One source of evidence for the phonemic level of processing has been drawn from the occasional "normal" errors which are quite common when talking spontaneously. For example, in the course of conversation one speaker intended to say "shops stay open till six," but instead produced "sops shay open till stix." This error reflects the "migrations" of the phonemes "s", "sh", and "t", and indicates that at some point in producing the utterance these phonemes were available but subsequently became "disorganised."

In addition to selecting the correct phoneme, fluent speech production is dependent on coordinated timing and anticipatory positioning of the complex speech musculature. In normal speech the "same" sound is often realised by a number of different combinations of articulatory movements. Take, for example, the words *geese* and *gas*. These are both three-phoneme words with the sounds "g" and "s" in common. However, these sounds are not produced identically in the two words. In *geese* the "g" sound is articulated with the tongue further forward in the mouth than in *gas*; furthermore, the "s" sound is often longer in duration in the word *geese*. (If you attempt to use the "g" pronunciation appropriate to *geese* in saying the word *gas* the sound is obviously distorted). These different patterns of articulation arise because speech production takes account of the context in which a particular phoneme is produced. The "ee" sound of *geese* is produced in a more anterior position in the mouth than is the "a" sound of *gas*, and the location in which the "g" sound is produced is accommodated in anticipation of these different vowel sounds. This ability to organise and integrate speech movements, namely the kinetic aspects of speech production, reflects a level of articulatory programming which is different from the "phonemic" level (see also Chapter 7.)

A high incidence of speech-production errors has been noted in patients with language disorders since the beginnings of the study of aphasia. Thus Broca (1861) focused on his patient's deficit in near "articulate speech" (see Chapter 1). Subsequent analyses suggested that there might be more than one type of impairment. Lichtheim (1885) pointed out that some patients were able to talk and, like Broca's cases, could also comprehend, but nevertheless muddled up word sounds in their spontaneous speech.

The broadly based analyses of the nineteenth-century neurologists have been refined, and it is now clear that there are two major subclasses of speech-production deficit which can be identified. Some patients show disorders in the organisation and sequencing of phonemes, despite adequate ability to produce the individual sounds of language (a phonemic disorder). Other patients may have adequate ability to select the appropriate phonemes, but they are impaired in the organisation and integration of the complex coordinated actions which are necessary for their production (a kinetic disorder).

The two major patterns of deficit, affecting the phonemic and kinetic levels of speech production, are differentiated from the *dysarthric* disorders. In dysarthria the muscles involved in speech production are affected by paralysis, weakness, or involuntary movements (e.g., Darley, Aronson, & Brown, 1975). The dysarthrias are not specific speech-production deficits, but are primary motor impairments affecting musculature. They can be considered as being similar in some respects to the effects of a hemiparesis or hemisensory loss on the patient's ability to use a limb. Dysarthric patients therefore have difficulties with all tasks for which the affected set of muscles are required (e.g., eating or swallowing). In the context of language; dysarthric disorders invariably affect all utterances requiring the participation of the affected muscle or muscle groups. The patient consistently makes mistakes on some sounds but may produce others correctly. By contrast, in primary disorders of speech production, the patient's deficit is confined to speaking and, moreover, the errors that an individual patient makes are typically quite inconsistent. The same words or sounds may be produced accurately on one occasion and inaccurately on another.

Empirical Characteristics

Phonemic Impairments

Patients may be impaired in their ability to organise phonemes in a sequence. This occurs despite adequate abilities to coordinate the articulatory movements necessary for their production. (Blumstein, 1988)

This type of impairment is perhaps one of the most common that is seen in aphasic patients (Goodglass & Kaplan, 1972). Speech may be produced at a normal or near normal rate, but it may be almost unintelligible due to errors in selection and ordering of the constituent sounds of the target word. In disorders of this type there may be no difficulty in retrieving the target word, but rather in producing it. These types of mistake can in principle be distinguished from errors of partial word retrieval (Kay & Ellis, 1987; see Chapter 7). In invoking a primary disorder of speech production there is at least an implicit assumption that word-retrieval procedures are intact.

If the patient's error has some resemblance in sound to the target word, such as when only one or two of the constituent phonemes are in error, then the patient's mistake is termed a *phonemic* (or "literal") *paraphasia* (e.g., *snail* → *stale; perhaps* → *perharst*). These errors are sometimes further subclassified into those which result in a real word (e.g., *snail* → *stale; name* → *mane*) and those which do not, or neologisms (*skeleton* → *skeffington; balloon* → *ballons*) (e.g. Lesser, 1978).

Evaluation of phonemic impairments of speech have mostly focused on paraphasic responses where there is a clear relationship between target and response (e.g., Lecours & Lhermitte, 1969; Blumstein, 1973; Pate, Saffran, & Martin, 1987). Both phonemically similar real-word errors and neologisms are typically observed in the same patients: it seems likely that the production of phonemically similar words has the same source of neologisms, since any phonemic transformation has a finite possibility of generating a "real" word.

Lecours & Lhermitte (1969) analysed the speech-production errors which were made (in a reading task) by two French speaking patients whose spontaneous speech was characterised by phonemic neologisms. They found that phonemic substitutions were frequent, and when they occurred, the target phoneme and the response were often very similar (e.g., *gratis* → *kradiss*) (see also Blumstein, 1973; Martin & Rigrodsky, 1974). Lecours & Lhermitte also found that there there was an increased likelihood of a sequencing error when the target contained two similar or identical phonemes. They found that sequencing errors which involved pairs of similar consonants were the most common and accounted for over 75% of the patients' paraphasic responses. These sequencing errors frequently involved the deletion of one of a pair of two similar phonemes (e.g., *descendant* → *esendant*; *complex* → *comples*) or changes in the position of similar phonemes (*detestable* → *tedestable*). The patients' errors also sometimes resulted in the creation of a similar pair of phonemes where none was present in the target (*abinominable* → *admoninabl*). Martin & Rigrodsky (1974) also noted that phoneme substitutions were not only similar to the target phoneme, but were also similar to another phoneme in the intended word in 80% of their patients' errors.

Joanette, Keller, & Lecours (1980) studied speech-production errors in French-speaking patients, focusing on the phenomenon of multiple attempts to realise a target word or "conduit d'approche. For example, a patient might accomplish production of the target word *crayon* (pencil) by four successive attempts (*"krava, kreber, krevon, krayon"*). Their analysis addressed the question of whether there was a systematic reduction of errors in the course of successive approximations. Joanette *et al.* found that this type of error was most common in patients with an impairment in speech production occurring in the context of normal or near normal comprehension (conduction aphasics). Second, in these cases, there was a trend for their successive responses to be a closer and closer approximation to the target (see Fig. 9.1). Blumstein (1973, 1988) has also noted that such changes are gradual and systematic often involving single phonemes at each step. This trend of increasing close approximations toward the target was not observed in patients with comprehension deficits.

Although there is good evidence that phonemic errors tend to involve similar phonemes, there is no evidence that specific phonemes are more or less vulnerable. Errors tend to be less common on vowels than on consonants but are by no means rare (e.g., Martin & Rigrodsky, 1974). Substitution errors involving single consonants may actually be more common than errors on consonant clusters (such as the "str" in string) (Blumstein, 1973). However, word length can be important, with longer polysyllabic words being more likely to lead to errors than short words. Furthermore, in some patients the production of low-frequency words may be more difficult than more common words (McCarthy & Warrington, 1984; Pate, Saffran, & Martin, 1987).

Detailed studies of the of acoustic characteristics of speech in patients who make phoneme errors has shown that their actual pronunciation of individual word sounds may be entirely normal (see Fig. 9.2: Blumstein, Cooper, Goodglass, Statlender, & Gottlieb, 1980). The characteristics of the individual phonemes produced by the patients con-

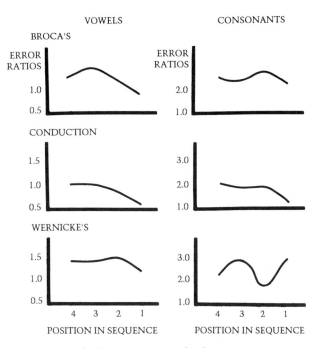

Figure 9.1. Schematic graph showing increasingly closer approximations to a target in patients with conduction aphasia (Joanette *et al.*, 1980).

form to the phoneme inventory of the language even though they are misselected and misordered. Furthermore the sequences of phonemes produced by the patients in their error responses also typically conform to the sequencing "rules" for phonemes in the relevant language (thus English speakers' responses do not begin a word with an illegal sequence such as "lk" or "sf").

Task-Specific Disorders

Phonemic disorders can be relatively task specific. In the classical syndrome of conduction aphasia, the patient's spontaneous speech is fluent and the incidence of phonemic errors is low. By contrast, in repetition tasks there is a very significant increase in the number of such errors. The converse pattern of preserved and impaired function is seen in one subtype of the classical syndrome of transcortical motor aphasia. Repetition of words and sentences may be normal, however spontaneous speech may be contaminated by numerous phonemic paraphasic errors (Goldstein, 1948). For example, McCarthy & Warrington (1984) reported one case of conduction aphasia (O.R.F.) who was able to achieve a score at the ninety-fifth percentile on an oral test of word definition (WAIS Vocabulary). However he was impaired in repeating

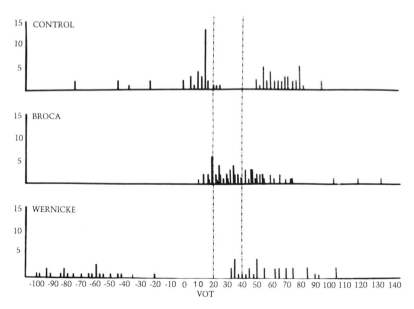

Figure 9.2. Examples of speech production in a control patient, a Broca's aphasic patient (probably kinetic disorder), and a Wernicke's aphasic patient (predominantly phonemic errors). This figure shows a clear distinction between different phonemes in the control and Wernicke's case, but much more overlap in the Broca's patient (Blumstein *et al.*, 1980).

even single high-frequency monosyllabic words (e.g., *base* → *vaysse*; *wash* → *fosh*). By contrast, in a case of transcortical motor aphasia (A.R.T.), spontaneous speech was so limited that he was unable to produce any comprehensible utterances, only paraphasic distortions. He failed to score on the expressive vocabulary test, but had no difficulty in comprehension. His deficit was attributable to his severe speech production impairment. In this context his near perfect ability to repeat single polysyllabic low-frequency words was quite remarkable.

The ability of two conduction aphasic patients (O.R.F. and R.A.N.) to repeat complete novel sentences was contrasted with their ability to repeat a different type of sentence, namely clichés. Clichés, whilst they obey the syntactic rules of English, have much in common with low-frequency polysyllabic words. A cliché is a "frozen" sentence whose syntax or word content cannot be changed without losing its meaning. For example, the cliché "He's as deaf as a post" loses its import if it is transformed into the "equivalent" sentence "A post is as deaf as he is." Furthermore, in many clichés the referents of the individual words are metaphorical, and the basis for the original metaphor is lost in history: why not "He's as deaf as a brick?" By contrast, in sentences the content words can be replaced by synonyms or the syntax can be altered without substantially affecting their meaning. The results showed that the conduction aphasic patients were capable of repeating short novel sentences accurately, however their performance on clichés was very impaired. The converse pattern applied to the transcortical motor aphasic patient (see Table 9.1). Pate *et al.* (1987) conducted a careful analysis of the errors made by a single case in reading words in a text and in reading familiar phrases (e.g., "Letter of the law"). They found that there were far more errors which crossed word boundaries in the case of clichés. This suggested that the patient was processing them as a single unit.

Kinetic Impairments

The realisation of a recognisable phoneme depends on the coordination of a number of precisely timed actions of the speech-production apparatus. Selective impairments at this level of speech production result in distorted speech sounds. The patient's speech is typically very slow, with abnormal timing and syllable stress. In attempting to produce individual speech sounds, some phonemes may be distorted to the point at which they are almost unintelligible. The sound produced by the patient may not have the characteristics of the phonemes of their native language; to the clinical examiner, they may sound "childlike," "foreign," or otherwise distinctly "abnormal."

The first systematic investigation of kinetic speech-production impairments was reported by Alajouanine, Ombredane, & Durand (1939). One of these patients (E.Fr.) had a severe impairment of speech production, but his other language functions including narrative writing were well preserved. His speech was characterised by slow, syllabic, and laboured production. He produced a written account of his difficulties as follows: "I can only talk syllabically because my articulation is sluggard. It is no longer automatic but has to be commanded, directed. I have to think of the word I am going to utter and the way in which to utter it. If I want to say 'bonjour' I can no longer do so out of habit. It is no longer automatic. If I am not very attentive I would say 'bouseu.' . . . . For this reason I must articulate each vowel each consonant, in short each syllable" (Lecours & Lhermitte, 1976 p. 93).

Alajouanine *et al.* (1939) used a simple technique for analysis of the acoustic aspects of the patients' speech, namely a tracing of variations

Table 9.1 Repetition of Cliches and Sentences[a]

Case	Cliché	Sentence	Cliché	Sentence
1	50	85	Take it with a pinch of salt	I like peanuts
			Down in the mouth	Everyone was in a hurry
2	18	45	Every Tom Dick and Harry	He finished his homework
			Nothing to write home about	The books were on the table
3	73	53	Thin end of the wedge	The carpet is grey

[a]Examples of clichés and sentences: percentage correct for two conduction aphasic patients (O.R.F. and R.A.N.) and one transcortical motor aphasic patient (A.R.T.) (from McCarthy & Warrington, 1984).

in air pressure emitted by the mouth and nose whilst the patient was producing a word. They contrasted the performance of the patients with those of normal control subjects and noted that there were abnormalities in the duration and timing of individual phonemes. They considered that the patients' errors were mostly on those speech sounds whose articulation required highly differentiated and very precise movements. The patients appeared to be relying on cruder or less precise movements. Alajouanine *et al.* also commented on the patients' ability to produce phonemes in different contexts. In an "easy" context, the patients were able to produce a sound (such as the "t" of *tap*) but had more difficulty when it was in the context of a consonant cluster (such as *trap*).

These early findings have been substantiated in more modern studies using direct measurement of the acoustic characteristics of the speech wave-form. Patients may be impaired in timing the movements required for speech (so that, for example, the sounds "b" and "p" as in *bat* and *pat* are not clearly distinguished from each other). Furthermore, patients may have particular difficulty in making the necessary rapid transitions between different speech sounds (e.g. Blumstein, Cooper, Zurif, & Caramazza, 1977; Freeman, Sands, & Harris, 1978; Shinn & Blumstein, 1983; Ziegler & Von Cramon, 1985; 1986 see Fig. 9.2).

Shankweiler & Harris (1966) investigated the relative difficulty of different speech sounds in five patients whose impairments were primarily kinetic in nature. They used a transcription technique, writing down the patients' responses, rather than a direct physical measurement of the acoustic pattern which the patients produced. They found that the patients' error rate was higher for consonants than for vowels and higher for clusters than for single consonants. Shankweiler & Harris also noted that certain consonants were particularly difficult: namely the sounds /v/ as in ga*v*e or *v*ery, /ʃ/ as in *sh*ut or da*sh* /ŋ/ as in ra*ng* /ʒ/ as in bei*g*e /θ/ as in ba*th* and /j/ as in *y*ou. By contrast the sounds /m/ as in *m*ack, /n/ as in k*n*ow and /p/ as in *p*art were relatively easy . Shankweiler & Harris pointed out that their patients' errors were often close approximations to the target phoneme.

These findings appear to be robust. Thus, the differential susceptibility of vowels as compared to consonants has been confirmed, except in the case of very severely impaired subjects. The gradation of consonant difficulty obtained by Shankweiler & Harris has also been confirmed. Patients do have particular difficulties with consonant clusters and, in order to cope, the patient may turn such a cluster into an "easier" syllabic group (*brother → burruther*) or might omit one element of the cluster (*brother → buther*) (e.g., Lebrun, Buyssens, & Henneaux, 1973).

The kinetic impairment of movement coordination and timing which has been documented in producing single sounds is also apparent in the patients' ability to produce longer utterances. Indeed their disorder may be exacerbated by the requirement to produce several words (e.g., Tuller, 1987). This may be a causal factor in giving rise to an overall impression of slow, syllable-paced speech (Lecours & Lhermitte, 1976). It appears as though short words are as likely to produce errors as are long words, however it is unclear whether this holds for all degrees of severity of the syndrome.

Patients have been described who speak as with a foreign accent (see also chapter 8)(e.g., Alajouanine *et al.*, 1939; Monrad-Krohn, 1947). One of the cases originally reported by Alajouanine *et al.* (1939) was subsequently discussed in greater detail by Lecours & Lhermitte, (1976). The patient was described as sounding "English" rather than French. This accent change occurred in the context of a more extensive set of difficulties with speech production. For some other patients, an accent change is the most prominent or pronounced deficit. Graff-Radford, Cooper, Colsher & Damasio (1986) described one such case. The patient's speech was slow and had an abnormal melody which some people thought was "Scandinavian." She made numerous systematic errors in pronouncing vowels (e.g., trip → treep, different → deeferent, back → bock, hospital → hoaspital). They commented that these errors were more frequent in spontaneous speech than in reading or repetition. A somewhat different type of "foreign accent" was reported by Blumstein, Alexander, Ryalls, Katz, & Dworetzky (1987). The patient, despite being a native Bostonian, was thought to sound like the speaker of a Romance language such as Italian or French. In addition to a prosodic deficit (see Chapter 8) the patient had a marked deficit at the level of the single word. In pronouncing single words she had a "non-American" accent. Individual syllables were given equal stress, resulting in a change in the timing of her speech. Individual sounds were also affected. For example, the words *butter* and *pretty* (pronounced like *buddur* and *priddy* in Boston) were articulated with clear medial "t" sounds (e.g., *but-er*, *pri-ty*). The disorder came on suddenly, and both the patient and her husband reported that there had been a very clear change in the way she pronounced words. By no means do all patients with a deficit in the coordination and timing of the articulatory system show a "foreign accent syndrome."

Anatomical Considerations

Phonemic Disorders

Errors in phoneme sequencing and selection are relatively common in aphasic disorders (e.g., Blumstein, 1973). As an isolated deficit they are associated with the classical syndromes of "conduction aphasia" and "transcortical motor aphasia" (see Chapter 1). The framework put forward by Wernicke and Lichtheim suggested that the critical lesion site in conduction aphasia (speech-production errors predominantly in repetition) should affect the main pathways between Wernicke's area in the temporal lobe and Broca's area in the frontal lobe. Geschwind (e.g. 1970) argued that damage to this tract, the arcuate fasciculus, was critical for the syndrome of conduction aphasia to arise. Green & Howes (1977) reviewed 25 published cases of conduction aphasia for whom pathological evidence was available either surgically or at post-mortem (from Lichtheim, 1885, to Benson, Sheremata, Bouchard, Segarra, Price, & Geschwind, 1973). Their findings are summarised in Table 9.2 and Fig. 9.3. The highest incidence of damage was found in the supramarginal gyrus and adjacent areas, consistent with

Table 9.2   Surgical and Post-mortem Reports of Lesions in 25 Cases of Conduction Aphasia
(Green & Howes, 1977)

Author and date of case report	Type of lesion	Locus[a]							
		1	2	3	4	5	6	7	8
Lichtheim (1884)	Infarct			1	2	2			1
Pick (1898)	Infarct			2					1
Pershing (1900)	Infarct					1		1	
Goldstein (1911)	Tumour			1					1
Liepmann & Pappenheim (1914)	Infarct	1		1	2	1	1		
Bonhoeffer (1923)	Infarct		1		2	2	1		
Pötzl (1925)	Infarct				2				
Hilpert (1930)	Abscess				2	2			
Stengel (1933)	Tumour			1	2		1		
Pötzl & Stengel (1937)	Infarct	1	1		2	2			1
Goldstein & Marmor (1938)	Infarct	1		2	1		1		1
Coenen (1940)	Infarct	1		1	2		2		
Stengel & Lodge Patch (1955)	Infarct			1	2	2	1	1	
Hécaen et al. (1955)	Tumour			1	2		1		
Hoeft (1957)	Infarct				2	2			
Konorski et al. (1961)	Tumour				2				
Kleist (1962)	Infarct		2	2	1		1		
Kleist (1962)	Infarct	1	1	2	2				
Caraceni (1962)	Tumour					2			
Warrington et al. (1971)	Tumour				2	2			
Warrington et al. (1971)	Tumour			2	2	2	1		
Brown (1972)	Tumour					1	2		
Benson et al. (1973)	Infarct				2	1	2		
Benson et al. (1973)	Infarct				2	2	1		
Benson et al. (1973)	Infarct			1	2		1		1
Total cases of partial damage		5	4	7	2	5	9	2	6
Total cases of severe damage		0	1	8	16	9	3	0	0
Total damage (out of possible 50)		5	6	23	34	23	15	2	6

[a]Key to locus numbers: 1, Heschl's gyrus; 2, planum temporale (posterior); 3, first temporal gyrus (posterior); 4, supramarginal gyrus; 5, supramarginal gyrus; 6, angular gyrus; 7, parietal operculum; 8, insula.

Key to cell numbers: 1, partial damage; 2, severe damage. All 1's and 2's are summed separately to obtain column totals for partial and severe damage. Figures for total overall damage were obtained by multiplying each total for severe damage by two and adding that total column's total for partial damage.

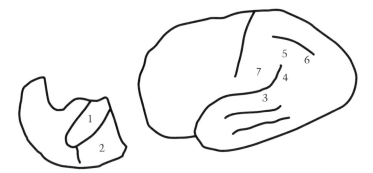

Figure 9.3. Areas of the dominant cortical hemisphere implicated in cases of conduction aphasia. 1, Heschl's gyrus; 2, planum temporale (posterior); 3, first temporal gyrus (posterior); 4, supramarginal gyrus; 5, supramarginal gyrus; 6, angular gyrus; 7, parietal operculum. For further explanation see Table 9.2. (Adapted from Green & Howes, 1977.)

Geschwinds's hypothesis. Subsequent single case reports are in accord with this analysis (e.g., Damasio & Damasio, 1980; McCarthy & Warrington, 1984; Caplan, Vanier, & Baker, 1986a).

Group studies have also been largely consistent with this localisation. Kertesz found both supra- and infra-sylvian lesions were present in 11 cases with clinically defined conduction aphasia. A comparable localisation was identified in three cases with chronic and persistent deficits (Kertesz, 1979).

There is very little evidence as to the precise localising significance of phonemic errors confined to spontaneous speech. Goldstein (1948) thought that this type of disorder could be attributed to mild damage affecting Broca's area, however, there is insufficient evidence from group studies or from single case studies to make this more than a plausible speculation.

Kinetic Deficits

The kinetic impairments of speech production appear to have a very precise localising significance. An autopsy study of one of the cases initially studied by Alajouanine *et al.* (1939) was reported by Lecours & Lhermitte (1976). The patient had a focal lesion with corticocortical softening of the inferior half of the left precentral gyrus. Schiff, Alexander, Naeser, & Galaburda (1983) presented an extensive review of all the published cases with a selective kinetic deficit (*aphemie* in their terminology) for whom anatomical evidence was available. They concluded that, without exception, all of these cases had anterior dominant hemisphere lesions involving the pars opercularis, the inferior prerolandic gyrus, or the white matter deep to these areas (see Fig. 9.4). An anterior left hemisphere locus has also been implicated in the "foreign accent syndrome." However, there are as yet too few cases on record to be more precise about its anatomical correlates.

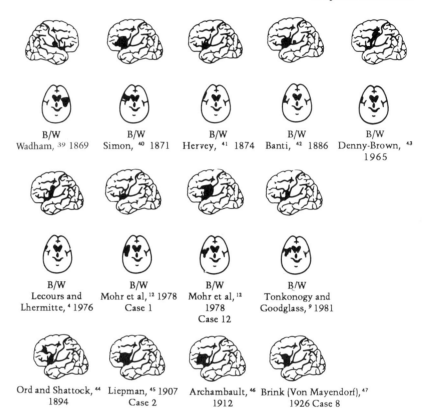

Figure 9.4. Locus of lesion in patients with selective kinetic impairments of speech (Schiff *et al.*, 1983).

Theoretical Considerations

The distinction which has been drawn between phonemic and kinetic disorders has not been consistently applied in the literature on speech-production impairments. These deficits are sometimes subsumed under the superordinate term *apraxia of speech* to designate a deficit in speech production which is out of proportion to other language difficulties. Whilst the concept of apraxia of speech is useful insofar as it differentiates disorders of speech production from other language deficits, it fails to draw a necessary distinction between phonemic and kinetic impairments. These disorders do not appear to reflect different degrees of severity of a single deficit. Impairments at both the phonemic level and the kinetic level can be highly selective. For example, patients with a phonemic impairment may produce normal phonemes but substitute, delete and misorder them. By contrast, patients with a kinetic deficit may produce "neophonemes," that is, word sounds which do not belong to their native language (see Fig. 9.2: Blumstein *et al.*, 1980).

Phonemic Impairments

The interpretation of phonemic impairments has focused on two main levels. The first has been concerned with relationship between phonemic processing and other components of the language system (disconnection models). The second has attacked the problem by an analysis of the characteristics of phonemic errors and their implications for normal speech production (process models). These frameworks are essentially compatible but have differed in their emphasis. The first has looked at different error rates in specific tasks. The second has been less concerned with "task" effects than a detailed analysis of error characteristics. These approaches are beginning to interact more closely as exemplified by the third position which will be considered here: the response buffer hypothesis.

Disconnection Models   Lichtheim (1884) first described a patient who could talk but who was unable to repeat what was said to him. This is the core feature of the classical syndrome of conduction aphasia. It contrasts with another type of deficit in which the patient can repeat but cannot talk spontaneously (Lichtheim, 1885; Goldstein, 1948). Lichtheim accounted for this double dissociation by proposing that there were two "routes" by which speech could be initiated. Using his now somewhat archaic terminology, he suggested that conduction aphasic patients who could talk but not repeat had damage to a route which linked the auditory images of words with the motor images of words. These cases had preserved links between their "concept centres" and the motor images of words (see Figs. 1.14 and 6.10). Lichtheim interpreted the complementary syndrome of transcortical motor aphasia in similar terms. These patients had damaged the links between the concept centres and the motor images of words, leaving the links between auditory images and motor images intact. Geschwind (1965) adopted Lichtheim's analysis of conduction aphasia in suggesting that such patients had disconnected the direct links between hearing and speaking. A comparable interpretation of conduction aphasia has been proposed by Friedrich, Glenn, & Marin (1984).

Lichtheim's theoretical account of these two syndromes was put to the test in a study which compared two conduction aphasics with a transcortical motor aphasic (McCarthy & Warrington, 1984; see above, p. 199). On Lichtheim's account the demands of a task should be critical in determining success or failure in speech production. Thus if a word has to be processed actively for its meaning, then patients with conduction aphasia should be facilitated whereas if it is simply repeated without active semantic processing then their performance should deteriorate. The converse would be expected in transcortical motor aphasia. The critical experiment required the subjects to repeat single polysyllabic words under two conditions. The words were either presented in isolation (as in a conventional test of repetition) or when they were the final item in a sentence. In order to encourage the patients to process the words for their meaning, they were asked to decide whether the sentence context in which the words were presented was sensible or nonsense (see Table 9.3). The results were unambiguous. The conduction aphasic patients were impaired when attempting to repeat polysyllabic words in isolation, and the transcortical motor aphasic showed near perfect levels of performance. By contrast, the conduction aphasics showed a significant benefit when asked to perform the dual task of judging the sentence and producing the final word. The transcortical motor aphasic was impaired under these conditions (Table 9.4).

The differential effects of sentence and cliché repetition (see p. 200) can be explained in similar terms. The conduction aphasics were more impaired in repeating familiar over-learned clichés than in repeating sentences. The converse trend was found for the transcortical motor aphasic. In the former task, repetition can be mediated by relatively passive processing, indeed, a cliché may have a similar status to a long polysyllabic word (Pate, *et al.* 1987). The task of sentence repetition, however, requires active semantic processing, and on this task the conduction aphasic patients showed well preserved speech production. This clear evidence of task-specific effects is entirely consistent with Lichtheim's original hypothesis. To express his ideas in more modern terms: there must be two distinct transcoding procedures or routes for speech production. One is a passive transcoding process between auditory input and phonemic processing for production, impaired in conduction aphasia. The other is a more actively mediated transcoding process between semantic input and phonemic processing, impaired in transcortical motor aphasia (see Fig. 9.5).

Table 9.3 Examples of Sensible and Nonsensible Sentences

Enforced Semantic Processing
The houses were built on a chosen location The houses were sailed on a chosen location
The portrait was a miniature The portrait saw a miniature
When something is upright it's vertical When something is smelly it's vertical
Glass is usually transparent Glass is never transparent
The man who pulls rabbits out of a hat is a magician The man who drowns rabbits out of a hat is a magician
The match was won by a last minute penalty The match was won by a last hour penalty
Athletes are often muscular Athletes are never muscular

Table 9.4   The Effects of Enforced
Semantic Processing[a]

Case	Sentence	Word
O.R.F.	63	45
R.A.N.	65	50
A.R.T.	27	87

[a]Figures show percentage correct repeating a word in context and a word in isolation.
(Adapted from McCarthy & Warrington,
1984.)

Process Models   These models have focused on the basis of phonemic
errors in speech production. Such models can be viewed as broadly
complementary to the "disconnection" (or "multiple routes) approach
rather than as strict alternatives. Two such models will be considered
here.

Kinesthetic Feedback—Luria (1966) used the term *afferent motor
aphasia* as a label for deficits which broadly correspond to the phonemic
subtype of speech-production disorder. Luria emphasised the role of
kinesthetic sensory information in speech production. In the absence of

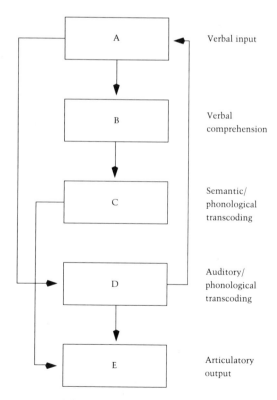

Figure 9.5.   Two-route model of speech production (McCarthy & Warrington, 1984).

such feedback, phonemic substitutions would arise. However, there is no evidence that sensory information from the articulatory apparatus is critical for normal speech production. Even when sensory input from the mouth and tongue is disrupted or distorted, speech may be normal. For example, following administration of a local Dentist's anaesthetic, sensory input may be markedly reduced, but nevertheless the resultant speech does not assume the characteristics of a phonemic impairment.

Phonemic Activation—Findings such as those of Lecours & Lhermitte (1969) indicated that phonemic errors were more common in certain contexts. Furthermore, phoneme substitutions are often very similar to the target (see page 197). These findings led Lecours & Lhermitte to propose a phoneme activation model. Specifically, they suggested that phonemes could be conceptualised as discrete units (or neural circuits) which were organised in terms of their similarities. Frequently occurring phoneme clusters might also be represented as specific units within the system. These phoneme and phoneme cluster units were selected by a process termed *activation* (by activation they meant an increase in the energy levels of units, analogous to the increase in firing rate which occurs in neurons when they are appropriately stimulated). Units, or representations at the level of the single word, were transcoded into phonemes by activating phoneme level units. However, if there was a disorder in such a system the activation of phoneme units might be abnormal: Lecours & Lhermitte discussed the possible effects which would arise if the system was disrupted so that there was abnormally brief or abnormally long-lasting activation of the phoneme units. Phonemic paraphasic errors such as transposition, deletion, and addition would be accounted for in terms of anomalous levels of activation in this hypothetical phoneme assembly system. The effects of word length and possibly even of word frequency could be accounted for within such a framework.

Response Buffer   An alternative view has been put forward by Caramazza, Miceli, Villa, & Romani (1986), who have argued that phonemic paraphasic errors are the product of an impairment in a specific type of memory store. This store, termed the *response buffer* (see also Chapter 13), is required to hold output from an earlier phonemic processing system so that speech can be produced fluently. Caramazza *et al.* have suggested that the response buffer may be reduced in capacity in patients who produce phonemic paraphasias. This account offers an alternative interpretation of the effects of word length in terms of a restriction in the number of units which can be held prior to production. There is evidence from normal speech errors that word strings are maintained in some form of temporary storage system prior to production. Thus, errors such as *clear blue sky → blear clue sky* suggests that more than one word is represented in a store prior to production. This type of highly constrained word-sound exchange has yet to be documented in patients with a phonological impairment of speech production (Caplan, 1987). Pate *et al.* (1987) reported a patient who made numerous phonemic errors across a wide range of tasks including reading, repetition, and in spontaneous speech. The patient, like the cases reported by McCarthy & Warrington (1984) showed effects of word length and word frequency in his speech production. However Pate *et al.* noted that their patient produced relatively few errors which crossed individual word boundaries in the production of unfamiliar sentences. This cross-boundary error was, however, far more common in familiar phrases and proper names. The patient also made more errors on polysyllabic words (e.g., *murderous*) than for pairs of words with an identical sound structure (e.g., *murder us*). A response-buffer account of this patient's disorder would therefore have to be modified to account for the different incidence of errors occurring within "words" but not across words.

Kinetic Impairments

Kinetic impairments affect the active control and modulation of the actions of speech. Three accounts of this class of disorder will be considered here.

Primary Motor Deficit   Alajouanine *et al.* (1939) originally hypothesised that the speech-production impairments of patients with this syndrome (which they termed *phonetic disintegration*) were the product of spasticity, dystonia, paralysis, or apraxia. These deficits resulted in a "regression" to more primitive or childlike articulatory patterns. They did not specify in any detail which of these deficits might be causal for particular patterns of speech error. This account does not appear to be adequate to encompass the selectivity of this deficit. For example, kinetic disorders are restricted to speech production whereas paralysis, spasticity or dystonia would affect any activity or which the affected muscles were required (the classical dyarthrias). Moreover patients with a kinetic impairment may have no difficulty in producing complex meaningless tongue and mouth movements on command so their disorder cannot simply be the result of an "oral apraxia" (see Chapter 5) (Schiff *et al.*, 1983).

Action Sequencing   Luria (1966) used the term *efferent motor aphasia* to label patients whose deficit broadly corresponded to the kinetic subtype. In efferent motor aphasia, Luria suggested that the patient's major deficit was in switching between different articulatory actions. Luria considered this deficit to be one manifestation of more general frontal lobe impairments in changing from one pattern of action to another (see also chapter 16). He accounted for the patient's difficulties in terms of the "pathological inertia" of a pattern of activity. The hypothesis that this disorder reflects "perseveration" of a previous articulation has been questioned; indeed there is no evidence that errors of perseveration characterise this syndrome (e.g., Alajouanine *et al.*, 1939).

Temporal Organisation Lecours & Lhermitte (1969, 1976) hypothesised that patients with kinetic impairments might have a deficit in selecting and utilising the component actions which were required to produce a single phoneme (as distinct from assembling a sequence of phonemes to form a word). Thus, in order to produce a phoneme it is necessary to coordinate several actions simultaneously (such as mouth closure and breath production in saying "p"). The patients were thought to have a difficulty in timing or coordinating these specific sets of speech actions. The hypothesis that patients with kinetic impairments have a deficit in the speech action dynamics has been expressed by a number of other workers, and appears to be well substantiated by empirical work (e.g., Freeman *et al.*, 1978; Sands, Freeman, & Harris, 1978). Blumstein (e.g., 1988) has argued that these impairments are not simply a generalised failure of speech timing, but of coordination. Production of sound durations may be relatively well preserved and maintain the timing contrasts appropriate to the individual's language. However, when the coordination of two components of the articulatory system is required to modify sounds in context (such as anticipatory lip rounding in the "s" sound of *Sue* as compared with lip widening in pronouncing *see*), then impairment of coordination is once again observed (e.g., Tuller, 1987; Ziegler & Von Cramon, 1985, 1986).

Blumstein has argued that the primary deficit is one of coordinating independent components of the speech production apparatus. This hypothesis is also well supported by direct measurements using X-ray microbeam analysis to examine lip, tongue, and velar movements in patients with kinetic disorders (Itoh, Sasanuma, & Ushijima, 1979; Itoh, Sasanuma, Hirose, Yoshioka, & Ushijima, 1980).

As has been noted above the "foreign accent syndrome" is unlikely to be a unitary disorder. The accent in the patient described by Graff-Radford, Cooper, Colsher, and Damasio (1986) was attributable to abnormalities in pitch control and a preferential pattern in her vowel substitutions. The case reported by Blumstein *et al.* (1987) had somewhat different characteristics, with near normal vowel production and a tendency to "insert" additional vowel-like sounds before and after consonants. Blumstein *et al.* argued that these aspects of the patients speech could be attributed to an impairment in the rhythmic aspects of speech timing. Her deficit was considered to be qualitatively distinct from disorders affecting the coordination of different articulatory movements. However, no single explanation is likely to be satisfactory for all cases of "foreign accent syndrome" and the extent to which these disorders reflect mild coordination impairments, compensatory strategies, or a qualitatively distinct class of deficits needs to be established.

Conclusion

Disorders of speech production have been considered here in terms of a single major discontinuity, First, there are impairments in the stage at which somewhat "abstract" entities, phonemes, are assembled, ordered, and stored prior to production. Second, there are impairments which affect the timing and coordination of those actions necessary for speech. Within one of these two broad classes it has been possible to distinguish two further subtypes of deficit implicating different types of phonological processing or transcoding. It seems almost certain that dissociations will also be documented in the case of kinetic deficits as well as phonemic ones.

10

Reading

Introduction

The ability to read is comparatively recent in the development of human skills. In relation to the development of cognitive abilities in the individual, there is a relatively long "lag" between the acquisition of a spoken word vocabulary and the development of a vocabulary for the written word. In learning to read most children acquire the ability to differentiate a large number of visually complex word patterns within 2 or 3 years. This results in the acquisition of a "sight vocabulary" and the development of the skill of "sounding out" unfamiliar letter strings.

Neurological Approach The ability to read can be selectively impaired by cerebral lesions. The systematic analysis of patterns of reading difficulty commenced with the work of the classical neurologists in the late nineteenth century. Neurologists such as Charcot (1884) and Dejerine (1892) were concerned first to establish the relationship between disorders of spoken language and disorders of reading, and second to establish the relationship between impairments of reading and of writing. The dissociation of dyslexia from language disorders was largely accepted by the beginning of the twentieth century. The neurological classification of the dyslexias then focused on whether patients' reading difficulties occurred together with writing impairments or not. Two major syndromes were identified, namely dyslexia with dysgraphia and dyslexia without dysgraphia. The syndrome of dyslexia without dysgraphia as described by Dejerine consisted of a severe impairment in reading single words and in naming single letters. Despite these impairments, the patient was able to write but could no longer read back what he had written. In dyslexia with dysgraphia, both reading and writing were impaired (e.g., Benson, 1979c). This typology of the dyslexias has gradually been replaced by information-processing analyses which focus more on the characteristics of individual patients' errors rather than on associated deficits: this framework will be the focus of this chapter.

Information-Processing Analyses   The starting point for the cognitive analysis of impaired reading was an influential pair of papers by Marshall & Newcombe (1966, 1973). They suggested that acquired reading disorders could reflect different types of breakdown within the subcomponents of a complex skill. In a development of this approach, Shallice & Warrington (1980) suggested that acquired dyslexias could be subdivided into those which affected the patients' ability to analyse the visual attributes of the written word and those which affected later stages of the reading process. Disorders affecting visual processing have been termed *peripheral* or *visual word form dyslexias;* those affecting the ability to derive sound or meaning from print have been termed *central dyslexias.* This broad classification will be adopted in the following discussion of reading impairments.

Empirical Characteristics

Visual Word-Form Dyslexias

Although there are only a very limited number of letters in any alphabetic writing system, they are combined and permuted into many thousands of meaningful words in any language. These are complex visual patterns but nevertheless they can be recognised in a fraction of a second by a fluent reader. In 1886 Cattel demonstrated that normal subjects could recognise whole words as rapidly as single letters. Recognition times for several letters which did not make up a word were slower than for single letters. Cattel's early findings have been replicated many times and have been interpreted as evidence that words are processed as visual units rather than as a series of single letters. Indeed, a whole word-recognition stage is incorporated in most contemporary models of the reading process (e.g., Morton, 1969; Allport, 1979; Henderson, 1982). It is now possible to identify at least three patterns of deficit which implicate dysfunction at this visual level of reading. These disorders have been termed *spelling dyslexia, neglect dyslexia,* and *attentional dyslexia.*

Spelling Dyslexia   One form of dyslexia without dysgraphia results in patients reading or attempting to read letter by letter. In such patients reading is gravely impaired, although their spelling and writing may be normal (see Fig. 10.1). Even severely affected patients may be capable of writing well-organised and coherent paragraphs. However, they are quite unable to read back what they have written. In those cases whose letter naming is preserved their residual reading capacities are typically

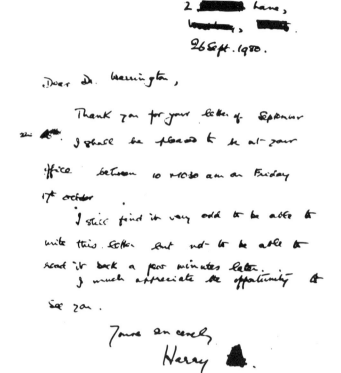

Figure 10.1. Letter written by a patient with a spelling dyslexia.

mediated by a strategy of spelling the word aloud and reconstructing the word letter by letter: literally the patient may say, "R,E,A,D spells read" (hence the term *spelling dyslexia:* Wolpert, 1924).

The phenomenon of letter-by-letter reading is clearly a strategy to which patients resort in order to overcome their difficulty in normal reading. Clinically it appears as though the patients are making use of their letter recognition and naming skills in order to spell the word to themselves. Patients with good spelling skills tend to be the most efficient letter-by-letter readers. Reading letter by letter is obviously very slow. Indeed, it is an order of magnitude slower than that of a normal reader. There is a direct relationship between the number of letters in a word and the patient's speed in reading: longer words are read far more slowly than short words. Staller, Buchanan, Singer, Lappin, & Webb (1978) reported the first case of letter-by-letter reading (B.Y.) in whom reading speed was documented using a word–nonword discrimination task (e.g., *cat* vs *cal*). He took over twice as long to discriminate 7-letter words as compared with 3-letter stimuli. Further cases in whom oral reading times have been well documented have firmly established this word-length effect (Warrington & Shallice, 1980; Patterson & Kay, 1982; Shallice & Saffran, 1986; Coslett & Saffran, 1989b; see Fig. 10.2).

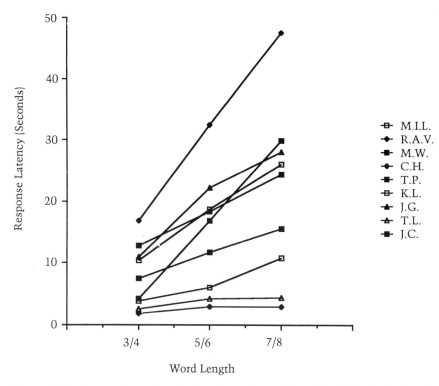

Figure 10.2. Range of word-length effects in patients with spelling dyslexia (for details of individual patients see text).

Warrington & Shallice (1980) used the technique of brief visual presentations to investigate the residual reading capacities of two patients who were only able to read letter by letter. Under these conditions their reading was very significantly impaired. For example, one case (J.D.C.) was unable to read any 6-letter words presented for 200 msec. When reading 3-letter words her score increased to 50% correct. Furthermore, there was no difference between her scores on reading 3-letter words as compared with reading 3-letter nonsense syllables (e.g., *sut*) or random consonant strings (e.g., *lkt*). Her ability to read briefly presented printed stimuli appeared to be entirely determined by the capacity of her visual span of apprehension (see Chapter 13).

Warrington & Shallice (1980) used these same brief visual presentation techniques to investigate a patient's ability to extract meaning from a printed word. The patient (R.A.V.) was quite unable to categorise, or match to a picture, words which were presented too briefly for him to read letter-by-letter. There was thus no evidence for any ability to extract meaning from these stimuli. Patterson & Kay (1982) obtained similar findings with three further cases. On tests requiring the subjects to make a two-choice semantic judgment such as "object vs. living thing" or "animal vs. fruit" the patients were uniformly bad. Patterson & Kay concluded that there was no evidence that these patients had even partial information about the meaning of words when they were prevented from reading letter by letter. However, there are other patients who are able to extract some partial meaning from words which are presented too quickly for them to read. A patient (M.L.) studied by Shallice & Saffran (1986) was able to perform two-choice semantic judgments and similar findings have been reported in three further cases by Coslett & Saffran (1989b).

The apparent loss of the ability to recognise words as coherent visual units has been investigated by contrasting patients' ability to read "joined up writing" (script) as compared with their ability to read print. Even in the clearest script, individual letters are often indecipherable without the supporting context of the adjoining letters; script therefore maximises reliance on whole-word reading. Two patients (J.D.C. and R.A.V.) who read using a letter-by-letter strategy were found to be much slower and less accurate in reading the clearest script than in reading print (see Table 10.1). This finding corroborates many earlier clinical reports that handwriting is particularly difficult for patients with a spelling dyslexia.

Neglect Dyslexia   In this type of dyslexia the patient misreads the initial (left neglect) or terminal (right neglect) parts of words. The errors are not simply "deletions" of the letter string, but typically consist of the production of an alternative real word of approximately the same length as the target. The clearest examples come from patients with left neglect (see Table 10.2). These errors can occur in reading single words in isolation, in reading columns of words, or in reading prose passages. In some cases the disorder may be so severe that normal reading is completely vitiated.

The first suggestion that there was a subtype of reading impairment which differentially affected one side of a word was reported in a brief single case report. Warrington & Zangwill (1957) noted that their patient (T.S.) had a marked "dyslexia without dysgraphia" which had

Table 10.1   Script Reading and Word Length[a]

	Word length (letters)		
	3	5	7
Script	7.9	12.1	14.0
Print	5.5	8.6	9.0

[a]Values reflect time in seconds to read columns of three words (patient R.A.V.). Adapted from Warrington & Shallice, 1980.

Table 10.2 Examples of Left-Neglect Dyslexia Errors Made by Three Patients[a]

J.A.F.		J.O.H.		V.B.	
HIS	this	IT	sit	ATE	date
LET	wet	AID	said	NUN	run
TRAIN	rain	HOW	brow	NEVER	lever
CLOCK	block	MAKE	cake	DREAM	cream
ANYONE	someone	WISH	dish	WORSE	horse
WINDMILL	sawmill	STORY	factory	WILLOW	pillow
SMOULDER	shoulder	MOUNT	discount	HADDOCK	paddock
PREFERENTIAL	deferential	RIGHT	fright	WHETHER	together

[a]See text for details of individual patients.

different characteristics from spelling dyslexia. He had a tendency to misread the final parts of words, producing alternative real words (e.g., *breaking* → *breakfast; registrar* → *registration; tongue* → *together*).

A series of six patients who made reading errors on the *beginning* of words were reported by Kinsbourne & Warrington (1962a). They frequently misread individual words, irrespective of whether they were presented in isolation, in columns, or in a connected passage. The majority of the patients' errors implicated the beginnings of words and consisted of substitutions of letters or groups of letters. The last few letters were almost invariably incorporated into the patients' response. In virtually every error, these letter substitutions changed the stimulus into an alternative real word. However, it was not related in meaning to the target.

Subsequent quantitative accounts of neglect dyslexia have confirmed and extended these clinical case reports. In a large corpus of reading responses reported in a single case (J.A.F.) it was observed that real-word neglect errors occurred on approximately one-quarter of the items which she attempted (Baxter & Warrington, 1983). There was a remarkable correspondence between the number of letters in the target word and the "length" of the response over a wide range of word lengths (see Table 10.2).

Ellis, Flude, & Young (1987) described a further single case in considerable detail (V.B.). They also showed that her errors were mostly substitutions of alternative letters rather than additions of letters or simple letter deletions (see Table 10.2). Thus the patient read *elate* as *plate* and not *late* and *peach* as *beach*, not *each*. They analysed their corpus of over 300 errors using a systematic method for classifying their patient's mistakes as "neglect" or due to other visual factors.

They defined as "neglect errors" those responses in which the word was identical to the target to one side of a "neglect point" but diverged *completely* from the target to the right of that point. Even using these very conservative criteria they found that over two-thirds of the patient's errors could be classified as neglect errors. The majority of nonneglect responses were also real-words that were based on "general visual similarity between target and error" (*slave* → *shave; screech* → *speech; abhor* → *labour; weather* → *sweater*).

A similar analysis using Ellis *et al.*'s definition of a neglect point was applied in the investigation of a further case of left-neglect dyslexia (J.O.H.) (Costello & Warrington, 1987). Although the incidence of non-word responses was by no means negligible in this patient, a detailed examination of the pool of real-word neglect errors showed that his errors closely matched the target words in length (with items ranging from two to seven letters). Indeed nearly half of his neglect errors were identical in length to the target (see Table 10.2). On those errors which did not conserve word length exactly, he was just as likely to increase the length of a word as to decrease it. Finally, his reading of short words was less accurate than his reading of long words.

Attentional Dyslexia   The syndrome termed *attentional dyslexia* has only been documented in two cases (F.M. and P.T.: Shallice & Warrington, 1977a). The patients were able to read individual words and name individual letters almost perfectly. They were, however, significantly impaired when more than one item of the same type was present in the visual field. For example, the patients' ability to read single letters presented in isolation was nearly perfect, whereas attempting to read an array or row of letters resulted in an increase in their error rates. A very similar effect was observed with words (see Table 10.3): the patients were able to read single 3-letter words almost perfectly but made multiple errors when attempting to read rows of only four words. Perhaps unsurprisingly, their reading of text was very severely compromised.

In one experiment the patients were simply required to name a single letter which was flanked by other differently coloured letters (e.g., *F/KSR*). In naming single letters in isolation the patients scored 91% and 100% correct, but their scores dropped to 73% in the flanking condition. Although the patients' performance was impaired when the target letter was flanked by other letters, their performance was considerably better when the target letter was flanked by numbers (88% and 98% correct, respectively).

Table 10.3   Reading Single and Multiple Targets[a,b]

	% Correct			
	Letters		Words	
	1	4	1	4
F.M.	92	83	92	80
P.T.	100	71	100	82

[a]Performance of two patients with an attentional dyslexia in naming letters and reading words.
[b]Adapted from Shallice & Warrington, 1977a.

Central Dyslexias

The central dyslexias are thought to depend on processing operations which follow the initial visual analysis of a printed word. Two main subtypes of central dyslexic disorders have been identified. In one disorder, the patient appears to read using the commonest print to sound rules of the language: reading by sound. In the other disorder, patients appear to rely on an established sight vocabulary of words and are unable to read by sound. These deficits have been the subject of extensive research by psychologists interested in their implications for the normal reading process. These disorders are thought to represent the loss of specific "central" components of the normal reading system.

Reading by Sound (Surface Dyslexia/Phonological Reading)   Normal skilled readers are typically able to attempt a reasonable pronunciation of words which have no meaning for them, such as those which are outside the range of their vocabulary. In general, the pronunciation that is given to an unfamiliar word reflects the "rules," or the more common correspondences between spelling and sound, which are found in the reader's language. For example, readers of this chapter may not know the meaning of words such as *shiboleth, chitterling,* or *herpetology* and yet would have no problem in giving them a convincing pronunciation (Nelson & O'Connell, 1978). Whilst these "rules" work for the majority of words in the English language, there are a number of English words which cannot be read using these spelling-to-sound correspondences. They are said to be "irregular." For example, *yacht, busy, debt, sew, ache,* and *quay* are irregular words, whereas *boat, time, cash, hike,* and *tree* are regular words.

Marshall & Newcombe (1973) described two cases (J.C. and S.T.) who were not only over-reliant on spelling-to-sound correspondences but who also misapplied them. The patients appeared to be "cobbling together" a pronunciation on the basis of their partial knowledge of the relationships between spelling and sound. For example, *lace* might be read as *lake* because the patient was unable to apply the very common rule that c + e results in an "s" pronunciation. These patients were able to understand spoken words and, in the case of mispronounced words, the patients appeared to interpret their mispronunciations rather than the printed word (e.g., *listen* → "Liston, the boxer"). Marshall & Newcombe introduced the term *surface dyslexia* to denote these patients' laborious attempts at reading by sound.

If a patient is reading by sound, then this should give rise to particular difficulties in reading irregular words which do not obey the common pronunciation rules of the language (such as *aunt, aisle, chord*). The selective impairment of irregular word reading with preservation of regular word reading was first recorded by Warrington (1975), who noted that two patients found it easier to read regular words (such as *classification*) than those which departed from the commoner pronunciation rules of the language (such as *nephew*). This difference was subsequently established quantitatively in a number of single case studies (e.g., Shallice & Warrington, 1980; Shallice, Warrington, & McCarthy, 1983; Bub, Cancelliere & Kertesz 1985; McCarthy & Warrington, 1986b).

Patients with this type of dyslexia may be able to read both single words and prose passages fluently provided that the words are regular. Indeed, their reading speed may be entirely normal (i.e., less than 1 second per word). Irregular words are read as if they were unfamiliar regular words by applying the commonest print/sound correspondences of the language. Thus *sew* might be read as *sue*, *busy* as *buzzy*, *ache* as *atchey*, etc. This type of error has been termed a *regularisation*. These patients, as would be predicted by their ability to read using print-to-sound correspondences, have no difficulty in pronouncing invented nonwords (e.g., *nin, dold, blean, sust*) (see Table 10.4).

There may be gradations in the severity of impairment in reading by sound. One patient (E.M.) who was studied over a number of years showed a progressive decline in the number of irregular words which could be read accurately, indicating a gradual increase in her reliance on print-to-sound correspondences (Shallice & Warrington, 1980). In other cases (e.g., W.L.P.; Schwartz, Saffran, & Marin, 1980b) the patient may only be impaired in reading a few irregular words, the majority being produced accurately. In another patient (M.P.) described by Bub, *et al.* (1985), regularisation errors mostly occurred on less common words. For another case (K.T.) regularisation errors were observed on words over a wide range of frequencies in the language: even very common irregular words such as *have* and *love* were read incorrectly as *hayve* and *lowve* (McCarthy & Warrington, 1986b).

Reading by Sight Vocabulary   Children not only learn the rules of print-to-sound correspondences, but they also build up a "sight" vocabulary. This is a repertoire of words which can be read and understood without recourse to "sounding out" procedures. In the skilled adult reader this repertoire may be enormous and may even encompass all the words which are in his or her spoken word vocabulary. Indeed for many people the range of written words which are understood exceeds those which can be pronounced correctly (e.g., *topiary, metamorphosis*).

Table 10.4   Regular/Irregular Word Reading[a]

	% Correct		
Reference	Regular words (e.g., *boat, time*)	Irregular words (e.g., *love, yacht*)	Nonwords (e.g., *nint*)
Shallice *et al.*, 1983 (H.T.R.)	79	48	84
McCarthy & Warrington 1986b (K.T.)	86	41	100

[a]Performance of two patients reading by sound.

There are patients whose reading is entirely reliant on their sight vocabulary.

One of the first systematic explorations of this pattern of impairment was a case reported by Low (1931). He described a patient who had lost the ability to read "meaningless" words, such as function words (e.g., *if, and, there, for, to, by, me, when*) and other grammatical units such as verb endings (giv*en*, give*s*, giv*ing*). Low established first, by inference, and second, by demonstration, that this patient read using "visual images" rather than by using "auditory images." Low noted that when the patient made errors, they were often similar in meaning or in visual appearance to the target and were never related in terms of their sound alone. From this evidence he inferred that visual images were likely to be more salient. Second, he demonstrated that the patient was very poor in reading nonwords—a finding which was quite consistent with his inference of a failure of "auditory images" in reading real words.

There are now a number of cases on record who are almost totally unable to read using print-to-sound correspondences. These patients are only able to read by using their sight vocabulary: this type of reading deficit is commonly termed *phonological dyslexia* (after Beauvois & Derouesné, 1979). Cases with a particularly selective impairment of this type may not appear dyslexic because they may have a full sight vocabulary and so would not be detected in most clinical assessments. Their deficit only becomes apparent when they are asked to read nonwords. A brief account of two such patients was given by Shallice & Warrington (1980). One patient (G.R.N.) was able to read a range of single words at a competent level, but nevertheless her reading of simple nonsense words was very significantly impaired. A further case (W.B.) reported by Funnell (1983) showed a comparable discontinuity between his ability to read a range of single words (approximately 90%) as contrasted with his complete inability to read nonwords (0%). A further replication was provided by Baxter & Warrington (1985).

In other patients the symptom of phonological dyslexia co-occurs with a loss of certain parts of the patient's sight vocabulary (as was observed in Low's original case). These patients have a double deficit, one affecting their ability to "sound out" the printed word and a second which compromises the sight vocabulary itself. Such cases have provided valuable evidence with regard to the organisation of the systems of sight reading. Beauvois & Derouesné (1979) and Derouesné & Beauvois (1979) reported a patient (R.G.) who had particular difficulty in reading grammatical function words (e.g., *and, if, for,*) and made errors on grammatical word endings (such as the *-ed* of *walked,* and the *-s* of *dances*). Subsequently Patterson (1982) described a further case (A.M.) with impairments in reading both of these classes of grammatical unit (technically termed *grammatical morphemes*).

In other patients, the reading deficit affects not only nonwords, function words, and grammatical units, but also extends to affect certain

Table 10.5 Performance of Four Deep Dyslexic Patients on Reading Aloud

	% Correct		
	Concrete	Abstract	Nonword
Marshall & Newcombe (1973) (G.R.)	50[a]	10[a]	—
Shallice & Warrington (1975) (K.F.)[b]	73[a]	14[a]	—
Patterson & Marcel (1977) (P.W.)	67	13	0
Patterson & Marcel (1977) (D.E.)	70	10	10

[a]Nouns.
[b]See Table 10.6

categories of substantive words (e.g., adjectives, nouns, verbs). Patients may show a difference between their reading of *abstract* and *concrete* words. Abstract words refer to concepts, states, or qualities (e.g., *idea, danger, peace*), whereas concrete words have tangible, imageable referents (e.g., *camera, table, monkey*). Marshall & Newcombe (1973) described a patient (G.R.) whom they designated a *deep dyslexic*. He was impaired in reading words with an abstract meaning, but his reading of concrete or imageable words was much more satisfactory. Subsequently a large number of cases (see Table 10.5 above) have been reported with substantially the same pattern of deficit (e.g., Shallice & Warrington, 1975; Patterson & Marcel, 1977; Saffran & Marin, 1977; and Kapur & Perl,1978).

These effects of word class (function words, grammatical morphemes) and effects of semantic class (abstract vs. concrete/imageable) might be thought of as reflecting a single dimension of task difficulty along which reading breaks down. Evidence that this is not necessarily valid comes from a single case studied by Warrington (1981a). The patient (C.A.V.: see Table 10.6) was unable to read words by sounding them out and was totally unable to read nonwords. As a consequence he was reliant on his residual sight vocabulary. However, his deficit was *not* for abstract words (as had been observed in all previous cases), but instead it affected his reading of *concrete* words.

Many investigations of deep dyslexia have included very detailed analyses of the various error types which occur. The major classes of error are as follows:

Visual errors. These consist of a visual approximation to the target in which partial information about its shape and letter properties is retained.

Semantic errors. The errors are sometimes related in meaning to the target word.

Derivational errors. This type of error involves modification of word endings or word beginnings, such as changing a verb into a noun. This label is also commonly used to classify errors on inflections, such as plurals or verb tenses.

The incidence of these different error types is very variable from case to case (see Table 10.7).

Table 10.6 Examples of Words That Could and Could Not Be Read by Two Patients Reading Using Their Residual Sight Vocabulary

Concrete word reader (K.F.)		Abstract word reader (C.A.V)	
Read	Not read	Read	Not read
ambulance	far	division	beef
aquarium	come	opposite	carrot
farmhouse	hurt	zero	fruit
manager	kind	excuse	head
needle	might	clumsy	city
spider	grow	apprehension	bird
treasure	you	description	salt
whiskey	never	accordance	daughter
		coward	hospital

In this section, the empirical characteristics of the major types of residual reading skills in the acquired dyslexias have been discussed. Some patients will show a more mixed pattern of deficit, whereas others may have a virtual or complete absence of any reading capacities.

Anatomical Considerations

Classical Neurological Syndromes

Patients with dyslexia without dysgraphia have been studied from a neuropathological rather than a neuropsychological point of view. This

Table 10.7 Examples of Errors Made by Deep Dyslexic Patients[a]

	Semantic	Derivational	Visual
G.R.	act — play	wise — wisdom	stock — shock
	close — shut	strange — stranger	quiz — queue
	dinner — food	pray — prayers	saucer — sausage
	uncle — cousin	birth — born	crowd — crown
	56%	11%	22%
P.W.	unit — one	warmth — warm	bush — brush
	occasion — event	speak — speech	gain — grain
	coast — seashore	height — high	bead — bread
	cemetery — burial	marriage — married	crab — crag
	54%	22%	13%
K.F.	tear — crying	English — England	fellow — falling
	gone — none	silence — silent	yet — yes
	study — student	golden — gold	come — comb
	services — forces	British — Britain	grew — green
	4%	19%	61%

[a]Percentage of each type of reading error and examples selected from three individual corpora.

enterprise dates back to Dejerine (1892). These patients have typically shown lesions involving the left occipital lobe and splenium (e.g., Greenblatt, 1973; Ajax, Schenkenberg, & Kasteljanetz, 1977; Friedman & Albert, 1985). To some extent, this syndrome may overlap with the deficit which has been variously termed *spelling dyslexia* and *letter-by-letter reading,* but this has not been empirically established in any single case.

Dyslexia with dysgraphia may overlap both with the visual word-form dyslexias and the central dyslexias. Once again, the focus of the investigation of patients with this neurological syndrome has been neuropathological rather than cognitive. There has been reasonable consensus that lesions of the angular gyrus are implicated in this syndrome (e.g., Hécaen & Kremin, 1976; Friedman & Albert, 1985).

Visual Word-Form Dyslexias

Spelling Dyslexia   Posterior regions of the left hemisphere were implicated in four cases of letter-by-letter reading reported by Kinsbourne & Warrington (1962b). Staller *et al.* (1978) described a parietotemporal lesion in a single case of this syndrome. A comparable lesion localisation was observed in another single case by Warrington & Shallice (1980). Autopsy evidence is consistent with this localisation. Kinsbourne & Warrington (1963b) described a patient (Mrs. B) who read letter by letter as a result of a vascular lesion (of 6 months duration). The area of infarction was found to be located in the inferior/anterior occipital lobe adjacent to the temporal lobe of the left hemisphere. This lesion was restricted to the lateral surface of the brain and the interhemispheric fibres (splenium and corpus callosum) were considered to be intact (see Fig. 10.3).

Neglect Dyslexia   In those cases of neglect dyslexia in whom a unilateral lesion has been demonstrated, the critical lesion site is contralateral to the side of the word which is neglected. Thus right neglect has been observed in association with left-hemisphere lesions and left neglect with right-hemisphere lesions (Warrington & Zangwill, 1957; Kinsbourne & Warrington, 1962a). Within the cerebral hemispheres damage to the parietal lobe has been documented in all cases.

Neglect dyslexia involving the left side of words appears to be more common than neglect of the right side. Although this may be yet another example of the higher incidence or greater severity of "neglect" errors in patients with right-hemisphere lesions (see Chapter 4), there are a number of other possibilities. For example, the damage to the left hemisphere which might result in a neglect dyslexia could also damage other systems involved in reading. Alternatively, the left-to-right constraints on English spelling (the orthography in which this syndrome has been most fully documented) might render neglect more difficult to detect in the context of a left-hemisphere lesion. Since there are

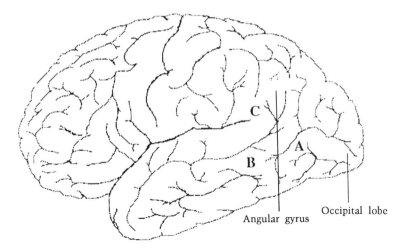

Angular gyrus   Occipital lobe

Figure 10.3. Schematic diagram of brain that indicates the probable loci of spelling dyslexia (A), reading by sound (B), and reading by sight vocabulary (C).

more alternative word beginnings than there are alternative endings, right-sided neglect would be less easy to detect clinically.

Attentional Dyslexia The two patients with this disorder had space-occupying tumours which were located in the posterior left hemisphere and extended deeply into subcortical structures (Shallice & Warrington, 1977a). The critical structures which are involved in this syndrome remain unknown.

Central Dyslexias

Reading by Sound Reading by sound has been recorded in a wide variety of pathological conditions including degenerative disorders, head injury, stroke, and tumour. The frequency of these reports suggests that this type of dyslexia may be a relatively common occurrence in patients with cerebral lesions. Vanier & Caplan (1985) assessed the locus of lesion in seven cases in whom reading by sound was a prominent symptom. They tentatively concluded that, although there was a wide variance in the precise locus of the lesions, "involvement of posterior structures, especially temporal lobe structures is necessary." The patient reported by Shallice *et al.* (1983) had a lesion located in the left temporal lobe, which is entirely consistent with Vanier & Caplan's conclusions (see Fig. 10.3).

Reading by Sight Vocabulary Patients who are reliant on reading via their sight vocabulary have lost the ability to read by sound. A patient (G.O.S.) described by Baxter & Warrington (1985) had a relatively isolated deficit in reading nonwords, with preservation of her sight vocabulary. She had a large temporoparietal lesion. Other cases with a deficit largely confined to reading by sound have either had poorly localised lesions (e.g., Warrington & Shallice, 1980) or have not been investigated from a neuropathological perspective (e.g., Funnell, 1983).

Turning now to those patients with a double deficit affecting both their ability to read by sound together with malfunction of components of the sight vocabulary itself. This may result in selective impairments in reading words belonging to certain semantic or grammatical categories (see above). The case (R.G.) described by Beauvois & Derouesne (1979) had a selective impairment in reading function words. He had a relatively restricted lesion affecting parieto-occipital regions of the left hemisphere including the angular gyrus with some extension into subcortical structures. The case of deep dyslexia (G.R.) with impaired function word reading and poor reading of concrete words described by Marshall & Newcombe (1973) had a lesion in the temporoparietal region. Marin (1980) reviewed five subsequent cases with this syndrome complex and concluded that in all cases the damage was quite extensive within the left hemisphere. The supramarginal gyrus was involved in all, but involvement of the angular gyrus was only significant in one patient. Autopsy evidence is available in one case (K.F.), who had a large traumatic lesion. This involved maximally the inferior parietal lobule and the temporo-occipital region of the left hemisphere (see Fig. 10.3).

Theoretical Considerations

The analysis of the reading process has possibly received more attention from psychologists than any other cognitive skill. In this regard the data from patients with acquired dyslexia has proven crucial in the development of models of normal reading. In this section the relationship between reading and other "language"-based skills will be considered briefly. This will be followed by an account of the basic organisation of the reading process from an information-processing perspective. Finally there will be a somewhat more detailed discussion of the theoretical relevance of each of the different types of dyslexic syndrome using this model as a basic framework.

Reading Disorders and Language There is good evidence that patients with very impaired comprehension of the printed word may have normal comprehension of the spoken word (e.g., Warrington & Shallice, 1979; Shallice & Warrington, 1980; Shallice & Coughlan, 1980). There is only tentative evidence for the converse pattern of deficit—a patient with adequate auditory perception who can comprehend the printed word but not the spoken word (see Chapter 6). Bramwell (1897) described a patient who apparently had lost all comprehension of spoken language. She could repeat what she heard, write it down, and then comprehend by reading her own writing!

In patients in whom language and reading difficulties coexist the deficits do not necessarily mirror each other. To give but one example: A patient (W.L.) described by Allport & Funnell (1981) had fluent spontaneous speech with appropriate use of function words, but he had marked difficulty in retrieving nouns. His reading showed the converse pattern of vulnerability: function words were impaired and concrete nouns were relatively well preserved.

Reading, Writing, and Spelling   It has been recognised since the time of Dejerine (1892) that impairments of reading can occur in patients with intact spelling and writing (hence the term *dyslexia without dysgraphia*). The converse dissociation has also been recorded (e.g., Basso, Taborelli, & Vignolo, 1978). Shallice (1981) systematically documented entirely normal reading of nonwords in a patient (P.R.) with a severe dysgraphia for the same nonwords. Even more striking is the observation that very different types of dyslexia and dysgraphia can co-occur. Beauvois, Derouesné, & Saillant (1980) reported that their patient (R.G.), who was dependent on his sight vocabulary for reading, was only able to use common sound-to-letter correspondences in his writing (see Chapter 11).

Information-Processing Framework for Dyslexia

In the early 1970s reading skills in normal subjects and reading disorders in patients began to be analysed in terms of information-processing models. Such models formalise the types of discontinuity and dissociations that occur within complex skills. The basic organisation of the reading system is shown in Fig. 10.4. This type of framework (or broadly similar ones) has been widely adopted by cognitive neuropsychologists (e.g., Patterson, Marshall, & Coltheart, 1985). The model outlined in the figure indicates that the visual analysis of letter strings precedes reading by sound or reading by a sight vocabulary. There is a long history of psychological theories that propose a stage of processing

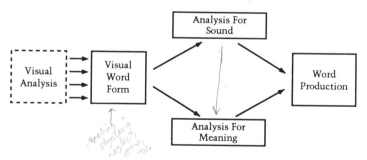

Figure 10.4.   Generic framework schematizing a two-route model of reading.

which is intermediate between the preliminary visual analysis of a word and reading a word for its meaning. This system processes words as whole units (the visual word-form system). Evidence for the existence and necessity of this stage has been provided by investigations of acquired dyslexic syndromes. Some patients who read letter by letter appear to have a primary impairment at this level of processing. They are unable to identify words any more rapidly than non-words and appear to be unable to process words as whole units in any reading task (e.g. Warrington & Shallice, 1980).

The evidence for parallel routes subsequent to the visual word form is based on the double dissociation between those cases who read primarily by sound and those who are reliant on the use of a sight vocabulary. As an aside, it might be noted that in languages which have "syllabic" and "idiographic" scripts (such as Kana and Kanji in Japanese) there are patients who become dyslexic for one type of script but not the other. The two types of script appear to be processed relatively independently by the two routes (e.g., Sasanuma, 1980, 1985).

In patients reading alphabetic scripts by the sound-based "phonological route," words which have uncommon print-to-sound correspondences are misread. In the extreme case all words departing from the most common correspondences between print and sound are misread; in more mildly affected patients, only the very irregular or uncommon words may give rise to errors. In cases with a selective deficit regular words and novel "nonsense" words can be read with normal speed and accuracy. The properties of this reading process will be elaborated below.

By contrast, patients whose reading is dependent on their established sight vocabulary are unable to read nonwords but do not have specific difficulties with words which have unusual spelling-to-sound correspondences. In those cases in whom the sight vocabulary disorder is partial rather than absolute, it has been possible to investigate in more detail the properties of the sight vocabulary itself. The subtypes of this "direct route" reading will be discussed below.

There are a number of variants of the scheme shown in Fig. 10.4 which differ in their details (e.g., Coltheart, 1985; Patterson & Coltheart, 1987; Ellis & Young, 1987; Shallice, 1988), but it is not too much of a distortion to suggest that there is broad agreement on the basic organisation of reading. To summarise: visually presented letter strings are first analysed by a visual word-form system. The output of the visual word form is subsequently processed by correspondences between print and sound or is processed for meaning directly. These two routes may operate in parallel in the normal reader.

Visual Word-Form Dyslexias

Spelling Dyslexia   There are three main explanations of spelling dyslexia. First, it has been thought of as a disconnection syndrome. Second, the deficit represents a component of more general failure of the ability to integrate visual elements into a coherent whole. Third, it implicates a specialised visual word-recognition system which is intermediate between early visual processing and the attainment of meaning: the visual word form.

Disconnection—The earliest account of the syndrome of dyslexia without dysgraphia was that of a disconnection. Because of the relative preservation of writing in these cases it was thought that there was a disconnection between visual input in the right-hemisphere and left-hemisphere centres for the images of words which supported both reading and writing (Dejerine, 1892). How well does such a formulation account for the more specific syndrome of spelling dyslexia?

It is fair to say that much, but perhaps not all, of the anatomical evidence is consistent with this interpretation (e.g., Friedman & Albert, 1985). Many patients with spelling dyslexia do indeed have damage which affects the major visual pathway between the right and left hemispheres (the splenium, see above). Furthermore, the majority of cases have shown impairment of visual input to the left hemisphere (right-sided hemianopia). However, the syndrome has also been documented in a patient without damage to the splenium (Kinsbourne & Warrington, 1963b). A dyslexia without dysgraphia which appears to correspond in its characteristics to spelling dyslexia has also been documented in patients whose visual fields were normal (Greenblatt, 1973; Vincent, Sadowsky, Saunders, & Reeves, 1977).

Quite apart from the possibility of an anatomical disconnection, it is necessary to consider the evidence for "disconnection" between components of a functional model (see also Chapters 2 and 6). This would entail a break in the links between early visual analysis and whole-word recognition systems (an explanation which parallels the neurological account but is not committed to a specific anatomical substrate). It has been argued that some variant of the disconnection hypothesis is able to account for the disorders shown by at least some patients. Any concept of functional disconnection requires elaboration in order to account for the absolute sparing of number and letter recognition which is common to all "pure" cases (e.g., case R.A.V., Warrington & Shallice, 1980). One possibility is that letter recognition and word recognition are mediated by separable processing systems, only one of which is disconnected. Alternatively it has been suggested that there may be a reduction in the amount of information which is transmitted (Patterson & Kay 1982). Words would require greater "channel capacity" and thus might fail to reach the whole-word recognition system. The observation that some letter-by-letter readers (i.e., patients who read even 3- and 4-letter words in this manner) may be able to report three or four briefly presented random letters is evidence against this variant of the disconnection hypothesis (Warrington & Shallice, 1980). [Performance on this type of task is thought to reflect the operation of a visual short-term memory (see Chapter 13).] In order to account for these patients' performance it would be necessary to postulate at least two separate pathways for transmitting information about visually presented letters. One would be responsible for transmitting information about letters when they were briefly presented. The other route would be implicated in transmission of this same information to visual word-recognition systems. Without this additional assumption the disconnection hypothesis fails as a general account of spelling dyslexia.

Failure to integrate visual information—Can spelling dyslexia be thought of as a component of a more general visual "agnosic" disorder? In 1924 Wolpert introduced the concept of a specific type of visual recognition deficit (termed *simultanagnosia*) which affected the patients' ability to integrate the parts of a whole into a coherent unit. Although the patients were able to identify the individual items in a complex scene and the letters in words, they were unable to integrate these elements into a coherent whole. This global deficit resulted in a piecemeal analysis of scenes and spelling dyslexia. However, patients with spelling dyslexia do not necessarily show piecemeal perception of complex scenes: for example, one patient with a marked spelling dyslexia (R.A.V.) actually obtained above an average score on tests of complex picture interpretation on the Wechsler Adult Intelligence Scale (Picture Completion, Picture Arrangement). These components of the syndrome of simultanagnosia would therefore appear to fractionate rather than cluster together in any meaningful way (Warrington & Shallice, 1980; Shallice & Saffran, 1986). An integrative agnosia (see Chapter 2) of this form therefore does not seem to offer a valid account of spelling dyslexia.

Visual Word-Form Impairment—Warrington & Shallice (1980) argued that the disorder of spelling dyslexia implicated damage to a system which is responsible for the visual analysis of letter strings as coherent units: the visual word form (see Fig. 10.4). This system was considered to be a processing stage which was *prior* to any derivation of meaning or sound from the printed letter string. They argued that the basis of the deficit in spelling dyslexia (at least in some cases) was in damage to the word form itself rather than to a disconnection or simultanagnosia.

The disorder of spelling dyslexia could not be accounted for in terms of an impairment in deriving meaning from written words with preservation of letter naming. For example, there was no evidence of any semantic errors (i.e., those based on word meanings) and no evidence of partial comprehension. Furthermore, there was no evidence of any difference between the patients' reading of nonwords or words with different levels of regularity. Were the patients' deficits simply attributable to failure to derive meaning from words (rather than to an impaired word form: see Fig. 10.4) reading by sound should have been fast and efficient. This was not the case: all classes of material were read slowly, and letter by letter. Warrington & Shallice proposed that their patients had a deficit at the level of the visual word form itself.

In introducing the term *visual word form system* Warrington & Shallice (1980) went beyond the concept of a processing stage which is solely responsible for recognising a sight vocabulary. They proposed that it should be viewed as a more complex system "which parses (multiply and in parallel) letter strings into ordered familiar units and categorises these units visually." Damage to this system would result in impairment on all tasks in which familiar letter strings had to be recognised as whole units. They emphasised that their patients were specifically impaired on those tasks which maximised whole-word reading and which prevented letter-by-letter reading. In particular, Warrington & Shallice stressed the patients' difficulty in reading script and in reading material presented for very short durations.

Patients with a spelling dyslexia may show a number of different patterns of impairment in deriving meaning from words presented too briefly for them to be read letter by letter. Quite possibly this reflects the heterogeneity of this "syndrome." Cases range from those who are unable to derive any information from the printed word through to those who are able to derive some approximate information about the meaning of the target (Shallice & Saffran, 1986; Coslett & Saffran, 1989b). Whether these different disorders reflect degrees of information loss within the visual word-form system itself or whether they reflect a partial disconnection between the visual word form and word meaning systems remains an open question (Shallice, 1988).

Neglect Dyslexia   Neglect dyslexic patients read at a normal rate but nevertheless make visual errors involving the beginnings or ends of words. Three theoretical issues will be discussed. First, whether the phenomena of neglect dyslexia can be accounted for in terms of a sensory impairment (such as failure to compensate for a hemianopia); second, how this disorder relates to other forms of neglect (see Chapter 4); and third, the implications of neglect dyslexia for visual word-form processing.

Relationship to Sensory Processing—It has been argued that neglect dyslexia might be due to a failure of early visual processing or, more specifically, a visual-field defect. In their discussion of a case with right-sided neglect dyslexia, Warrington & Zangwill (1957) suggested that the deficit might be accounted for in terms of a failure to compensate for a hemianopia. However, subsequent cases of neglect dyslexia have been reported to have full visual fields (Kinsbourne & Warrington, 1962a). (As an aside it should be noted that patients with hemianopia do not necessarily show neglect in reading, even in the acute stages of their illness.)

The characteristics of the neglect-dyslexic patient's errors are also quite different from those that would be expected if the impairment were at a very early stage in visual information processing. For example there is frequently a close relationship between the length of the stimulus word and the length of the word produced as a response (see Table 10.2). It might perhaps be argued that this could still be due to failure to process words at an early sensory level combined with a guessing strategy. This however, fails to account for the preservation of compound-word reading and the inverse effects of word length (Costello & Warrington, 1987; see above).

The relationship between neglect dyslexia and other forms of spatial neglect (see Chapter 4) has also been debated. Ellis *et al.* (1987) suggested that there might be a continuum of task difficulty with neglect dyslexia representing an extreme point. It is true that a number of the reported cases of neglect dyslexia have also shown a range of other neglect phenomena, including reading only the last few words of a line of print.However, neglect on visuospatial tasks and neglect in text reading dissociate from neglect in single-word reading. A dramatic example of the fractionation of neglect dyslexia from other types of neglect is that of a patient (J.O.H.) who showed neglect of the right in copying arrays of simple shapes but had a left-sided neglect dyslexia (Costello & Warrington, 1987). Two of the neglect-dyslexic patients reported by Kinsbourne & Warrington (1963a) were unimpaired in their ability to follow lines in printed text *despite* making neglect errors on words in the text. The converse is also shown. A patient (V.S.N.) with a pronounced neglect on spatial tasks (including missing the left most words when reading lines of text; see Fig. 4.15) was quite normal in reading single words and the individual words in text (Kartsounis & Warrington 1989). There is thus a double dissociation between spatial neglect and neglect dyslexia. Clearly, neglect dyslexia cannot be considered as being on a continuum with other forms of neglect.

How then should neglect dyslexia be accounted for? The deficit appears to affect a stage of processing which is prior to any assignment of meaning to the written word. For example Ellis *et al.* (1987) asked a patient (V.B.) to define words which she had misread. They noted that her definitions were appropriate to her dyslexic error rather than to the target. There are a number of plausible alternative stages of processing which might be implicated by this type of response. Ellis *et al.* argued that since their patient maintained word length in her errors, her deficit might be accounted for in terms of an impairment in the coding of the specific *identities* of letters. Information about the *spatial* extent of the letter string was preserved.

An alternative possibility has been put forward by Costello & Warrington (1987). They noted that their patient showed an inverse effect of word length—longer words were actually read more accurately than were short words. Moreover, although word length was commonly preserved in the patient's error responses, where it was not, additions of letters were more common than were letter deletions. They suggested that the patient's impairment might lie within the procedures required for *selection* of the appropriate targets within the visual word form system itself.

Attentional Dyslexia   In attentional dyslexia, patients are able to read letters, and even words, with the important proviso that these are the only similar stimuli in view. This highly specific difficulty has been identified with a failure in selective attention (Shallice & Warrington, 1977a).

In all sense modalities, the normal individual has the ability to filter out irrelevant information so that attention can be focused or targeted appropriately. We tend to take for granted this ability to ignore the unnecessary information which bombards our senses and the ease with which we selectively attend to a small part of the environment. For example, when reading text or in naming a letter present in an array, it is necessary to focus attention so that one is not "flooded" with information from elsewhere in the visual field. It is thought that patients with attentional dyslexia have lost the ability to focus their attention when they are required to attend to one item among other items of the same class.

For the normal subject there must be a "gate" or selective attention "filter" that achieves an orderly transfer of information from early visual processing systems, which operate rapidly, spatially, and in parallel, to later recognition systems that operate more slowly. It was suggested that this transmission of information was faulty in attentional dyslexia. However, attentional dyslexia has not been sufficiently explored for any explanation to be more than a speculative possibility. Precise characterisation of this pattern of deficit awaits further and more detailed investigation.

Central Dyslexias

Reading by Sound: The Phonological Route   This type of dyslexic impairment is characterised by over-reliance on the common spelling–sound correspondences of language, resulting in difficulty in reading irregular words which flout the common rules of pronunciation (see above). At the same time, the patient's reading of nonwords may be normal. In discussions of this pattern of acquired dyslexia, the major issues have been the relationship between phonological reading and other components of the reading system and the properties of the phonological reading process itself.

Visual Word Form in Phonological Readers.—There is now good evidence that visual word-form processing (see above) can be intact in at least some patients who read by sound. First, cases have been described (e.g., H.T.R., M.P., K.T.) whose reading *speed* is entirely normal both for long words and for words presented in script. This profile is quite unlike that of those patients with a spelling dyslexia who read slowly, letter by letter, and show massive word-length effects. In some cases it has been possible to demonstrate the relative integrity of the visual word form in phonological readers using more direct techniques. Bub *et al.* (1985) asked their patient (M.P.) to judge whether stimuli were words or nonwords ("lexical decision"). The patient was able to discriminate words from nonwords, even succeeding on those words which she misread. A different procedure was used with another case (K.T.). He was told that there were three words in a string of "joined up words" such as *orangechickenred*. He was asked both to read them aloud and also to copy them with the appropriate spaces in between (McCarthy & Warrington, 1986b). His performance was excellent on this task, despite his *complete* failure to comprehend the target words. These findings indicate that in the purest cases of patients who can only read by sound, visual processing of the letter string is intact.

In other cases there may be additional disorders of visual form word processing. This seems the most likely explanation of the slow, laborious process of "cobbling together" words sound by sound shown by patients such as those studied by Marshall & Newcombe (1973) and by Newcombe & Marshall (1985). Indeed, patients with this type of reading have been considered as showing a more complex form of spelling dyslexia (Shallice & McCarthy, 1985).

Relationship to Processing for Meaning—The majority of fluent phonological readers have had grave impairments of written (and spoken) language comprehension (e.g., Warrington, 1975; Shallice *et al.*, 1983; Bub *et al.*, 1985; McCarthy & Warrington, 1986b). That these patients read by sound whilst showing no comprehension of the written or spoken word indicates that translating, or transcoding, between print and sound can proceed independently of any processing for meaning. This class of disorder therefore provides very clear evidence for the existence of a print-to-sound reading system or "route" which is independent of written word comprehension.

Some patients who read by sound have intact comprehension of the spoken word. In such cases patients may have difficulty in discriminating between the meanings of written "homophonic" words (e.g., *peel, peal*) (Coltheart, 1985; Masterson, Coltheart, & Meara, 1985). There is thus a failure to comprehend the written word, with preservation of auditory comprehension, suggesting a dissociation of these types of verbal knowledge (see also Chapters 6 and 11).

Properties of Phonological Reading—The patterns of errors which are made by phonological readers have been used to guide models of the functioning of the normal system which translates (or transcodes) print into sound. The earliest suggestion was that this process operated at the level of "grapheme–phoneme conversion." Specifically, it was argued that the basic units involved in transcoding were single letters or common letter clusters (e.g., "sh," "ck," "ee," "oo") which typically map onto a single word sound or phoneme.

A number of observations have called this simple and intuitively plausible account into question. First, there are a number of words which are technically "irregular" which can be read correctly by (at least some) phonological readers (e.g., K.T.; H.T.R.). Words such as *leather* and *weather* are technically "irregular" words since they do not have the commonest pronunciation of the grapheme "ea" in which it rhymes with "ee" (e.g., *heat, leaf, seat*, etc.). However, when "ea" is followed by the letters "th" the commonest pronunciation is actually the so-called irregular one in which it rhymes with the "e" of *bet* (*weather, leather, feather*, etc.). These words are only "moderately irregular," and contrast with "very irregular" words (such as *have* and *come*) in which highly unusual pronunciations are given to the critical vowels. Phonological readers make most of their errors on this latter class of words. This profile of reading difficulty has been termed the "levels of regularity" effect. This pattern is in clear contradiction to the predictions made by a grapheme–phoneme position. What appears to be happening is that the patients are sensitive to the overall letter context in which graphemes occur. This has led to the revision and elaboration of the earlier model to include the possibility that transcoding rules apply not just to single graphemes, but over larger grapheme and letter groupings (Shallice *et al.*, 1983; Shallice & McCarthy, 1985; Patterson & Morton, 1985).

The size of the units over which print-to-sound translation operates may be quite large. One patient (K.T.) was able to read many polysyllabic words rapidly and correctly including the appropriate assignment of word stress (e.g., *department, president,*). He had absolutely *no* comprehension of these long words yet they were clearly more than a string of letters. A further example of multiple-letter processing was demonstrated with "affixed" words such as "desig*nate*," "magi*cian*," "resig*nation*." The changes in pronunciation between words such as *design* and *designate* are quite systematic in English and represent "regularity" patterns which operate over the entire word. The patient was able to read such root words and their derivations equally accurately and with a very low error rate, despite misreading such common words as *come* as *comb*, *move* as *mauve*, and *break* as *breek*.

Reading via the phonological route has been shown to be independent of meaning systems. It is also a complex process which can operate over a range of different sizes of spelling unit.

Reading by Sight Vocabulary   It has been established that some patients rely on a sight vocabulary for reading. Unlike those patients who read by sound, who were discussed in the previous section, these dyslexics are *unable* to make use of print-to-sound correspondences (the phonological route, see above). This is shown by their very poor ability to read nonwords.

Most investigators would accept that reading which was based on the use of a sight vocabulary was mediated by "direct" links, or a direct route, from the visual word-form system to meaning representations (see Fig. 10.4). Those patients who show impairment in reading certain classes or categories of word are thought to demonstrate *additional* deficits within the meaning (or the semantic processing) route itself. The different patterns of breakdown which are observed in this broad class of patients appear to reflect the component (or components) of the semantic route which are damaged. There are two main classes of theoretical interpretation. First, there are those which have considered the possibility that these patients are reading using a right-hemisphere system. The alternative position is that reading by a sight vocabulary implicates damage to a component or subcomponent of a left-hemisphere reading system.

The Right-Hemisphere Hypothesis—Patients with the cluster of deficits which has been labeled "deep dyslexia" have in common the inability to read nonwords, the occurrence of semantic errors, and impairment in reading grammatical words and in reading abstract rather than concrete words. It is held that these deficits are not an "arbitrary" cluster, but rather that they reflect the properties of a different reading system in the right hemisphere (e.g., Coltheart, 1980; Saffran, Bogyo, Schwartz, & Marin, 1980; Patterson, Varga-Khadem & Polkey, 1989). Concrete or imageable words have been suggested to benefit from a dual encoding and a dual representation in the brain (Paivio, 1971). Unlike abstract words, it is argued that concrete or imageable words are encoded in a visual form as well as in a verbal form. Expressing this dual-encoding hypothesis in neuropsychological terms it has been proposed that the right hemisphere has a lexicon/dictionary which is limited to concrete words. Both abstract *and* concrete words are represented in the left hemisphere. Reading in deep dyslexia was thought to reflect the operation of the right hemisphere system rather than a symptom complex which reflected dysfunction within a normal left-hemisphere reading system.

According to the right-hemisphere hypothesis the syndrome of deep dyslexia should always form a coherent entity rather than have a variable pattern, but this is not the case. Deep dyslexic readers differ considerably in the degree and characteristics of their dyslexia and in their vulnerability to semantic errors (Shallice & Warrington, 1980: see Table 10.7). Perhaps most crucially for the right-hemisphere hypothesis there should never be a patient who is better at reading abstract words than concrete words. Such a case was described by Warrington (1981a). This patient (C.A.V.) was significantly worse at reading words with a high rating of concreteness than words with high abstract rating. Since the right-hemisphere hypothesis cannot account for the diverse phenomena which are shown by patients reading by their sight vocabulary, alternative interpretations are viable.

The Left-Hemisphere Hypothesis—The major alternative to the right-hemisphere hypothesis is the view that patients dependent on their sight vocabulary are reading by the use of their residual left hemisphere vocabulary. Deficits have been identified at the stages of access to the meaning (semantic) system, degradation within this system, and word retrieval.

One case (A.R.) was impaired on matching a printed word to a picture and was unreliable in producing an appropriate pantomime to words which he could not read (e.g., *bend, bow*). This patient was frequently able to achieve a *partial* understanding of the words which he was unable to read. For example, when shown the word *ostrich* he responded "I get the impression of an animal." He was able to categorise written words on semantic dimensions (e.g., animal/not animal; see also Chapter 6) at a level which was well above chance, although he still showed a significant impairment. His deficit clearly implicated a failure of semantic processing. His disorder was identified as being one of failure to *access* a full semantic specification of the written word. The deficit, was highly variable, resulting in unpredictability in the words which could be read from one occasion to the next (Warrington & Shallice, 1979; see also Chapter 6). The very variability of this patient's reading abilities indicated that he had not "lost" the words he was unable to read. His *potential* sight vocabulary was very large. However, only a restricted subset of his vocabulary was accessible at any one time. His dyslexia was attributed to an instability in the procedures required for accessing a full semantic specification of the written word.

Some patients have a highly *stable* but *depleted* reading vocabulary. That is, the words which they can read and the words which they fail to read are consistent from one testing session to another. It is the presence of a stable deficit which differentiates this type of dyslexia from one of access to semantic representations. One patient (K.F.) was tested on 216 words on two separate testing occasions. He scored 66% and 63% correct on the two tests, respectively. A measure of his consistency was highly significant (Kendall's coefficient of concordance). Not only was he consistent; he also showed an impairment in comprehension of the same words which he failed to read (Shallice & Warrington, 1975).

There are other patients who appear to have relatively preserved comprehension of written words which they cannot *read aloud*. Their deficit may be selective for reading and not attributable to some more general speech-production impairment (Marshall & Newcombe, 1973). The patient's deficit appears to be somewhat like the "word-finding difficulty" which is observed in the syndrome of nominal aphasia (see Chapter 7). Indeed, the patient's disorder could be considered as analogous to a nominal aphasia which is specific for written material. Patients are often able indicate that a full semantic specification of the target has been accessed. For example, a patient (V.S.) studied by Saffran & Marin (1977) was able to define a large number of written words and performed at an above-average level on a written word–picture matching test (Peabody Picture Vocabulary) despite having a 20% error rate when reading very common short words aloud. Patterson (1978, 1979) has also documented two cases with this pattern of dyslexia (D.E. and P.W.) and has demonstrated that their comprehension was creditable when they were reading to themselves. They were able to judge the meaningfulness of sentences (e.g., spaghetti moves around searching for food) and answer written questions despite having a marked "dyslexic" impairment. This pattern of dyslexia is therefore considered to be at the spoken-word *retrieval* stage of the reading process.

Conclusion

The relationship between the different subtypes of dyslexia has been discussed here from a purely cognitive perspective. The anatomical evidence also indicates a degree of independence of these different syndromes. In this regard commonly co-occurring cognitive deficits, *neuropsychological syndromes,* are of relevance. Thus spelling dyslexia is associated not only with hemianopic deficits in many cases; it may also co-occur with a degree of visual associative agnosia and impaired visual short-term memory, implicating the anterior left occipital lobe (see Chapters 2 and 13). Reading by sound is very commonly observed in patients with impaired word comprehension and left temporal lobe lesions (see Chapter 5). By contrast, reading via the sight vocabulary is frequently associated with another left parietal syndrome of impaired auditory–verbal short-term memory (see Chapter 13). these different clusters of commonly associated deficits should not be considered causal for the patient's reading disorder (since in some cases they do dissociate). Rather, by implicating different anatomical loci, they lend further weight to the behavioural evidence for dissociation between these components of the reading system.

The evidence from the acquired dyslexic syndromes has been used to refine and modify models of the normal reading process. Investigators have made the reasonable assumption that patients have "lost" some component or components of the normal reading system. If this assumption is valid then the profile of patients' performance should be instructive with regard to the way in which normal reading is organised. Justification for this assumption comes from the convergence of evidence between experimental psychology and neuropsychology (e.g., Coltheart, 1985; Shallice, 1988). Models such as that shown in Fig. 10.4 have been thought of as reasonable (if approximate) descriptions of the way in which normal reading is organised, and not simply as formal descriptions of neuropsychological deficits.

11

Spelling and Writing

Introduction

Writing and spelling are less well-practiced skills for most people than
reading or even calculation. Even in the case of the highly educated
individual, the ability to write may be only exercised rarely: business
letters are often dictated rather than written by hand and communication is more frequently conducted by telephone rather than by letter.
Nevertheless, in the course of schooling the majority of people in our
society achieve a modicum of competence in writing and spelling
skills. Unlike spoken language, the skills of spelling and writing are
relatively late in their acquisition and usually require formal teaching.
Learning to write is a complex task. Not only must the ability to spell
words be learned, but it is necessary to acquire the appropriate degree
of motor control so that letter shapes are recognisable and can be
produced fluently. These components of the skill of writing must be
brought together in order to produce a correctly written word.

In the earliest accounts of disorders of writing two approaches were
taken. On one, written and spoken expression were thought to lie on a
continuum. The other position argued that these skills were independent. The "continuum" viewpoint considered that the processes of
spoken and written language were very highly interrelated, with written
language being more vulnerable. Thus, patients with acquired disorders
of language (aphasia) would be expected to show a somewhat more
severe impairment in their written language than in their speech. Even
the motor aspects of writing were thought to be directly dependent
on the integrity of "internal" language processes or "inner speech"
(Wernicke, 1874; Lichtheim, 1885; Dejerine, 1892).

The independence position was first expressed by Ogle (1869; cited
by Hécaen & Albert, 1978); who coined the term *agraphia* to designate
acquired disorders of writing. He described a number of agraphic patients, the majority of whom were also aphasic. However, one patient

was agraphic but not aphasic, and another case was aphasic but not agraphic. On the basis of these dissociations Ogle concluded that although agraphia and aphasia often occurred together, a separate writing "centre" could be identified. The possibility that there might be a separable writing centre was also expressed by Bastian (1898) (who designated it by the somewhat grandiose term of the cheiro-kinesthetic centre.) Exner (1881), however, is usually regarded as the major proponent of the view that there might be a specific centre for the motor skill of writing (analogous to Broca's centre for articulate speech).

The distinction between agraphia arising as a consequence of a specific disorder of motor skill and an agraphia secondary to language impairments appears to be an oversimplification. Patients may have specific difficulties in *spelling* rather than in *writing* the target word and vice versa. They may be able to produce written letters and put them together into a sequence, however their choice of letters or letter order is wrong. Gerstmann (1927), was the first writer to emphasise the theoretical significance of a spelling disorder. He proposed a "syndrome complex" of agraphia, acalculia, left–right disorientation, and finger agnosia. A major component of this syndrome was an agraphia characterised by errors of spelling rather than of the actions of writing. This agraphia could not be attributed to a primary language disorder. Gerstmann's observations were replicated and extended by the demonstration that agraphic patients with and without aphasia made qualitatively different types of error (Kinsbourne & Warrington, 1964b). The selective impairment of spelling skills is now a well recognised, albeit rare, phenomenon. It is also clear that there may be important differences between patients in terms of the precise characteristics of their deficit. As an aside, it might be noted that the terms "agraphia" and "dysgraphia" are used interchangeably to describe these disorders.

Empirical Characteristics

The agraphias can be subdivided into those which affect the processes of spelling and those which affect writing. Within these two broad classes there are further subtypes of disorder; these will be considered in turn..

Disorders of Spelling

Patients may show marked difficulties in the spelling of words which were once clearly within their spelling vocabulary. These spelling disorders have been broadly subdivided into two main types depending on the pattern of the patient's errors. These are spelling which appears to be based on word-sound information and spelling which is dependent on an established vocabulary of words.

Spelling by Sound   When confronted with a word which is not in one's normal spelling vocabulary, it is usually possible to generate a "reasonable" approximation of the spelling. In producing such an approximation, use is made of the sound (or phonology) of the word, which is in turn translated into a spelling pattern. Whilst this works for some words, in many languages there are a number of words whose spelling pattern is very different from that which would be expected on the basis of their pronunciation. The problem of translating from the word's sound into the correct sequence of letters is a complex one. Some words are quite "exceptional" in the way that sound and spelling relate to one another. The correspondence between sound and spelling appears to be almost arbitrary. For example, even the common English words *come, said,* and *onion* are "exceptions" in that they break the conventional sound-to-letter correspondences (correct sound-based spellings might be *kum, sed,* and *unnyun*). In addition to the complex exception words of the language, there are also a very large number of "ambiguous" words in which the identical word sound is commonly represented by two or more different spellings. For example the sound of *"e"* is realised very differently in common words such as t*ea*m, s*ee*n, th*e*se, and f*ie*ld. Unless one "knows" which spelling pattern is appropriate to each of these words it would be impossible to produce all of them correctly.

Patients who spell by sound have particular difficulties with exception words, and words for which there are a number of alternative spelling patterns. The patient appears to spell by translating the sounds of words directly into those spelling patterns which are appropriate in the language. Beauvois & Derouesné (1981) reported a French speaking patient (R.G.) with this type of impairment, which they termed *lexical* or *orthographical agraphia*. By this terminology they meant that the patient appeared to have lost the ability to retrieve word-specific (lexical) spelling patterns (orthography) and was reliant on the use of common sound-to-spelling correspondences, resulting in numerous errors (agraphia). Beauvois & Derouesné tested their patient on words which were exceptional in their correspondences between sound and spelling and also on words for which there were a number of alternative spelling patterns. The patient made most errors on words with unusual sound-to-spelling correspondences and was also impaired on words containing sounds for which there were alternative plausible spellings. If there were no alternative ways of spelling a particular sound (the pattern was unambiguous), then the patient made very few mistakes. (In English, examples of these types of word would be as follows. unusual: *island;* ambiguous: *team;* unambiguous: *hat*). The patient was also very good, scoring 90% correct, when producing plausible spelling patterns for invented nonwords (an English example would be *lat*). The patient's errors were biased in favour of the commoner sound-to-spelling correspondences of the French language, however, the same sound or the same word was not consistently translated into the same spelling. This indicated that the patient was able to use a limited number of alternative translations between sound and spelling. Beauvois & Derouesné's original observations have been confirmed and extended in a number of subsequent cases (see Table 11.1). In all of these cases there has been evidence of an impairment in spelling words with unusual, rule-breaking correspondences between sound and spelling (e.g. Hatfield & Patterson, 1983; Roeltgen & Heilman, 1984; Goodman & Caramazza, 1986a, 1986b; Baxter & Warrington, 1987).

Patients who spell by sound make a characteristic error which is termed a *regularisation* (see Table 11.2). This consists of plausible renditions of sound-to-letter correspondences appropriate to the language. In many cases the patient's error can be "read back" as the target item. Errors may be particularly prominent in multisyllablic words which include "unstressed" sounds (such as the "i" in *pencil*, the "e" in *panel*, and the "o" in *carol*). This unstressed sound is actually the same in all of these words (try pronouncing them to yourself if you need to be convinced), and in fact it can be represented by virtually any of the vowel letters of the language.

Unambiguous words can be spelled correctly, regardless of how common or rare they are in the language. With ambiguous or irregular words, some cases, may find common words easier to spell correctly (Goodman & Caramazza, 1986a; Coltheart & Funnell, 1987). However, the relative preservation of the ability to spell common words is by no means an invarient characteristic of this type of spelling disorder. Baxter & Warrington's (1986) case (K.T.) did not show any effect of word frequency on items which were matched for their degree of ambiguity. However, if a patient with a bias toward spelling by sound *does* have some residual word-spelling knowledge, then common words are be more likely to be preserved than rare words. Indeed the relative sparing of common words is the more common empirical observation (e.g. Goodman & Caramazza, 1986a).

Table 11.1 Results of Lexical Agraphic Patients on Writing Nonwords and Words of Different Levels of Ambiguity (% Correct)

		Level of ambiguity		
	Nonwords	Low (e.g., *splash*)	Medium (e.g., *brain*)	High (e.g., *city*)
Beauvois & Derouesné (1981) (R.G.)	100	93	67	36
Hatfield & Patterson (1983) (P.T.)	—	93	—	38
Roeltgen & Heilman (1984) (L.A., 1)	90	100	90	30
Roeltgen & Heilman (1984) (L.A., 2)	90	100	88	70
Roeltgen & Heilman (1984) (L.A., 3)	100	100	100	90
Goodman & Caramazza (1986a) (J.G.)	100	90	—	70
Goodman & Caramazza (1986b) (M.W.)	100	100	—	88
Baxter & Warrington (1987) (K.T.)	95	86	—	19
Controls	90	100	100	98

Table 11.2 Types of Spelling Errors Made by Different Classes of Dysgraphic Patients[a]

Regularisation (K.T.)	Semantic (J.C.)	Visual/order (G.O.S.)	Neglect (O.R.F.)
knock — nok	time — clock	advantage — advangate	brush — rush
build — bild	sky — sun	cobweb — coweb	route — soute
mighty — mite	desk — chair	orchestra — orchestro	joy — doy
juice — juse	chair — table	provide — provise	think — fink
nought — nort	yacht — boat	illusion — illuised	club — llub
door — dor	give — take	kneel — kneed	money — yoney
stay — stai	they — their	threat — streak	sick — cick
yes — yess	yours — our	seige — seize	class — glass
plate — plait	laugh — smile	stretch — strecht	choir — shoir
hound — hownd	appear — magic	belief — beleif	crime — mrime

[a]See text for individual patient details.

Vocabulary-Based Spelling In the previous section patients whose spelling was partially or totally reliant on sound-based spelling procedures were described. In this section the converse pattern of impairment will be discussed. This consists of the patient being partially or totally reliant on an established spelling vocabulary, the ability to spell by sound being gravely compromised. This type of spelling impairment has been termed *phonological agraphia*.

Shallice (1981) described a patient (P.R.) whose ability to spell many familiar real words was at an above-average level. On routine testing he would probably not have been diagnosed as dysgraphic since he could spell words such as *genealogy, cupola,* and *coniferous*. However, more detailed investigation showed that he had a relatively selective dysgraphic impairment: he was unable to spell by sound. He was very poor at the simple task of producing a letter corresponding to a conventionalised sound (e.g. /Bə/ for B). His writing of nonwords was also markedly impaired. His attempts to spell these stimuli indicated that he was attempting to use "analogies" with words which were in his extensive and multilingual vocabulary. On some occasions this was a successful strategy: for example, when asked to spell "ji" he did so, commenting that it was Hindustani! However other errors such as "na" → "gn" (via *gnat*) illustrate that this form of mediation was by no means invariably successful.

Spelling which is dependent on an established vocabulary has since been documented in a considerable number of other cases. All of these patients have shown a disproportionate impairment in the spelling of nonwords, with relative preservation of their spelling vocabulary for many real words (e.g., Assal, Buttet, & Jolivet, 1981; Bub & Kertesz, 1982b; Nolan & Caramazza, 1982; Roeltgen, Sevush, and Heilman, 1983; Baxter & Warrington, 1983, 1985; Kremin, 1987; see Table 11.3).

Patients who are dependent on the use of a spelling vocabulary may have additional deficits within the vocabulary itself. As in the case of reading (see Chapter 10), such deficits are of interest because of the light which they can shed on the organisation of established spelling vocabularies. The patient (P.R.) reported by Shallice (1981) showed

Table 11.3 Word-Class Effects (% Correct[a]) in Patients Spelling Using Their Established Vocabulary

Reference	Concrete	Abstract	Nonword
Shallice (1981) (P.R.)	100	92	5–25
Bub & Kertesz (1982a) (J.C.)	75–80	33–45	0–5
Bub & Kertesz (1982b) (M.H.)	100	96	0–5
Baxter & Warrington (1985) (G.O.S.)	97	69	0
Kremin (1987) (Michel)	60	28	0

[a]Range of performance on each type of stimulus.

specific difficulties in spelling grammatical function words and grammatical word endings (and, if, for, by; loveliness, mittens). His errors were mostly omissions, with occasional substitutions (e.g., as → has; how → why). He had no difficulty in using these same words in his spontaneous speech and was mostly accurate when he was asked to generate a spoken sentence containing a function word (e.g., as: "They went home as it was late"). His word-ending errors were mostly substitutions (loveliness → lovely, injure → injury). In addition he had some difficulty in spelling uncommon words with an abstract meaning (i.e., words which refer to concepts or ideas, for example, amenable, entity, habituate. See Table 11.3.). In the case of abstract words his failures could be traced back to a more fundamental deficit in auditory comprehension (Shallice, 1981).

Bub & Kertesz (1982a) described a patient (J.C.) who was quite unable to spell nonwords. Her spelling vocabulary for concrete words was more intact than that for abstract words. Unlike the case described by Shallice (1981), her errors were often substitutions of alternative real words with a similar meaning to the target, i.e., semantic errors (see Table 11.2). A similar (French) case was described by Kremin (1987). The patient (Michel) also produced real-word errors, often with a semantic relationship to the target word. Kremin established that there was a parallel between spoken words which he could not comprehend and those which gave rise to errors on spelling tests.

One case (G.O.S.) has been reported who had entirely normal comprehension of the words which she was unable to spell (function words, low-frequency abstract words, and verbs) (Baxter & Warrington 1985). Thus she was able to define abstract words, was able to comprehend sentences in which function words and verbs were critical, and was able to include the words she was unable to spell within a spoken sentence. For example, although she was unable to spell the word connect she was able to include the word connect in the spoken sentence: "If you put a plug on a sewing machine then you would connect it to the electricity."

Disorders of Spelling Assembly Other patients may have grave impairments of spelling, but their disorder appears to be orthogonal to (and even independent of) the linguistic distinctions discussed above. Gerstmann (1927) first observed that the sequencing of letters in spellings could be specifically impaired. In a quantitative analysis of spelling errors Kinsbourne & Warrington (1964b) confirmed Gerstmann's observations. Dubois, Hécaen, & Marcie (1969) described patients with similar spelling difficulties. The patients made errors of letter order and letter substitution; in five cases these mistakes were most prominent in the middle of words.

Subsequent studies have confirmed and extended these findings. It has been noted that patients' difficulties are typically related to word length, with longer words being more vulnerable than shorter words (see Fig. 11.1). Error analysis has shown that letter-position effects may vary in individual patients. Errors may predominate at the beginnings, ends, or middles of words. An (Italian) patient (F.V.) was described by Miceli, Silveri, & Caramazza (1987) who made errors of letter substitution, addition, omission or order. A similar (but more severely affected) case (L.B.) was reported by Caramazza, Miceli, Villa, & Romani (1987; see Table 11.4). In both of these patients, (like those studied by Dubois *et al.*, 1969), errors were more common in the middle of words (a serial position effect which is an exaggeration of the normal pattern in "slips" of the pen; Wing & Baddeley, 1980). Hillis & Caramazza (1989) reported different positional errors in two further cases. One patient had relatively greater difficulty with word endings (D.H.), and in the other case errors predominated in word beginnings (M.L.) (Fig. 11.2).

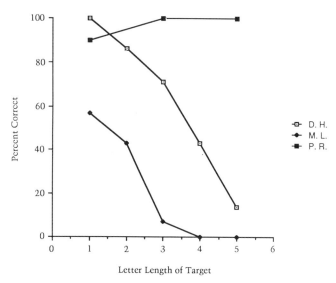

Figure 11.1. Word-length effects in two cases (□, D.H., and ◆, M.L.). A third dysgraphic case (■, P.R.) without word-length effects is included for comparison. (Adapted from Hillis & Caramazza, 1989, and Shallice, 1981.)

Table 11.4 Types of Errors Produced in Writing to Dictation by Two
Spelling Assembly Cases[a]

	F.V.		L.B.	
Type of Error	Words (%)	Nonwords (%)	Words (%)	Nonwords (%)
Substitutions	46	46	37	36
Additions	16	10	8	9
Omissions	7	10	34	37
Order-transpositions	3	—	21	19
Mixed	27	34	—	—

[a]Percent correct responses.

Deficits in spelling assembly and effects of word length can and do
co-occur with other types of spelling impairment. One patient (O.R.F.)
who was unable to spell by sound, also showed a marked positional
bias in his spelling (Baxter & Warrington 1983). He often spelled words
backwards and made errors of letter repetition and letter order which
were most prominent at the beginnings of words (see Table 11.2 and
Fig. 11.2).

Modality-Specific Impairments of Spelling   Spelling of a word can be
achieved orally, in writing, or (for some people) by typing. Whereas for
most of the patients described above there is little difference reported

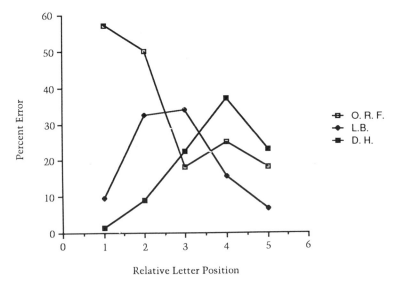

Figure 11.2.   Relative letter-position effects showing left neglect (□, O.R.F.), errors predominantly in the middle of words (♦, L.B.), and errors predominantly at the end of
words (■, D.H.) (see text for individual patient details).

between the various means of spelling output, other cases show a marked discrepancy.

Oral spelling alone is insufficient for the vast majority of purposes, and indeed there are cultures in which the concept of "spelling aloud" is entirely alien (e.g., Italian). This is not the case in English and American educational systems, where spelling aloud is often used in teaching children the complexities of the language's spelling patterns. Patients may show a selective impairment of their oral or written spelling: the two skills appear to be independent of each other. Kinsbourne & Warrington (1965) reported a single case study of a nonaphasic patient (J.P.): the patient was able to spell words using written output at an average level but made numerous errors when attempting to spell orally (and indeed he only scored 2/100). The converse dissociation, namely a selective impairment in written spelling with a preservation of oral spelling, was reported by Kinsbourne & Rosenfeld (1974). Although their patient had no difficulty in producing single written letters, numerous mistakes occurred when he attempted to write words. At the same time his ability to spell orally was intact. These complementary observations indicate that these two forms of spelling production are distinct.

Disorders of Writing

Writing is a complex skill which is acquired only through considerable effort and practice. The individual's handwriting probably takes at least 10 years to develop its personal and characteristic style. The ability to write may be selectively impaired, with preservation of the ability to spell orally or with the use of "block" letters. This deficit is termed an *apraxic agraphia*. This disorder is usually considered to represent one subclass of those deficits in organising and producing voluntary actions which are termed the *apraxias* (see Chapter 5).

Letter-Form Selection The normal person is able to select and organise the movements necessary to write the letters of the alphabet. Moreover, they are able to produce the appropriate letter form, regardless of whether cursive script or printing is being used. Disorders of letter-form selection are termed *ideational agraphia* (by analogy with ideational apraxia: see Chapter 5). In the pure form of this syndrome, the patient may be unable to write letters or words to dictation yet at the same time be capable of producing legible copies of the same material.

Zangwill (1954) provided the first systematic case study of a patient with a relatively selective impairment in letter-form production. Despite a good average level on a standard oral spelling test, the patient was gravely impaired in writing, whether spontaneously or to dictation. "In writing the alphabet which the patient could recite without error, about one quarter of letters were malformed, omitted, or transposed. . . . On the other hand numerals from one to twenty were always written correctly and in the proper sequence." The patient made "outspoken malformations and substitutions of letters but never of whole words. In writing to dictation, errors multiplied rapidly and the outcome was illegible." Remarkably, "the patient could copy words and letters with normal speed and accuracy!"

The selective impairment of letter formation was present in an even more severe form in a patient (I.D.T.) described by Baxter & Warrington (1986). His spelling abilities (tested by oral production) were at a good average level. However he was very impaired both in writing spontaneously and in writing to dictation. His difficulty was so severe that not a single legible written word was produced. When attempting to write letters the patient frequently produced a single vertical line; other errors included incomplete letters or combinations of two letters. He was also very impaired in tasks where he was required to convert words or letters from upper to lower case (e.g., HOUSE → house) and in converting print into script (see Fig. 11.3). In contrast to his profound impairment in changing letter case and writing to dictation, he was able to copy individual letters and words with near normal fluency. Perhaps most remarkably there was a relative preservation of his ability to draw pictures from memory.

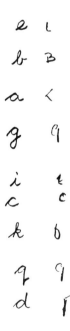

Figure 11.3. Example of a dysgraphic patient (I.D.T.) attempting to transpose lower case to upper case letters.

Crary & Heilman (1988) have also described a patient with a disproportionately severe impairment in the production of written letters.
When asked to write letters to dictation she would frequently refuse
complaining that she could not "see" them. In addition, she also made
errors of letter substitution. She had no difficulty in copying letters and
even words. The patient's deficit was clearly one of writing rather than
spelling, since when given block letters her performance was substantially improved (from 0 to 83%).

There is evidence of even more fine-grained dissociations in letter
production. A case (D.K.) described by Patterson & Wing (1989) showed
a disproportionate degree of impairment in writing lower case letters as
compared with upper case letters. On some occasions he appeared to
have "forgotten" the shape of the target; on others his response latency
for lower case letters was particularly slow.

Spatial Agraphia   Patients may show a range of different spatial distortions in their writing. This is often considered a secondary impairment rather than a primary agraphia. (see Chapter 4). Hécaen & Marcie
(1974) classified spatial errors in writing into the following groups.

1. Orientation errors: Writing was not properly oriented on the page,
but tended to slope or undulate.
2. Neglect errors: Writing was crowded onto one side of the page
leaving an excessively wide "margin" on the other side.
3. Reiteration of strokes: Patients would make errors in which additional strokes were added. This was particularly prominent with the
letters "m," "n," and "u."
4. Spacing errors: Extra-large "gaps" were left between the letters of a
word.

Writing disorders with these broad characteristics have been documented in a number of subsequent studies (e.g., Lebrun, 1985; Ellis,
Young, & Flude, 1987). An example of a spatial agraphia is given in Fig.
11.4.

Anatomical Considerations

There is a general consensus that primary impairments of both spelling
and writing are typically associated with posterior lesions of the left
(or language) hemisphere. The prevalence of these disorders is less
certain and is likely to vary according to the spelling system of the
language in which spelling is assessed. In an Italian study, Basso,
Taborelli, & Vignolo (1978) found a very low incidence of selective
agraphia in a consecutive series of 500 patients with lesions of the left
hemisphere. In this sample only 2 patients had an isolated impairment
(i.e., agraphia without aphasia). A higher incidence of selective spelling

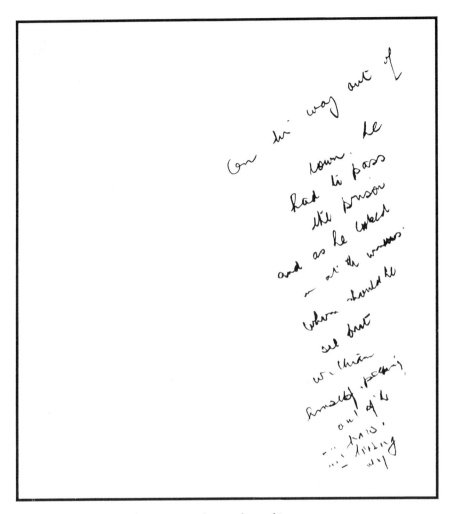

Figure 11.4. Example of a patient with spatial agraphia.

deficits was reported for a series of English patients studied by Baxter-Versi (1987). She reported three cases with a disproportionate deficit in spelling in a series of 26 left-hemisphere-lesioned patients.

Disorders of Spelling

Spelling by Sound Patients whose spelling is characterised by an over-reliance on the commoner sound-to-spelling correspondences of the language (the lexical agraphics) have all had lesions involving the parietal lobe. Roeltgen & Heilman (1984) reported four patients with this type of deficit. They reported that a small area at the junction of the posterior angular gyrus and the parieto-occipital lobule was com-

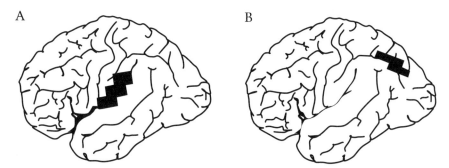

Figure 11.5. Schematic diagrams indicating the common sites of lesion in (A) spelling by established vocabulary, and (B) spelling by sound. (Adapted from Roeltgen & Heilman, 1984.)

mon to all of the patients (see Fig. 11.5). Baxter-Versi's (1987) study (see above) also included two similar cases. Whilst one patient's lesion localisation overlapped with that identified by Roeltgen & Heilman, the other patient appeared to have sparing of this area.

Vocabulary-Based Spelling In the case of patients who are reliant on the use of their spelling vocabulary (and are unable to spell nonwords), the critical lesion also appears to implicate parietal lobe structures. However, in the majority of cases the lesions have been extensive. On the basis of a review of the literature, together with four cases studied personally, Roeltgen & Heilman (1984) argued that regions near the supramarginal gyrus or the insula medial to it were implicated in all cases with this syndrome (see Fig. 11.5). In the case of patients with additional impairments within their spelling vocabulary, lesions have extended to include the temporal lobe (Bub & Kertesz, 1982a; Baxter & Warrington, 1985; Kremin, 1987).

Disorders of Spelling Assembly Gerstmann (1927) contended that damage to the left parietal lobe was critical in giving rise to deficits in letter sequencing. In one case studied by Miceli, Silveri, & Caramazza (1985), a very restricted lesion was observed which involved "the superior parietal lobule and perhaps the superior portion of the angular gyrus."

Patients who make errors primarily confined to one end of words (neglect spellers) have had lesions contralateral to the side of words which they neglect in spelling. The two cases with errors predominating on the left side of words had right-hemisphere lesions involving the parietal lobe. However, in these patients (O.R.F. and M.L.) language was also lateralised to the right hemisphere (Baxter & Warrington, 1983; Hillis & Caramazza, 1989). Right-sided neglect spelling has been recorded following a left frontoparietal lesion in a case (D.H.) with normal language lateralisation (Hillis & Caramazza, 1989).

Disorders of Writing

There have been very few cases reported whose impairments have confined to writing, and the lesion localisation is correspondingly uncertain. Exner (1881) proposed that lesions at the foot at the second frontal convolution would give rise to a specific disorder of writing. In a single case study, Gordinier (1899) reported an autopsy of a patient (Lizzie W.) who had presented with a total inability to write and no other apparent cognitive or motor deficits. Her lesion was located in the site predicted by Exner.

Those cases with disproportionate difficulties in the retrieval of appropriate letter forms with preservation of fluent copying of letter forms have had damage including the parietal regions of the language hemisphere. The patient reported by Zangwill (1954) had a parieto-occipital lesion, and a posterior parietal locus was also implicated in the cases reported by Auerbach & Alexander, 1981; Baxter & Warrington, 1986; and Crary & Heilman, 1988.

Spatial Agraphia   Hécaen & Marcie (1974) reported a retrospective survey of 82 patients with unilateral lesions (verified either surgically or at post mortem). They found that repetition of letter strokes was associated with lesions of the right hemisphere, as was the tendency to crowd words on the right side of the page. Within the right-hemisphere group, both of these errors were associated with more posterior lesions. Patients with left-hemisphere lesions showed a tendency to enlarge the right margin.

Theoretical Considerations

Until the papers of Beauvois & Derouesné (1981) and Shallice (1981), acquired disorders of spelling were either considered in terms of their relationship to language impairments or for their possible localising significance. In their analyses, Beauvois & Derouesné and Shallice adopted a framework similar to that which had proven successful in characterising the acquired disorders of reading (see Chapter 10). This information-processing approach to the analysis of acquired dysgraphic syndromes has since been elaborated to include both disorders of writing and disorders of spelling.

Disorders of Spelling

Disorders of spelling can be thought of as affecting one of two processes, both of which are available to the normal individual. One process is concerned with translating, or transcoding between the sound of a word and a spelling. The second allows spelling from a stored vocabulary of known words. There is a general consensus that these two major types of spelling impairment reflect the operation of two distinct routes for spelling. These are shown schematically in Fig. 11.6. As is proposed in the two-route models of reading (see Chapter 10), spelling can be mediated either via a sound-to-spelling route and/or by a route to an established spelling vocabulary.

The impairment of spelling can occur as a relatively isolated deficit. First, it may dissociate from the ability to comprehend or retrieve the spoken word (Beauvois & Derouesné, 1981; Goodman & Caramazza, 1986a). There is also no necessary parallel between impairments of spelling and reading (see Chapter 10). Even if reading difficulties do occur in patients who spell by sound, these are not necessarily of the same severity or of the same type [e.g., Beauvois & Derouesné, 1981; Goodman & Caramazza, 1986a,b). For example, Beauvois & Derouesné's case (R.G.) read using his sight vocabulary but spelled by sound. Such dissociations pose the question as to the status of knowledge of spellings in relation to other verbal "vocabularies" of knowledge. This problem will be discussed below when considering patients who spell without recourse to sound-based information (Vocabulary-Based Spelling).

Sound-Based Spelling   A major theoretical issue has been the question of how "sound-based" spelling is organised. (In this regard, the theoretical debate has many similarities to that which has been raised with regard to the form of dyslexia in which patients read by sound; see Chapter 10). This process appears to implicate an initial analysis of the constituent sounds of the word and their translation into some set of "spelling units" for production. The question remains as to the size of the constituent units in this translation process. Goodman & Caramazza (1986a, 1986b) analysed the errors made by two patients spelling

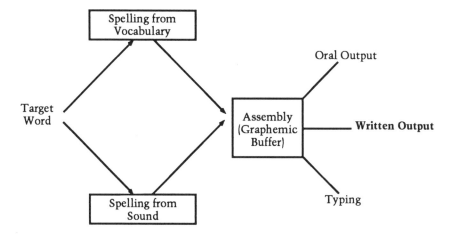

Figure 11.6.   A basic model of the two-route model of spelling.

by sound and argued that translation was between single sounds (i.e. phonemes: see Chapters 6 and 9) and letters. For example, the word *clamp* has five distinct sounds corresponding to the letters "c," "l," "a," "m," and "p," and the word *ship* has three phonemes corresponding to the letters "sh," "i," and "p." They suggested that the target word would be broken up into its constituent sounds, and each individual sound would be mapped onto the appropriate letter or letter cluster (technically, this is termed *phoneme–grapheme correspondence* processing).

For other patients, the situation appears to be more complex. In a study of a single case (K.T.), Baxter & Warrington (1987, 1988) argued that he used spelling-to-sound correspondences which "spanned" two or more word sounds (phonemes). They conducted a detailed analysis of his correct and incorrect spellings, taking account of units larger than a single sound. For example the sound "k" as in "can" is ambiguous since it can be written with four different spelling patterns, namely, "k," "c," "ck," and "ch." However, when there is an initial cluster sound "cl" then it is almost always spelled with a "c": the letter combination "kl" almost never occurs in this first position (e.g., *clamp, cling, clear,* but note: *Kleenex!*). The patient (K.T.) used this relatively complex letter-cluster and letter-position "rule" and almost never made errors on a word-initial "cl" (*click, clamp,* and *cleft* were correct, but *quick → kwic, trek → treck, knock → nok,* and *rank → wrank*). Such evidence indicates that, for this patient at least, spelling by sound uses correspondences which are larger than single phoneme-to-letter mappings.

Vocabulary-Based Spelling   Patients reliant on their spelling vocabulary are unable to spell words by using sound–spelling rules. In the extreme case such patients might have a virtually intact spelling vocabulary but at the same time be unable to spell simple, easy non-words. However, such a "dysgraphia" would probably pass undetected on most routine clinical assessments. Patients typically come to the clinician's attention when the spelling vocabulary itself is also somewhat impaired. For all reported patients there has been evidence of difficulty in spelling uncommon words and words from particular grammatical or semantic categories (e.g., Shallice, 1981; Bub & Kertesz, 1982b; Roeltgen & Heilman, 1984; Baxter & Warrington, 1985; Kremin, 1987).

For some patients, impairments affecting subcategories of the spelling vocabulary broadly parallel those observed in auditory comprehension (e.g., Shallice, 1981). The question arises as to whether there is a necessary relationship between spoken comprehension and spelling. Some patients have been reported who appear to show relative preservation of spelling in the absence of spoken-word comprehension. In a clinical report, Yamadori & Albert (1973) described a patient who was unable to comprehend the names of indoor objects but was nevertheless able to spell them. Thus when asked to point to a chair the patient responded "c,h,a,i,r, . . . c,h,a,i,r" "I have to double check that word later, I don't know." Further evidence for the dissociation between spelling and spoken-word comprehension has been provided in a number of single case studies (Saffran & Marin, 1977; Roeltgen, Rothi, & Heilman, 1986; Kohn & Friedman, 1986; Patterson, 1986). These studies raises the possibility that the spelling vocabulary is independent of auditory comprehension.

The evidence for independence of a vocabulary for comprehending the spoken word and a vocabulary for spelling is strengthened by the converse dissociation. Patients may retain the ability to comprehend the very words which they are unable to spell. The patient (J.C.) described by Bub & Kertesz (1982a) was unable to spell by sound and made numerous semantic errors in spelling (see above). He also showed a category effect, with function words and abstract words being significantly worse than concrete words. However, his comprehension was considered to be intact. A comparable dissociation was documented in the patient (G.O.S.) described by Baxter & Warrington (1985, see above). She could clearly comprehend the verbs which she was unable to spell.

The category-specific gaps in these patients' spelling vocabularies indicate that their spelling deficit arises following successful comprehension of the target. In this regard, such cases parallel those with category-specific anomias and dyslexias with intact comprehension (see Chapters 7 and 10). Their deficit could arise either retrieving the appropriate spelling from the spelling vocabulary system or perhaps (as argued by Baxter & Warrington) within the spelling vocabulary itself.

Disorders of Spelling Assembly   However intact the spelling system is, it would be quite useless without some means of producing the target word. Patients with a disorder in spelling assembly can be thought of as showing a disorder at a stage in processing which is intermediate between retrieval and production of spelling. It has been argued that in order to translate between the spelling vocabulary and either oral or written spelling it is necessary to hold information in a temporary memory store, the spelling, or "graphemic," buffer. It is suggested that this store is required to allow for a time lag between rapid retrieval of a spelling and the slower process of spelling production.

Certain patients have been described whose impairments appear to reflect a deficit at this level of processing. They make errors of letter order suggesting that the whole word has been retrieved but that crucial order information is lost during the course of writing or spelling the word aloud (Kinsbourne & Warrington, 1964b). Experimental studies of single cases with this type of disorder have shown that there are marked effects of target length and, furthermore, that there are serial position effects (see above Figs. 11.1 and 11.2). In some patients the serial position effects are an exaggeration of the normal pattern, with errors predominating in the middle of words. Caramazza and his colleagues (e.g., 1987, 1989) have argued that this type of serial position curve is to be expected if there is an impairment retrieving information from the buffer store. Indeed, they drew an analogy between these serial position effects and those which are observed in auditory "short-term memory" (see Chapter 13).

A spelling deficit confined to the oral modality has been described in one case (Kinsbourne & Warrington, 1965). This patient's deficit has been interpreted as one which affected a specific processing system that is required for spelling aloud (see above). Why one should need such a functionally useless spelling "route" (except perhaps as a relic of school training) is not obvious!

Neglect Spelling—Patients sometimes report using a "visualisation" strategy for spelling (Shallice, 1981). Hillis & Caramazza (1989) have suggested that this may involve "reading" from the memory buffer store which is used in producing spellings. A marked left–right gradient was apparent in a case (O.R.F.) reported by Baxter & Warrington (1983). Regardless of the direction in which he attempted to spell words (his preference was backwards!), he made a very significant number of mistakes on the word beginnings. This patient did *not* show a neglect pattern in his reading of single words, indicating that the deficit cannot simply be interpreted as a complex secondary effect of neglect dyslexia. Neglect spelling has since been reported in three further cases (Barbut & Gazzaniga, 1987; Hillis & Caramazza, 1989). It has been interpreted as evidence for an interaction between attentional processes and spelling procedures. This interaction might occur at the level of *access* to a spelling vocabulary or in *retrieval* from a buffer store required for spelling assembly, or perhaps even in secondary "imagery" procedures (see also Chapter 4).

Disorders of Writing

Patients may have a disorder which is specific to writing with preservation of their oral spelling. This disorder is often considered as a specific subtype of the apraxic disorders of voluntary movement (see Chapter 5). The relationship between writing and other types of voluntary action was explored in a group study by Hécaen, Angelergues, & Douzenis (1963). The majority of patients diagnosed as "apraxic" were also agraphic. However, in five patients with apraxia, writing was considered to be intact. The converse dissociation, namely of impaired writing and preservation of other "praxic" abilities was more common. The impairment of praxic skills with preservation of writing has been documented in some detail in a single case (M.D.) by Cipolotti & Denes (1989). The patient was unable to imitate simple hand postures, and even the most elementary graphic copying tasks were beyond his capacity, nevertheless his spontaneous writing and writing to dictation were preserved. Most remarkably in this case, despite preservation of fluent writing there was a complete failure to copy letters or words (see Fig. 11.7).

Figure 11.7. Example of relative preservation of writing and impairment of copying in a patient (M.D.) with a severe apraxia (Cipolotti & Denes, 1989).

The converse dissociation, namely the impairment of writing with preserved praxis, has been more frequently described. There are at least four cases on record with impairment in writing in whom other types of voluntary action were relatively well preserved. The patient described by Zangwill (1954) was able to imitate meaningless hand movements and could pantomime the use of objects; Rothi & Heilman (1983) and Coslett, Rothi, Valenstein, & Heilman (1986) described two further cases with a profound impairment in writing who were able to produce gestures and pantomimes on command. Perhaps the most

Figure 11.8. Free drawing of a cat by a patient (I.D.T.) with a grave ideational dysgraphia.

clearcut example of this dissociation is the patient (I.D.T.) described by Baxter & Warrington (1986). The patient was quite unable to write but nevertheless produced relatively good drawings (see Fig. 11.8).

Patients with impairments in writing show a variety of different characteristics. Their errors may range from substitutions of alternative real letters in writing (e.g., Rothi & Heilman, 1981) through to cases who are unable to produce anything except a "squiggle" when attempting to write (e.g., Margolin & Wing, 1983). Patients also differ in the extent to which they benefit from having a model to copy from. For some cases, copying is well preserved, and even fluent, despite impairment in the voluntary recall of the actions necessary to form letters ("ideational agraphia"). In other cases, copying may be as impaired as spontaneous writing (Kinsbourne & Rosenfeld, 1974). These types of deficit by no means exhaust the disorders which are seen clinically; some patients appear to have lost the automaticity of their writing (Dubois *et al.*, 1969), whereas others appear to have a selective loss of particular letter forms (e.g., lower case letters, Patterson & Wing, 1989).

Is it possible to go beyond a mere taxonomy of writing disorders and develop a theoretical framework? A number of information-processing frameworks have been proposed which attempt to systematise the diverse types of writing impairment (e.g., Ellis, 1982, 1988; Margolin,

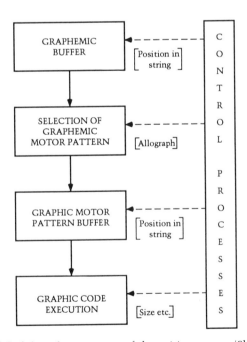

Figure 11.9. Model of the subcomponents of the writing process (Shallice, 1988).

1984; Shallice, 1988; see Fig. 11.9). Central to these models is the concept of established sets of motor programmes for writing (graphemic motor patterns in Shallice's terminology). Patients may fail to select the appropriate graphemic motor pattern, or they may have difficulty in implementing a skilled writing action (disorders at the "Buffer" and "Execution stages of Shallice's model). This analysis has much in common with the framework proposed for other disorders of voluntary action: the apraxias (see Chapter 5). Such accounts would appear to offer a potentially powerful framework for analysing acquired disorders of writing.

Conclusion

A major distinction has been drawn in this chapter between disorders of the spelling process and disorders of writing. Disorders of spelling take three major forms. The "linguistic" or central spelling deficits reflect impairment in either a sound-based or a vocabulary-based spelling "route." The impairments which have been classified here as disorders of spelling assembly can be thought of as affecting a stage which is subsequent to these central processes but prior to the actions of writing. The disorders of writing may be viewed as a highly specific form of apraxia. However, they dissociate from other impairments of voluntary action and have been thought of as implicating a specific set of stored motor patterns for writing.

12

Calculation

Introduction

Although competence in dealing with abstract mathematical concepts is only achieved by a relatively few, highly educated members of the population, a basic facility with calculation is achieved by most people before leaving school. This skill is, in fact, a prerequisite for independent existence in our culture. For example, the ability to count, add, subtract, and multiply is essential for using money, the calendar, and measuring instruments. Perhaps because of their routine application, the vast majority of adults have attained a considerable degree of sophistication in the skills of arithmetic and calculation. The application of basic arithmetic skills is constantly required and, as such, they are possibly even more central to most people's daily lives than are the skills of reading and writing.

The ability to perform routine arithmetic calculations breaks down selectively in patients with cerebral lesions. In early attempts to classify disorders of language and literacy, a disorder of calculation was not identified as a coherent pattern of deficit in its own right. Rather it was viewed as a direct consequence of disturbed language or reading skills. The first systematic investigation of disorders of calculation was reported by Henschen (1919). He conducted an investigation of 110 patients with cerebral lesions and subsequently reviewed an even larger series of patients' impairments of calculation (305 cases), drawing both on published cases and on his own patients (Henschen, 1920). He noted the frequent (although by no means invariant) co-occurrence of language and reading difficulties with impairments in calculation. In view of these dissociations Henschen argued that a specific impairment of calculation could be identified, which he termed *acalculia*.

The concept of acalculia was refined by Berger (1926). He drew a distinction between primary and secondary acalculic deficits on the basis of his investigations of a series of 18 patients with relatively selective impairments of calculation. In 15, calculation difficulties could be attributed to disorders of language, reading, memory, or attention. Berger considered the impairment of calculation in these patients to be a secondary, rather than a true or primary, acalculia. A primary acalculia was identified in the remaining three cases in whom the processes of calculation themselves were impaired, a disorder Berger termed *anarithmetria*.

Empirical Characteristics

Hécaen, Angelergues, & Houillier (1961) proposed a tripartite classification of the acalculias. In this classification they distinguished a failure of calculation *per se* from impairments in other aspects of number processing.

1. *Anarithmetria*, a primary deficit in calculation corresponding to that identified in Berger's classification.
2. *Alexic and/or agraphic acalculia*, in which failure on tests was attributable to specific deficits in reading or writing numbers.
3. *Spatial acalculia*, in which errors arose because of spatial disorganisation of written calculations (see Fig. 12.1).

Hécaen *et al.* (1961) documented all three types of impairment. Specific anarithmetria was less common than a calculation disorder due to dyslexia, dysgraphia, or spatial difficulties. However, alexic and

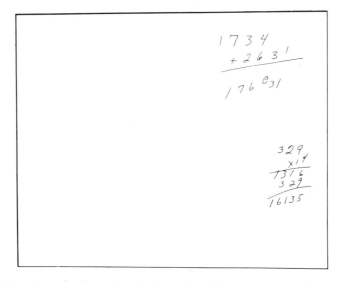

Figure 12.1. Example of spatial acalculia. (Adapted from Hécaen & Albert, 1978.)

agraphic acalculia could be high selective and therefore constituted a form of "primary" or number-specific impairment. Such disorders were documented in 10% of cases. Spatial acalculia could take the form of neglect of numbers on one side of the calculation or failure to maintain spatial organisation of the numbers in their appropriate columns. It appeared to be a truly "secondary" disorder in that it occurred in the context of spatial impairments on a range of visual tasks (Hécaen et al., 1961).

Even within the primary acalculias, which are the focus of this chapter, a range of dissociations have been documented. Specific deficits in number processing can be considered from the perspective of whether they implicate disorders at the level of *comprehension* of written or spoken numbers, disorders in the *retrieval* of written or spoken numbers, or a deficit in the *basic operations* of calculation themselves.

Comprehension and Retrieval of Numbers

Spoken Number Comprehension   The selective impairment of spoken number comprehension has only been quantitatively documented in a single case reported by Warrington (1982c). The patient (S.T.H.) was gravely impaired in the comprehension of spoken numbers, having difficulties with judging which of two spoken numbers was the larger or smaller (e.g., "Is nine greater or smaller than three?"). Remarkably, her ability to to make comparative judgments of visually presented Arabic numerals was intact. Thus she was able to point to the larger of two written numbers (e.g., 7 or 9) perfectly. She also failed on simple spoken tests of number knowledge such as "How many toes on each foot?". Her difficulties could not be explained in terms of a generalised deficit in comprehending the spoken word since she was able to achieve an above-average score on a standardised test of auditory vocabulary (Peabody Picture Vocabulary).

Written Number Comprehension   The impairment of written number comprehension [both in Arabic form (e.g., 5) and number words (e.g., five)] can occur as a selective deficit, with other types of written word or symbol being adequately comprehended (Hécaen et al., 1961). Within the domain of written number processing there is evidence of further dissociations: the comprehension of Arabic numerals may dissociate from the ability to comprehend written number words (e.g., 7 vs. seven). This dissociation has been reported by McCloskey & Caramazza (1987). One case (H.Y.) was unable to judge comparative sizes of written numbers but was able to comprehend Arabic numerals. Impairment in reading Arabic numerals or written number words may also dissociate from the ability to read arithmetic signs (e.g., +, ×, −). Hécaen et al. (1961) found 16 patients with impaired ability to read arithmetic signs but preserved ability to read numbers. Ferro & Bothello

(1980) documented another two patients with this pattern of difficulty.

Retrieval of Numbers Disorders in retrieving number names do not necessarily implicate a deficit in using these same numbers in oral calculation. Benson & Denckla (1969) reported a patient who made errors in reading numbers aloud and who had difficulty in retrieving the correct number word to answer either an oral or a written calculation. She was unable to write the appropriate number or speak it; her errors were "wrong" numbers rather than a simple failure to respond. Nevertheless, she was capable of selecting the correct answer to a calculation when given a choice of visually presented numerals. For example, when given the written problem "4 + 5" the patient said "eight," wrote "5," and chose "9"!

Alexia for Numbers McCloskey & Caramazza (1987) identified two qualitatively distinct impairments in Arabic number reading tasks. Some patients made errors involving the order or the magnitude of number strings but read the actual number names correctly (see Table 12.1, case J.E.). Other patients were impaired in naming individual Arabic numerals, but showed preserved knowledge of the way that numbers were organised in terms of thousands, hundreds, tens, and units (see Table 12.1, case A.T.).

Calculation

Evidence for a fractionation of computational skills was presented by Cohn (1961); he described eight cases whose disorders of calculation were all somewhat different. His patients were all tested on written multiplication tasks. He observed that there were two common sub-

Table 12.1   Alexia for Numbers[a]

Stimulus	J.E.	A.T.
5900	five thousand ninety	nine thousand nine hundred
750	seven thousand five hundred	seven hundred fifty
3108	three thousand one hundred eight	three thousand one hundred six
602	six thousand two	six hundred three
5600	five thousand sixty	five thousand six hundred
8900	eight thousand ninety	eight thousand eight hundred
8360	eight thousand three hundred sixty	nine thousand two hundred sixty
6030	six thousand three hundred	six thousand thirty
163	one hundred sixty-three	nine hundred sixty-two
1200	one thousand twenty	one thousand two hundred
1034	one thousand thirty-four	two thousand thirty-four
5097	five thousand nine hundred seven	five thousand ninety-seven

[a]Example of errors made in reading arabic numbers aloud. Adapted from McCloskey & Caramazza (1987).

types of acalculic error. In one group of patients Cohn considered that the deficit was attributable to failure to recall the overlearned facts of arithmetic tables. For example, one case had "forgotten" the multiplication tables, but was nevertheless capable of addition and subtraction (albeit with errors in "carrying" operations). The second group of patients showed a secondary (spatial) acalculia.

The specific impairment of arithmetical skills, in a patient with normal number comprehension, was documented in a single case (D.R.C.) by Warrington (1982c). Although the patient had previously worked as a consultant physician and research scientist he was no longer able to add, subtract, or multiply with any semblance of efficiency. He described his calculation skills as having "lost all automaticity." He also commented that he frequently had to reach the solution of arithmetic problems by a laborious counting process. His performance was very slow and he had a significant error rate, particularly when he attempted to work at speed. Despite these impairments the patient's ability to retrieve and apply appropriate arithmetical steps was intact. Indeed, given time, he was able to perform complex calculations utilising the correct operations in their correct order. For example, he could solve three of the four most difficult items on the WAIS arithmetic test (e.g., "A man earns £60 a week. If 15% is withheld for taxes, how much does he receive each week?").

His response times were systematically recorded on a series of tests designed to evaluate his ability to perform simple additions, subtractions, and multiplications. Any response to these calculations taking over 2 seconds was regarded as being of "long latency" (on the basis of the performance of a control group of consultant physicians matched for age). Overall there was a very high incidence of long-latency responses. For example, on the easiest task, that of adding all combinations of numbers between 1 and 9 the incidence of his long-latency responses was as high as 33%. On a more demanding addition task, (using all combinations of numbers between 1 and 9 and 11 to 19,) his error rate and the number of long-latency responses increased (see Fig. 12.2). He had particular difficulty when the smaller number in the addition was presented first (e.g., 4 + 12). This increase in difficulty reflects an exaggeration of the normal pattern of slowed responses with this unconventional presentation of an addition problem. The patient never gave an impermissible response, and indeed many of his answers were good approximations to the target (see Fig. 12.3). This pattern of deficit has since been replicated in other patients (Benton, 1987; Caramazza & McCloskey, 1987).

The evidence for selective impairments affecting the steps and procedures of arithmetic is less secure. Such disorders are however, relatively common in the context of more pervasive difficulties with problem solving (Luria, 1966; see Chapter 16). Caramazza & McCloskey (1987) have given a brief clinical account of two cases who

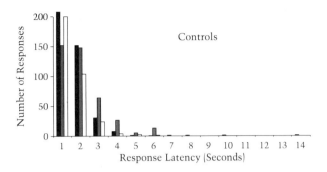

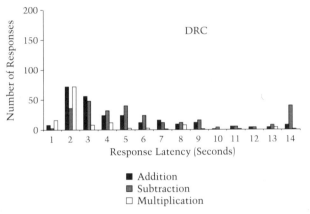

■ Addition
■ Subtraction
□ Multiplication

Figure 12.2. Comparison of controls and an acalculic patient (D.R.C.) in their speed of response in oral arithmetic tasks. (Adapted from Warrington, 1982c.)

were specifically poor at operations such as "carrying" in addition and shifting the intermediate products in long multiplication.

Anatomical Considerations

Comprehension and Retrieval of Numbers

Henschen (1919) implicated the left parietal lobe, and in particular the angular gyrus, in impairments of reading and writing numbers. Hécaen et al. (1961) conducted a retrospective survey of a large series of patients with posterior lesions of either or both cerebral hemispheres. Of the patients with unilateral lesions, left parietal damage was associated with alexic & agraphic acalculia.

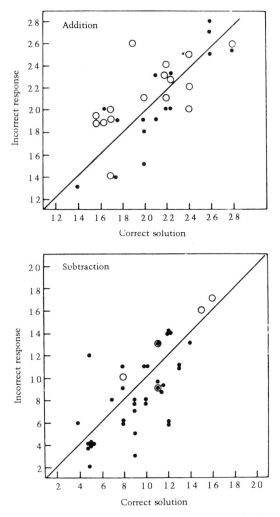

Figure 12.3. Relationship between target and response in an acalculic patient (D.R.C.) (Warrington, 1982c).

Calculation

Group studies have consistently found that impaired calculation is associated with damage to the posterior sectors of the left hemisphere (e.g. Levin & Spiers, 1985). Hécaen *et al.* (1961) reported a high incidence of calculation impairments in patients with postrolandic lesions of the left hemisphere. Grafman, Passafiume, Faglioni, & Boller (1982) used a test of written arithmetic with patients whose reading and writing of numbers was intact. They found that posterior lesions of the left hemisphere (as defined by the presence of a visual-field defect) gave rise to greater impairment. This held true even when scores on a demanding test of sentence comprehension were taken into account (the Token Test: see Chapter 8). Jackson & Warrington (1986) developed a graded difficulty test of oral addition and subtraction. Their results were very similar to those of Grafman *et al.* (1982). Once again, patients with left-hemisphere damage were significantly more impaired than patients with right-hemisphere lesions, all of whom scored within the range of the controls. Warrington, James, & Maciejewski (1986) reported a retrospective study of 656 patients with localised unilateral cerebral lesions who had been tested on the arithmetic subtest of the WAIS. They found that patients with left-hemisphere lesions were significantly more impaired than those with right-hemisphere lesions. Moreover, within the left-hemisphere group, patients with left parietal involvement were more impaired than were those without parietal involvement.

The findings from single case studies are all entirely consistent with these group investigations in implicating damage to the posterior sectors of the left hemisphere, and most especially the left parietal lobe, as being crucial in the aetiology of disorders of calculation. Henschen's (1920) review of selected cases with acalculia emphasised the role of the left hemisphere. He also went somewhat further in contending that lesions to structures in the region of the boundary between the parietal and temporal lobes were common to these patients. A lesion involving the left parietal lobe but encroaching on the left occipital lobe was documented in a single case (D.R.C.) with a highly specific deficit in calculation (Warrington, 1982c). A similar localisation was reported for a case described by Benton (1987).

Theoretical Considerations

Calculation is a complex and multicomponent skill. It is necessary first to be able to comprehend the elements of a calculation (numbers, arithmetic signs), second, to actually compute a solution, and third, to retrieve the correct number word for an answer. The comprehension and retrieval of numbers are in some sense peripheral to the operations and procedures of "calculation." In this regard, they are comparable to the relationship between the comprehension and retrieval of words and the ability to solve verbal problems. Failure to comprehend or retrieve number words can be most constructively viewed as highly specific aphasic, dyslexic, or dysgraphic deficits. Indeed the selective impairment and preservation of these skills have been cited as evidence for category-specific impairments of verbal knowledge (see Chapters 6 and 7). Goodglass, Klein, Carey, & Jones (1966) established that both comprehension and naming of numbers could be selectively spared or selectively impaired in aphasic patients (see Figs. 6.4 and 7.4).

Comprehension and Production of Numbers

Although there are a number of interesting clinical observations on disorders of number comprehension (see above) the data has not been integrated into any coherent theoretical account. Whilst there are pointers toward multiple dissociations in comprehension of written numbers, spoken numbers, and Arabic numerals, this evidence is only tentative. The evidence for a dissociation between the comprehension and retrieval of numbers is more secure. As with other forms of "word-retrieval deficit" (e.g., aphasia, dyslexia, and dysgraphia), patients may be able to comprehend numbers which they are unable to produce (Benson & Denckla, 1969; McCloskey & Caramazza, 1987). However, the theoretical relationships between different types of number "production" and different types of number naming task (with the various permutations of Arabic, Roman, and alphabetic notation as well as speech) have yet to be articulated (see McCloskey & Caramazza, 1987).

Detailed error analyses have been conducted based on patients' responses to tasks requiring them to read Arabic numbers. In reading a number such as "2302" some cases make errors of number order and magnitude, whereas others make errors on the number words (see above). These two types of impairment have been termed the *syntactic* (or number sequence rule) and the *lexical* (number word) subtypes.

Alexia for Numbers: Syntax   Although the term *syntax* is probably most familiar when used in the context of sentences, analogous conventional syntactic rules are also applied in multinumeral strings. Thus it is necessary to know that Arabic numerals are organised from left to right, with the leftmost position representing the largest power of 10 in the decimal system. The symbol "0," for example, has the status of raising the preceding numeral by a power of 10, and only in the case where there is no preceding numeral does it have the status of "zero." Failure to take account of these rules results in errors of number magnitude (i.e., with preservation of number names) or number order when multidigit numbers are presented. This pattern of deficit implicates a disorder in processing the conventional "zero" rules and ordering rules of number organisation, that is, a failure of number syntax (Deloche & Seron, 1987; McCloskey & Caramazza, 1987).

Alexia for Number Names   Other patients do not make errors of syntax, but do make errors of number word substitution. McCloskey, Sokol, & Goodman (1986) investigated the naming errors made by a single case (H.Y.) and observed a remarkable pattern in his substitutions (see Fig. 12.4). Numbers having their values in the range 1 to 9 were preferentially substituted with other "1 to 9" numbers; numbers having "teen" values were substituted by other numbers in the range 10 to 19. Numbers in the range 20 to 90 were also interchanged.

McCloskey *et al.* argued that multidigit strings are first processed for

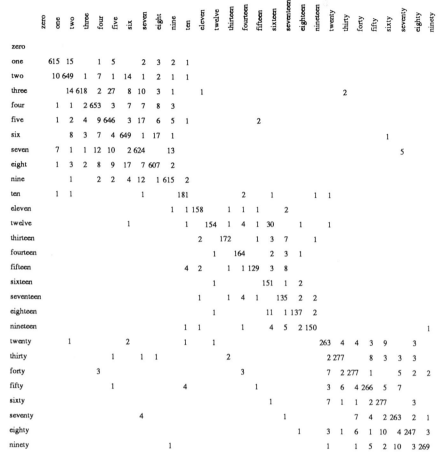

Figure 12.4. Number of word-substitution errors showing the one, teens, and tens effect in an acalculic patient (H.Y.) (McCloskey *et al.*, 1986).

their syntactic structure, and number names are then produced in the appropriate "slots" within this basic framework. The patient's errors occurred in retrieving the appropriate number items to fill the "slots." The highly constrained pattern of substitution errors was considered to reflect the organisation of the number-production system into three major categories, namely "ones," "teens," and "tens." Two further cases with this error pattern have since been described (McCloskey & Caramazza, 1987).

Disorders of Calculation

Henschen's (1920) pioneering analysis of acquired disorders of calculation clearly differentiated them from the comprehension and production numbers. He viewed the process of calculation as reflecting the operation of a unitary "faculty." This unitary view of the processes of calculation persisted for many years, the major issues being those of how this process should be conceptualised. For some writers, the fundamental deficit was considered to be one in the ordered spatial representation of numbers (e.g., Lange, 1933). This viewpoint was based on formal mathematical analyses of the organisation of the number system in which numbers were viewed as being spatially distributed. Thus the numbers "two" and "seven" can be thought of as being located on a spatial line of numbers, and the processes of addition might consist of spatial manipulations resulting in an increment in the spatial extent of the number line. Patients who had generalised spatial difficulties were noted to perform poorly on tests of written arithmetic, and this was considered as supporting the notion of a central spatial representation of the number system. However, this is far from convincing evidence.

Hécaen and his colleagues (1961, 1962) clearly differentiated visuospatial disorders affecting the performance of written arithmetic from primary deficits in calculation. Patients with general spatial difficulties were impaired in the analysis and execution of written arithmetic problems (e.g., Fig. 12.1). However, patients with a primary acalculia showed impaired calculation despite having intact spatial skills. Indeed the anatomical evidence is consistent with there being a double dissociation between impairments on spatial tasks (associated with right-hemisphere dysfunction: see Chapter 4) and failure on tests of spoken arithmetic (associated with left-hemisphere lesions: see above).

Calculation does not appear to be a unitary "faculty": Within the primary acalculias a broad subdivision can be drawn between (1) knowledge of arithmetic procedures, and (2) knowledge of arithmetic facts. By arithmetic procedures is meant the operations required for carrying out a specific calculation. By arithmetic facts is meant a vocabulary of number combinations (e.g., that $4 + 5 = 9$, that $10 - 1 = 9$, and that $3 \times 3 = 9$).

There is only sparse evidence for the selective impairment of arithmetic procedures, i.e., in the organisation of the steps and sequences of calculation. Cohn (1961a) cited one convincing example. The patient, when given the written calculation "963×69," carried out the steps in reverse order but obtained the appropriate intermediate products and wrote her solutions in the reverse order making only minor errors. Caramazza & McCloskey (1987) provided a further example of this type of failure (case D.L.).

The evidence for impaired arithmetic facts is more secure. One case with a severe acalculia (D.R.C.) was capable of defining arithmetic operations precisely (e.g., "Subtraction is the reduction of the magnitude of a particular number by the magnitude stated of another number and that is it!") (Warrington, 1982c). Given sufficient time he was capable of performing multidigit and multistep calculations and solving complex problems. However, he was unable to add, subtract, or multiply with any semblance of efficiency.

Warrington considered these deficits from the perspective of Groen & Parkman's (1972) model of calculation. Parkman & Groen (1971) noted that children took far longer to add 5 + 4 as compared with 5 + 2 (approximately half a second per increment). Similarly, in subtraction, 7 − 3 took longer than 7 − 2. In adults, the increments in response latency (as a function of the size of the addend or subtrahend) were smaller by a different order of magnitude (20 ms per increment). This led to Groen & Parkman's (1972) "retrieval–counting" model of arithmetic. This states that in skilled adult calculation most response times reflect direct access to memorised information. On those occasions where direct access fails, the subject reverts to a slow "counting" process which is operative in the early stages of the acquisition of the skill.

Warrington observed that the proportion of long-latency responses in her patient (D.R.C.) was of a different order of magnitude than those of a control group (see Fig. 12.2). Following Groen & Parkman it was hypothesised that in the case of this patient there was a failure of direct access to the stored facts of arithmetic. When direct access failed, a slow, counting-like procedure was adopted. In this respect he resembled young children. For young children a vocabulary of arithmetic facts have yet to be acquired, but in the case of the acalculic patient (D.R.C.) the ability to utilise these facts was impaired.

In an analysis of the accuracy and latency of the patient's responses it was found that on some occasions he was able to retrieve "facts" quickly and accurately. however, on other occasions the identical calculation was carried out slowly and sometimes inaccurately. Since the same arithmetic facts could be retrieved on some occasions but not on others, it was argued that his deficit was attributable to a failure to access the facts of arithmetic rather than to their loss or degradation. A similar degree of inconsistency was observed on addition, subtraction, and multiplication tasks. (For further discussion of access disorders see Chapters 6 and 10.)

Conclusion

The ability to read numbers appears to be quite a different skill from that required in reading words and letters. It appears that at least some of the discontinuities in the Arabic decimal system used in our culture are mirrored in the discontinuities observed in patients with brain lesions. For English-speaking patients this is particularly striking in the distinction to be observed between the numbers 1 and 9, the "teens," and the "tens."

With regard to the manipulation of numbers it has been suggested that numeracy represents a specific category of semantic knowledge

(Warrington, 1982c). It is a specific subdomain which is analogous to other established knowledge bases (e.g., verbal and visual semantic knowledge; see Chapters 2 and 6). In some acalculic patients subcategories of this system may be inoperative, inaccessible, or degraded. For any individual this vocabulary of arithmetic facts and arithmetic procedures will range from the most basic through to a rich and elaborate knowledge base.

13

Short-Term Memory

Introduction

There is a clear limit to the amount of verbal material which we can retain in memory for long enough to reproduce it *exactly*. For example, most people can remember about seven (plus or minus two) random digits, but only four or five random words or letters. This restriction, in what has become known as the "span of apprehension," was first investigated in the nineteenth century. In 1887, Jacobs reported a novel experiment on the auditory span of apprehension in which he asked people to write down from memory sequences of numbers which he had read aloud to them. He found that the maximum span of the normal individual was about seven or eight. He also noted that there was an increase in the size of the individual's span between the ages of 8 and 19, suggesting that it might in some way be linked with the growth of intellectual abilities which occurred at the same time. Subsequently, Binet & Simon (1908) incorporated the digit-span task in their tests of intelligence, and it is still a component of most measures of verbal intellectual abilities (e.g., the WAIS).

More recently, performance on span tasks has been interpreted as a measure of *short-term memory*. In the experimental study of short-term memory it has become conventional to differentiate between limitations on *capacity* and limitations on *duration*. Studies of capacity have been concerned with the limitation on the number of items or amount of information which can be retained and reproduced following a single presentation. Investigations of the duration of short-term memory have focused on the rate at which material is forgotten in the absence of conscious attention and rehearsal.

Empirical Characteristics

Auditory–Verbal Short-Term Memory

Luria, Sokolov, & Klimkowski (1967) described two patients with a selective impairment in their ability to repeat spoken lists of numbers, words, and syllables. Indeed, their spans were only reliable for one item from these different types of list. Luria *et al.* noted that the patients tended to reproduce the last item in the series first and were unable to recall the earlier items. Thus one case (B.), when given the spoken words *house, night* to repeat, could only recall *night.* This tendency persisted, even when the patient was instructed to repeat the items in their correct order: "He complained that it is only the last element he can retain, and that the former elements disappeared from his memory." When the same material was presented visually the patients were more successful. Furthermore, under these conditions they attempted to reproduce the information in the order in which it was presented.

Following Luria *et al.*, Warrington & Shallice reported a series of detailed studies of a single case (K.F.) who had a particularly limited span for auditory material (Warrington & Shallice, 1969; Shallice & Warrington, 1970; Shallice & Warrington, 1977b). Presented with single numbers, letters, and words, his repetition was virtually error free, but when the load was increased to two items there was a dramatic drop in his ability to recall the material (see Table 13.1). Typically, he would repeat one of the two items correctly and then omit or make a substitution error on the other. He had equivalent difficulty on a task in which speech production was not required. Presented with one letter he was error free in pointing to the target in an array of letters. When presented with two items his performance deteriorated. However, his span improved substantially when numbers and letters were presented visually (at the same rate as the spoken stimuli) (see Table 13.1). Also, when given a series of "blocks" of 10 trials of repeating two spoken digits, his performance deteriorated from 75% correct on the first trial to 35% correct on the last trial. The impairment of auditory–verbal span has since been documented in a large and growing number

Table 13.1 Repetition of Numbers and Letters Presented Auditorially and Visually (Case K.F.)[a]

	Auditory presentation			Visual presentation		
	1 Item	2 Items	3 Items	1 Item	2 Items	3 Items
Numbers						
Items correct	20/20	28/40	37/60	20/20	39/40	48/60
Strings correct	20	12	6	20	19	10
Letters						
Items correct	19/20	21/40	26/60	20/20	37/40	48/60
Strings correct	19	7	2	20	17	11

[a]Adapted from Warrington & Shallice (1969).

of cases. Caplan & Waters (1990) provide a detailed account which compares the abilities of some 16 cases.

Capacity   For normal subjects, the capacity of short-term memory (i.e., the number of items which can be immediately recalled exactly) is not determined by the physical properties of the stimulus. Rather it is affected by the subjects' ability to "chunk" or "recode" it into higher-order units. For example, the letters "h," "c," "a," "t," "y" would load the capacity of the system to a similar (or even greater) extent than the word *five, one, four, eight, six,* despite there being more acoustic information in the number string. Similarly, a string of random words would load the system to a greater extent than a meaningful sentence (e.g., *far, house, light, got* vs. *Children like playing games.*).

Patients' repetition of lists of random stimuli has typically been used as an index of their short-term memory capacity. Such measures have permitted clinicians and researchers alike to actually cite measurements of the capacity of this system. Patients are cited as having "a span of 1" or "a span of 3.5 items." However, it has emerged that whilst span for lists is a useful and reliable index, span for sentences cannot be so clearly defined. Saffran & Marin (1975) noted that a patient (I.L.) could repeat some sentences which were considerably longer than her reduced (3.6 item) digit span. When errors in sentence repetition occurred, they were close approximations to the target sentence and retained its gist. Thus the patient repeated, "The residence was located in a peaceful neighbourhood" as "The residence was situated in a quiet district."

Patients have been reported whose "sentence span" is up to seven times as long as their "list span." A patient (O.R.F.) who was only able to repeat one list item reliably could repeat six and seven word sentences with remarkable consistency, scoring 34/40 (McCarthy & Warrington, 1984). A subsequent investigation made a direct comparison between sentence and word-list repetition in two cases (R.A.N. and N.H.A.) with digit spans restricted to one item. The patients' ability to repeat six-word sentences was reliably better than their repetition of three words (in a predictable sequence) which were taken from the same sentence. Thus the patients were able to repeat the sentence "He took care with the law," but not *took, care, law* (see Table 13.2). Further investigation showed that their repetition of complete sentences was better than their repetition of incomplete sentences (e.g., "London is a very busy" vs. "London is a very busy city"). Whilst in standard list-span tasks a reduction in the length of the stimulus improved their performance, the opposite was true in the case of sentences (McCarthy & Warrington, 1987a).

The relative preservation of sentences as compared with short lists of digits or words was emphasised in these patients. It has also been shown that this relationship can be reversed. One patient (N.H.B.) whose repetition of lists was within the normal range (digit span of 5)

Table 13.2 Repetition of Sentences and Key Words in Two Span-Impaired Cases (R.A.N. and N.H.A.)[a]

	Case 1	Case 2
Complete sentence	55	60
Complete list	15	40
Key words in sentence	88	90
Key words in list	50	77

[a]Adapted from McCarthy & Warrington (1987a).

was impaired in repeating sentences. He had impaired comprehension of single words but was able to repeat lists regardless of whether he "knew" the words or had "lost" them from his vocabulary (see also Warrington, 1975). Like normal control subjects he had a smaller span for words than for digits and showed a reduced span for invented non-words. His list span therefore appeared to be determined by his prior experience of word sounds rather than their meaningfulness. By contrast, his repetition of sentences appeared to be determined by his ability to *comprehend* the constituent words: Meaningfulness was critical. When all the words were known to him he was able to repeat sentences of six and seven words in length (e.g., "Men sit in chairs all day long.") However if one word was unknown (e.g., *flag* in the sentence "The flag was coloured bright red.") he was only able to repeat the first words of the sentence and made sound-based errors on the remainder (e.g., "The blag was fullered with a right breg."). These findings suggest that whereas list span is dependent on the auditory "familiarity" of the stimulus superior sentence span demands intact comprehension of the sentence.

Duration Short-term memory is not only limited in terms of the amount of information which can be stored, but also in terms of its duration. Verbatim information appears to be retained for a relatively short time unless one is able to "rehearse" it. For example, when taking down an unfamiliar address or telephone number it is necessary to "say" the information to oneself, to mentally rehearse it, so that it will be retained for long enough to write the information down or dial a number.

The investigation of "forgetting" in short term memory gained considerable momentum as the result of the development of a technique for investigating the storage and decay of information. In what has become known as the *Brown–Petersen* task, the subject is presented with some material to be remembered and is then asked to perform a "distracting" task continuously for a set period of time (Pillsbury and Sylvester, 1940; Brown, 1958; Petersen & Petersen, 1959). The idea behind this technique is to prevent the subject from attending to or rehearsing information in short-term storage. Since rehearsal can boost memory (as in the above example of taking down an address or telephone number), an adequate measure of the absolute duration of short-term storage is dependent on eliminating such rehearsal strategies. Using the retention-with-distraction methodology, Petersen & Petersen were able to demonstrate that normal subjects forgot a significant proportion of "meaningless" information in less than a minute.

It has been established that patients with a reduced short-term memory capacity may also have an exceptionally transient storage of auditory–verbal information. They may be unable to retain even a single letter following a few seconds of interpolated activity (such as counting). Indeed, the clinical impression may be that if the patients had to cough they would forget the stimulus! Warrington & Shallice (1972) first documented this effect in their single case (K.F.). Although he could repeat single spoken letters without error, his performance deteriorated following as little as 5 seconds of distracting activity. There was no decrement with visual presentation of the same material. Although the patient's span improved somewhat over the course of their investigations, the identical pattern of results was later obtained with two-item lists (see Fig. 13.1). After relatively short delays there was a very significant drop in his scores following auditory presentation (but not, however, following visual presentation). Reduced span for verbal material together with extremely rapid forgetting following distraction has since been documented in a number of cases (e.g., J.B. and W.H., Warrington, Logue, & Pratt, 1971; P.V., Basso, Spinnler, Vallar, & Zanobia, 1982; M.C., Caramazza, Berndt, & Basili, 1983; M.K., Howard & Franklin, 1988; R.A.N. and N.H.A., McCarthy & Warrington, 1987a).

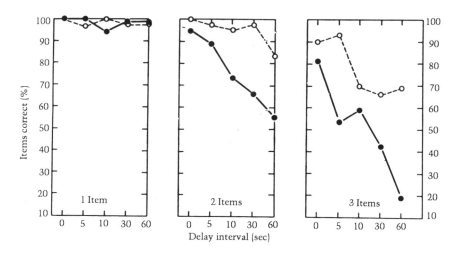

Figure 13.1. Forgetting of one-, two-, and three-item lists with auditory and visual presentation in a single case (K.F.). ○ = visual; ● = auditory (Adapted from Warrington & Shallice, 1972.)

Material-Specific Effects Span-impaired patients have difficulty in retaining auditory-verbal material. However, in at least some cases the retention of *non-verbal* auditory information may be preserved. Shallice & Warrington (1974) investigated the retention of meaningful sounds in two patients (J.B. and K.F.). Lists of 3 meaningful sounds were selected from a pool of 12 familiar sounds (e.g., footsteps, cow lowing, telephone ringing, bell chiming, etc.). The patients' performance was within normal limits on this task. Performance on nonverbal auditory-span tasks can be entirely normal even when the stimuli are meaningless. Friedrich, Glenn, & Marin (1984) tested a patient (E.A.) for recall of lists of tones which were presented rapidly (two per second). Her tone span was a very satisfactory 6 despite a digit span of less than 2. A further case (E.D.E.) has been tested on a series of computer-generated noises presented in lists of 4. The patient's ability to recognise a single probe item presented following the list was within the normal range (Berndt & Mitchum, 1990).

Visual Short-Term Memory

The evidence discussed so far has focused on impairments in retaining auditory material. In such cases the retention of visually presented material may be relatively spared. Selective impairments of visual short-term memory have also been documented. Furthermore (as was the case with auditory span), the deficit may be specific to particular types of material. Two main classes of material have been investigated—visual–verbal and visual–spatial.

Visual–Verbal Visual span for symbolic or otherwise meaningful stimuli can be tested by using brief exposure durations of stimulus arrays (of the order of 100–200 ms). The use of such brief exposure durations prevents subjects from "recoding" stimuli into a spoken form. Under these conditions normal subjects can report between four and five items. Kinsbourne & Warrington (1962b) investigated four patients who had particular difficulty in reporting more than one briefly presented visual stimulus. These patients were able to report single geometric shapes, silhouettes, and letters shown for 160 ms. However, when pairs of stimuli were presented, the patients could only report one of the items. The patients claimed that they could not recall a second item and made errors of omission and substitution. The impairment of this type of visual short-term memory has since been replicated in other patients (J.D.C., Warrington & Shallice, 1980; M.L., Shallice & Saffran, 1986).

Kinsbourne & Warrington dismissed any primary "perceptual" or "attentional" explanation of these effects since it did not appear to matter whether the stimuli were large or small or whether they were horizontally or vertically aligned. Remarkably, the patients' impairment was specific to verbal symbolic material and did not extend to spatial arrays of dots. They were normal in reporting the number of briefly presented scattered dots, performing accurately with arrays of up to six items.

It should be noted that auditory–verbal short-term memory can be within the normal range for patients with an impaired visual–verbal span. Subsequent corroboration of this dissociation may be drawn from a group study by Warrington & Rabin (1971) using tachistoscopic span tasks in which subjects were shown brief (160-ms) exposures of arrays of five simple symbolic stimuli. These included numbers, letters, and arrays of lines selected from a set of four possible targets [i.e., C, ∪, /, −]. A comparatively high incidence of impairment was noted on all these tasks. However, as in the single case studies, those patients who were impaired on the tachistoscopic span tasks did not necessarily have a comparable auditory digit-span deficit.

Visual–Spatial   The visual span tasks which have been discussed so far have all used stimuli which are meaningful or symbolic. These types of task appear to dissociate from tests which require the subject to retain information about the spatial organisation of stimuli. In one of the first tasks of this type, Alajouanine (1960) used arrays of three symbols which were shown briefly to patients. They were subsequently tested for recognition using a four-choice test in which the items remained the same but their spatial location was systematically varied.

Kimura (1963) also used brief-presentation procedures in a spatial task in which patients were required to report the number of dots which were presented in an array. (This test is substantially the same as the task which was performed normally by the patients with a selective impairment in visual–verbal span: see above). She found that some patients were impaired on this task. Similar findings were reported by Warrington & James (1967b), who noted that patients made errors both of underestimation and of overestimation (see also Chapter 4).

A different type of visual–spatial span task was developed by Corsi (Milner, 1971). In this task the subject is confronted with an array of nine identical blocks distributed so that there is no definable pattern in their arrangement (see Fig. 13.2). In presentation of the task, the examiner taps a sequence of blocks at a rate of one per second. The subject is required to reproduce the sequence immediately afterward. Sequences of between two and eight items are typically tested. Patients may show a selective impairment in performing this task with spans reduced to three items rather than the normal five or six. If the identical spatial arrangement of blocks is presented with numbers visible on the stimuli then patients may show normal levels of performance (De Renzi & Nichelli, 1975; De Renzi, Faglioni, & Previdi, 1977).

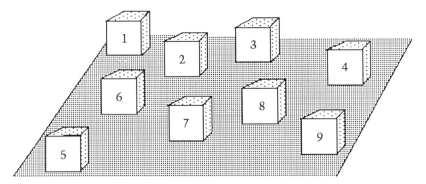

Figure 13.2.   Corsi Blocks Test showing array of blocks from the viewpoint of the examiner. (Adapted from Milner, 1971.)

Anatomical Considerations

The anatomical correlates of impaired auditory and visual span are reasonably well established.

Auditory–Verbal Short-Term Memory

Warrington *et al.* (1971) reported that for three cases (K.F., J.B., and W.H.) with severe auditory–verbal short-term memory deficits, the critical lesion site was in the inferior parietal lobe of the left hemisphere (see Fig. 13.3). Damage to the inferior parietal lobe of the left or language hemisphere has been demonstrated in all those subsequent cases of impaired auditory verbal span with focal lesions (e.g., I.L., Saffran & Marin, 1975; O.R.F. and R.A.N., McCarthy & Warrington, 1984).

De Renzi & Nichelli (1975) used a digit span task in a group study of patients with unilateral vascular lesions. They found that patients with left-hemisphere lesions were more impaired than right-hemisphere cases. However, reduced span was associated with lesions in both anterior and posterior sectors. Other group studies have used the digit-span subtest of the WAIS, which requires the subject to repeat lists of digits both forward (as in standard span tasks) and backward. In a study of 215 cases with unilateral cerebral lesions, McFie (1975) found that patients with left parietal lesions were most impaired on this task. A trend for patients with left parietal involvement to be the most impaired was also noted in a retrospective survey of 656 unilateral lesion cases (Warrington, James, & Maciejewski, 1986). In that study, the highest incidence of impairment was noted in cases with left temporoparietal lesions.

Overall, this data is broadly consistent with the observations on single cases with a selective impairment of span in indicating the importance of left parietal lobe lesions, particularly those affecting the inferior parietal lobe where it conjoins with the left temporal lobe.

Visual Short-Term Memory

Visual–Verbal   On the basis of clinical and radiological evidence Kinsbourne & Warrington (1962b) suggested that impairments on their visual–verbal span tasks implicated lesions of the left occipital lobe. This hypothesis was supported in an autopsy study of a single case with a visual span of apprehension which was reliable for only one item (Kinsbourne & Warrington, 1963b). The patient was found to have a small area of infarction in the inferior/anterior occipital lobe close to the junction with the left temporal lobe (see Fig. 13.3). In a subsequent case studied by Shallice & Saffran (1986), the C.T. scan showed focal damage to the left occipital lobe.

A group study has strengthened the evidence from these single cases and confirmed that damage to the posterior left hemisphere is implicated in visual–verbal short-term memory impairments. In a study of patients with unilateral lesions Warrington & Rabin (1971) found that the left-hemisphere group was significantly worse than the right. With-

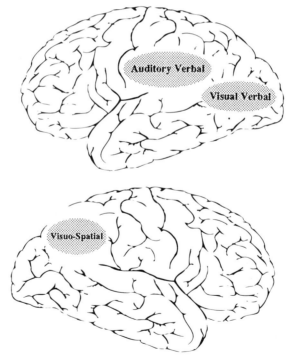

Figure 13.3.   Diagram showing approximate locus of lesion in cases with impairments of short term memory.

Table 13.3 Performance by Patients (% Correct) with Localised Cerebral Lesions on Visual–Verbal Span Tasks[a]

Groups	Random digits	Random letters	2nd-Order letters	4th-Order letters	Lines
Control (N = 20)	80	69	90	92	56
Right (N = 27)	74	68	88	92	55
Left (N = 39)	55	50	73	77	43
Right posterior (N = 7)	65	65	85	88	49
Left posterior (N = 13)	44	41	62	62	35

[a]Adapted from Warrington & Rabin (1971).

in the left hemisphere, patients in the "posterior" group (i.e., with parietal and/or occipital lobe involvement) were the most impaired (see Table 13.3).

Visual–Spatial The anatomical correlates of spatial span appear to differ from those of visual–verbal span. In a single-trial recognition memory test Alajouanine (1960) noted that patients with lesions of the right occipital-parietal regions were most likely to make errors. Kimura (1963) contrasted the effects of right and left temporal lobe lesions on her dot-enumeration task. She found that patients with right temporal lobe damage were the most impaired. Warrington & James (1967b) used a similar task in a study which contrasted patients with lesions in all cerebral sectors. They found that patients with right parietal lesions were the most impaired (see also Chapter 4).

The Corsi Blocks Test has somewhat more ambiguous anatomical correlate results. In a study of patients with lateralised lesions subdivided into those with visual-field defects (posterior lesions) and those without (anterior lesions) De Renzi & Nichelli (1975) found that posterior lesions of either hemisphere could result in impaired performance. When a delay was interposed between presentation of the sequence and subsequent recall, De Renzi *et al.* (1977a) reported a somewhat more pronounced deficit in the group with posterior right-hemisphere lesions suggesting that this group had greater difficulty in retaining spatial information.

Theoretical Considerations

The major focus of theoretical interest in the literature on short-term memory has been a search for the function of short-term memory. As this endeavour has primarily been concerned with auditory–verbal short-term memory, this topic will be the focus of this section. First, however, it is necessary to make a few brief comments about the relatively neglected problem of the role of visual–verbal or visual–spatial span in normal information processing.

Visual Short-Term Memory

The evidence suggests that verbal and spatial impairments of visual short-term memory may be dissociable in terms of their anatomical correlates, selective verbal-span impairments are primarily associated with damage to posterior sectors of the left hemisphere and spatial-span impairments primarily with damage to posterior sectors of the right hemisphere. With regard to the functions of visual–verbal span, the only clearly established fact is that it is not required for reading single words or recognising complex pictures. Although patients with a reduced visual span for briefly presented letters or symbols may show additional impairments in reading (spelling dyslexia: see Chapter 10), this is not inevitably the case (Warrington & Rabin, 1971). Conversely, patients with spelling dyslexia may have normal visual–verbal span (Warrington & Shallice, 1980).

Impairments on the Corsi Blocks Test can occur independently of any primary deficit in spatial perception (see Chapter 4; De Renzi & Nichelli, 1975). Patients may also show selective impairment of their spatial span with preservation of the ability to learn and retain spatial information over the long term. Conversely, a patient with impaired spatial long-term memory (topographical amnesia, see Chapter 15) had preserved spatial span (De Renzi & Nichelli, 1975). A functional role for visual spatial span has been incorporated into the model of working memory proposed by Baddeley and his colleagues. In this model, visual–spatial span is held to be important for subserving visual imagery and imagery-mediated problem solving (Baddeley & Hitch, 1974).

Auditory–Verbal Short-Term Memory

Two main issues have been considered in theoretical discussions of impairment on span tasks. First, the possibility that span impairment is the consequence of deficits in perception or speech production has been debated. Second, the function of auditory–verbal short-term memory has been considered. This latter debate has focused on the relationship between auditory–verbal short-term memory and other aspects of cognitive processing.

Relationship to Language Disorders   Patients with language disorders (aphasia) frequently have impaired ability to repeat auditory–verbal material verbatim and also score poorly on tests requiring them to recall lists of digits or letters (span tasks). Impairment of performance on span tasks need not, however, be accompanied by any other language difficulty and can occur as a remarkably isolated and selective deficit. It was this dissociation that first led Luria *et al.* (1967) to consider that impairment on span tasks was the consequence of a specific memory deficit rather than the secondary consequence of an aphasia.

Perceptual Disorders—If a patient is unable to hear or perceive the sounds of language, then it seems likely that this would have consequences for the patient's ability to retain spoken information (see Chapter 6). It has been suggested that subtle deficits in speech perception may account for failure on span tasks (Allport, 1984). However, word recognition may be quite normal in patients with reduced auditory–verbal span. Warrington & Shallice (1969) used a test of word detection in which a patient (K.F.) was presented with lists of 40 words spoken at the same fast (one per second) rate as in span tasks. He was asked to tap every time he heard a word belonging to a specific category (i.e., colours, countries, animals). The patient performed this task very competently (96% correct). This result was replicated in two further cases (Warrington *et al.*, 1971).

Patients' ability to discriminate similar language sounds (phonemes) may be entirely normal despite a grave impairment of their auditory–verbal span. For example, patients have been tested on discrimination tasks in which they are asked to decide whether two words are the same or different (e.g., *choke/joke* see also chapter 6). Their ability to make these subtle distinctions may be within the range of normal controls (Vallar & Baddeley, 1984a; McCarthy & Warrington, 1984). In other cases, there may be a moderate degree of difficulty with stringent discrimination tasks (Friedrich *et al.*, 1984). However, it is uncertain whether this is sufficient to account for the patient's marked deficit on span tests.

Speech-Production Disorders—An alternative reason for failure on span tasks might be some difficulty in producing a verbal response rather than in retaining information. Patients have been described who have a very limited span on conventional repetition tests. Nevertheless if they are tested using recognition procedures (e.g., pointing to items in an array) their span may be within the normal range (Kinsbourne, 1972; Caplan, Vanier, & Baker, 1986a).

However, in many cases short-term memory impairment is clearly not the consequence of a primary speech-production deficit. First, there are a number of patients on record who show equivalent difficulties regardless of whether they are required to respond orally, by pointing or in probed recognition. Second, patients frequently show improved performance with visual presentation of the same class of material despite being required to produce a spoken response. Third, they may show rapid forgetting on the Brown–Petersen task (retention with distraction) even though speech-production requirements are identical at all retention intervals (see Vallar & Shallice, 1990).

There is a thus a broad consensus that for some patients failure on span tasks may reflect a primary impairment in retaining spoken verbal information rather than in perceiving or producing it. Such cases are described as having a deficit in their short-term memory for spoken information. However, the function of short-term memory in cognitive information-processing has proven surprisingly elusive.

Function of Auditory–Verbal Span

Experimental psychologists have hypothesised that short-term memory is an integral component of the normal information processing system. The evidence from patients has been important in attempts to define its function. First, it has been argued that short-term memory is a gateway to more permanent memory representations, second, that it is a component of cognitive problem-solving abilities, and third, that it is a critical part of the language-processing system. These three possibilities will be considered in turn.

Gateway Theory The gateway theory of memory organisation postulated that information was initially held in a short-term store (STS) and subsequently transferred from STS into longer-term memory storage by a process of rehearsal. This account was sufficiently established in the late 1960s to be regarded as the dominant model of memory (Murdoch, 1967; Atkinson & Shiffrin, 1968). However, the evidence from patients with selective impairment of short-term storage called into question the idea that entry to long-term memory was achieved via short-term store, i.e., that these forms of memory were organised in series.

In their original studies of a short-term memory case (K.F.), Warrington & Shallice (1969; Shallice & Warrington 1970) established that his auditory–verbal learning was not only normal, but well above average on some tests. He was tested on the Wechsler "paired associate" learning test. In this task he was presented with 10 pairs of spoken words. Retention was tested by presenting the first word of the pair and requiring recall of the second. On this stringent test he scored within the average range.

He was also required to learn a list of 10 spoken words using a cumulative learning technique described by Luria (1966). Ten words were presented at the same rate as in the digit-span task (i.e., one per second) and he was asked to recall them immediately. Learning was measured in terms of trials to a criterion of perfect recall. Remarkably he was slightly better than a matched control group on this task. He was also tested on a "free-recall" task in which there was a single spoken presentation of a 10-word list (see also Chapter 14). In normal subjects there is a clear "serial position effect," with recall being best for items at the beginning and end of the list (the primacy and recency effect). He showed normal levels of performance with early and middle items on the list, but his "recency" effect was reduced to one item.

This pattern is to be expected on theoretical grounds if verbal long-term memory is intact (primacy and middle portions of the list) but short-term memory is impaired (the recency effect). A fourth test of long-term memory, which is more like everyday learning, is that of story recall (Wechsler "logical memory"). The patient was read a short passage and asked to recall as much as possible about its content. His recall was as good as that of normal control subjects.

These four tests of verbal learning and verbal retention have been attempted by three other cases with impaired auditory–verbal short-term memory. In these patients, at least, verbal long-term memory has been shown to be at entirely normal levels (e.g. Warrington et al., 1971; De Renzi & Nichelli, 1975; Basso et al., 1982).

These findings effectively eliminate the "gateway" model of memory processing. Were short-term memory a gateway to longer-term storage, it follows that an impairment in short-term memory tasks should *necessarily* lead to an impairment in verbal learning tasks. Since long-term memory can be normal in span-impaired cases, there must be a degree of independence between the processing systems which are involved in long- and short-term memory. Shallice & Warrington (1970) proposed a model of the relationship between long- and short-term verbal memory which allowed for parallel input into both systems (see Fig. 13.4).

Working Memory Baddeley and his colleagues have developed a model in which the ability to hold verbal material verbatim plays an important role in problem solving (e.g., Baddeley, 1986). The working-memory model consists of three major components: the "articulatory loop," the "visuospatial sketchpad" (or "scratch pad," see above), and

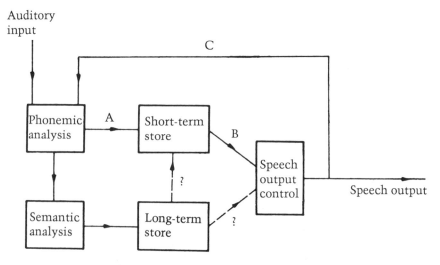

Figure 13.4. Model of the relationship between auditory–verbal short-term memory and long-term memory (Shallice & Warrington, 1970).

the "central executive." Performance on auditory-verbal span tasks requires the operation of this articulatory loop under the directing control of the central executive system. The articulatory loop is held to consist of two main components, a phonological storage system and a rehearsal loop (Baddeley, 1986; see Fig. 13.5). In the terms of this model, at least some patients with a selective impairment of auditory–verbal span can be thought of as having a deficit in the phonological store and/or the rehearsal loop (Vallar & Baddeley, 1984b).

In normal people, verbal problem solving is also thought to make use of the temporary storage capacities of the "articulatory loop." Evidence in favour of this position is derived from tasks in which subjects are required to perform visually presented arithmetic or reasoning tests whilst simultaneously holding spoken lists in memory. Under these "concurrent task" conditions performance deteriorates and subjects become slower and make more errors (Baddeley & Hitch, 1974).

If the temporary storage of verbatim information is necessary for verbal problem solving, then patients with selective impairments of span should be disproportionately impaired on tests such as mental arithmetic. It is fair to say that the majority of patients with an impaired digit span have shown weak performance on graded-difficulty arithmetic tests. However, the presentation of these tasks is typically spoken and therefore places considerable demands on retention in addition to problem-solving operations. Despite these demands, some cases are on record with arithmetic scores within the normal range (Warrington *et al.*, 1971; McCarthy & Warrington, 1984). Furthermore,

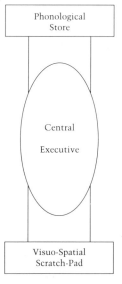

Figure 13.5. Baddley's model of "working memory" showing the relationship between the "articulatory loop," "visuospatial scratchpad," and "central executive." (Baddeley, 1986.)

in (the possibly more demanding) conditions of everyday life, patients may be entirely capable of dealing with verbal "problems" routinely. For example, patients may be capable of holding down demanding jobs, including working as a senior secretary or running a business (e.g., Warrington *et al.*, 1971; Basso *et al.*, 1982). Impaired span clearly does not necessarily compromise the patient's ability to perform verbal reasoning operations themselves. However, it may be still be critical for those very specific types of problem solving that require the maintenance of an exact verbatim record of the spoken input (see below).

Fluent Language Production   It has been argued that short-term memory may be important for dealing with fluent language production (and/or language comprehension; see below). In language production it is often necessary to retain "chunks" of several words of the language so that fluent production can occur. If short-term memory were involved in these processes then patients should have difficulty in producing fluent speech.

In producing speech it is not only necessary to be able to use single words; these words have to be organised and produced in an acceptable order so as to convey the speaker's ideas. People do not speak "word by word" but in chunks as large as phrases or sentences, with minute, imperceptible gaps between the words in each of these large chunks. Normal fluent speech appears to require the maintenance of several words in a short-term "buffer" store prior to their utterance (see Chapters 8 and 9), and it has been argued that the functioning of this store is measured by span tasks (Morton, 1970).

However, patients with an impaired span do not necessarily show difficulties with the production of normal fluent speech. Shallice & Butterworth (1977) conducted a careful psycholinguistic analysis of the spontaneous speech of one case (J.B.). On clinical testing she gave the impression of having entirely normal spontaneous speech. Indeed her occupation as a senior secretary would not have been possible without good language and literacy skills. Shallice & Butterworth found that her total speech time, pauses, and errors ("slips of the tongue") were within the range of normal control subjects. Normal or near normal levels of spontaneous fluent speech have also been documented in other cases (Saffran & Marin, 1975; Basso *et al.*, 1982). These findings indicate that there is no necessary relationship between impairment on short-term span tasks and fluent speech production.

Whether impaired speech fluency by itself would have adverse effects on span tasks (e.g., by reducing the rate of "inner speech" or rehearsal) is not certain. It has been established that subcortical damage leading to a complete loss of the ability to use the muscles required for speech does not affect span performance on recognition tasks (Baddeley & Wilson, 1985). It has also been shown that patients with gravely impaired single-word production may have normal spans (Kinsbourne, 1972; see above). However, the question remains as to whether other types of speech fluency impairment can directly lead to impaired performance on span tasks.

Language Comprehension   Auditory–verbal span provides a verbatim record of a spoken utterance. This rather obviously suggests that this short-term verbal record might be required for some aspect of normal language comprehension. Although this hypothesis has been toyed with from time to time it has long been clear that there is no simple relationship between performance on span tasks and the ability to process spoken language. The simplest form of the hypothesis that span is required for all forms of language comprehension can be rejected. First, patients with gravely impaired span do not necessarily show any difficulties in coping with conversations. Indeed, three cases whose impairments have been studied in detail (J.B., V.B., and N.H.A.) hold demanding jobs for which good language comprehension is a prerequisite (Shallice & Butterworth, 1977; Vallar & Baddeley, 1984a; McCarthy & Warrington, 1987a,b). Second, they may be able to respond appropriately to long non redundant questions (e.g., "What is the name of the glass or polished surface that you can look into to see a reflection of yourself?") (Warrington *et al.*, 1971).

The idea that auditory–verbal span impairment should lead to general reduction in the size of the "window" over which verbal utterances are analysed can also be rejected. Sentence repetition may be relatively well preserved in patients with impaired digit and word span. This suggests that the ability to extract information "on line" from a spoken sentence was relatively spared. The observation that patients may be *more* impaired in repeating partial sentences as compared with complete sentences suggests that they were dependent on the use of a dynamic and anticipatory system for processing meaningful spoken material.

Order-Dependent Processing—So, it appears that the processing of "everyday" language can be normal in patients with a grave impairment of span, might they be impaired in processing more specific types of linguistic information? It has been suggested that short-term storage is required so that the syntactic aspects of language can be parsed and structured as words are heard. A short-term record is required for order-dependent language processing (e.g., Frazier & Fodor, 1978; Hitch, 1980; Ellis & Beattie, 1986; Baddeley & Wilson, 1985).

Conversational speech typically contains many clues which aid in comprehension. There is only very limited ambiguity in what is said, since much of "message" is conveyed by the meanings of the words, and information is usually relevant to the context of the conversation. Such comprehension may not place any great demands on a verbatim record of speech. However, it has been suggested that a verbatim record may be necessary for comprehending sentences in which word order and syntax are critical (e.g., Caramazza, Basili, Koller, & Berndt 1981; Schwartz, Saffran, & Marin, 1980a; Caplan, Vanier, & Baker, 1986b).

Sentences such as "The girl phoned the boy" require retention of the order of nouns so that the hearer knows who did what to whom. They cannot be interpreted by making use of word meanings alone (see also Chapter 8). Vallar & Baddeley (1984b) used the Parisi & Pizzamiglio (1970) test of sentence comprehension in their single case (P.V.). The test contains order-dependent sentences such as "The cat is behind the tree" (see Chapter 8). The patient scored at a normal level on this task. A more stringent test of word order and syntactic processing devised by Schwartz *et al.* (1980a) was administered to two cases whose auditory spans for words and digits were only reliable for one item (McCarthy & Warrington, 1987b). This test requires the subject to choose the appropriate picture for sentences such as "The boy was phoned by the girl." Order information is crucial for successful performance on this task since the distractor picture shows the girl being phoned by the boy. The patients obtained very satisfactory scores *despite* their grave impairment of auditory span. These findings indicate that the ability to process word order *per se* may not be compromised by an impaired auditory–verbal short-term memory.

It has also been suggested that sentence length may be critical: long sentences may exceed the patient's "span" and so result in errors, perhaps more especially when word order is important (Vallar & Baddeley, 1984a; Baddeley, Vallar, & Wilson, 1987). Vallar & Baddeley found that their patient (P.V.) had no difficulty in detecting the anomaly in sentences such as "It is true that physicians comprise a profession that is manufactured in factories from time to time." Such sentences contain a frank "semantic" mistake: professions are never "manufactured." However, the patient had more difficulty with a different set of long sentences in which the anomaly hinged on reversal of semantically related nouns (e.g., "One cannot reasonably claim that sailors are often lived on by ships of various kinds"). Vallar & Baddeley argued that the patient was adversely affected by sentence length. When sentences exceeded her span then she was at a disadvantage in processing this type of "order" information. However, there does not appear to be any simple relationship between the number of words in a sentence and difficulty in comprehension. Patients with a gravely impaired auditory verbal span may succeed in comprehending long sentences but fail to comprehend shorter ones such as "Show me the red circle" or "The bird was watched" (McCarthy & Warrington, 1987b; Saffran, 1990).

Backup Resource An alternative hypothesis has been that this verbatim record is only required as a "back-up" resource. It is not a critical part of normal "on-line" language processing but may be called on to "replay" a spoken message in the event that normal understanding fails (e.g., Shallice & Warrington, 1970; Saffran & Marin, 1975; McCarthy & Warrington, 1987b). Shallice & Warrington (1970) speculated that this record might be required for replaying complex sentences so that a "second pass" could be made when initial attempts at comprehension failed. Evidence in favour of this hypothesis is the difficulty that patients with an impaired span have on sentences with a high information load, such as Token Test instructions (e.g., "Before picking up the green circle, touch the red square" De Renzi & Nichelli, 1975; see also Chapter 8). By contrast, span impaired patients may have no difficulty with sentences in which the information is cumulative and conveys a single major proposition (such as "What is the name of the thin grey dust that remains after something has burned such as a cigarette?) (Warrington *et al.*, 1971). In performing the Token Test one is aware by introspection of "replaying" and "backtracking" over the spoken message so as to understand the instructions and carry them out adequately. In the other types of sentence, the information seems to be understood immediately as it is heard on line. The question therefore arises as to when such a backup resource is required.

In a detailed study of two cases (R.A.N. and N.H.A.) comprehension was explored over a range of sentence types (McCarthy & Warrington, 1987b). In these cases neither syntactic complexity nor sentence length per se appeared to be critical for sentence comprehension. It appeared that there were three types of sentence-comprehension task on which they were impaired. First, in common with all well-documented cases of severe short-term memory impairment, their performance on the Token Test was extremely poor. This was attributed to their difficulty in dealing with large amounts of condensed (and relatively arbitrary) information in a relatively brief auditory message.

Second, the patients were impaired when sentences broke conventional conversational "rules." This was observed on a task originally devised by Huttenlocher, Eisenberg, & Strauss (1968). The task requires the subject to move tokens according to simple instructions which are presented in either a conventional or an unconventional form. For example, if one is shown a black and a white token and asked to arrange the display so that "black is above the white" (see Fig. 13.6A) the sentence is easy provided that the black token can be moved. This is a conventional way of giving instructions (by placing the word "black" at the beginning of this sentence attention is drawn to something which can be moved). With this type of instruction the patients performed the task well. However, conversational conventions are contravened if the black token is fixed and the subject is handed the white token and told "black is above white" (Huttenlocher *et al.*, 1968). Attention is drawn to the "wrong" item by these instructions and the sentence therefore requires mental reorganisation (see Fig. 13.6B). This unconventional form of instruction was impossible for the two patients and they scored at chance. It was argued that the ability to "mentally reorganise" a sentence requires the retention of a verbatim record of what has been said so that it can be replayed and reanalysed for comprehension (i.e., "black above white" "I must put the white below the black").

Third, these patients were very impaired in responding to simple spoken comparative judgments (e.g., "Which is green, a poppy or a

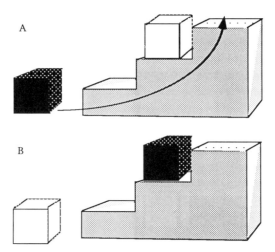

Figure 13.6. For the sentence "Black above white" (A) schematically shows the "easy" condition in which the black token is movable and the white token fixed and (B) shows the difficult condition in which the black token is fixed. (Huttenlocher *et al.*, 1968)

lettuce?"). One scored only 75% correct and the other obtained a chance score of 49%. Such sentences are not order dependent and have only three critical words. However, it was argued that the supplementary cognitive operation of comparison requires verbatim retention of the three critical words so that the judgment can be made. It is necessary to backtrack over a verbatim record whilst making the judgment. The patients found this apparently simple task extremely difficult (even though they had no difficulty in comprehending the constituent words) (McCarthy & Warrington, 1987b).

In considering the overall profile of the patients' performance it was argued that three conditions were likely to impose constraints upon normal "immediate" or "on-line" language comprehension and require backtracking operations dependent on auditory–verbal short-term memory;

1. When the rate of information presentation was too great for the development of a sufficiently unambiguous cognitive representation of sentence content (e.g., the Token Test)
2. When expectancies and assumptions biased the interpretation of the spoken message in the wrong way (e.g., the Huttenlocher *et al.* test)
3. When an understanding of the sentence appropriate to the task required supplementary cognitive operations to be performed on the spoken input (e.g., simple comparative judgments).

It was considered that these three conditions were unlikely to be mutually independent, or even exhaustive. Rather, they were highlighted as crucial characteristics of those sentence-comprehension tasks in which the backup resources of a verbatim record were likely to be necessary. Short-term memory provides this resource and allows a message to be reanalysed in the absence of continued external auditory input.

On this account auditory verbal span is not an integral part of a "general-purpose" verbal problem-solving system. Rather, it is required for only a very specific set of cognitive operations: those in which a verbatim record must be replayed in order to restructure and reorganise information contained in the spoken message. This explanation has the advantage of being able to account for the paradox that patients may be able to comprehend order-dependent sentences but fail on apparently simpler tasks such as moving a single token or making a comparative judgment.

Conclusion

The evidence from neuropsychological analyses has indicated that there are several dissociable short-term memory systems. Furthermore, selective disorders of these systems have relatively good localising significance. Five possible functional roles for auditory–verbal span have been considered. First, it has been established that short-term memory is not a gateway to the longer-term storage of information. Second, it is not a necessary component of general verbal problem-solving abilities. Third, it is not a necessary component of normal fluent language production. Fourth, the view that the verbatim record provided by span is a necessary component of normal sentence comprehension has been seriously questioned. Finally, it has been suggested that this record may have a role as a backup resource when backtracking over a spoken message is required. Specifically this system appears to be necessary under circumstances in which additional cognitive "work" has to be performed so that the message can be fully understood.

14

Autobiographical Memory

Introduction

The normal individual is able to maintain a constantly changing and updated record of salient personal and public events. With the passage of time these records may be modified, amalgamated, or even forgotten. The recollection of events which occurred yesterday is far more detailed than that of the events of the same day last week, and it may be almost impossible to recollect the events which occurred on the same date a year ago. This running autobiographical record is a constructive, and reconstructive, "long-term" memory which is unique to the individual. Impairment of the ability to use or maintain an adequate autobiographical, personalised record of events is relatively common in cerebral disease. However, such disorders may arise for a wide variety of reasons. In considering "long-term" memory impairments the first major subdivision which will be drawn here is that between global impairments of *autobiographical* memory and disorders affecting the patient's ability to remember certain classes of material (*material-specific* impairments). Disorders of autobiographical memory will be considered in this chapter. Material-specific disorders will be the focus of Chapter 15.

Global Impairments of Autobiographical Memory The patient may have such a dense memory deficit that it would appear to be virtually absolute for the past, present, and future. In some cases, this impairment of memory may be attributable to (or made worse by) other deficits affecting the patient's intellect or alertness (e.g., in the context of widespread cerebral malfunction). Memory deficits occurring in the context of more generalised cognitive failure are differentiated from those impairments which occur in the context of normal levels of intellect and alertness. It is this latter group of selective autobiographical memory impairments which will be the focus of this chapter. Selective autobiographical memory disorders also vary in their severity. Thus in some other cases there may be some residual ability to recall events of the past, register the present, or anticipate the future. Whether or not mild, moderate, or severe disorders of autobiographical memory should be viewed as lying on a continuum is controversial.

Subtypes of "Amnesia" Within these selective and global memory deficits patients may also vary in terms of the *qualitative aspects* of the memories which can be retrieved. In the pure *amnesic* syndrome, the patient's memory appears to be virtually contentless. By contrast, other patients appear to have a fluent recall of information. However, that information has little relationship to objective reality. In some instances, recall may seem to be based on actual events and occurrences. These memories are produced in a disorganised manner and muddled with regard to their time or location of occurrence. When recall is based on "invented" or "muddled" events the deficit is termed *paramnesia*.

The amnesic syndrome, in its pure form, has been extensively researched and is one of the most fully documented syndromes in the neuropsychological literature. Clinical accounts date back to at least the latter half of the nineteenth century (e.g., Korsakoff, 1889). There are two major components of the amnesic syndrome. First, patients may have difficulty in recalling or recognising events which have occurred since the onset of illness—*anterograde amnesia*. Second, patients may be impaired in recalling events which occurred before the onset of their amnesic condition—*retrograde amnesia*. These two components typically co-occur in the amnesic patient.

Empirical Characteristics

Anterograde Amnesia

The first quantitative experimental investigations of a patient (H.M.) with severe and selective anterograde memory deficit were conducted by Milner and her colleagues (e.g., Scoville and Milner, 1957; Milner, Corkin and Teuber, 1968). The patient had a grave impairment of his ongoing memory following an operation to relieve intractable epileptic seizures. "He could no longer recognise the hospital staff, apart from Dr. Scoville himself, whom he had known for many years; he did not remember and could not relearn the way to the bathroom, and he seemed to retain nothing of the day-to-day happenings in the hospital. . . . A year later, H.M. had not yet learned the new address, nor could he be trusted to find his way home alone, . . . He is unable to learn where objects constantly in use are kept" (Milner, 1966, p. 113). Despite these difficulties, he had a high average level of "intelligence" as measured on a standard test (Wechsler Bellvue Scale, IQ 112) and was alert and cooperative. On a standard clinical test of memory

(Wechsler Memory Scale) his scores were very impaired (memory quotient 67). "His immediate recall of stories and drawings fell far below the average level and on the 'associate learning' subtest of this scale he obtained zero scores for the hard word associations, low scores for the easy associations and failed to improve with repeated practice. . . . Moreover, on all tests we found that once he had turned to a new task the nature of the preceding one could no longer be recalled, nor the test recognised if repeated" (Scoville and Milner, 1957, p. 17).

Milner and her colleagues used conventional experimental tests of memory in to quantify his deficit. In a series of experiments they documented his severe impairment on tests of verbal and nonverbal memory (Milner, Corkin, & Teuber, 1968). Thus he failed to recognise faces in a delayed matching test in which he was presented with 12 faces and asked to select the ones he had seen before after a delay of 90 seconds filled with distracting activity. He also failed on delayed recall of a complex drawing. Drachman & Arbit (1966) also documented his impairment on tests of verbal and visual learning. They found that he was unable to learn a series of digits or a sequence of light flashes which was longer than his immediate memory span despite repeated presentations. (In this respect he differs markedly from patients with a selective impairment of short-term memory; see Chapter 13.)

The selective impairment of performance on formal tests of verbal and nonverbal learning and memory are now accepted as diagnostic criteria for identifying an anterograde amnesic deficit. A large number of studies have been carried out which have extended and replicated the original findings with case H.M. For example, in one subsequent study Baddeley & Warrington (1970) assessed six amnesic patients on two tests of verbal memory. The first test evaluated the patient's ability to learn associations between word pairs (paired associate learning). Following presentation of a list of word pairs, recall was tested by presentation of the first item of each pair and requiring recall of the second. The patients were uniformly bad at this task. The second test involved the presentation of 10 item lists. Recall was required either immediately, or following 30 min. of interpolated "distracting" activity. On the immediate-recall test, patients were able to reproduce the last few items in the list at the same level as controls. However, for the items at the beginning and the middle of the list their recall rate plummeted. (This serial position effect is quite the reverse of that observed in patients with an impaired short-term memory; see Chapter 13). In the delayed-recall condition, their performance was disastrous and only the last item was reproduced at the same level as controls (see Fig. 14.1).

Patients with a severe anterograde amnesia are not only impaired on recall tests, but also on the easier task of recognition memory. Warrington (1974) tested a group of four amnesic patients using recognition-memory tests for words and faces. In each test there were 50 items, and recognition was tested by pairing each item with a very similar distractor. The amnesic group scored at a chance level on both

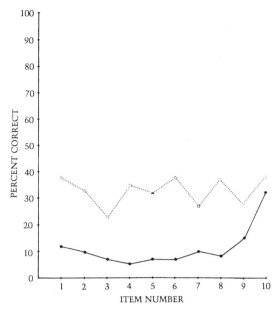

Figure 14.1. Serial position curve for amnesic ●——● and control ○----○ patient groups (Baddeley & Warrington, 1970).

tests. In these tasks which permit a direct comparison between verbal and nonverbal memory (see Chapter 15) the amnesics were globally impaired.

There is now no dispute that these quantitative measures of memory function provide an index of the impairment of event memory which corresponds with the difficulties which the patients experience in everyday life.

Preserved Memory in Anterograde Amnesia

As has been noted, patients with an anterograde amnesia perform very poorly on conventional tests of event memory. In this context the discovery that there were certain types of task which amnesics could perform at a normal or near normal level represented a breakthrough. Performance on these tasks could not simply be explained away in terms of their being easier than the tests on which the amnesics were globally impaired. Rather, these findings suggested that there were some types of memory preserved in amnesic patients. These findings have led to an analysis of the types of memory or learning task in which amnesics show evidence of both the acquisition of new information and its later retention. There is now a vast literature on the types of task in which amnesics show normal levels of learning. The major types of preserved learning are summarised below.

Conditioning   Classical conditioning is one of the most basic forms of learning and is observed in all vertebrates. Naturally occurring reflexes can be "conditioned" to occur to a stimulus which would not normally provoke them without a learning experience (e.g., dogs can "learn" to salivate on presentation of a tone alone if food and tones have been presented together sufficiently often). Amnesic patients can also learn such associations. Weiskrantz & Warrington (1979) used a procedure in which a puff of air to the eye (eliciting a reflex eye-blink) was paired with a sound and a flash of light. The amnesic patients were able to acquire a conditioned eye-blink response and to retain it for at least 1 day. When questioned about the task only 10 minutes after the trials had finished, the patients were unable to recall any relevant details. Preservation of conditioning has since been replicated by Daum, Channon, & Canavan (1989). However, whether or not amnesics condition at a normal rate has not been established.

Motor-Skill Acquisition   Milner (1962, 1965) first demonstrated that H.M. was able to learn and to retain a motor skill: he learned how to trace an outline drawing when looking in a mirror rather than when looking at his hand. This is a surprisingly difficult task, and H.M. showed slow, but progressive improvement in his performance over a number of successive trials. Moreover, when H.M. was retested 2 and 3 days later he still showed the benefit of his earlier practice despite being unable to recall having performed the task before. Since this first experiment there have been further demonstrations of this type of learning and memory in amnesic patients. Corkin (1968) demonstrated that H.M. was able to learn to keep a stylus in contact with a patch of light moving in a predictable pattern on a display (the "pursuit rotor" task). His rate of learning was slower than controls and his level of performance was somewhat lower. Corkin attributed his slow learning to slowed reaction time rather than to a memory deficit *per se*. Subsequent investigations have shown that amnesic patients may acquire this skill at a normal rate (e.g., Cermak, Lewis, Butters, & Goodglass, 1973; Brooks & Baddeley, 1976; see Fig. 14.2). On the slightly less artificial task of piano playing, a patient studied by Starr & Phillips (1970) was taught a new melody and could play it the following day if he was prompted with the first few bars.

Perceptual Learning   Tasks which tap some aspects of skill acquisition but which do not have a manual-motor component can also be intact in amnesia. Warrington & Weiskrantz (1968) studied a group of six patients with a global and severe memory deficit (five of whom were also reported by Baddeley & Warrington, 1970; see above). Warrington & Weiskrantz demonstrated that, despite their dense amnesia, the patients showed remarkably good learning and long-term retention of pictorial and verbal material under certain conditions. The testing technique involved presenting fragmented or degraded stimuli in increasing degrees of "completeness." The incomplete-picture stimuli were those devised by Gollin (1960) (see Fig. 2.7). An example of an incomplete-

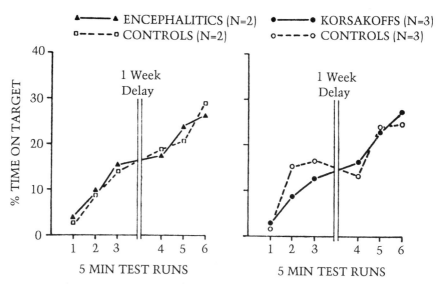

Figure 14.2. Acquisition of skill on the pursuit rotor task by two subgroups of amnesics (encephalities and Korsakoffs) and control subjects (Brooks & Baddeley, 1976).

word stimulus is given in Fig. 14.3. In one experiment, the degraded stimuli were presented for five acquisition trials in order to determine cumulative learning. Normal subjects and amnesics alike learned to identify the stimulus at significantly lower degrees of completeness over the repeated presentations. The amnesics, although not as good as normal controls, showed highly competent learning when tested on subsequent days. An example of the performance of one case from this series (N.T.) is shown in Fig. 14.4. This same profoundly amnesic patient showed savings of 20% over a 3-month interval (Warrington & Weiskrantz, 1968). These basic findings were replicated by Milner *et al.* (Case H.M., 1968). In a subsequent experiment Warrington & Weiskrantz (1970) established that the method of testing retention was crucial, rather than the method of acquisition. Patients were presented with whole words and subsequently tested for retention using either a free-recall task, a yes/no recognition test, or by identification of the most fragmented version of the word. The amnesic patients were (as expected) gravely impaired on the recall and recognition conditions. However, they showed normal levels of retention when they were asked to identify a fragmented word (see Fig. 14.5).

Other forms of perceptual learning can also be intact in amnesia such as the normal ability to learn and retain reading of transformed text (Moscovitch, 1982). In this task (devised by Kolers, 1968) subjects are presented with mirror transformed text and asked to read it as quickly as possible. Normal subjects improve their performance on this task with practice, and so do amnesic patients. The gain shown by amnesic patients was not specific to particular texts or words and therefore appears to be a very general perceptual skill-acquisition

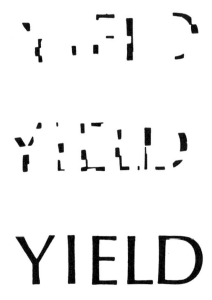

Figure 14.3. Example of an incomplete-word stimulus (Warrington & Weiskrantz, 1968).

effect. Using a somewhat more naturalistic task, Brooks & Baddeley (1976) found that amnesic patients were able to improve their speed in solving jigsaw puzzles.

Word Completion Warrington & Weiskrantz (1970) demonstrated that amnesic patients benefited from initial-letter cues in a recall task.

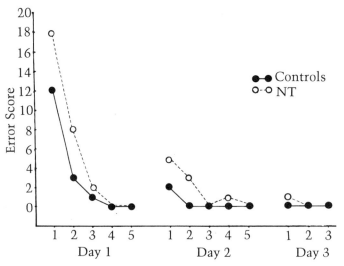

Figure 14.4. Learning on Gollin's pictures by a single amnesic (N.T.) (Warrington & Weiskrantz, 1968 unpublished data).

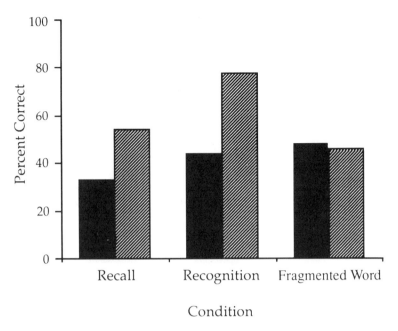

Figure 14.5. The effects of different types of retention test (recall, yes/no recognition, and fragmented words) in amnesics (solid bars) and controls (cross-hatched bars). (Adapted from Warrington & Weiskrantz, 1970.)

They presented subjects with printed lists of words and tested their retention either by standard recall and recognition techniques or by presenting the first three letters of the target item in a word-completion task. In this task the subjects were asked to retrieve a word beginning with the first three letters provided by the examiner (e.g., "cha," *chair*). As expected, the amnesics were severely impaired on the recall and recognition conditions. However, they were as good as normal control subjects on word completion (see Fig. 14.6). This method of testing retention in amnesic patients gives highly reliable effects (e.g., Warrington & Weiskrantz, 1974; Warrington & Weiskrantz, 1978; Graf & Schacter, 1985; Schacter, 1985). This technique has been extensively employed in studies designed to explore the characteristics and limitations of memory in amnesic subjects (see below and Schacter, 1987). Other related types of task include presentation of words followed by a task of "filling in the missing letter" (e.g., "P"-"N"-"C"-"L" for PENCIL), on which amnesics are facilitated by prior exposure to the target word (e.g., Tulving, Schacter, & Stark, 1982).

Verbal Facilitation   There are a number of effects of prior-exposure facilitation which can be demonstrated in amnesic patients. Jacoby & Witherspoon (1982) showed facilitation of spelling in amnesic and con-

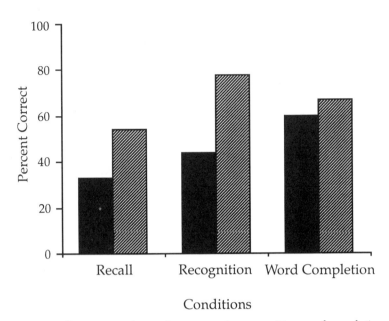

Figure 14.6. Different types of retention test: yes/no recognition, word completion, and recall in amnesics (solid bars) and controls (cross-hatched bars) (Adapted from Warrington & Weiskrantz, 1970).

trol subjects. Homophones (e.g., *bear/bare*) were presented for spelling; subjects typically produced the more frequent word (e.g., *bear*). However, after a series of trials inducing biasing contexts for the less common words (e.g., "What would you call somebody without any clothes on?"), both amnesics and control subjects spelled that version in a subsequent "spelling test." In a recognition-memory test for the same items, the amnesic patients scored at chance.

Warrington & Weiskrantz (1982) observed that amnesic patients showed "repetition effects" in naming, category identification (e.g., object/animal), and generation of opposites (e.g., black/white). Subjects were presented with target words and asked to respond as rapidly as possible. On a second presentation of the same stimuli in these tasks, the reaction times of both the amnesics and the control subjects were faster, thereby showing facilitation. Similar effects were documented by Cermak, Talbot, Chandler, & Wolbarst (1985) who showed that the threshold for identification of words (but not of nonwords) was lowered on a second attempt in amnesic patients.

Problem-Solving Skills The first report of preserved learning of a more complex problem-solving skill in amnesic patients was made by Kinsbourne & Wood (1975). They found that amnesic patients were able to learn the rule of generating numbers in a Fibonacci series (i.e., a series of numbers in which each successive term is the sum of the two preceding terms). Subsequently, Cohen (1984) claimed that H.M., and a further group of 11 amnesics were normal in their progressive improvement over trials on the "Tower of Hanoi" problem. Follow-up with H.M. 1 year later indicated that he had still retained the ability to solve the problem.

Facilitation on problem solving tasks is not necessarily dependent on multiple learning trials. McAndrews, Glisky, & Schacter (1987) observed that amnesic patients showed substantial facilitation on a sentence completion task following a single presentation. The task consisted of sentences with "difficult" completions (e.g., the person was unhappy because the hole closed? answer—pierced ears). Severely amnesic patients showed highly significant facilitation in producing the solution to these sentences after a one week delay.

A more practically relevant problem-solving skill with direct implications for the rehabilitation of amnesic patients was investigated by Glisky, Schacter, & Tulving (1986). They showed that a group of amnesic patients was able to learn the rudiments of computer operation following extensive practice. In a follow-up study Glisky & Schacter (1987) reported successful training of a severely amnesic patient (H.D.) on a complex task of computer data entry. She was trained extensively (both in the laboratory and in the work environment) using cuing techniques and extensive repetitions of all components of the task. The training programme was so effective that she was able to "perform the job in the real-world work environment as quickly and as accurately as experienced data-entry employees" (p. 893).

Short-Term Memory   Despite failure to maintain an ongoing autobiographical record, amnesic patients may be able to retain and reproduce verbatim information normally in immediate-recall tasks. Both Zangwill (1946) and Talland (1965) noted that profoundly amnesic patients scored at a level comparable to normal subjects on tests of sentence repetition. In one of the first quantitative studies, Drachman & Arbit (1966) found that H.M. had a normal auditory memory span for spoken lists of digits and a normal visual immediate memory span for sequences of lights presented in an array. These findings have since been replicated in other investigations. For example, Baddeley & Warrington (1970) also found that amnesic subjects had normal digit spans, and in a subsequent study Warrington & Baddeley (1974) found that amnesic patients had normal scores on a test of the immediate recall of spatial positions. The capacity of their short-term memory is clearly normal (see Chapter 13).

Short-term memory (as its name suggests) does not last for more than 20 or 30 seconds for normal subjects in the absence of rehearsal. Thus, the recall of three random consonants or words deteriorates if the subject is distracted and prevented from rehearsing them during the retention interval (e.g., by giving the patient a mental arithmetic task to perform; see Chapter 13). Although clinical experience suggests that amnesic patients are particularly susceptible to distraction, they may show exactly the same "forgetting" rates as normal subjects on measures of short-term retention.

The original experiment by Baddeley & Warrington (1970) showed that with intervals as long as 60 seconds, an amnesic group demonstrated a completely normal rate of forgetting on the Brown–Petersen task. These findings were considered as somewhat anomalous when they were first reported, because it was widely accepted that amnesic patients inevitably required "constant rehearsal" in order to bridge the shortest of time intervals (Milner, 1966). This need for "constant rehearsal" was ostensibly supported by the clinical observation that amnesic patients did indeed appear to have a memory which lasted for seconds rather than for minutes. Although a number of failures to replicate were initially reported (e.g., Cermak & Butters, 1972), later work has substantiated these counterintuitive findings (see Fig. 14.7). It is now generally accepted that in patients with a *selective* amnesic syndrome (i.e., without other cognitive deficits) normal forgetting curves can be obtained with the specific, albeit artificial, conditions of

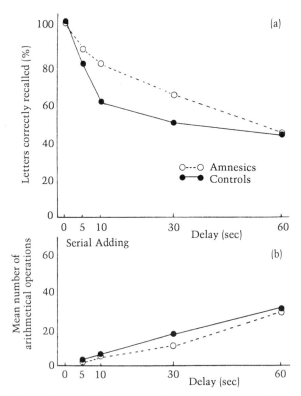

Figure 14.7(a) Normal rates of forgetting on Brown–Peterson task by amnesic subjects. **(b)** Normal performance on intervening distracting task by amnesic subjects (Warrington, 1982b).

the Brown–Petersen task (e.g., Cermak, 1976; Warrington, 1982b; Moscovitch, 1984).

Retrograde Amnesia

Retrograde amnesia refers to the inability to recall information about events which occurred prior to the onset of amnesia. The ability to recall events appears to differ from the ability to recall (or recognise) context-free factual information. Thus patients with an organic retrograde amnesia (in the absence of other cognitive deficits) typically retain their linguistic knowledge and salient personal facts such as their names. They may also retain a *very* basic outline of their career, marital status, and family. The case of the patient who has simply lost his or her personal identity which pervades fictional and "newsworthy" accounts of amnesia usually describes people with psychological rather than neurological problems (Kopelman, 1987).

One case of organic amnesia (R.F.R.) appeared to have little recall of the most salient events in his life on clinical testing. He knew he was stationed in Egypt during his service with the Royal Air Force, but he commented "I'm not sure that I got to Cairo." Asked about his honeymoon he replied, "Europe somewhere, I don't know where" (Warrington & McCarthy, 1988, p. 188). His autobiographical memory was more formally tested by requiring him to write an account of his life given four headings: Schooldays, Time in the Services, Career, Marriage and Family. This task was repeated on seven different days. He was encouraged to take as long as he wanted and to provide as much detail as he could. Two of his attempts at this task are given (verbatim) in Table 14.1. His recall was stereotyped, with little change in content over repeated attempts. It was as if he had a skeletal "C.V." which he could not elaborate.

The Status of Old Memories   Quantitative research on retrograde amnesia has largely focused on the issue of whether there is some sparing of older memories in amnesic patients. On the basis of clinical observation, Ribot (1882) proposed a law of regression in memory loss suggesting that the dissolution of memory was inversely related to the recency of the event. The notion that the more long standing the memory, the less vulnerable it is to the effects of organic disease has some superficial plausibility. However, it is based on anecdotal and informal observation rather than on a quantitative assessment of memories from different periods in an individual's past. The apparent preservation of old memories may reflect the reiteration of stereotyped stories rather than a fresh act of remembering.

The clinical approach to assessing retrograde memories has investigated patients' ability to recall salient items from their own autobiographies. This is sometimes tested by presenting patients with a target word (e.g., *Letter*) and asking them to recall any discrete episodes

Table 14.1 Autobiographical Recall by an Amnesic Patient (R.F.R.) on Two Consecutive Days[a]

Third attempt
  Schooldays
  Basic school education until the age of 11 years when I passed the "scholarship examination" and was accepted into a Higher Education Grammar School where I remained until the age of 17 years. I passed the "matriculation examination" with "languages" as my specialised category.
  Services
  I was a regular serviceman in the Royal Air Force for a little under 4 years. I served with the Photographic Intelligence Section, mainly in the U.K. and the Middle East.
  Career
  I joined the police service in 1954.
  Marriage and Family
  I married in December—I think! My wife is of Irish descent. I have three children, viz. two sons and a daughter.
Fourth attempt
  Schooldays
  Attended elementary school until the age of eleven, when I entered grammar school where I remained until I was sixteen or seventeen. I left after matriculating, etc.
  Services
  I served with the R.A.F. as a photographic intelligence photographer, working mainly in the Middle East.
  Career
  (no response)
  Marriage and Family
  I married my wife in December 1966. I have three children, viz. two boys and a daughter.

from their past which are associated with the word (Crovitz & Schiffman, 1974; Zola-Morgan, Cohen, & Squire, 1983; Baddeley & Wilson, 1986). When this task has been used with amnesic patients it has been found that recall is typically confined to events described as occurring in childhood, whereas normal control subjects produce memories from throughout their life spans. Cermak & O'Connor (1983) found that one severely amnesic patient (S.S.) could relate anecdotes about his childhood and young adult years. With regard to the quality of the patient's recall they commented that "In truth, such conversation is often perseverative in that he relies on a limited repertoire of stories, though it always seems that other memories could be evoked if the appropriate cues were known" (p. 230). This stereotyped pattern of recall was also noted informally for case H.M. by Milner (1966) and more formally for another case (R.F.R.) by Warrington & McCarthy (1988). (see above).

The quantitative approach to the assessment of retrograde deficits has examined patients' ability to recall or recognise public events. This has the advantage of providing an independently verifiable pool of memoranda on which the performance of amnesics can be directly contrasted with controls. Warrington & Sanders (1971) explored methods of obtaining objective measures of remote memories spanning a 30-year time period. They devised questionnaires about public events and pictures of famous personalities. Items matched for their salience at the time of occurrence were assembled for different time periods for both the "events" and the "faces" versions of the task. Memory for events was assessed both by recall and by recognition (see Table 14.2). In the faces version of the test, if a subject failed to name a photograph of a famous person (e.g., Truman, Johnny Ray) they were offered a choice of three equally famous names (Truman, Roosevelt, Menzies; Jim Reeves, Johnny Ray, Bill Haley). In their control sample, Warrington & Sanders found that there was a clear time-related decrement in performance, on both the events and faces tasks with the more contemporary items being easier to remember than more remote items. There was no evidence of any relative sparing of old memories in the older age groups, and amnesic patients were severely impaired across all time periods sampled (Sanders & Warrington, 1971).

Quantitative methods of assessing retrograde amnesia have since been extensively used particularly famous faces tests. Somewhat different patterns of retrograde memory impairment have been observed in

Table 14.2 Events Questionnaire[a]

Events circa 1950
1. The Truculent sank in the Thames; what kind of craft was it?

(a) submarine	(b) motor torpedo boat	(c) destroyer

2. What was the nationality of Seretse Khama's wife?

(a) English	(b) German	(c) American

3. What was stolen from Westminster Abbey?

(a) altar cloth	(b) Edward II's chair	(c) Stone of Scone

4. To what cause did Bernard Shaw leave his money?

(a) Anti-vivisectionist Society	(b) Society of Vegetarians	(c) The reform of English spelling

5. What British scientist was imprisoned for telling the Russians how to make the atomic bomb?

(a) Oppenheim	(b) Fuchs	(c) Braun

6. What was found in Tobermory Bay?

(a) German submarine	(b) Spanish galleon	(c) Viking longboat

Events circa 1965
1. Where was Churchill's funeral service held?

(a) St. Paul's	(b) Westminster Abbey	(c) Blenheim Chapel

2. In which Welsh village was there a disaster causing the death of many children?

(a) Abertillery	(b) Abergavenny	(c) Aberfan

3. What happened to Gerald Brooke?

(a) Imprisoned in China	(b) Imprisoned in Russia	(c) Imprisoned in Spain

4. What was the Sea Gem?

(a) trawler	(b) oil rig	(c) pleasure boat

5. What did Beeching report on?

(a) docks	(b) railways	(c) trade unions

6. Who was Mr. Shastri?

(a) Indian Prime Minister	(b) Pakistani Prime Minister	(c) Ceylonese Prime Minister

[a]Examples from Events Questionnaire used by Warrington & Sanders (1971): if the subject failed to recall the answer to the question, a subsequent choice of three items (a, b, or c) was given to assess recognition memory.

these various studies. The most common finding has been of apparently better recall or recognition of very old memories (e.g., Seltzer & Benson, 1974; Albert, Butters, & Levin, 1979; Squire & Cohen, 1982; Cermak & O'Connor, 1983; Shimamura & Squire, 1986). Meudell, Northern, Snowden, & Neary (1980) introduced a further test making use of archival recordings of famous voices. They noted that only the oldest memories were preserved. The patients had "an impaired memory for voices which extends over both the recent and remote past. The retrograde amnesia. . . extends as far as the second decade of their lives, that is into the time of their youth" (p. 136). Warrington & McCarthy (1988) replicated the original "famous faces" findings of Sanders & Warrington (1971) in a single case (R.F.R.) with a very profound retrograde amnesia. This dense and long-enduring retrograde amnesic deficit has also been observed by Snowden (1983, cited by Kapur, Heath, Meudell & Kennedy, 1986).

There are a number of methodological problems inherent in the testing of "old" memories. A major difficulty lies in equating the salience of memories over various time periods sampled. The problem here is that normal people forget and it is difficult to avoid producing an "impossible" task when testing for events which occured 30 years ago which are also matched for their salience with more recent occurrences. Good levels of performance for old memories can be achieved, but only at the risk of abandoning any attempt to match for salience. Indeed, some tests have deliberately chosen items so that normal subjects function at an 80% level for all decades in the past. For example, the loser in a recent American presidential election (Dukakis, Hart) might be included as a contemporary item, but equivalent performance on previous decades could only be achieved by contrasting these "ephemeral" people with household names such as Roosevelt or Truman. When memory for different time periods is tested by items matched for their salience, there is little evidence of temporal gradients in amnesics. Thus, when normal subjects are shown to "forget," amnesics fail to score. When normal subjects show no evidence of forgetting, amnesics show a temporal gradient, with increasing vulnerability of recent events (see Fig. 14.8) The relative preservation of old memories in amnesic patients appears to depend on knowledge of established cultural information rather than ephemeral events.

Butters & Cermak (1986) documented a severe retrograde amnesia and anterograde amnesia in a unique single case (P.Z.) The patient was an eminent scientist (born 1914) who had written his autobiography only 2 years before he became amnesic. They concluded, "First PZ has a very severe retrograde amnesia for autobiographical events with sparing of information only from the very remote past. Second, PZ's retrograde amnesia cannot be secondary to a deficiency in original learning. The fact that all questions were drawn from his own autobiography eliminates the possibility that he had never acquired the information"

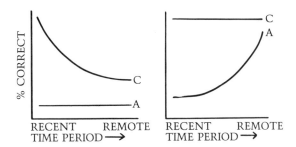

Figure 14.8. Schematic representation of two types of finding in studies of retrograde amnesia. When controls (C) forget, amnesics (A) score at "floor" levels; When there is no gradient in controls amnesics show relative preservation of "old" memories.

(p. 267). The temporal gradient of impairment in this patient is shown in Fig. 14.9.

Fractionation of Retrograde Memory?   As was found to be the case for anterograde memory impairments, it appears as though methods of testing the retention of remote memories are crucial. Marslen-Wilson & Teuber (1975) investigated remote memory using prompts to recall names of famous faces in H.M. and a group of other amnesic patients. The subjects were given the Christian name and the initial syllable of the surname and asked to recall the famous personality. For all of the

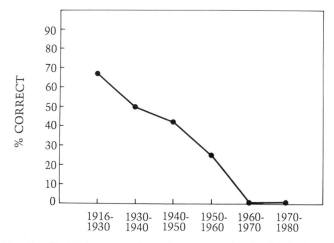

Figure 14.9. Recall of information from the patient's (P.Z.) published autobiography (Butters and Cermak, 1986).

Figure 14.10.   Triplet of faces from the "face-selection" test (Warrington & McCarthy, 1988).

amnesics there was a massive gain under these conditions. Indeed, their performance was at ceiling when this technique was used. A similar result was obtained by Sanders & Warrington (1975). Subsequently this technique was incorporated into a retrograde memory test battery by Albert *et al.* (1979) and once again a benefit from cues was reported.

These observations were replicated and extended in a study of a single case (R.F.R.) (Warrington & McCarthy, 1988). The patient was tested for recall of the name of a famous personality either when given a picture of the individual or when prompted by the Christian name and initial letter of their surname (e.g., "Neil K?" for Neil Kinnock; "Shirley W.?" for Shirley Williams). The patient scored at a "floor" level in naming the famous faces, but was within normal limits on the prompted recall condition. In a second experiment, he was tested for his ability to discriminate familiar and unfamiliar names (name-selection). He was presented with three names: one was that of a famous personality and the other two were similar names of unknown people (e.g., Robert Kennedy, Michael Driscoll, Eric Blythe; Indira Gandhi, Paneer Singh, Shuli Patel). On a visual analogue of the name-selection task, R.F.R. was presented with three photographs, only one of which was of a famous personality (see Fig. 14.10). His score was within the control range on this task, despite his grave impairment when tested using recall and forced-choice recognition techniques (Warrington & McCarthy, 1988) (see Table 14.3).

These experiments, in which different methods of testing were contrasted, reinforce the complexities which are inherent in testing remote memories. On certain measures, retrograde memory may appear to be abolished. Using other techniques to assess memory for the identical event, retrograde knowledge may give the appearance of being intact.

Table 14.3 The Effects of Different Types of Retention Test on Retrograde Knowledge of Famous Personalities in an Amnesic Patient[a], [b]

	R.F.R.		Controls ($N = 8$)	
	1980–1985	1970–1980	1980–1985	1970–1980
Face naming	2	1	10.1	8.1
			(S.D. 2.93)	(S.D. 2.6)
Face selection	13	12	13.25	13.75
			(S.D. 1.47)	(S.D. 1.28)
Name selection	15	14	—	—

[a] Maximum = 15.
[b] Data from Warrington & McCarthy (1988).

Paramnesic Disturbances

Confabulation   The disorder of confabulation is distinguished from classical amnesia in that the patient may produce "memories" which have no basis in "actual" events or occurrences (e.g., Bonhoeffer, 1904; Berlyne, 1972; Stuss, Alexander, Lieberman, & Levine, 1978; Shapiro, Alexander, Gardner, & Mercer, 1981; Baddeley & Wilson, 1986). Although it can occur as a complication in cases of global memory impairment (e.g., Berlyne, 1972; Mercer, Wapner, Gardner, & Benson, 1977), confabulation is by no means a characteristic of a classical selective amnesia. Indeed, confabulation may arise in patients whose performance on standard tests of anterograde memory and learning is within the normal range (Stuss *et al.*, 1978; Kapur & Coughlan, 1980). For these reasons confabulation can be considered a paramnesic disorder rather than a variant of a severe form of amnesia.

For example, one patient (S.B.) described by Kapur & Coughlan (1980) "would claim to have fictitious appointments when in fact he was attending a day centre and he would frequently dress for dinner in the evening in the mistaken belief that guests were coming. He would also attempt to take cups of tea outside saying these were for his foreman who had discontinued employment with him several years earlier" (p. 461).

Two classes of confabulation have been identified, termed *fantastic confabulation* and *provoked* (or *momentary*) *confabulation* (Berlyne, 1972). Fantastic confabulation is characterised by spontaneously produced "stories" about events or occurrences, sometimes, although not invariably, with a grandiose or bizarre content. For example, one 72-year-old patient reported by Berlyne (E.E.L.) "stated that she had just been playing cricket for the ladies eleven, that she was a doctor in charge at Manchester University, and that her son was a Field Marshall and a V.C."

Momentary confabulation, or provoked confabulation, consists of a fabricated event or occurrence which is elicited by the investigator in response to direct questioning. For example, in response to the question "What did you do yesterday?" the patient may produce a plausible, but invented, series of events. Provoked confabulation may be confined to a limited range of questions drawing on autobiographical memory or events that the patient "should" know. In a study of patients with both provoked and fantastic confabulation, Mercer *et al.* (1977) and Dalla Barba, Cipolotti, & Denes (1989) observed that confabulatory responses were mostly elicited with easy questions about events which "should" be known (e.g., "Why are you in Hospital?", "What have you been doing?"). On more difficult questions that elicited a "don't know" response from controls (e.g., "Who won the Super Bowl last year?"), these same patients were also likely to respond "don't know" rather than produce a confabulation. The patients knowledge of what they should know was intact, but their retrieval of "should know" information was impaired.

Shapiro *et al.* (1981) used a structured recall test in order to investigate confabulation. They presented subjects with three-component pictures for inspection (e.g., a man in a boat fishing). Recall of the pictures was tested after some unrelated interpolated activity. Shapiro *et al.* found that this task reliably elicited confabulation in "severe" cases. Furthermore, the amount of confabulation could be reduced by presenting the subject with cues following erroneous recall (e.g., "There was a man in the picture. . .").

Reduplicative Paramnesia In this syndrome, the patient may believe that certain places are "duplicated" (Pick, 1903) or transposed in place (Benson, Gardner, & Meadows, 1976; Ruff & Volpe, 1981). One patient described by Kapur, Turner, & King (1988) insisted that his house was not his real home and remarked how striking it was that the owners of this house even had the same ornaments as he had! Other cases may "relocate" the hospital (in which they are staying as patients). The relocation frequently results in locating the hospital in places near their own homes or actually within their houses (Weinstein, Kahn, & Sugarman, 1952; Benson *et al.* (1976).

Anatomical Considerations

It is now established that there are a number of critical lesion sites that give rise to a global amnesic deficit. Global amnesias arise following bilateral lesions of the medial surface of the temporal lobes, particularly the hippocampus and amygdala. Global amnesias also arise following lesions to more central areas of the brain (diencephalic regions), namely the thalamus and the mamillary bodies. These are all structures in the limbic system, a set of closely interconnected structures first identified by Papez (1937) (see Fig. 14.11).

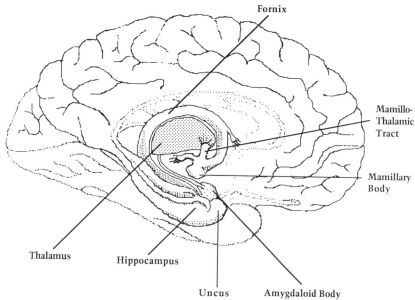

Figure 14.11. Diagram showing the major structures in Papez circuit which give rise to the amnesic syndrome when damaged bilaterally.

Medial Temporal Lobe Lesions

Case H.M. had radical surgery in an attempt to reduce his severe and disabling epilepsy. Scoville & Milner (1957) described his operation as follows. "On September 1, 1953, bilateral medial temporal lobe resection was carried out, extending posteriorly for a distance of 8 cm. from the midpoints of the tips of the temporal lobes with the temporal horns constituting the lateral edges of resection" (p. 16). This resulted in ablation of the anterior two-thirds of the hippocampal complex, the uncus, the amygdala, and the hippocampal gyrus. He was subsequently found to have a marked amnesic impairment. One further surgical temporal lobe case has been described (Dimsdale, Logue, and Piercy, 1964). The patient (N.T.) had a unilateral right medial temporal lobe resection which produced an unexpected and very profound global amnesia (subsequently her memory impairment was extensively documented by Warrington and colleagues from 1968 through 1978). At post mortem, in addition to her unilateral surgical ablation, it was found that she had a long-standing atrophic lesion confined to the left hippocampus (Duchen, unpublished data).

Profound global amnesic deficits have also been documented following bilateral medial temporal lobe damage arising from other causes. These include herpes-simplex encephalitis, (e.g., Parkin & Long, 1988; Warrington & McCarthy, 1988) and vascular lesions involving both posterior cerebral arteries (e.g., Dejong, Itabashi, & Olson, 1969; Benson, Marsden, & Meadows, 1974; Muramuto, Kuru, Sugishita, & Togokura, 1979; Trillet, Fisher, Serclerat, & Schott, 1980).

Diencephalic Damage

Loss of neurons in the thalamus and the mamillary bodies may also give rise to a profound global amnesia. This pattern of pathology is frequently associated with a disorder known as the Korsakoff syndrome. This neurological condition most commonly occurs as a consequence of heavy and chronic alcohol abuse together with a thiamine deficiency. In the acute phase, patients typically present with a confusional state, together with other signs of central nervous system dysfunction. Some patients recover to show a chronic amnesic syndrome (Victor, et al., 1971, 1988). Focal diencephalic damage may also arise in other pathological conditions (e.g., Von Cramon, Hebel, & Schuri, 1985 Dall'Ora, Della Sala and Spinnler, 1989).

Victor *et al.* (1971, 1988), conducted a retrospective post-mortem review of a series of patients with diagnosis of Korsakoff psychosis and claimed that degeneration of the dorsal medial nucleus was a common feature of those who were clinically described as amnesic. Mair, Warrington, & Weiskrantz (1978) reported post-mortem evidence from two further Korsakoff cases (E.A. & H.J.) whose amnesia had been extensively studied during life. They found that these patients had two lesion sites: first, bilateral mamillary body degeneration (particularly affecting the medial nuclei), and second, a bilateral area of gliosis in medial thalamus, between the medial dorsal nucleus and the subependymal zone. This localisation of the minimal lesion in Korsakoff amnesia has since been replicated in two further cases (Mayes, Meudell, Mann, & Pickering, 1988).

Some supporting evidence for the critical role of these structures in memory processing has been provided on the basis of CT scan evidence by Von Cramon *et al.* (1985). They reported a series of four cases who had sustained bilateral vascular lesions in the region of the diencephalon. Three of the patients were found to have a dense and global amnesia on formal neuropsychological assessment. The fourth case was not impaired on memory tests. In a detailed analysis of the radiological evidence it was concluded that lesions of the mamillothalamic tract were critical for chronic amnesic impairments. Similar lesion sites have been implicated in cases of "thalamic amnesia" for whom there was adequate radiological evidence (e.g., Schott, Mauguière, Laurent, Serclerat, & Fischer, 1980; Barbizet, Degos, Louran, Nguyen, & Mas, 1981; Michel, Laurent, Foyatier, Blanc, & Portafaix, 1982). Von Cramon *et al.* noted that in their patient without an amnesia the mamilla-thalamic tracts were spared.

Is Amnesia a Single Syndrome?

The foregoing discussion has implied that "global memory impairments," or amnesia, are fundamentally similar regardless of the site of damage. This is a working assumption that has been adopted by some researchers but seriously questioned by others. The main contrast which has been drawn is that between amnesia resulting from bilateral medial temporal lobe damage and that arising from diencephalic damage.

In some investigations, both diencephalic and medial temporal lobe cases have been combined into a single small group of amnesics on the grounds that they did not differ on any clinical criterion. For example, Warrington & Weiskrantz (e.g., 1970, 1974) used groups of amnesics who were not differentiated according to the site of their lesions and included the temporal lobe case (N.T.: see above). as well as the Korsakoff cases reported by Mair et al. (1978) (E.A. and H.J.). Empirical support for the assumption that there is no difference between diencephalic and medial temporal lobe amnesias is provided by Brooks & Baddeley (1976: see Fig. 14.2), who investigated both types of case. They found that the pattern of preserved and impaired memory functions was identical in the two types of patient.

Adherents of the "two amnesias" hypothesis have suggested that there are qualitative differences between diencephalic and medial temporal lobe cases (e.g., Parkin, 1984; Squire, 1986). Specifically, it is suggested that medial temporal lobe cases have a disorder affecting the retention of new information, whereas diencephalic patients have a more pervasive memory disorder. First, it is claimed that medial temporal lobe lesions give rise to a disproportionate impairment of anterograde memory, with preservation of old memories. Diencephalic lesions result in anterograde amnesia, and a retrograde amnesia characterised by a temporal gradient, with only the oldest memories being spared. Second, it has been suggested that the anterograde amnesia of medial temporal lobe cases is characterised by abnormally fast forgetting rates. Neither of these points is unequivocally supported by empirical evidence.

Milner reported that case H.M. had a very limited degree of retrograde amnesia. For example, he has been described as having no recall of an uncle who died 3 years before his operation and to be unclear about people and events that first came into prominence in the decade before his operation. Earlier memories from his childhood and teens were considered to be relatively spared. (Scoville & Milner, 1957; Marslen-Wilson & Teuber, 1975). However, there are at least two medial temporal lobe cases with intact cognitive skills in whom a profound retrograde amnesia was documented [Sanders & Warrington, 1971 (N.T.); Warrington & McCarthy, 1988 (R.F.R.)].

The hypothesis that forgetting rates differ in the two pathologies has also been difficult to assess. Huppert & Piercy (1979) suggested that Korsakoff patients had normal forgetting of material (once it had been registered), whereas H.M. forgot more rapidly. In order to equate initial learning, memory stimuli were presented for different lengths of time to the amnesic and control subjects. This technique is problematic in that it is extremely difficult to ensure initial levels of learning. Indeed, an attempted replication of these findings was unsuccessful (Freed, Corkin, & Cohen, 1987).

Evaluation of the two-amnesias hypothesis has also been complicated by the fact that the critical patient groups may differ in more than one respect. Unless the severity of the global memory deficit and the co-occurrence of additional cognitive impairments is adequately matched, then it is not possible to test the two-amnesias hypothesis. Diencephalic cases are most usually long-term chronic alcoholics who are commonly impaired on a wide range of cognitive tasks (e.g., Butters & Cermak, 1980; Oscar-Berman, 1980). The severity of their global memory deficit varies, from the apparently absolute (e.g., Mair *et al.*, 1979) to mild or moderate deficits which may be specific to particular classes of material (Winocur, Oxbury, Roberts, Agnetti, & Davis, 1984; Squire & Shimamura, 1986). Bilateral medial temporal lobe cases may also vary in the severity of their memory impairment and in the incidence of associated cognitive deficits. (e.g., Warrington & Shallice, 1984; Greenwood, Bhall, Gordon, & Roberts, 1983).

Paramnesic Impairments

The paramnesic deficits of confabulation and reduplication may be observed in both focal and more generalised cerebral disease. As an aside, it should be noted that deficits superficially resembling organic paramnesia are sometimes seen in "psychiatric" disturbances such as hypomania (Weinstein & Kahn, 1955). In the case of focal cerebral lesions, the disorder may be most marked following damage to those medial aspects of the frontal lobes which are closely linked anatomically to the limbic system and basal forebrain nuclei (Damasio, Graff-Radford, Eslinger, Damasio, & Kassell, 1985). Damage to these areas is not uncommon in cases of infarction resulting from ruptured anterior communicating artery aneurism. Logue, Durwood, Pratt, Piercy, & Nixon (1968) noted confabulation in 18 of 79 consecutively studied patients with this pathology. Reduplicative phenomena may be more frequent following right-hemisphere damage including the frontal lobe (Kapur *et al.*, 1988). However, bilateral frontal pathology has been documented in the majority of cases.

Theoretical Considerations

The implications of the amnesic syndrome for theories of normal memory were recognised following the early descriptions of case H.M. His selective impairment in memory for events was seen as having the potential to cast light on the normal processes involved in day-to-day memory. It was assumed that one critical process had been disrupted, giving rise to his amnesia, and that an understanding of that process would provide valuable insights into normal memory functioning. The first models to be explored were those which considered memory as consisting of three interlinked component processes of *input, storage,* and *retrieval.* There was considerable debate as to which of these components was specifically disrupted in the amnesic syndrome. Each of these components could (arguably) account for some of the data, but no account cast in these terms could account adequately for the selective preservation of memory on certain types of task. This has led to the development of a different emphasis within theoretical accounts of amnesia: the question is now less one of "why they forget" than "why they remember some things and forget others."

First, those theories of amnesia which focused on one of the component stages of memory will be briefly considered. This will be followed by a more detailed account of the more cognitive models of the amnesic syndrome. Although the documentation of systematic patterns of preservation of memory has resulted in a redefinition of the characteristics of amnesia, the issues raised by the earlier theories remain valid and must be accounted for in any viable theory of amnesia.

Component Stage Models

Input Theories   The hypothesis that amnesics were specifically impaired in the acquisition of new memory traces despite normal perception and short-term memory was initially cast in terms of a "consolidation" hypothesis. The idea of consolidation was based on the physiological thesis that a certain finite period of time was necessary for a memory trace to become fixed or established (Hebb, 1949). Milner argued that for H.M. "The essential deficit is one of consolidation so that no stable learning can take place" (Milner, 1966). The clinical presentation of an absolute failure of ongoing memory together with the relative sparing of older memories almost demanded such an explanation.

The concept of consolidation has also been expressed in psychological terms by Craik & Lockhart (1972). They suggested that the relative "strength" of a memory trace was dependent on the type of processing which the individual performed on the information to be remembered at the time of learning. If a stimulus was processed only to a "shallow" level, by restricting attention to its superficial aspects (e.g., the sound of a word, whether a face was male or female), then memory was worse than if "deeper" or more "elaborative" encoding had been carried out (e.g., focusing on the meaning of a word, on the friendliness of a face). Normal subjects show strong and significant effects of manipulations designed to increase depth or elaborativeness of processing in memory tasks.

Cermak and his colleagues (e.g., Cermak & Moreines, 1976; Cermak & Reale, 1978) suggested that amnesic patients failed to consolidate memories because they were unable to achieve deeper levels of processing. Cermak & Moreines presented Korsakoff subjects with a list of words and asked them to perform different types of decision on the stimuli in an attempt to vary the level of processing. Subjects were asked to detect the occurrence of rhyming words or pairs of semantically related words occurring in a long spoken list. Korsakoff patients scored at the same level as controls on rhyming words, but were differentially impaired in detecting pairs of words belonging to the same semantic category. These findings appear consistent with "consolidation" theory.

Whilst both the physiologically based consolidation theory of Milner and the levels-of-processing approach taken by Cermak and his colleagues could account for some aspects of the amnesic deficit, they are inadequate to account for others. First, were "consolidation" the critical problem in amnesic subjects it is unclear why they should be so sensitive to different types of retention tests. The preservation of performance under one set of conditions and impairment under others is hardly compatible with either a psychological or physiological account of consolidation. Second, there should be no memory deficit for events that have been "consolidated" before the onset of amnesia. Profound retrograde amnesias may, however, be of many years duration, if not lifelong. This notion could only be salvaged by assuming that consolidation itself was lifelong or retrograde amnesia was attributable to an independent impairment.

Retrieval: Interference Theory   Overall consolidation theory appears to offer only a partial explanation of the amnesic syndrome. An alternative hypothesis was put forward by Warrington & Weiskrantz (1970, 1974), who favoured an interpretation in terms of a disorder caused by interference within the processes of retrieval. There were two critical observations which led to the adoption of this position: the differential effects of methods of testing retention (see above) and the formal documentation of retrograde amnesia which in some cases appeared to affect all of a patient's adult life.

Warrington & Weiskrantz suggested that, at retrieval, amnesics might be particularly vulnerable to interference effects. In normal memory processing, interference from prior or subsequent information has been found to produce massive decrements in performance. For example, normal subjects may find it difficult to learn the number of their latest car or a new telephone number. These interference effects extend over many time periods (e.g., Underwood, 1945; Barnes & Underwood, 1959; Postman, 1961). Since amnesics were normal when they were given prompts in the word-completion paradigm, it was argued that their memory impairment could not have been due to failure in input or storage.

The interference hypothesis was formally tested in a series of experiments which manipulated the amount of interference in learning tasks, with retention being tested by word completion (Warrington & Weiskrantz, 1978). Amnesics were no more or less prone to interference effects than normal subjects. This series of experiments led to Warrington and Weiskrantz to reject the retrieval-interference theory of amnesia.

Storage Theory   This hypothesis represents one variant of the "consolidation" perspective. It is suggested that one subgroup of amnesics (medial temporal lobe cases) can input information adequately and have no deficit in retrieval. Rather the duration for which memories are stored is abnormally brief. This hypothesis has proven difficult to test empirically (see page 317). Since the amnesic syndrome is defined in terms of impaired (floor level) performance on formal learning and memory tests then rates of forgetting are necessarily confounded by other variables. On those few tasks in which amnesic patients show normal learning (e.g., incomplete pictures) there is no evidence that information is forgotten abnormally quickly, even in the critical medial temporal lobe cases (e.g., cases H.M. and N.T.: see Fig. 14.4).

Cognitive Theories

The most striking phenomena that have come to light in studies of both anterograde and retrograde amnesia are the contrasts between an almost absolute deficit on certain kinds of memory task and normal or near normal levels of performance on others. These dissociations cannot be accounted for by any of the simple "input," "storage," or "retrieval" hypotheses discussed above. It is now widely held that the key to the amnesic syndrome lies in a model or theory that gives priority to the preserved/impaired character of the syndrome. There are three major theoretical positions which have focused on this aspect of amnesia. Two of the accounts have focused on an appropriate specification of the impaired/preserved dichotomy and the third has, in addition, attempted to formulate a dynamic model of normal memory based on the evidence from amnesia.

Procedural/Declarative Cohen & Squire (1982) have argued that the concepts of procedural and declarative knowledge (borrowed from the artificial intelligence literature) capture the distinction between what is preserved and what is impaired in amnesia. Procedural knowledge is defined as *knowing how*. For example, one may learn how to perform the mirror drawing task or know how to increase the speed of a car. Declarative knowledge is defined as *knowing that* and refers to operations such as the ability to recall or recognise discrete facts or events. Amnesic patients are considered to show preservation of procedural knowledge and procedural learning. Their deficit is in the recall or recognition of declarative knowledge and the learning of declarative information. This viewpoint is supported by the observation that amnesics are able to demonstrate knowledge of how to do something (e.g., mirror drawing) whilst being unable to recall that they have done so within the past few minutes. This framework has been popular as a shorthand descriptive characterisation of the amnesic syndrome.

However the distinction between preserved procedural knowledge and impaired declarative knowledge is both too broad and too narrow as a general theory of amnesia. Consider first the construct of procedural knowledge. This term is usefully and meaningfully applied to the acquisition and retention of procedures (e.g., motor skills and problem-solving routines: see Chapters 5 and 16). However the usefulness of the concept of procedural knowledge is considerably lessened by extending its range to encompass the powerful and long-lasting effects of prompts on recall (the word-completion effect).

Turning to the construct of declarative knowledge, this is too broad insofar as it encompasses abilities that are entirely normal in the amnesic subject. For example, the ability to retrieve the names of objects would be accepted as an instance of declarative knowledge. However, amnesic patients may have no difficulty on vocabulary or naming tests; indeed their reaction times have been shown to be quite normal on word-retrieval tasks (Meudell, Mayes, & Neary, 1981; Warrington & Weiskrantz, 1982). It has been argued that normal word retrieval in amnesia can be accounted for in terms of the overlearned status of the stimuli. Memory for words may simply be "stronger" than memory for events. If the "strength" of memory for word meanings were an adequate explanation for their preservation in amnesia then the selective impairment of word comprehension should not occur: strong memories should be less vulnerable than weak ones. However, there are patients whose memory for words may be gravely disrupted (see Chapter 6) but who are nevertheless capable of maintaining a normal autobiographical record. Such patients attest to the fact that word knowledge and the ability to retrieve knowledge of events do not lie on a continuum. For example, there are patients with a very profound impairment of knowledge of word meanings who are nevertheless capable of verbal learning tasks (Coughlan & Warrington, 1981), of giving a coherent description of their personal history (De Renzi, Liotti, & Nichelli, 1987; and of leading an independent working life (Warrington, 1975; McCarthy & Warrington, 1987a). Clearly these achievements are quite beyond the capabilities of a patient with a global amnesia.

Second, and more crucially, in a case with profound retrograde amnesia for events (R.F.R.) there was evidence of preservation of the vocabulary which had been acquired during this same retrograde period. Thus the patient failed to recognise a photograph of his wife, did not know whether or not his parents were alive, and could only produce a generic and skeletal autobiography. However he had no difficulty whatsoever in defining words and acronyms which had recently come into the language: for example, he defined "AIDS" as "illness or disease, the AIDS virus" and "The Shuttle" as a "passenger-carrying space vehicle, it's both for landing and re-taking off."

Perhaps even more impressive is the evidence for the acquisition of a new vocabulary and other types of declarative knowledge in patients following the onset of their amnesia. A patient (H.D.) described by Glisky & Schacter (1987) was successfully retrained in computer data entry, necessitating the acquisition of a vocabulary of new technical words and acronyms (e.g., "DOC" and "YMD"). Another patient described by Wood, Brown, & Felton (1989) became amnesic in childhood. Despite a persisting and severe amnesia she showed a cumulative acquisition not only of vocabulary, but also of the conceptual information contained in "school subjects." The converse syndrome, semantic amnesia, the loss of school knowledge has also been described (Grossi, Trojano, Grasso, & Orsini, 1988).

It is clear that the skills subsumed by the concept of declarative knowledge may have multiple components: being able to recollect a salient personal event and being able to define a word are dissociable in amnesic and aphasic patients. Although the constructs of procedural and declarative knowledge appear to offer a neat dichotomy and a useful shorthand, a more elaborate scheme is clearly required to encompass the pattern of preserved and impaired function in amnesia.

Implicit vs. Explicit Memory It has been suggested that the things amnesics can and cannot do reflect qualitatively different types of retrieval from a *single* memory store, rather than different types of memory (e.g., Jacoby, 1984). The distinction has been conceptualised in terms of the degree to which retrieval is dependent on conscious voluntary procedures (*explicit memory*) rather than on automatic processes (*implicit memory*). The word-completion task is one example of an "automatic" or "implicit" test of memory. Graf, Squire, & Mandler (1984) demonstrated that amnesic patients only showed benefit from cues if they were encouraged to guess rather than when they attempted active recall. This was interpreted as evidence that there were two different types of retrieval for the same memory, only one of which was available to the amnesic. Subsequently, Graf & Schacter (1985) reported that these effects could also be observed in a paired-associate learning task. Patients were presented with lists of word pairs for learning (e.g., *house, chair*). In the recall phase of the task, the second word was cued using the first three letters (e.g., "cha?"). However, it could either be paired with the same word as had been seen in the learning phase (*house*, "cha?") or with a new stimulus (e.g., *book*, "cha?"). Graf & Schacter found that their amnesic group obtained higher overall scores when the target word was paired with the same stimulus as in the learning phase of the test. This suggested that amnesic patients could form memories for new associative information provided they were tested using an "implicit" task. However, when the data was reevaluated, the effects were seen to be confined to patients with a "mild to moderate" memory impairment. Severe global amnesics did not show the effect (Schacter & Graf, 1986). Overall, the implicit–explicit distinction does not seem to offer a full account of amnesic memory deficits and is too narrow in scope to encompass much of the data on preserved abilities in amnesics. Indeed, Schacter (1985, 1987) has suggested that this distinction be applied in a "theoretically neutral" way to characterise different types of task, rather than different forms of memory process.

Episodic/Semantic Tulving (1973) drew a distinction between two types of long-term memory: one involved the retention of day-to-day events or episodes and the other was implicated in the processing of semantic knowledge such as word meanings. At the time this theory was proposed, the general view was that long-term memory was a unitary, if complex, system. In principle, its properties could be investigated either by testing the subjects to recall the name of an item (e.g., "small yellow bird") or by asking them to recall items from a recently presented word list. Tulving criticised this approach and argued on theoretical grounds that a distinction should be drawn between the ability to remember culturally established facts and the ability to remember which instance of such a fact occurred in a specific episode.

This distinction between episodic and semantic memory is broadly supported by neuropsychological evidence: the evidence for the selective impairment of semantic knowledge has already been discussed (see Chapters 2 and 6). Many patients with an impairment in comprehending word meanings can be thought of as having a deficit in their semantic memory, with preservation of their autobiographical memory (see above). It has been argued that the amnesic syndrome provides the double dissociation, in that the amnesic is specifically impaired in the acquisition and retrieval of episodic information, with semantic memory being intact (Kinsbourne & Wood, 1975; Cermak & O'Connor, 1983; Tulving, 1983).

This theory has the advantage of being able to account for many of the characteristics of retrograde memory impairments. Indeed, it can account both for the quantitative aspects of retrograde amnesia and for the relative preservation of old memories documented on some tests. First, amnesic patients typically fail to recall many salient events from their past and only produce a few stereotyped autobiographical accounts. It has been argued that these "memories" can be considered as being retrieved from a personalised set of facts which, although unique to the individual, have acquired the status of semantic knowledge (Cermak & O'Connor, 1983; Warrington & McCarthy, 1988). Second, with regard to the relative preservation of old memories, gradients may arise as a consequence of the type of memory that is being assessed rather than according to differences in the "strength" of older information (see Fig. 14.9). Butters & Cermak (1986) have suggested that newly acquired knowledge may be the episodic in nature, but with the time and continual rehearsal memories become "independent of specific temporal and spatial contexts i.e. semantic memory. From this point of view the gradients evidenced by PZ and other alcoholic Korsakoff patients are due to the relatively greater vulnerability of episodic rather than of semantic memory" (p. 268).

Although the dichotomy of episodic and semantic memory accounts for many features of the amnesic syndrome, this framework, as was the case with the procedural declarative dichotomy, cannot account for all the known phenomena of the amnesic syndrome. For example, it provides no account of motor-skill learning or the retention of problem-solving routines. Indeed the strengths of the procedural/declarative dichotomy are the weaknesses of the episodic/semantic dichotomy. More critically, the view that amnesics simply have an impairment of "episodic memory" is too simplistic and cannot account for the variables that affect verbal recall.

Cognitive Mediation   Rather than focus on dichotomies, other theorists have been more concerned with the dynamic aspects of memory (e.g., Wickelgren, 1979; Mandler, 1980, 1985; Baddeley, 1982; Morton, Hammersley, & Bekerian, 1985; Shallice, 1988). Perhaps the most explicit development of this approach in the context of the amnesic syndrome is the disconnection hypothesis put forward by Warrington & Weiskrantz (1982).

Warrington & Weiskrantz used Tulving's basic distinction between episodic and semantic memory as the starting point for their theoretical approach. They hypothesised a dynamic *cognitive mediational memory* system which they argued was inoperative in the amnesic syndrome. By cognitive mediational memory they implied a system in which "memoranda could be manipulated, inter-related and stored in a continually changing record of events. It may be by recourse to this memory system that normal subjects recall or recognise events" (p. 242).

In considering the amnesic syndrome, they focused not so much on what was special about what amnesics *could* learn, but what characterised those tasks on which they failed to show a normal benefit from cognitive processing (e.g., Cermak & Moreines, 1976: see above). The critical evidence in this regard was those tasks in which the conditions of testing were held constant and the "memoranda" (i.e., test material and cognitive strategies) were manipulated. Three experiments illustrate this perspective.

Baddeley & Warrington (1973) manipulated different encoding strategies in a verbal free-recall task. In one condition subjects were instructed to form a visual image (e.g., the *dog* chased the *thief* through the *street* in the *village*). Whereas the control subjects showed substantial gains when they were instructed to form a visual image, the amnesic patients did not (see Fig. 14.12). In a second experiment using a somewhat different technique, Warrington (1982b) found that amnesic patients failed to benefit from meaningful relationships between words in a retention-with-distraction task (see above). Random noun–verb–adjective combinations (e.g., *pipe–cold–frighten*; *walk–shiny–pools*) were contrasted with word triplets linked by their meaning (e.g., *crack–nut–hard*; *birds–south–fly*). The amnesics and controls performed at identical levels with the random words, however on meaningful triplets the amnesic patients failed to show the gain which was observed in all controls.

The third experiment was one of learning to make associations between pairs of words presented in a list (paired-associate learning) (Warrington & Weiskrantz, 1982). There were three conditions, rhyme

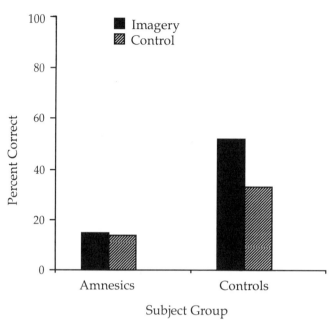

Figure 14.12. Histogram showing failure of amnesic subjects to benefit from imagery instructions (Baddeley & Warrington, 1973).

pairs (*ring–sing*), semantic-category pairs (*bird–owl*) and meaningful noun-verb pairs (*floor–wash*). Both controls and amnesics scored at the same level on the rhymes condition (40% correct). However, the amnesics were much worse than controls on the semantic category and the noun–verb conditions (see Fig. 14.13).

Warrington & Weiskrantz pointed out that a common feature of those tasks on which amnesics failed to show the normal gain were those in which there was a requirement to use cognitive operations. The preserved memory abilities of amnesics were viewed as reflecting a set of conditions in which learning and memory could be demonstrated without the necessity for involving cognitive mediation. The amnesics were unable to use a cognitive mediational memory system.

What might be the cause of this deficit? Warrington & Weiskrantz drew on the neuroanatomical evidence and postulated that lesions involving Papez circuit (see Fig. 14.11) gave rise to the classical amnesic syndrome. It was viewed as a disconnection syndrome rather than as a degradation or failure of access to a specific memory store. As discussed in the anatomical section, the sufficient lesion for global amnesia is one (and possibly two) small and circumscribed areas of damage in midline diencephalic structures. The small size of the lesion, together with its devastating effects, is consistent with an anatomical disconnection within a highly integrated circuit.

These critical diencephalic structures are linked directly to anterior

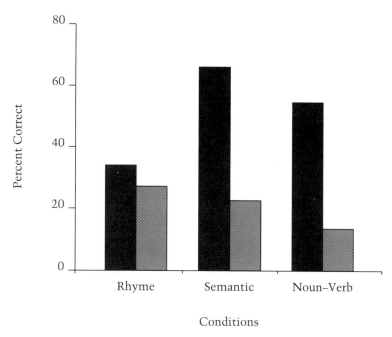

Percent Correct

Conditions

Figure 14.13.   Paired-associate learning for rhyme, semantic, and noun–verb pairs in amnesic (cross-hatched bars) and control (solid bars) subjects (Warrington & Weiskrantz, 1982).

and posterior cerebral cortex. Posterior cerebral cortex is implicated in processing vocabularies of verbal and nonverbal information (see Chapters 2 and 6) and the acquisition of skills (see, e.g., Chapter 5). Anterior cortex has been implicated in the modulation and control of cognitive skills (see Chapter 16). Structures in the frontal lobes are therefore a likely candidate for subserving the cognitive mediational memory system or some crucial component of it.

This interpretation is supported to some extent by the paramnesic phenomena of confabulation and reduplication associated with frontal lobe damage. The frontal memory impairment can perhaps be thought of as a failure of a system which is required to organise the search, modulation, editing, and reconstruction of memories. In such cases, unlike in the pure global amnesic patient, cognitive mediational memory processing is itself disorganised or even degraded.

The disconnection hypothesis predicts that there should be a close correlation between the severity of anterograde and retrograde memory impairments in patients with the critical bilateral medial temporal or diencephalic lesions. It leaves open the very likely possibility that isolated anterograde or retrograde deficits might occur in other types of pathology (e.g., following closed head injury or diffuse brain damage). Indeed, an isolated retrograde memory impairment has been documented by Kapur *et al.* (1986) in the context of a patient following multiple transient episodes of confusion and memory loss.

Conclusion

The analysis of the amnesic syndrome has perhaps posed more questions than answers for theories of the organisation of normal memory. The paradox that certain "memory" tasks can be performed by patients "without memory" has led to a revision of simplistic views of autobiographical memory as a "box" into which information was input, stored, or retrieved. In this regard it has served as a corrective to theories of normal memory function. At the very least it is necessary to make a distinction between the dynamic and reconstructive aspects of memory, and a knowledge base of overlearned information. However this distinction is hardly new. Bartlett, who could be credited with being one of the first cognitive psychologists, first pointed out that normal memory is not simply a direct read-out of stored information. Rather, it involves constructive and reconstructive activities (Bartlett, 1932). Active cognitive mediation does appear to be required both for the establishment of memories, and for their subsequent retrieval. It is this type of memory processing which is impaired in the amnesic and paramnesic disorders.

15

Material-Specific Memory

Introduction

There is abundant evidence which shows that the memory for an event can be laid down in more than one way (e.g., Paivio, 1971). For example, when recounting a visit to a city or town, one can recall the names of the people one has met, the name of the hotel, names of streets, names of important landmarks, and names of districts or neighbourhoods (verbal memory). One can also recall the appearance of people, buildings, their locations, the view out of the window, and routes to places of interest (nonverbal memory). Memory for these different types of material dissociates in patients with cerebral lesions. The majority of evidence for material specific-impairments of memory has been documented in group studies. The techniques for investigation have been derived from experimental methods used in cognitive psychology. These involve the presentation of an artificial "event" for testing immediate or delayed retention.

Empirical Characteristics

Verbal Memory

Studies of verbal memory impairment have been concerned to establish the specificity and selectivity of the impairment. Many studies have included a direct comparison between performance on tests of verbal learning and memory and performance on nonverbal tests. These investigations have firmly established that not only can verbal memory impairments be differentiated from aphasia; they can also be distinguished from impairments in learning and memory for nonverbal material (see below).

Zangwill (1946) reported that performance on tests of verbal recall could be markedly impaired. He used two tasks. One required the patient to learn one of the Babcock (1930) sentences. ("One thing a nation must have to become rich and great is a large secure supply of wood.") The sentence was spoken by the examiner, and the patient attempted to repeat it. Up to 10 trials were given for learning and Zangwill informally noted that some patients had marked difficulties with this task. These findings were replicated by Ettlinger & Moffett (1970). Zangwill's' second task consisted of immediate or delayed recall of a story. Although this test was failed by a significant number of patients normal levels of story recall could occur in the context of poor sentence learning.

Milner (1958, 1967) also used the task of short-story recall. Patients were presented with a short passage and asked to reproduce it immediately and again following a delay of 1 hour filled with other cognitive tests. She found that some patients were impaired both on immediate recall and on the delayed recall test. However, milder impairments were only apparent following a delay. Milner also noted that patients with impaired verbal memory were slower to read stories on their initial presentation. Since the patient group was not dyslexic, Milner attributed their deficit to difficulties in keeping track of the verbal information, necessitating more "double checking" of the paragraph.

A task taken directly from the experimental literature on verbal memory is that of paired-associate learning (see Chapters 13 and 14). This test can be presented for recall following a single trial, but most commonly several (e.g., three) learning trials were given. This test appears to be sensitive to specific and clinically mild difficulties with verbal learning (Meyer & Yates, 1955). In patients without a primary dyslexia or aphasia it does not appear to matter whether the material is presented in spoken or written form (Milner, 1967).

Coughlan (1979) compared recall and recognition using 10 and 35 word lists respectively. These were constructed so that the frequency and concreteness/ imageability (see Chapter 10) of the stimuli were systematically (orthogonally) varied. For normal subjects high-frequency words are easier to recall, whereas low-frequency words are easier when tested by recognition (Brown, 1976). Coughlan found the same pattern in his patients with cerebral lesions whose overall level of performance was much worse than controls.

Warrington (1984) documented specific impairments in verbal recognition memory. Patients were presented with lists of 50 common words (printed individually on cards). Recognition was subsequently assessed by asking the patient to choose the target word when paired with one similar distractor item. Similar findings were obtained by Vilkki (1987) in a 3-choice recognition memory test.

Nonverbal Memory

In the case of nonverbal material, a wide range of recall, recognition, and learning tasks have been employed. These range from tasks of "pictorial" recall and recognition, in which the subject is shown relatively complex two-dimensional stimuli, to tests requiring the subject to learn and recall the spatial organisation of simple or identical items. Pictorial recall tasks have used drawing of complex abstract patterns (Osterreith, 1944) or arrays of shapes (Wechsler, 1945, 1987; Benton, 1974). Recognition tasks have permitted a wider range of material to be investigated. One of the earliest attempts to quantify recognition memory for nonverbal material was a test of recurring nonsense figures developed by Kimura (1963). A fixed subset of 8 cards recurred throughout a list of 160 nonsense-figure stimuli. Kimura found that some patients were impaired in detecting these recurrences.

Spatial learning has been assessed using a variety of methods. Milner (1965) introduced a maze-learning task in which the subject must discover, through trial and error, the appropriate "stepping stones" to follow through a 10 × 10 array of metal boltheads (see Fig. 15.1). Touching a bolthead which was not a "stepping stone" resulted in closure of an electrical circuit, and an auditory tone. She noted that failure on this test could arise in two distinct ways. Patients either failed to follow the rules of the task, or failed to learn despite following the rules. Corkin (1965) developed a tactile version of the maze test (see Fig. 15.2). This consisted of a more conventional "labyrinth" maze which the subject was required to learn without making false turns when blindfolded. A number of investigators have used very similar methods to assess spatial memory (e.g., Newcombe & Russell, 1969; Hécaen, 1972; Ratcliffe & Newcombe, 1973; De Renzi, Faglioni, & Villa, 1977b).

A somewhat different spatial learning task has been devised by Corsi (quoted by Milner, 1971). The task consists of learning a sequence of positions. The subject is shown an unpatterned array of identical wooden blocks which are tapped in a predetermined sequence by the examiner (see Fig. 13.2). Control subjects find that long sequences of

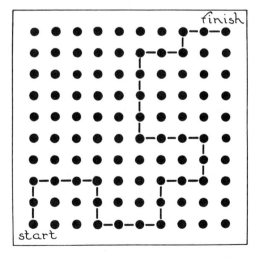

Figure 15.1. Milner's (1965) visual maze-learning task (see text for detailed description).

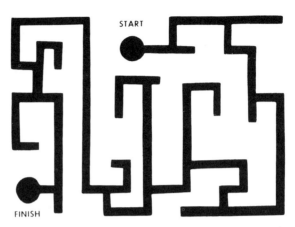

Figure 15.2. Corkin's (1965) tactile maze (see text for details).

positions cannot be recalled following one presentation, whereas short lists can be reproduced from short-term memory (see Chapter 13). Indeed, several learning trials are required to learn sequences which exceed their span by one or two items. Patients may show a selective impairment in learning on this task (De Renzi, Faglioni, & Previdi, 1977a). In a somewhat more naturalistic task, Smith & Milner (1981, 1984) have investigated patients' ability to recall the spatial locations of objects following a "learning" phase in which the subject is oriented to each item in turn by giving an estimate of its cost.

Patients with impaired spatial memory and impaired spatial learning do not necessarily show difficulties on stringent tests of spatial analysis which were described in Chapter 4 (De Renzi *et al.*, 1977a; Hécaen, Tzortzis, & Masure, 1972). The question remains as to whether there is a (counterintuitive) double dissociation between perception and memory for spatial material. There are pointers toward this dissociation. Taylor (cited in Milner, & Teuber, 1968) showed that impaired spatial analysis does not necessarily lead to a *disproportionate* loss of spatial information from memory. Two patients were described, one of whom (J.A.D.) showed a specific difficulty in recall of a spatially complex figure with normal copying. By contrast, another case (J.Du) had difficulties with spatial organisation in copying the figure but, in recall, her drawing retained nearly all of the relevant detail which had been present in the copy (see Fig. 15.3). These findings suggest that the relationship between perception and memory for spatial information is not a direct one.

Face Memory Memory for familiar and unfamiliar faces has been more extensively investigated than any other class of nonverbal stimuli (see also Chapter 3). Tests have required subjects to memorise unfamiliar faces for subsequent recognition (e.g., De Renzi & Spinnler, 1966; Warrington & James, 1967c). Milner (1968) gave subjects arrays of 12 faces to memorise. Recognition was tested either immediately or

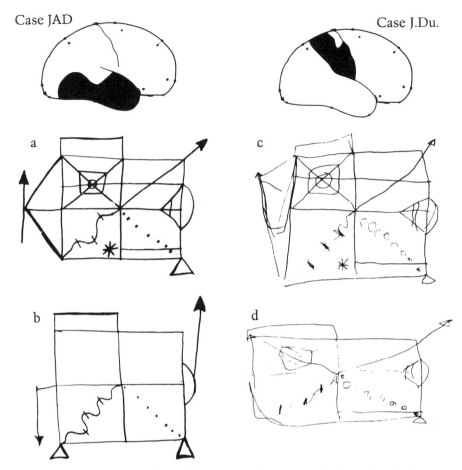

Figure 15.3. Impairment of spatial memory with intact copying (J.A.D.) and relative preservation of memory with impaired copying (J.Du) a and c, copy from model; b and d, delayed recall (Taylor cited by Milner & Teuber, 1968).

following a delay filled with intervening activity. The subjects were asked to select the "old" faces from a larger array of 25 faces. She found that a substantial number of patients were disproportionately impaired on this task in both delay conditions. Warrington (1984) used a different technique. Fifty faces were presented sequentially and recognition memory for these faces was tested by a forced-choice procedure in which the target face was paired with a similar new face. Warrington also found a high incidence of selective impairment on this test. Similar findings were reported by Vilkki (1987).

Topographical Memory Patients may be selectively impaired in their ability to recall or recognise routes or buildings. This type of memory deficit is sufficiently common and sufficiently handicapping to have earned the status of a syndrome: *topographical amnesia.* Perhaps because of the inherent difficulties in designing tests suitable for groups, investigation of this disorder has been limited to a few single case studies. Two main subtypes of topographical memory loss have been reported. Patients may either have difficulty in recognising places or buildings or else in recalling "routes" (Paterson & Zangwill, 1945).

Pallis (1955) gave a very clear clinical description of a patient (A.H.) who failed to recognise places. He stated

> My reason tells me that I must be in a certain place yet I don't recognise it. It all has to be worked out each time. . . . It's not only the places that I knew before all this happened that I can't remember. . . . Take me to a new place now, and tomorrow I couldn't get there myself. My difficulty with buses is to know where to get off. Two colleagues of mine once got on at the same stop. One of them was a totally blind man. I told them I wanted to get off at P. Square. The blind man offered to put me down there which he did without trouble. I have to keep the idea of the route in my head the whole time and have to count turnings as if I were following instructions that had been memorised." (p. 219)

Pallis observed "He could outline on a plan of Cardiff the appropriate route for getting from the Hospital to the Railway Station or football stadium. Yet when confronted with the concrete task of doing so his performance was poor." Specific buildings and places appeared to have lost their individual significance.

Whiteley & Warrington (1978) described a very similar case (J.C.) in whom there was a selective impairment in recognising individual buildings and streets. They described him as "Looking at a building, being able to see and describe it clearly, yet, if he looks away and then looks back again it looks different as though someone had put another unfamiliar building in its place. The street in which he lives seems unfamiliar and each day he might be going along it as if for the first time" (p. 575). In spite of these difficulties the patient was described as being able to use a map easily and follow verbal instructions relying heavily on street names, house numbers, and other verbal clues (e.g., Odeon Cinema). On testing the only deficits of note were a marked impairment on a recognition memory test for buildings and some difficulty in identifying well-known London buildings. Impairments in recognising familiar places and buildings with preservation of the ability to recall routes and use verbal "cues" has since been reported by Landis, Cummings, Benson, & Palmer, 1986).

De Renzi *et al.* (1977b) described a patient (M.A.) with a somewhat different type of topographical memory loss. During her time in hospital "she was not self confident and looked hesitantly to left and right in search of some familiar landmark. If she went downstairs to the ground floor, on her return to the first floor she was uncertain whether she had to turn to the right or the left in order to come back to the female ward. . . . when shown more complex paths in the garden outside the clinic she always got lost" (pp. 501–502). She was given an extensive series of learning and memory tests and her only significant deficit was her extremely slow learning on a visual maze test. Even after 275 trials she was still making a significant number of errors and she never reached criterion. A very similar case was described by Hécaen, Tzortzis, & Rondot (1980). He too had great difficulty on a spatial learning test unless highly distinctive landmarks were present. However, Habib & Sirigu (1987) have reported a "route finding" case with normal performance on Milner's (1965) maze learning test. These findings suggest that the deficit may affect a very specific aspect of spatial memory: locomotor space.

Anatomical Considerations

Material-specific memory deficits have been documented in group studies of patients with unilateral cerebral lesions. In general, these studies have shown that damage to the left hemisphere impairs verbal memory, whereas nonverbal memory is affected by lesions of the right hemisphere.

Milner and her colleagues have studied patients following elective surgery for epilepsy. On tests of recognition it was consistently found that material-specific deficits were associated with damage to the temporal lobes. Within the temporal lobe group, larger lesions involving the hippocampus (see Fig. 14.11) rather than the lateral temporal cortex gave rise to more severe deficits. Milner and her colleagues emphasised the role of medial temporal lobe structures in giving rise to these recognition memory impairments (see Milner, 1978, for discussion).

Whilst left temporal lobe lesions may give rise to selective verbal memory deficits, studies of patients with other types of pathology have indicated that such impairments can occur following lesions in virtually any sector of the left hemisphere (e.g., McFie & Piercy, 1952; Newcombe, 1969; Coughlan, 1979). The reason for this conflict of evidence may arise from the nature of the lesions (relatively well circumscribed in elective surgery cases), the duration of the pathology (often perinatal in chronic epilepsy), or perhaps due to the specific nature of the memory task. Thus, "Broca's area" (see Fig. 1.1) is typically spared with left temporal lobectomies, and there are very few cases with parietal lobe lesions of either hemisphere. In the case of nonverbal learning and memory there is also evidence that lesions of all sectors of the right hemisphere may give rise to significant material-specific deficits (Newcombe, 1969). Milner (1967) has drawn attention to the qualitative differences between "failures" on memory tests arising from lesions in frontal and temporal lobe cases (see below).

One of the problems with determining the relative anatomical correlates of verbal and nonverbal memory deficits is the practice of using tasks which differ not only in terms of material, but also in terms of the methods used for assessing memory. This was controlled in a study by Warrington (1984). Tests of recognition memory for visually presented words and faces were given to a series of 279 patients with unilateral lesions which were classified into groups with frontal, temporal, or occipitoparietal involvement. It was found that whilst there was a trend for temporal lobe lesions to result in a higher incidence of deficit (i.e., scores below the 5th percentile), material-specific memory disorders were also relatively common following lesions of the parietal or frontal lobes (see Fig. 15.4). Although some patients with unilateral cerebral lesions tended to show weaker than normal scores on both tests, the incidence of *selective* memory impairments (those in which there was a discrepantly low score on one of the two tests) showed a clear laterality effect. Selective impairments were also observed in all sectors of the relevant hemisphere. Similar findings were reported by Vilkki (1987).

In a further group of patients with generalised cerebral atrophy established on CT scanning, Warrington found that there was an unexpect-

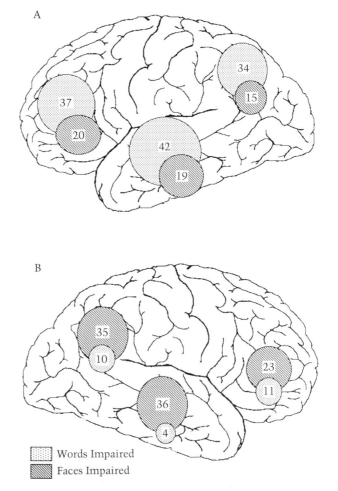

Figure 15.4. Incidence on impairment of Recognition Memory for Words and Faces (RMT) in patients with unilateral lesions (Warrington, 1984).

edly high incidence of material-specific memory impairments. In a group of patients with memory impairments arising as a consequence of chronic alcohol abuse but no asymmetry on CT scanning (Korsakoff syndrome: see Chapter 14), Squire & Shimamura (1986) have also demonstrated material-specific disorders. Thus, even in cases without clearly lateralised brain disease (at least as visualised on CT scanning) there may nevertheless be evidence for disproportionate, material-specific impairments of memory.

Landis *et al.* (1986b) reviewed 20 published cases of impaired "topographic familiarity" and added 16 cases of their own. They noted that whilst "patients with loss of environmental familiarity often have bilateral posterior hemispheric lesions. . . . a unilateral right-sided postero-medial lesion is sufficient to produce the syndrome." The locus which they identified is similar to that implicated in disorders of face recognition (prosopagnosia: see Chapter 13). An even more precise localisation was suggested by Habib and Sirigu (1987) in their study of four cases. They noted that all cases had lesions involving "part of a cortical–subcortical area situated below the calcarine fissure, including most of the lingual and parahippocampal gyri" (see Fig. 3.4). The lesion site common to all of their cases was a small area of the right parahippocampal gyrus, its adjacent white matter and subiculum, but sparing the hippocampus. It is as yet unclear whether there are distinct anatomical correlates corresponding to different subtypes of topographical memory loss.

Theoretical Considerations

It has been noted that there may be a comparable incidence of failure on material-specific memory tests following lesions to all sectors of cortex. Does this mean that material specific memory should be viewed as a viable candidate for "mass action" (see Chapter 1)? No, most probably not. Patients fail on memory tasks for a variety of fundamentally different reasons. A priori it seems reasonable to expect that a skill as complex and powerful as memory should consist of many component processes which should (in principle) dissociate. In approaching this problem, research (primarily conducted by Milner and her colleagues) has focused on the constraints imposed by different tasks and their relationship to memory deficits in patients with unilateral frontal and temporal lobe lesions.

Spatial memory provides an example of the complexity of assigning specific anatomical correlates to impaired performance on memory tasks. First, it has already been noted that there is a double dissociation between patients' ability to recall or recognise places as compared with routes. Both of these components of memory appear necessary for everyday "navigation" in the environment. Using laboratory tasks it has been shown that there are even more complications: patients with differently localised lesions may show different types of difficulty with the same task. Furthermore, these impairments appear to have less to do with the material to be learned than with the types of processing which the task requires.

Task Specific Memory Disorders

In a study of maze learning, Milner (1965) noted that both right frontal and right temporal lesions could result in poor learning of mazes—but for different reasons. Patients with right frontal lesions failed to comply with the rules of the task and thus showed impaired learning (see also Chapter 16). By contrast, patients with right temporal lesions were slow to learn the maze but obeyed the rules of the task.

Prisko (1963: cited in Milner and Teuber, 1968) showed that patients with frontal lobe lesions were specifically impaired in a delayed-response task. This test (which was adapted from experimental studies of brain-lesioned animals), required the subject to judge whether two successively presented stimuli (clicks, flashes, tones, colours, and nonsense patterns) were the same or different. Prisko found that when the comparison stimuli were drawn from a very limited (and therefore repeated) set of stimuli, namely the clicks, flashes, tones, and colours, frontal lobe patients were impaired. By contrast, on the nonsense pattern stimuli which were drawn from a large (and therefore less repetitive) set, the frontal patients performed normally, but right temporal lobe cases were impaired.

Prisko (cited in Milner, 1971) found that patients with frontal lobe lesions were impaired in judging which of two stimuli had occurred most recently. Verbal, simple pictorial, and abstract design versions of the task were used.

> In the verbal form of the recency task the subject is given a pack of 184 cards, on each of which two spondaic words are inscribed (e.g., cowboy railroad). He must read the words aloud and then turn to the next card. From time to time a test card appears bearing two words with a question mark between them and the subject must say which of the two words he read more recently. . . . . In the limiting condition one of them will be new, at which point the task becomes a simple test of recognition, with the subject indicating which word he has seen before. (Milner, 1982, pp. 222–223)

The frontal lobe impairment in making a "recency" judgment occurred despite the patients having good recognition of the stimuli when one of the pair of words was new. By contrast, patients with temporal lobe lesions were impaired on the recognition memory test but not on the recency task (see Fig. 15.5). The temporal lobe deficit was considered to be attributable to faulty memory storage, whereas the frontal deficit could not be explained in these terms.

Related findings were reported by Smith & Milner (1988). They presented subjects with a series of nonverbal nonsense design stimuli, some of which were repeated between three and nine times during the course of the test. Following presentation of the stimuli the patients were tested for recognition of the stimuli and also asked to estimate how frequently an item had been presented. Patients with right temporal lesions were impaired on the recognition test, whereas those with frontal lobe lesions scored at a normal level. When the patients were asked to estimate the frequency of stimulus presentations, the temporal lobe group were significantly better than patients with frontal lobe lesions.

Petrides & Milner (1982) devised a task which maximised the strategic aspects of memory processing. In their "self-ordered pointing" task patients were presented with a series of arrays in which the same items were presented in a different location. Verbal (words), pictorial, and nonverbal (abstract design) arrays were used (see Fig. 15.6). The patient's task was to point to one item on each array until all of the items had been touched once only. Patients with frontal lobe lesions were significantly impaired on this task. Those with left frontal lesions were impaired on both the verbal and nonverbal versions of the task. Those with right frontal lesions showed a deficit only on the abstract designs (see Fig. 15.7).

Petrides (1985) has also noted that frontal lobe patients may have particular difficulty with a task termed *conditional associative learning*. In this task, the subject is required to learn to associate a previously neutral stimulus (such as a coloured light) to a specific response: either a set of spatial locations (see Fig. 15.8) or a simple hand

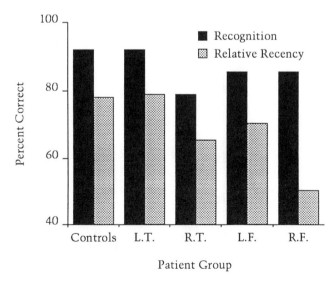

Figure 15.5. Histogram showing relative impairment of right frontal group on recency judgments for nonverbal stimuli. (Adapted from Prisko, cited by Milner, 1971.)

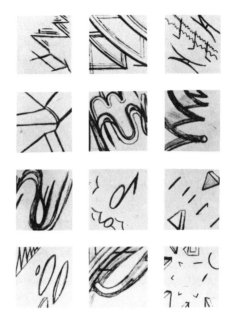

Figure 15.6. Example of abstract design stimuli from Petrides & Milner's (1982) self-ordered pointing task.

posture. Learning of the association was achieved by trial and error. Petrides found that patients with lesions of either the right or the left frontal lobes were impaired on both versions of the task. Those with left temporal lobe lesions had difficulties with the hand position task, and those with right temporal lesions were impaired on the spatial version. Petrides & Milner attributed the frontal lobe patients' deficit

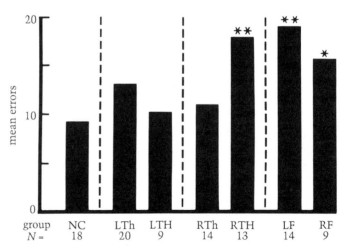

Figure 15.7. Histogram showing impairment of left and right frontal lobe cases on self-ordered pointing for abstract designs (Petrides and Milner, 1982).

Figure 15.8. Experimental procedure for spatial condition of associative learning (Petrides, 1985).

to a disorder in the appropriate utilisation of external cues in order to acquire the association.

In the case of patients with frontal lobe lesions the effects of task demand largely appear to override the more clear-cut material specific effects that are observed in more posterior lesions. Milner & Petrides (1984) have argued that there is an association between the type of demands placed by different memory tasks and the laterality of the frontal lobe lesion. Patients with right frontal lesions are particularly impaired on tasks requiring them to take account of the information provided by external signals on maze-learning tasks and in judging recency. Milner & Petrides suggest that the right frontal patients' deficit affects the coding and time-tagging of external events. Patients with left frontal lesions were worst on the self-ordered pointing task, suggesting that they were primarily impaired on the organisation of action and the generation of strategies. Tasks such as conditional associative learning require both external and "internal" sources of information to be coordinated, hence the generally weak performance of patients with lesions of either frontal lobe.

Conclusion

The deficits shown by patients with unilateral frontal lobe lesions bears some relationship to the paramnesic disturbances discussed in Chapter 14. Patients with unilateral frontal lobe damage can be thought of as being impaired in the cognitive operations, or cognitive mediation of memory. Can the analogy be stretched further, to consider the paramnesic disorders as merely being an aggregate of material and task-specific frontal lobe memory impairments? Whilst this remains a viable possibility, the evidence is far from clear.

It would also be premature to consider the consequences of "posterior" cerebral lesions as giving rise to a partial amnesic syndrome, or of a global amnesic syndrome fractionating into multiple material-specific deficits. The alternative, and one which seems a priori the more plausible, is that material-specific disorders are qualitatively different. To even consider post-rolandic material-specific disorders as "homogeneous" is a gross oversimplification. There may be multiple functional deficits which give rise to poor performance on material-specific memory tests. For example, in more lateral left temporal lesions, verbal semantic processing may be too "shallow" to permit effective long-term memory (Coughlan & Warrington, 1981). Mild or subclinical word-finding difficulties can also potentially result in impairment which might be particularly apparent on recall tasks (Zangwill, 1946; Coughlan, 1979). In a similar vein, different types of primary impairment in perceptual or spatial abilities may interact with the demands of "nonverbal" memory systems. For whatever reason, material-specific memory deficits, even in their gravest form, do not cause the devastation of a global amnesia.

16

Problem Solving

Introduction

The overview of cognitive abilities which has been given so far has concentrated on the organisation of a number of cognitive skills and their interrelationships. Such an account of human cognitive function is very incomplete: it leaves open the issues of how such abilities are brought into action in everyday life so as to achieve one of a number of goals, that is, how they are utilised in "problem solving." "Problem solving" encompasses a vast range of normal cognitive activity. At its most basic, the ability to "problem solve" requires the modulation and control of more fundamental or routine cognitive skills. The right skill has to be harnessed at the right time and changing between skills has to be flexible. Psychologists distinguish between two main ways in which the organisation of cognitive skills is controlled: habitual routines and novel reorganisation. Habitual well-established routines (such as the series of acts required to get from home to work in the morning) are thought to be established in memory. Like a computer program, the various component skills can be "called up" as and when the time is appropriate. This type of skill organisation is not strictly problem solving. Problem solving comes into play when we initiate nonhabitual or novel patterns of behaviour which require the reorganisation of sets of established cognitive skills or when we have to change our habits.

In a clinical context patients may be impaired when habitual or automatic cognitive routines are inadequate for the task at hand. Paradoxically, this may result in difficulties which are more apparent in everyday life than on structured tests of "intelligence" taken during a clinical examination. Normal scores on intelligence tests do not mean that the patient's problem-solving abilities are intact. Tests such as the WAIS have multiple components, and the problems which they present can often be performed in a number of different ways. If the patient has some residual problem-solving capabilities or is only handicapped by one type of problem solving procedure they may be able to compensate for their deficit in the formal context of a clinical assessment. Furthermore, "intelligence tests" are frequently biased toward an evaluation of the sophistication and development of established cognitive skills. Despite normal scores on such tests patients may have marked difficulty in thinking or in controlling their behaviour appropriately when they are challenged with a situation which requires the generation of novel patterns of behaviour. A wide range of tasks has been developed in an attempt to bring the complex processes of problem solving under experimental control. At the outset it needs to be said that the attempt to quantify patients' impairments has met with only a very limited degree of success.

Empirical Characteristics

The following aspects of problem solving will be considered here: (1) focused attention, (2) higher-order inferences, (3) formulation of strategies, (4) flexibility, and (5) evaluation of the outcome.

Focused Attention

It is almost a truism to state that in order to solve a problem it is first necessary for the individual to notice that a problem exists in the first place! We need to notice events and to direct attention and/or action toward them as appropriate. For example, when driving we can scan the road regularly to monitor oncoming and overtaking traffic. Our attention is not not necessarily "demanded" by the stimuli which we are monitoring, rather we have to make an effort to distribute our attention appropriately. This aspect of problem solving has been investigated in studies of patients' ability to monitor the environment and sustain their concentration and in studies of selective attention.

Sustained Attention Some patients may be highly distractable (Rylander, 1939). They appear unable to ignore trivial events in the environment and may have difficulties in concentration. Luria and his colleagues have shown that some patients may show normal physiological responses (the orienting response) to stimuli which are sudden or attention demanding. However, when the stimuli are not intrinsically attention grabbing but require attention to be paid *voluntarily* then the patient may fail to show normal patterns of attentional "arousal" (Luria, 1966; 1969). Behavioural aspects of concentration have been assessed using boring tasks. Salamaso & Denes (1982) used a reaction-time task to assess concentration. Their test required the subject to detect *rare* occurrences of a target which occurred in a long series of similar stimuli. The stimuli were briefly presented sloping lines or pairs of letters. Subjects were simply asked to respond on those occasional trials when pairs of stimuli were different. Some patients were unable to detect the targets reliably. An impairment in concentration was particularly apparent in a simple counting test (Wilkins, Shallice, & McCarthy, 1987). Patients were presented with a short series of auditory clicks or tactile pulse stimuli presented at a regular rate. Patients had difficulty in counting slow, monotonous stimuli (i.e., presented at a rate of one per second) but performed normally with faster, attention-demanding stimuli. A deficit has also been observed in a relatively slowly paced reaction-time task by Alivisatos & Milner (1989).

Selective Attention Tests requiring the selective allocation of attention have been used in order to investigate patients' ability to avoid producing the most automatic or habitual form of response. Perret (1974) reported that patients were impaired on the Stroop Colour Word task. In this test the subject is required to name the colour of the ink in which a colour name is printed. In the experimental condition the name of the ink colour is in conflict with the printed colour name, so that the word GREEN might be printed in red letters. Normal subjects find it difficult to suppress their habitual reading responses when asked to name the colour of the print in which a word is written. This is reflected in slower responses for the conflicting stimuli as compared with their speed at naming colour patches. Patients may have specific difficulties with this task, either making a large number of errors or being abnormally slow.

Drewe (1975) examined patients' ability to withhold responses to one of two stimuli: the subjects were required to press a button when one light was illuminated but to withhold their responses when another light was shown. Some patients were particularly impaired in withholding responses to stimuli. In a somewhat more complex "conflict" condition, in which subjects had to press a blue button when a red light was illuminated and a red button to a blue light, their performance was worse. At the same time, these same patients had no difficulty in performing a task in which every stimulus required a rapid choice reaction (discriminating right- and left-sided stimuli).

In another type of task, Teuber and his colleagues (Teuber, 1964, 1966) found that patients were impaired in setting a line to the gravitational vertical when they were seated in a chair which was tilted. The patients' difficulty could not be accounted for in terms of any primary deficit in spatial analysis or spatial perception since the orientation of the rod could be correctly aligned with the vertical when the chair was not tilted (a task which was very difficult for patients with a spatial impairment). The specific difficulty shown by patients under conditions in which the chair was tilted away from the vertical could be attributed to the demands in focusing on gravitational rather than other sensory information.

Higher-Order Inferences

The ability to draw a higher-order inference requires that the individual be able to abstract the necessary information from the elements of the problem. To abstract is to go beyond the constellation of concrete or physical properties of a single exemplar and to analyse how certain of its properties may be related to those of others. For example, although a saucepan and a pair of scissors can differ in colour, shape, and function, they are both instances of the higher-order or more abstract classes of "metal things," "household objects," "small manipulable objects," and "personal possessions."

The ability to form abstract concepts has been tested using both verbal and nonverbal test material. Perhaps the most widely used test of abstraction using verbal material is the task of proverb definition. The patient is asked to give the meaning of sayings such as "A bird in the hand is worth two in the bush" or "Too many cooks spoil the broth" (e.g., Benton, 1968). Concrete definitions take the content of the proverb literally and might consist of a description of the complexities of catching birds or of putting too much salt in the soup.

Another test which may require verbal abstraction is the Similarities subtest of the WAIS. In this test the subject must say how two words are "alike" (e.g., orange and banana; dog and lion). Concrete responses usually consist of a very superficial physical resemblance (e.g., an orange and a banana are the same sort of colour; a dog and a lion both bite). In other cases the patient may fail to produce any similarities and persist in listing differences despite repeated reminders (an orange is round, a banana isn't; a dog is tame and a lion is wild). Word-definition tasks, such as the Vocabulary subtest of the WAIS, can also elicit difficulties in abstraction. In the extreme case the patient may simply include the stimulus word in the definition (repair might be defined as "you repair a car or a bicycle" or conceal as "you conceal something"). Whilst responses such as these are often accepted by clinicians as evidence for impairment in abstraction, the use of such tests has not been formally validated. Clinical observation suggests that few patients give "concrete" responses to all items and therefore may even achieve "normal" scores on the overall test.

The principal nonverbal tests which are used to assess abstraction are classification or sorting tasks. Halstead (1940) used a collection of 62 miscellaneous objects and asked patients to sort them so that items that were similar in some way were in separate groups. He found that some patients included less than half of the objects in their groupings. Furthermore, they tended to group together objects which did not have a coherent (or, to use Halstead's terms, a stable) organising principle.

More commonly, versions of the sorting task are used in which the patient is asked to classify an array of tokens which vary in dimensions such as shape and colour (Weigl, 1927; Goldstein & Scheerer, 1941). In the widely used Weigl–Goldstein–Scheerer sorting task, the patient is simply asked to "put the pieces into groups so that the ones that are alike in one way are grouped together." Having sorted the pieces on one dimension the patient is asked to reorganise them (see below). In the extreme case, the patient may be unable to detect a single classificatory principle. He may simply attempt to organise the tokens into patterns or fit them together like the pieces of a jigsaw (Goldstein & Scheerer, 1941).

Cicerone, Lazar, & Shapiro (1983) examined patients' ability to abstract a single relevant dimension from multidimensional stimuli. They used a display which consisted of two symbols that varied in size, colour, location, and background colour (see Fig. 16.1). The subject's task was to determine the correct dimension (e.g., by focusing on background colour rather than on the symbol or on its location). Each choice was followed by feedback as to whether it was right or wrong. Cicerone *et al.* found that some patients were relatively insensitive to being told their choice was "wrong" and persisted in using the same criterion on subsequent trials, a failure which might be attributable to disorders of abstraction, flexibility, or processing of feedback (see below).

Formulation of Strategies

The formulation of a strategy implies that the individual is able to produce a plan of action which is suitable for the problem at hand. The types of task which have been studied include those of generating a relatively "simple" strategy and those which draw upon the patient's ability to anticipate the outcome of a series of steps in solving a

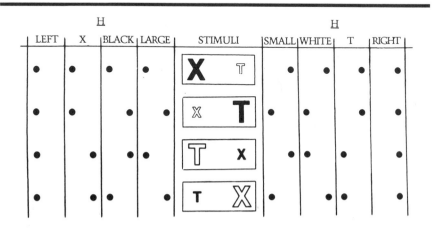

Figure 16.1. Stimuli for Cicerone *et al.*'s (1983) task requiring patients to learn to abstract a single relevant dimension.

problem. The generation of strategies has been assessed using problems with different requirements for "anticipatory" processing.

Simple Strategy Generation   Karpov, Luria, & Yarbuss (1968) described a patient with difficulties in the modulation of his eye movements in response to task demands (see Fig. 16.2). Regardless of the specific question that was being asked (e.g., "Is the family rich or poor?", "What is the age of each person in the painting?"), the patient made relatively aimless eye movements. This contrasted with the normal type of search in which eye movements were modulated according to the specific question. This was considered to be a failure of appropriate strategy generation.

A very different form of strategy-mediated "search" task which places demands upon the patient's ability to generate an appropriate strategy without any external stimulus is that of "verbal fluency" (e.g., Milner, 1964; Benton, 1968). The patient is asked to generate as many words as possible beginning with a particular letter of the alphabet ("B", "F," "A,", "S," and "T" are frequently used clinically). The task is

Figure 16.2.   Eye-movement recordings during picture inspection by a control subject (a and b) and a patient with frontal lobe lesions (c and d). (Adapted from Karpov *et al.*, 1968.)

generally given a time limit of 60 or 90 seconds. Patients may fail this task by producing a very limited number of responses or giving the same words repeatedly (perseveration). Fluency for words belonging to a particular semantic category may also be a sensitive measure, particularly in patients without any primary language deficit (e.g., Ramier & Hécaen, 1970; Perret, 1974; Hécaen & Ruel, 1981; Benton, Hamsher, Varney, & Spreen, 1983).

Jones-Gotman & Milner (1977) have devised a nonverbal analogue of verbal fluency: design fluency. The patient is asked to produce as many different nonsense shapes or doodles as possible in a limited time period. Some patients may show a reduction in the number of designs which they produce. Individual differences in this task are quite large, so that it has limited clinical applicability.

Impaired generation of strategies may also underpin a deficit in making cognitive estimates, (Shallice & Evans, 1978). In this task the patient is required to make estimates such as "What is the largest object normally found in a house?", "What is the length of the average man's spine?", and "How fast do racehorses gallop?" These questions cannot be answered directly from general knowledge. They require novel reasoning, perhaps by search and comparison with information in the individual's repertoire. Patients may give bizarre answers. For example, cases on National Hospital files have given responses such as "a ceramic toilet seat" for the largest object; a man's spine was given as "5 feet long," racehorses were thought to gallop at "70 miles an hour" and the age of the oldest person alive "older than you" (E.K.W.). Clinical observation also suggests that when patients are questioned about extreme answers and asked to "try again" they may only revise their estimates by a small amount. For example, the length of a man's spine might be revised from 5' to 4'9". A similar type of task involving the estimation of the price of objects has been devised by Smith & Milner (1984). They found that patients might wildly over- or underestimate the current price of common goods (pricing a sewing machine gave particular difficulty).

Strategy generation has also been investigated in the context of memory tasks (see also Chapter 15). Petrides & Milner (1982) presented subjects with a series of arrays of pictures, words, or abstract designs. Each array in a particular series contained the same items placed in different spatial locations. When shown the first array in the series patients were simply asked to point to any item. On the second and subsequent trials they were required to point to a different item in each array (without repeating a location choice of consecutive trials). They found that some patients had a very specific impairment on this task regardless of the type of stimulus material.

Anticipatory Processing (Lookahead)   In order to solve many problems it is necessary to anticipate, and keep in mind the consequences of one action on others. Such nonindependence of elements in a multicomponent problem is characteristic of many everyday situations. For example, in organising a meal it is necessary to decide to prepare and start the cooking of some ingredients before others. One can consider the processes of "lookahead" as consisting of the ability to organise a coherent series of steps or subgoals so that the overall goal can be achieved (e.g., Shallice, 1982, 1988).

Difficulties with lookahead may be observed in some patients when solving arithmetic problems. The subject may fail to take a necessary intermediate step [e.g., given the problem "There are twice as many books on one shelf as on another, and there are eighteen books altogether, how many books on each shelf?", the patient may simply respond "9" (Luria, 1966)]. In this case, the patient fails to utilise the information in the expression "twice as many" and simply proceeds with the question as if it were a simple division by two.

One test has been devised specifically in order to examine the processes of lookahead in greater detail (Shallice, 1982). The "Tower of London" task is a graded-difficulty problem which requires the subject to move beads placed in one configuration on an apparatus to a different position. The beads must only be moved one at a time and must always be kept on the apparatus pegs (which can hold one, two, or all three beads, respectively). The problems are graded in terms of the number of moves which are required for solution (see Fig. 16.3). Impairment on this task was characterised by slow and inaccurate performance. A number of the errors made by patients consisted of failure to appreciate the necessity for using a (non-obvious) intermediate goal position in order to solve the problem (such as moving a bead away from its final position in order to hold it temporarily whilst other moves were being carried out).

Flexibility

The ability to shift comparatively rapidly between different concepts and to adopt different perspectives on a concept is a prerequisite for carrying out the operations necessary for much problem solving. One must be capable of changing and of modifying one's responses flexibly.

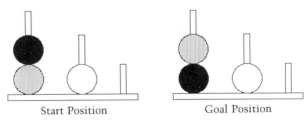

Figure 16.3. Example of problem from the Tower of London (Shallice, 1982).

Patients may have difficulties when a number of consecutive reversible cognitive operations are required on a mental image. Semmes, Weinstein, Ghent, & Teuber (1963) used a task in which the patient was required to match positions on his (or her) body with those indicated on a line drawing of the human body. The line drawing could be presented in any one of four different orientations (as if facing toward or away from the subject and either upside-down or standing upright). They documented a selective impairment on this task which they attributed to the requirements of a rapid switching between different perspectives (rather than to any primary problems with language or spatial processing). Subsequently Kim, Morrow, Passafiume, & Boller (1984) reported similar findings.

A pronounced lack of flexibility may also be shown in a range of "abstraction" tasks (see above). Category-sorting tasks such as the Weigl-Goldstein-Scheerer test have been recognised as a useful indicator of flexible problem-solving abilities since the 1930s (e.g., Rylander, 1939). Although patients may succeed on the first classification, they may nevertheless fail to switch to another categorisation on the second. They may also verbalise the alternative solution whilst persisting with the same sorting response on the second trial (Luria, 1966). Failure to shift a sorting criterion (termed *perseveration*) can be very prominent in the Wisconsin Card Sorting Test (see below).

Evaluation of Outcome

The ability to evaluate the outcome of an action or a problem-solving procedure may be impaired. This has been investigated in two related ways: first, the patient's ability to take account of feedback or comments from the examiner, and second, the ability to solve a problem "according to the rules."

Feedback   The Wisconsin Card Sorting Task (Berg, 1948) is widely used as a test of flexibility in problem-solving strategies (see above) and also as a means of evaluating a patient's sensitivity to feedback about his or her performance. Three dimensions are used for classification of a series of cards (number, colour, and shape; see Fig. 16.4). The patient is required to sort the cards according to one dimension and, having maintained the classification for a criterion number of trials, is subsequently required to shift to each of the other dimensions in turn (six shifts is usual). In one version of this task the patient is not directly informed that changes in the sorting criteria will be required (Milner, 1963). Once the subject has achieved 10 consecutive correct classifications, previously correct responses are simply designated "wrong" until the patient shifts to an alternative dimension. Milner (1964) found that some patients showed "perseverative" responding. Despite being told that their previous classification was now "wrong" they persisted with the old classification for several trials. Nelson (1976) used a

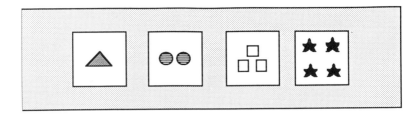

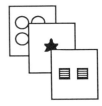

Figure 16.4. Wisconsin Card Sorting stimuli (e.g., Berg, 1948).

simplified version of the task in which the patients were explicitly informed of a change in sorting criterion, rather than the examiner simply saying "wrong" to a previously correct choice. Even under these simplified conditions a significant number of patients failed to switch their sorting criteria.

Perseveration Milner's study showed that a number of patients failed on the Wisconsin test because they perseverated and continued to produce a response even though it was no longer appropriate. Perseveration can occur in much less intellectually demanding situations. In some cases patients may continue to repeat a single movement continuously (motor perseveration). If asked to draw a circle they may perseverate with drawing circles until the pen or pencil is removed from their hands (see Fig. 16.5). In other patients, perseveration is more "conceptual." This may take the form of a "blending" of responses. Thus if a patient is first asked to write to dictation and then asked to draw on command, letters or words may be incorporated into the drawing. In other cases the command to draw a cross followed by the command to draw a cross followed by the command to draw a circle may result in the cross being repeated inside the circle (e.g., Luria, 1965, 1966, 1969; Goldberg & Tucker, 1979; Goldberg & Bilder, 1987).

Rule Following Adaptive behaviour frequently requires one to limit one's activity in accordance with "rules." The most "obvious" course of action may be inappropriate or even dangerous and therefore has to be modified or inhibited. Milner (1964) reported that some patients were unable to follow the rules of a task in learning to trace a path through a stylus maze (see also Chapter 15). The task consists of an

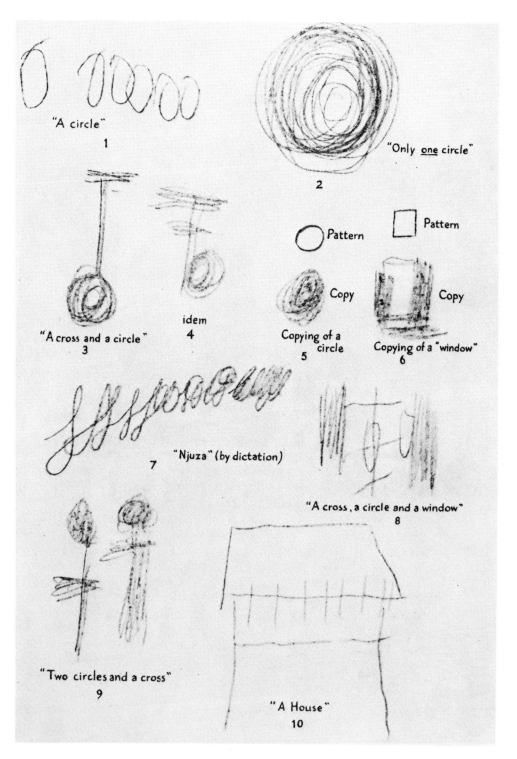

Figure 16.5. Examples of different types of perseveration. (Adapted from Luria, 1965.)

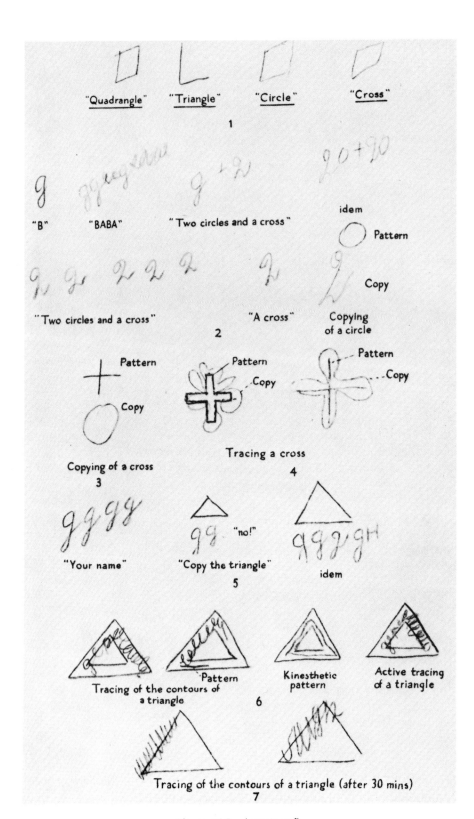

"Quadrangle" "Triangle" "Circle" "Cross"

1

"B"   "BABA"   "Two circles and a cross"

idem

Pattern

"Two circles and a cross"   "A cross"   Copying of a circle

Copy

2

Pattern   Pattern   Pattern

Copy   Copy   Copy

Copying of a cross   Tracing a cross

3   4

"Your name"   "Copy the triangle"   idem

"no!"

5

Tracing of the contours of a triangle   Pattern   Kinesthetic pattern   Active tracing of a triangle

6

Tracing of the contours of a triangle (after 30 mins)

7

Figure 16.5. *(continued).*

array of metal bolt heads which provide a series of "stepping stones" through which a path must be traced (see Fig. 15.1). Wrong turns on the maze are signalled by loud "clicks." Milner noted that some patients "broke the rules" by ignoring the clicks and continuing to trace their own idiosyncratic path. She commented, "The patient . . . appears to simplify the problem, adopting the set of trying to get from the start to the finish as quickly as possible, without regard to the one permissible route" (p. 326). These findings have been replicated with a tactile version of the maze-learning task (Corkin, 1965).

Patients may also be impaired in inferring regularities, or rules governing the behaviour of others. Stevenson (1967) reported that some patients had particular difficulty in determining that a sequence of events was regular. In one task the subject was presented with a row of egg cups in which either the extreme right or the extreme left egg cup covered a coin. The subject's task was initially to "guess" where the coin was hidden. The subject was then shown which egg cup covered the coin. On subsequent trials the coin was moved one step at a time to the right or to the left. Although this task was easy for controls, patients had difficulty in inferring any regularity in the examiner's behaviour. This deficit was also quite pronounced in a simple alternation task in which a coin was alternatively hidden under one of two egg cups. Patients had difficulty in working out the regularity of the alternation. Even when the solution had been reached in practice, some patients described their solution as "just guessing," whilst one patient stated that "she was trying to read the examiner's mind."

The disorders of problem solving which have been discussed in this section are diverse. For any individual patient it is typically impossible to predict the occurrence of one deficit on the basis of failure or preservation of function on another task.

Anatomical Considerations

Impairments in this heterogeneous range of tasks, which have been broadly subsumed under the heading of "problem solving," have been attributed to dysfunction of the more anterior sectors of the brain as compared with more posterior sectors. However, failure on problem-solving tasks can, and not infrequently does, arise in patients with posterior lesions or more diffuse cerebral damage. For many of the tasks which were cited in the empirical section the evidence for localisation is dependent on investigations of small number of patients, some of whom have not even been compared with patients with lesions in other sectors of the cerebrum. Replication of these findings has only been attempted in a few instances and attempts at replication have not always been successful (Shallice, 1982).

The evidence for anatomical correlates of the disorders discussed in the empirical section is summarised in Table 16.1. The table shows

Table 16.1 Summary of Localisation Studies for Problem-Solving Tasks

Investigation	Task	Impaired group
Wilkins et al. (1987)	Slow counting	Right frontal
Jones-Gotman & Milner (1977)	Design fluency	Right frontal
Robinson et al. (1980)	Wisconsin Card Sorting	Right frontal
Smith & Milner (1984)	Price estimation	Right frontal
Milner (1964)	Visual maze following	Right frontal
Corkin (1965)	Tactile maze following	Right frontal
Perret (1974)	Stroop	Left frontal
McFie & Piercy (1952)	Weigl sorting	Left frontal
Benton (1968)	Weigl sorting	Left frontal
Hécaen & Ruel (1981)	Weigl sorting	Left frontal
Milner (1964, 1971)	Verbal fluency	Left frontal
Ramier & Hécaen (1970)	Verbal fluency	Left frontal
Perret (1974)	Verbal fluency	Left frontal
Petrides & Milner (1982)	Self-ordered pointing	Left frontal
Shallice (1982)	Tower of London	Left frontal
Semmes et al. (1963)	Mannikin test	Left frontal (and R.P.)[a]
Kim et al. (1984)	Mannikin test	Left frontal (and R.P.)[a]
Milner (1971)	Wisconsin Card Sorting	Left frontal
Drewe (1974)	Wisconsin Card Sorting	Left frontal
Taylor (1979)	Wisconsin Card Sorting	Left frontal
Salamaso & Denes (1982)	Vigilance	Right and left frontal
Alivisatos & Milner (1989)	Reaction time	Right and left frontal
Halstead (1940)	Category sorting	Right and left frontal
Cicerone et al. (1983)	Concept formation	Right and left frontal
Stevenson (1967)	Inferring sequences	Right and left frontal
Stevenson (1967)	Delayed alternation	Right and left frontal
Shallice & Evans (1978)	Cognitive estimates	Right and left frontal
Nelson (1976)	Wisconsin Card Sorting	Right and left frontal

[a]R.P., right parietal.

that there are a number of conflicting results. Also, by default, this table does not include studies in which findings have been entirely negative. The almost chaotic profile of results accurately mirrors clinical experience: it is often difficult to infer the lateralisation or localisation of a lesion on the basis of failures in problem solving. Possibly, failure on those tasks which require the internal generation of strategies and/or control of motor-executive functions shows a greater tendency to be associated with damage to the left frontal lobe rather than to the right. But overall there are remarkably few tasks which appear to be sensitive to unilateral damage of the right frontal lobe. A considerable proportion of tasks appear to be affected by damage to either the right or left frontal regions. It is unclear whether the general lack of asymmetry reflects a higher incidence of bilateral pathology in frontal lobe lesions and/or a relative lack of asymmetric organisation of the frontal lobes. More likely is the possibility that the tasks which have been used are complex and necessarily involve multiple processing systems.

Luria analysed the stages of problem solving and their breakdown in frontal lobe damage, distinguishing between disorders of concentration and those which affected problem-solving procedures. He considered that these two types of disorder were distinguishable and, moreover, that they implicated different anatomical loci. The medial zones of the frontal lobes were involved in concentration and "paying" attention. The more lateral aspects of the frontal lobes were implicated in failures of problem solving.

Milner has argued that within the frontal lobes cognitive impairments are most pronounced following damage to the dorsolateral areas. She found that on the Wisconsin Card Sorting Test patients with dorsolateral lesions of the left hemisphere were more impaired, finding fewer categories and making more perseverative errors. "The critical lesion is dorso-lateral, not orbital and a small left frontal excision involving this area causes lasting impairment" (Milner, 1971, p. 275). Drewe (1975), however, argued that patients with lesions involving the medial surface of the frontal lobes were more impaired than those with

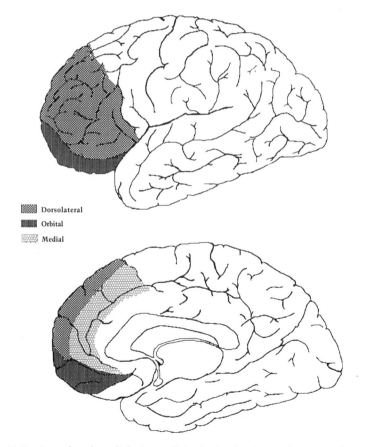

Dorsolateral
Orbital
Medial

Figure 16.6. Lateral and medial views of the brain showing major cytoarchitectonic subdivisions of the frontal lobes (after Stuss & Benson, 1986).

lesions confined to the dorsolateral regions. It is unclear to what extent this apparent conflict of evidence reflects these investigators' differing definitions of "medial" and "dorsolateral" (Stuss & Benson, 1986). Figure 16.6 shows that according to at least one definition, dorsolateral frontal cortex in fact extends onto the medial aspect of the frontal lobes.

There are also suggestions that certain deficits may be correlated with lesions of specific zones within dorsolateral frontal cortex. It has been argued that perseverative responding on the Wisconsin task and the breaking of rules in maze learning are associated with superior dorsolateral lesions, whereas verbal fluency is more affected by inferior dorsolateral lesions (Milner, 1963, 1964; Taylor, 1979).

Theoretical Considerations

Theoretical interpretations of problem solving impairments have tended to give more emphasis to anatomical-functional levels of analysis (i.e., what do the frontal lobes do?) rather than to particular types or dissociations of cognitive deficit (i.e., what can go wrong with problem solving?). In this respect, the neuropsychological analysis of problem solving has lagged behind that of the more "routine" cognitive skills. Prior to any consideration of the theoretical frameworks which have been advanced, it needs to be said that, whereas their level of analysis is often elaborate, the empirical data base is less than robust.

Goldstein (1944) thought that there was single common factor implicated in primary disorders of problem solving. He suggested that damage in the frontal lobes resulted in a specific impairment of "abstraction." He used the term in a very broad sense to incorporate a number of seemingly disparate functions. These included the ability to adopt a mental set, to grasp the whole of a situation and to analyse its component parts, the capacity for flexibility in evaluating aspects of a situation, and the ability to plan ahead. Goldstein's analysis of the types of deficit which can be observed following frontal lobe damage provides a fairly comprehensive descriptive list of problem-solving impairments. However it is unclear that his account does any more than simply subsume a set of empirical observations under a single verbal label.

Luria's Theory

Luria has provided the most comprehensive framework for analysing disorders of problem solving (e.g., Luria, 1966; 1969; 1973). His work has been a major influence in the field and will therefore be considered in some detail. Luria took as his starting point the clinical observation that primary impairments of problem solving were associated with frontal lobe lesions. He then developed a theory of frontal lobe function and problem solving based upon these different types of disorder. He considered that the frontal lobes were directly implicated in the formation of plans and programs of action. They were capable of recruiting "lower" activating systems of the brain and so permitted the modulation of activity.

Focused Attention   Luria postulated that impairments in the modification and modulation of the individual's waking state or level of activation were distinguishable from cognitive impairments of planning and reasoning. The empirical data base for this hypothesis was derived from studies of autonomic responses in patients and normal people (skin conductance). By contrast with normal subjects and patients with damage to other areas of the brain, patients with medial frontal lesions showed little change in autonomic responsivity when tasks required them to "make an effort." For example, when normal subjects or patients with posterior cerebral lesions were given instructions to count a series of "clicks" or tones, increases in skin conductance were observed. These changes were not as marked in patients with medial frontal lobe damage. Luria attributed this abnormality to an impairment in the voluntary control of attention rather than to a general lack of responsivity since these same patients were normally responsive to surprising stimuli.

Luria considered that voluntary attention was mediated via verbal processing or inner speech. He therefore attributed these abnormalities to a failure of the *verbal* control of voluntary attention. Luria's concept of the failure of voluntary attention would appear to be entirely applicable to the deficits which frontal lobe-lesioned patients have shown on tests of sustained attention or distractibility (see above). However, it is unclear to what extent his emphasis on the verbal control of attentional processes is critical since impairments of voluntary attention may occur in patients with right frontal lesions (and no language deficits).

Stereotyped Behaviour   Luria (e.g., 1966, 1973) considered that a number of the more cognitive disorders of problem solving could be interpreted in terms of the replacement of more complex types of reasoning and behaviour by simpler and more basic forms ("stereotypes"). Luria's concept of a stereotype was in fact quite broad and encompassed deficits such as motor inertia and perseveration as well as failures on more complex cognitive tasks. Stereotyped cognitive behaviour was shown in experiments in which the patient was required to perform a task in which there was incompatibility, or conflict between the stimulus and the response. Luria and his colleagues used a simple tapping task in which the subject was told, "When I tap once, you tap twice." They found that some patients had difficulties in following this rule. The patients persisted in giving the most "compatible" or "obvious" response, simply echoing the taps made by the examiner. Luria also described a simple rule-based drawing task. The patient was asked to "Always draw the one on top first" and then given the instruction "Cross below circle." Patients would break the rules as a consequence of their reliance on stereotypes by simply drawing the symbols in their spoken order. Luria's concept of stereotyped behaviour can easily be extended to account for the failures on more conventional tests of selective attention such as the Stroop task (see above). By its very breadth it can also encompass failures of flexibility in problem solving and insensitivity to feedback.

Planning   Luria attributed failure on problem-solving tasks to different types of planning impairment. Patients might act impulsively without analysing the constituent elements of a problem. Logical operations were not abolished; they were simply not generated appropriately. He claimed that with the aid of discursive argument provided by the clinical examiner complex operations such as analogical reasoning could be performed. "As a rule patients with lesions of the frontal lobes with their distinctive impulsiveness never start with a preliminary analysis of the task's conditions but immediately attempt to solve. This leads to typical errors in planless solving attempts that usually remain uncorrected" (Luria, 1973, p. 15). In discussing abnormal searching strategies he commented

> . . .that organised visual analysis of the material is here fully absent. Patients with massive lesions of the frontal lobes do not perform any preliminary orienting activity. They do not single out the most informative details of the picture and do not confront them. The gaze of such a patient wanders chaotically about the whole picture without changing its focus under the influence of the task set; sometimes it assumes the character of inertly repeating movements that in no way reflect any thinking activity. It is clear therefore that the patient's answers do not result from active analysis but present occasional guesses that come into his mind. (Luria, 1973, p. 18).

He pointed out once again that these deficits were sometimes overcome by the examiner's provision of external supporting cues.

Patients might not only lose control of the *production* of actions; they might also lose the ability to check the *consequences* of an action (see above). Luria noted that this might be restricted to processing the consequences of the patient's own actions. If the same mistakes were made by the examiner, then the patient would notice them. Once again, Luria highlighted the controlling function of language in this type of deficit. Patients lost the ability to modulate their behaviour in response to verbal commands or even in response to their own overtly spoken instructions.

Evaluation   Luria's account of impairments in problem solving was largely based on clinical observation of patients rather than on controlled quantitative experiments. However, his theoretical analysis provides a first approximation for characterising the diverse deficits in problem solving which were discussed in the empirical section. Many of his speculations have been made more secure in the context of quantitative group studies. In particular, tests discussed above, which have demonstrated disorders in planning (such as the Tower of London and Self-Ordered Pointing) and in strategy generation (such as verbal fluency and cognitive estimates) are entirely consistent with his framework.

However, Luria's emphasis on the regulatory function of speech in attention and planning (which was borrowed from Russian learning theory and developmental psycholinguistics, e.g., Vygotsky, 1962) has received less support. Some patients do show a dramatic dissociation between speech and action, either verbalising the correct solution to a problem whilst failing to solve it in action or failing to verbalise a solution whilst solving the problem in action (Stevenson, 1967). However, such cases may be relatively rare (Drewe, 1975). Furthermore, patients with severe aphasic difficulties do not necessarily show impairment on tests of planning. Lesions of the left parietal and temporal lobes may give rise to grave impairments of language (see, e.g., Chapter 8). However, such patients are not necessarily impaired on tests of problem solving (Warrington, 1975; Warrington, James, & Maciejewski, 1986). Furthermore, planning disorders may be task- and material-specific. For example, Costello & Warrington (1989) have shown that failures of planning can be specific to the verbal domain (see Chapter 8). The dissociations between speech and action which are seen in some patients are probably best viewed as a specific subtype of disorder rather than as a fundamental cause of disturbances of planning and the control of action.

A number of subsequent formulations of the role of the frontal lobes in problem solving have been heavily influenced by Luria's work. For example, Damasio (1985) has commented that deficits in problem solving are attributable to "impairment of the cognitive programs . . . that allow the coherent organisation of mental contents on which creative thinking and language depend and permit . . . the planning of future actions." He also commented that "the potential for multiple lines of cognitive activity . . . appears lost" (p. 369). A central aspect of current concepts of primary impairments of problem solving is the idea that they may be interpreted as failure of a high-level "executive" (or board of executives) which normally subserves the selection and modulation of different programmes for problem-solving behaviour.

Modulatory Function

Milner (1964) developed Luria's concept of the replacement of more complex types of behaviour by "stereotypes." She suggested that complex behaviour "is dependent on the simultaneous functioning of many complex sets any one of which can take over the action system when the appropriate signals verbal or otherwise arise . . . The effects of frontal lobe lesions suggest a disturbance of this modulatory function" (p. 331). The concept of impairments of modulatory function has since been refined; specifically it has been suggested that there are two dissociable types of deficit (Milner, 1982; Milner & Petrides, 1984). One is attributable to a failure in the monitoring of external events, and the other to failures in the modulation of active self-generated planning. This hypothesis was primarily based on data from studies of memory impairments (see Chapter 15). These studies had shown that, over and above any material-specific effects, there were dissociable disorders of recency discrimination (right frontal lesions) and self-ordered pointing (left frontal lesions). The disorder of recency discrimination was attributed to a failure to monitor external events, and failures on self-ordered pointing to a deficit in the generation and control of self-generated plans and strategies. Milner & Petrides' hypothesis appears to encompass at least some of the "lateralised" disorders of problem solving which have been documented. For example, it can easily account for the deficit in maze performance associated with right frontal lesions in terms of a failure to monitor external events. It might also account for deficits on the "Tower of London" planning task (associated with left frontal lesions) in terms of a failure to initiate and modulate self-generated plans of action.

Supervisory Attentional System   Norman & Shallice (1980) and Shallice (1982) have adopted a computational information-processing approach to modeling disorders of "executive" function. Norman & Shallice took as their starting point the distinction between habitual and novel action routines (see above). They suggested that the selection and integration of these two classes of action were based on different principles.

Norman & Shallice proposed that control over the sequencing and integration of the components required for complex but well-established patterns of behaviour is mediated by hierarchically organised "schemas" or memory representations (e.g., Lashley, 1951: see also Chapter 5). In driving to work the highest level of the schema might be a comparatively abstract representation of the route. Such high-level schemas can call up subordinate "programs" or subroutines; thus "driving to work" will have component schemas including at the lowest level instructions to muscles to press pedals and turn the steering wheel.

Norman & Shallice suggested that under many conditions we can function on "auto pilot," selecting and integrating cognitive or behavioural skills on the basis of established schemata. Once a schema has been triggered it "competes" for dominance and control of action by a process of inhibiting other schemas which would be likely to conflict with it: the power of the schema to inhibit others would reflect the strength of its "activation" (a process which they termed *contention scheduling*). When one needs to suppress an automatically attractive alternative source of stimulation, to plan novel solutions to problems, or to change flexibly from one pattern of behaviour to another, the selection of schemas on the basis of the strength of their initial activation might be disastrous. Norman & Shallice argued that, under these circumstances, the selection of schemas was modulated by the operation of a *supervisory attentional system*. The supervisory attentional system can provide a boost to a schema's level of activation, thereby enabling it to "get ahead" in the competition for dominance despite starting from a handicapped position.

How then does this relate to impairments of problem solving? Shallice's (1982) argument goes as follows. Frontal lobe lesions lead to a deficit at the level of the supervisory attentional system. The apparently diverse phenomena of impaired sustained attention (distractibility) and perseveration (see above) are attributed to a failure of the supervisory attentional system. Distractibility would arise because the patient was unable to inhibit "attractive" input, and perseveration would arise because one schema gained abnormal levels of dominance over others.

Whilst this account is parsimonious, it is underspecified and likely to require elaboration (Shallice, 1988). For example, double dissociations of deficits in problem solving would not be easily encompassed within a framework in which there was no differentiation of function of the "supervisory" system. Milner's report of dissociations between verbal fluency and Wisconsin Card Sorting provides some evidence for such fractionations. In addition, there is evidence for dissociations which can be derived from reports of lateral asymmetries and of very different types of deficit following lesions to orbital, medial, and dorsolateral regions of the frontal lobes well beyond the range of phenomena considered in this book. At the very least these findings are pointers towards a multicomponent "executive" system.

Conclusion

The analysis of deficits in problem solving has itself been a problem solving exercise for both theoreticians and clinicians alike. This may be at least partially attributable to the assumption that "problem solving" must be cognitively "difficult" and therefore requires complex tasks which place demands on many cognitive skills. However, a patient's deficit may be most "obvious" in tasks which are (superficially at least) remarkably "undemanding" in terms of their intellectual requirements (such as verbal fluency, Weigl sorting, etc.). The critical factors appear to be the requirement for the modulation and control of established cognitive skills in a problem-solving situation rather than the primary intellectual difficulty of the task at hand.

A multicomponent view of the complex modulatory and attentional systems which are necessary for problem solving seems plausible.

Indeed, drawing on the neuroanatomical evidence, a multicomponent system is suggested by the diverse anatomical connections which the frontal lobes have with all other parts of the cerebrum (e.g., Stuss & Benson, 1986). On one level, account must be taken of the necessity for modulating activation and effort, for maintaining a stable state of affect, and for sustaining concentration. At another level, cognitive skills have to be integrated and adapted so that they comply with situational constraints and yet are optimally coordinated so that the goals of the individual are achieved as efficiently as possible. As summarised by Luria (1973):

> Man not only reacts passively to incoming information but creates intentions, forms plans and programmes of his actions, inspects their performance and regulates his behaviour so that it conforms to these plans and programmes; finally he verifies his conscious activity comparing the effects of his actions with the original intentions and correcting any mistakes he has made. (page 79–80)

Any viable theory of problem solving will need to encompass these complex variables.

17

Conclusion

The cognitive approach to neuropsychology has proven a highly productive "paradigm" for research on brain behaviour relationships. By taking as its starting point the detailed analysis of cognitive skills and abilities, it has been possible to undertake a fine-grain investigation of individual patients' difficulties, to evaluate the localising significance of a specific class of deficit, and to develop and modify theoretical models. There are, however, a number of veiled assumptions and methodological issues intrinsic to this approach which are appropriate to consider in this concluding chapter.

Empirical Evidence

Clinical cognitive neuropsychology takes as its starting point the complex phenomena which may be observed in patients with cerebral lesions. The primacy of these clinical observations is reflected in the organisation of the material in this book. The range and variety of disorders often seems almost infinite to the clinician. However, operating within the cognitive information-processing framework the evaluation of such disorders is a logical and constrained procedure.

Neuropsychology is a *methodology* rather than a theoretically coherent domain of enquiry. Its level of scientific development is akin to that of "natural history" in its focus on description and classification. This by no means implies that it is an atheoretical field of study; without an adequate theoretical framework appropriate observations would not be made or their significance appreciated. However, by contrast with standard teaching on scientific method, hypothesis testing and theoretical development are unashamedly "data driven" in this type of clinical research. One only rarely begins a study with the intention of testing a specific formulation derived on the basis of a priori theorising. Rather, a patient may be observed with a profile of impairments which challenges a specific theoretical position and it is at that stage that the more conventional hypothetico-deductive method of scientific enquiry begins. The background of cognitive theory provides the constraints on which *cognitive* neuropsychology is based. In this domain questions of the incidence of impairments and localisation of lesions are in a sense secondary to the enterprise of obtaining a coherent understanding of the difficulties shown by individual patients. They require a different methodology (group studies) and a different set of clinical skills.

Theoretical issues come and go, and today's area of intensive research may be considered as peripheral and irrelevant tomorrow. Nevertheless, the strong empirical data base of clinical research means that information remains valid regardless of any specific theoretical bias. This means that in considering impairments of skills and abilities it has been possible to give weight to observations made a century ago as well as to papers published in the last few weeks. Thus Lissauer's observations on "Gottlieb L.," Liepmann's documentation of the "Reichsungurat," and Salomon's "agrammatic" patient speak as loudly to theoretical models of today as they did to those of the early researchers. In reviewing the literature pertinent to cognitive neuropsychology one is struck not so much by the changes in interpretation as in the overall continuity of the enterprise. Unlike many other areas one is dealing with "facts," which do not have a "sell by" date and, given adequate quantitative documentation, need to be incorporated within any coherent or general framework.

Anatomical Considerations

For some researchers establishing the anatomical correlates of impairments is perceived as being the primary goal of neuropsychology. By contrast, in the "ultracognitive" tradition anatomical considerations are regarded as being peripheral, and neurological evidence is only produced "by default." Both of these views are unnecessarily extreme. It goes without saying that without a relatively sophisticated analysis of "function" there would be no function to localise. It is, of course, also perfectly possible to address questions of "function" without knowledge of lesion localisation. However, knowledge of clinico–anatomical correlates adds considerable power to the neuropsychological method on a number of fronts.

First, lesion localisation may provide convergent evidence for dissociations of function deduced on behavioural grounds. If a double dissociation (see Chapter 1) is documented on cognitive tests, and this behavioural dissociation is mirrored by different anatomical correlates, then this adds considerable strength to theoretical interpretations. Thus, in domains as diverse as "object recognition," "speech production," and "material-specific memory" dissociations at the behavioural level are associated with very different lesion localisations. These findings not only indicate that one is dealing with different components of complex skills and abilities, but they also effectively eliminate the argument that neuropsychological dissociations are explicable in terms of premorbid individual differences. The conditional probability that those individuals who are premorbidly "deficient" in specific skills and abilities would also sustain the appropriate lesions is very small. In this regard, the evidence from patients selected according to lesion localisation rather than because of their "peculiar" cognitive abilities is crucial. The data from the group-study approach permits such inferences to be drawn.

Second, knowledge of neuroanatomical correlates often provides a useful starting point for clinical and research work. In a clinical context, knowledge of the types of deficit associated with specific lesion sites allows the investigator to be a more effective diagnostician. Knowledge of lesion locus also provides a convergent and partially independent criterion for patient selection in research. Thus the selection of patients according to lesion locus or pathology often permits replication and extension of findings. For example, knowledge that the types of temporal lobe lesion associated with herpes-simplex encephalitis may give rise to category-specific impairments (see Chapter 8, Warrington & Shallice, 1984) has allowed the testing of specific hypotheses about the way semantic memory is organised. This has been possible because researchers are now aware both of the deficit and of the patient subgroup in whom the deficit is not infrequently observed.

Third, lesion localisation may suggest, or constrain, theoretical accounts at the "cognitive" level. This is not a case of confusing levels of explanation, but rather an important example of interaction *between* levels of explanation. One example of this interaction is the "disconnection" theory of amnesia (see Chapter 14, Warrington & Weiskrantz, 1982). The observation that profound and permanent impairments of memory could arise as a consequence of damage to a very restricted area of the diencephalon in principle eliminated any interpretation of this impairment in terms of damage to a "store" of memories. Rather, taken in conjunction with the cognitive-behavioural evidence, this restricted and critical lesion localisation suggested that what had been lost were the links between essential subcomponents of the autobiographical memory system.

Theoretical Considerations

Working Assumptions

Cognitive neuropsychology provides a powerful tool for investigating the subcomponents of cognitive skills. It has been most effective in its documentation of the dissociation of deficits and in providing a convergent methodology for evaluating schemes and models of function based on studies of normal subjects. In developing theoretical frame-works for analysing cognitive skills it is usual to assume that patients have "lost" a specific subcomponent (or "links" between subcompo-nents) and that their deficit reflects the functioning of a normal system "minus" one or more critical elements. Whilst this "subtractive" as-sumption is a useful working hypothesis, it is not without its problems (Kolb & Whishaw, 1985; Shallice, 1988). Not the least of its difficulties is the troubling propensity which people have for developing strategies and coping with their deficits. The use and availability of compensato-ry strategies is sometimes considered as a distraction from the major focus of research. However, future developments are likely to take their use more seriously, not only for the evaluation of theoretical models but also for the very real problems of developing appropriate rehabilita-tion techniques.

Problems for analyses at the theoretical level arise when the com-pensatory strategy is viewed as an intrinsic property of the impaired cognitive skill. To take but one example; in the case of "spelling dys-lexia" (see Chapter 10) patients may resort to the common compen-satory strategy of spelling words aloud to themselves. Focus on the compensatory strategy (rather than on the basis of the individual pa-tient's recourse to it) only results in rather empty theoretical debates as to whether spelling dyslexia per se is most properly considered as a deficit within one or other subcomponents of the skill of reading. It is inappropriate to take such compensatory strategies too literally within the subtractive framework. In reality, the disorder is not in the com-pensatory strategy (which by definition is "working" for the patient!), but may lie anywhere between an early stage of visual analysis and the final stages of word utterance.

Another assumption intrinsic to the "subtractive" method is that the residual skills and abilities of patients with cerebral lesions are mediated by the same processing systems as those of "intact" subjects. Much has been written on this particular topic. The validity of this assumption has been most critically called into question in the debate as to whether there is a qualitatively distinct right-hemisphere lan-guage system which only comes into operation following extensive left-hemisphere damage (e.g., Coltheart, 1980; Saffran, Bogyo, Schwartz, & Marin, 1980; Patterson, Varga-Khadem, & Polkey, 1989; see Chapter 10). Were this the case then there would be little point in conducting much cognitive neuropsychological research, since the def-icits shown by patients would only bear a remote relationship to the functioning of the normal system. However the weight of the evidence appears to favour of the validity of the "subtractive" assumption rather than the "alternative system" hypothesis, at least in patients who have sustained their lesions in adulthood (see Chapter 1). First, there is no sound biological basis for postulating even partial duplication of "high-er" cognitive skills such as language. From the perspective of evolutionary theory it is hard to see what selective advantages would accrue by filling up "expensive" neural space with a spare system. In all but the more advanced societies brain lesions tend to be fatal. Second, the very diversity of neuropsychological impairments, their association with specific lesion sites, and their presentation in both acute and chronic cases argues against any simple variant of this framework.

Models and Modules

The fractionation and dissociation of cognitive skills and abilities poses numerous theoretical and philosophical issues. Neuropsychology has provided a useful taxonomy of deficits and has contributed extensively to the understanding of the functional architecture of cognitive skills and abilities. It is sometimes tempting to think of the "box and arrow" models of cognitive function as being an accurate account of encapsulated subsystems or modules. This leads on to the dangerous road of "organology" and is in principle only a refined version of the phrenological theorising of Gall & Spurzheim. It is necessary to bear in mind that the models of "functional architecture" which abound in this area of research are highly abstract formalisms rather than something which is "out there" waiting to be localised. The only evidence in favour of encapsulated subsystems applies to elementary sensory and motor function; beyond this level, things are considerably more complicated (Shallice, 1984).

To take a concrete example, consider the puzzling question of why abilities such as reading and writing (which are in biological terms a very recent development), might break down in highly selective ways following brain damage. We can construct formal models of their organisation; however, it seems implausible to suggest that specific neural systems were left "empty" prior to the development of these advanced skills, that there were modules just waiting to be filled at the appropriate stage of cultural development. The most likely answer to this riddle comes from considering these functions as *skills*, which in the course of their acquisition have become differentiated from more biologically "established" abilities such as object recognition, speech, and action. Clinical evidence is broadly in favour of such a hypothesis, with common co-occurrences of disorders in object recognition and written-word recognition, impairments of word meaning and of sight or spelling vocabularies, and failures of voluntary action and spontaneous writing to cite but a few examples. That these skills dissociate in other cases indicates a degree of autonomy, however their co-occurrence suggests that they *may* have a common developmental core. The "box and arrow" formalisms of cognitive psychology speak to the issue of how these skills are organised; what they cannot tell us is how they have developed and how they are integrated with other cognitive abilities.

Conclusion and Prospects

Can neuropsychology go further than the "carving of cognition at its seams"? In principle and practice the answer to this question must be "yes." Because of its interdisciplinary nature neuropsychology has continuously juggled with multiple levels of theoretical analysis, ranging from questions of phenomenology and consciousness at one end of the scale through to pharmacology at the other. However, the domains of cognitive function which have been the focus of this book are particularly well suited to questions of the organisation of skills rather than the more broad-ranging questions of their development and integration. Within this framework it has already been possible to extend this general approach to investigate the fine-grain properties of component processing systems. Although it is a limited perspective on the complex processes of cognition, it is one which has proven remarkably fruitful. It is our firm belief that the core body of knowledge which has been derived from the cognitive approach to neuropsychology provides an essential prerequisite for addressing these wider issues.

References

Abadi, R.V., Kulikowski, J.J., & Meudell, P. (1981). Visual performance in a case of visual agnosia. In M.W. Van Hoff & E. Mohn (Eds.), *Functional recovery from brain damage* (p. 275–286). Amsterdam: Elsevier.

Ajax, E.T., Schenkenberg, T., & Kasteljanetz, M. (1977). Alexia without agraphia. *Archives of Neurology (Chicago)*, **17**, 645–652.

Ajuriaguerra de, J., Hécaen H., & Angelergues, R. (1960). Les Apraxies: Variétés cliniques et latéralisation lésionnelle. *Revue Neurologique*, **102**, 566–594.

Akelaitis, A.J. (1944). A study of gnosis, praxis and language following section of the corpus callosum. *Journal of Neurosurgery*, **1**, 94–102.

Alajouanine, T. (1960). *Les grandes activités du lobe occipital*. Paris: Masson.

Alajouanine, T. (1968). *L'aphasie et le langage pathologique*. Paris: Baillière.

Alajouanine, T., Ombredane, A., & Durand, M. (1939). *Le syndrome de désintégration phonétique dans l'aphasie*. Paris: Masson.

Alajouanine, T., Sabouraud, O., & de Ribacourt, B. (1952). Le jargon des aphasiques. Désintégration anosonagnosique des valeurs sémantiques de langage. *Journal Psychologique*, **45**, 158–180, 293–329.

Albert, M.L. (1973). A simple test of visual neglect. *Neurology*, **23**, 658–664.

Albert, M.L., & Bear, D. (1974). Time to understand. A case study in word deafness with reference to the role of time in auditory comprehension. *Brain*, **97**, 383–394.

Albert, M.L., Reches, A., & Silverberg, R. (1975a). Hemianopic colour blindness. *Journal of Neurology, Neurosurgery and Psychiatry*, **38**, 546–549.

Albert, M.L., Reches, A., & Silverberg, R. (1975b). Associative visual agnosia without alexia. *Neurology*, **25**, 322–326.

Albert, M.S., Butters, N., & Levin, J. (1979). Temporal gradients in the retrograde amnesia of patients with alcoholic Korsakoff's disease. *Archives of Neurology (Chicago)*, **36**, 211–216.

Alexander, M.P., Hiltbrunner, B., & Fischer, R.S. (1989). Distributed anatomy of transcortical sensory aphasia. *Archives of Neurology (Chicago)*, **46**, 885–892.

Alivisatos, B., & Milner, B. (1989). Effects of frontal or temporal lobectomy on the use of advance information in a choice reaction time task. *Neuropsychologia*, **27**, 495–504.

Allport, D.A. (1979). Word recognition in reading. In P.A. Kolers, M.E. Wrolstad, & H. Bouma (Eds.), *Processing of visible language* (Vol. 1, pp. 227–257). New York: Plenum.

Allport, D.A. (1984). Auditory verbal short term memory and conduction aphasia. In H. Bouma & D.G. Bouwhuis (Eds.), *Attention and performance: X. Control of language processes* (pp. 313–325). Hillsdale, NJ: Erlbaum.

Allport, D.A. (1985). Distributed memory, modular systems and dysphasia. In S.K.

Newman & R. Epstein (Eds.), *Current perspectives in dysphasia* (pp. 32–60). Edinburgh: Churchill-Livingstone.

Allport, D.A., & Funnell, E. (1981). Components of the mental lexicon. *Philosophical Transactions of the Royal Society of London, Series B* **295,** 397–410.

Annett, M. (1985). *Left, right, hand and brain: The right shift theory.* Hillsdale, NJ: Erlbaum.

Arena, R., & Gainotti, G. (1978). Constructional apraxia and visuo-perceptive disabilities in relation to laterality of cerebral lesions. *Cortex,* **14,** 463–473.

Arrigoni, G., & De Renzi, E. (1964). Constructional apraxia and hemispheric locus of lesion. *Cortex,* **1,** 170–197.

Assal, G. (1969). Régression des troubles de la reconnaissance des physiognomies et de la mémoire topographique chez un malade opéré d'un hématome intracérébral pariéto-temporal droit. *Revue Neurologique,* **121,** 184–185.

Assal, G., Buttet, J., & Jolivet, R. (1981). Dissociations in aphasia: A case report. *Brain and Language,* **13,** 223–240.

Assal, G., Faure, C., & Anderes, J.P. (1984). Non-reconnaissance d'animaux familiers chez un paysan: zooagnosie ou prosopagnosie pour les animaux. *Revue Neurologique,* **140,** 580–584.

Atkinson, R.C., & Shiffrin, R.M. (1968). Human memory: A proposed system and its control processes. In K.W. Spence & J.T. Spence (Eds.), *The psychology of learning and motivation: advances in research and theory* (Vol. 2, pp. 90–195). New York: Academic Press.

Auerbach, S.H., & Alexander, M.P. (1981). Pure agraphia and unilateral optic ataxia associated with a left superior parietal lobe lesion. *Journal of Neurology, Neurosurgery and Psychiatry,* **44,** 430–432.

Auerbach, S.H., Allard, T., Naeser, M., Alexander, M.P., & Albert, M.L. (1982). Pure word deafness: An analysis of a case with bilateral lesions and a deficit at the pre-phonemic level. *Brain,* **105,** 271–300.

Babcock, H. (1930). An experiment in the measurement of mental deterioration. *Archives of Psychology,* **117,** 1–93.

Baddeley, A.D. (1982). Implications of neuropsychological evidence for theories of normal memory. In D.E. Broadbent & L. Weiskrantz (Eds.), *The neuropsychology of cognitive function* (pp. 59–72). London: The Royal Society.

Baddeley, A.D. (1986). *Working memory.* Oxford: Clarendon Press.

Baddeley, A.D., & Hitch, G. (1974). Working memory. In G.H. Bower (Ed.), *The psychology of learning and motivation* (Vol. 8, pp. 47–89). Hillsdale, NJ: Erlbaum.

Baddeley, A.D., Vallar, G., & Wilson, B. (1987). Sentence comprehension and phonological memory: Some neuropsychological evidence. In M. Coltheart (Ed.), *Attention and performance: XII. the psychology of reading* (pp. 509–529). Hove, London: Erlbaum.

Baddeley, A.D., & Warrington, E.K. (1970). Amnesia and the distinction between long- and short-term memory. *Journal of Verbal Learning and Verbal Behavior,* **9,** 176–189.

Baddeley, A.D., & Warrington, E.K. (1973). Memory coding and amnesia. *Neuropsychologia,* **11,** 159–165.

Baddeley, A.D., & Wilson, B. (1985). Phonological coding and short term memory in patients without speech. *Journal of Memory and Language,* **24,** 490–502.

Baddeley, A.D., & Wilson, B. (1986). Amnesia, autobiographical memory and confabulation. In D.C. Rubin (Ed.), *Autobiographical memory* (pp. 225–252). Cambridge: Cambridge University Press.

Barbieri, C., & De Renzi, E. (1989). Patterns of neglect dissociation. *Behavioural Neurology,* **2,** 13–24.

Barbizet, J., Degos, J.D., Louran, F., Nguyen, J.P., & Mas, J.L. (1981). Amnésie par lésion eschemique biothalamique. *Revue Neurologique,* **137,** 415–424.

Barbut, D., & Gazzaniga, M.S. (1987). Disturbances in conceptual space involving language and speech. *Brain,* **110,** 1487–1496.

Barnes, J.M., & Underwood, B.J. (1959). "Fate" of first-list associations in transfer memory. *Journal of Experimental Psychology,* **58,** 97–105.

Bartlett, F.C. (1932). *Remembering: A study in experimental and social psychology.* Cambridge: Cambridge University Press.

Barton, M., Marwjewski, M., & Urrea, D. (1969). Variation of stimulus context and its effect on word finding ability in aphasia. *Cortex,* **5,** 351–365.

Basso, A., Capitani, E, & Laiacona, M. (1988). Progressive language impairment without dementia: a case with isolated category specific semantic defect. *Journal of Neurology, Neurosurgery & Psychiatry,* **51,** 1201–1207.

Basso, A., Lecours, A.R., Moraschini, S., & Vanier, M. (1985). Anatomicoclinical correlations of the aphasias as defined through computerized tomography: Exceptions. *Brain and Language,* **26,** 201–229.

Basso, A., Spinnler, H., Vallar, G., & Zanobia, E. (1982). Left hemisphere damage and selective impairment of auditory-verbal short term memory. *Neuropsychologia,* **20,** 263–274.

Basso, A., Taborelli, A., & Vignolo, L.A. (1978). Dissociated disorders of speaking and writing in aphasia. *Journal of Neurology, Neurosurgery and Psychiatry,* **41,** 556–563.

Bastian, H.C. (1898). *Aphasia and other speech defects.* London: Lewis.

Bauer, R.M. (1984). Autonomic recognition of names and faces in prosopagnosia: A neuropsychological application of the guilty knowledge test. *Neuropsychologia,* **22,** 457–469.

Baxter, D.M., & Warrington, E.K. (1983). Neglect dysgraphia. *Journal of Neurology, Neurosurgery and Psychiatry,* **46,** 1073–1078.

Baxter, D.M., & Warrington, E.K. (1985). Category specific phonological dysgraphia. *Neuropsychologia,* **23,** 653–666.

Baxter, D.M., & Warrington, E.K. (1986). Ideational agraphia: A single case study. *Journal of Neurology, Neurosurgery and Psychiatry,* **49,** 369–374.

Baxter, D.M., & Warrington, E.K. (1987). Transcoding sound to spelling: Single or multiple sound unit correspondences. *Cortex,* **23,** 11–28.

Baxter, D.M., & Warrington, E.K. (1988). The case for biphoneme processing: A rejoinder to Goodman-Schulman. *Cortex,* **24,** 137–142.

Baxter-Versi, D.M. (1987). *Acquired spelling disorders.* Unpublished doctoral dissertation, London University, London.

Bay, E. (1950). Agnosie und Funktionswandel. *Monographien aus dem Gesamtgebiete der Neurologie und Psychiatrie,* **73,** 1–94.

Beauvois, M.-F. (1982). Optic aphasia: A process of interaction between vision and language. *Philosophical Transactions of the Royal Society of London, Series B,* **298,** 35–47.

Beauvois, M.-F., & Derouesné, J. (1979). Phonological alexia: Three dissociations. *Journal of Neurology, Neurosurgery and Psychiatry,* **42,** 1115–1124.

Beauvois, M.-F., & Derouesné, J. (1981). Lexical or orthographic agraphia. *Brain,* **104,** 21–49.

Beauvois, M.-F., Derouesné, J., & Saillant, B. (1980). Syndromes neuropsychologiques cognitif trois exemples: Aphasie tactile, alexie phonologique et agraphie lexicale. *Cahiers de Psychologie,* **23,** 211–245.

Beauvois, M.-F., & Saillant, B. (1985). Optic aphasia for colour and colour agnosia: A distinction between visual and visuo-verbal impairments in the processing of colours. *Cognitive Neuropsychology,* **2,** 1–48.

Beauvois, M.-F., Saillant, B., Meninger, V., & Lhermitte, F. (1978). Bilateral tactile aphasia: A tacto-verbal dysfunction. *Brain,* **101,** 381–401.

Behrens, S.J. (1988). The role of the right hemisphere in the production of linguistic stress. *Brain and Language,* **33,** 104–127.

Behrens, S.J. (1989). Characterising sentence intonation in a right hemisphere damaged population. *Brain and Language,* **37,** 181–200.

Benson, D.F. (1967). Fluency in aphasia: Correlation with radio isotope scan localisation. *Cortex,* **3,** 373–394.

Benson, D.F. (1979a). Aphasia. In K.M. Heilman & E. Valenstein (Eds.), *Clinical Neuro-psychology* (pp. 22–58). New York: Oxford University Press.

Benson, D.F. (1979b). Neurologic correlate of anomia. In H. Whitaker & H.A. Whitaker (Eds.), *Studies in neurolinguistics* (Vol. 4, pp. 293–328). New York: Academic Press.

Benson, D.F. (1979c). *Aphasia, alexia, agraphia.* New York: Churchill-Livingstone.

Benson, D.F. (1985). Aphasia. In K.M. Heilman & E. Valenstein (Eds.), *Clinical Neuropsy-chology* (pp. 17–47). New York: Oxford University Press.

Benson, D.F., & Denckla, M.B. (1969). Verbal paraphasia as a source of calculation distur-bance. *Archives of Neurology (Chicago), 21,* 96–102.

Benson, D.F., Gardner, H., & Meadows, J.C. (1976). Reduplicative paramnesia. *Neurology (NY), 26,* 147–151.

Benson, D.F., & Geschwind, N. (1985). The aphasias and related disturbances. In A.B. Baker & R.J. Joynt (Eds.), *Clinical neurology* I (pp. 1–34). New York: Harper & Row.

Benson, D.F., & Greenberg, J.P. (1969). Visual form agnosia: A specific deficit in visual recognition. *Archives of Neurology (Chicago), 20,* 82–89.

Benson, D.F., Marsden, C.D., & Meadows, J.C. (1974). The amnesic syndrome of posteri-or cerebral artery occlusion. *Acta Neurologica Scandinavica, 50,* 133–145.

Benson, D.F., Sheremata, W.A., Bouchard, R., Segarra, J.M., Price, D., & Geschwind, N. (1973). Conduction aphasia: A clinicopathological study. *Archives of Neurology (Chicago), 28,* 339–346.

Benton, A.L. (1961). The fiction of the "Gerstmann Syndrome." *Journal of Neurology and Neurosurgical and Psychiatry, 24,* 176–181.

Benton, A.L. (1962). The visual retention test as a constructional praxis test. *Confina Neurologica, 22,* 141–155.

Benton, A.L. (1964). Contributions to aphasia before Broca. *Cortex, 1,* 314–327.

Benton, A.L. (1968). Differential behavioural effects in frontal lobe disease. *Neuropsych-ologia, 6,* 53–60.

Benton, A.L. (1974). *The revised visual retention test.* New York: Psychological Corporation.

Benton, A.L. (1984). Hemispheric dominance before Broca. *Neuropsychologia, 22,* 807–811.

Benton, A.L. (1985). Perceptual and spatial disorders. In K. Heilman & E. Valenstein (Eds.), *Clinical Neuropsychology* (2nd ed.). New York: Oxford University Press.

Benton, A.L. (1987). Mathematical disability and the Gerstmann syndrome. In G. Deloche & X. Seron (Eds.), *Mathematical disabilities* (pp. 111–120). Hillsdale, NJ: Erlbaum.

Benton, A.L., & Fogel, M.L. (1962). Three-dimensional constructional praxis. *Archives of Neurology (Chicago), 7,* 347–354.

Benton, A.L., Hamsher, K. de S., Varney, N.R., & Spreen, O. (1983). *Contributions to neuropsychological assessment.* New York: Oxford University Press.

Benton, A.L., Hannay, J., & Varney, N.R. (1975). Visual perception of line direction in patients with unilateral brain disease. *Neurology, 25,* 907–910.

Benton, A.L., & Hécaen, H. (1970). Stereoscopic vision in patients with unilateral cere-bral disease. *Neurology, 20,* 1084–1088.

Benton, A.L., & Joynt, R.J. (1960). Early descriptions of aphasia. *Archives of Neurology (Chicago), 3,* 205–221.

Benton, A.L., Smith, K.C., & Lang, M. (1972). Stimulus characteristics and object naming in aphasic patients. *Journal of Communication Disorders, 5,* 19–24.

Benton, A.L., & Van Allen, M.W. (1968). Impairment in facial recognition in patients with cerebral disease. *Cortex, 4,* 344–358.

Benton, A.L., & Van Allen, M.W. (1972). Prosopagnosia and facial discrimination. *Journal of Neurological Science, 15,* 167–172.

Benton, A.L., Varney, N.R., & Hamsher, K. de S. (1978). Visuo-spatial judgement: A clinical test. *Archives of Neurology (Chicago), 35,* 364–367.

Berg, E.A. (1948). A simple objective technique for measuring flexibility in thinking. *Journal of General Psychology, 39,* 15–22.

Berger, H. (1926). Über Rechenstörungen bei Herderkrankungen des Grosshirns. *Archiv für Psychiatrie und Nervenkrankheiten*, **78**, 238–263.

Berlyne, N. (1972). Confabulation. *British Journal of Psychiatry*, **120**, 31–39.

Berndt, R.S. (1987). Symptom co-occurence and dissociation in the interpretation of agrammatism. In M. Coltheart, G. Sartori, & R. Job (Eds.), *The cognitive neuropsychology of language* (pp. 221–233). London: Erlbaum.

Berndt, R.S., & Mitchum, C. (1990). In G. Vallar & T. Shallice (Eds.), *Neuropsychological impairments to short term memory*. Cambridge: Cambridge University Press.

Binet, A., & Simon, T. (1908). Le développement de l'intelligence chez les enfants. *Année Psychologique*, **14**, 1–94.

Bisiach, E. (1966). Perceptual factors in the pathogenesis of anomia. *Cortex*, **2**, 90–95.

Bisiach, E., Capitani, E., Colombo, A., & Spinnler, H. (1976). Halving a horizontal segment: A study on hemisphere damaged patients with focal lesions. *Archives Suisses de Neurologie Neurochirurgie et de Psychiatrie*, **118**, 119–206.

Bisiach, E., & Luzzatti, C. (1978). Unilateral neglect of representational space. *Cortex*, **14**, 129–133.

Bisiach, E., Luzzatti, C., & Perani, D. (1979). Unilateral neglect, representational schema and consciousness. *Brain*, **102**, 609–618.

Bisiach, E., Nichelli, P., & Spinnler, H. (1976). Hemispheric functional asymmetry in visual discrimination between univariate stimuli: An analysis of sensitivity and response criterion. *Neuropsychologia*, **14**, 335–342.

Blumstein, S.E. (1973). *A phonological investigation of aphasic speech*. The Hague: Mouton.

Blumstein, S.E. (1988). Approaches to speech production deficits in aphasia. In F. Boller & J. Graffman (Eds.), *Handbook of neuropsychology* (Vol. 1, pp. 349–365). Amsterdam: Elsevier.

Blumstein, S.E., Alexander, M.P., Ryalls, J.H., Katz, W., & Dworetzky, B. (1987). On the nature of the foreign accent syndrome: A case study. *Brain and Language*, **30**, 305–320.

Blumstein, S.E., Baker, E., & Goodglass, H. (1977a). Phonological factors in auditory comprehension in aphasia. *Neuropsychologia*, **15**, 19–30.

Blumstein, S.E., Baker, E., & Goodglass, H. (1977b). The perception and production of voice onset time in aphasia. *Neuropsychologia*, **15**, 371–383.

Blumstein, S.E., Cooper, W.E., Goodglass, H., Statlender, S., & Gottlieb, J. (1980). Production deficits in aphasia: A voice-onset time analysis. *Brain and Language*, **9**, 153–170.

Blumstein, S.E., Cooper, W.E., Zurif, E.B., & Caramazza, A. (1977). The perception and production of voice onset time in aphasia. *Neuropsychologia*, **15**, 371–383.

Blumstein, S.E., Tarter, V.C., Nigro, G., & Statlender, S. (1984). Acoustic cues for the perception of place of articulation in aphasia. *Brain and Language*, **22**, 128–149.

Bodamer, J. (1947). Die Prosopagnosie. *Archiv für Psychiatrie und Zeitschrift für Neurologie*, **179**, 6–54.

Bogen, J.E. (1985). The callosal syndromes. In K. Heilman & E. Valenstein (Eds.), *Clinical Neuropsychology*, (pp. 295–338). New York: Oxford University Press.

Bogen, J.E., & Vogel, P.J. (1962). Cerebral commissurotomy: A case report. *Bulletin of the Los Angeles Neurological Society*, **27**, 169.

Bonhoeffer, K. (1904). Der korsakowsche Symptomenkomplex in seinen Beziehungen zu den verschiedenen Krankheitsformen. *Allgemeine Zeitschrift für Psychiatrie und Psychisch-Gerichtliche Medicin*, **61**, 744–752.

Bonhoeffer, K. (1923). Zur Klinik und Lokalisation des Agrammatismus und der Rechts-Links-Desorientierung. *Monatsschrift für Psychiatrie und Neurologie*, **54**, 11–42.

Bornstein, B. (1963). Prosopagnosia. In L. Halpern (Ed.), *Problems of dynamic neurology* (pp. 283–318). Jerusalem: Hadasseh Medical Organization.

Bornstein, B., Sroka, M., & Munitz, H. (1969). Prosopagnosia with animal face agnosia. *Cortex*, **5**, 164–169.

Bowers, D., Bauer, R.M., Coslett, H.B., & Heilman, K.M. (1985). Processing of faces by patients with unilateral hemisphere lesions. I. Dissociation between judgements of facial affect and facial identity. *Brain and Cognition, 4*, 258–272.

Bowers, D., Coslett, H.B., Bauer, R.M., Speedie, L.J., & Heilman, K.M. (1987). Comprehension of emotional prosody following unilateral hemispheric lesions. Processing defect versus distraction defect. *Neuropsychologia, 25*, 317–328.

Brain, W.R. (1941). Visual disorientation with special reference to lesions to the right cerebral hemisphere. *Brain, 64*, 244–272.

Bramwell, B. (1897). Illustrated cases of aphasia. *Lancet, 1*, 1256–1259. [Edited and reprinted with commentary by D. Howard (1984). *Cognitive Neuropsychology, 1*, 245–258.]

Brick, J.F., Frost, J.L., Schochett, S.S., Gutman, L., & Crosby, T.W. (1985). Pure word deafness. C.T. localisation of the pathology. *Neurology (Cleveland), 35*, 441–442.

Broca, P. (1861). Remarques sur le siège de la faculté du langage articulé suivie d'une observation d'aphémie. *Bull. Soc. Anat., Paris, 6*, 330. [Translated in R. Herrnstein & E.G. Boring, (1965). *A source book in the history of psychology*. Cambridge, MA: Harvard University Press.]

Brooks, D.N., & Baddeley, A.D. (1976). What can amnesic patients learn? *Neuropsychologia, 14*, 111–122.

Brown, J. (1958). Some tests of the decay theory of immediate memory. *Quarterly Journal of Experimental Psychology, 10*, 12–21.

Brown, J. (1976). An analysis of recognition and recall of problems and their comparison. In J. Brown (Ed.), *Recall and recognition* (pp. 11–35). London: Wiley.

Brown, J.W. (1972). *Aphasia apraxia and agnosia*. Springfield, IL: Charles C. Thomas.

Brown, R., & McNeil, D. (1966). The "tip of the tongue" phenomenon. *Journal of Verbal Learning and Verbal Behavior, 5*, 325–337.

Brown, W.P., & Ure, D.M.N. (1969). Five rated characteristics of 650 word association stimuli. *British Journal of Psychology, 60*, 223–250.

Bruce, V., & Young, A. (1986). Understanding face recognition. *British Journal of Psychology, 77*, 305–327.

Bruyer, R., Laterre, C., Seron, X., Feyereisen, P., Strypstein, E., Pierrard, E., & Rectem, D. (1983). A case of prosopagnosia with some preserved covert remembrance of familiar faces. *Brain and Cognition, 2*, 257–289.

Bub, D., Black, S., Hampson, E., & Kertesz, A. (1988). Semantic encoding of pictures and words: Some neuropsychological observations. *Cognitive Neuropsychology, 5*, 27–66.

Bub, D., Cancelliere, A., & Kertesz, A. (1985). Whole word and analytic translation of spelling-to-sound in a non-semantic reader. In K.E. Patterson, J.C. Marshall, & M. Coltheart (Eds.), *Surface dyslexia: Neuropsychological and cognitive studies of phonological reading* (pp. 15–34). Hove, London: Erlbaum.

Bub, D., & Kertesz, A. (1982a). Deep agraphia. *Brain and Language, 17*, 146–165.

Bub, D., & Kertesz, A. (1982b). Evidence for lexicographic processing in a patient with preserved written over oral single word naming. *Brain, 105*, 697–717.

Buckingham, H.W. (1981). Where do neologisms come from? In J.W. Brown (Ed.), *Jargon aphasia* (pp. 39–62). New York: Academic Press.

Butters, N., & Cermak, L.S. (1980). *Alcoholic Korsakoff's syndrome: An information processing approach to amnesia*. New York: Academic Press.

Butters, N., & Cermak, L.S. (1986). A case study of the forgetting of autobiographical knowledge: Implications for the study of retrograde amnesia. In D.C. Rubin (Ed.), *Autobiographical memory* (pp. 253–272). Cambridge: Cambridge University Press.

Butterworth, B. (1979). Hesitation and the production of verbal paraphasias and neologisms in jargon aphasia. *Brain and Language, 8*, 133–161.

Butterworth, B., Howard, D., & McLoughlin, P. (1984). The semantic deficit in aphasia: The relationship between semantic errors in auditory comprehension and picture naming. *Neuropsychologia, 22*, 409–426.

Calvanio, R., Petrone, P.N., & Levine, D.N. (1987). Left visual spatial neglect is both environment-centered and body-centered. *Neurology, 37*, 1179–1183.

Campbell, D.C., & Oxbury, J.M. (1976). Recovery from unilateral visual-spatial neglect. *Cortex*, **12**, 303–312.

Campbell, R., Landis, T., & Regard, M. (1986). Face recognition and lip reading: A neuropsychological dissociation. *Brain*, **109**, 509–521.

Campion, J., & Latto, R. (1985). Apperceptive agnosia due to carbon monoxide poisoning. An interpretation based on critical band masking from disseminated lesions. *Behavioural Brain Research*, **15**, 227–240.

Caplan, D. (1985). Syntactic and semantic structures in agrammatism. In M.-L. Kean (Ed.), *Agrammatism* (pp. 125–152). New York: Academic Press.

Caplan, D. (1987). *Neurolinguistics and linguistic aphasiology: An introduction*. New York: Cambridge University Press.

Caplan, D., & Hildebrandt, G. (1988). *Disorders of syntactic comprehension*. Cambridge, MA: M.I.T. Press.

Caplan, D., & Waters, G.S. (1990). Short-term memory and language comprehension: A critical review of the neuropsychological literature. In G. Vallar & T. Shallice (Eds.), *Neuropsychological impairments of short term memory*. (pp. 337–389). Cambridge: Cambridge University Press.

Caplan, D., Vanier, M., & Baker, C. (1986a). A case study of reproduction conduction aphasia. I. Word production. *Cognitive neuropsychology*, **3**, 99–128.

Caplan, D., Vanier, M., & Baker, C. (1986b). A case study of reproduction conduction aphasia. II. Sentence comprehension. *Cognitive Neuropsychology*, **3**, 129–146.

Caraceni, T. (1962). L'afasia di conduzione. *Rivista di Patologia Nervosa e Mentale*, **83**, 531–551.

Caramazza, A., Basili, A., Koller, J., & Berndt, R.S. (1981). An investigation of repetition and language processing in a case of conduction aphasia. *Brain and Language*, **14**, 235–271.

Caramazza, A., Berndt, R.S., & Basili, A.G. (1983). The selective impairment of phonological processing: A case study. *Brain and Language*, **18**, 128–174.

Caramazza, A., & McCloskey, M. (1987). Dissociation of calculation processes. In G. Deloche & X. Seron (Eds.), *Mathematical disabilities* (pp. 221–234). Hillsdale, NJ: Erlbaum.

Caramazza, A., Miceli, G., Villa, G., & Romani, C. (1986). The role of the (output) phonological buffer in reading, writing and repetition. *Cognitive Neuropsychology*, **3**, 37–76.

Caramazza, A., Miceli, G., Villa, G., & Romani, C. (1987). The role of the graphemic buffer in spelling: Evidence from a case of acquired dysgraphia. *Cognition*, **26**, 59–85.

Caramazza, A., & Zurif, E.B. (1976). Dissociation of algorithmic and heuristic processes in language comprehension. *Brain and Language*, **3**, 572–582.

Carmon, A. (1971). Disturbance in tactile sensitivity in patients with cerebral lesions. *Cortex*, **7**, 83–97.

Cattel, J.M. (1886). The inertia of the eye and brain. *Brain*, **8**, 295–312.

Cermak, L.S. (1976). The encoding capacity of a patient with amnesia due to encephalitis. *Neuropsychologia*, **14**, 311–326.

Cermak, L.S., & Butters, N. (1972). The role of interference encoding in the short-term memory deficits of Korsakoff patients. *Neuropsychologia*, **10**, 89–96.

Cermak, L.S., Lewis, R., Butters, N., & Goodglass, H. (1973). Role of verbal mediation in the performance of motor skills by Korsakoff patients. *Perceptual and Motor Skills*, **37**, 259–262.

Cermak, L.S., & Moreines, J. (1976). Verbal retention deficits in aphasic and amnesic patients. *Brain and Language*, **3**, 16–27.

Cermak, L.S., & O'Connor, M. (1983). The anterograde and retrograde retrieval ability of a patient with amnesia due to encephalitis. *Neuropsychologia*, **21**, 213–233.

Cermak, L.S., & Reale, L. (1978). Depth of processing and retention of words by alcoholic Korsakoff patients. *Journal of Experimental Psychology*, **5**, 164–175.

Cermak, L.S., Talbot, N., Chandler, K., & Wolbarst, L.R. (1985). The perceptual priming phenomenon in amnesia. *Neuropsychologia*, **23**, 615–622.

Chain, F., Leblanc, M., Chedru, F., & Lhermitte, F. (1979). Négligence visuelle dans les lésions postérieures de l'hemisphere gauche. *Revue Neurologique*, **135**, 105–126.

Charcot, J.M. (1883). Un cas de suppression brusque et isolée de la vision mentale des signes et des objets (formes et couleurs). *Progrés Medicale*, **11**, 568–571.

Charcot, J.M. (1884). *Differenti forme d'afasia*. Milan: Vallardi.

Chedru, F., Leblanc, M., & Lhermitte, F. (1973). Visual searching in normal and brain damaged subjects. Contribution to the study of unilateral inattention. *Cortex*, **9**, 94–111.

Cicerone, K.D., Lazar, R.M., & Shapiro, W.R. (1983). Effects of frontal lobe lesions on hypothesis sampling during concept formation. *Neuropsychologia*, **21**, 513–524.

Cipolotti, L., & Denes, G. (1989). When a patient can write but not copy: Report of a single case. *Cortex*, **25**, 331–337.

Coenen, W. (1940). Klinischer und anatomischer Beitrag zur Frage der Leitungsaphasie. *Archiv für Psychiatrie*, **112**, 664–678.

Cohen, N.J. (1984). Preserved learning capacity in amnesia: Evidence for multiple memory systems. In L.R. Squire & N. Butters (Eds.), *Neuropsychology of memory* (pp. 83–103). New York: Guildford Press.

Cohen, N.J., & Squire, L.R. (1982). Preserved learning and retention of pattern analysing skill in amnesia: Dissociation of "knowing how" and "knowing that." *Science*, **210**, 207–209.

Cohn, R. (1961a). Dyscalculia. *Archives of Neurology (Chicago)*, **4**, 301–307.

Cohn, R. (1961b). *The person symbol in clinical medicine*. Springfield, IL: Charles C. Thomas.

Cole, M., & Perez-Cruet, J. (1964). Prosopagnosia. *Neuropsychologia*, **2**, 237–246.

Cole, M., Schutta, H.S., & Warrington, E.K. (1962). Visual disorientation in homonymous half fields. *Neurology*, **12**, 257–263.

Collingnon, R., & Rondeaux, J. (1974). Approche clinique des modalités de l'apraxie constructive secondaire aux lésions corticales hémispheriques gauches et droites. *Acta Neurologica Belgica*, **74**, 137–146.

Colombo, A., De Renzi, E., & Faglioni, P. (1976). The occurrence of visual neglect in patients with unilateral cerebral disease. *Cortex*, **12**, 221–231.

Coltheart, M. (1980). Reading, phonological recoding and deep dyslexia. In M. Coltheart, K.E. Patterson, & J.C. Marshall (Eds.), *Deep dyslexia* (pp. 197–226). London: Routledge.

Coltheart, M. (1985). Cognitive neuropsychology and the study of reading. In M.L. Posner & O.S.M. Marin (Eds.), *Attention and performance* (Vol. 11, pp. 3–37). Hillsdale, NJ: Erlbaum.

Coltheart, M., & Funnell, E. (1987). Reading and writing: One lexicon or two? In D.A. Allport, D.G. MacKay, W. Prinz, & E. Scheerer (Eds.), *Language perception and production: relationships between listening, reading and writing* (pp. 313–339). London: Academic Press.

Conrad, K. (1949). Uber aphasische Sprachstörungen bei hirnverletzten Linkshändern. *Nervenarzt*, **20**, 148–154.

Cooper, W.E., Soares, C., Michelow, D., & Goloskie, S. (1984). Clausal intonation after unilateral brain damage. *Language and Speech*, **27**, 17–24.

Corkin, S. (1965). Tactually-guided maze learning in man: Effects of unilateral cortical excisions and bilateral hippocampal lesions. *Neuropsychologia*, **3**, 339–351.

Corkin, S. (1968). Acquisition of motor skill after bilateral medial temporal-lobe excision. *Neuropsychologia*, **6**, 225–265.

Corlew, M.M., & Nation, J.E. (1975). Characteristics of visual stimuli and naming performance in aphasic adults. *Cortex*, **11**, 186–191.

Coslett, H.B., Rothi, L.J.C., Valenstein, E., & Heilman, K.M. (1986). Dissociations of writing and praxis: Two cases in point. *Brain and Language*, **28**, 357–369.

Coslett, H.B., & Saffran, E.M. (1989a). Preserved object recognition and reading comprehension in optic aphasia. *Brain*, **112**, 1091–1110.

Coslett, H.B., & Saffran, E.M. (1989b). Evidence for preserved reading in "pure alexia." *Brain, 112,* 327–360.

Costa, L.D., Vaughan, H.G., Horwitz, M., & Ritter, W. (1969). Patterns of behavioural deficit associated with visual spatial neglect. *Cortex, 5,* 242–263.

Costello, A. de L., & Warrington, E.K. (1987). The dissociation of visuo-spatial neglect and neglect dyslexia. *Journal of Neurology, Neurosurgery and Psychiatry, 50,* 1110–1116.

Costello, A. de L., & Warrington, E.K. (1989). Dynamic aphasia. The selective impairment of verbal planning. *Cortex, 25,* 103–114.

Coughlan, A.K. (1979). Effects of localised cerebral lesions and dysphasia on verbal memory. *Journal of Neurology, Neurosurgery and Psychiatry, 42,* 914–923.

Coughlan, A.K., & Warrington, E.K. (1978). Word comprehension and word retrieval in patients with localised cerebral lesions. *Brain, 101,* 163–185.

Coughlan, A.D., & Warrington, E.K. (1981). The impairment of verbal semantic memory: A single case study. *Journal of Neurology, Neurosurgery and Psychiatry, 44,* 1079–1083.

Craik, F.I.M., & Lockhart, R.S. (1972). Levels of processing: A framework for memory research. *Journal of Verbal Learning and Verbal Behavior, 11,* 671–684.

Crary, M.A., & Heilman, K.M. (1988). Letter imagery deficits in a case of pure apraxic agraphia. *Brain and Language, 34,* 147–156.

Critchley, M. (1953). *The parietal lobes.* London: Edward Arnold.

Crovitz, H.F., & Schiffman, H. (1974). Frequency of episodic memories as a function of their age. *Bulletin of the Psychonomic Society, 4,* 517–518.

Dalla Barba, G.F., Cipolotti, L., & Denes, G. (1990). Autobiographical memory loss and confabulation in Korsakoff's syndrome: An experimental case study. *Cortex.* In press.

Dall'Ora, P., Della Sala, S., & Spinnler, H. (1989). Autobiographical memory. Its impairment in amnesic syndromes. *Cortex, 25,* 197–217.

Damasio, A.R. (1985). The frontal lobes. In K. Heilman & E. Valenstein (Eds.), *Clinical neuropsychology* (2nd ed., pp. 339–375). New York: Oxford University Press.

Damasio, A.R., Damasio, H., & Van Hoesen, G.W. (1982). Prosopagnosia: Anatomic basis and behavioural mechanisms. *Neurology, 32,* 331–341.

Damasio, A.R., & Damasio, H. (1986). The anatomical substrate of prosopagnosia. In R. Bruyer (Ed.), *The neuropsychology of face perception and facial expression* (pp. 31–38). Hillsdale, NJ: Erlbaum.

Damasio, A.R., Graff-Radford, N.R., Eslinger, P.J., Damasio, H., & Kassell, N. (1985). Amnesia following basal forebrain lesions. *Archives of Neurology (Chicago), 42,* 263–271.

Damasio, A.R., Yamada, T., Damasio, H., Corbett, J., & McKee, J. (1980). Central achromatopsia: Behavioural, anatomic and physiological aspects. *Neurology, 30,* 1064–1071.

Damasio, H. (1981). Cerebral localisation of the aphasias. In M.T. Sarno (Ed.), *Acquired aphasia* (pp. 27–50). New York: Academic Press.

Damasio, H., & Damasio, A.R. (1980). The anatomical basis of conduction aphasia. *Brain, 103,* 337–350.

Darley, F.L., Aronson, A.E., & Brown, J.R. (1975). *Motor speech disorders.* Philadelphia, PA: Saunders.

Daum, I., Channon, S., & Canavan, A.G.M. (1989). Classical conditioning in patients with severe memory problems. *Journal of Neurology, Neurosurgery and Psychiatry, 52,* 47–51.

De Bleser, R. (1987). From agrammatism to paragrammatism: German aphasiological traditions and grammatical disturbances. *Cognitive Neuropsychology, 4,* 187–256.

De Haan, E.H.F., Young, A.W., & Newcombe, F. (1987a). Face recognition without awareness. *Cognitive Neuropsychology, 4,* 385–415.

De Haan, E.H.F., Young, A.W., & Newcombe, F. (1987b). Faces interfere with name classification in a prosopagnosic patient. *Cortex, 23,* 309–316.

Dejerine, J. (1892). Contribution à l'étude anatomoclinique et clinique des différentes variétés de cécité verbal. C.R. Hebdomadaire des Scéances et *Mémoires de la Sociéte de Biologie,* **4,** 61–90.

Dejerine, J. (1914). *Sémeiologie des affections du système nerveux.* Paris: Masson.

Dejong, R.N., Itabashi, H.H., & Olson, J.R. (1969). Memory loss due to hippocampal lesions. Report of a case. *Archives of Neurology (Chicago),* **20,** 339–348.

De Kosky, S.T., Heilman, K.M., Bowers, M.D., & Valenstein, E. (1980). Recognition and discrimination of emotional faces and pictures. *Brain and Language,* **9,** 206–214.

Deloche, G., & Seron, X. (1987). Numerical transcoding: A general production model. In G. Deloche & X. Seron (Eds.), *Mathematical disabilities* (pp. 137–170). Hillsdale, NJ: Erlbaum.

Dennis, M. (1976). Dissociated naming and locating of body parts after left anterior temporal lobe resection: An experimental case study. *Brain and Language,* **3,** 147–163.

Dennis, M., & Whitaker, H.A. (1977). Hemisphere equipotentiality and language acquisition. In S.J. Segalowitz & F.A. Gruber (Eds.), *Language development and neurological theory.* New York: Academic Press.

Denny-Brown, D. (1958). The nature of apraxia. *Journal of Nervous and Mental Disease,* **126,** 9–33.

De Renzi, E. (1983). *Disorders of space exploration and cognition.* Chichester: Wiley.

De Renzi, E. (1985). Methods of limb apraxia examination and their bearing on the interpretation of the disorder. In E. Roy (Ed.), *Neuropsychological studies of apraxia and related disorders* (pp. 45–64). Amsterdam: Elsevier-North-Holland.

De Renzi, E. (1986a). Prosopagnosia in two patients with CT scan evidence of damage confined to the right hemisphere. *Neuropsychologia,* **24,** 385–389.

De Renzi, E. (1986b). Current issues in prosopagnosia. In H.D. Ellis, M.A. Jeeves, K.F. Newcombe, & A. Young (Eds.), *Aspects of face processing (pp. 243–252).* Dordrecht, Holland: Martinus Nijhoff.

De Renzi, E. (1986c). The apraxias. In A.K. Asbury, G. McKhann, & W.I. McDonald (Eds.), *Diseases of the nervous system* (pp. 848–854). Philadelphia, PA: Ardmore Medical Books.

De Renzi, E., Bonacini, M.G., & Faglioni, P. (1989). Right posterior brain damaged patients are poor at assessing the age of a face. *Neuropsychologia,* **27,** 839–848.

De Renzi, E., & Faglioni, P. (1967). The relationship between visuo-spatial impairment and constructional apraxia. *Cortex,* **3,** 194–216.

De Renzi, E., & Faglioni, P. (1978). Normative data and screening power of a shortened version of the token test. *Cortex,* **14,** 41–49.

De Renzi, Faglioni, P., Lodesani, M., & Vecchi, A. (1983). Performance of left brain damaged patients on imitation of simple movements and movement sequences. Frontal and parietal injured patients compared. *Cortex,* **19,** 333–343.

De Renzi, E., Faglioni, P., & Previdi, P. (1977a). Spatial memory and hemispheric locus of lesion. *Cortex,* **13,** 424–433.

De Renzi, E., Faglioni, P., & Scotti, G. (1970). Hemispheric contribution to exploration of space through the visual and tactile modality. *Cortex,* **6,** 191–203.

De Renzi, E., Faglioni, P., & Scotti, G. (1971). Judgment of spatial orientation in patients with focal brain damage. *Journal of Neurology, Neurosurgery and Psychiatry,* **34,** 489–495.

De Renzi, E., Faglioni, P., & Scotti, G. (1972a). Impairments of colour sorting behaviour after hemispheric damage: An experimental study with the Holmgren skein test. *Cortex,* **8,** 147–163.

De Renzi, E., Faglioni, P., & Scotti, G. (1972b). Impairment in associating colour to form concommitant with aphasia. *Brain,* **95,** 293–304.

De Renzi, E., Faglioni, P., & Sorgato, P. (1982). Modality specific and supramodal mechanisms of apraxia. *Brain,* **105,** 301–312.

De Renzi, E., Faglioni, P., & Spinnler, H. (1968). The performance of patients with unilateral brain damage on face recognition tasks. *Cortex,* **4,** 17–34.

De Renzi, E., Faglioni, P., & Villa, P. (1977b). Topographical amnesia. *Journal of Neurology, Neurosurgery and Psychiatry, 40,* 498–505.

De Renzi, E., & Ferrari, C. (1978). The Reporter's test: A sensitive test to detect expressive disturbances in aphasics. *Cortex, 14,* 279–293.

De Renzi, E., Gentilini, M., & Barbieri, C. (1989). Auditory neglect. *Journal of Neurology, Neurosurgery and Psychiatry, 52,* 613–617.

De Renzi, E., Gentilini, M., Faglioni, P., & Barbieri, C. (1989). Attentional shifts towards the rightmost stimuli in patients with left visual neglect. *Cortex, 25,* 231–237.

De Renzi, E., Liotti, M., & Nichelli, P. (1987). Semantic amnesia with preservation of autobiographical memory. A case report. *Cortex, 23,* 575–597.

De Renzi, E., & Lucchelli, F. (1988). Ideational apraxia. *Brain, 111,* 1173–1188.

De Renzi, E., Motti, F., & Nichelli, P. (1980). Imitating gestures: A quantitative approach to ideomotor apraxia. *Archives of Neurology (Chicago), 37,* 6–10.

De Renzi, E., & Nichelli, P. (1975). Verbal and nonverbal short term memory impairment following hemispheric damage. *Cortex, 11,* 341–353.

De Renzi, E., Pieczuro, A., & Vignolo, L.A. (1968). Ideational Apraxia: A quantitative study. *Neuropsychologia, 6,* 41–52.

De Renzi, E., & Scotti, G. (1970). Autotopagnosia: Fiction or reality? *Archives of Neurology (Chicago), 23,* 221–227.

De Renzi, E., Scotti, G., & Spinnler, H. (1969). Perceptual and associative disorders of visual recognition: Relationship to the site of lesion. *Neurology, 19,* 634–642.

De Renzi, E., & Spinnler, H. (1966). Visual recognition in patients with unilateral cerebral disease. *Journal of Nervous and Mental Disease, 142,* 513–525.

De Renzi, E., & Spinnler, H. (1967). Impaired performance on color tasks in patients with hemispheric damage. *Cortex, 3,* 194–216.

De Renzi, E., & Vignolo, L.A. (1962). The token test: A sensitive test to detect receptive disturbances in aphasia. *Brain, 85,* 665–678.

Derouesné, J., & Beauvois, M.-F. (1979). Phonological processing in reading: Data from alexia. *Journal of Neurology, Neurosurgery and Psychiatry, 42,* 1125–1132.

Dimsdale, H., Logue, V., Piercy, M. (1964). A case of persisting impairment of recent memory following right temporal lobectomy. *Neuropsychologia, 1,* 287–298.

Drachman, D.A., & Arbit, K. (1966). Memory and the hippocampal complex. II. *Archives of Neurology (Chicago), 15,* 52–61.

Drewe, E.A. (1974). The effect of type and area of brain lesion on Wisconsin Card Sorting Test performance. *Cortex, 10,* 159–170.

Drewe, E.A. (1975). An experimental investigation of Luria's theory on the effects of frontal lobe lesions in man. *Neuropsychologia, 13,* 421–429.

Dubois, J., Hécaen, H., & Marcie, P. (1969). L'agraphie "pure." *Neuropsychologia, 7,* 271–286.

DuCarne, B., & Pillon, B. (1974). La copie de la figure complexe de Rey dans les troubles visuo-constructifs. *Journal Psychologie Normale et Pathologique, 4,* 449–469.

Dunn, L.M. (1965). *Peabody picture vocabulary test.* Circle Pines, MN: American Guidance Service Inc.

Efron, R. (1968). What is perception? In R.S. Cohen & M. Wartofsky (Eds.), *Boston studies in the philosophy of science* (Vol. 4, pp. 137–173). New York: Humanities Press.

Ellis, A.W. (1982). Spelling and writing (and reading and speaking). In A.W. Ellis (Ed.), *Normality and pathology in cognitive functions* (pp. 113–146). New York: Academic Press.

Ellis, A.W. (1985). The production of spoken words: A cognitive neuropsychological perspective. In A.W. Ellis (Ed.), *Progress in the psychology of language* (Vol. 2, pp. 107–145). London: Erlbaum.

Ellis, A.W. (1988). Normal writing processes and peripheral acquired dysgraphias. *Language and Cognitive Processes, 3,* 99–127.

Ellis, A.W., & Beattie, G. (1986). *The psychology of language and communication.* London: Weidenfield & Nicolson.

Ellis, A.W., Flude, B.M., & Young, A.W. (1987). "Neglect dyslexia" and the early visual processing of letters in words. *Cognitive Neuropsychology*, **4**, 439–464.

Ellis, A.W., & Young, A.W. (1987). "Neglect dyslexia" and the early visual processing of letters and words. *Cognitive Neuropsychology*, **4**, 439–464.

Ellis, A.W., & Young, A.W. (1988). *Human cognitive neuropsychology*. Hove, London: Erlbaum.

Ellis, A.W., Young, A.W., & Flude, B.M. (1987). Afferent dysgraphia in a patient and in normal subjects. *Cognitive Neuropsychology*, **4**, 465–486.

Etkoff, N.K.L. (1984). Selective attention to facial identity and facial emotion. *Neuropsychologia*, **22**, 281–295.

Ettlinger, G. (1956). Sensory deficits in visual agnosia. *Journal of Neurology, Neurosurgery and Psychiatry*, **19**, 297–307.

Ettlinger, G., & Moffett, A.M. (1970). Learning in dysphasia. *Neuropsychologia*, **8**, 465–474.

Ettlinger, G., Warrington, E.K., & Zangwill, O.L. (1957). A further study of visual-spatial agnosia. *Brain*, **80**, 335–361.

Exner, S. (1881). Untersuchungen über die Lokalisation der Funktionen in der Grosshirnrinde des Menschen. Wien: Braumuller.

Faglioni, P., Scotti, G., & Spinnler, H. (1969). Impaired recognition of letters after hemisphere damage. *Cortex*, **5**, 120–133.

Faglioni, P., Spinnler, H., & Vignolo, L.A. (1969). Contrasting behaviour of right and left hemisphere damaged patients on a discriminative and semantic test of auditory recognition. *Cortex*, **5**, 366–389.

Farah, M.J., Hammond, K.M., Mehta, Z., & Ratcliff, G. (1989). Category specificity and modality specificity in semantic memory. *Neuropsychologia*, **27**, 193–200.

Farnsworth, D. (1957). *Farnsworth–Munsell 100-hue test for color vision*. Baltimore, MD: Munsell Color Company.

Faust, C. (1955). *Die zerebralen Herdstörungen bei Hinterhauptsverletzungen und ihre Beurteilung*. Stuttgart: Thieme.

Ferro, J.M., & Bothello, M.H. (1980). Alexia for arithmetical signs: A cause of disturbed calculation. *Cortex*, **16**, 175–180.

Ferro, J.M., & Santos, M.E. (1984). Associative visual agnosia: A case study. *Cortex*, **20**, 121–134.

Foix, C. (1916). Contribution à l'étude de l'apraxie idéomotrice. *Revue Neurologique*, **1**, 285–298.

Frazier, L., & Fodor, J.D. (1978). The sausage machine: A new two-stage parsing model. *Cognition*, **6**, 291–325.

Freed, D.M., Corkin, S., & Cohen, N.J. (1987). Forgetting in HM: A second look. *Neuropsychologia*, **25**, 461–471.

Freeman, F.J., Sands, E.S., & Harris, K.S. (1978). Temporal coordination of phonation and articulation in a case of verbal apraxia: A voice onset time study. *Brain and Language*, **6**, 106–111.

Friedman, S., & Albert, M.L. (1985). Alexia. In K.M. Heilman & E. Valenstein (Eds.), *Clinical neuropsychology* (pp. 49–73). New York: Oxford University Press.

Friedrich, F.J., Glenn, C., & Marin, O.S.M. (1984). Interruption of phonological coding in conduction aphasia. *Brain and Language*, **22**, 266–291.

Freud, S. (1891). Zur Aufassung der Aphasien. Wien: Deuticke.

Freund, D.C. (1889). Über optische Aphasie und Seelenblindheit. *Archiv für Psychiatrie und Nervenkrankheiten*, **20**, 276–297.

Funnell, E. (1983). Phonological processing in reading: New evidence from acquired dyslexia. *British Journal of Psychology*, **74**, 159–180.

Gainotti, G. (1972). Troubles de dessin et lésions hemispheriques retrolandiques unilatérales gauches et droites. *Encéphale*, **61**, 245–264.

Gainotti, G., Caltagirone, C., & Ibba, A. (1975). Semantic and phonemic aspects of auditory language comprehension in aphasia. *Linguistics*, **154/155**, 15–29.

Gainotti, G., D'Erme, P., Monteleone, D., & Silveri, M.C. (1986). Mechanisms of unilateral spatial neglect in relation to laterality of cerebral lesions. *Brain,* **109**, 599–612.

Gainotti, G., Messerli, P., & Tissot, R. (1972). Qualitative analysis of unilateral spatial neglect in relation to laterality of cerebral lesion. *Journal of Neurology, Neurosurgery and Psychiatry,* **35**, 545–550.

Gainotti, G., Miceli, G., Caltagirone, C., Silveri, M.C., & Masullo, C. (1981). The relationship between the type of naming error and semantic-lexical discrimination in aphasic patients. *Cortex,* **17**, 401–409.

Gainotti, G., Silveri, M.C., Villa, G., & Miceli, G. (1986). Anomia with and without comprehension disorders. *Brain and Language,* **29**, 18–33.

Gainotti, G., & Tiacci, C. (1970). Patterns of drawing disability in right and left hemisphere patients. *Neuropsychologia,* **8**, 289–303.

Gall, F., & Spurzheim, G. (1809). Research on the nervous system in general and on that of the brain in particular. [Reprinted in K. Pribram (Ed.). (1969). *Brain and behaviour: Vol. 1. Mood states and mind.* Harmondsworth: Penguin Books.]

Gardner, H. (1973). The contribution of operativity to naming capacity in aphasic patients. *Neuropsychologia,* **11**, 213–220.

Gazzaniga, M.S. (1970). *The bisected brain.* New York: Appleton Century Crofts.

Gazzaniga, M.S. (1983). Right hemisphere language following bisection: A 20-year perspective. *American Psychologist,* **38**, 535–537.

Gerstmann, J. (1927). Fingeragnosie und isolierte Agraphie: Ein neues Syndrom. *Zeitschrift für Neurologie und Psychiatrie,* **108**, 152–177.

Geschwind, N. (1965). Disconnection syndromes in animals and man. *Brain,* **88**, 237–294.

Geschwind, N. (1967). The varieties of naming errors. *Cortex,* **3**, 97–112.

Geschwind, N. (1970). The organisation of language and the brain. *Science,* **170**, 940–944.

Geschwind, N. (1975). The apraxias: Neural mechanisms of disorders of learned movement. *American Scientist,* **63**, 188–195.

Geschwind, N., & Fusillo, M. (1966). Colour naming deficits in association with alexia. *Archives of Neurology (Chicago),* **15**, 137–146.

Geschwind, N., & Kaplan, E. (1962). A human cerebral deconnection syndrome. *Neurology,* **12**, 675.

Geschwind, N., Quadfasel, F.A., & Segarra, J.M. (1968). Isolation of the speech area. *Neuropsychologia,* **6**, 327–340.

Gil, R., Pluchon, C., Toullat, G., Micheneau, D., Rogez, R., & Lefevre, J.P. (1985). Disconnexion visuo-verbale (aphasie optique) pour les objets, les images, les couleurs et les visages avec alexie "abstractive." *Neuropsychologia,* **23**, 333–349.

Glisky, E.L., & Schacter, D.L. (1987). Acquisition of domain specific knowledge in organic amnesia: Training for computer-related work. *Neuropsychologia,* **25**, 893–906.

Glisky, E.L., Schacter, D.L., & Tulving, E. (1986). Computer learning by memory-impaired patients: Acquisition and retention of complex knowledge. *Neuropsychologia,* **24**, 313–328.

Gloning, I., Gloning, K., & Hoff, H. (1968). *Neuropsychological symptoms and syndromes in lesions of the occipital lobe and the adjacent areas.* Paris: Gauthier-Villars.

Gloning, K., & Quatember, R. (1966). Methodischer Beitrag zur Untersuchung der Prosopagnosie. *Neuropsychologia,* **4**, 133–144.

Godwin-Austin, R.B. (1965). A case of visual disorientation. *Journal of Neurology, Neurosurgery and Psychiatry,* **28**, 453–458.

Goldberg, E., & Bilder, R.M. (1987). The frontal lobes and hierarchical organisation of cognitive control. In E. Perecman (Ed.), *The frontal lobes revisited* (pp. 159–187). New York: IRBN Press.

Goldberg, E., & Tucker, D. (1979). Motor perseveration and long term memory for visual forms. *Journal of Clinical Neuropsychology,* **1**, 273–288.

Goldberg, G. (1985). Supplementary motor area structure and function: Review and hypotheses. *Behavioural and Brain Sciences*, **8**, 567–616.

Goldstein, K. (1911). Die amnestische und die zentrale Aphasie (Leitungsaphasie). *Archiv für Psychiatrie und Neurologie*, **48**, 314–343.

Goldstein, K. (1915). *Die transkortikalen Aphasien. Ergebnisse Neurologie und Psychiatrie*. Jena: Fischer.

Goldstein, K. (1944). The mental changes due to frontal lobe damage. *Journal of Psychology*, **17**, 187–208.

Goldstein, K. (1948). *Language and language disturbances*. New York: Grune & Stratton.

Goldstein, K., & Marmor, J. (1938). A case of aphasia with special reference to the problems of repetition and word finding. *Journal of Neurology and Psychiatry* [New Series], **1**, 329–339.

Goldstein, K., & Scheerer, M. (1941). Abstract and concrete behaviour: An experimental study with special tests. *Psychological Monographs*, **53** (Whole No. 239).

Gollin, E.S. (1960). Developmental studies of visual recognition of incomplete objects. *Perceptual and Motor Skills*, **11**, 289–298.

Goodglass, H., Barton, M., & Kaplan, E. (1968). Sensory modality and object naming in aphasia. *Journal of Speech and Hearing Research*, **3**, 257–267.

Goodglass, H., & Blumstein, S. (1973). *Psycholinguistics and aphasia*. Baltimore, MD: Johns Hopkins University Press.

Goodglass, H., & Budin, C. (1988). Category and modality specific dissociations in word comprehension and concurrent phonological dyslexia. *Neuropsychologia*, **26**, 67–78.

Goodglass, H., Gleason, J.B., & Hyde, M.R. (1970). Some dimensions of auditory language comprehension in aphasia. *Journal of Speech and Hearing Research*, **13**, 595–606.

Goodglass, H., Hyde, M.R., & Blumstein, S. (1969). Frequency picturability and availability of nouns in aphasia. *Cortex*, **5**, 104–119.

Goodglass, H., & Kaplan, E. (1963). Disturbance of gesture and pantomime in aphasia. *Brain*, **86**, 703–720.

Goodglass, H., & Kaplan, E. (1972). *The assessment of aphasia and related disorders*. Philadelphia, PA: Lea & Febiger.

Goodglass, H., Kaplan, E., Weintraub, S., & Akerman, N. (1976). The "tip of the tongue" phenomenon in aphasia. *Cortex*, **12**, 145–153.

Goodglass, H., Klein, B., Carey, P., & Jones, K. (1966). Specific semantic word categories in aphasia. *Cortex*, **2**, 74–89.

Goodglass, H., & Quadfasel, F.A. (1954). Language laterality in left-handed aphasics. *Brain*, **77**, 521–548.

Goodglass, H., Quadfasel, F.A., & Timberlake, W.H. (1964). Phrase length and the type and severity of aphasia. *Cortex*, **1**, 133–152.

Goodglass, H., & Stuss, D.T. (1979). Naming to picture versus description in three aphasic subgroups. *Cortex*, **15**, 199–211.

Goodglass, H., Wingfield, A., Hyde, M.R., & Theurkauf, J.C. (1986). Category specific dissociations in naming and recognition by aphasic patients. *Cortex*, **22**, 87–102.

Goodman, R.A., & Caramazza, A. (1986a). Dissociation of spelling errors in written and oral spelling: The role of allographic conversion in writing. *Cognitive Neuropsychology*, **3**, 179–206.

Goodman, R.A., & Caramazza, A. (1986b). Aspects of the spelling process: Evidence from a case of acquired dysgraphia. *Language and Cognitive Processes*, **1**, 263–296.

Gordinier, H.C. (1899). A case of brain tumor at the base of the second left frontal convolution. *American Journal of Medical Science*, **117**, 526–535.

Gorelick, P.B., & Ross, E.D. (1987). The aprosodias: Further functional-anatomic evidence for the organisation of affective language in the right hemisphere. *Journal of Neurology, Neurosurgery and Psychiatry*, **50**, 553–560.

Graf, P., & Schacter, D.L. (1985). Implicit and explicit memory for new associations in normal and amnesic subjects. *Journal of Experimental Psychology*, **11**, 501–518.

Graf, P., Squire, L.R., & Mandler, G. (1984). The information that amnesic patients do not forget. *Journal of Experimental Psychology, 10*, 164–178.

Graff-Radford, N.R., Cooper, W.E., Colsher, P.L., & Damasio, A.R. (1986). An unlearned foreign "accent" in a patient with aphasia. *Brain and Language, 28*, 86–94.

Grafman, J., Passafiume, D., Faglioni, P., & Boller, F. (1982). Calculation disturbances in adults with focal hemispheric damage. *Cortex, 18*, 37–50.

Green, E., & Howes, D.H. (1977). The nature of conduction aphasia: A study of anatomic and clinical features and underlying mechanisms. In H. Whitaker & H.A. Whitaker (Eds.), *Studies in neurolinguistics* (Vol. 3, pp. 123–156). New York: Academic Press.

Greenblatt, S.H. (1973). Alexia without agraphia or hemianopia: anatomical analysis of an autopsied case. *Brain, 96*, 307–316.

Greenwood, R., Bhall, A., Gordon, A., & Roberts, J. (1983). Behaviour disturbances during recovery from herpes simplex encephalitis. *Journal of Neurology, Neurosurgery and Psychiatry, 46*, 809–817.

Groen, G.J., & Parkman, J.M. (1972). A chronometric analysis of simple addition. *Psychological Review, 29*, 329–343.

Grossi, D., Trojano, L., Grasso, A., & Orsini, A. (1988). Selective semantic amnesia after closed head injury: A case report. *Cortex, 24*, 457–464.

Gurd, J.M., Bessel, N.J., Bladon, R.A.W., & Bamford, J.M. (1988). A case of foreign accent syndrome with follow-up clinical neuropsychological and phonetic descriptions. *Neuropsychologia, 26*, 237–251.

Habib, M., & Sirigu, A. (1987). Pure topographical disorientation: A definition and anatomical basis. *Cortex, 23*, 73–85.

Halligan, P.W., & Marshall, J.C. (1988). How long is a piece of string? A study of line bisection in a case of visual neglect. *Cortex, 24*, 321–328.

Halligan, P.W., & Marshall, J.C. (1989). Perceptual cueing and perceptuo-motor compatability in visuo-spatial neglect: A single case study. *Cognitive Neuropsychology, 6*, 423–435.

Halstead, W.C. (1940). Preliminary analysis of grouping behaviour in patients with cerebral injury by the method of equivalent and non-equivalent stimuli. *American Journal of Psychiatry, 96*, 1263–1294.

Hannay, H.J., Varney, N., & Benton, A.L. (1976). Visual localisation in patients with unilateral brain disease. *Journal of Neurology, Neurosurgery and Psychiatry, 39*, 307–313.

Hardie, R., & Lees, A. (1985). The control of movement and its clinical disorders. In A. Crockard, R. Hayward, & J.T. Hoff (Eds.), *Neurosurgery: Scientific basis of clinical practice* (pp. 158–179). Oxford: Blackwell.

Hart, J., Berndt, R.S., & Caramazza, A. (1985). Category specific naming deficit following cerebral infarction. *Nature (London), 316*, 439–440.

Hatfield, F.M., Barber, J., Jones, C., & Morton, J. (1977). Object naming in aphasics—the lack of effect of context or realism. *Neuropsychologia, 15*, 717–727.

Hatfield, F.M., & Patterson, K.E. (1983). Phonological spelling. *Quarterly Journal of Experimental Psychology, 35A*, 451–468.

Head, H. (1926). *Aphasia and kindred disorders of speech.* Cambridge: Cambridge University Press.

Hebb, D.O. (1949). *The organization of behaviour.* New York: Wiley.

Hécaen, H. (1962). Clinical symptomatology in right and left hemisphere lesions. In V.B. Mountcastle (Ed.), *Interhemispheric relations and cerebral dominance* (pp. 215–243). Baltimore, MD: Johns Hopkins University Press.

Hécaen, H. (1972). *Introduction à la Neuropsychologie.* Paris: Larousse.

Hécaen, H. (1978). Les Apraxies idéomotrices essai de dissociation. In H. Hécaen & M. Jeannerod (Eds.), *Du contrôle moteur à l'organisation du geste* (pp. 333–358). Paris: Masson.

Hécaen, H., & Albert, M.L. (1978). *Human neuropsychology.* New York: Wiley.

Hécaen, H., & Angelergues, R. (1962). Agnosia for faces. *Archives of Neurology (Chicago), 7*, 92–100.

Hécaen, H., & Angelergues, R. (1963). *La cécité psychique.* Paris: Masson.

Hécaen, H., & Angelergues, R. (1964). Localisation of symptoms in aphasia. In A.V.S. De Rueck & M. O'Connor (Eds.), *Disorders of language* (pp. 223–260). London: Churchill.

Hécaen, H., Angelergues, R., Bernhard, C., & Chiarelli, J. (1957). Essai de distinction des modalités cliniques de l'agnosie des physionomies. *Revue Neurologique, 96,* 125–144.

Hécaen, H., Angelergues, R., & Douzenis, J.A. (1963). Les agraphies. *Neuropsychologia, 1,* 179–208.

Hécaen, H., Angelergues, R., & Houillier, S. (1961). Les variétés cliniques des acalculias au cours des lesions retrolandiques: Approche statistique du problème. *Revue Neurologique, 2,* 85–103.

Hécaen, H., & Ajuriaguerra de, J. (1956). Agnosie visuelle pour les objets inanimés par lésion unilatérale gauche. *Revue Neurologique, 94,* 222–223.

Hécaen, H., & Ajuriaguerra de, J. (1963). *Les gauchers, prévalence manuelle et dominance cérébrale.* Paris: P.U.F.

Hécaen, H., Dell, M.B., & Roger, A. (1955). L'aphasie de conduction (leitungsaphasie). *Encéphale, 2,* 170–195.

Hécaen, H., Goldblum, M.C., Masure, M.C., & Ramier, A.M. (1974). Une nouvelle observation d'agnosie d'objet. Déficit de l'association ou de la catégorisation, spécifique de la modalité visuelle. *Neuropsychologia, 12,* 447–464.

Hécaen, H., & Kremin, H. (1976). Neurolinguistic research on reading disorders resulting from left hemisphere lesions: aphasic and "pure" alexia. In H. Whitaker & H.A. Whitaker (Eds.), *Studies in neurolinguistics* (Vol. 2, pp. 269–329). New York: Academic Press.

Hécaen, H., & Marcie, P. (1974). Disorders of written language following right hemisphere lesions: Spatial dysgraphia. In J. Beaumont & S. Dimond (Eds.), *Hemisphere function in the human brain* (pp. 345–366). London: Elek.

Hécaen, H., & Rondot, P. (1985). Apraxia as a disorder of signs. In E. Roy (Ed), *Neuropsychological studies of apraxia and related disorders* (pp. 75–98). Amsterdam: Elsevier-North-Holland.

Hécaen, H., & Ruel, J. (1981). Sièges lésionnels intrafrontaux et déficit au test de "fluence verbale." *Revue Neurologique, 137,* 277–284.

Hécaen, H., & Sauget, J. (1971). Cerebral dominance in left handed subjects. *Cortex, 7,* 19–48.

Hécaen, H., Tzortzis, C., & Masure, M.C. (1972). Troubles de l'orientation spatiale dans une épreuve de recherche d'itinerairie lors des lésions corticales unilatérales. *Perception, 1,* 325–330.

Hécaen, H., Tzortzis, C., & Rondot, P. (1980). Loss of topographical memory with learning deficits. *Cortex, 16,* 525–542.

Heilbronner, K. (1906). Über Agrammatismus und die Störung der inneren Sprache. *Archiv für Psychiatrie und Nervenkrankheiten, 41,* 653–683.

Heilman, K.M. (1973). Ideational apraxia: A redefinition. *Brain, 96,* 861–864.

Heilman, K.M. (1975). A tapping test in apraxia. *Cortex, 11,* 259–263.

Heilman, K.M. (1979). Apraxia. In K.M. Heilman & E. Valenstein (Eds.), *Clinical Neuropsychology* (1st ed.) (pp. 159–185). New York: Oxford University Press.

Heilman, K.M., & Rothi, L.J. (1985). Apraxia. In K.M. Heilman & E. Valenstein (Eds.), *Clinical Neuropsychology* (pp. 131–150). New York: Oxford University Press.

Heilman, K.M., Rothi, L.J., & Valenstein, E. (1982). Two forms of ideomotor apraxia. *Neurology, 32,* 342–346.

Heilman, K.M., & Scholes, R.J. (1976). The nature of comprehension errors in Broca's conduction and Wernicke's aphasics. *Cortex, 12,* 258–265.

Heilman, K.M., Scholes, R.J., & Watson, R.T. (1975). Auditory affective agnosia: Disturbed comprehension of affective speech. *Journal of Neurology, Neurosurgery and Psychiatry, 38,* 69–72.

Heilman, K.M., Schwartz, H.D., & Geschwind, N. (1975). Defective motor learning in ideomotor apraxia. *Neurology, 25,* 1018–1020.

Heilman, K.M., Tucker, D.M., & Valenstein, E. (1976). A case of mixed transcortical aphasia with intact naming. *Brain, 99,* 415–426.

Heilman, K.M., & Valenstein, E. (1979a). Mechanisms underlying hemispatial neglect. *Annals of Neurology, 5,* 166–170.

Heilman, K.M., & Valenstein, E. (1979b). *Clinical Neuropsychology.* New York: Oxford University Press.

Heilman, K.M., & Valenstein, E. (1985). *Clinical Neuropsychology* (2nd ed.). New York: Oxford University Press.

Henderson, L. (1982). *Orthography and word recognition in reading.* London: Academic Press.

Henschen, S.E. (1919). Über Sprach-, Musik-und Rechenmechanismen und ihre Lokalisation im Gehirn. *Zeitschrift für die Gesamte Neurologie und Psychiatrie, 52,* 273–298.

Henschen, S.E. (1920). *Klinische und anatomische Beiträg zur Pathologie des Gehirns.* Stockholm: Nordiske Bokhandein.

Heywood, C.A., Wilson, B., & Cowey, A. (1987). A case study of cortical colour "blindness" with relatively intact achromatic discrimination. *Journal of Neurology, Neurosurgery and Psychiatry, 50,* 22–29.

Hier, D.B., & Mohr, J.P. (1977). Incongruous oral and written naming. Evidence for a subdivision of the syndrome of Wernicke's aphasia. *Brain and Language, 4,* 115–126.

Hillis, A.E., & Caramazza, A. (1989). The graphemic buffer and attentional mechanisms. *Brain and Language, 36,* 208–235.

Hilpert, P. (1930). Die Bedeutung des linken Parietallappens für das Sprechen. *Journal für Psychologie und Neurologie, 40,* 225–255.

Hinton, G.E., & Sejnowski, T.J. (1986). Learning and relearning in Boltzmann machines. In D.E. Rummelhart & J.L. McClelland (Eds.), *Parallel distributed processing: explorations in the microstructure of cognition* (Vol. 1, pp. 282–317). Cambridge, MA: M.I.T. Press.

Hitch, G. (1980). Developing the concept of working memory. In G. Claxton (Ed.), *Cognitive psychology: New directions.* London: Routledge.

Hoeft, H. (1957). Klinisch-anatomischer Beitrag zur Kenntnis der Nachsprechaphasie (Leitungsaphasie). *Deutsche Zeitschrift für Nervenheilkunde, 175,* 560–594.

Holmes, G. (1918). Disturbances of visual orientation. *British Journal of Ophthalmology, 2,* 449–468.

Holmes, G., & Horrax, G. (1919). Disturbances of spatial orientation and visual attention with loss of stereoscopic vision. *Archives of Neurology and Psychiatry, 1,* 385–407.

Howard, D., & Franklin, S. (1988). *Missing the meaning? A cognitive neuropsychological study of the processing of words by an aphasic patient.* Cambridge, MA: M.I.T. Press.

Howard, D., & Orchard-Lisle, V. (1984). On the origin of semantic errors in naming: Evidence from the case of a global aphasic. *Cognitive Neuropsychology, 1,* 163–190.

Howard, D., Patterson, K., Franklin, S., Morton, J., & Orchard-Lisle, V. (1984). Variability and consistency in picture naming by aphasic patients. *Advances in Neurology, 42,* 263–276.

Howes, D., & Geschwind, N. (1964). Quantitative studies of aphasic language. *Res. Publ. Ass. Nerv. Ment.Dis. 42,* 229–244.

Hughlings Jackson, J. (1876). Reprinted in J. Taylor (Ed.), *Selected writings of John Hughlings Jackson.* London: Hodder & Stoughton, 1932.

Humphreys, G.W., & Riddoch, M.J. (1984). Routes to object constancy: Implications from neurological impairments of object constancy. *Quarterly Journal of Experimental Psychology, 26A,* 385–415.

Humphreys, G.W., & Riddoch, M.J. (1987a). *To see but not to see: A case study of visual agnosia.* London: Erlbaum.

Humphreys, G.W., & Riddoch, M.J. (1987b). The fractionation of visual agnosia. In G.W. Humphreys & M.J. Riddoch (Eds.), *Visual object processing* (pp. 281–306). London: Erlbaum.

Humphreys, G.W., Riddoch, M.J., & Quinlan, P.T. (1988). Cascade processes in picture identification. *Cognitive Neuropsychology*, **5**, 67–104.

Huppert, F.A., & Piercy, M. (1979). Normal and abnormal forgetting in organic amnesia: Effects of locus of lesion. *Cortex*, **15**, 385–390.

Huttenlocher, J., Eisenburg, K., & Strauss, S.I. (1968). Comprehension: Relation between perceived actor and logical subject. *Journal of Verbal Learning and Verbal Behavior*, **7**, 527–530.

Hyvarinen, L., & Rovamo, J. (1981). Acquired blindness for achromatic stimuli. *Documenta Opthalmolosica Proceedings Series* **30**, 94–99.

Ishihara, S. (1983). *Ishihara's tests for color blindness*. Tokyo: Kanehara.

Itoh, M., Sasanuma, S., & Ushijima, T. (1979). Velar movements during speech in a patient with apraxia of speech. *Brain and Language*, **7**, 227–239.

Itoh, M., Sasanuma, S., Hirose, H., Yoshioka, H., & Ushijima, T. (1980). Abnormal articulatory dynamics in a patient with apraxia of speech: X-ray microbeam observation. *Brain and Language*, **11**, 66–75.

Jackson, J.H. (1870). Remarks on non-protrusion of the tongue in some cases of aphasia. *Lancet*, **1**, 716. [Reprinted in Taylor, J. (Ed.). (1932). *Selected writings of John Hughlings Jackson*. London: Hodder & Stoughton.]

Jackson, J.H. (1876). Case of large cerebral tumor without optic neuritis and with left hemiplegia and imperception. *Royal Opthalmological Hospital Reports*, **8**, 434–444.

Jackson, J.H. (1879). On affectations of speech from diseases of the brain. I. *Brain* **1**, 304–330. [Reprinted in J. Taylor (Ed.). (1932). *Selected writings of John Hughlings Jackson*. London: Hodder & Stoughton.]

Jackson, J.H. (1880). On affectations of speech from diseases of the brain. II. *Brain*, **2**, 323–356. [Reprinted in J. Taylor (Ed.), 1932. *Selected writings of John Hughlings Jackson*. London: Hodder & Stoughton.]

Jackson, M., & Warrington, E.K. (1986). Arithmetic skills in patients with unilateral cerebral lesions. *Cortex*, **22**, 610–620.

Jacobs, J. (1887). Experiments on "prehension." *Mind*, **12**, 75–79.

Jacobson, R. (1971). Studies on child language and aphasia. *Janua Linguarum Series Minor 114*. The Hague: Mouton.

Jacoby, L.L. (1984). Incidental vs. intentional retrieval: Remembering and awareness as separate issues. In L. Squire & N. Butters (Eds.), *The neuropsychology of memory* (pp. 145–156). New York: Guilford Press.

Jacoby, L.L., & Witherspoon, D. (1982). Remembering without awareness. *Canadian Journal of Psychology*, **32**, 300–324.

Jason, G.W. (1983). Hemispheric asymmetries in motor function. I. Left hemisphere specialisation for memory but not performance. *Neuropsychologia*, **21**, 35–45.

Jeannerod, M. (1988). *The neural and behavioural organisation of goal directed movements*. Oxford: Clarendon Press.

Joanette, Y., Keller, E., & Lecours, A.R. (1980). Sequences of phonemic approximation in aphasia. *Brain and Language*, **11**, 30–44.

Jones, L.V., & Wepman, J.M. (1965). Dimensions of language performance in aphasia. *Journal of Speech and Hearing Research*, **4**, 220–232.

Jones-Gotman, M., & Milner, B. (1977). Design fluency: The invention of nonsense drawings after focal cortical lesions. *Neuropsychologia*, **15**, 653–674.

Kapur, N., & Coughlan, A.K. (1980). Confabulation and frontal lobe dysfunction. *Journal of Neurology, Neurosurgery and Psychiatry*, **43**, 461–463.

Kapur, N., Heath, P., Meudell, P.R., & Kennedy, P. (1986). Amnesia can facilitate memory performance: Evidence from a patient with dissociated retrograde amnesia. *Neuropsychologia*, **24**, 215–221.

Kapur, N., & Perl, N.T. (1978). Recognition reading in paralexia. *Cortex*, **14**, 439–443.

Kapur, N., Turner, A., & King, C. (1988). Reduplicative paramnesia: Possible anatomical and neuropsychological mechanisms. *Journal of Neurology, Neurosurgery and Psychiatry*, **51**, 579–581.

Karpov, B.A., Luria, A.R., & Yarbuss, A.L. (1968). Disturbances of the structure of active perception in lesions of the posterior and anterior regions of the brain. *Neuropsychologia*, **6**, 157–166.

Kartsounis, L.D., & Warrington, E.K. (1989). Unilateral visual neglect overcome by cues implicit in stimulus arrays. *Journal of Neurology, Neurosurgery and Psychiatry*, **52**, 1253–1259.

Kay, J., & Ellis, A.W. (1987). A cognitive neuropsychological case study of anomia: Implications for psychological models of word retrieval. *Brain*, **110**, 613–629.

Kerschensteiner, M., Hartje, W., Orgass, B., & Poeck, K. (1972). The recognition of simple and complex realistic figures in patients with unilateral brain lesions. *Archiv für Psychiatrie und Nervenkrankheiten*, **216**, 118–200.

Kertesz, A. (1979). *Aphasia and associated disorders*. New York: Grune & Stratton.

Kertesz, A., & Benson, D.F. (1970). Neologistic jargon—a clinicopathological study. *Cortex*, **6**, 362–386.

Kertesz, A., Ferro, J.M., & Shewan, C.M. (1984). Apraxia and aphasia. The functional anatomical basis for their dissociation. *Neurology*, **30**, 40–47.

Kertesz, A., Lesk, D., & McCabe, P. (1977). Isotope localisation of infarcts in aphasia. *Archives of Neurology (Chicago)*, **34**, 590–601.

Kertesz, A., Harlock, W., & Coates, R. (1979). Computer tomographic localisation and prognosis in aphasia and nonverbal impairment. *Brain*, **102**, 34–50.

Kertesz, A., & Shephard, A. (1981). The epidemology of aphasic and cognitive impairments in stroke. *Brain*, **104**, 117–128.

Kim, Y., Morrow, L., Passafiume, D., & Boller, F. (1984). Visuoperceptual and visuomotor abilities and locus of lesion. *Neuropsychologia*, **22**, 177–185.

Kimura, D. (1963). Right temporal lobe damage: Perception of unfamiliar stimuli after damage. *Archives of Neurology (Chicago)*, **8**, 264–271.

Kimura, D. (1977). Acquisition of a motor skill after left hemisphere damage. *Brain*, **100**, 527–542.

Kimura, D. (1982). Left hemisphere control of oral and brachial movements and their relationship to communication. *Philosophical Transactions of the Royal Society of London, Series B*, **298**, 135–149.

Kimura, D., & Archibald, Y. (1974). Motor functions of the left hemisphere. *Brain*, **97**, 337–350.

Kinsbourne, M. (1972). Behavioural analysis of the repetition deficit in conduction aphasia. *Neurology*, **212**, 1126-1132.

Kinsbourne, M. (1977). Hemi-neglect and hemisphere rivalry. In E.A. Weinstein & R.P. Friedland (Eds.), *Advances in neurology* (Vol. 18, pp. 41–49). New York: Raven Press.

Kinsbourne, M., & Rosenfeld, D.B. (1974). Agraphia selective for written spelling: an experimental case study. *Brain and Language*, **1**, 215–225.

Kinsbourne, M., & Warrington, E.K. (1962a). A variety of reading disability associated with right hemisphere lesions. *Journal of Neurology, Neurosurgery and Psychiatry*, **25**, 339–344.

Kinsbourne, M., & Warrington, E.K. (1962b). A disorder of simultaneous form perception. *Brain*, **85**, 461–486.

Kinsbourne, M., & Warrington, E.K. (1963a). Jargon aphasia. *Neuropsychologia*, **1**, 27–37.

Kinsbourne, M., & Warrington, E.K. (1963b). The localising significance of limited simultaneous form perception. *Brain*, **85**, 697–702.

Kinsbourne, M., & Warrington, E.K. (1964a). Observations on colour agnosia. *Journal of Neurology, Neurosurgery and Psychiatry*, **27**, 296–299.

Kinsbourne, M., & Warrington, E.K. (1964b). Disorders of spelling. *Journal of Neurology, Neurosurgery and Psychiatry*, **27**, 224–228.

Kinsbourne, M., & Warrington, E.K. (1965). A case showing selectively impaired oral spelling. *Journal of Neurology, Neurosurgery and Psychiatry*, **28**, 563–567.

Kinsbourne, M., & Wood, F. (1975). Short-term memory processes and the amnesic syndrome. In D. Deutsch & J.A. Deutsch (Eds.), *Short-term memory* (pp. 258–291). New York: Academic Press.

Klein, R., & Harper, J. (1956). The problem of agnosia in the light of a case of pure word deafness. *Journal of Mental Science*, **102**, 112–120.

Kleist, K. (1912). Der Gang und der gegenwärtige Stand der Apraxie-forschung. *Ergebnisse der Neurologie und Psychiatrie,* **1,** 342–452.

Kleist, K. (1916). Über Leitungsaphasie und grammatische Störungen. *Monatschrift für Psychiatrie und Neurologie,* **40,** 118–199.

Kleist, K. (1934). *Gehirnpathologie.* Leipzig: Barth.

Kleist, K. (1962). *Sensory aphasia and amusia.* (T.J. Fish & J.B. Stanton, Trans.). Oxford: Pergamon.

Koffka, K. (1935). *Principles of gestalt psychology.* London: Routledge.

Kohn, S.E., & Friedman, R.B. (1986). Word meaning deafness: A phonological-semantic dissociation. *Cognitive Neuropsychology,* **3,** 291–308.

Kolb, B., & Milner, B. (1981). Performance of complex arm and facial movements after focal brain lesions. *Neuropsychologia,* **19,** 491–503.

Kolb, B., & Wishaw, I.Q. (1985). *Fundamentals of human neuropsychology.* San Francisco, CA: Freeman.

Kolers, P.A. (1968). The recognition of geometrically transformed text. *Perception and Psychophysics,* **3,** 57–64.

Kolk, H.H.J., Van Grunsven, M.J.F., & Kuper, A. (1985). On parallelism between production and comprehension in agrammatism. In M.L. Kean (Ed.), *Agrammatism* (pp. 165–206). New York: Academic Press.

Konorski, J., Kozniewska, H., & Stepien, L. (1961). Analysis of symptoms and cerebral localization of the audio-visual aphasia. *Proceedings of the VII International Congress of Neurology II* (pp. 234–236). Rome: Societa Grafica Romana.

Kopelman, M.D. (1987). Amnesia: Organic and psychogenic. *British Journal of Psychiatry,* **150,** 428–442.

Korsakoff, S.S. (1889). Uber eine besondere Form psychischer Störung combiniert mit multipler Neuritis. Archiv für Psychiatrie und Nervenkrankheiten, **21,** 669–704. [Translation by M. Victor and P.I. Yakovlev (1955). *Neurology,* **5,** 394–406.]

Kremin, H. (1986). Spared naming without comprehension. *Journal of Neurolinguistics,* **2,** 131–148.

Kremin, H. (1987). Is there more than ah-oh-oh? Alternative strategies for writing and repeating lexically. In M. Coltheart, R. Sartori, & R. Job (Eds.), *The cognitive neuropsychology of language* (pp. 295–335). London: Erlbaum.

Kussmaul, A. (1877). Die Störungen der Sprache. *Ziemssens Handbuch der Speziellen Pathologie und Therapie,* **12,** 1–300.

Ladavas, E. (1987). Is the hemispatial deficit produced by right parietal lobe damage associated with retinal or gravitational coordinates. *Brain,* **110,** 167–180.

Landis, T., Cummings, J.L., Christen, L., Bogen, J.E., Imhof, H-G.(1986). Are unilateral right posterior lesions sufficient to cause prosopagnosia? Clinical and radiological findings in six additional patients. *Cortex,* **22,** 243–252.

Landis, T., Cummings, J.L., Benson, F., & Palmer, E.P. (1986). Loss of topographic familiarity: An environmental agnosia. *Archives of Neurology (Chicago),* **43,** 132–136.

Landis, T., Regard, M., Bliestle, A., & Kleihues, P. (1988). Prosopagnosia and agnosia for noncanonical views. *Brain,* **111,** 1287–1297.

Lange, J. (1933). Probleme der Fingeragnosie. *Zeitschrift für die gesamte Neurologie und Psychiatrie,* **147,** 594–610.

Laplane, D., Talairach, J., Meininger, V., Bancaud, J., & Orgogozo, J.M. (1977). Clinical consequences of corticectomies involving the supplementary motor area in man. *Journal of Neurological Science,* **34,** 301–314.

Lashley, K. (1929). *Brain mechanisms and intelligence.* Chicago, IL: University of Chicago Press.

Lashley, K. (1951). The problem of serial order in behavior. In L.A. Jeffries (Ed.), *Cerebral mechanisms in behavior* (pp. 112–136). New York: Wiley.

Layman, S., & Greene, E. (1988). The effect of stroke on object recognition. *Brain & Cognition,* **7,** 87–114.

Lebrun, Y. (1985). Disturbances of written language and associated abilities following damage to the right hemisphere. *Applied Psycholinguistics,* **6,** 231–260.

Lebrun, Y., Buyssens, E., & Henneaux, J. (1973). Phonetic aspects of anarthria. *Cortex*, **9**, 126–135.

Lecours, A.R., & Lhermitte, F. (1969). Phonemic paraphasias: Linguistic structures and tentative hypotheses. *Cortex*, **5**, 193–228.

Lecours, A.R., & Lhermitte, F. (1976). The "pure" form of the phonetic disintegration syndrome (pure anarthria): Anatomo-clinical report of a single case. *Brain and Language*, **3**, 88–113.

Lecours, A.R., & Lhermitte, F. (1979). *L'aphasie*. Paris: Flammarion.

Lehmkuhl, G., Poeck, K., & Willmes, K. (1983). Ideomotor apraxia and aphasia: An examination of types and manifestations of apraxic symptoms. *Neuropsychologia*, **21**, 199–212.

Leicester, J., Sidman, M., Stoddard, L.T., & Mohr, J.P. (1969). Some determinants of visual neglect. *Journal of Neurology, Neurosurgery and Psychiatry*, **32**, 580–587.

Lesser, R. (1974). Verbal comprehension in aphasia: An English version of three Italian Tests. *Cortex*, **10**, 247–263.

Lesser, R. (1978). *Linguistic investigations of aphasia*. London: Arnold.

Levin, H.S., & Spiers, P.A. (1985). Acalculia. In K.M. Heilman & E. Valenstein (Eds.), *Clinical Neuropsychology* (2nd ed., pp. 97–114). New York: Oxford University Press.

Lhermitte, F., & Beauvois, M.-F. (1973). A visual-speech disconnexion syndrome. Report of a case with optic aphasia, agnosic alexia and colour agnosia. *Brain*, **96**, 695–714.

Lhermitte, F., Chain, F., Aron, D., Le Blanc, M., & Soaty, O. (1969). Les troubles de la vision des couleurs dans lésions postérieures du cerveau. *Revue Neurologique*, **121**, 5–29.

Lhermitte, F., & Pillon, B. (1975). Prosopagnosie. Role de l'hémisphere droit dans la perception visuelle. *Revue Neurologique*, **131**, 791–812.

Lichtheim, L. (1884). Über Aphasie. *Deutsches Archiv für Klinische Medizin*, **36**, 204–268. [Reprinted and translated in *Brain*, **7**, 433–484 (1885).]

Lichtheim, L. (1885). On aphasia. *Brain*, **7**, 433–484.

Liepmann, H. (1898). *Ein Fall von reiner Sprachtaubheit*. Breslau: Psychiatrische Abhandlugen.

Liepmann, H. (1900). Das Krankheitsbild der Apraxie (motorische Asymbolie). *Monatschrift für Psychiatrie und Neurologie*, **8**, 15–44, 102–132, 182–197. [Reprinted in D.A. Rottenberg & F.H. Hochberg (Eds.), *Neurological classics in modern translation*. New York: Hafner Press.

Liepmann, H. (1905). Der weitere Krankheitsverlauf bei dem einseitig Apraktischen und der Gehirnbefund auf Grund von Serienschnitten. *Monatsschrift für Psychiatrie und Neurologie*, **17**, 283–311.

Liepmann, H. (1920). Apraxia. *Ergebnisse der Gesamten Medizin*, **1**, 516–543.

Liepmann, H., & Pappenheim, M. (1914). Über einen Fall von sogenannter Leitungsaphasie mit anatomischem Befund. *Zeitschrift für die Gesamte Neurologie und Psychiatrie*, **27**, 1–41.

Linebarger, M.C., Schwartz, M.F., & Saffran, E.M. (1983). Sensitivity to grammatical structure in so-called agrammatic aphasics. *Cognition*, **13**, 361–392.

Lissauer, H. (1890). Ein Fall von Seelenblindheit nebst einem Beitrag zur Theorie derselben. *Archiv für Psychiatrie*, **21**, 222–270. [Edited and reprinted in translation by Jackson, M. (1988). Lissauer on agnosia. *Cognitive Neuropsychology*, **5**, 155–192.]

Logue, V., Durwood, M., Pratt, R.T.C., Piercy, M., & Nixon, W.L.B. (1968). The quality of survival after rupture of an anterior cerebral aneurism. *British Journal of Psychiatry*, **114**, 137–168.

Low, A.A. (1931). A case of agrammatism in the English language. *Archives of Neurology and Psychiatry*, **25**, 556–597.

Lund, E., Spliid, P.E., Anderson, E., & Møller, M. (1986). Vowel perception. A neuro-radiological localisation of the perception of vowels in the human cortex. *Brain and Language*, **29**, 191–211.

Luria, A.R. (1964). Factors and forms of aphasia. In A.V.S. de Rueck & M. O'Connor (Eds.), *Disorders of language* (pp. 143–167). London: Churchill.

Luria, A.R. (1965). Two kinds of motor perseveration in massive injuries of the frontal lobes. *Brain*, **88**, 1–10.

Luria, A.R. (1966). *Higher cortical functions in man*. London: Tavistock.

Luria, A.R. (1969). Frontal lobe syndromes. In P.J. Vinken & G.W. Bruyn (Eds.), *Handbook of clinical neurology* (Vol. 2, pp. 725–757). Amsterdam: Elsevier-North Holland.

Luria, A.R. (1970). *Traumatic aphasia*. The Hague: Mouton.

Luria, A.R. (1973). *The working brain*. New York: Basic Books.

Luria, A.R. (1976). *Basic problems in neurolinguistics*. The Hague: Mouton.

Luria, A.R., Sokolov, E.N., & Klimkowski, M. (1967). Towards a neurodynamic analysis of memory disturbances with lesions of the left temporal lobe. *Neuropsychologia*, **5**, 1–11.

Luria, A.R., & Tsetskova, L. (1978). The mechanism of dynamic aphasia. *Foundations of Language*, **4**, 296–307.

Mack, J.L., & Levine, R.N. (1981). The basis of visual constructional disability in patients with unilateral cerebral lesions. *Cortex*, **17**, 515–532.

Mair, W.G.P., Warrington, E.K., & Weiskrantz, L. (1978). Neuropathological and psychological examination of 2 patients with Korsakoff's psychosis. *Brain*, **102**, 749–783.

Malone, D.R., Morris, H.H., Kay, M.C., & Levin, H.S. (1982). Prosopagnosia: A double dissociation between the recognition of familiar and unfamiliar faces. *Journal of Neurology, Neurosurgery and Psychiatry*, **45**, 820–822.

Mandler, G. (1980). Recognizing: The judgment of previous occurrence. *Psychological Revue*, **87**, 252–271.

Mandler, G. (1985). *Cognitive psychology: An essay in cognitive science*. Hillsdale, NJ: Erlbaum.

Margolin, D.I. (1984). The neuropsychology of writing and spelling: Semantic, phonological, motor and perceptual processes. *Quarterly Journal of Experimental Psychology*, **36A**, 459–489.

Margolin, D.I., & Wing, A.M. (1983). Agraphia and micrographia: Clinical manifestations of motor programming and performance disorders. *Acta Psychologica*, **54**, 263–283.

Marie, P. (1906a). Revision de la question de l'aphasie: La troisième convolution frontale gauche ne joue aucun rôle spéciale dans la fonction du langage. *Semaine Medicale (Paris)*, **21**, 241–247. [Reprinted in M.F. Cole & M. Cole (Eds.) (1971). *Pierre Marie's papers on speech disorders*. New York: Hafner.]

Marie, P. (1906b). Revision de la question de l'aphasie. Que faut-il penser des aphasies sous corticales (aphasies pures)? *Semaine Medicale (Paris)*, **42**, 493–500.

Marie, P., and Foix, C. (1917). Les aphasies de guerre. *Revue Neurologique*, **24**, 53–87.

Marin, O.S.M. (1980). CAT scans of five deep dyslexic patients. Appendix 1. In M. Coltheart, K.E. Patterson, & J.C. Marshall (Eds.), *Deep dyslexia* (pp. 407–433). London: Routledge.

Marr, D. (1982). *Vision*. San Francisco, CA: Freeman.

Marshall, J.C., & Halligan, P.W. (1988). Blindsight and insight in visuo-spatial neglect. *Nature (London)*, **336**, 766–767.

Marshall, J.C., & Halligan, P.W. (1989). Does the midsaggital plane play any privileged role in "left neglect." *Cognitive Neuropsychology*, **6**, 403–422.

Marshall, J.C., & Newcombe, F. (1966). Syntactic and semantic errors in paralexia. *Neuropsychologia*, **4**, 169–176.

Marshall, J.C., & Newcombe, F. (1973). Patterns of paralexia: A psycholinguistic approach. *Journal of Psycholinguistic Research*, **2**, 175–199.

Marslen-Wilson, W.D., & Teuber, H.-L. (1975). Memory for remote events in anterograde amnesia: Recognition of public figures from news photographs. *Neuropsychologia*, **13**, 347–352.

Martin, A.D., & Rigrodsky, S. (1974). An investigation of phonological impairment in aphasia. Parts I and II. *Cortex*, **10**, 317–346.

Masterson, J., Coltheart, M., & Meara, P. (1985). Surface dyslexia in a language without irregularly spelled words. In K.E. Patterson, J.C. Marshall, & M. Coltheart (Eds.),

Surface dyslexia: neuropsychological and cognitive studies of phonological reading (pp. 215–223). Hove, London: Erlbaum.

Mateer, C., & Kimura, D. (1977). The impairment of nonverbal oral movements in aphasia. *Brain and Language, 4,* 262–276.

Mayes, A.R., Meudell, P.R., Mann, D., & Pickering, A. (1988). Location of lesions in Korsakoff's syndrome. Neuropsychological and neuropathological data on two patients. *Cortex, 24,* 367–388.

McAndrews, M.P., Glisky, E.L., & Schacter, D. (1987). When priming persists: Long lasting implicit memory for a single episode in amnesic patients. *Neuropsychologia, 25,* 497–506.

McCarthy, R.A., & Warrington, E.K. (1984). A two route model of speech production: Evidence from aphasia. *Brain, 107,* 463–485.

McCarthy, R.A., & Warrington, E.K. (1985). Category specificity in an agrammatic patient: The relative impairment of verb retrieval and comprehension. *Neuropsychologia, 23,* 709–727.

McCarthy, R.A., & Warrington, E.K. (1986a). Visual associative agnosia: A clinico-anatomical study of a single case. *Journal of Neurology, Neurosurgery and Psychiatry, 49,* 1233–1240.

McCarthy, R.A., & Warrington, E.K. (1986b). Phonological reading: Phenomena and paradoxes. *Cortex, 22,* 359–380.

McCarthy, R.A., & Warrington, E.K. (1987a). The double dissociation of short term memory for lists and sentences: Evidence from aphasia. *Brain, 110,* 1545–1563.

McCarthy, R.A., & Warrington, E.K. (1987b). Understanding: A function of short term memory? *Brain, 110,* 1565–1578.

McCarthy, R.A., & Warrington, E.K. (1988). Evidence for modality specific meaning systems in the brain. *Nature (London), 334,* 428–430.

McCloskey, M., & Caramazza, A. (1987). Cognitive mechanisms in normal and impaired number processing. In G. Deloche & X. Seron (Eds.), *Mathematical disabilities* (pp. 201–219). Hillsdale, NJ: Erlbaum.

McCloskey, M., Sokol, S.M., & Goodman, R.A. (1986). Cognitive processes in verbal number production: inferences from the performance of brain-damaged subjects. *Journal of Experimental Psychology, General, 115,* 307–327.

McCrae, D., & Trolle, E. (1956). The defect of function in visual agnosia. *Brain, 79,* 94–110.

McFie, J. (1961). The effects of hemispherectomy on intellectual function in cases of infantile hemiplegia. *Journal of Neurology, Neurosurgery and Psychiatry, 24,* 240–249.

McFie, J. (1975). *Assessment of organic intellectual impairment.* London: Academic Press.

McFie, J., & Piercy, M. (1952). The relationship of laterality of lesion to performance on Weigl's sorting test. *Journal of Mental Science, 98,* 299–308.

McFie, J., & Zangwill, O.L. (1960). Visual-constructive disabilities associated with lesions of the left cerebral hemisphere. *Brain, 82,* 243–259.

McFie, J., Piercy, M.F., & Zangwill, O.L. (1950). Visual spatial agnosia associated with lesions of the right cerebral hemisphere. *Brain, 73,* 167–190.

McGurk, H., & MacDonald, J. (1976). Hearing lips and seeing voices. *Nature (London), 264,* 746–748.

McKenna, P., & Warrington, E.K. (1978). Category specific naming preservation: A single case study. *Journal of Neurology, Neurosurgery and Psychiatry, 41,* 571–574.

McKenna, P., & Warrington, E.K. (1980). Testing for nominal dysphasia. *Journal of Neurology, Neurosurgery and Psychiatry, 43,* 781–788.

McKenna, P., & Warrington, E.K. (1983). *The graded naming test.* Windsor: Nelson.

Meadows, J.C. (1974a). Disturbed perception of colours associated with localised cerebral lesions. *Brain, 97,* 615–632.

Meadows, J.C. (1974b). The anatomical basis of prosopagnosia. *Journal of Neurology, Neurosurgery and Psychiatry, 37,* 489–501.

Mercer, B., Wapner, W., Gardner, H., & Benson, D. (1977). A study of confabulation. *Archives of Neurology (Chicago)*, **34**, 429–433.

Meudell, P.R., Mayes, A.R., & Neary, D. (1981). Amnesia is not caused by cognitive slowness. *Cortex*, **16**, 413–419.

Meudell, P.R., Northen, B., Snowden, J.S., & Neary, D. (1980). Long term memory for famous voices in amnesic and normal subjects. *Neuropsychologia*, **18**, 133–139.

Meyer, J.S., & Barron, D.W. (1960). Apraxia of gait: A clinico-physiological study. *Brain*, **83**, 261–284.

Meyer, V., & Yates, H.J. (1955). Intellectual changes following temporal lobectomy for psychomotor epilepsy. *Journal of Neurology, Neurosurgery and Psychiatry*, **18**, 44–52.

Miceli, G., Caltagirone, C., Gainotti, G., & Payer-Rigo, P. (1978). Discrimination of voice versus place contrasts in aphasia. *Brain and Language*, **6**, 47–51.

Miceli, G., Mazzucchi, A., Menn, L., & Goodglass, H. (1983). Contrasting cases of Italian agrammatic aphasia without comprehension disorder. *Brain and Language*, **19**, 65–97.

Miceli, G., Silveri, M.C., & Caramazza, A. (1985). Cognitive analysis of a case of pure agraphia. *Brain and Language*, **25**, 187–212.

Miceli, G., Silveri, M.C., & Caramazza, A. (1987). The role of the phoneme-grapheme conversion system and of the graphemic buffer in writing. In M. Coltheart, R. Sartori, & R. Job (Eds.), *The cognitive neuropsychology of language* (pp. 235–252). London: Erlbaum.

Miceli, G., Silveri, M.C., Romani, C., & Caramazza, A. (1989). Variation in the pattern of omissions and substitutions of grammatic morphemes in the spontaneous speech of so-called agrammatic patients. *Brain and Language*, **36**, 447–492.

Miceli, G., Silveri, M.C., Villa, G., & Caramazza, A. (1984). On the basis of the agrammatic's difficulty in producing main verbs. *Cortex*, **20**, 207–220.

Michel, D., Laurent, B., Foyatier, N., Blanc, A., & Portafaix, M. (1982). Infarctus thalamique paramédian gauche étude de la mémoire et du langage. *Revue Neurologique*, **138**, 533–550.

Milner, B. (1958). Psychological deficits produced by temporal-lobe excision. *Research Publications—Association for Research in Nervous and Mental Disease*, **36**, 244–257.

Milner, B. (1962). Les troubles de mémoire accompagnant des lésions hippocampiques bilaterales. *Physiologie de l'hippocampe* (Report No. 107). Paris: CNRS.

Milner, B. (1963). Effects of different brain lesions on card sorting. *Archives of Neurology (Chicago)*, **9**, 90–100.

Milner, B. (1964). Some effects of frontal lobectomy in man. In J.M. Warren & K. Akert (Eds.), *The frontal granular cortex and behaviour* (pp. 313–331). New York: McGraw-Hill.

Milner, B. (1965). Visually-guided maze learning in man: Effects of bilateral hippocampal, bilateral frontal and unilateral cerebral lesions. *Neuropsychologia*, **3**, 317–338.

Milner, B. (1966). Amnesia following operations on the temporal lobes. In C.W.M. Whitty & O.L. Zangwill (Eds.), *Amnesia* (pp. 109–133). London: Butterworth.

Milner, B. (1967). Brain mechanisms suggested by studies of the temporal lobes. In F.L. Darley (Ed.), *Brain mechanisms underlying speech and language* (pp. 122–145). New York: Grune & Stratton.

Milner, B. (1968). Visual recognition and recall after right temporal-lobe excision in man. *Neuropsychologia*, **6**, 191–209.

Milner, B. (1971). Interhemispheric differences and psychological processes. *British Medical Bulletin*, **27**, 272–277.

Milner, B. (1975). Psychological aspects of focal epilepsy and its neurosurgical management. *Advances in Neurology*, **8**, 299–321.

Milner, B. (1978). Clues to the cerebral organisation of memory. *INSERM Symposium*, **6**, 139–154.

Milner, B. (1982). Some cognitive effects of frontal-lobe lesions in man. *Philosophical Transactions of the Royal Society of London, Series B*, **298**, 211–226.

Milner, B., Branch, C., & Rasmussen, T. (1964). Observations on cerebral dominance. In

A.V.S. de Rueck & M. O'Connor (Eds.), *Disorders of language (pp. 200–222)*. London: Churchill.

Milner, B., Corkin, S., & Teuber, H.-L. (1968). Further analysis of the hippocampal amnesic syndrome: 14-year follow-up of H.M. *Neuropsychologia, 6*, 215–234.

Milner, B., & Petrides, M. (1984). Behavioural effects of frontal lobe lesions in man. *Trends in Neuroscience, 7*, 403–407.

Milner, B., & Teuber, H.-L. (1968). Alteration of perception and memory in man: Reflections on methods. In L. Weiskrantz (Ed.), *Analysis of behavioural change* (pp. 268–375). New York: Harper & Row.

Mohr, J.P. (1976). Broca's area and Broca's aphasia. In H. Whitaker & H.A. Whitaker (Eds.), *Studies in neurolinguistics* (Vol. 1, pp. 201–235). New York: Academic Press.

Mohr, J.P., Leicester, J., Stoddard, L.T., & Siman, M. (1971). Right hemianopia with memory and colour deficits in circumscribed left posterior cerebral artery infarction. *Neurology, 21*, 1104–1113.

Mollon, J.D., Newcombe, F., Polden, P.G., & Ratcliff, G. (1980). On the presence of three cone mechanisms in a case of total achromatopsia. In G. Verriest (Ed.), *Color vision deficiencies* (Vol. 5, pp. 130–135). Bristol, England: Hilger.

Monrad-Krohn, G.H. (1947). Dysprosody or altered "melody" of language. *Brain, 70*, 405–415.

Morlaas, J. (1928). *Contribution à l'étude de l'apraxie*. Paris: Amedée Legrand.

Morton, J. (1969). The interaction of information in word recognition. *Psychological Review, 76*, 165–178.

Morton, J. (1970). A functional model of memory. In D.A. Norman (Ed.), *Models of human memory* (pp. 203–254). New York: Academic Press.

Morton, J. (1980). A new attempt at an interpretation, or, an attempt at a new interpretation. In M. Coltheart, K.E. Patterson, and J.C. Marshall (Eds.), *Deep Dyslexia* (pp. 91–118). London: Routledge.

Morton, J., Hammersley, R.H., & Bekerian, D.A. (1985). Headed records: A model for memory and its failure. *Cognition, 20*, 1–23.

Moscovitch, M. (1982). Multiple dissociations of function in amnesia. In L.S. Cermak (Ed.), *Human memory and amnesia* (pp. 337–370). Hillsdale, NJ: Erlbaum.

Moscovitch, M. (1984). The sufficient conditions for demonstrating preserved memory in amnesia: A task analysis. In L. Squire & N. Butters (Eds.), *The neuropsychology of memory* (pp. 104–114). New York: Guilford Press.

Muramuto, O., Kuru, Y., Sugishita, M., & Togokura, Y. (1979). Pure memory loss with hippocampal lesions. *Archives of Neurology (Chicago), 36*, 34–56.

Murdoch, B.B., Jr. (1967). Recent developments in short term memory. *British Journal of Psychology, 58*, 421–433.

Myers, D.M., & Goodglass, H. (1978). The effects of cuing on picture naming in aphasia. *Cortex, 14*, 178–189.

Nelson, H.E. (1976). A modified card sorting task sensitive to frontal lobe defects. *Cortex, 12*, 313–324.

Nelson, H.E., & O'Connell, A. (1978). Dementia: The estimation of premorbid intelligence levels using the new adult reading test. *Cortex, 14*, 234–244.

Nespoulos, J.L., Dordain, M., Perron, C., Ska, B., Bub, D., Caplan, D., Mehler, J., & Lecours, A.R. (1988). Agrammatism in sentence production without comprehension deficits: Reduced availability of syntactic structures and/or of grammatical morphemes? A case study. *Brain and Language, 33*, 273–295.

Newcombe, F. (1969). *Missile wounds of the brain: A study of psychological deficits*. London: Oxford University Press.

Newcombe, F. (1979). The processing of visual information in prosopagnosia and acquired dyslexia: functional versus physiological interpretation. In D.J. Oborne, M.M. Gruneberg, & J.R. Eiser (Eds.), *Research in psychology and medicine*. (Vol. 1, pp. 315–322). London: Academic Press.

Newcombe, F., & Marshall, J.C. (1985). Sound-by-sound reading and writing. In M. Coltheart, K.E. Patterson, & J.C. Marshall (Eds.), *Surface dyslexia* (pp. 35–51). London: Routledge.

Newcombe, F., Oldfield, R.C., & Wingfield, A. (1965). Object naming by dysphasic patients. *Nature (London)*, **207**, 1217–1218.

Newcombe, F., & Russell, W.R. (1969). Dissociated visual perceptual and spatial deficits in focal lesions of the right hemisphere. *Journal of Neurology, Neurosurgery and Psychiatry*, **32**, 73–81.

Newcombe, F., Young, A.W., & De Haan, E.H.F. (1989). Prosopagnosia and object agnosia without covert recognition. *Neuropsychologia*, **27**, 179–191.

Nielsen, J.M. (1937). Unilateral cerebral dominance as related to mind blindness. *Archives of Neurology and Psychiatry*, **38**, 108–135.

Nielsen, J.M. (1946). *Agnosia, apraxia, aphasia: their value in cerebral localisation* (2nd ed.). New York: Harper (Hoeber).

Nolan, K.A., & Caramazza, A. (1982). Modality independent impairments in word processing in a deep dyslexic patient. *Brain and Language*, **16**, 237–264.

Norman, D.A., & Shallice, T. (1980). *Attention to action: Willed and automatic control of behavior*. (Report no. 99). San Diego, CA: Centre for Human Information Processing, University of California. [Reprinted in revised form in R.J. Davidson, G.E. Schwartz, & D. Shapiro (Eds.) (1986). *Consciousness and self regulation* (Vol. 4). New York: Plenum.

Ogden, J.A. (1985a). Contralesional neglect of constructed visual images in right and left brain damaged patients. *Neuropsychologia*, **23**, 273–277.

Ogden, J.A. (1985b). Autotopagnosia: Occurrence in a patient without nominal aphasia and with an intact ability to point to parts of animals and objects. *Brain*, **108**, 1009–1022.

Ogden, J.A. (1987). The 'neglected' left hemisphere and its contribution to visuospatial neglect. In M. Jeannerod (Ed.), *Neurophysiological and neuropsychological aspects of spatial neglect* (pp. 215–233). Amsterdam: Elsevier-North-Holland.

Ogle, J.W. (1869). Aphasia and agraphia. *Report of the Medical Research Council of St. George's Hospital, London*, **2**, 83–122.

Oldfield, R.C. (1966). Things, words and the brain. *Quarterly Journal of Experimental Psychology*, **18**, 340–363.

Oldfield, R.C., & Wingfield, A. (1965). Response latencies in naming objects. *Quarterly Journal of Experimental Psychology*, **17**, 273–281.

Oscar-Berman, M. (1980). Neuropsychological consequences of long term alcoholism. *American Scientist*, **68**, 410–419.

Osterreith, P.A. (1944). Le test de copie d'une figure complèxe. *Archives de Psychologie*, **30**, 206–356.

Oxbury, J.M., Campbell, D.C., & Oxbury, S.M. (1974). Unilateral spatial neglect and impairments of spatial analysis and visual perception. *Brain*, **97**, 551–564.

Oxbury, J.M., Oxbury, S.M., & Humphrey, N.K. (1969). Varieties of colour anomia. *Brain*, **92**, 847–860.

Paivio, A. (1971). *Imagery and verbal processes*. New York: Holt, Rinehart & Winston.

Pallis, C.A. (1955). Impaired identification of faces and places with agnosia for colours. Report of a case due to cerebral embolism. *Journal of Neurology, Neurosurgery and Psychiatry*, **18**, 218–224.

Papez, J.W. (1937). A proposed mechanism of emotion. *Archives of Neurology and Psychiatry*, **38**, 725–743.

Parisi, D. (1987). Grammatical disturbances of speech production. In M. Coltheart, G. Sartori, & R. Job (Eds.), *The cognitive neuropsychology of language* (pp. 201–219). London: Erlbaum.

Parisi, D., & Pizzamiglio, L. (1970). Syntactic comprehension in aphasia. *Cortex*, **6**, 204–215.

Parkin, A.J. (1984). Amnesic syndrome, a lesion specific disorder. *Cortex*, **20**, 479–508.

Parkin, A.J., & Long, N.R.C. (1988). Comparative studies of human amnesia; syndrome or syndromes? In H. Markowitsch (Ed.), *Information processing by the brain* (pp. 107–124). Toronto: Huber.

Parkman, J.N., & Groen, G.J. (1971). Temporal aspects of simple addition and comparison. *Journal of Experimental Psychology*, **89**, 335–342.

Pate, D.S., Saffran, E.M., & Martin, N. (1987). Specifying the nature of the production impairment in a conduction aphasic: A case study. *Language and Cognitive Processes*, **2**, 43–84.

Paterson, A., & Zangwill, O.L. (1944). Disorders of visual space perception associated with lesions of the right cerebral hemisphere. *Brain*, **67**, 331–358.

Paterson, A., & Zangwill, O.L. (1945). A case of topographical disorientation associated with a unilateral cerebral lesion. *Brain*, **68**, 188–211.

Patterson, K.E. (1978). Phonemic dyslexia: Errors of meaning and meaning of errors. *Quarterly Journal of Experimental Psychology*, **30**, 587–601.

Patterson, K.E. (1979). What is right with "deep" dyslexic patients. *Brain and Language*, **8**, 111–129.

Patterson, K.E. (1982). The relation between reading and phonological coding: Further neuropsychological investigations: In A.W. Ellis (Ed.), *Normality and pathology in cognitive functions* (pp. 77–111). London: Academic Press.

Patterson, K.E. (1986). Lexical but nonsemantic spelling? *Cognitive Neuropsychology*, **3**, 341–367.

Patterson, K.E., & Coltheart, V. (1987). Phonological processes in reading: A tutorial review. In M. Coltheart (Ed.), *Attention and performance XII: the psychology of reading* (pp. 421–447). Hove, London: Erlbaum.

Patterson, K.E., & Kay, J. (1982). Letter-by-letter reading: Psychological descriptions of a neurological syndrome. *Quarterly Journal of Experimental Psychology*, **34A**, 411–441.

Patterson, K.E., & Marcel, A.J. (1977). Aphasia, dyslexia and the phonological coding of written words. *Quarterly Journal of Experimental Psychology*, **29**, 307–318.

Patterson, K.E., Marshall, J.C., & Coltheart, M. (1985). *Surface dyslexia: Neuropsychological and cognitive studies of phonological reading.* Hove, London: Erlbaum.

Patterson, K.E., & Morton, J. (1985). From orthography to phonology: An attempt at an old interpretation. In K.E. Patterson, J.C. Marshall, & M. Coltheart (Eds.), *Surface dyslexia: neuropsychological and cognitive studies of phonological reading* (pp. 335–359). Hove, London: Erlbaum.

Patterson, K.E., Varga-Khadem, F., & Polkey, C.E. (1989). Reading with one hemisphere. *Brain*, **112**, 39–64.

Patterson, K.E., & Wing, A.M. (1989). Processes in handwriting: A case for case. *Cognitive Neuropsychology*, **6**, 1–23.

Perenin, M.T., & Jeannerod, M. (1978). Visual function within the hemianopic field following early cerebral hemidecortication in man. I. Spatial localisation. *Neuropsychologia* **16**, 1–13.

Perenin, M.T., & Vighetto, A. (1983). Optic ataxia a specific disorder in visuomotor coordination. In A. Hein & M. Jeannerod (Eds.), *Spatially oriented behaviour* (pp. 305–326). New York: Springer-Verlag.

Perenin, M.T., & Vighetto, A. (1988). Optic ataxia: A specific disruption in visuomotor mechanisms. *Brain*, **111**, 643–674.

Perret, E. (1974). The left frontal lobe of man and the suppression of habitual responses in verbal categorical behaviour. *Neuropsychologia*, **12**, 323–330.

Pershing, H.T. (1900). A case of Wernicke's conduction aphasia with autopsy. *Journal of Nervous and Mental Disease*, **27**, 369–374.

Petersen, L.R., & Petersen, M.J. (1959). Short term retention of individual items. *Journal of Experimental Psychology*, **91**, 341–343.

Petrides, M. (1985). Deficits on conditional associative-learning tasks after frontal and temporal lobe lesions in man. *Neuropsychologia*, **23**, 601–614.

Petrides, M., & Milner, B. (1982). Deficits on subject-ordered tasks after frontal and temporal lobe lesions in man. *Neuropsychologia*, **20**, 249–262.

Pick, A. (1898). *Beiträge zur Pathologie und pathologischen Anatomie des Zentralnervensystems* (pp. 134–149). Berlin: Karger.

Pick, A. (1903). On reduplicative paramnesia. *Brain*, **26**, 260–267.

Pick, A. (1905). Studien über motorische Apraxie und ihr nahestehende Erscheinungen. Deuticke: Leipzig.

Pick, A. (1908). *Über Störungen der Orientierung am eigenen Körper. Arbeiten aus der Deutschen Psychiatrischen Universitätsklinik in Prag.* Karger: Berlin.

Pick, A. (1922). Störung der Orientierung am eigenen Körper. Beitrag zur Lehre vom Bewusstsein des eigenen Körpers. *Psychologische Forschung*, **1**, 303–318.

Pick, A. (1931). Aphasie. *Handbuch d. Norm. u. Path. Physiol*, **15**(2), 1416–1524. [Reprinted in translation by Brown, J.W. (1973). *Aphasia*. Springfield, IL: Charles C. Thomas.]

Pieczuro, A.C., & Vignolo, L.A. (1967). Studio sperimentale sulla aprassia ideomotoria. *Sistema Nervoso*, **19**, 131–143.

Piercy, M., Hécaen, H., & Ajuriaguerra de, J. (1960). Constructional apraxia associated with unilateral cerebral lesion, left and right sided cases compared. *Brain*, **83**, 225–242.

Pillsbury, W.B., & Sylvester, A. (1940). Retroactive and proactive inhibition in immediate memory. *Journal of Experimental Psychology*, **27**, 532–565.

Pitres, A. (1898). *L'aphasie amnésique et ses variétés cliniques.* Paris: Aléan.

Podroza, B.L., & Darley, F.L. (1977). Effect of auditory pre-stimulation on naming in aphasia. *Journal of Speech and Hearing Research*, **20**, 669–683.

Poeck, K., De Bleser, R., & Von Kanenlingk, D.G. (1984). Neurolinguistic status and localisation of lesion in patients with exclusively consonant-vowel recurring utterances. *Brain*, **107**, 199–217.

Poeck, K., Hartje, W., & Kerschensteiner, M. (1973). Sprachverständnisstörungen bei aphasischen und nichtaphasischen Hirnkranken. *Deutsche Medizinische Wochenschrift*, **98**, 139–147.

Poeck, K., & Lehmkuhl, G. (1980). Das Syndrom der ideatorischen Apraxie und seine Localisation. *Nervenarzt*, **51**, 217–225.

Poeck, K., & Stachowiak, F.J. (1975). Farbennennungsstörungen bei aphasischen und nicht aphasischen Hirnkranken. *Journal of Neurology*, **209**, 95–102.

Poizner, H., Klima, E.S., & Bellugi, U. (1987). *What the hands reveal about the brain. A bradford book.* Cambridge, MA: M.I.T. Press.

Poppelreuter, W. (1914–1917). *Die psychischen Schädigungen durch Kopfschuss im Kriege 1914/16 mit besonderer Berücksichtigung der pathopsychologischen, pädagogischen, gewerblichen und sozialen Beziehungen: Vol. 1. Die Störungen der niederen und höheren Sehleistungen durch Verletzungen des Okzipitalhirns.* Leipzig: Voss.

Poppelreuter, W. (1923). Zur Psychologie und Pathologie der optischen Wahrnehmung. *Zeitschrift für die Gesamte Neurologie und Psychiatrie*, **83**, 26–152.

Posner, M.I., Cohen, Y., & Rafal, R.D. (1982). Neural systems control of spatial orienting. *Philosophical Transactions of the Royal Society of London, Series B*, **298**, 60–70.

Posner, M.I., Walker, J.A., Friedrich, F.J., & Rafal, R.D. (1984). Effects of parietal injury on covert orienting of attention. *Journal of Neuroscience*, **4**, 1863–1874.

Postman, L. (1961). The present status of interference theory. In C.N. Cofer (Ed.), *Verbal learning and verbal behavior* (pp. 152–179). New York: McGraw-Hill.

Pötzl, O. (1925). Über die parietal bedingte Aphasie und ihren Einfluss auf das Sprechen mehrerer Sprachen. *Zeitschrift für die Gesamte Neurologie und Psychiatrie*, **96**, 100–124.

Pötzl, O., & Stengel, E. (1937). Über das Syndrom Leitungsaphasie-Schmerzasymbolie. *Jahrbücher für Psychiatrie*, **53**, 174–207.

Quensel, F. (1908). Über Erscheinungen und Grundlagen der Worttaubheit. *Deutsche Zeitschrift für Nervenkrankheiten*, **35**, 25.

Ramier, A.M., & Hécaen, H. (1970). Róle respectif des atteintes frontales et de la latéralisation lésionnelle dans les déficits de la "fluence verbale." *Revue Neurologique*, **123**, 17–22.

Rapcsak, S.Z., Kaszniak, A.W., & Rubens, A.D. (1989). Anomia for facial expressions: Evidence for a category specific visual-verbal disconnection syndrome. *Neuropsychologia*, **27**, 1031–1041.

Rapcsak, S.Z., Verfaellie, M., Fleet, W.S., & Heilman, K.M. (1989). Selective attention in hemispatial neglect. *Archives of Neurology (Chicago)*, **46**, 178–182.

Rasmussen, T., & Milner, B. (1977). The role of early left brain injury in determining lateralisation of cerebral speech functions. *Annals of the New York Academy of Sciences*, **229**, 355–369.

Ratcliff, G., & Davies-Jones, G.A.B. (1972). Defective visual localisation in focal brain wounds. *Brain*, **95**, 46–60.

Ratcliff, G., & Newcombe, F. (1973). Spatial orientation in man: Effects of left, right and bilateral posterior cerebral lesions. *Journal of Neurology, Neurosurgery and Psychiatry*, **36**, 448–454.

Ratcliff, G., & Newcombe, F. (1982). Object recognition: Some deductions from the clinical evidence. In A.W. Ellis (Ed.), *Normality and pathology in cognitive function* (pp. 147–171). London: Academic Press.

Raymond, F., & Egger, M. (1906). Un cas d'aphasie tactile. *Revue Neurologique*, **14**, 371–375.

Ribot, T.A. (1882). *The diseases of memory*. New York: Appleby.

Riddoch, G. (1935). Visual disorientation in homonymous half-fields. *Brain*, **58**, 376–382.

Riddoch, M.J., & Humphreys, G.W. (1983). Perceptual and action systems in unilateral neglect. In M. Jeannerod (Ed.), *Neurophysiological and neuropsychological aspects of spatial neglect* (pp. 151–181). Amsterdam: Elsevier-North-Holland.

Riddoch, M.J., & Humphreys, G.W. (1986). Neurological impairments of object constancy: The effects of orientation and size disparities. *Cognitive Neuropsychology*, **3**, 207–224.

Riddoch, M.J., & Humphreys, G.W. (1987a). A case of integrative visual agnosia. *Brain*, **110**, 1431–1462.

Riddoch, M.J., & Humphreys, G. (1987b). Visual object processing in optic aphasia: A case of semantic access agnosia. *Cognitive Neuropsychology*, **4**, 131–185.

Riddoch, M.J., Humphreys, G.W., Coltheart, M., & Funnell, E. (1988). Semantic systems or system? Neuropsychological evidence re-examined. *Cognitive Neuropsychology*, **5**, 3–25.

Robinson, A.L., Heaton, R.K., Lehman, R.A.W., & Stilson, D.W. (1980). The utility of the Wisconsin Card Sorting test in detecting and localising frontal lesions. *Journal of Consulting and Clinical Psychology*, **48**, 605–614.

Rochford, E., & Williams, M. (1962). Studies in the development and breakdown of the use of names. Part I. The relationship between nominal dysphasia and the acquisition of vocabulary in childhood. *Journal of Neurology, Neurosurgery and Psychiatry*, **25**, 222–233.

Rochford, E., & Williams, M. (1963). Studies in the development and breakdown of the use of names. Part II. Recovery from nominal dysphasia. *Journal of Neurology, Neurosurgery and Psychiatry*, **26**, 377–381.

Rochford, G., & Williams, M. (1965). The development and breakdown of the use of names. IV. The effects of word frequency. *Journal of Neurology, Neurosurgery and Psychiatry*, **28**, 407–443.

Roeltgen, D.P., & Heilman, K.M. (1984). Lexical agraphia. Further support for the two strategy hypothesis of linguistic agraphia. *Brain*, **107**, 811–827.

Roeltgen, D.P., Rothi, L.J., & Heilman, K.M. (1986). Linguistic semantic agraphia: A dissociation of the spelling system from semantics. *Brain and Language*, **27**, 257–280.

Roeltgen, D.P., Sevush, S., & Heilman, K.M. (1983). Phonological agraphia: Writing by the lexical-semantic route. *Neurology*, **33**, 755–765.

Rondot, P., & Tzavaras, A. (1969). La prosopagnosie après vingt années d'études cliniques et neuropsychologiques. *Journal of Psychological and Normative Pathology*, **2**, 133–165.

Ross-Russell, R.W., & Bharucha, N. (1978). The recognition and prevention of border zone ischemia during cardiac surgery. *Quarterly Journal of Medicine, New Series XLVII*, **187**, 303–323.

Ross-Russell, R.W., & Bharucha, N. (1984). Visual localisation in patients with occipital infarction. *Journal of Neurology, Neurosurgery and Psychiatry, 47,* 153–158.

Rothi, L.J., & Heilman, K.M. (1981). Alexia and agraphia with spared spelling and letter recognition abilities. *Brain and Language, 12,* 1–13.

Rothi, L.J., & Heilman, K.M. (1983). Apractic agraphia in a patient with normal praxis. *Brain and Language, 18,* 35–46.

Rubens, A.B. (1976). Transcortical motor aphasia. In H. Whitaker & H.A. Whitaker (Eds.), *Studies in neurolinguistics* (Vol. 1, pp. 293–303). New York: Academic Press.

Rubens, A.B., & Benson, D.F. (1971). Associative visual agnosia. *Archives of Neurology (Chicago), 24,* 305–316.

Rudge, P., & Warrington, E.K. (1990). Selective impairment of memory and visual perception in splenial tumours. *Brain* (in press).

Ruff, R.L., & Volpe, B.T. (1981). Environmental reduplication associated with right frontal and right parietal lobe injury. *Journal of Neurology, Neurosurgery and Psychiatry, 44,* 382–386.

Rylander, G. (1939). Personality changes after operations on the frontal lobes. *Acta Psychiatrica et Neurologica Scandinavica, Supplementum,* No. 20.

Sacks, O. (1985). *The man who mistook his wife for a hat.* New York: Summit Books.

Saffran, E.M. (1990). In G. Vallar & T. Shallice (Eds.), *Neuropsychological impairments to short term memory* (in press).

Saffran, E.M., Bogyo, L.C., Schwartz, M.F., & Marin, O.S.M. (1980). Does deep dyslexia reflect right hemisphere reading? In M. Coltheart, K.E. Patterson, & J.C. Marshall (Eds.), *Deep dyslexia* (pp. 381–406). London: Routledge.

Saffran, E.M., & Marin, O.S.M. (1975). Immediate memory for word lists and sentences in a patient with a deficient auditory short-term memory. *Brain and Language, 2,* 420–433.

Saffran, E.M., & Marin, O.S.M. (1977). Reading without phonology. *Quarterly Journal of Experimental Psychology, 29,* 515–525.

Saffran, E.M., Marin, O.S.M., & Yeni-Komshian, G.H. (1976). An analysis of speech perception in word deafness. *Brain and Language, 3,* 209–228.

Saffran, E.M., Schwartz, M.F., & Marin, O.S.M. (1980a). The word order problem in agrammatism production. *Brain and Language, 11,* 263–280.

Saffran, E.M., Schwartz, M.F., & Marin, O.S.M. (1980b). Evidence from aphasia: Isolating the components of a production model. In B. Butterworth (Ed.), *Language production* (Vol. 1, pp. 221–241). London: Academic Press.

Salamaso, D., & Denes, G. (1982). Role of the frontal lobes on an attention task: A signal detection analysis. *Perception and Motor Skills, 55,* 1147–1150.

Salomon, E. (1914). Motorische Aphasie mit Agrammatismus und sensorisch-agrammatischen Störungen. *Monatsschrift für Psychiatrie und Neurologie, 35,* 181–208, 216–275.

Sanders, H.I., & Warrington, E.K. (1971). Memory for remote events in amnesic patients. *Brain, 94,* 661–668.

Sanders, H.I., & Warrington, E.K. (1975). Retrograde amnesia in organic amnesic patients. *Cortex, 11,* 397–400.

Sands, E.S., Freeman, F.J., & Harris, K.S. (1978). Progressive changes in articulatory patterns in verbal apraxia: A longitudinal case study. *Brain and Language, 6,* 97–105.

Sartori, G., & Job, R. (1988). The oyster with four legs: A neuropsychological study on the interaction of visual and semantic information. *Cognitive Neuropsychology, 5,* 105–132.

Sasanuma, S. (1980). Acquired dyslexia in Japanese: Clinical features and underlying mechanisms. In M. Coltheart, K.E. Patterson, & J.C. Marshall (Eds.), *Deep dyslexia* (pp. 48–90). London: Routledge.

Sasanuma, S. (1985). Surface dyslexia and dysgraphia: How are they manifested in Japanese? In K.E. Patterson, J.C. Marshall, & M. Coltheart (Eds.), *Surface dyslexia: Neuropsychological and cognitive studies of phonological reading* (pp. 225–249). Hove, London: Erlbaum.

Schacter, D.L. (1985). Priming of old and new knowledge in amnesic patients and normal subjects. *Annals of the New York Academy of Science*, **144**, 41–53.

Schacter, D.L. (1987). Implicit memory: History and current status. *Journal of Experimental Psychology*, **13**, 501–518.

Schacter, D.L., & Graf, P. (1986). Preserved learning in amnesic patients: Perspectives from research on direct priming. *Journal of Clinical and Experimental Neuropsychology*, **8**, 727–743.

Schenkenberg, T., Bradford, D.C., & Ajax, E.T. (1980). Line bisection and unilateral visual neglect in patients with neurological impairment. *Neurology*, **30**, 509–517.

Schiff, H.B., Alexander, M.P., Naeser, M.A., & Galaburda, A.M. (1983). Aphemia: Clinical-anatomic correlations. *Archives of Neurology (Chicago)*, **40**, 720–727.

Schott, B., Mauguière, F., Laurent, B., Serclerat, O., & Fischer, C. (1980). L'amnésie thalamique. *Revue Neurologique*, **136**, 117–130.

Schuell, H., Jenkins,J., & Jimenez-Pabon, E. (1964). *Aphasia in adults: diagnosis, prognosis and treatment*. New York: Harper & Row.

Schuell, H.R., Jenkins, J.J., & Landis, L. (1961). Relationships between auditory comprehension and word frequency in aphasia. *Journal of Speech and Hearing Research*, **4**, 30–36.

Schwartz, M.F., Linebarger, M.C., & Saffran, E.M. (1985). The status of the syntactic deficit theory of agrammatism. In M.L. Kean (Ed.), *Agrammatism* (pp. 83–124). Orlando, FL: Academic Press.

Schwartz, M.F., Saffran, E.M., & Marin, O.S.M. (1980a). The word order problem in agrammatism. I. Comprehension. *Brain and Language*, **10**, 249–262.

Schwartz, M.F., Saffran, E.M., & Marin, O.S.M. (1980b). Fractionating the reading process in dementia: Evidence for word-specific print-to-sound associations. In M. Coltheart, K.E. Patterson, & J.C. Marshall (Eds.), *Deep dyslexia* (pp. 259–269). London: Routledge.

Scoville, W.B., & Milner, B. (1957). Loss of recent memory after bilateral hippocampal lesions. *Journal of Neurology, Neurosurgery and Psychiatry*, **20**, 11–21.

Selnes, O.A., Rubens, A.B., Risse, G.L., & Levy, R.S. (1982). Transient aphasia with persistent apraxia: Uncommon sequelae of massive left-hemisphere stroke. *Archives of Neurology (Chicago)*, **39**, 122–126.

Seltzer, B., & Benson, D.F. (1974). The temporal pattern of retrograde amnesia in Korsakoff's disease. *Neurology*, **24**, 527–530.

Semenza, C., & Zettin, M. (1988). Generating proper names: A case of selective inability. *Cognitive Neuropsychology*, **5**, 711–721.

Semmes, J., Weinstein, S., Ghent, L., & Teuber, H-L. (1963). Correlates of impaired orientation in personal and extrapersonal space. *Brain*, **86**, 747–772.

Sergent, J. (1987). A new look at the human split brain. *Brain* **110**, 1375–1392.

Shallice, T. (1979). Case study approach in neuropsychological research. *Journal of Clinical Neuropsychology*, **1**, 183–211.

Shallice, T. (1981). Phonological agraphia and the lexical route in writing. *Brain*, **104**, 413–429.

Shallice, T. (1982). Specific impairments of planning. *Philosophical Transactions of the Royal Society of London, Series B*, **298**, 199–209.

Shallice, T. (1984). More functionally isolable subsystems but fewer "modules"? *Cognition*, **17**, 243–252.

Shallice, T. (1988). *From neuropsychology to mental structure*. New York: Cambridge University Press.

Shallice, T., & Butterworth, B. (1977). Short term memory impairment and spontaneous speech. *Neuropsychologia*, **15**, 729–735.

Shallice, T., & Coughlan, A.K. (1980). Modality specific comprehension deficits in deep dyslexia. *Journal of Neurology, Neurosurgery and Psychiatry*, **43**, 866–872.

Shallice, T., & Evans, M.E. (1978). The involvement of the frontal lobes in cognitive estimation. *Cortex*, **14**, 294–303.

Shallice, T., & McCarthy, R.A. (1985). Phonological reading: From patterns of impairment to possible procedures. In K.E. Patterson, J.C. Marshall, & M. Coltheart (Eds.), *Surface dyslexia: neuropsychological and cognitive studies of phonological reading* (pp. 361–397). Hove, London: Erlbaum.

Shallice, T., & Saffran, E.M. (1986). Lexical processing in the absence of explicit word identification. Evidence from a letter-by-letter reader. *Cognitive Neuropsychology*, **3**, 429–458.

Shallice, T., & Warrington, E.K. (1970). Independent functioning of the verbal memory stores: A neuropsychological study. *Quarterly Journal of Experimental Psychology*, **22**, 261–273.

Shallice, T., & Warrington, E.K. (1974). The dissociation between short-term retention of meaningful sounds and verbal material. *Neuropsychologia*, **12**, 553–555.

Shallice, T., & Warrington, E.K. (1975). Word recognition in a phonemic dyslexic patient. *Quarterly Journal of Experimental Psychology*, **27**, 187–199.

Shallice, T., & Warrington, E.K. (1977a). The possible role of selective attention in acquired dyslexia. *Neuropsychologia*, **15**, 31–41.

Shallice, T., & Warrington, E.K. (1977b). Auditory-verbal short term memory impairment and spontaneous speech. *Brain and Language*, **4**, 479–491.

Shallice, T., & Warrington, E.K. (1980). Single and multiple component central dyslexic syndromes. In M. Coltheart, K.E. Patterson, & J.C. Marshall (Eds.), *Deep dyslexia* (pp. 119–145). London: Routledge.

Shallice, T., Warrington, E.K., & McCarthy, R.A. (1983). Reading without semantics. *Quarterly Journal of Experimental Psychology*, **35A**, 111–138.

Shankweiler, D., & Harris, K. (1966). An experimental approach to the problem of articulation in aphasia. *Cortex*, **2**, 277–292.

Shapiro, B.E., Alexander, M.P., Gardner, H., & Mercer, B. (1981). Mechanisms of confabulation. *Neurology*, **31**, 1070–1076.

Shapiro, B.E., & Danley, M. (1985). The role of the right hemisphere in the control of speech prosody in propositional and affective contexts. *Brain and Language*, **25**, 19–36.

Shimamura, A.P., & Squire, L.R. (1986). Korsakoff's syndrome: A study of the relation between retrograde amnesia and remote memory impairment. *Behavioral Neurosciences*, **100**, 165–170.

Shinn, P., & Blumstein, S. (1983). Phonetic disintegration in aphasia: Acoustic analysis of spectral characteristics for place of articulation. *Brain and Language*, **20**, 90–114.

Silveri, M.C., & Gainotti, G. (1988). Interaction between vision and language in category specific semantic impairment. *Cognitive Neuropsychology*, **5**, 677–709.

Sitdis, J.S., & Volpe, B.T. (1988). Selective loss of complex pitch or speech discrimination after unilateral lesion. *Brain and Language*, **34**, 235–245.

Sittig, O. (1921). Störungen im Verhalten gegunüber Farben bei Aphasischen. *Monatsschrift für Psychiatrie und Neurologie*, **49**, 159–187.

Sittig, O. (1931). *Über Apraxie*. Berlin: Karger.

Smith, A. (1966). Speech and other functions after left (dominant) hemispherectomy. *Journal of Neurology, Neurosurgery and Psychiatry*, **29**, 467–471.

Smith, A., & Sugar, O. (1975). Development of above normal language and intelligence 21 years after left hemispherectomy. *Neurology*, **25**, 813–818.

Smith, M.L., & Milner, B. (1981). The role of the right hippocampus in the recall of spatial location. *Neuropsychologia*, **19**, 781–795.

Smith, M.L., & Milner, B. (1984). Differential effects of frontal-lobe lesions on cognition estimation and spatial memory. *Neuropsychologia*, **22**, 697–705.

Smith, M.L., & Milner, B. (1988). Estimation of frequency of occurrence of abstract designs after frontal or temporal lobectomy. *Neuropsychologia*, **26**, 297–306.

Spellacy, F.J., & Spreen, O. (1969). A short form of the Token Test. *Cortex*, **5**, 390–397.

Sperry, R.W., Gazzaniga, M.S., & Bogen, J.E. (1969). Interhemispheric relationships: the neocortical commissures; syndromes of hemispheric disconnection. In P.J. Vinken & G.W. Bruyn (Eds.), *Handbook of clinical neurology* (Vol. 4, pp. 273–290). Amsterdam: Elsevier-North Holland.

Spreen, O., Benton, A.L., & Van Allen, H.W. (1966). Dissociation of visual and tactile naming in amnesic aphasia. *Neurology, 16,* 807–814.

Squire, L.R. (1986). The neuropsychology of memory dysfunction and its assessment. In I. Grant & K.M. Adams (Eds.), *Neuropsychological assessments of neuropsychiatric disorders* (pp. 268–299). New York: Oxford University Press.

Squire, L.R., & Cohen, N.J. (1982). Remote memory, retrograde amnesia, and the neuropsychology of memory. In L.S. Cermak, I. Grant, & K.M. Adams (Eds.), *Human memory and amnesia* (pp. 275–303). Hillsdale, NJ: Erlbaum.

Squire, L.R., & Shimamura, A.P. (1986). Characterizing amnesic patients for neurobehavioral study. *Behavioral Neurosciences, 100,* 866–877.

Staller, J., Buchanan, D., Singer, M., Lappin, J., & Webb, W. (1978). Alexia without agraphia: An experimental case study. *Brain and Language, 5,* 378–387.

Starr, A., & Phillips, L. (1970). Verbal and motor memory in the amnesic syndrome. *Neuropsychologia, 8,* 75–88.

Steinthal, H. (1871). Cited by Hécaen and Rondot (1985).

Stengel, E. (1933). Zur Lehre von der Leitungsaphasie. *Zeitschrift für die Gesamte Neurologie und Psychiatrie, 149,* 266–291.

Stengel, E. (1948). The syndrome of visual alexia with colour agnosia. *Journal of Mental Science, 94,* 46–58.

Stengel, E., & Lodge Patch, I.C. (1955). 'Central' aphasia associated with parietal symptoms. *Brain, 78,* 401–416.

Stevenson, J.F. (1967). *Some psychological effects of frontal lobe lesions in man.* Unpublished master's thesis, University of Cambridge.

Street, R.F. (1931). *A Gestalt completion test. A study of a cross section of intellect.* New York: Bureau of Publications, Columbia University, The Teachers College.

Strohmeyer, W. (1903). Über subkortikale Alexie mit Agraphie und Apraxie. *Deutsche Zeitschrift für Nervenheilkunde, 24,* 372–380.

Stuss, D.T., Alexander, M.P., Lieberman, A., & Levine, H. (1978). An extraordinary form of confabulation. *Neurology, 28,* 1166–1172.

Stuss, D.T., & Benson, D.F. (1986). *The frontal lobes.* New York: Raven.

Sutherland, N.S. (1973). Object recognition. In E.C. Carterette & M.P. Friedman (Eds.), *Handbook of perception* (Vol. 3, pp. 157–185). New York: Academic Press.

Talland, G.A. (1965). *Deranged memory.* New York: Academic Press.

Tanaka, Y., Yamadori, A., & Mori, E. (1987). Pure word deafness following bilateral lesions: A psychophysical analysis. *Brain, 110,* 381–403.

Taylor, A.M., & Warrington, E.K. (1971). Visual agnosia: A single case report. *Cortex, 7,* 152–161.

Taylor, A.M., & Warrington, E.K. (1973). Visual discrimination in patients with localised cerebral lesions. *Cortex, 9,* 82–93.

Taylor, L. (1968). Cited by Milner and Teuber.

Taylor, L. (1979). Psychological assessment of neurosurgical patients. In T. Rasmussen & R. Merino (Eds.), *Functional Neurosurgery* (pp. 165–180). New York: Raven.

Teuber, H.-L. (1955). Physiological psychology. *Annual Review of Psychology, 6,* 267–296.

Teuber, H.-L. (1964). The riddle of frontal lobe function in man. In J.M. Warren & K. Akert (Eds.), *The frontal granular cortex and behavior* (pp. 410–441). New York: McGraw-Hill.

Teuber, H.L. (1965). Some needed revisions of the classical views of agnosia. *Neuropsychologia, 3,* 371–378.

Teuber, H.L. (1966). The frontal lobes and their function: Further observations on rodents, carnivores, subhuman primates, and man. *International Journal of Neurology, 5,* 282–300.

Tiberghen, G., & Le Clerc, I. (1986). The cognitive locus of prosopagnosia. In R. Bruyer (Ed.), *The neuropsychology of face perception and facial expression* (pp. 39–62). Hillsdale, NJ: Erlbaum.

Tissot, R., Mounin, G., & Lhermitte, F. (1973). *L'agrammatisme*. Paris: Dessart.

Todor, J.I., & Smiley, A.L. (1985). Performance differences between the hands: implications for studying disruption to limb praxis. In E.A. Roy (Ed.), *Neuropsychological studies of apraxia and related disorders* (pp. 309–344). Amsterdam: Elsevier/North-Holland.

Tognola, G., & Vignolo, L.A. (1980). Brain lesions associated with oral apraxia in stroke patients: A clinico-neuroradiological investigation with the C.T. scan. *Neuropsychologia, 18*, 257–271.

Torii, H., & Tamai, A. (1985). The problem of prosopagnosia. Report of three cases with occlusion of the right posterior cerebral artery. *Journal of Neurology, 232*, Supplement 140.

Tranel, E., & Damasio, A.R. (1985). Knowledge without awareness: An autonomic index of facial recognition by prosopagnosics. *Science, 228*, 1453–1454.

Trillet, M., Fisher, C., Serclerat, D., & Schott, B. (1980). Le syndrome amnésique des schémes cérébrales postérieures. *Cortex, 16*, 421–434.

Tucker, D.M., Watson, R.T., & Heilman, K.M. (1977). Discrimination and evocation of affectively toned speech in patients with right parietal disease. *Neurology, 27*, 947–950.

Tuller, B. (1987). Anticipatory co-articulation in aphasia. In J.H. Ryalls (Ed.), *Phonetic approaches to speech production in aphasia and related disorders* (pp. 243–260). Hillsdale, NJ: Erlbaum.

Tulving, E. (1973). Episodic and semantic memory. In E. Tulving & W. Donaldson (Eds.), *Organization of memory* (pp. 382–404). New York: Academic Press.

Tulving, E. (1983). *Elements of episodic memory*. Oxford: Clarendon Press.

Tulving, E., Schacter, D., & Stark, H. (1982). Priming effects in word-fragment completion are independent of recognition memory. *Journal of Experimental Psychology, 8*, 336–342.

Tyrrell, P.J., Warrington, E.K., Frackowiak, R.S.J., & Rossor, M.N. (1990). Heterogeneity in progressive aphasia due to focal cortical atrophy: A clinical and PET study. *Brain, 113*, 1321–1336.

Tzavaras, A., Hécaen, H., & Le Bras, H. (1970). Le problème de la spécificité du déficit de la reconnaissance du visage humain lors de lésion hémisphérique unilatérales. *Neuropsychologia, 8*, 403–417.

Tzavaras, A., Hécaen, H., & Le Bras, H. (1971). Trouble de la vision des couleurs après lésions corticales unilatérales. *Revue Neurologique, 124*, 316–402.

Underwood, B.J. (1945). The effect of successive interpolations on retroactive and proactive inhibition. *Psychological Monographs 59* (Whole No. 273).

Vaina, L. (1987). Visual texture for recognition. In L.M. Vania (Ed.), *Matters of intelligence: conceptual structures in cognitive neuroscience* (pp. 89–114). Dordrecht, Holland: Reidel.

Vallar, G., & Baddeley, A.D. (1984a). Phonological short term store, phonological processing and sentence comprehension: A neuropsychological case study. *Cognitive Neuropsychology, 1*, 121–141.

Vallar, G., & Baddeley, A.D. (1984b). Fractionation of working memory: neuropsychological evidence for a phonological short-term store. *Journal of Verbal Learning and Verbal Behaviour, 23*, 151–161.

Vallar, G., & Shallice, T. (Eds.). (1990). *Neuropsychological impairments to short term memory*. New York: Cambridge University Press.

Vanier, M., & Caplan, D. (1985). CT scan correlates of surface dyslexia. In K.E. Patterson, J.C. Marshall, & M. Coltheart (Eds.), *Surface dyslexia: Neuropsychological and cognitive studies of phonological reading* (pp. 511–525). Hove, London: Erlbaum.

Verrey, D. (1888). Hemiachromatopsie droite absolue. *Archives d'Ophthalmologie (Paris), 8*, 239–300.

Victor, M., Adams, R.D., & Collins, C.-H. (1971). *The Wernicke-Korsakoff Syndrome*, First edition. Philadelphia, PA: Davis.

Victor, M., Adams, R.D., & Collins, C.-H. (1988). *The Wernicke-Korsakoff syndrome,* Second edition. Philadelphia, PA: Davis.

Vignolo, L. (1982). Auditory agnosia. *Philosophical Transactions of the Royal Society of London, Series B,* **298,** 49–57.

Vilkki, J. (1987). Incidental and deliberate memory for words and faces after focal cerebral lesions. *Neuropsychologia,* **25,** 221–230.

Vincent, F.M., Sadowsky, C.H., Saunders, R.L., & Reeves, A.G. (1977). Alexia without agraphia or colour naming deficit: A disconnection syndrome. *Neurology,* **27,** 689–691.

Von Cramon, D.Y., Hebel, N., & Schuri, U. (1985). A contribution to the anatomical basis of thalamic amnesia. *Brain,* **198,** 993–1008.

Von Stockert, T.R. (1974). Aphasia sine aphasia. *Brain and Language,* **1,** 277–282.

Vygotsky, L.S. (1962). *Language and thought.* Cambridge, MA: M.I.T. Press.

Wada, J., & Rasmussen, T. (1960). Intra-carotid injection of sodium amytal for the lateralisation of cerebral speech dominance. *Journal of Neurosurgery,* **17,** 266–282.

Warrington, E.K. (1974). Deficient recognition memory in organic amnesia. *Cortex,* **10,** 289–291.

Warrington, E.K. (1975). The selective impairment of semantic memory. *Quarterly Journal of Experimental Psychology,* **27,** 187–199.

Warrington, E.K. (1981a). Concrete word dyslexia. *British Journal of Psychology,* **72,** 175–196.

Warrington, E.K. (1981b). Neuropsychological studies of verbal semantic systems. *Philosophical Transactions of the Royal Society of London, Series B,* **295,** 411–423.

Warrington, E.K. (1982a). Neuropsychological studies of object recognition. *Philosophical Transactions of the Royal Society of London, Series B,* **298,** 15–33.

Warrington, E.K. (1982b). The double dissociation of short and long-term memory deficits. In L.S. Cermak (Ed.), *Human memory and amnesia* (pp. 61–76). Hillsdale, NJ: Erlbaum.

Warrington, E.K. (1982c). The fractionation of arithmetic skills: A single case study. *Quarterly Journal of Experimental Psychology,* **34A,** 31–51.

Warrington, E.K. (1984). *Recognition memory test.* Windsor: Nelson.

Warrington, E.K. (1986). Visual deficits associated with occipital lobe lesions in man. *Experimental Brain Research Supplementum,* **11,** 247–261.

Warrington, E.K., & Baddeley, A.D. (1974). Amnesia and memory for visual location. *Neuropsychologia,* **12,** 257–263.

Warrington, E.K., & James, M. (1967a). Disorders of visual perception in patients with localised cerebral lesions. *Neuropsychologia,* **5,** 253–266.

Warrington, E.K., & James, M. (1967b). Tachistoscopic number estimation in patients with unilateral cerebral lesions. *Journal of Neurology, Neurosurgery and Psychiatry,* **30,** 468–474.

Warrington, E.K., & James, M. (1967c). An experimental study of facial recognition in patients with unilateral cerebral lesions. *Cortex,* **3,** 317–326.

Warrington, E.K., & James, M. (1986). Visual object recognition in patients with right hemisphere lesions: axes of features? *Perception,* **15,** 355–366.

Warrington, E.K., & James, M. (1988). Visual apperceptive agnosia: A clinico-anatomical study of three cases. *Cortex,* **24,** 13–32.

Warrington, E.K., James, M., & Kinsbourne, M. (1966). Drawing disability in relation to the laterality of cerebral lesion. *Brain,* **89,** 53–82.

Warrington, E.K., James, M., & Maciejewski, C. (1986). The WAIS as a lateralising and localising diagnostic instrument: A study of 656 patients with unilateral cerebral lesions. *Neuropsychologia,* **24,** 223–239.

Warrington, E.K., Logue, V., & Pratt, R.T.C. (1971). The anatomical localisation of selective impairment of auditory verbal short-term memory. *Neuropsychologia,* **9,** 377–387.

Warrington, E.K., & McCarthy, R.A. (1983). Category specific access dysphasia. *Brain,* **106,** 859–878.

Warrington, E.K., & McCarthy, R.A. (1987). Categories of knowledge: further fractionation and an attempted integration. *Brain*, **110**, 1273–1296.

Warrington, E.K., & McCarthy, R.A. (1988). The fractionation of retrograde amnesia. *Brain and Cognition*, **7**, 184–200.

Warrington, E.K., & Pratt, R.T.C. (1973). Language laterality in left handers assessed by unilateral E.C.T. *Neuropsychologia*, **11**, 423–428.

Warrington, E.K., & Rabin, P. (1970). Perceptual matching in patients with cerebral lesions. *Neuropsychologia*, **8**, 475–487.

Warrington, E.K., & Rabin, P. (1971). Visual span of apprehension in patients with unilateral cerebral lesions. *Quarterly Journal of Experimental Psychology*, **23**, 423–431.

Warrington, E.K., & Sanders, H.I. (1971). The fate of old memories. *Quarterly Journal of Experimental Psychology*, **23**, 432–444.

Warrington, E.K., & Shallice, T. (1969). The selective impairment of auditory verbal short-term memory. *Brain*, **92**, 885–896.

Warrington, E.K., & Shallice, T. (1972). Neuropsychological evidence of visual storage in short term memory tasks. *Quarterly Journal of Experimental Psychology*, **24**, 30–40.

Warrington, E.K., & Shallice, T. (1979). Semantic access dyslexia. *Brain*, **102**, 43–63.

Warrington, E.K., & Shallice, T. (1980). Word-form dyslexia. *Brain*, **103**, 99–112.

Warrington, E.K., & Shallice, T. (1984). Category specific semantic impairments. *Brain*, **107**, 829–853.

Warrington, E.K., & Taylor, A.M. (1973). Contribution of the right parietal lobe to object recognition. *Cortex*, **9**, 152–164.

Warrington, E.K., & Taylor, A.M. (1978). Two categorical stages of object recognition. *Perception*, **7**, 695–705.

Warrington, E.K., & Weiskrantz, L. (1968). New method of testing long-term retention with special reference to amnesic patients. *Nature (London)*, **277**, 972–974.

Warrington, E.K., & Weiskrantz, L. (1970). Amnesic syndrome: Consolidation or retrieval? *Nature (London)*, **228**, 628–630.

Warrington, E.K., & Weiskrantz, L. (1974). The effect of prior learning on subsequent retention in amnesic patients. *Neuropsychologia*, **12**, 419–428.

Warrington, E.K., & Weiskrantz, L. (1978). Further analysis of the prior learning effect in amnesic patients. *Neuropsychologia*, **16**, 169–177.

Warrington, E.K., & Weiskrantz, L. (1982). Amnesia: A disconnection syndrome. *Neuropsychologia*, **20**, 233–249.

Warrington, E.K., & Zangwill, O.L. (1957). A study of dyslexia. *Journal of Neurology, Neurosurgery and Psychiatry*, **20**, 208–215.

Wasserstein, J., Zappulla, R., Rosen, J., Gerstman, L., & Rock, D. (1987). In search of closure: Subjective contour illusions, Gestalt completion tests, and implications. *Brain & Cognition*, **6**, 1–14.

Watson, R.T., & Heilman, K.M. (1983). Callosal apraxia. *Brain*, **106**, 391–403.

Wechsler, I.S. (1933). Partial cortical blindness with preservation of colour vision. *Archives of Ophthalmology (Chicago) [New Series]*, **9**, 957–965.

Wechsler, D.A. (1945). A standardized memory scale for clinical use. *Journal of Psychology*, **19**, 87–95.

Wechsler, D.A. (1987). *Wechsler memory scale revised*. New York: Harcourt Brace Jovanovich.

Weigl, E. (1927). Zur Psychologie sogenannter Abstraktionsprozesse. *Zeitschrift für Psychologie*, **103**, 2–45. [Translated by M. Rioch and reprinted, (1948). On the psychology of so called processes of abstraction. *Journal of Abnormal and Social Psychology*, **36**, 3–33.]

Weinstein, E.A., & Cole, M. (1963). Concepts of anosopagnosia. In L. Halpern (Ed.), *Problems of dynamic neurology* (pp. 254–273). Jerusalem: Jerusalem Post Press.

Weinstein, E.A., & Kahn, R.L. (1955). *Denial of illness, symbolic and physiological aspects*. Springfield, IL: Charles C. Thomas.

Weinstein, E.A., Kahn, R.L., & Sugarman, L.A. (1952). Phenomenon of reduplication. *Archives of Neurology and Psychiatry*, **67**, 808–814.

Weisenburg, T., & McBride, K.E. (1935). *Aphasia: A clinical and psychological study.* New York: Commonwealth Fund.

Weiskrantz, L. (1968). Some traps and pontifications. In L. Weiskrantz (Ed.), *Analysis of behavioural change* (pp. 415–429). New York: Harper & Row.

Weiskrantz, L. (1980). Varieties of residual experience. *Quarterly Journal of Experimental Psychology,* **32,** 365–386.

Weiskrantz, L., & Warrington, E.K. (1979). Conditioning in amnesic patients. *Neuropsychologia,* **17,** 187–194.

Weiskrantz, L., Warrington, E.K., Sanders, M.D., & Marshall, J.C. (1974). Visual capacity in the hemianopic field following a restricted occipital ablation. *Brain,* **97,** 709–728.

Wepman, J.M., Bock, R., Jones, L., & Van Pelt, D. (1956). Psycholinguistic study of aphasia: A revision of the concept of anomia. *Journal of Speech and Hearing Disorders,* **21,** 468–477.

Wernicke, K. (1874). Der aphasische Symptomenkomplex. Breslau. [Translated in *Boston Studies in Philosophy of Science,* **4,** 34–97.]

Whitaker, H. (1976). A case of isolation of the language function. In H. Whitaker & H.A. Whitaker (Eds.), *Studies in Neurolinguistics* (Vol. 2, pp. 1–58). New York: Academic Press.

Whitaker, H.A., & Ojemann, G.A. (1977). Lateralisation of higher cortical functions: A critique. *Annals of the New York Academy of Sciences,* **299,** 459–473.

Whiteley, A.M., & Warrington, E.K. (1977). Prosopganosia: A clinical, psychological and anatomical study of three patients. *Journal of Neurology, Neurosurgery and Psychiatry,* **40,** 395–403.

Whiteley, A., & Warrington, E.K. (1978). Selective impairment of topographical memory: A single case study. *Journal of Neurology, Neurosurgery and Psychiatry,* **41,** 575–578.

Wickelgren, W.A. (1979). Chunking and consolidation: A theoretical synthesis of semantic networks, configuring in conditioning, S-R versus cognitive learning, normal forgetting, the amnesic syndrome, and the hippocampal arousal system. *Psychological Review,* **86,** 44–60.

Wilkins, A.J., Shallice, T., & McCarthy, R.A. (1987). Frontal lesions and sustained attention. *Neuropsychologia,* **25,** 359–365.

Willbrand, H. (1887). *Die Seelenblindheit als Herderscheinung und ihre Beziehung zur homonymen Hemianopsie, zur Alexie und Agraphie.* Wiesbaden: Bergmann.

Williams, S., & Canter, G. (1982). The influence of situational context on naming performance in aphasic syndromes. *Brain and Language,* **17,** 92–106.

Williams, S., & Canter, G. (1987). Action naming performance in four syndromes of aphasia. *Brain and Language,* **32,** 124–136.

Wing, A.M. (1984). Disorders of movement. In M.M. Smith & A.M. Wing (Eds.), *The psychology of human movment* (pp. 269–296). London: Academic Press.

Wing, A.M., & Baddeley, A.D. (1980). Spelling errors in handwriting: A corpus and a distributional analysis. In U. Frith (Ed.), *Cognitive processes in spelling* (pp. 251–285). London: Academic Press.

Winocur, G., Oxbury, S., Roberts, R., Agnetti, V., & Davis, C. (1984). Amnesia in a patient with bilateral lesions to the thalamus. *Neuropsychologia,* **22,** 123–143.

Wolpert, I. (1924). Die Simultanagnosie—Störung der Gesamtauffassung. *Zeitschrift für die Gesamte Neurologie und Psychiatrie,* **93,** 397–415.

Wood, F.B., Brown, I.S., & Felton, R.H. (1989). Long term follow-up of a childhood amnesic syndrome. *Brain & Cognition,* **10,** 76–86.

Woods, B.T. (1980). The restricted effects of right hemisphere lesions after age one; Wechsler test data. *Neuropsychologia,* **18,** 65–70.

Wulfeck, B.B. (1988). Grammaticality judgements and sentence comprehension in agrammatic aphasia. *Journal of Speech and Hearing Research,* **31,** 72–81.

Wyke, M. (1967). The effect of brain lesions on the rapidity of arm movement. *Neurology,* **17,** 1113–1130.

Yamadori, A., & Albert, M.L. (1973b). Word category aphasia. *Cortex,* **9,** 112–125.

Yaqub, H., Gascon, G., Al-Nosha, M., & Whitaker, H. (1988). Pure word deafness (acquired verbal auditory agnosia) in an Arabic speaking patient. *Brain,* **111,** 457–466.

Zaidel, E. (1976). Auditory vocabulary of the right hemisphere after brain bisection or hemidecortication. *Cortex,* **12,** 191–211.

Zaidel, E. (1983a). A response to Gazzaniga: Language in the right hemisphere, convergent perspectives. *American Psychologist,* **38,** 542–546.

Zaidel, E. (1983b). Disconnection syndrome as a model for laterality effects in the normal brain. In J.B. Hellige (Ed.), *Cerebral hemisphere asymmetry: method, theory and applications* (pp. 95–151). New York: Praeger.

Zangwill, O.L. (1946). Some qualitative observations on verbal memory in cases of cerebral lesion. *British Journal of Psychology,* **37,** 8–19.

Zangwill, O.L. (1954). Agraphia due to a left parietal glioma in a left handed man. *Brain,* **77,** 510–520.

Zangwill, O.L. (1960a). *Cerebral dominance and its relation to psychological function.* Edinburgh and London: Oliver & Boyd.

Zangwill, O.L. (1960b). Le problème de l'apraxie idéatroie. *Revue Neurologique,* **102,** 595–603.

Zangwill, O.L. (1964). Intelligence in aphasia. In A.V.S. de Rueck & M. O'Connor (Eds.), *Disorders of language* (pp. 261–284). London: Churchill.

Zarit, S.H., & Kahn, R.L., (1974). Impairment and adaptation in chronic disabilities: Spatial inattention. *Journal of Nervous and Mental Disease,* **159,** 63–72.

Zeigler, D.K. (1952). Word deafness and Wernicke's aphasia. *AMA, Archives of Neurology and Psychiary,* **67,** 323–331.

Ziegler, W., & Von Cramon, D. (1985). Anticipatory co-articulation in a patient with apraxia of speech. *Brain and Language,* **26,** 117–130.

Ziegler, W., & Von Cramon, D. (1986). Disturbed co-articulation in apraxia of speech: Acoustic evidence. *Brain and Language,* **29,** 34–47.

Zihl, J., Von Cramon, D., & Mai, N. (1983). Selective disturbance of movement vision after bilateral brain damage. *Brain,* **106,** 313–340.

Zingeser, L.B., & Berndt, R.S. (1988). Grammatical class and context effects in a case of pure anomia: Implications for models of language production. *Cognitive Neuropsychology,* **5,** 473–516.

Zola-Morgan, S., Cohen, N.J., & Squire, L.R. (1983). Recall of remote episodic memory in amnesia. *Neuropsychologia,* **21,** 487–500.

Author Index

Subject Index

Thinking Inside the Block Schedule

Thinking Inside the Block Schedule

Strategies for Teaching in Extended Periods of Time

Pam Robbins
Gayle Gregory
Lynne E. Herndon

CORWIN PRESS, INC.
A Sage Publications Company
Thousand Oaks, California

For information:

Corwin Press, Inc.
A Sage Publications Company
2455 Teller Road
Thousand Oaks, California 91320
E-mail: order@corwinpress.com

CORWIN
PRESS

Sage Publications Ltd.
6 Bonhill Street
London EC2A 4PU
United Kingdom

Sage Publications India Pvt. Ltd.
M-32 Market
Greater Kailash I
New Delhi 110 048 India

Printed in the United States of America

Library of Congress Cataloging-in-Publication Data

Robbins, Pamela.
   Thinking inside the block schedule: Strategies for teaching in
extended periods of time / by Pam Robbins, Gayle Gregory,
Lynne E. Herndon.
   p. cm.
Includes bibliographical references and index.
   ISBN 0-8039-6782-9 (cloth: acid-free paper)
   ISBN 0-8039-6783-7 (pbk.: acid-free paper)
   1. Block scheduling (Education). 2. Lesson planning.
3. Classroom management. I. Gregory, Gayle. II. Herndon, Lynne E.
III. Title.

This book is printed on acid-free paper.

03 04 05 10 9 8 7 6 5 4 3 2

Corwin Editorial Assistant:	Julia Parnell
Production Editor:	Denise Santoyo
Editorial Assistant:	Cindy Bear
Typesetter/Designer:	Janelle LeMaster
Cover Designer:	Oscar Desierto

Contents

Foreword

For the past 10+ years, it has been demonstrated in hundreds of schools across the nation that a school's climate and environment can be improved rather quickly just by altering the school's schedule. For example, the number of referrals to the office is reduced when students each day spend fewer minutes under a time deadline in crowded spaces such as hallways, dressing rooms, and lunchrooms; obviously, the number of class tardies is reduced if each day students report to four blocks of classes rather than to eight single periods of classes!

Although modifications have been made to some of the types of block schedules that Michael Rettig and I proposed in our 1995 book *Block Scheduling: A Catalyst for Change in High Schools*, the concept of block scheduling continues to be accepted by many administrators, teachers, parents, and students. There is a growing collection of data from hundreds of individual schools that report increases in student performance based on factors such as improved grade point averages, attendance, and graduation rates, along with increases in the number of students taking Advanced Placement (AP) classes and in ACT test scores.

Despite reported successes in a relatively large number of schools, we still believe that the continued success of the block scheduling movement will be determined largely by the ability of teachers and administrators to work together to improve instruction. Regardless of a school's time schedule, what happens between individual teachers and students in classrooms is still most important. A well-designed school schedule can be a catalyst for crucial changes—including instructional changes in classrooms—needed in high schools across the United States. We contend that staff development remains the key to the success of these instructional changes. Teachers must have multiple opportunities to develop active learning strategies in their various disciplines. Long periods of lecturing do not work. Teachers must know how to make a lecture more interactive. They need a repertoire of approaches to convey content in

a lively, engaging way so that students develop both deep and long-term understandings of the concepts and skills that will make them successful not only in school
but also after they leave today's classrooms.

In this book, the authors provide an array of strategies that teachers, administrators,
and staff development personnel will find useful as they work in planning, developing,
and delivering content within extended periods of instructional time. Throughout this
volume, the metaphor of a play is used. Teachers, students, and administrators—the
actors on this new stage of extended time—will find that their "lines" must be different
than they were in the traditional classroom setting if their instruction is to be engaging
and challenging for students.

These chapters address a variety of considerations crucial to teaching in the block.
Chapter 1 begins with key decisions related to program implementation. Chapter 2
exams "the players"; in this chapter, the reader is introduced to the related brain
research on learning and how that information can be considered when teaching
students during extended class periods. The remaining chapters address such topics
as developing a positive classroom climate, designing appropriate curriculum, planning lessons, generating and sustaining the attention of students, implementing active
instructional strategies, using technology in the lesson design, modifying homework
expectations, providing for inclusion students, managing the classroom, and assessing
student performance.

The suggestions in this book are practical, and the authors report that the strategies
have been used successfully by practitioners in various types of school settings.
Although this text can be read from cover to cover, I think that most teachers would
choose to read it selectively by topics. Regardless of how the content is read, teachers
working in schools with block schedules will find the ideas helpful in designing
meaningful, engaging lessons, particularly in classes containing many active, diverse
students.

Robert Lynn Canady
Professor Emeritus, University of Virginia
Senior Education Consultant for State and National Programs
for Educators, Continuing Education, University of Virginia

Acknowledgments

This book was conceptualized by three educators: Pam Robbins, an educational consultant; Gayle Gregory, an educational consultant; and Lynne E. Herndon, a veteran classroom teacher. It represents a response to educators who have expressed a need for an organized, practical, and comprehensive way to plan for all aspects of classroom instruction during extended periods of instructional time.

We are indebted to many professional educators and family members who, by their example, have helped steer the direction of this book.

To our husbands—Ray, Joe, and Paul—we express our thanks for understanding the long hours of writing, for editorial suggestions, and for "the push" it took to get us to the finish line. To D. D. Dawson, a special thanks for her patience, friendship, technical assistance, and many hours of labor. To her husband, Tom, thanks for letting her do this.

As professionals, our lives have been touched by many grand teachers—the late Judy Arin Krupp, the late Madeline Hunter, Bruce Joyce, Marsha Weil, Dennis Sparks, Howard Gardner, Jane Scott, Pat Wolfe, Thomas Armstrong, Daniel Goleman, Maurice Elias, Tony Gregorc, Kent Peterson, Jay McTighe, and Jane Bailey, to mention a few.

We dedicate this book to committed educators all over the world who are rising to the challenge of meeting the needs of learners in an increasingly diverse landscape of educational practice and helping them—with enthusiasm, insight, knowledge, energy, and creativity—achieve their highest potential.

About the Authors

Pam Robbins consults internationally in the areas of instructional strategies for block scheduling, brain-compatible teaching approaches, emotional intelligence, peer coaching, supervision, leadership, school improvement, and presentation skills. Her clients include local school districts, state departments of education, universities, leadership academies, the Department of Defense Education Activity, and corporations throughout the world. She also works with professional organizations such as the National Staff Development Council, the Association for Supervision and Curriculum Development, Phi Delta Kappa, the American Association of Administrators in South America, and the American Society for Training and Development. This former classroom teacher has written or cowritten three books: *How to Plan and Implement a Peer Coaching Program* (1991); *The Principal's Companion* (with Harvey Alvy, 1995); *If I Only Knew* (with Harvey Alvy, 1998); and *Thinking Inside the Block: The Teacher's Day-Planner* (with Lynne E. Herndon, 1998). She has also developed *Professional Inquiry Kit on Emotional Intelligence* (with Jane Scott, 1997). Her educational background includes a bachelor's degree in English from the University of California, a master's degree in education from California State University, Sacramento, and a doctorate from the University of California, Berkeley. She is dedicated to providing meaningful, research-based professional growth opportunities for all organizational members to accomplish their long- and short-range goals. She may be contacted by calling (540) 828-0107, or by email: probbins@shentel.net.

Gayle Gregory has been a teacher in elementary, middle, and secondary schools. For many years, she taught in schools with extended periods of instructional time (block schedules). She has had extensive districtwide experience as a curriculum consultant and staff development coordinator. Most recently, she was course director at York University for the Faculty of Education, teaching in the teacher education program. She now consults internationally with teachers, administrators, and staff developers in the areas of brain-compatible learning, block scheduling, emotional intelligence, instructional and assessment practices, collaborative learning, presentation skills, coaching and mentoring, and managing change. She is affiliated with many organizations, such as the Association for Supervision and Curriculum Development and the National Staff Development Council, and is the coauthor of *Designing Brain Compatible Learning*. She is committed to lifelong learning and professional growth for herself and others. She may be contacted by calling (905) 336-6565, or by email: gregoryg@haltonbe.on.ca.

Lynne E. Herndon taught science for 16 years at Fort Dodge Senior High School, Fort Dodge, Iowa. Fort Dodge Senior High implemented a block schedule during the last three years that she taught at this school. She has conducted workshops at the local, state, and national levels in the areas of classroom management, lesson planning for extended periods, and development of instructional strategies for teaching in a block schedule. She has also worked as a staff development consultant and currently works as a school improvement consultant for Heartland Education Agency, area 11, in Johnston, Iowa. She may be contacted by calling (515) 222-5842, or by e-mail: lherndon @AEA11.k12.ia.us.

1

Making the Right Choices

Which Play Is Appropriate, Considering the Audience, Schoolhouse, and Resources?

Block scheduling, simply defined, creates large segments of instructional time for staff and students. These longer-than-usual periods provide several opportunities. Many teachers have used this extended time as a resource to integrate the curriculum, providing enriched student learning experiences. Others have used the additional minutes of instructional time to afford students the chance to delve deeper into subject areas, creating enhanced student understandings. Schools have used block scheduling to increase the number of credits that students may take in a given year. Many schools report several benefits derived from longer periods of instructional time: fewer discipline referrals, better student attendance, enhanced staff-student relationships, more students on the honor roll. Students report that block scheduling has prepared them for college and is "less stressful" than a traditional schedule. One major factor affecting block scheduling success relies heavily on how instructional time is used. It is to this factor that the book is devoted. In the chapters that follow, specific attention is given to enhancing the use of instructional time with respect to a variety of dimensions: what is known about how the brain learns, teaching strategies, ways to promote attention, working with inclusion students, active participation, review strategies, grouping techniques, approaches to curriculum, assessment practices, classroom

1

management, dealing with student absences, promoting student responsibility, time management, and using technology. A second major factor affecting block scheduling success is the selection of a schedule conducive to the needs and goals of the particular school and its community.

In many settings, staff, students, and parents report that once they experienced block scheduling, they would never return to a traditional schedule. These settings are frequently sites where staff, students, parents, and community studied block scheduling formats and carefully planned, implemented, and monitored block scheduling efforts. A review of the research, conducted by Rettig and Canady (1999), as well as their collective experiences in working with hundreds of schools throughout the United States, revealed the following 12 findings regarding block scheduling:

1. The two major types of block scheduling that have developed in high schools throughout the United States are the alternate-day schedule (A/B schedule) and the 4/4 semester schedule. A few schools have developed modifications of a trimester block, but that format is not common.

2. Ample data support the fact that schools experiencing the most success with block scheduling involved teachers, students, and parents in the decision to change the schedule.

3. The majority of administrators, teachers, parents, and students support block scheduling after at least two years of implementation.

4. A block schedule changes the school environment positively, especially in the form of fewer disciplinary referrals to the office and less tardiness. In general, the school day becomes less stressful for both teachers and students.

5. The A/B schedule is much easier to implement than the 4/4 schedule because the A/B schedule has fewer political and administrative problems.

6. Few schools have successfully implemented a pure 4/4 block schedule in which students take four classes, each running for about 1 ½ hours, per semester. In most cases, schools, using a 4/4 schedule, have made modifications to accommodate year-long classes in band and Advanced Placement courses. The most practical adaptation involves using an A/B format embedded in the 4/4 schedule for such success.

7. For maximum student success, 4/4 schools should provide students with a balanced load of classes each semester.

8. The 4/4 schedule provides greater instructional flexibility than the A/B format. In the 4/4, students may repeat failed classes and still graduate with their class, and high achievers may complete eight sequential courses in mathematics or foreign language during the four years of high school.

9. Staff development is critical for successful implementation of any block scheduling model. Teachers must have multiple opportunities to develop active teaching strategies in their various disciplines. Lecturing for large amounts of time becomes a major problem with a block schedule.

10. Whether block scheduling helps or hinders student achievement on standardized tests remains an open question. Many individual schools have reported gains. Larger studies in both Canada and the United States have reported conflicting results.

11. Few schools to date have returned to the single-period schedule after adopting the A/B or 4/4 block. Only one of the 201 schools that implemented a block schedule in Virginia during the last nine years has returned to a traditional schedule.

12. Evidence suggests that schools are more likely to move from an A/B schedule to the 4/4 model than they are to move from the 4/4 to an A/B schedule.

SOURCE: Reprinted with permission from the March 1999 issue of *The School Administrator* magazine.

Frequently, in those sites in which block scheduling was imposed or was not studied carefully to ensure a match between the schedule selected and the school context in which it was to be implemented, negative experiences were reported, as well as a desire to return to a familiar, more traditional schedule. The decision to go to "the block" involves change—for all stakeholders in the schoolhouse and the community it serves. The decision should not be approached lightly because of its far-reaching consequences.

To Block or Not?

How a schedule is selected, what takes place during the planning process, and how staff and students perceive block scheduling have major implications for curriculum delivery, instruction, assessment practices, staff morale, parents, and students. Many possible scheduling configurations exist. When the needs, goals, and desires of the stakeholders are considered in relation to scheduling options, the chances for instructional success are immeasurably greater.

Conceptually, the decision to go to a block schedule should include a planning phase and an implementation and maintenance phase. The *planning phase* should involve all potential stakeholders. In this phase, careful consideration of needs and wants should take place. Then, a variety of schedules should be identified and studied before a specific schedule is selected. The planning matrix that follows is one in which these decisions can be played out.

The Planning Phase

During the planning phase, key stakeholders meet. This group might consist of teachers, administrators, students, support staff, parents, and community members—

individuals who will ultimately be affected by the selection of a block schedule. This group is the planning committee. Together, they brainstorm "considerations," or attributes of a schedule they would like to have—for example, classes that meet daily, the flexibility to have two 45-minute shorter classes within a block of 90 minutes, and the potential to have a seminar or adviser base class.

Often, specialists such as physical education instructors or choir or band teachers would like to have specific considerations honored. After considerations are brainstormed, they might be shared with the faculty at large to be sure all possible factors are generated. Once this list is developed, a variety of scheduling options can be identified; for example, the 4 × 4, modified 4 × 4, A/B, parallel, or Copernicus plans might be considered.

Frequently, schools in the planning phase form study groups to identify schedule configurations and then study them. If the timeline permits, some innovative staff members may initiate and implement small pilot programs in their subject areas to be used the next year. Pilot programs allow staff to gain insights into the transition to the block so that others may follow a less stressful and more guided path. These "trailblazers" may identify challenges that can be worked out beforehand and may serve as valuable resources during the initial implementation process. For instance, at one high school, two science teachers worked together to develop a ninth-grade science program and time-tabled a double period every other day. Two social studies teachers used extended time blocks on alternate days to implement a pilot program in their disciplines. They identified issues to be considered, such as the need for an increased instructional repertoire for teachers, more variety in the learning experiences designed for students, and changes in assessment practices. This information was helpful in identifying the staff development needs to be considered during readiness building activities for the block.

Many times, visits are arranged to those sites whose schedules appear to be most appealing. Professional journals, professional organizations, and the Internet may provide additional resources to this part of the planning process. After options have been identified and shared with the staff at large, the next step in using the planning matrix is to examine "importance" scores.

To begin, each listing under "Considerations for Selecting a Schedule" is reviewed and its value or "importance" to the planning committee members is assessed. Considerations that are very important are assigned a 3, those that are rather important are assigned a 2, and those that are somewhat important are assigned a 1. Consensus building is used to arrive at an importance score. Hence, the left column of the planning matrix may look like that shown in Figure 1.1.

Figure 1.1. Planning Matrix

Scheduling options →		4×4 block	A/B block	Modified block
Considerations for selecting a schedule ↓				
Seminar	2			
Adviser base	3			
Flexibility to have two 45-min. classes within the 90 block	3			
Classes meet daily	2			
ROTC	2			
Band all year	3			
A.P. all year	3			
Foreign language all year	2			
Math all year	2			
P.E. all year	1			
Embedded electives	1			
Opportunity for students to obtain Carnegie units	2			
Planning time for collaboration	3			

NOTE: The numbers in the small boxes indicate "importance scores" designated by the planning committee.

Importance scores are placed in the boxes to the right of the considerations. Obviously, there might be several more considerations than those listed in the example, depending on the specific context in which the block was to be implemented. Involving in the planning process as many stakeholders as possible who will be affected by the block will provide an important array of considerations to ponder.

Next, each scheduling option is assessed for the degree to which it meets each consideration. If a scheduling option meets a consideration well, it is assigned a 3; if it somewhat does, it is assigned a 2; if it barely does, it is assigned a 1; and if it clearly does not address a consideration, it is assigned a 0. Figure 1.2 illustrates how the scores might multiply out.

Figure 1.2. Sample Filled-In Planning Matrix

Scheduling options →		4×4 block	A/B block	Modified block
Considerations for selecting a schedule ↓				
Seminar or adviser base	2	1×2	2×2	3×2
Flexibility to have two 45-min classes within the 90-min block	3	1×3	2×3	3×3
Classes meet daily	1	3×1	0×1	2×1
Totals		8	10	17

The schedule that receives the highest number in the totals row is assumed to be the most desirable schedule, given the planning group's list of considerations and the scheduling options studied. At this stage, the staff at large may meet to examine the planning matrix and the results of tallying importance scores. They consider whether the scheduling option with the highest importance score is a viable schedule for their school, their students, faculty, and parents.

The Implementation and Maintenance Phases

Ensuring Success

Once the schedule has been adopted and the implementation process has begun, it is helpful to have members of each department come together to review successful practices and problem-solve challenges that have emerged. The discussion should include, but is not limited to, needed training, time for planning, and assessment practices. Thoughtful evaluation of how the schedule is addressing the essential learnings embodied in the curriculum for each discipline is a key aspect of ensuring success in the block. Often, midcourse corrections are necessary, once implementation is initiated, to meet a variety of stakeholders' needs—hence, the importance of evaluating each phase of implementation. School-level activities during the implementation phase of block scheduling that will contribute to success include curriculum mapping, analysis of assessment data across disciplines and related strategic planning, seminars in which staff generate and explain a list of teaching strategies, problem-solving sessions, opportunities to co-plan and possibly co-teach, and time to develop interdisciplinary units. The maintenance phase engages staff in assessing the total impact of the block and prescribing necessary changes.

Learnings About Change

The decision to go to block scheduling and the selection of a specific schedule involves large-scale change for all organizational members and the community at large. Therefore, it is essential to consider the change literature and the implications for practice it offers:

- Remember that change involves the entire system. Don't neglect to include all the stakeholders in dialogue. Listen to others for suggestions and cautions.
- Seek to understand the change process. Consider the emotions that change evokes in those affected by the change. Provide forums for these emotions to be expressed and addressed. Then, get started and solve problems along the way.
- Consult those who have traveled the road before you. Don't reinvent the wheel, but rather learn the strategies and recognize the pitfalls that others have discovered.
- Budget should be examined. Think creatively about how to manipulate resources to achieve the desired outcomes. Don't be constrained by the status quo.

- Be sure to include an evaluation component. Establish baseline data at the beginning of the process and collect data along the way. Both hard and soft data will be useful. Chronicle the journey so that lessons learned can be shared. Evaluation should be ongoing.

- Take time to stop and reflect throughout the process. Change is hard work. Celebrate incremental successes to generate continued momentum. Don't spend too long on the failures, other than to analyze and learn from them.

Using Instructional Time

Another influence affecting block scheduling success is how instructional time is used. Instructional decisions will ultimately affect the pace of instruction, the rate of content coverage, student time on task, the motivation of staff and students, and most important, student learning and achievement. This book outlines and details key areas of focus to be addressed to facilitate block considerations.

The book is organized into 14 chapters. As we pondered the essence of each chapter, we were struck by the similarity of these chapters to acts in a play. For example, the next chapter addresses preproduction considerations. As it pertains to the block, the chapter examines who the cast of characters in the block are, what the set on which their lives unfold is like, and what is going on in the world that will influence their lives on this stage. Lest we reveal the entire play before the reader has the opportunity to become immersed in its individual scenes, let's stop here and let the play begin.

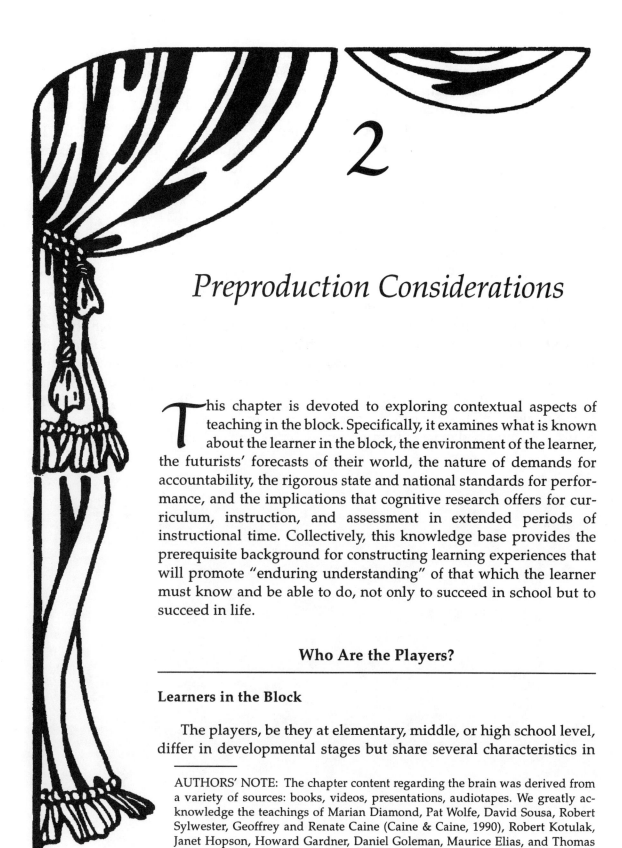

2

Preproduction Considerations

This chapter is devoted to exploring contextual aspects of teaching in the block. Specifically, it examines what is known about the learner in the block, the environment of the learner, the futurists' forecasts of their world, the nature of demands for accountability, the rigorous state and national standards for performance, and the implications that cognitive research offers for curriculum, instruction, and assessment in extended periods of instructional time. Collectively, this knowledge base provides the prerequisite background for constructing learning experiences that will promote "enduring understanding" of that which the learner must know and be able to do, not only to succeed in school but to succeed in life.

Who Are the Players?

Learners in the Block

The players, be they at elementary, middle, or high school level, differ in developmental stages but share several characteristics in

AUTHORS' NOTE: The chapter content regarding the brain was derived from a variety of sources: books, videos, presentations, audiotapes. We greatly acknowledge the teachings of Marian Diamond, Pat Wolfe, David Sousa, Robert Sylwester, Geoffrey and Renate Caine (Caine & Caine, 1990), Robert Kotulak, Janet Hopson, Howard Gardner, Daniel Goleman, Maurice Elias, and Thomas Armstrong, who have informed our practice as writers and teachers.

common. Research and experience tell us that the following considerations need to be taken into account when designing learning experiences for these individuals regardless of grade level. Students must feel that they

Matter

Belong

Are empowered and capable

Are safe and sheltered emotionally, intellectually, and physically

Have some choice and influence over what happens to them

Are connected to someone, a group, or a cause beyond themselves

Are contributing members of society

Are loved, cared for, and valued

Can be successful

When these aspirations are honored in the teaching/learning process, students are more likely to be highly engaged, active learners and will most likely succeed at high levels.

Designer Brains

Cognitive research tells us that no two brains are exactly the same. In fact, Robert Sylwester (1995) has referred to this phenomenon, suggesting that each individual possesses a unique "designer brain." Every brain in the classroom is characterized by several specific, "one of a kind" traits. For instance, every brain has a preferred style for learning. Some brains prefer visual stimuli, others auditory or kinesthetic. Some prefer a combination of these. Some brains like music during the learning process; some need quiet. Some like light; others prefer a dimly lit setting. Some brains like information presented in sequential order; to others, this matters not. Some brains need words; other brains like pictures or symbols. Some brains like humor; others value a more serious stance. Some brains need real-life examples; others enjoy story, metaphor, or analogy. Some crave food or drink during the learning process; others find this unnecessary or even distracting. Some need movement to integrate new information; others favor a more passive stance. Some brains prefer solitude during the learning process; other thrive when afforded the opportunity to interact collaboratively with others. All are motivated by a quest for meaning.

The talents of these unique brains differ dramatically as well. Howard Gardner (1995) suggests that people have a least eight different intelligences, or ways of processing information (see Figure 2.1).

Figure 2.1. Gardner's Eight Intelligences

Verbal/Linguistic	Ability to use language effectively to communicate
Musical/Rhythmic	Sensitivity to rhyme
Visual/Spatial	Ability to perceive accurately one's world visually and symbolically
Logical/Mathematical	Predisposition to numbers and logical process
Naturalist	Desire and ability to function in nature and to categorize phenomena in the environment
Bodily/Kinesthetic	Expertise to use the body to express oneself and perform a range of physical skills
Interpersonal	Being attuned to the emotions and feelings of others and respond accordingly
Intrapersonal	Having an accurate knowledge of oneself and the ability to act on that knowledge

Each brain is unique in its profile of strengths in these areas. Plasticity with regard to the ability to develop these competencies exists throughout life. Another distinguishing characteristic that makes brains unique is one's *emotional intelligence* (Goleman, 1995), or ability to use one's emotions intelligently. This intelligence includes five domains (see Figure 2.2). Students differ dramatically with respect to demonstrating competencies in each of these domains.

Figure 2.2. Five Domains of Emotional Intelligence (Salovey, in Goleman, 1995)

Self-awareness	Ability to recognize one's own emotions
Managing emotions	Ability to express and control emotions as the situation dictates
Motivation	Ability to persist in the face of setbacks or obstacles
Empathy	Ability to recognize emotions in others and to feel with others
Social arts	Ability to deal with and manage the emotions of others

Designer brains come to the schoolhouse with a variety of experiences. Some have been raised in poverty, others in wealth, and still others in middle-class settings. Some have grown up in a neurally stimulating context, having been read to, talked with, cuddled, played with, and given opportunities to explore the world within the confines of a safe, nurturing environment. In such environments, an individual has the opportunity "to develop a broad range of skills—mental, physical, aesthetic, social and emotional" (Diamond & Hopson, 1998, p. 108). Other brains have been raised in an environment characterized by deprivation in terms of nurturing, touch, and opportunities to interact with books, ideas, other human beings, and the environment. They have frequently been subsumed by television viewing, "sitting alone and passive, dreaming eyes of wonder glazed over, imagination shelved, and exploratory energy on hold" (Diamond & Hopson, 1998, p. 109).

In some environments where brains have developed, parents have taken an active positive role. In others, this has not been the case. Some brains have been raised in environments characterized by stress, fear, and pressure, whereas others have had safe, joyful, secure environments. Students whose brains have grown up in homes where family members may be "crippled by emotional problems including alcoholism, drug dependence, food disorders, chronic rage, anxiety, and depression" (Armstrong, 1998, p. 30) are particularly at risk. Exposure to these conditions often sets up "patterns of stress that come out as behavioral or learning problems" (Armstrong, 1998, p. 30).

It has long been said, "You are what you eat." Research has documented the positive impact of a diet rich in protein, vitamins, minerals, and calories appropriate to the stature of the individual. The brains of learners who lack this nutritional edge will have difficulty focusing, staying on task, and being active, successful participants in the learning environment. Armstrong (1998) notes that "problems such as poor prenatal care, malnutrition and other factors commonly associated with poverty can damage the child's brain from the start of life hereby limiting the potential to develop natural genius qualities" (p. 32). To add to the complexity of this scene, individual brains are placed in a learning environment with 20 to 30 other brains, all of which have different needs and experiences. Their interests differ as well. Some are moved to act by romance, others by cars, sports, music, art, technology, video, fashion, or relationships. Teachers have observed that class composition is becoming increasingly diverse and a reflection of society, with many backgrounds and cultures. Students differ widely with the expectations they bring to school, parental support, drive for success, perseverance, work ethic, baseline knowledge, reading level, self-esteem, social skills, and personal goals. These differences contribute to the already complex portrait of diversity. No wonder some have commented in the past that teaching is second in stress level only to that of air traffic controllers! But oh, what an opportunity a teacher has to touch the future by contributing to each learner's developing brain!

What Is the Set Like?

The Environment

Some who view the stage on which youths' and adolescents' lives are unfolding see a dark side.

> The typical American child does not experience an enriched environment. He or she watches three to four hours of television each day while in preschool and in day school. Is rather sedentary. Doesn't read very well. Doesn't particularly like school. Doesn't do much homework. Doesn't have many hobbies. Eats a less than optimal diet. Drops out of sports by 9th or 10th grade. Experiments in high school with alcohol and drugs which can potentially

stunt brain development. Listens to rock or rap music from two to six hours per day. Spends far more time dating and earning pocket money than studying, volunteering, or engaging in new and challenging activities. And overall, grows up with a disenchanted mind that never reaches its full potential or even comes close. (Diamond & Hopson, 1998, p. 5)

Daniel Goleman, in his foreword to *Emotionally Intelligent Parenting* (Elias, Tobias, & Friedlander, 1999, pp. xv, xvi) adds to this scenario:

I believe that children are the unintended victims of two forces at large on the stage, one economic, the other technological. The ratcheting up of global competitiveness means that today's generation of parents has to work longer and harder to maintain a decent standard of living than was true for their own parents' generation—it's not that parents love their children less, but they have less free time to spend with their children than their own parents did with them. At the same time, increased mobility for families means that fewer and fewer have relatives like a grandmother in the neighborhood to take up the slack. All too many families live in neighborhoods where they are afraid to let their younger children play outside unsupervised—let alone go into a neighbor's home. On the technological side, there is an unprecedented experiment going on with the world's youth; more children than ever before in human history are spending more hours of their lives than ever staring at a video monitor. Whether they are absorbed in an educational CD-ROM or watching junk TV, the fact is they are not playing with other children.

This quote foreshadows the reality that many teachers observe: Students who lack the interpersonal skills typically developed as a result of child's play and critical for success in communicating, resolving conflicts, and decision making in school and in life.

To add to this dismaying portrait, the media remind us daily about unprecedented violence in the schools and in the streets. Many parents fear exposing their children to such dangerous reality and therefore require them to spend time alone in the safety of their homes. This solitude, however, often contributes further to a lack of opportunity to practice vital social skills. Indeed, it is a dilemma.

Lest we paint a scene of total malaise, this set also has a bright side. Considerable evidence suggests that, despite all odds, some students not only prevail but flourish. We know from the brain research that meaningful, lively interaction in the classroom can teach students vital academic, social, and emotional lessons that positively influence their lives not only during the time they spend within the schoolhouse but forever. The literature on resilience suggests that among the many internal and external factors fostering resilience are a positive sense of self-esteem and a significant relationship with an adult. These are two characteristics that teachers and schools can influence, especially within extended periods of instructional time (Henderson & Milstein, 1996).

Standards and Benchmarks

Standards and benchmarks have influenced both policy and practice worldwide. Globally, educators and policymakers have sought to establish visionary, consistent guidelines for high-performing students and schools. This action has produced standards and benchmarks of performance in key curricular areas, with the goal of promoting student success in higher education, the workplace, and life. This movement has required teachers to look more analytically at the content areas for which they are responsible and, as one teacher put it, "clean the closet" so that those topics that are nice to teach but not essential will receive less priority in the teaching process. The expected targets or benchmarks also provide a measure of clarity for students and staff who, in the past, may not have been clear about curriculum expectations. As students strive to meet or exceed specified benchmarks and standards rather than just pass tests, these targets have also provided a measure of consistency and perceived fairness. The continuum of skills leading to the specified benchmarks and standards provides an essential guide that reminds both students and staff about the continuous nature and interrelatedness of curriculum.

In most contexts, earnest efforts are being made to meet these noble ends. Yet, reality tells us that not all students learn in the same way on the same day. Although this would be the ideal scene, it plays out differently, depending on the location of the stage. In many schools, the play's characters are enveloped by a great force that affects them and influences their teachers: rigorous state and national standards. In some settings, students and teachers find support from parents and the community for helping students meet these specified ends. In other settings, such support may be lacking. In some states, these high-stakes measures will determine whether students will advance or repeat a grade—whether they spend summers in school, in leisure time, or in a vocational position. Many teachers feel pressured, with this new accountability, to make every moment count in the classroom. They worry about having quality time to address essential learnings in a way that promotes long-term retention. Both students and teacher feel, at times, a sense of performance anxiety, as well as the optimism that springs from great expectations. In classrooms where teachers have extended periods of instructional time, if time is well used and if nonessential components of the curriculum are "selectively abandoned," students and teachers have the opportunity to delve deeply within target areas to foster long-term learning.

The World of the Future

Futurists enter the scene. They forecast attributes of the world that the cast of students will encounter. To some, it is a world unfamiliar. For example, Alvin Toefler, a well-known futurist, offers that the "literacy of the future" will not be the ability to read and write, but rather the ability to learn, unlearn, and relearn. This prediction is based on the forecast that new information will emerge and transform rapidly. Other futurists tell us that a person under age 25 will be expected to change careers every 10

years and jobs every 4 years. The Secretary's Commission on Achieving Necessary Skills (1991) outlines five competencies that will be essential to thrive in the future:

An ability to
    Identify, organize, plan, and allocate resources
    Work with others
    Acquire and use information
    Understand complex interrelationships (systems)
    Work with a variety of technologies

Extended periods of instructional time provide the potential for these "life skills" to be developed.

> In a national survey of what employers are looking for in entry-level workers, specific technical skills are now less important than the underlying ability to learn on the job. After that, employers listed:
> - Listening and oral communication
> - Adaptability and creative responses to setbacks and obstacles
> - Personal management, confidence, motivation to work toward goals, a sense of wanting to develop one's career and take pride in accomplishments
> - Group and interpersonal effectiveness, cooperativeness and teamwork, skills at negotiating disagreements
> - Effectiveness in the organization, wanting to make a contribution, leadership potential (Goleman, 1998, p. 13)

As one reflects on the workplace realities of the present and the future, it becomes apparent that the rigorous academic standards have been constructed to assist students in meeting the challenges the future will bring. Several schools are recognizing that it will take unconventional means—like restructuring time and varying teaching methodology—to prepare students to meet these necessary ends.

How Will Lines Be Learned?

Cognitive Research and Teaching in the Block

Even though every brain is unique, some common principles derived from cognitive research should inform classroom- and school-level practices regarding how brains are taught and how they learn. Ultimately, these principles will influence which "lines" of the curriculum the cast of characters learn, how well the lines are learned, how the characters are able to apply them, and how long the characters remember them.

Probably the most astonishing finding of recent brain research is that the brain is the one organ that needs external stimulation from the environment to develop and thrive (Kotulak, 1996). Another related phenomenon is that the brain is remarkably plastic. The term *plasticity* refers to the ability of the brain to change continually and grow new branchlike connections, called *dendrites*, between neurons as a result of external environmental stimulation and experience. Thus, classrooms that provide students with meaningful, engaging, active learning experiences have the capacity to change students' brains physically!

When information first enters the brain, it enters through the senses. This input registers initially in the sensory memory. There, it lingers for 0.75 second. This means that rich sensory stimuli should be used to capture the attention of students and that opening activities should be designed to engage students at once. Here, it is important that the stimuli be reflective of a multitude of senses. Worthy of note is that a good percentage of learners are visual or kinesthetic, yet ironically, many classrooms are dominated by auditory input. (Could this possibly explain why many teachers complain that students "do not pay attention"?)

Once in the sensory memory, one of two things happens to the input. It either is dumped and forgotten or is passed on to the working memory. What determines what gets passed on versus what gets dumped? It's what the student pays attention to. Thus, for the student in the classroom, attention is enhanced when lessons have meaning—relevancy or real-life connections. Novelty, color, humor, and hands-on experiences all have the potential of increasing attention. It has been said that "emotion drives attention, which drives learning and memory" (Sylwester, 1995, p. 86), Hence, if, on the one hand, students bring emotional baggage to the classroom, their ability to focus and attend will be hampered because they are thinking of what is most urgent and pressing to them at the moment (e.g., a fight at the locker, a problem at home, a lost love). If, on the other hand, the content provides an enticing "emotional hook," it will generate attention and engagement. A simulation, a challenging problem or question, and an engaging story or artifacts from time past all are examples of emotional hooks that help focus attention and produce learning. Strongly charged emotional content will go directly into long-term memory. One reason why key events in life stand out in our minds is that they are generally highly charged with emotion.

If attention is garnered, then data moves from the sensory memory to the next part of the memory system, short-term memory, which is the only place where conscious thought occurs. Here, information lingers from 3 to 20 seconds, unless it is rehearsed or elaborated, to sustain it in working memory. The process of *rehearsal* increases the chances that the brain will organize, retain, and send the information into long-term memory, to be retrieved at a later date when needed. The term *rehearsal* is synonymous with *practice.* It can involve rote repetition of information (repeating it in its original form), or it can be elaborative, or associated with something else familiar to the learner; for example, using the mnemonic device "Eat good bread dear father!" or "Every good boy does fine" helps students remember the names of the lines in the treble clef. The sentence is far easier to remember for most students than the string of five letters.

Elaborative rehearsal is so powerful because long-term memory is organized in networks of association. Hooking new information to something that is familiar generates a valuable "memory hook." Although rote rehearsal or simple repetition works in the short run, because there is nothing to "hook" it onto the information is often difficult to store and retrieve. Organizing information through elaboration sets up files in long-term memory that, when opened in the future, will help the learner access prior knowledge and experiences. To enhance the impact of rehearsal, when students are offered a variety of ways to process information (auditory, visual, kinesthetic), the chances of retention are increased. For example, some students find rhymes and raps easy to recall, whereas others find visual symbols, pictures, and graphics more useful. Still others find that hands-on experiences cement new learnings best. Because of these properties of short-term memory, projects, performances, and exhibitions help students both deepen their understandings and relegate information to long-term memory. Rehearsal can provide a prime opportunity to employ the eight intelligences and develop them further while simultaneously enhancing the memory of that which has been rehearsed.

Because the brain is a pattern-seeking organ, studies have shown that when information is presented in the natural context in which it occurs, it is remembered more vividly. For example, transforming the classroom into a rain forest to immerse students in the environment they are studying can provide valuable insights and create a meaningful context to solidify learnings. Or, following a geometry lesson on shapes, taking a walk in the neighborhood to locate these shapes in the environment in which they naturally occur can provide new learnings about the relationship between form and function. When the students are tested later on the concepts they learned, memories are more likely to flow back vividly into conscious thought if they can recall the experience in which they were immersed.

It appears that the capacity of short-term memory is limited. Its capacity is influenced by developmental age. The 5-year-old can remember two bits of information (plus or minus two). Every other developmental year, memory space is increased by one. From 15 years old to adult, the capacity appears to be seven bits or chunks (plus or minus two) (Miller, 1956; Pascal-Leon, 1980). Although this appears to be a simple formula for delivering information, in fact it is much more complex. What might be one chunk or bit for a given learner may be five or six for the inclusion student or the student who lacks foundational prior experiences. The limited memory spaces people have can be augmented by employing the concept of *chunking* to expand the capacity of the memory system. Most people think of their Social Security number, not as nine bits, but rather as three sections—three numbers, then two numbers, then four numbers. They "chunk" the information to facilitate its memorization. In teaching, an example of this is designing curriculum around key concepts as organizers (as opposed to conveying a series of unrelated facts). This provides a powerful way to increase student memory. For example, two teachers used a theme of "Conflict" in social studies and language arts to help students gain deeper insights into the concept of conflict as it related to conflict in war, opinion, and literature. This approach to organizing bits of information can provide "memory files" that are more easily retrieved and remem-

bered. This technique also helps students comprehend the connections between disciplines. When teachers integrate the curriculum in this way, understanding is enhanced and deepened. Having longer periods of instructional time provides the stage for this to occur. Understanding the capacity of short-term memory has important implications for the design, delivery, and follow-up review of curriculum. When new information is being presented, the developmental age of the learner should influence decisions about how much content should be introduced at one time.

Research and experience tell us that the brain remembers best what comes first, and next best what comes last. Therefore, the more "firsts" and "lasts" in an instructional sequence (provided that the activities are related and build upon one another), the greater the chances that the information will be remembered. For example, students in a biology class were invited to complete a crossword puzzle reviewing the previous day's vocabulary lesson (students were immediately engaged and their attention maximized). Following this, they paired with partners and compared answers. The teacher then asked the students to respond to oral prompts in unison. Then, the students were given physical models to assemble. Following this, they watched a video in which they compared and contrasted the models they created with those they viewed. Finally, they wrote in their learning journals about their experience, using both words and graphics to explain their insights. At the end of class, each of the students wrote on a file card one question or comment that had come to mind and handed it to the teacher as they left the room. The next time the class met, the teacher began the session with a discussion using, as a springboard for dialogue, the cards the students had completed.

After spending time in short-term memory, one of three things can happen to the information: It can be (a) rehearsed once again, (b) dumped and forgotten (if it didn't have enough meaning or wasn't rehearsed long enough), or (c) sent to long-term memory. Once in long-term memory, information stays forever; if it is not frequently used or reviewed, though, it may be difficult to recall. Have you ever taken a statistics class, studied, and passed the exam? If 6 months later someone had asked you to demonstrate a chi-square test, could you have done it? Most people would say no! This reality has major implications for classroom practice. Frequent opportunities to review content that has been taught in a meaningful way facilitates long-term retention. This relates to the saying, "If you don't use it, you lose it!" The more opportunities a student has to review and revisit content, the greater the chance that enduring understanding will be developed (Wiggins & McTighe, 1998).

All information in long-term memory is stored unconsciously in networks of association. For example, think about the word *ocean*. What associations flow into your mind as a result of this train of thought? Some might picture an ocean; others might associate it with vacations, water sports, or maps. Were you aware of any connections you associated with *ocean* 5 minutes ago? Probably not (unless you were daydreaming) because these associations are stored unconsciously and do not become conscious until they are retrieved and brought to short-term memory, where conscious thought occurs. Generally, the retrieval process takes 3 to 5 seconds to access (some learners may take longer or shorter, depending on how vividly the information was initially introduced,

how frequently the material has been reviewed, or the learner's mental or emotional state). This is important to know when asking students questions. By providing "thinking time" before asking students to respond, teachers give learners more time to access information housed in networks within long-term memory. As a result, responses tend to be more elaborate, more diverse, and well thought out. Teachers who understand the existence of these neural networks of association also appreciate how vital it is to use strategies like brainstorming and dialogue to add to students' neural networks. They also understand how important it is to begin teaching episodes by inviting students to access what is in their neural networks of associations related to the topic of the day. Teachers have intuitively known that activating prior knowledge often facilitates the learning process. Now they know why.

Long-term memory is actually of two kinds: declarative and procedural. *Declarative memory* is where, who, what, when, and why facts, as well as episodes from one's past (e.g., dates in history, vocabulary, memories from childhood), are stored. *Procedural memory* is the brain's "autopilot." Skills and processes that one can do without thinking (e.g., driving a car, keyboarding, skiing, tying one's shoes) are a part of procedural memory. This is why some people can drive to work on some days, arrive, and ponder, "How did I get here?"

How information becomes procedural in nature is a function of how frequently it has been retrieved, rehearsed, or practiced. All procedural knowledge begins as declarative knowledge. For instance, when one first learns to drive a vehicle with a manual transmission, each position of first, second, and third gear is a distinct "factlet" within declarative memory. Once one rigorously practices shifting gears, eventually the process becomes automatic; that is, one can do it without thinking. Could this possibly explain why some students never relegate to automaticity the multiplication tables? That is, they have not had sufficient practice in the way(s)—visual, auditory, kinesthetic—they learn best. Information has a greater chance of becoming part of long-term memory if it has been practiced or rehearsed in a variety of ways, such as embedded in rhyme, rhythm, or music; used in narrative or story; depicted visually; introduced in a hands-on way; discussed as it relates to students' lives; taught to someone else; or conveyed through simulation.

Additional strategies that teachers can use to help students relegate content and skills to long-term memory are explored throughout the book. In subsequent chapters, "brain compatible" instructional, curricular, and assessment strategies are introduced, explained, and modeled. Cognitive research is revisited and referenced to validate why these strategies work in practice and to model their importance in the learning process.

Scene, Backdrop, Ambiance
Creating the Climate

The Scene

The sun shines brightly on the medieval costumes donned by the sixth-grade students of Thomas Harrison Middle School (Harrisonburg City Schools, Harrisonburg, Virginia) as they file by their cheering seventh- and eighth-grade colleagues and enter a huge tent. Beneath the canopy, music is being played by students who roam among those in the tent. Booths feature a variety of crafts and activities. Before visitors can partake in the festivities, however, they must cash in U.S. dollars for medieval currency. After all, these are medieval times!

This Medieval Faire was the culminating event for an integrated unit of study about medieval times. Teams of teachers planned together to create a dynamic context in which to teach concepts and skills from mathematics, social studies, science, art, music, and language arts curricula. Through a variety of simulations and classroom-based tasks leading up to this event, students were able to experience firsthand what it was like to live, play, and work in medieval society.

As a visitor from the local business community left the faire, she noticed a slight-framed boy standing alone outside the tent. She approached him, told him she had

enjoyed her visit to the faire, and offered him the medieval currency she had not spent. The student looked up and seemed amazed at this gesture of kindness. "Really?" he inquired. She smiled and handed him the currency. "Yippee!" he yelled as he darted off. "I have currency!"

Implications

This scenario reminds us of the strong need that all students have to feel included, valued, and a sense of belonging. It also illustrates that sometimes a random deed of kindness may touch a student, not just for a day, but for a lifetime. The emotional climate of this schoolhouse—whether students feel accepted and connected—has a profound effect on their academic performance and social relationships. This chapter addresses key considerations for creating this ambiance.

Newspaper reports, magazines, television, and radio have carried many detailed stories of school violence. In several of these incidents, those who committed the horrific crimes were students who felt ignored, rejected, or teased by others. Although these accounts immediately remind us of how crucial it is to provide skills training in anger control and conflict resolution, it also reminds us of a window of opportunity the classroom can provide—by ensuring that the schoolhouse becomes a home for both the heart and the mind. The emotional context in which a student spends time learning plays a crucial role in determining that child's success—both in school and in life.

The Backdrop: The Schoolhouse as a
Home for the Heart and the Mind

Teachers and administrators today are experiencing tremendous pressure to help students meet or exceed rigorous national- and state-level academic standards. At the same time, they are facing an educational landscape that is increasingly diverse—culturally, academically, socially, and emotionally. This complex backdrop puts schools in the difficult position of being compelled to focus on academics with a population of youths who often lack prerequisite skills or who are emotionally or socially needy. That is, the students may come from households where emotional stress is high as a result of failed relationships, where family members are in trouble with the law, where substance abuse takes place, or where financial support is unstable. Sometimes these burdens weigh heavily on students' minds, providing a cloud of preoccupation that often precludes students' ability to concentrate on what a teacher places before them. Remarkably, these are often students perceived by teachers as "hard to like." Ironically, the one place where these same students may find a source of solace is in school.

Classrooms and schools that function as homes for the heart and the mind go beyond recognizing the harsh realities that may affect youths in providing a context where both academics and emotions can be addressed simultaneously. Admittedly, to chart such a course is not always easy, and at times efforts will be swamped by waves

of despair. But several principles can, when attended to, make a profound difference in the learning environment and in the lives of those who spend time there.

The Ambiance: The School and Classroom Climate

The "feeling tone," or ambiance, of an environment where students spend time has a significant impact on their perceptions of activities that occur within that setting and on their learnings that evolve as a consequence of engagement in those activities. Caine and Caine, in *Education on the Edge of Possibility* (1997), refer to a desirable state of *relaxed alertness*, which they define as a setting in which the learner experiences "low threat and high challenge at the same time. Threat and fatigue inhibit brain functioning, whereas challenge accompanied by safety and belief in one's abilities leads to peak performance" (p. 153).

Relaxed alertness has several components. Some are a function of what the teacher does; others are attributes of the classroom and school.

Teacher Behaviors

An old adage professes, "People don't care how much you know until they know how much you care." This certainly holds true in the classroom. One volunteer in an alternative school in Allentown, Pennsylvania, remarked, "Children need to know that they matter. If they don't, nothing else does." An atmosphere of caring can be created in several ways. Six ways are described below:

1. *Treat each student as a whole person*—someone who is respected for his or her input, opinions, viewpoints, and contributions, as well as cherished for his or her personal qualities. Often, when adults recall a teacher who has made a significant difference in their lives, they remember attributes such as, "He (She) believed in me and respected me as a person." This stance produces an influence that goes well beyond the academic school year.

2. *Celebrate differences as a gift.* Each person's window on the world provides a valuable and unique perspective. When these uniquenesses are combined within the classroom and school community, they add a dimension of richness. Differences can be a function of background experiences, cultural heritage, learning styles, personality styles, or intelligences. Students feel valued when these traits are viewed as gifts. This stance often decreases potential confrontations and conflicts because everyone brings something of worth to the learning community.

3. *Provide roles and responsibilities for each student.* This teacher-bestowed gift often helps a student feel connected to classmates and the classroom, providing a sense that he or she matters, as well as a sense of contribution that emerges from responsibility.

Roles and responsibilities often produce a source of structure that, in some home settings, is sorely lacking. Recognition for both roles and responsibilities often contributes to students' self-esteem and provides a sense of ownership in what goes on within the classroom.

4. *Offer choices.* As one teacher recently reflected, "Learning doesn't occur on the same day in the same way for every learner. So, saying it slower and louder will not usually make a difference." When learners are provided with choices about how they might learn and process information (and perhaps different timelines or time allocations for tasks), they perceive that their differences are influencing the teaching/learning process and that they have a greater ability to reach designated benchmarks because they can work toward them through areas of strength. For instance, one teacher invited students to choose among reading a text, working in a cooperative group, doing a research project, or using talking books (books on tape) during a recent assignment. Although choice will not always be possible—given the topic, available resources, or the teacher's planning time—when it is possible, it can help all learners feel as if their differences and needs are being respected and addressed. When different learners share their learnings, acquired through a variety of pathways, diversity once again becomes valued as an attribute rather than viewed as a detriment.

5. *Engage learners in contributing to the physical environment or ambiance of the classroom.* Some teachers have invited students to create murals, mobiles, poetry, or sayings to post on the walls. One teacher took individual photographs of students and invited them to post their pictures on colored paper and write on the paper three positive words they would like to be recognized as portraying in their thoughts and actions. These posters were placed on a wall that became the Wall of Fame. Other teachers have invited students to bring in pictures, writings, or objects important to them and have decorated the room with these objects. Another benefit results from these activities as well. As one elderly gentleman once reflected, "Teach students to appreciate beauty, and they will be less likely to destroy it."

Students feel cared for when their contributions are valued. One teacher was teaching an integrated unit involving music, social studies, and language arts. Students brought in "their music," and the teacher brought in his. They compared world events and what was going on in society when the music was produced. They examined the stories the songs conveyed. They analyzed the plots of the stories—and learned more about each other in the process! After this experience, the teacher reflected, "They didn't think my music was weird after this activity. In fact, some students even said they liked it!"

6. *Model emotional intelligence and emotionally intelligent behavior.* Simply defined, *emotional intelligence* is the ability to use one's emotions intelligently. As Maurice Elias (Elias et al., 1999) reminds us, referring to Goleman's 1995 best seller *Emotional Intelligence: Why It Can Matter More Than IQ,*

We have neglected the role of feelings in our children's healthy growth. We are now paying the price, as families and as society, with a higher incidence of violence and disrespectful behavior. . . . We are paying when we emphasize the intellect of students but forget their hearts. And, of course, our children pay as well as their unhappiness and troubled behaviors continue to grow" (p. 3).

In Chapter 2, five domains of emotional intelligence set forth in Goleman's 1995 book are introduced and described. These domains can be both modeled and addressed in the classroom in a variety of ways.

1. *Self-awareness is the ability to recognize a feeling as it happens.* Feelings play a crucial role in personal decision making. "People with greater certainty about their feelings are better pilots of their lives" (Goleman, 1995, p. 43). In addition to recognizing feelings, those with a well-developed sense of self-awareness are able to describe their feelings with words. They possess strategies to deal productively with moods. For example, if circumstances trigger a bad mood, they have several ways to transform that mood—exercise, talking with a friend, listening to music. In classrooms, teachers can articulate their feelings and encourage students to do the same. This also helps build an emotional vocabulary.

In one block scheduling setting, a teacher allocates time twice a week for a class meeting. Students are encouraged to use a 10-point rating scale to describe their moods that day and to articulate what they believe contributed to that mood. Students reach out to each other, as when one student expresses feeling "down in the dumps," and collaborate in suggesting strategies to banish the bad mood and create a positive, uplifting one in its stead. "While students initially balked at the idea of a class meeting, now they look forward to them. It's brought the class closer, and they seem to care more for one another. They're much more kind in their interactions," noted the teacher.

2. *Managing emotions* is a skill that builds on self-awareness. It represents a capacity to handle feelings so that they are appropriate, given a particular circumstance. This domain of emotional intelligence includes the ability to soothe or calm oneself, control anger, deal with irritability or failure, and dispel feelings of anxiety. Teachers report that many students have not had experience managing emotions or seen it modeled. One teacher organized several lessons around this domain. She located popular videos with scenes in which individuals did either a good or poor job of managing their emotions. After showing each clip, the class analyzed the decision making embedded in each scenario. When an actor "lost it" and emotions flared, the class problem-solved what alternatives might have been pursued and the potential consequence of each. This series of lessons led the class to a study of conflict resolution. The teacher noted that, after a few weeks of focusing on this topic, conflicts among class members became fewer, and those that did unfold were handled much more skillfully.

3. *Motivation* is the ability to persist in the face of setbacks or obstacles. Motivating oneself and delaying gratification underlie students' abilities to focus, to resist the urge to give up when the "going gets tough," and to pursue goals. These abilities are closely linked to the spirit of optimism and accomplishment. Implicit in this domain is the concept of a "flow state." Goleman (1995) states,

> Being able to enter flow is emotional intelligence at its best; flow represents perhaps the ultimate in harnessing emotions in the service of performance and learning. . . Flow is a state of self-forgetfulness. . . [P]eople in flow are so absorbed in the task at hand that they lose all self-consciousness, dropping the small preoccupations. . . [I]n flow, people exhibit a masterly control of what they are doing, their responses perfectly attuned to the changing demands of the task. And although people perform at their peak while in flow, they are unconcerned with how they are doing, with thoughts of success or failure—the sheer pleasure of the act itself is what motivates them. (pp. 90, 91)

One teacher asked students to bring in examples of people who had been observed in a state of flow. They brought in examples of artists, athletes, writers, musicians, and mechanics. Then she asked students to ponder, "Have you ever experienced a flow state?" After some dialogue, students were asked to write about flow states they had encountered or imagined.

4. *Empathy*—the ability to "walk a mile in another's shoes"—is predicated on self-awareness. Criminal investigators of violent crimes note that this domain in particular is lacking in murderers, rapists, child molesters, and psychopaths. Many teachers have commented on how worried they are about the number of students who don't seem to model empathy for others. One teacher explained that, after reading a story about child abuse, in which a father ran over his son's legs with a car, the students laughed! She was horrified at their reactions. In follow-up readings, she asked students to read stories from a particular character's point of view. This began to change their perceptions. "With many standards addressing point of view or perspective taking," observed one teacher, "this is a natural way that one can approach teaching empathy while simultaneously building critical competencies in language arts and reading."

5. *Social arts*, or handling relationships, involves the skill of managing emotions in other people. It is the ability to read body language, to anticipate individual's needs. Individuals who do this well are often described as "social stars." They are popular, well liked. Others gravitate toward them. They are often in leadership roles and frequently demonstrate an adeptness at interpersonal relationships. Students in one classroom created a display of individuals who they believed demonstrated this fifth domain of emotional intelligence. Each student wrote a paragraph that represented an assertion of why this particular individual qualified to be one of those who represented competence in handling relationships.

Some readers may have read this section on emotional intelligence and wondered to themselves, Is it really worth the time, given all that must be taught? According to Daniel Goleman, in *Working With Emotional Intelligence* (1998), international surveys of employers revealed data that suggest "emotional competencies were found to be twice as important in contributing to excellence as pure intellect and expertise" (p. 31).

In addition to teacher behaviors, several school- and classroom-level attributes contribute to creating a climate.

School and Classroom Factors

School-Level Factors

- Teachers share similar beliefs and collaborate with students in developing and reinforcing "rules to live by." They are consistent in implementing them.
- The school is perceived as a learning community, and teachers share collective responsibility for students.
- The environment of the school is orderly and inviting. Displays of all students' work—not just superb examples—decorate the halls. Students are openly acknowledged for their contributions.
- Students perceive that the environment of the school is safe. After recent incidents of school violence, many students expressed concern about personal safety. At one school where student concern was high, teachers volunteered to post themselves at entrances to the school to greet students and to survey the environment for evidence of danger. Safety also implies that the adults in the school will also provide psychological safety; teasing, for example, will not be tolerated.

Classroom-Level Factors

- Teachers and students have mutual respect.
- Students and teachers have time to conference together.
- Students have opportunities to work alone and with peers.
- Time is allocated for reflection.
- Risk taking is encouraged. Being able to take risks and to make mistakes are a large part of the learning process. One teacher used a motto to communicate this to her students: "Failure is the opportunity to begin again more intelligently." Another said to the class, "Why do you think pencils have erasers? You're supposed to make mistakes!"
- Anxiety is absent. One can reduce student anxiety by placing around the room statements focused on relaxing students and on giving them confidence. One teacher posted sayings around the room, such as: "Everyone needs time to think and learn." "Everyone learns—but in his or her own way, and not on the same day." "It's OK to ask for help. You don't have to go it alone."

Merrill Harmin (1993, 1994), quoting the work of Grace Pilon (1988), calls these "truth signs." Truth signs are intended to communicate important truths about learning. "They are intended to help students become wise, balanced, self-responsible learners" (p. 49). They are also intended to encourage students. For instance, "human nature is ever capable of improvement and never able to being made perfect" (John Clare, as quoted in Harmin, 1993, p. 52). These truths can be reassuring to individuals and provide a way for students to support each other in their work and creative endeavors.

- A classroom creed is established. Developing a classroom creed may be a way of having students identify what a safe environment is for thinking and learning. In small groups, students may contribute one idea that they think would be helpful to create an optimal learning environment. Through group discussion and grouping and classifying ideas, students can come to consensus about two or three norms.

- The class has a spirit of "invitational learning." In working with a group of students, one teacher was overhead saying, "I invite you to take out your math text and take a look at the odd-numbered problems today." When someone asked about her use of the word *invite*, she said, "So often when you command students to do things, it inspires resistance. So, I believe it's more powerful to use what I call invitational learning. I've discovered that a lot more students come my way with this approach."

- Strong interpersonal bonds exist between students and between teachers and students. It's important for each player in the classroom to feel valued as a human being and connected to others. Some teachers in the block schedule took time to administer a personality profile. Students scored their profiles and discussed the implications for interpersonal relationships, how conflicts are handled, how others are perceived, and preferences for learning. Following this activity, they used the computer to generate a graph that depicted the frequency of distribution of class members by personality style. In this activity, students had the opportunity to apply math skills as they learned about themselves.

The Physical Environment

What did you have for dinner last Saturday night? Did you have to think of where you were before you could think of what was on your plate? This example illustrates how human brains store information "in context." Hence, the context in which learning occurs—especially the physical environment and whether it is welcoming or sterile—makes a difference for students.

Interesting and relevant material on classroom bulletin boards helps focus the learners' attention on the content and processes of the curriculum. Displays of student work send overt or covert messages that student work is valued and highlighted in this

classroom. Materials and artifacts pertinent to the topic or subject are great motivators for hands-on kinesthetic learners who want and need to go beyond "sit and git" lessons (a setting in which the student sits and listens and gets the message from the teacher) to develop understanding. Orderly yet "resource rich" classrooms provide an invitation to learners to explore their environment. As they do, their brains actually change as well, growing dendrites and making connections as a consequence of the active learning process.

One teacher papered the walls of her classroom with butcher paper and, after every unit of study, invited the class to select a recorder and an artist. The recorder led a discussion with the class about the key points of the unit and recorded these on the butcher paper, along with the date of the unit. The artist led the class in reflecting about what images or graphics came to mind regarding the content of the unit. These were graphically depicted on the wall. Students could, as a result of this "time line" of sorts, see the connectedness of what they learned in February with what they were currently learning in April.

In another classroom, a giant "idea" box was located near the door. The teacher let students know about an upcoming unit—for example, one on the Civil War. She invited students to contribute ideas about how different subject areas might be integrated within the unit and asked what students were curious about. The Friday before the unit was to be introduced, the class gathered around the idea box and helped the teacher empty it, sharing the ideas as they were pulled from the box. This process built anticipation for the learning about to occur and gave the class a sense of ownership, or influence, on what would be delivered within the unit.

Another aspect of the physical environment is furniture, lighting, and the "stage area." Furniture needs to be arranged in accordance with how a teacher wants students to interact. It should also be positioned so that students have visual access to main instructional areas and should facilitate teacher monitoring.

For some students, lighting makes a big difference. Some are particularly annoyed by florescent lights and the low level buzz they sometimes emit. Natural light is great, when possible. When it is not, making sure the lighting does not glare is essential. Some students sensitive to light find that laying a blue or yellow transparency over a page can be helpful in reducing glare.

Finally, the "stage area" is where most of the teaching takes place. This area should be as free from distraction as possible. Even if a poster with a motorcycle rider on the front board of the classroom with a noble message like "Be cool . . . stay in school" is in the students' visual field, chances are that one day a student or two may go on an imaginary trip with the motorcycle and wonder, "What colors do these come in? How many cylinders does this bike have?" Hence, side and back walls provide better areas for display while keeping the main areas of the room where presentations are made relatively plain.

Summary

When a playwright begins to write a play, he or she envisions a setting. The set design will enhance the play, creating an ambiance and feeling that depicts the mood and emotions the characters are to identify with and function within. This is crucial in a classroom, too, where the environment plays a big part in influencing learners. Current cognitive research tells us that sensory memory is constantly scanning the environment and receiving sensory input. If the brain deems the input important, that, in turn, captures attention and influences conscious thought in short-term and, ultimately, working memory. Learners can be overstimulated or "swamped" with stimuli or, conversely, be unfocused because of lack of stimulation. Hence, the amount and quality of stimuli are a contributing factor to focusing attention and, ultimately, learning. Teachers who are conscious of creating key attributes in a learning environment not only facilitate learning but also develop students' sense of self-worth and belonging. This is a gift that will make its mark well beyond the end of the school year and influence students' perception of self and well-being in years to come. It will also impact their lingering impression of the schooling experience.

4

Organizing the Script

Designing the Curriculum

Successful productions have well-written, well-designed scripts. Playwrights the world over initially identify their expectations and the impact they intend to have on the audience. Without that intention, the production would be unfocused and meaningless to the audience and would not have the positive and long-lasting effect that was intended. Similarly, curriculum (a plan for learning) must be designed (as is a script) with a vision of the desired outcomes for specific learners and the structure to reach that end. Without this vision and structure, curriculum would be a random scene with meaningless acts toward no specific end. *Curriculum* is derived from the Latin *currere,* meaning "to run." Curriculum without purpose or intention becomes a random race without a course, a seemingly pleasurable or contrastingly onerous experience with no focused end.

The Cheshire Cat cautioned Alice, "If one doesn't know where one is going, then it doesn't matter which way one goes." If teachers are intentional and "begin with the end in mind" (Covey, 1989, p. 97), they will have a clear understanding of what they are trying to help their students achieve and will be more thoughtful in targeting standards, designing learning experiences directed at achieving those standards, and selecting assessment tools appropriate to measure growth.

Designing Down

The standards movement has increased educator awareness of curriculum design connected to expectations and related competencies desired for all learners. This standards-based focus or approach has caused many to revisit and reexamine the practice of designing curriculum. Figure 4.1 presents two ways of approaching the learning process—the "old" and the "new."

Figure 4.1. Planning Paradigms

Old Way	New Way
Teachers used to:	Now teachers:
Consider topics: • Content • Materials • Texts • Curriculum guides	Select content based on: • Specific standards • Knowledge of content (what's essential) • Skills needed for the future • Values, behaviors, or traits to succeed in school and life
Design learning activities: • Lecture • Presentations/demonstration • Didactic/Socratic method • Text, questions, and answers	Describe what success might look like: • Establish criteria and indicators • Communicate what the criteria and indicators might look like to the learner
Evaluate learning: • Test • Quiz • Exam	Design assessment processes: • Informal assessments—dialogue • Teacher tests and quizzes • Peer observation and feedback • Self-Assessment and metacognition • Performance tasks
	Design learning experiences activities that will enable learners to reach standards. Consider: • Brain research • Multiple intelligences • Active learning • Processing channels (auditory, visual, kiknesthetic) • A "match" with standards and assessment

The new way has often been called "designing down" or backward mapping (Wiggins & McTighe, 1998). It enables the teacher to streamline the planning process and maximize the quality of instructional time.

"Coverage" or Mastery?

One dilemma in education is that so much content/knowledge must be covered. It can come down to the daily grind of "teach, test, and hope for the best." Madeline Hunter, a well-known educator, used to caution teachers that covering curriculum was like a dash to the airport: You may get there, but some passengers who weren't ready may have been left behind. With information exploding almost daily, it will be impossible for schools to "pour and store" every bit of information available into every learner. That is not to say that one should abandon content for standards and processes, but rather that one should carefully select the content appropriate as the vehicle to achieve the standards and competencies. Each discipline will always need to define and refine its content objectives targeted for students and to include what is essential in the curriculum as a foundation for that particular discipline. To do this, first, expectations are carefully selected and content is identified. Second, appropriate strategies for data collection and feedback (assessment tools) are designed and shared with students so that expectations are clear. Third, students are immersed in learning activities and experiences that will explore the content and develop the skills targeted. During the learning process, data are collected on how students are progressing toward the standards. These data collected as feedback information are valuable to teachers and students in assessing what has been learned, what changes must be made in the curriculum, and what must be done next in the learning process. Figure 4.2 shows this *learning cycle* as a seamless process of targeting, planning, and assessing student growth toward targeted standards.

A planning model for the learning cycle is given in Chapter 13 (see Figure 13.1), the assessment chapter, so that the designing down process can be completed. Over the years, much has been added to the curriculum in all disciplines, but little has been removed. As a result, teachers and students often observe that much more content is to be taught than time allows for in depth and breadth. Careful exploration of standards and thoughtful consideration of content help teachers decide what should be "selectively abandoned" and what should be "judiciously included." One teacher referred to this process of selective abandonment as "benign neglect"! He went on to explain that one tool to help in the decision-making process was standards. Another tool was college-level freshman textbooks and exit expectations. If curriculum is to include that which students need for life and will endure beyond the test, it is essential that teachers within and across departments go through this culling out process. In doing so, many teachers often come to recognize that they have missed opportunities to integrate subjects across disciplines and to facilitate movement toward standards. Doyle and Strauss (1976, p. 25) have used the analogy that gum is the content teachers bring to the learners and that chewing the gum is the process of understanding and learning. Bob Garmstom, a well-known educator and organizational change consultant, suggests that, for learners to internalize and understand, they should be provided with perhaps less gum (content) and more time to chew (process the information). As a result of the analysis of the Third International Mathematics and Science Study (TIMSS) testing,

Figure 4.2. Seamlessly Informing and Facilitating Learning

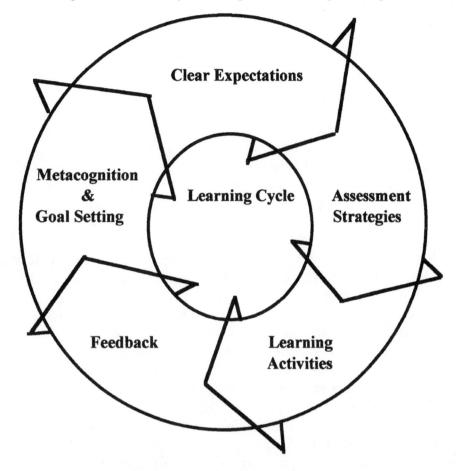

told that the curriculum is a "mile wide and an inch deep." With extended time blocks, learners can have time "to chew and construct meaning," thus enhancing understanding. Many teachers and students who have experienced the block say that the frantic classroom pace is slowed, that teachers can be more intentional about targeting standards, and that students can delve more deeply into the curriculum through a variety of meaningful learning activities. This observation reminds us of how crucial it is to focus on facilitating mastery of key concepts rather than on trying to cover all that is in the curriculum.

The Problem of Fragmented Curriculum

Another issue adding to the complexity of the teaching and learning process is that curriculum is often fragmented and delivered in a piecemeal fashion, topic by topic, discipline by discipline, with no connections or links to help students make real meaning or see where the new information fits in their world. David Perkins (1986) refers to this as the "Bo Peep" method of instruction (leave them alone, and they will

come home), wherein teachers teach the students and then the students are left alone to make their own sense, meaning, and connections or to transfer their new learning to the real world. He suggests that perhaps teachers should be more like "good shepherds," who facilitate the journey and help students make connections and see relevance in the learning as they apply it to situations in their lives. Following a textbook chapter by chapter or topic by topic is not always the best vehicle to help students in the learning process. Although the brain is a pattern-seeking organ, learners find it much easier to make connections if the process is facilitated by a skillful instructor who poses questions that beg exploration and who facilitates links between and among disciplines and processes. It takes time to do this. Extended periods of time can allow for this dialogue and exploration to occur. This process engages the learner in actively constructing meaning, which in turn develops new neural connections and promotes long-term memory of that which has been taught.

Constructivism

Cognitive research suggests that, to be stored most efficiently in mental files, new information must be linked to previous information. This linkage facilitates retrieval as well. Increasingly, however, teachers are noting that students come to school without the previous experiences or "files" one used to be able to count on; for example, students often are unfamiliar with folklore. Therefore, many teachers find themselves providing experiences out of which students can construct meaning. This is the basis of *contructivism*, a theory that was developed out of the work of Jean Piaget. The principles of contructivism (Brooks & Brooks, 1993) are as follows:

- Teachers pose questions that are relevant to the learner.
- Teachers use concepts as organizers for learning.
- Teachers value and encourage students' points of view.
- Teachers encourage students to challenge their suppositions.
- Teachers embed real assessments in the learning process.

An example of constructing meaning is illustrated in an eighth-grade classroom that was beginning to explore the concept of circumference of a circle and its relationship to diameter. In this classroom, students used string to measure around various round containers, such as food cans and garbage pails, and then they measured the diameter of each container. After charting these figures, students explored the commonality among the figures and discovered that the relationship is constant between the diameter of a circle and the circumference. They identified that relationship as 3.14 and understood π from having constructed that knowledge for themselves. Thus, using the formula for calculating the circumference $\pi \times d$ made sense to them because they had discovered it themselves. These principles conform to how the brain makes connections, grows dendrites, and stores information in mental files constructed when opportunities are provided to explore content in enriched environments through hands-on

manipulation and interactive dialogue. This approach is consistent with the notion that the brain is a pattern-seeking organ trying to make sense of new material by relating it to previous information or experience.

Relevance

Knowledge the learner perceives as relevant facilitates and increases attention, and with attention, learning can take place. Humans are driven by an innate curiosity to solve problems, accept challenges, and create things that are new and useful. This theory of learning, if embraced in classrooms, could make these settings vibrant, engaging places to spend time. It would also perhaps change the observation that "most students enter school as 'question marks' and for the most part leave as 'periods.'" This reality has been observed, for example, in classrooms taught with the "sit and git" method. Part of the relevance issue is that, frequently, students are unable to relate school and many of their classroom activities to the real world. The question "Why do I have to learn this?" is an all too common refrain in many classrooms. In fact, these words are addressed eloquently in the book with the same title by Dale Parnel (1995). He refers to the "freezer approach" to teaching: handing out information to be "frozen" in mental freezers until needed. The reality, however, is that the brain pays attention to what it finds meaningful, useful, or engaging. It filters out what it perceives as meaningless, irrelevant, or useless. If teachers can embed skills, knowledge, and applications in a real-world context, learners will have "emotional and relevancy hooks" to produce long-term memory files.

Sue Berryman and Thomas Bailey state:

> Traditional education and training misses the point that human beings are inquisitive, sense-making animals who learn best when they are fully and actively engaged in solving problems that mean something to them. Because it violates the way that people learn most effectively, our current approach to education and training simply does not work. (as quoted in Parnel, 1995, p. 78)

An example of building in relevance is the third-grade class that was designing a butterfly garden. This science project took the children out into the school garden to investigate the space available, research the flowers that would attract butterflies, visit a plant nursery in the community, and learn to plan on paper and then plant their garden. The children became engrossed in the task and diligently worked on the garden, respecting nature and learning many interrelated concepts and skills. Mathematics in measuring area and depth; language arts in planning, recording, and journal entries; and science content all integrated in a meaningful task that, when completed, gave great satisfaction to each child who participated. It also beautified the school and community and gave the children a personal sense of pride and contribution.

The Complexity in Designer Brains

The teacher as curriculum designer must consider the diversity of students in each class. In teaching, as well as in clothing, frequently one size doesn't fit all. Teachers often comment that students don't all learn in the same way on the same day. In short instructional time periods, teachers often only have time to give information (mostly stand and deliver). In extended instructional time periods, diverse learners can be allowed the options they need to make meaning and, ultimately, to make the new learning stick in their minds. In extended time periods, students can have opportunities to question, induce, examine, pose hypotheses, make models, and experiment with and manipulate materials. Honoring the multiple intelligences of students and allowing time for application, analysis, and assimilation of concepts and ideas is feasible in extended class periods. Longer blocks of time not only give teachers the opportunity to vary the approaches to topics and help students construct meaning but also allow students more time to dialogue and truly get to know one another. Students' interests, passions, and talents can be discovered, and teachers can then adapt curriculum to address the interests, needs, and concerns, as well as particular learning preferences and multiple intelligences, of their students. Students in block schedules often report that they think their teachers know them better and have more time to talk with them and respond to their questions. Surveys of schools on block schedules often reveal an enhanced climate at both the school and classroom levels.

Putting the Pieces Together

Figure 4.3 displays some curriculum considerations based on the principles of constructivism, principles of brain research, and classroom techniques. It invites curriculum designers to consider both research and practice when designing classroom learning experiences. Hence, theory is the lens through which one filters decisions when designing thoughtful curriculum.

Jack Miller from the Ontario Institute for Studies in Education (OISE) suggests that these considerations move us to a more holistic view of curriculum. He suggests that the process of changing curriculum moves through states beginning with a traditional *transmission model* of curriculum delivery, a more "stand and deliver" model, to a second phase referred to as the *transition model*, which is more teacher facilitated, possibly somewhat "command and control." The third phase is the *transformational model*, which is more student centered and brain compatible.

In Figure 4.4, the three models are shown with descriptors of their aims, teaching/learning strategies, and assessment techniques. In extended periods of time, teachers are more able to move toward the transformational model; students interact and take time to work on engaging projects and products wherein skills are embedded in context and a variety of more student-centered learning and assessment techniques are facili-

Figure 4.3. Curriculum Considerations

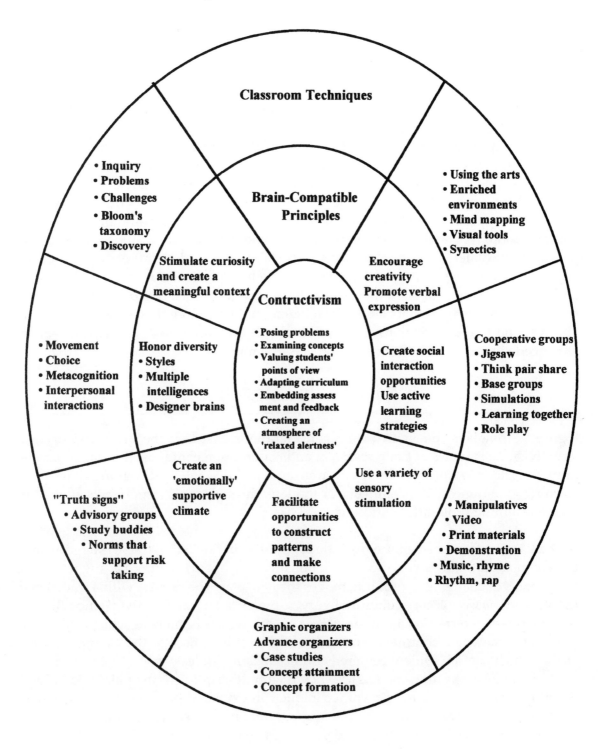

tated. Figure 4.4 may be helpful for teacher dialogue around the philosophical issues of curriculum orientation.

Figure 4.4. Curriculum Approaches

Aim	Teaching strategies	Assessment techniques
Transmissional Model: "Stand and deliver"		
Acquire and accumulate knowledge and skills	• Lecture • Program learning • Practice/drill • Recitation • Memorization	Tests Multiple choice True-false Fill in the blanks Matching
Transitional model: "Command and control"		
Develop problem-solving and decision-making skills	• Inquiry • Decision-making models • Independent study • Case study • Moral dilemmas	Checklists Observations Interviews Questionnaires Evaluation of problem solving
Transformational model: Brain Compatible . . . Learner Centered		
Individual and collective learning around crucial issues, questions, and projects	• Critical and creative thinking • Cooperative learning • Imagery • Whole language • Multiple intelligences • Concept development • Problem based	Interviews Metacognition Logs, journals Portfolios Exhibitions Performances

SOURCE: Adapted from Miller (1990).

Curriculum Design

To plan for a block schedule, initially one needs to take a look at the big picture. In designing the curriculum, it is important to start with clearly articulated standards and then design assessment tools and learning experiences to enable all students to reach the standards. Considering all that is available to enrich the teaching/learning process, teachers in extended time blocks have at their disposal more time to design the curriculum that will reach more learners.

In a selected course, first the teacher would list the units to be taught. Second, she would identify the number of weeks allowed for the course. Third, she would decide how many weeks to spend on each unit. Now that those decisions are made, the teacher has a place to start the unit planning. The teacher would then select resources to enhance the learning in this unit. She must also identify the chapters and page numbers

Figure 4.5. Long-Range Planning

Standards			Learning Experiences	Assessment	Data Collection	Metacognition
Expectations	Content objectives	Skills	Strategies to Foster Learning	Measures	Approaches	Reflections
			• Cooperative learning • Teacher directed • Jigsaw • Lecture • Demonstration • Think pair share • Laboratory experiments	• Project • Problem • Case study • Presentation • Rubric • Poster • Exhibition • Model • Performance	• Checklist • Observation • Video • Audio • Portfolio • Test • Quiz • Essay	• Log, journal • PNI (Plus, Negative, Interesting) • Six Hats • 3-2-1 • Portfolio • Dialogue • Visualization • Graphic organizers

Robbins, P., Gregory, G., & Herndon, L. E. *Thinking Inside the Block Schedule: Strategies for Teaching in Extended Periods of Time.* Copyright Corwin Press, Inc.

of the text and all other resources that would be available to students. This is also a good place to list any Web sites relative to the topic.

Figure 4.5 may be used in planning the scope and sequence of the curriculum. Planners can add strategies that they use or could use in their curriculum.

Using Long-Range Planning Guides

Having had an opportunity to create a long-range plan, teachers are better able to assess the scope and sequence of the curriculum and to analyze the parts and interpret the whole. This long-range plan invites teachers to regulate the pace of curriculum delivery. Teacher may fill in Figure 4.5 as they plan for the term, targeting standards and then aligning assessment and learning experiences. It is often called the *intended curriculum*. Throughout the year, as teachers modify and adjust the curriculum to meet the needs of their particular groups of learners, they should also modify and change the data to reflect the actual or *taught curriculum*. The following list of questions can be perused by individual teachers or groups to analyze and redesign the curriculum as a work in progress.

- Are the essential learnings included?
- Do the topics connect with one another? Are transitions provided between topics?
- What transitional bridges are or could be used?
- Would this order make sense to the learner?
- Have standards been sufficiently explored?
- Are thinking skills built in?
- Are the assessment tools appropriate for collecting data to show growth with respect to standards?
- Do the instructional processes/learning strategies have enough variety to reach a diverse group of learners?
- Are metacognition, self-reflection, and goal setting built in?
- Do the curriculum models interest, intrigue, and capture the attention of the learners?
- Are the opportunities for making connections, relating and developing understanding, and demonstrating competencies adequate?
- Has appropriate time for practice and feedback been built in?

Thus, individual teachers or teams of teachers can reflect on the curriculum and identify those areas where good curriculum design has created conditions for student learning to take place and standards to be met and those areas that need adjustment or modification of the learning and assessment strategies to result in student success. These individual long-range plans can also be shared with other teachers at the same

grade level and analyzed together. Sharing these planning guides across disciplines and grade levels will facilitate an understanding among faculty members about what students at different grade levels and subject areas are experiencing as a whole. With this added awareness, teachers can begin to integrate topics such as report writing in language arts to report writing in science or concepts such as conflict across the curriculum in language arts, social science, art, and so on as a linking or overriding theme.

These more natural emerging connections make more sense to students than force-fitting all disciplines under a thematic umbrella. Integrating curriculum should be a process of reinforcing natural, thoughtful, and practical connections between and among concepts, topics, disciplines, and cross-curricular skills (e.g., technology, thinking, language). Integration should not be trivialized to the point of putting a daffodil on the math ditto and making it part of the spring unit. In one social studies class during a unit on the Boston Tea Party, students were asked to keep journals as if they were living during this time. In geometry, students were to pick an interest area, such as flight, art, or dance, and explore how geometry affected or was part of this area. Longer time blocks in classrooms allow teachers to play out the curriculum in a way that helps students facilitate connections, make meaning, and reinforce concepts. It allows students not only to receive input but also to manipulate, analyze, apply, synthesize, and evaluate material and ideas and relate these learnings to their own lives and the context in which they live. This facilitates transfer and the appropriate use of the new learning, not only to be "tossed back" on the test but also to be remembered and accessed when needed to solve problems, create things of value, and handle complex situations.

Classroom Resources

As teachers think differently about instruction and assessment and begin to redesign and implement new curriculum, different resources will be needed in the classroom. If the mode has been "stand and deliver," a chalkboard, an overhead projector, and a textbook would probably be the extent of the resources needed. With longer class periods and the need for a context in which students can work cooperatively, problem-solve, and share, however, teachers will need to consider what new resources are needed. If teachers are to provide opportunities for interaction and small-group work, for example, different room configurations and often different furniture will be needed. If more active learning will be taking place, perhaps not only will the room arrangement differ but posting space for charts that students may construct will be needed. The following list of considerations may serve as a springboard for thinking about new resource needs. Notice that some of these resources will be particularly helpful for inclusion students, who may not read at the same grade level as their counterparts, or the child who manifests ADHD (attention deficit and hyperactivity disorder) tendencies and who may find it difficult to focus for extended periods of time.

Print and resource books beyond
the text
Videos and CD-ROMs
Library/resource materials
Computer/Internet access
Pictures, charts, bulletin boards
Flip chart pads
Colored paper and pens
Manipulatives

Models
Tape recorders
Camcorders
Digital cameras
Flexible table and chair
arrangements for group work
and/or experimentation
Materials for creative projects

Managing Change

Change is a process, not an event (Hord, Rutherford, Huling-Austin, & Hall, 1987). A new curriculum is not suddenly put into use; it requires careful planning, reflection, and dialogue among users. In doing this, gradually, mental models of what curriculum is and what it could be can change and evolve. Teachers need to envision and articulate their pictures of involved, engaged students, who may be actively constructing models, exploring concepts and ideas, and, ultimately, moving toward achieving standards. With this shared vision in place, teachers can move toward a new classroom for learning. Teachers also need support as they redesign their curriculum. It can be a challenging or "downshifting" experience to let go of the familiar "control" of the classroom and move from the "sage on the stage" role to the "guide on the side." It can be somewhat risky and perhaps even daunting to "take one's hands off the wheel" metaphorically and allow students to discover new learnings by using inductive processes rather than by always listening to the expert. Such new approaches to curriculum represent a paradigm shift for students as well, who at first may be dismayed with the new approach and may express a desire to return to the more familiar.

Administrators, colleagues, parents, and students need to be partners in the process of change. They will need to work together to understand, as well as support, the rationale for the change. This association will help all those involved be tolerant, empathic, and supportive of one another throughout the implementation process. Patience is needed to make informed decisions and collect data along the way. The path is not always clear, and the journey may not necessarily go just the way it was planned. But with a collective vision to guide the process, adjustments can be made as information becomes available or problems emerge. The old adage "Rome wasn't built in a day" can be applied to school reform. Real change takes time. Everyone involved in the change process will benefit from being in a state of relaxed alertness, aware of and stimulated by the challenge and also feeling safe and supported throughout the process.

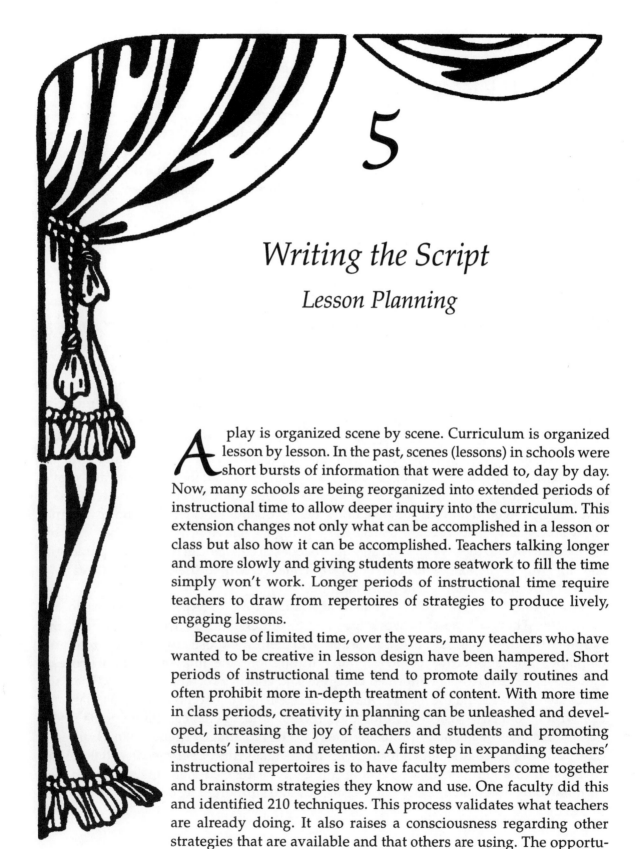

5

Writing the Script
Lesson Planning

A play is organized scene by scene. Curriculum is organized lesson by lesson. In the past, scenes (lessons) in schools were short bursts of information that were added to, day by day. Now, many schools are being reorganized into extended periods of instructional time to allow deeper inquiry into the curriculum. This extension changes not only what can be accomplished in a lesson or class but also how it can be accomplished. Teachers talking longer and more slowly and giving students more seatwork to fill the time simply won't work. Longer periods of instructional time require teachers to draw from repertoires of strategies to produce lively, engaging lessons.

Because of limited time, over the years, many teachers who have wanted to be creative in lesson design have been hampered. Short periods of instructional time tend to promote daily routines and often prohibit more in-depth treatment of content. With more time in class periods, creativity in planning can be unleashed and developed, increasing the joy of teachers and students and promoting students' interest and retention. A first step in expanding teachers' instructional repertoires is to have faculty members come together and brainstorm strategies they know and use. One faculty did this and identified 210 techniques. This process validates what teachers are already doing. It also raises a consciousness regarding other strategies that are available and that others are using. The opportu-

nity to converse with other teachers and to observe them using different teaching techniques strengthens interdependence and collaboration within and among faculty colleagues. It also allows staff to identify training and staff development needs they would like to have addressed.

Knowing that short-term memory, or conscious memory, has a limited number of chunks, given the developmental age of the learner, the teacher needs to consider how much content to present within a lesson and how to organize it to facilitate optimal learning. The process of chunking content is an important consideration in extended class time periods. *Chunking* is the term used for grouping or connecting content and skills together because of some linking thread, such as a concept or theme.

Another important understanding about how the brain learns is the concept of *beginning, ending, and middle* (*BEM*; Fitzgerald, 1996), or the *primacy-recency effect:* The brain pays attention to what it encounters first and remembers it best; it remembers second what comes last, and remembers least what is in the middle. In longer periods of time, therefore, teachers must divide the time into "chunks" so that the lesson contains several "firsts" and "lasts" to capture and sustain the attention of the learners.

This chunking also allows teachers to vary the activities, which, in turn, often provides a medium to meet a wider variety of learner needs. For example, one teacher began a lesson with a crossword puzzle that reviewed the previous day's biology vocabulary. Students paired and shared. Following this, the teacher read a prompt from the crossword, and students responded. The teacher then provided an overview of the class period. Students were to watch a video, construct a graphic organizer, use kits to build models, and write about their learnings in their learning journals. Within these lesson chunks, the activities are varied from active to metacognitive, individual to interactive. Such a design provides variety and engages or recaptures student attention to rejuvenate the learner.

A variety of lesson-planning models have been proposed. Whichever model one chooses, the following considerations for lessons in the block should be kept in mind:

- Divide the time into three or four chunks to provide several beginnings, ends, and middles (BEMs). Consider changing topics or activities related to a particular standard. This promotes alertness, attention, and engagement.

- Chunk the content so that students can develop "mental files" of connected, related ideas and information.

- Vary teaching strategies so that the diversity of learners in the class is addressed and honored.

- Provide a variety of learning experiences so that each learner is in a state of "flow" (Csikszentmihalyi, 1991) at some time during the period. Consider selecting activities representative of the multiple intelligences in the group.

- Build in opportunities for interactive dialogue, movement, and hands-on tasks, as well as for intrapersonal moments of reflection.

- Consider the cognitive research on how humans make meaning and develop memories of key learnings.

- Consciously select assessment strategies that are built into the learning cycle to give the learners ongoing feedback based on their progress toward targeted standards. Vary the type of assessment strategies so that all learners may thrive.

Decision Making

Teachers deal with a constant stream of decision making. In fact, it has been said that teachers make upwards of 1,500 decisions each day, either conscious or unconscious. As they pertain to lesson planning, teacher decisions hover around three areas: content of lessons, behavior of the learners, and behavior of the teacher.

Content of Lessons

As decision making relates to content concerns, focus on the following:

- Standards and benchmarks
- Stair steps of skills leading to outcomes
- Where each student is on the stair steps

Behavior of the Learners

Teachers are concerned about how students will get the information into their heads. How will auditory, visual, and kinesthetic learners receive and understand the information? Of the many strategies available (e.g., lecture, cooperative learning), which will be appropriate? Teachers must also decide how students will show what they know, be it through dialogue, demonstration, performance, writing, role playing, or modeling.

Behavior of the Teacher

These questions arise: How will I manipulate the variables of motivation to promote my students' enthusiasm? How will I organize and deliver information? How will I assess?

Undergirding these questions and determining success is class environment, for if the classroom is tense or unruly, not much learning will take place. In contrast, a welcoming atmosphere in which students can experience relaxed alertness is preferable.

Let's examine the process of lesson design, focusing on some key considerations for ensuring success. These considerations, as well as the brain research shared in the previous chapters, provide crucial "checkpoints" for the selection of lesson strategies best suited to both the learners and the content.

Lesson-Planning Models

One of the most familiar lesson-planning models is Madeline Hunter's (Russell & Hunter, 1976) 7-step lesson plan. As we look at each step of this lesson approach, we can see that these steps link very much to what has been learned about how the brain learns and makes meaning. The seven steps are as follows.

Motivation

1. *Anticipatory or mental set.* This step of the lesson is to capture student attention through *sensory* stimulation (visual, auditory, tactile, or olfactory). It sets the stage for the learning that is to come. Teachers can also provide an "emotional hook" for the new learning by introducing a *challenge, question, or problem* that is compelling or intriguing to students. As each learner is unique with respect to background, knowledge, and experience, so is the key that unlocks or opens each learner's latent mental files. To facilitate learning, teachers must *access prior knowledge* or *provide a shared experience* on which to build the new learning. If a learner has scant prior knowledge, setting the context will create a focus for the learning that is to come. This approach inspires curiosity and motivation. *So it is important to* use a mental set at the beginning of any learning segment. Strategies such as think pair share, K-W-L, brainstorming, advance organizers, videos, or field trips may be used to accomplish this.

2. *Sharing the purpose.* This step gives an overview of the lesson or unit to provide a sense of security about the lesson's direction and how one will get there. Changes will occur at some point, depending on the interests or preferences of the learners in the group, but *direction and purpose* are important elements in lesson design. Many learners want to know "Why would I need to learn this?" The mental set helps establish the *relevance* of the learning, which is a key ingredient in capturing student attention. The objective and purpose of the learning should be shared so that students are clear about what will be examined in the lesson, as well as why one would need to know the information for use in the *real world.* Linking learning to students' reality is an important aspect of the anticipatory set. The brain likes the "big picture." With this in focus, the little pieces are better understood. *So it is important to* provide written agendas or agenda maps. These are helpful in that they reveal the big picture. Providing rubrics, targets, or standards may help balance the anxiety of challenging expectations and presents students with a reason for their being immersed in certain activities.

The Instructional Process

3. *Providing input.* The input of the lesson is the "meat and potatoes," or content that is necessary to present or provide to the learners. Considering the broad standards

targeted and the subject discipline expectations, teachers choose content or subject material to create a high-quality and meaningful learning experience.

In short periods of class time, teachers are somewhat restricted in how they can present input. For the sake of efficiency and expediency, teachers often resort to lecture as a basic input tool. Although lecture is one tool for giving input, for many students it is not optimal. When teachers consider the capacity of the individual to take in more information by seeing and hearing, touching and talking, they expand their strategies. Some experts suggest that 67% of the population learns best visually! Hence, if enduring understanding of content is a goal, the teacher may want to explore approaches such as demonstrations, case studies, experiments, or cooperative learning tasks. With extended periods of time, teachers are freed from the constraints of "stand and deliver" to use a richer variety of input strategies to meet the needs of diverse learners.

Recognizing that the brain has a limited amount of memory space in short-term, or working, memory, teachers need to examine content for both quality and quantity. This examination should include decisions about which information to include selectively, how it should be presented, and which order is preferable. This process is referred to as *task analysis*. Task analysis requires a concept or body of information to be broken down into its component parts. These parts are then ordered according to what the learner must perform first, second, third, and so on. Presenting information in a logical, sequential way helps the brain learn because the brain looks for patterns. *So it is important to* conduct a task analysis to consider the best order and how the content should be chunked to help learners make the most sense of the information. Consideration should also be given to the complexity of the task and how the chunks can be sequenced to increase the chances that students can achieve mastery. Short lectures may be one choice for giving input. Information can also come from other students through a cooperative structure such as Jigsaw. The teacher might use a video clip, invite a guest speaker, provide a reading, use drama, or role-play. Input strategies should accommodate the diversity of learners and address multiple intelligences.

As in the mental set, sensory stimulation will engage the learner, capturing and sustaining the learner's attention. As always, the input should relate to the competencies that are to be achieved and should be presented in a way that makes the content relevant to students' lives.

4. *Demonstrating and modeling. Modeling* refers to the visual representation of what is being taught. In most cases, modeling is presented after or with information being presented. Modeling helps students retain in memory what is learned by adding visually to what has been presented verbally. It provides variety and creates interest, as well as offers, in some cases, a hands-on experience. *So it is important to* recognize the value of concrete materials and try to include models that relate to the content of the lesson. This gives students the opportunity to see, touch, and examine materials that will help deepen understanding. Models and demonstrations in science, manipulatives in mathematics, mind maps to depict character sketches in language arts, demonstrations in physical education, and maps and charts in social science are all strategies that provide visual and kinesthetic hooks to foster student learning.

5. *Checking for understanding.* During the *checking for understanding* step, the teacher monitors students to determine whether they understand the material presented. The teacher assesses students' competency in using the skills that have been introduced. On the basis of this assessment, the teacher then makes adjustments in the learning process. Adjustments may include reteaching by using an alternative strategy, rethinking the task analysis, reteaching the steps, or abandoning the lesson for the moment and coming back with a fresh approach. This step is generally done before the application or practice so that when asked to practice, students can do so masterfully. *So it is important to* check for understanding in ways that require students to demonstrate a skill or understanding of a concept. Often, a teacher asks students whether they understand and the students nod their heads. The teacher then proceeds to the next step of asking whether anyone has any questions. To this, most often, students shake their heads. All the teacher really knows at this point is that the students can still move their heads. Students should instead be involved in an activity or task that checks their understanding beyond a nod or shake of the head. They may be involved in a brainstorming or a think pair share, wherein they explain their thinking, address a question, or answer prompts posed by the teacher or questions generated by students. Any of these strategies will help students clarify their thinking. At the same time, it helps the teacher redirect the learning or facilitate the correction of any misconceptions or misunderstandings. Checking for understanding increases the chances that students will be successful when they apply their learnings.

Checking for understanding may be part of the mental set in which teachers will check that students are clear in their understanding before presenting the next step. Sometimes teachers will again check for understanding during the closure phase of the lesson. This can be accomplished with a journal entry or an "out the door" or "exit slip," wherein students jot down key learnings on a ticketlike slip of paper and hand it to the teacher as they leave.

6. *Guided and perfect practice. Practice* is that step of the lesson where students get a chance to apply or rehearse what they have learned. *Guided practice* includes coaching with or by peer groups or through teacher observation and monitoring. Without guided practice, students may practice incorrectly. It has been said that "Practice doesn't make perfect, only perfect practice makes perfect." If students have received coaching and feedback and have developed a clear understanding of the material or procedures, they can proceed to independent or group practice, confident that they are on the right track to developing a skill or knowledge base that is accurate. *So it is important to* provide an opportunity for students to explore and apply knowledge and skills in a supportive atmosphere where constructive guidance and feedback are given. Two examples are (a) structuring situations in which students try one example of a math problem or work one example with a partner and (b) taking students on a walk in a nearby neighborhood to identify geometric shapes in the real world. Asking students to use a Venn diagram to compare and contrast their own personalities with that of the main character in a piece of literature may be a way of checking whether students understand the character and/or can use the skill of comparing and contrasting. After the teacher assesses during

practice that students are able to work independently to apply the new learning, students should have the opportunity to apply the learning in a variety of ways. They may work alone or collaborate on a teacher-directed task. Some teachers invite students to select how they wish to practice. Students' flexibility to choose how they will "show what they know" will increase the chances of high interest and engagement with the new learning and thus enable students to develop long-term retention.

7. *Closure.* This step is usually the "final check" to determine whether students clearly understand the learning and can demonstrate this in a meaningful way. Closure generally revisits the purpose of the lesson and the expectations or targets. Often, closure addresses the transfer process and helps students reflect on where this new information or skill will be useful in the real world. What else might they want to know pertaining to the concepts or procedures learned? Discussion at this point may intrigue learners to investigate some aspect of the lesson further and more deeply. Personal questions may arise that some learners may want to pursue. *So it is important to* invite students to summarize their learning during closure activities. Socratic and open-ended questions stimulate higher levels of thinking to help students analyze, synthesize, and evaluate the learning. Students can be encouraged to predict or form hypotheses about what may come next in the learning, based on current information. A community circle (Gibbs, 1995), where students sit in a circle and reflect on a key aspect of their learning or a key question that puzzles or intrigues them, is another strategy for closure. Students may be assigned homework to consolidate their skills after they have reviewed the steps in the process. They may use a page divided down the middle, with a log on one side and reactions and reflections on the other side, to record new learnings and suggest a use for them in their daily world.

Typically, *independent practice* follows closure. This engages students in developing fluency and speed in applying new learnings on their own.

Summary

As outlined above, the 7-step lesson plan may seem linear and straightforward. It can, however, be as creative as the repertoire the teacher has at his or her disposal. The steps do not have to be in a specific order, and the time spent on each step is not necessarily the same in each lesson. Recalling the primacy-recency effect and the need for several beginnings, ends, and middles chunked during the class period, the teacher can be flexible in designing learning by using a variety of strategies and tools to reach the desired standards. The teacher must consider not only the variety of instructional strategies but also the importance of varying the learning experiences to include active, passive, kinesthetic, and reflective tasks.

With this information, teachers can design lessons that will appeal to the diverse learners they serve in a way that reflects the learners' interests, preferences, and multiple intelligences. With the techniques and strategies shown in Figures 5.1 in their repertoire, teachers will be more able to select and use that

which enables more learners to reach the standards. Teachers can select from the categories to create lessons that are engaging and dynamic for extended periods of instructional time. All the strategies are described in the chapters in this book.

Figure 5.1. Tools for Success When Teaching in Extended Instructional Blocks

Instructional models	Collaborative structures	Grouping strategies
Concept attainment	Think pair share	Cards
Concept formation	Think pair share write draw	Counting off
Inquiry	Wheel in a wheel	Statistics
Advance organizer	Take a stand	Chairs
Mnemonics	Check mate	Smell your way to a group
Role play	Interview team	Assignments
Synectics	Round the block	Name tags
Direct instruction	Collaborative corners	Candy
Lecture	Take a stand	Team formation
Simulations	Jigsaw	
Group investigation	Brainstorming	

Roles	Collaborative skills	Active learning
Encourager	Listening	Carousel brainstorming
Questioner	Taking turns	Shaping up a review
Clarifier	Encouraging others	Ticket out
Summarizer	Using positive statements	Rhyme
Prompter	Using quiet voices	Divide and conquer
Gatekeeper	Participating equally	Talk walk
Recorder	Staying on task	Experiments
Reporter	Asking for help	Dramatization
Materials manager	Checking for understanding	Crosswords
Timekeeper	Asking for clarification	Graphic organizers
Researcher	Following directions	Investigations
Liaison	Accepting difference	
Observer	Disagreeing agreeably	

Multiple intelligences	Assessment tools	Authentic tasks
Verbal linguistic	Rubrics	Exhibitions
Musical rhythmic	Contracts	Presentations
Bodily kinesthetic	PNI	Demonstrations
Logical mathematical	Six hats	Debates
Naturalist	Logs and journals	Speeches
Visual spatial	3-2-1	Models
Intrapersonal	Reflection stems	Products
Interpersonal	Portfolio	Posters
	Conferences	Projects

Figure 5.2 is an example of a lesson a teacher could use in an extended period of time, selecting from the array of techniques and strategies available.

Figure 5.2. Nutrition Lesson

Lesson topic: Nutrition: Healthy choices

Standard: Students will make informed decisions for a healthy life.

Expectations: Students will identify options for healthy snacking based on knowledge of good nutrition.

Beginning a Lesson:

How will I engage or motivate the learner? capture attention? How can the senses be engaged?

Choices?	Have students in **small groups** examine a selection of snacks and prioritize their preferences.
or	Suggest a **think pair share** in which students share with their partners the snacks they had yesterday and record on self-sticking notes. Develop a **web** as a large-group activity.
or	**Small groups** can examine several advertisements and list the snacks recommended and the reasons given for eating these choices.

Presenting Content:

How can I present information in a clear, interesting way?

Choices?	Students view a **short video** outlining the nutritional requirements and suggestions for healthy snacking. Students list key points to remember. They take a **talk walk** with a partner to share the information.
or	A **guest speaker** from the local health department visits to talk about healthy eating. Students go to **collaborative corners** selected on the basis of whether they practice healthy snacking as compared to the information given.
or	Students engage in a **jigsaw** to share information from texts.

Active engagement of the learner:

How will I hook the learner to rehearse or become involved with the information?

Choices?	Students will design a **poster** sharing the information about selecting healthy snacks.
or	Students will create a **rap or song** to encourage others to choose healthy snacks.
or	A **role play** will be presented to share information about healthy choices.

Checking for understanding:

How will I check to make sure students have the correct information?

Choices?	Students will **explain** their poster to the class.
or	Students will **present** their rap or song.
or	Students will **act out** their role play.

Application and practice:

How will students apply their new learnings?

Students will record their snacks for the next 3 days. They will bring in their recorded lists and analyze their snacks, using their knowledge of nutrition. They may use a **computer** program to analyze their snack intake.

Closure:

Students will reflect on their analysis and write a response in their journal.

Students will set goals for themselves about their snack choices.

Extension:

In a few weeks, the activity can be carried out again to see whether students' snacking habits have improved or changed in any other way.

Assessment:

Posters can be graded. Feedback can be given on presentations based on a rubric. A quiz can be given to test knowledge of nutrition.

Figures 5.3 (p. 52) and 5.4 (p. 53) are variations of block lesson plans for consideration. One of these may be useful for planning. These forms may be adapted and modified to suit individual teachers' preferences.

Figure 5.3. Block Lesson Plan I

Motivation:

Activate prior knowledge

Review or homework

Engage the learners

Providing the context
and
Sharing the purpose

Giving the "big picture"

Instructional Process

Presentation:
• Input

• Modeling

• Check for clarity

• Guided and perfect practice

Closure:

Figure 5.4. Block Lesson Plan II

The "Big" Picture

What is the standard of learning I am going to address in designing, teaching, and assessing this lesson?

_____

_____

Lesson expectation

What will students know and be able to do as a consequence of this lesson?

_____

_____

What strategies will I use to:

Activate prior knowledge?

_____

_____

Motivate and engage the attention of the learner?

_____

_____

Set the context?

_____

_____

Deliver instruction? (input, modeling, rehearsal opportunities)

_____

_____

Check for understanding?

_____

_____

Provide opportunities for perfect practice?

_____

_____

Assess student learning?

_____

_____

Foreshadow next steps?

_____

_____

Robbins, P., Gregory, G., & Herndon, L. E. *Thinking Inside the Block Schedule: Strategies for Teaching in Extended Periods of Time.* Copyright Corwin Press, Inc.

Other ways of organizing lessons are shown in Figure 5.5.

Figure 5.5. Teaching in the Block

Welcome	Lecturette (no more than 10-15 min)	Processing time	Report out	Students summarize learnings.
Introduction to the *outcomes* for the day	or	Options: • Think pair share	Options: • Random	Next class is foreshadowed.
	Quiet activity (e.g., reading, working problems, viewing a video)	• Check mate • Round the block • 1-2-4 • Write pair share	• Card deck • Select reporters	Homework is assigned.
Sponge activity (to sop up time that might be wasted while roll is taken)				
or				
Discussion of a current event in relation to today's content				

Additional lesson design formats are available, such as the two shown in Figure 5.6. Various instructional strategies and assessment tasks may be selected, depending on targeted standards and content.

Figure 5.6. Visual "Chunking" of a Block Lesson

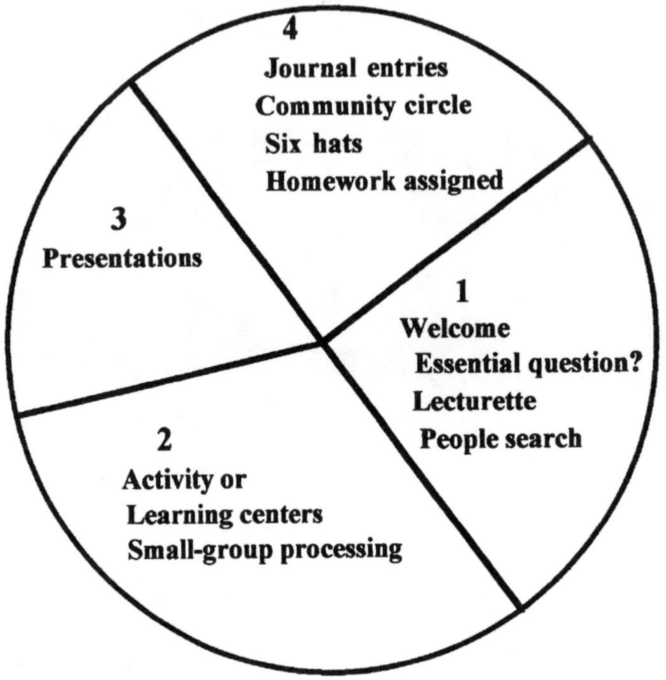

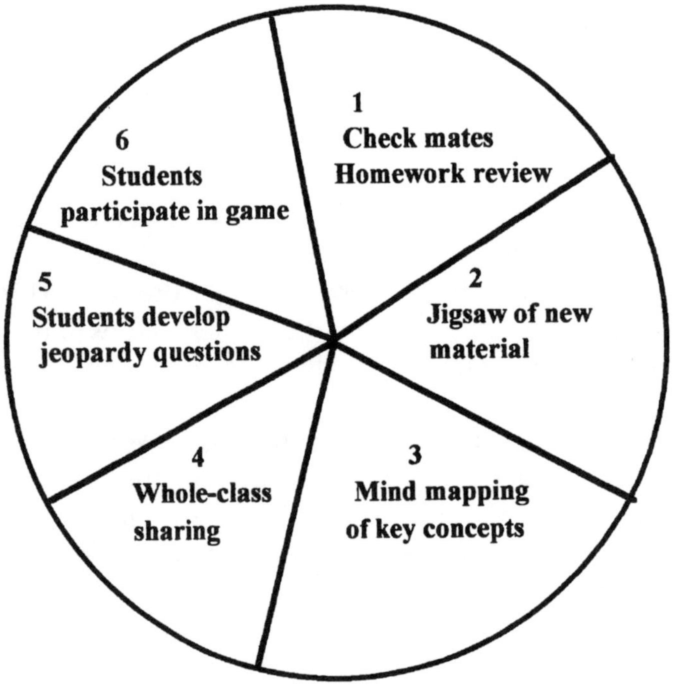

The Opening Scene
Generating and Sustaining Attention

Imagine that you walk into a theater. The usher invites you to "choose any seat in the house"! Surprised, your eyes search for the perfect seat. You spot one—an open seat, second row from the stage, right in the center of the theater! You move quickly toward it. You sit down and settle in. Soon, the lights go down, the curtain rises, and the spotlight shines on a lone player who deftly tells the audience in a hushed voice what is about to occur.

As you read this scenario, was your attention focused? When? Was it when you were looking for a place to sit? when the spotlight focused on the person onstage? when the player spoke in a hushed voice? all three times? Why was your attention focused? Was it a desire to find a seat to your liking? darkness blotting out distractions, the spotlight drawing your focus? the unusual tone of a hushed voice?

We all know from personal experience that a variety of things influence attention—likes, dislikes, novelty, color, need, and interest, to name a few. In the classroom, attention is critical, for if there is no attention, there is no learning. Many teachers who have worked in a block scheduling setting say that one of the biggest dilemmas they've

faced is generating and maintaining students' attention during extended periods of instructional time. This is particularly true with students who have attention deficit disorder (ADD), they add. Because of the importance of attention in the block, this book devotes a chapter to the subject, examining what influences attention and strategies to initiate and sustain students' attention over time.

Portraits of Success

One way to glean insight about attention during long periods of instructional time is to analyze successful practice. Imagine that you are sitting at the back of a classroom. The bell rings, signaling the beginning of a 90-minute period. As students file into the room, they move to one of two boxes and pull out file cards with their names. They proceed to their seats and begin marking these cards. As you peer over one student's shoulder, you notice that she is recording data about her attendance; whether she came to class prepared with text, notebook, and a writing implement; and whether she completed the homework assignment from the previous evening. At the end of the period, she will mark her participation in class in a space on her card. While students are engaged with their cards,[1] the teacher takes roll and circulates among the students, making welcoming comments as she goes. After a few minutes, the teacher invites students to put their cards aside and to take out a sheet of paper and something to write with. "In a moment," she says, "we will play the Age Game. Then you'll have 5 minutes to work with a partner to see whether you can figure out why this game works! Listen carefully and follow these steps:

1. Think of the number of days you would like to go out—for example, to play ball, to shop, to visit with friends, to eat—in a week. Write down that number 1 through 7.
2. Multiply that number by 2.
3. Add 5.
4. Multiply your answer by 50.
5. If you have already had your birthday this year, add 1,750. If you have not yet had your birthday, add 1,749.
6. Last, subtract the four-digit number of the year you were born.

You should now have a three-digit number. The first digit of this should be your original number. The second two digits should be your age![2]"

"Did it work?" the teacher asks with a smile. The class seems amazed. "Now you have 5 minutes to work with a partner to see whether you can figure out this game. And remember to use your '6-inch voices' [voices so soft that they don't carry farther than 6 inches] so that your neighbors won't hear your ideas and you won't distract them! Ready? Go!" Immediately, students put their heads together and begin trying to

figure out the formula. After 4 minutes, a clock placed on the overhead projector and visible on the front projection screen beeps, reminding students they have 1 minute to go! Students let out moans and utterances like, "Yikes—we gotta hurry!" When 5 minutes are up, the teacher calls for volunteers to approach the overhead projector and explain their thinking in writing, using transparencies and transparency pens. Because the workings of the Age Game can be explained in more than one way, several partner pairs share their work. The teacher asks students to stand if they agreed with an explanation after it is presented. This serves to engage the class and gives those who stand a chance to stretch their legs. Following the students' explanations, the teacher displays a flip chart with a state standard for problem solving written on it. She gestures to the standard and then to a picture of a target. "When we do activities like this one, we are developing skills to address targeted standards that will be on the state assessment. Two aspects of this are important. First, make sure you have the skills in math to pull this off! Second, make sure you have the power to stick with a problem when the answer is not immediately apparent. It's tough, but I saw most of you doing an excellent job of attending to the task!"

The teacher then leads the class through an agenda, posted on the right side of the chalkboard, informing them of the plan for the remainder of the period.

Following this, students check homework by using the "move and schmooze" strategy, wherein they get out their homework and have 3 minutes to mingle with their colleagues and compare answers. Homework questions are then entertained and resolved. Homework is turned in.

Next, the teacher introduces a lesson, working from the overhead, explaining, demonstrating, and giving students examples to work on and report out. This cycle of explanation, demonstration, and student work lasts about 20 minutes. Then, students watch a humorous video clip in which the concepts they had learned were applied in "real world" settings. After this, the class is invited to move to standing groups of three, each group having a piece of flip chart paper to write on. On the chart, they have to summarize their understandings of the lesson and generate a problem related to today's lesson content for another group to work on. After 10 minutes have passed, student trios are instructed to move to the right one chart and to work the problem the previous group left for them. Following this, the groups do a carousel walk, proceeding around the room, looking at each chart as they move.

After students return to their seats, homework is assigned and students have 10 minutes to begin working. As they do, the teacher circulates, monitoring student work and stopping periodically to provide assistance so that homework will, in fact, ensure a measure of "perfect practice," rather than reinforce errors. Many teachers have found that, by having students begin homework in class, students are more likely to finish it at home, and the error rate is reduced significantly.

During the last 3 minutes of class, students are instructed to rate their class participation on their cards, using the rubric the class had previously developed. As the bell rings, students are dismissed. Several students comment on how quickly the time passed as they filed their cards in the box and walked out of the classroom.

Analysis of Practice

The teacher in this scenario used several strategies to foster student attention throughout the lesson. Students first focused attention on a *timed task* that had become *routine.* The teacher *monitored* students as they marked their attendance cards. Then, they *participated* in the Age Game. *Games* tend to imply fun, and this one posed somewhat of a *mystery:* Why did the end turn out the way it did? The game had to do with one's age; most individuals like activities that *relate to them personally. Timed pair work* that included a measure of accountability (showing one's work on the overhead projector) fostered attention. Without accountability, pair work may often lead to off-task discussions among colleagues. The beeping *visible timer* inspired students to pay attention to the time allocated for task completion. In addition, when the teacher revealed the standard to which this task applied, attention was enhanced because the *need* for this skill was demonstrated.

The homework-checking "move and schmooze" activity engaged students in a *novel* way of exchanging homework answers. This teacher had several in her repertoire. Attention is often generated by *movement* and *variety.* When the teacher taught, she used explanation, demonstration, and student examples. *Changing activities* frequently generates and sustains attention. Attention is also fostered by *using examples with students' names or interests.* More often than not, because so many students are accustomed to watching television, the *video clip,* as well as the *humor* it evoked, drew the students' attention. *Flip charts with colored markers* can focus attention as well, especially because each trio had to *develop a problem* for the next group of students to work. Time for starting homework with the teacher *monitoring to ensure "perfect practice"* also tended to be an attention grabber. Finally, attention was focused once again when students paid attention to *marking their class participation cards.*

Another Look at Attention

Apart from the specific examples cited in the classroom scenario analysis, attention is also generated by emotion. Emotion may emanate from a variety of sources: It may be fostered by the relationship students have with a teacher; as one teacher once said, "I believe in working with kids from the inside out." Emotion may also be generated by students' interest in a particular activity or task; this phenomenon was observed in a biology class, for instance, where students were absorbed in observing baby chicks hatch from eggs the class had carefully incubated and monitored. Emotion may also be a function of the learning environment, discussed in Chapter 3, or the social context of the work group. Finally, the emotion a student brings to school can be the result of the home environment; it can promote or hinder attention to learning. Some students come to school to find a source of solace, lacking in their homes. Others come to school burdened with emotional distress, which inhibits their ability to focus on or attend to

academic tasks. Still other students come from homes that are so supportive and enthusiastic about school events and activities that this positive spirit flows from the home to the classroom and enhances attention.

As explained in Chapter 2, teachers have 0.75 second to capture a student's attention. And if they don't, the student's brain will select its own focus, which may or may not be what the teachers desire!

Teachers in the block have offered the following additional tips for promoting attention and added, "In small ways, we can make big differences in learning."

- *Provide advance organizers.* This strategy invites students to learn what they will be expected to do before they are asked to do it—for example, "After watching this video clip, you will be expected to describe, in writing, key events leading up to the Civil War" or, "After reading the two stories, I would like you to use a Venn diagram to display their similarities and differences with respect to plot, character development, setting, and voice."

- *Post outcomes* or standards toward which students are working in a designated place.

- *Use bracketing.* Bracketing invites students to put mental brackets around those thoughts that threaten to take them off task—for example, "Jot down on an index card anything that is begging for your attention. Then put it in an envelope and sit on it! You may come back to those thoughts at the end of our period."

- *Eliminate distractors* in the classroom. One way to focus attention is to minimize distractions that threaten to compete with what is intended as the central area of focus. To do this, keep in mind where one usually stands when teaching or facilitating groups. Make sure that interesting posters or objects are not in these places, but rather are in other areas of the room.

- *Ask for expectations.* When students perceive that their interest areas are being addressed, they are more likely to pay attention. For example, before a unit of study, ask students to peruse the materials and to generate a list of expectations or particular interest areas within those materials. Generate a class list of expectations (e.g., If this unit is to meet my needs, I expect that we will address these subtopics . . .). Post this list and check them off as they are addressed.

- *Generate previous experiences that relate to the topic.* Most students love to share their experiences verbally, graphically, or in writing. When they are asked to do this, they focus attention on information stored in their neural networks of association that relate to a topic about to be taught.

- *Use K-W-L charts.* The K in a K-W-L chart stands for "What do you think you already *know* about the topic to be taught?" The W stands for "What do you *want* to know?" (The answers "I don't know" and "I don't care" are not acceptable.) At the end of the unit, students are invited to reflect on the L, "What did you *learn*?" Asking students to complete K-W-L charts collaboratively prior to and after a learning experience increases attention to a particular topic and extends their learnings.

- *Use stories.* Stories that have engaging characters and events appeal to all learners—visual, auditory, or kinesthetic. They focus attention because the words require the learner to create mental pictures of what is going on and because they usually evoke emotion.

- *Use novelty.* The mind is always seeking patterns. Anything that stands out from the ordinary focuses attention because it is novel, often unexpected. In some classes, for example, teachers dress up as literary or historical characters. In others, novelty may involve students experiencing simulation; for instance, in one classroom, the teacher engaged students in constructing an assembly line in which they learned, firsthand, what it might have been like to work during the Industrial Revolution. "Sometimes the smallest thing can focus attention!" one teacher explained. Students in her class who have 5 weeks of perfect papers get to write in a special colored ink—red, purple, green—as a treat. They can continue doing so as long as they have perfect papers! Another teacher, Melanie Coody, in the Coppell Independent School District (Coppell, Texas), focused student attention when she turned her language arts classroom into a cafe. Reflecting on her purpose in selecting a restaurant theme for the year, she said, "I wanted to make the classroom an energetic, unique, motivating place for students to learn." In Melanie's classroom, students are greeted each day with a display board outside the classroom. It reveals to students "Today's Specials." This board immediately draws students' attention to what they will be experiencing in class—be it "Apple Adjective Pie, Simile Spaghetti, Narrative Nachos, or Silent Reading Rolls!"

- *Invite students to use 1- to 3-minute pauses.* These short time segments focus the attention of the students on what they have just learned. A 1- to 3-minute pause provides students with an opportunity to revisit content and summarize key points. Some teachers ask students to write their summaries on index cards; others, in learning journals. Still others may hand out shapes, such as a triangle, and ask students to note three key points of the lesson. These short, intense review segments focus attention (once students are taught how to use them) and promote long-term memory of content.

Summary

As a reader, you may now reflect on your attention as you read this chapter. Did your mind wander, or did it focus? If your mind wandered, perhaps you had other things on your mind competing for your attention. Or, perhaps many of the examples were familiar to you so they lacked novelty. The same is true in the classroom. What is uppermost in a student's mind gets attention. If a student perceives that she has "been there, done that," attention may be lacking.

If your mind focused, perhaps it did so because content was relevant or perceived to be useful, examples were novel, or the sections of the chapter provided interest and practicality and were relatively short. These are all conditions that motivate students to attend in the classroom:

provided interest and practicality and were relatively short. These are all conditions that motivate students to attend in the classroom:

- Relevance
- Perceived usefulness
- Novelty
- Interest
- Practical information
- Information or activities that invoke an "I can do this" stance
- Comfortable, engaging pace

Lest we lose your attention as a reader at this intermission, let's move on to the next chapter to see how this plot will develop and unfold.

Notes

---

1. Blackline masters for these cards are included in Robbins and Herndon, 1998.

2. This problem was designed to work in the year 2000. In 2001, change the 1,750 to 1,751 (in Step 5) and 1,749 to 1,750.

7

Developing the Plot
Selecting Instructional Strategies

In the theater, the playwright decides on the setting and characters. He or she must consider developing the plot with situations that the players will encounter as they move toward the climax and that tie the ideas together with a satisfying conclusion designed to please the audience and leave them with a message.

Although in the classroom the teacher does not have much choice about the characters, he or she can influence the setting. In addition, the teacher as curriculum designer has a choice of many strategies that will enable learners to move forward, achieving the targeted standards.

Joyce and Weil, in their book *Models of Teaching* (1986), outline four families of instruction: (a) the information processing family, (b) the personal family, (c) the social family, and (d) the behavioral systems family. These families were developed as a result of observing approaches to teaching and learning. *Teaching,* in this context, is what the teacher does to facilitate learning; *learning* is what students do in the process of making meaning and developing understanding as a consequence of the learning experience constructed by the teacher. The strategies included in *Models of Teaching* were selected because of their ability to help students reach educational goals. Each family contains several strategies. The range and diversity of these strategies give teachers an expanded repertoire that will have the potential to reach more learners. Teachers can help students

deepen and intensify their learnings by selecting a strategy that will match with the curriculum and the way students learn best. Each family has distinct goals and intents; for example, strategies within the social family have as their mutual goals the target of developing both social and academic skills.

Figure 7.1 shows the various strategies in each family. This chapter briefly describes all the strategies listed and more deeply explores what, why, and how to use those in **boldface type.**

Figure 7.1. Strategies of the Four Families of Instruction

Information Processing Family	Personal Family
• **Concept attainment** • **Concept formation** • **Inquiry** • **Advance organizers** • **Memorization** • Constructivism	• Learner centered • **Synectics** • Expanding personal horizons • Class meetings
Social Family	Behavioral Systems Family
• Group investigation • **Role play** • Jurisprudential inquiry • Simulations • **Cooperative group learning**	• **Direct instruction** • Lectures

SOURCE: Joyce & Weil (1986).

Instructional decisions are based on a consideration of content, desired behavior of the learner, and behavior of the teacher. A key aspect of the decision-making process is based on standards or expectations. The learning activity in which the student is to be involved should be selected so that the student will be engaged in a meaningful way with the content while developing the skills, processes, and values set out in the curriculum. As you read through the following family and strategy descriptions, you might also ask yourself, Under what conditions would I use each of these?

Information Processing Family

The *information processing family* includes strategies that help students construct meaning through processing information in a variety of ways, such as concept development and inquiring, to make personal meaning.

Concept Attainment

The teaching strategy of *concept attainment* is based on the work of Jerome Bruner and his colleagues Jacqueline Goodnow and George Austin. Their research, published in *The Study of Thinking* (1967), focused on two of the most basic human cognitive acts—categorizing and conceptualizing. Concept attainment helps students learn a concept by asking them to compare and contrast examples that do and do not contain those attributes. Concept attainment is an effective method for teaching concepts in different disciplines. Most people develop an understanding of a new concept by examining attributes they think are common in that category and by identifying other things that also fit the category. For example, a boy may develop an understanding of horses by observing and analyzing the attributes of horses and comparing those attributes with those of other animals. Attributes that are common to horses and that differ from attributes of other animals help the boy differentiate what characteristics are unique to horses, compared with cows, donkeys, or other four-legged animals.

The steps to concept attainment are these:

1. The instructor explains to students the process of concept attainment.
2. The instructor presents labeled examples of the concept (positive examples and negative examples).
3. Students compare attributes in positive and negative examples.
4. Students generate and test hypotheses.
5. Students identify the concept (confirmed by the instructor, if correct).
6. Students generate additional positive examples of the concept.
7. Students analyze their thinking patterns and strategies.

An example is a social skill concept that can be presented through concept attainment. The teacher would say, "Today, we are going to learn about a behavior that we can use when we are working together in groups. Your task is to identify the name for this behavior by examining positive and negative examples of it." The teacher, using a pocket chart or strips of masking tape (sticky side out) on the wall or board, would present a statement on a strip of paper that is a positive example of the verbiage one might use, such as "That's a neat idea," and place it in the left-hand column. (The teacher could also just write the phrase in the left-hand column on a chalkboard or whiteboard.) Then, the teacher would give a negative example (an example that does not reflect the concept the teacher is trying to communicate). The teacher would place the strip of paper with "That's dumb" on it in the right-hand column. After showing several positive and negative examples, the teacher would ask students to look at the positive examples and identify the commonalities of this group. Some students might be able to form a hypothesis as to the name for the type of behavior the positive examples communicate. Next, the teacher would present other examples, and students would identify whether they thought these were positive or negative examples. Then, a student would be asked to state his or her hypothesis. Next, students would generate

additional examples of their own to test their understanding. Last, students would discuss their thinking and identify how and when they came to understand the concept and its critical attributes. They could then discuss how the concept of encouragement is useful as a skill when working in groups. Following this, they could practice using statements of encouragement appropriately in a group situation. Examples of positive and negative examples of encouragement are listed below:

Positive/Negative Examples

Positive	Negative
That's a neat idea!	That's dumb!
You can do it!	Don't bother.
Try it your way.	Do it yourself.
Sounds like a good suggestion.	You can't do it.
What do you think?	No way!

Concept attainment can be used in any subject area to have students develop an understanding of the attributes of a concept. Concepts such as adverbs, homophones, and similes can be developed in language arts. In art, the concepts of abstract paintings and realist paintings can be explored by using copies of actual paintings. In social science, the concepts of islands and democratic countries can be analyzed by using concept attainment. In mathematics, concept attainment may be used to examine attributes of prime and nonprime numbers or the concept of geometric figures. In science, it might be used to explore electrical conductors and nonconductors. Primary students can develop the concept of heavy or light by examining real objects that represent yes and no examples. This process may take more time, but the understanding developed through discussion and analysis and by having students develop or construct their own meaning will probably be retained longer in mental files. This process may serve well as an advance organizer prior to the lesson or to clarify thinking during the lesson. It might also be used to review previously taught content.

Concept Formation

Concept formation is an inductive strategy developed by Hilda Taba (1967). The steps in the process are as follows:

1. Data collection
2. Interpretation of the data
3. Concept formation
4. Labeling of the concepts
5. Application of the principles

The teacher can give the data set to students, or students can create their own from previous knowledge and experience. For example, students may generate examples of events leading to the Civil War. Generalization and manipulation of data give students more ownership and choice in this process than in concept attainment, wherein the teacher controls the process.

In the first phase, students explore the data. In the second phase, students explore the relationships between and among the items in the data set. Next, students organize the data into groups based on relationships and crucial attributes and then label those groups. This strategy is consistent with the brain's ability to recognize patterns and its need to make meaning. It is also a way of chunking information to be filed as concepts based on commonalities rather than as discrete bits.

The power of this strategy is in the thinking that must take place to classify, label, and then use the principles. An example at the elementary level is students collecting items on a nature walk in the woods. Back at the school or camp, they examine their materials and the characteristics of each and begin to see the relationships between some of the items. Students will begin to organize the items into groups based on similarities. Once the groups are organized, they can be named or labeled. Having constructed knowledge of seeds and leaves and so on, students can use this information to identify other items that might fit into the category and understand the attributes and principles involved. Data can be generated by, discovered by, or given to learners. At the middle school level, students could use small self-sticking notes to generate all the attributes they can think of that would help a student be successful in school. Students can then share their ideas with a small group and examine and sort their ideas into groups of related items. Students can then label these groups and develop a list of the attributes of a successful student. As a result of this process, students will be more cognizant of what it takes to be a successful student. An understanding garnered in this way is much more powerful than one acquired by listening to the teacher just give the information. Students will tend to own the principles they have personally generated and are thus more likely to try to respect and work with them as their guide for behavior.

Students at the secondary level may generate the attributes of communism or a safe science lab or a quality presentation.

This strategy works well with small cooperative groups. It can be used as an advance organizer, a check for understanding, or a closure activity.

Inquiry

The *inquiry* process was designed to allow students to be active participants who generate quality questions, solve problems, and develop creative solutions. Students use creative and critical thinking, as well as their imagination, to problem-solve and to research. A climate that fosters inquiry enables higher order thinking to take place, as well as data-driven, substantive conversations.

Several conditions are needed to promote successful inquiry for students:

- Ask open-ended questions during the regular course of the school day.
- Begin to introduce some discovery lessons, in which students try to answer a class question.
- Evolve, over time, to group questions.
- Have students develop a personal question or develop one with a partner.
- Let students hear teacher questions that model curiosity or possibility.
- Use language that encourages thinking, such as, "I wonder why?" "How can we find out?" "What if . . . ?"

Inquiry helps students develop lifelong learning skills. It teaches students the following:

- A process for solving problems
- How to collect, analyze, and synthesize data
- A process for creative and critical thinking that fosters curiosity

Inquiry helps teachers do the following:

- Attend to students' natural curiosity
- Respond to individual differences
- Engage learners in their particular interests
- Integrate multiple standards (technology, research skills, language arts, and a combination of the expectations and competencies of several disciplines)

The following steps may be helpful in facilitating the inquiry process with students:

1. The teacher involves students in an initial experience or exploration.
2. The teacher poses a suitable question within the study.
3. Students generate reasonable alternatives to answer the question.
4. Students collect data to respond to the alternatives.
5. Students select the best answer to the question by exploring the data.
6. Students assess the accuracy of the conclusion.
7. Students communicate and evaluate their findings.

Advance Organizers

The *advance organizer* model of instruction was designed by David Ausubel (1960). It is the skill of providing learners with cognitive structures so that they have "mental hooks" on which to "hang" new concepts and information from a lecture or other presentation. It can be done in three phases. The first phase is to clarify the aims or

objectives of the lesson. The second is to present the organizer. The third is to develop an awareness of the content or information.

Memorization

Some things have to be memorized and do not lend themselves to learning in context. When a learner has no prior experiences that will help him or her learn new information, sometimes using a strategy such as mnemonics (which include acrostics and acronyms) will help hook new information to familiar words.

For example, as children, many adults learned HOMES as an acronym to remember the names of the Great Lakes—Huron, Ontario, Michigan, Erie, and Superior. A music teacher may use the phrase "Eat good bread dear father" to help students remember the names of the lines in the treble clef. Using associations in this way when material is unfamiliar helps students remember information.

Constructivism

Constructivism is an approach that invites learners to construct meaning as a consequence of being immersed in experiences. It is addressed in greater depth in Chapter 4, on curriculum.

Personal Family

Strategies in the *personal family* emphasize the individual and the uniqueness of every learner. They foster student understanding of self and others, as well as personal expression. Outcomes of lessons in this family often produce creativity, self-confidence, and a sensitivity toward others.

Learner Centered

A *learner-centered* strategy stresses the teacher's role as facilitator, developing a personal relationship with the learner. In this mode, the teacher helps students examine new ideas about themselves, their interpersonal relationships with others, and their education. The teacher helps students accept more of the responsibility for their own learning through open dialogue and honest communication. This can be facilitated through conferencing, interviewing, and the portfolio process.

Synectics

Synectics is a model for teaching creativity developed by William Gordon and his associates. Gordon (1961) originally developed this teaching system to train engineers and scientists confronted with problems that did not respond well to conventional problem-solving approaches. He later adapted this model for use in schools. Gordon

uses metaphoric activity and analogy to cultivate emotional responses, to break set, to gain distance, and to stimulate associations that are beyond the ordinary logical, problem-solving processes to afford new insights and inspire creative responses.

In developing this model, Gordon made the following assumptions:

- The process of creativity is not mysterious; the steps of creativity can be identified and taught.
- Creativity is necessary to many tasks and fields: science, engineering, the arts, writing, and everyday life.
- Group work and cooperation advance the acquisition and use of creative skills.

Synectics is a process, based on the use of metaphorical forms, for developing creativity. Synectics may be used to clarify concepts by making the strange seem familiar and to create uncommon and deeper meanings. The process also forces people to think along lines and channels not commonly used. Synectics is used in business to generate new images by relating unlike objects, images, and ideas. In the classroom, it can be used as a warm-up before writing, to solve problems, to create something unique, to investigate social issues, and to help students develop empathy through comparing and contrasting familiar and unfamiliar ideas and feelings.

The steps to synectics are as follows:

1. *Description of current condition:* The teacher has students describe the situation as they see it now.
2. *Direct analogy:* Students generate direct analogies and select one to explore further.
3. *Personal analogy:* Students become the analogy they selected in Step 2.
4. *Compressed conflict:* Students take descriptions from direct analogies and personal analogies, suggest several compressed conflicts, and choose one.
5. *Direct analogy:* Students generate and select another direct analogy based on the compressed conflict.
6. *Reexamination of the original task:* The teacher has students reexamine the original situation or problem, using the entire synectics experience.

For example, a teacher might invite students to write about winter (original condition). Then, he might ask students to put their writings aside and "break set" with the familiar by thinking about what animals or other living things come to mind when the topic of winter is mentioned. Students could brainstorm these and post them on butcher paper (direct analogy). The teacher would then ask students to generate a list of nonliving objects they associate with winter. These, too, would be recorded (direct analogy). Next, the teacher would ask students to "become" one of the objects on their list. For instance, perhaps students have "snow shovel" on their list. The teacher could

ask, "If you were a snow shovel, how would you look? How would you feel? How would people regard you?" Student responses to these questions would be recorded (personal analogy). Once this list was recorded, students would be invited to identify words that "seem to fight each other" (compressed conflict). For example, on the list might be *useful* and *abandoned.* After these combinations of words are identified, the teacher would ask students to find a direct analogy; for example, something that was "useful" and "abandoned" might be an "antique" or a "take-out food container." After this process is completed, as the final step the teacher would invite students once again to write about winter, but this time to use some of the brainstorming they generated or to incorporate new ideas or associations that emerged as a consequence of making the familiar strange. Student writings tend to be more creative and often include more metaphors, similes, and analogies as a result of the process.

Direct Analogy

Direct analogy is a basic form of analogy. Students could be directed to select a topic they wished to explore in depth and then examine how it is similar to something that is, on the surface, quite different. For example, the teacher could ask the class, "How is thinking like a pinball machine," or, "How is anger like a strawberry?" In subject areas, the teacher might ask, "How is an election like a submarine?" "How is a test like a space shuttle?" "How is happiness like a potato?" or "How is the Renaissance like a video game?"

Direct analogy is useful for defining concepts and for checking for understanding. It is also useful as an informal assessment to see whether students have thoroughly developed concepts; it causes students to think deeply about a topic and its attributes.

Personal Analogy

A *personal analogy* is often used to help students develop empathy and connections to identities outside themselves. They may identify with an inanimate object, an animal, a person, or something else. For example, sometimes to express feeling students can describe themselves as a broom or doorknob. They can relate personally to a kangaroo or platypus, a character in a novel or a historical figure in a particular situation, or a volcano or a wilted tulip. It may give them a vehicle for expressing feelings and emotions and help them develop empathy to have a deeper understanding of themselves and others.

Conflicting Analogies

Conflicting analogies are generated out of opposing ideas. They may almost be a "war of words" that helps people clarify their thinking, look at the upside and downside of ideas, and employ analytical thinking. This can include oxymorons such as "focused diversity," "random target," "civilized hostility," or "detailed irrelevance." Teachers can explore two opposite ideas, such as (a) How is the lottery an enabling hindrance?

(b) How is solitude a blessing and a detriment? and (c) How is welfare a necessary evil and a blessing? By looking at conflicting viewpoints, students develop a deeper understanding, rather than just get one point of view.

Expanding Personal Horizons

The focus of *expanding personal horizons* is on developing personal awareness. This awareness of one's own behavior is helpful in setting goals for specific growth. Self-awareness also leads to identifying strengths and weaknesses in others. This is often facilitated through encounter groups.

Class Meetings

William Glasser (1969) proposed a method of developing a caring, supportive classroom environment in which students can take ownership for the decision making and problem solving that must occur to have the class function with consideration and empathy for others. This inclusive atmosphere fosters an enabling, empowering climate where all learners can flourish.

The steps in the model are as follows:

1. Develop a climate with norms that will create an optimal learning environment.
2. Present the problem or issue.
3. Examine the personal values involved.
4. Explore alternative solutions.
5. Develop a commitment to solve the problem.
6. Assess the impact of the solution.

The teacher is key to facilitating the process toward a consensus. This model stresses the need for students to take responsibility for their learning and their personal needs in the learning environment. It empowers students to be cognizant of their individual role and the power of the group to solve their own problems. An issue such as the noise level in the classroom could be examined and discussed and solutions generated that could be implemented and evaluated.

Social Family

The *social family* builds on what is known about the concept of *synergy:* "2 + 2 = 5." The collective wisdom of individuals within a group is greater than just the sum of the group. The outcome of the collaborative experience is generally greater when minds think and create together. The social family has several strategies: group investigation, role play, jurisprudential model, and cooperative group learning. A brief description

of group investigation and role play is given below. A definition of jurisprudential model follows, and cooperative group learning is dealt with extensively.

Group Investigation

Group investigation is a cooperative inquiry into engaging challenges and problems. The process is as follows:

- Identifying the problem
- Collecting and exploring the data
- Creating hypotheses
- Verifying and testing the hypotheses

Often, an intriguing idea or challenge is key to engaging students with problems and issues.

Role Play

Role play is a strategy designed to help students practice skills in realistic situations and receive feedback on their performances. It allows them to explore their values and reflect on them. It helps students collect and organize data about many social issues and develop empathy as they role-play. It is useful for acting out conflicts and taking on the role of others in controversial situations. In role play, students may need direction at first in the following areas.

Setting the Stage. Students may need help providing space for the role play. They need to understand the purpose of the role play and be given some guidance in how to prepare for it. Simple signals and stage directions will need to be learned.

Providing Dialogue. Scripts may sometimes be provided initially to help students engage productively in a role play. Over time, with more experience, students may begin to write their own dialogue appropriate for the situation.

Developing Appropriate Audience Behavior. To help the role play be successful and the actors be comfortable, teachers may invite students to brainstorm positive behaviors for audience members to practice. Teachers should also establish routines for giving feedback in positive and nonjudgmental language. They will want to encourage self-reflection and emotional response to the scenario that is depicted and give helpful suggestions for future role plays.

Coaching Actors. Teachers may initially provide scripts, warm-up activities, and rehearsal time for the actors. Teachers may want to provide or suggest props and scenery

that would enhance the role play. A discussion concerning the focus and purpose of the role play will help students remain within the expectations and parameters of the roles.

Jurisprudential Inquiry

Jurisprudential inquiry is a secondary model that brings the legal case study approach to the classroom. Students analyze cases and identify issues. Options are generated for these issues. Then, the options are debated. Policy issues that relate to sports, economics, social science, and the physical and health sciences can be used as topics. This approach generates critical thinking and provides avenues for students to think at higher levels of Bloom's taxonomy (analysis, synthesis, and evaluation).

Cooperative Group Learning

The social model of cooperative group learning is one of the most researched strategies that improves student achievement. Many outstanding educators (e.g., Aronson, 1978; Bellanca & Fogarty, 1991; Bennett, Bennett-Rolheiser, & Stevhan, 1990; Cantelon, 1991a, 1991b; Clarke, Wideman, & Eadie, 1990; Johnson, Johnson, & Holubec, 1988; Kagan, 1992) have shared their expertise in cooperative group learning with other educators. Cooperative group learning is reported to facilitate building positive relationships among students in class, as well as boost academic achievement. These positive relationships help students feel connected and cared about in the classroom. The strategy helps students achieve mastery of content and skills and develop the thinking processes necessary for problem solving and higher order reasoning. It increases their competencies in social and interactive skills, which helps them get along with others in their families, the workplace, and the community.

Major studies in corporations show that the number one reason why people lose their jobs is not that "they don't know and can't do," but that they have interpersonal problems in the workplace (Johnson, Johnson, & Holubec, 1984). The processing of information and ideas in a group helps students deepen their understanding through the articulation of ideas and the variety of perspectives that group members shed on the topic or problem. The dialogue, rationale, and restating help participants make sense of the ideas and help "Velcro" the information into long-term memory through elaborative and sometimes rote rehearsal. Teachers who have been working in the block identify cooperative learning as one of the most useful strategies to promote learning in extended periods of instructional time.

Basics of Cooperative Learning

William Glasser (in Fogarty, 1995) reminds us that we learn

10% of what we read

20% of what we see

30% of what we hear

50% of what we see and hear

70% of what is discussed with others

80% of what we experience personally

95% of what we teach to someone else

Cooperative learning experiences foster students' abilities to retain what has been taught as a consequence of several opportunities to rehearse or practice content. Although cooperative group learning is a simple concept to grasp, it is more complicated to implement than one would think. For successful implementation, some foundations need to be constructed to support these collaborative structures in the classroom. The first is a climate conducive to learning and thinking. As discussed in Chapter 3, classrooms need to offer an atmosphere that is collaborative and supportive and that encourages risk taking and thinking. Then, trust needs to be established between and among students in the classroom. To build trust, students must be helped to know one another better and understand each other's strengths and weaknesses so that they can be vulnerable and yet also feel safe and supported.

Trust building can be accomplished simultaneously while teaching students simple structures that can also be used to process academic content and achieve standards in the curriculum. Simple cooperative structures can be used in a personal context to build trust. When the process is understood and internalized, it can be used with academic content in the curriculum. The following examples exemplify strategies that can be used both to foster trust and to address academic outcomes.

Think Pair Share. This strategy provides a simple structure (Lyman & McTighe, 1988) that is fairly easy to implement and that has a very positive impact on learners. Students are given a question or problem (concept, idea, homework) and are asked to think about it. They are then asked to pair with a partner and discuss the issue. Then, the pairs share with the whole class. This is a great strategy for processing every 10 to 15 minutes throughout a lecture. It allows information to be discussed and questions to be answered before "cumulative ignorance" takes place or students are lost or confused at the end of the lecture. It is a useful strategy for taking up homework and deepening understanding through articulation.

A Variation of Think Pair Share: Write Draw Make. This strategy invites students to write, draw (e.g., word webs, mind maps, graphic organizers), or create something, such as a model, poster, collage, or diorama. It provides visual-kinesthetic learners with an active way of processing information and enhancing understanding.

Wheel in a Wheel. This strategy is excellent for having students articulate their understanding, problem-solve, or rationalize their position. It is useful for verbal-linguistic and bodily kinesthetic learners who are able to clarify their thinking in an interpersonal way. Students form two concentric circles, with the inner circle of students facing the students in the outer circle, who are facing toward the center. Each facing pair responds to questions and issues and discuss them. Then, each student in the outer circle moves to the next person, who becomes a new partner, and the conversation continues. This is a useful strategy for trust-building activities, as well as for mastering information. It can be used as a review strategy in which the inner circle people ask questions of the outer circle people and then the process is reversed. Using strategies such as these develops the expressive and receptive verbal language skills of students as well.

Interview Teams. Two pairs of students work together. Each partner in every pair interviews the other. Then, each of the four, in turn, shares with the group of four what he or she has heard from his or her partner. This activity can be used to access prior knowledge at the beginning of a lesson or unit, to check for understanding midway through a lesson, or to bring closure or consolidate new learnings. Interview teams can also be used as a strategy to facilitate review of previously taught content/skills. It helps students practice the skills of active listening and paraphrasing.

Round the Block. Students form small groups of three or four students. Each small group has one sheet of paper and a marker for jotting down ideas. Individuals within the group get a chance to jot down an idea on the paper and pass it to the next person. This process fosters equal participation. It helps students focus on the task and is a useful strategy for brainstorming. It can be used as an anticipatory set at the beginning of a lesson or to review information. Sometimes teachers just have students share orally, rather than pass a paper.

Collaborative Corners. Students select a corner, go there, and discuss a question, issue, or problem. Their selection may be based on a preference, an opinion, or a strongly held value. This can be used as a trust-building or "getting to know you" activity or to consolidate thoughts and develop a rationale. Students could go to the corner to discuss their favorite vacation: camping, a tropical beach, a visit to an exciting city or the family cottage. In each corner, students put their heads together and develop a rationale for their choice. Collaborative corners could be used to signify a reaction to a statement that may be controversial—for example, "We need to change the gun laws." Students go to the corner of choice: Agree, Strongly Agree, Disagree, or Strongly Disagree. Then, they develop a rationale with the group that assembles in their particular corner to articulate their position. Students could also choose a favorite character from a story and go to the corner and develop a character sketch with the group: Charlotte, Wilbur, Fern, or Templeton (from *Charlotte's Web*). It could be used as a prewriting activity to generate ideas, vocabulary, and rationale. This physical move-

ment helps provide options for kinesthetic learners, raises students' energy and oxygen levels, and reduces stress.

Take a Stand. Another kinesthetic simple structure is having students take a stand on an issue. The teacher makes a statement and asks students to respond by standing in a row related to a particular response to the issue. It could be using the agree/disagree variations as in collaborative corners, or it could be standing in the rows designated "I know a lot about the topic," "I'm not too sure about the topic," "I know one thing about the topic," "I know very little about the topic," and "I've never heard anything about this before." It could also be to stand on a number from 1 to 10, according to how much they agree with a particular statement, such as "Every parent needs to take a parenting course." After the students have lined up, they can discuss with their line-mates why they chose that particular row and what they know or why they agree or disagree. This makes a good anticipatory set at the beginning of a lesson and can be used at the end of a learning experience as a chance to discuss what has been learned in this particular area.

Check Mate. Students pair up, and one partner answers the question or problem or practices the skill that has been taught. The other partner coaches and encourages. Then, they reverse roles. After they are finished, they can meet with another pair to share their expertise. They show their appreciation of each other and celebrate their success. This activity works well with math problems and in taking up homework in any subject.

Name Your Team. Sometimes it's a good idea to have students develop a name for their team or their base group if they will work together over time or on an extended project. This helps them explore their commonalities and develop a group identity. It is a further opportunity to bond and develop trust. They might do this by looking at their personal multiple intelligences profiles, their hobbies and interests, and/or their personal characteristics. Students often realize that they are more similar than different. In cooperative learning, students need to know each other at a deeper level than just what academic success they have had. That personal knowledge of each other helps students realize that everyone is vulnerable in some areas and has strengths or talents in others. This realization enables tolerance and empathy to develop in the group so that while they are working they will be more understanding and able to make allowances for the diversity within the group.

Team Portrait. To further build trust and a spirit of teamness, teachers may ask students to create a poster, collage, or banner for their team. They can use symbols and pictures with a slogan to symbolize their unique team. Those students who like to use visual representations may prefer this form of expression. Teachers "on the block" comment that because students will be spending extended periods of time together, a variety of team-building and trust-building strategies is essential for classroom har-

Figure 7.2. How Jigsaw Groups Meet

Home base groups (individuals are assigned a task according to their letters or numbers)	1 2 / 3 4	1 2 / 3 4	1 2 / 3 4	1 2 / 3 4

Home base groups (individuals are assigned a task according to their letters or numbers)				
	1 2 3 4	1 2 3 4	1 2 3 4	1 2 3 4
Expert groups (individuals help each other learn the material)	1 1 1 1	2 2 2 2	3 3 3 3	4 4 4 4
Home base groups (each individual within the group teaches his or her piece of the content)	1 2 3 4	1 2 3 4	1 2 3 4	1 2 3 4

mony and academic pursuits. In addition, these strategies provide vital opportunities for students to practice key skills needed in the workplace. National surveys of employers conducted by the U.S. Department of Labor cite team building and communication as two key skills for success in the workplace.

Jigsaw. This useful strategy includes the use of expert groups as part of the process. This strategy was first introduced by Elliot Aronson in 1978, as well as by Johnson et al. (1988), and Kagan (1992). Although this is an interesting and engaging as well as efficient technique for examining a large amount of content, it is a much more involved strategy than those previously outlined and should not be attempted until students have developed adequate social skills to cope with larger groups and complex tasks.

Initially, students are organized into groups of three, four, or five members, often referred to as the base group. Each group member is given a letter or number (e.g., 1, 2, 3, 4, 5). The material to be examined is divided into the same number of pieces as there are members in the group (e.g., 3, 4, 5). Then, the material is distributed to each member of the group. The next step is forming expert groups in which all the 1s meet together, all the 2s, and so on (see Figure 7.2). In the expert groups, the members examine the material, information, or model; analyze the critical points (the what); and decide how to share that information back in their base group (the how). After the experts have finished their dialogue and have reached a level of understanding, they return to their base groups and each group member, in turn, teaches teammates what he or she has learned.

This strategy is powerful in fostering interdependence as each person has a key piece to the whole that is valuable for a shared understanding. Having to understand new information thoroughly enough to share it with others requires careful examination and critical-thinking skills. The ability to articulate, explain, or interpret helps the individual with long-term and enduring understanding.

An example of using Jigsaw in action is as students are studying a new topic, such as the countries of Africa. They would be assigned the areas of geography, people,

wildlife, food, and agriculture. The expert groups would meet and explore these five areas and, once their expertise was developed, they would return to their home or base groups and teach each other. Jigsaw can be used in any subject discipline with almost any content. It can serve as an advance organizer, as an strategy for presenting information (input phase), or as a closure activity to consolidate student learning.

Teacher Considerations in Designing Cooperative Activities

It is important that teachers be cognizant of certain considerations when planning to use cooperative structures. Paying attention to these considerations will increase the chances that the groups will function well and achieve their academic goals, as well as develop the social skills and thinking skills they need for life (Johnson et al., 1988).

The acronym TASK may be a way to remember these ideas:

T   hinking is built into the process.

A   ccountability is essential. Goal achievement: both individual and group.

S   ocial skills for team success.

K   eeping everyone on TASK. Roles, tasks, resources, novelty, simulations, and clear expectations.

Thinking Skills Are Built Into the Process

Educators are always looking for ways to build thinking skills into lessons and tasks. Cooperative learning is a wonderful strategy as it lends itself to interactive thinking. Teachers can use concept formation or synectics, Venn diagrams or other graphic organizers to help students think together in cooperative groups. Teachers can deliberately build in all levels of thinking by using Bloom's taxonomy so that students are exploring ideas and issues from all perspectives.

Brainstorming is often used to generate data and to problem-solve in cooperative learning. Guidelines for brainstorming techniques are shown in Figure 7.3.

Figure 7.3. Guidelines for Brainstorming Techniques

Group Brainstorming
- The teacher sets a quantity target to keep the group moving.
- The teacher stipulates a short time frame; this helps keep the group on task.
- The teacher appoints a recorder.
- Each member thinks of a few ideas prior to group brainstorming.
  (This is referred to as "priming the pump.")
- The recorder jots down the groups' ideas large enough for all to see.
- No criticism is allowed.
- No debate is allowed; just keep the others' ideas flowing.

(continued)

Round the Room Brainstorming
- The teacher posts large sheets of chart paper around the room. Each sheet is accompanied by a different colored marker.
- The teacher writes a different topic, idea, or question on each one.
- In small groups at each sheet, groups generate ideas for 45 seconds or so and then move to the next chart, taking their colored marker with them (this provides a measure of accountability).
- When a group returns to the original chart, group members peruse, clarify, and summarize.
- Students can take out notebooks and record key ideas from the completed charts.

Four S's for Brainstorming
S   peed—rapid fire
S   top criticism
S   illiness is OK
S   upport and build on others' ideas

Dot Jot—Paper Pass
- Each group has a piece of butcher paper at their table.
- Each group brainstorms around a topic, issue, or question.
- Each idea is jotted down on the paper, following a dot.
- After a minute or two, each paper is passed to the next group so that the new groups can add more ideas.
- When the paper returns to the group where it started, the members organize a summary of ideas to be discussed and presented.

Accountability Is Essential

In any cooperative learning task, students must achieve an academic goal to be successful. As a result of any learning experience, students are assessed on what they know, what they can do, and how they function. They may be held accountable by testing or through a quiz. They may be held accountable orally, through randomly asked questions, or in a large-group discussion. They could be asked to model, demonstrate, or exhibit a new skill they have acquired.

Checklists provide feedback to students on their growth in the area of social skills. Reflection forms may be filled in by groups or individuals to dialogue about their use of social skills. The following list of questions may be used two or three at a time for *reflection and dialogue* by group members:

What word would you like people to use to describe your group?

If they watched you today, what word would they use?

Did you listen to each other? What evidence do you have?

Did you respect ideas from other people? How did you do that?

Did you disagree in a "polite way"? What did you say?

Did you ask clarifying questions?

Did you extend other people's answers? What did that sound like?

Did you all participate equally? What evidence do you have?

Some *personal reflection* questions:
What were you being asked to do?
What information did you have?
Had you solved a problem like this before?
What strategies did you use?
What problems did you encounter?
What was your plan?
What can you predict?
How are you feeling about this experience?
What would you do differently next time?
Where can you get some help if you need it?

Students may also process the social skill growth they have made and set goals by using a *pluses and wishes* format (see Figure 7.4). Students list all the pluses, or positive aspects, of their working together and then all their wishes and plans for the next time they work together.

Figure 7.4. Pluses and Wishes Format

Pluses	Wishes	Plans for Next Time

Sometimes students are asked to reflect on their working relationships and to respond to questionnaires like the one shown in Figure 7.5.

Figure 7.5. Working Relationship Questionnaire

How well did you work together?

We listened to each other.	☺	😐	☹
We helped each other.	☺	😐	☹
We got our work done.	☺	😐	☹
As a result of working together, we feel . . .	☺	😐	☹

Social Skills for Team Success

After attending to the building of a positive, inclusive climate and developing trust, students must develop social skills to be successful in group work. Many students come to school with well-developed social skills that they have seen modeled for them in

family situations and that they have practiced and received feedback on in their early and formative years. Their emotional intelligence is high. They are at ease with themselves. They manage their emotions and are self-motivated, seeking intrinsic rewards for learning. Not only are they self-aware but they also are aware of others and can show empathy and have the skills to manage others and interact with others successfully (Goleman, 1995)

These abilities are not always innate, however. If students have not had opportunities to encounter positive role models and learn from them, or if they have not been taught these skills, they may be lacking in this area of development. Although they have perhaps missed the optimal window of opportunity for developing these competencies, it is not too late if a focus is placed on social skills development and if situations are provided for practice and feedback.

Here are some *fundamental social skills:*
- Listening to others
- Taking turns
- Encouraging others
- Using positive statements
- Using quiet voices
- Participating equally
- Staying on task
- Asking for help
- Using polite language

Here are some skills for *maintaining group process:*
- Checking for understanding
- Asking for clarification
- Following directions
- Disagreeing/Agreeably
- Resolving conflicts
- Accepting differences
- Encouraging one another

Teaching Social Skills

It is important that teachers help students learn the appropriate social skills needed to work successfully in collaborative groups and to accomplish their academic goals. Students need to be able to understand the following in relation to any social skill that has been targeted:

- Why the skill is needed
- What the skill is—what it looks, sounds, and feels like
- How to practice the skill

- The importance of practice
- The need for opportunities to debrief the learning process and reflect on the practice

Following are suggestions for the steps in the process of teaching social skills.

Why the Skill Is Needed. Often, at some point in group work, the need for a particular skill clearly presents itself. At this moment, it is ideal to analyze the situation to identify what is going on in the group and to see the need for a skill that will help the group function better. As the teacher or one group observes another, students can see a problem and suggest a skill that might be helpful for the group to learn and practice.

What the Skill Is. Any learning target must be clear and comprehensible to the learner. Often, the teacher can facilitate the opportunity to highlight a particular positive social skill needed for successful collaboration. The use of the skill can be illustrated through a story, video, or current event. Students can role-play to get a sense of how the skill looks, sounds, and feels in action. Teachers can also facilitate the development of a *T chart* that looks at what the skill "Sounds like" and "Looks like." A third column may be added to the chart to include what the skill "Feels like" (Hill & Hancock, 1993).

Thinking about feelings helps students with the skill of self-awareness and the ability to identify personal feelings and then helps with the ability to be empathic to others. Students can generate these indicators as a class, contributing statements in their own verbiage so that, in group situations, the language is comfortable and familiar to use.

Figure 7.6 is an example of a chart that describes "using names." It was generated by students during a discussion of the importance of calling one another by name.

Figure 7.6. Social Skill: Using Names

Sounds like	Looks like	Feels like
I hear my name.	Smiles	I'm important.
Names are said nicely.	Looking at the person	People care about me.
Everyone's name is heard.		

Students can show that they understand the skill by drawing about it, role-playing a situation where the skill is used appropriately, using puppets to play out the skill in a particular scenario, or writing about themselves or others using this skill in real-life situations. Using a concept attainment lesson that gives attributes of the behavior may help students understand the skill and give them language to use as they practice.

The Importance of Practice. Teachers need to organize group interactions and select the appropriate social skill that could be practiced during an activity. Using names is important in activities where everyone needs to be involved, feel included, and participate equally. The skill to be practiced should fit the situation. For example, *equal*

participation is an important skill to use when the group is trying to share opinions and come to consensus.

The Need for Gathering Feedback and Debriefing the Skill. In this case, students can use a checklist to check off each time their names were used during the group activity, like the one shown in Figure 7.7. An observer may collect the data. After the group has finished, the data can be shared and discussed. Students can then celebrate the progress they have made, if that is the case, or set realistic goals for the next time they work together. Figure 7.3 is a blackline master that can be used and adapted with groups to collect data and debrief the learning experience.

Figure 7.7. Reflecting on Our Group Work Together

Social skill we focused on: _____

We did a great job at: _____

Most of us: _____

We need to work on: _____

Personally, I need to work on: _____

In the space below, individuals sign and indicate what skill they will work on the next time the group is together.

Name _____   _____

Name _____   _____

Name _____   _____

Name _____   _____

Each member signs to show agreement with the information on the form.

WE AGREE _____ _____ _____ _____

Keeping Students on TASK Roles

Roles. To increase the possibility that students stay on task, roles can be assigned so that each member of the group has a role to perform that is necessary for the group to be successful and achieve their group goal. The following are some roles that can be assigned:

Encourager:	Encourages each member of the group
Questioner:	Asks questions to help the work proceed
Clarifier:	Uses language to ensure clarity and understanding
Summarizer:	Restates information for the group
Prompter:	Uses language to keep discussion moving
Gatekeeper:	Monitors the group process to include all members

The *book marks* shown in Figure 7.8 may be given to students so that they have some language to use when performing their roles.

Figure 7.8. Book Mark

Encourager	Questioner	Clarifier
Helpful language:	Helpful language:	Helpful language:
Great idea	Who could . . . ?	Is this what you meant?
Thanks for sharing	What's a first step?	Explain your idea to me. . .
What do you think?	How could we . . . ?	Say again . . .
Interesting idea	What's the best plan?	Did I hear . . . ?
Right on! . . . What else . . . ?	When can we . . . ?	I think you said . . .
Thank you . . .	Any ideas . . . ?	Do you mean . . . ?

Summarizer	Prompter	Gatekeeper
Helpful language:	Helpful language:	Helpful language:
I think we agree that . . .	Perhaps . . .	Whose turn is it?
Most of us said . . .	I think . . . I	Has everyone given an idea?
Some of us . . .	My idea . . .	We have ___ minutes left.
Others differ . . .	Suppose . . .	That's three done
It seems to me . . .	Another idea . . . ?	Let's check all the steps.
In summary . . .	Anyone else . . . ?	

Other roles that may be assigned are as follows:

Recorder: Takes notes or records ideas, completes necessary forms

Reader: Reads all directions to the group

Reporter: Reports out to the large group after the group activity

Materials Manager or "Go For": Gets supplies and resources and materials needed

Timekeeper: Keeps track of time to make sure the task is completed in the appropriate time

Researcher: Carries out research necessary for the task and reports back to the group

Liaison: Reports to the teacher on behalf of the group

Observer: Keeps track of the group's activities and collects data on how well the group is functioning and using the skills expected

In assigning roles, teachers need to know the students well enough to assign roles that will either capitalize on their strengths or provide practice in areas where they need to grow. For instance, one teacher assigned a student who often monopolized conversations an observer role, in which he focused on the group's interactions, but did not speak. After playing this role for several class periods, he was assigned a new role. At one point, he began to blurt out a comment, realized what he was doing, and placed his own hand over his mouth and ceased speaking out of turn! Sometimes students can select their roles from those suggested by the teacher or group. This ensures a comfort level and further develops a commitment to the task.

Sequence of Tasks. If each member of the group has an individual task to do within the group task, individuals feel needed and perceive that they are necessary members of the group. Tasks such as cutting, gluing, illustrating, researching, keyboarding, and editing may be assigned in the sequence they will occur during an activity. Sometimes students may rotate the tasks to give every member an opportunity to contribute at some time with each of the tasks.

Resources. To increase interdependence among the group members, the teacher can limit resources so that group members must share and rely on one another to make the learning experience successful. Resources such as texts, computer, scissors, readings, and paper are shared by the group to help them focus, collaborate, and complete the task.

Novelty. The brain loves novelty and intriguing situations. Sometimes the group task will lend itself to simulations in which students are asked to take on an identity as a "research team" or to assume a fantasy situation. They may take on the role of a real team that exists outside school. Problem-solving situations with scientists or environmentalists can be enticing for students. They may work in a real-world environment at the science or computer lab of a local business or industry. These simula-

tions often give students an understanding of how the learning is relevant in the real world and helps them explore career options.

Questions Frequently Asked

How Do We Group Students?

Students may be grouped for many reasons and in many ways. Sometimes, for quick activities, students are randomly grouped by just getting a partner of choice with whom they will work. Sometimes random grouping can be done by the teacher, using a counting-off technique. The following grouping techniques offer an array of options.

Counting-Off. Divide the number of students by the number of members you want in each group (e.g., 24 students divided by 3, which is 8). Have the students count off 1 to 8. Then tell all the 1s, 2s, 3s, and so on to form groups of three and to move to a place to work together.

Cards. Some teachers use cards with different information or stickers on them and distribute these to the class. Students then need to find other students whose cards go with theirs—for example, (a) find the cards that have the same math answer, 2 + 3, 1 + 4, 6 − 1; (b) find the cards that have the same color of dot or the same symbol or geometric shape, (c) find the other three pieces to form a complete comic strip, or (d) find the others who are singing or humming the same nursery rhyme, camp song, or popular tune.

Statistics. Another grouping strategy is to have students form a line around the room alphabetically or by birth dates. Students may be grouped by statistics based on similarities, such as those with birthdays in the same month, those of the same age, same color of eyes, same color of hair, same number of family members, same shoe size, or same height. This will take some preparation at the beginning of the semester. Teachers will need to give students a questionnaire to fill out and thus gather the relevant information. Engaging students in analyzing the data they have generated can be instructive, as well as fun.

Chairs. Chairs offer another creative way of grouping students. Colored yarn can be tied on the chairs, and students can be given a piece of colored yarn as they come in the door. Another approach is to assign numbers or names of animals, flowers, songs, places, or other things on the chairs. The labels used (e.g., numbers, animals, flowers) can be written on pieces of paper which students can pick out of a box as they enter the classroom. One advantage of handing students pieces of colored yarn is that teachers can be selective in how students are placed without the students being aware of this happening. The grouping is planned, but it appears random. Whenever possible, it is helpful to rotate the grouping strategy to the content of a lesson. One science

teacher used the following activity to group students and also introduce a lesson on the olfactory sense.

Smell Your Way to a Group. This is an excellent way to use up those 35-mm film canisters. Soak cotton balls with liquids of the same odor or scent and put each into a separate canister. If groups of four are needed, four canisters are used for each scent. Suggestions for scents are perfumes, peppermint, vanilla, pine, coffee, cough medicine, and rose petals. Be creative. Distribute the canisters to the class and then instruct students to locate others who have the same scent as theirs. That will be their working group. This activity is time-consuming to set up but well worth the effort as this strategy is always one of the students' favorites.

Assignments. Teachers hand students the assignments with a number or symbol already on them. Students are asked to find classmates with the identical number or symbol. Another way of doing this is to print the assignments on colored paper and then have students locate others with the same color of paper to form a group.

Name Tags. Place name tags on the tables where students are to be seated. Since some students are self-conscious about wearing name tags, names can be assigned that tie into the content of study. Examples include characters in a play or book, names of rocks and minerals, politicians, composers, artists, foods, muscles, bones, states, countries, theorems, greetings or statements in foreign languages, software names, and tools. Teachers who have used this approach suggest it is easiest and more affordable to use plastic name tag holders so that they can be reused.

Candy. Different types of wrapped candy may be used. Count out candy ahead of time, noting how many of each kind are needed for the number of groups. As students enter the room, give each a piece of candy. (Remember to tell students not to eat the candy just yet!) When the class is ready to start, tell students to find their group peers who have the same kind of candy. After this task, they may eat the candy.

Grouping Sticks. Some teachers use a wooden craft stick for each student. Each stick has a student's name and a different colored square, circle, and triangle. When sticks are given out, teachers can ask students to find the other three with the same color of triangle and to form a group. Another day, it may be partners with the same color of circle. This activity facilitates the quick formation of random groups.
Caution: As much fun as grouping creatively can be, more energy should be put into the planning of the learning experience than into the grouping experience. Select approaches that take a minimum of time to orchestrate so that as much time as possible can be allocated to the learning task.
If teachers want to develop truly heterogeneous groups based on varied ability, *team formation wheel,* developed by Sheila Silversides (in Kagan, 1992), can be used to ensure that teams consist of low-, middle-, and high-achieving students. Four circles of four sizes are attached in the center with a paper fastener so that they can rotate (see Figure

Figure 7.9. Team Formation Wheel

L =Low achieving student
M =Middle achieving student
H =High achieving student

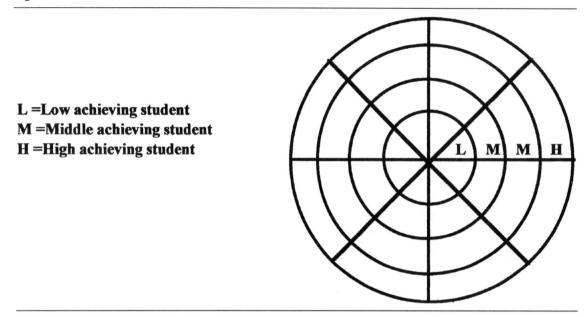

7.9). Circles can be rotated to create new teams with a balance of all three types of learners in each group of four.

How Do I Arrange the Room for Optimum Positive Interaction?

Students need to be "eye to eye" and "knee to knee" to facilitate dialogue when they are working in groups. It is much easier to make this happen if the tables and chairs are moved into various formations as groups need to change. It may be a chore for teachers to set up the room by themselves; however, students can be a great help in reorganizing the classroom. The teacher can display a room design on the overhead, and students can organize the room as the initial task of the day. If only desks are available, then desks need to be pulled together to get students in close proximity to complete a task successfully. To lessen the noise of rearranging, cut an X into tennis balls and slip them onto the legs of the desks like casters. In this way, desks can be slid into place quickly and quietly.

What Do We Do When Problems Arise?

A variety of problems can arise when students work in cooperative groups. Some of these are summarized below, along with suggestions for resolving these problems.

Conflicts. When students work together, conflicts are inevitable. Building in social skills, such as disagreeing in an agreeable way, may help head off some conflicts. Providing students with insights about why conflicts usually occur—more often than not from differences in wants and needs of individual group members—can also be

helpful. Formal training in conflict resolution can develop powerful social and emotional skills which will be valuable tools for a lifetime.

Tuning Out. Sometimes students seem not to be able to stay on task. Giving them a specific role may be helpful. Giving someone in the group the encourager role may help the unfocused student stay included. Reminding students of their interdependence may entice other students to tell the individual who has strayed how important he or she is to the group.

Overbearing Student. The teacher could ask the overbearing student to be the observer and to collect data during the process. Using a "talking stick" may help because the student can only talk when he or she has the stick. Some teachers give each student five poker chips. Every time they speak, they must give up a poker chip. After all a student's chips are gone, the student must simply observe and let other students have a turn to speak (Kagan, 1992).

Absent Student. The student who is absent may need a buddy to keep him or her informed or on track with the work missed. A class and/or team folder with copies of work missed may also be a resource. As technology availability increases, students can use e-mail and team Web sites to keep connected. Some teachers have students, on a rotating basis, use a laptop computer to take notes. These notes are provided to students who have been absent or to students who have physical challenges that make note taking difficult.

Teacher Collaboration. No matter what the problem is, no one answer is guaranteed to work. Each collaborative scenario and each student is unique. Thus, problem solving will involve trial and error. Other teachers who teach a particular student may be a good resource with additional strategies that may work for that individual. Many teachers who are implementing cooperative group learning can post their problems in faculty lounges or workrooms, and other teachers can brainstorm and make suggestions or share strategies that have worked for them in similar situations. As a faculty, this activity reinforces that "we are in this together" working for student success.

How Do We Grade?

To grade or not to grade, that is the question! Again, no one answer or rule about assigning grades applies when one uses cooperative group learning. Often, teachers can use cooperative group learning as the vehicle for learning and accomplishing standards and then evaluate individually with more traditional methods of evaluation, such as tests and quizzes, or on each student's individual portion of the group project.

Experience has taught many teachers that moving too quickly to a group grade before groups are functioning well or students and parents understand and appreciate the value of cooperative group learning can be a disaster that may cause resentment toward the strategy. Here are some questions teachers should ask themselves:

- Is there one group product?
- Is there an individual portion of the task?
- Is there a social skill to be given a grade?

It may not be necessary or even considered fair to assign a grade if the groups have just been formed and are just beginning to work together. Evaluation may not be necessary if the activity is simple and short lived. Checklists, observation forms, and reflections may be more appropriate to encourage students to set personal and team goals and plan strategies for improvement. In time, sharing grades will be more acceptable and probably reinforcing of the concept of collaboration when the product is a collective one and a true spirit of collaboration exists. Clear criteria and an understanding of how the grades will be given must be explained up front. Teachers may decide to use a combination of grading practices based on the standards targeted in the learning experience and the social skills students are working on.

Some possible combinations are listed below:

Grade for
- Group product
- Individual part of the product
- Test or quiz mark
- Demonstration
- Presentation

Grade for
- Academic product
- Social grade
- Individual role

Grade
- 30% for participation
- 35% group academic grade
- 35% individual academic score

Your own combination:
-
-

As teachers work at implementing cooperative groups, they start small with simple structures, building trust and developing teamwork skills. It is a new process for teacher and students, and it will take time to master processes and work through problems and issues. The planner shown in Figure 7.10 may be used in thinking

Figure 7.10. Planning a Lesson

This organizer may be helpful in helping teachers think about all the aspects of the cooperative lesson			

Standards	Content Objectives/Benchmarks

Academic activity	Social behavior
Assessment tool	Data/Feedback

Materials	Grouping	Roles	Accountability

Steps in lesson (directions, expectations)

- •
- •
- •

- •
- •
- •

Debriefing: Who? How?	Grading?

Robbins, P., Gregory, G., & Herndon, L. E. *Thinking Inside the Block Schedule: Strategies for Teaching in Extended Periods of Time.* Copyright Corwin Press, Inc.

through the decisions that need to be made when planning a cooperative group learning.

Behavioral Systems Family

The *behavioral systems family* is founded on the belief that humans thrive in situations where the task and the feedback are clear (Skinner, 1953). In any learning experience in which the expectations are outlined, the desired strategy is explained and modeled, and practices and feedback mechanisms are built in, learners will modify their behavior to move toward specific goals. Among the strategies discussed below, no doubt some will be familiar!

Direct Instruction

Direct instruction is probably best known with reference to Madeline Hunter and the 7-step lesson plan (Russell & Hunter, 1976). This approach has seven components:

1. Anticipatory or mental set
2. Sharing the purpose
3. Providing input
4. Demonstrating and modeling
5. Checking for understanding
6. Guided and perfect practice
7. Closure

During the *anticipatory or mental set*, students' minds are being prepared for the learning about to occur. This preparation sometimes involves accessing students' prior knowledge that will help them during the lesson, sharing the outcomes and intent of the lesson in a way that has meaning for the learners, and diagnosing what the students already know in relation to the intended lesson.

Next, during *sharing the purpose*, the teacher gives an overview of the lesson or unit so that students have a sense of security about the lesson's direction. Then, in *providing input*, the teacher provides information. This can be in a variety of forms: explanation, mini-lecture, video clip, or a reading. Following this, the teacher provides *demonstrating and modeling* of what students will be required to know or be able to do. At this point in the lesson, the teacher wants to be sure that students understand what has been taught. Typically, the teacher provides an opportunity for students to practice what has been modeled. As students engage in the task, the teacher monitors to *check for students' understanding*. If students appear to perform appropriately, additional *guided practice*, in which students practice under a teacher's guidance, may be assigned. If students demonstrate that they are having difficulty, however, the teacher may have to go back and reteach, model, or demonstrate.

Finally, at the end of the lesson for the component called *closure*, the teacher provides students with a task in which they have to demonstrate perfect practice or understanding of what has been taught. This may be in the form of a quiz, test, interview, performance, or development of a product. Independent practice follows, in which students practice newly learned skills and concepts on their own (the intent of this practice being to develop fluency and speed).

In the 7-step lesson plan, each component leads logically to the next. The pace of the lesson, however, is predicated on student performance. The decision to move from one step to the next is a function of feedback from students. In contrast with cooperative learning strategies, this approach tends to be much more teacher directed. The decision to use this approach will be a function of the content to be taught, standards for performance, student characteristics and styles, the learning environment, teacher beliefs, and behavior.

Lectures

Lectures have long been used as a vehicle for imparting information to students. Lectures generally have been a "pour and store" model of instruction in which the teacher talks and students listen. Lectures can be enriched, however, with a variety of techniques that help students focus their attention, that engage them in thinking, and that facilitate connections between new knowledge and prior learning.

Introducing the Lecture

Because emotion drives attention and attention drives learning, structuring the lecture so that students are engaged with the topic is essential. This may be accomplished by the following:

- Posing an intriguing question, challenge, or problem
- Telling a short story or personal anecdote
- Showing an interesting object or model
- Introducing a pertinent quotation
- Demonstrating something intriguing
- Engaging students in personal reflection or examining personal attitudes or preferences
- Playing a video clip

Once the lecture is introduced, the context can be created and the purpose explained. This provides valuable background information for students. Sharing the context and purpose helps enhance a lesson's meaning and promotes understanding of where a particular skill or concept might be applicable in the "real world."

Setting the Context and Purpose

The old adage "Tell them what you're going to tell them, tell them, and then tell them what you've told them" is useful to remember when designing a lecture—with one exception. At the end of the lesson, students, rather than the teacher, should summarize learnings because it is the students who need to practice or rehearse the content. Students need to see the "big picture," as well as the pieces that will be examined.

Teachers often provide students with an overview and the expected results of the lecture:

- What is going to be covered
- Where it fits with previously learned information
- Why it is relevant to the student
- How it may be useful in the real world

Using Organizers

To provide a context that maximizes learning for students, teachers can use organizers to help students sort and classify information and to make note taking meaningful, creative, and useful. Students may use the organizers during the lecture or as a check for understanding after the lecture has concluded.

Various organizers may be used. The window pane lecture, described below, provides an opportunity for students to take notes in window pane boxes during the lesson, and once the lecture has ended, they can re-create the content of the window panes to check their comprehension. Students can use words or symbols in each box under different headings to organize information. Figures 7.11 and 7.12 are blackline masters that provide a sample of two organizers that may be used. *Notes to Me* (Figure 7.11) lets students "dot jot" key items as they listen. *What's New About . . .* (Figure 7.12) can also be useful if information during the lecture lends itself to a format that addresses Who? What? When? Where? and Why? A fill-in-the-blanks format can also be designed to facilitate note taking during a lecture. This approach involves the teacher providing students with a handout in which they have an opportunity to fill in blanks within sentences. This approach focuses learner attention. Collectively, all the organizer strategies provide opportunities for students to be actively engaged in the lecture. This ingredient is sorely lacking in the traditional lecture. It may also explain why students remember more of what they have heard when they use the strategy. Active involvement through notetaking also engages all three sensory channels: auditory, visual, and kinesthetic. Hence, the approach addresses a wide variety of learners' styles.

Figure 7.11. Notes to Me

Topic: _____

Source: _____

-
-
-
-
-

Summary:

_____

_____

_____

Questions:

-
-
-

Figure 7.12. What's New About . . .

Topic or Issue: _____

Who?

What?

When?

Where?

Why?

So what . . . _____

_____

_____

Presenting the Lecture

Once the context and purpose are set and the learners are engaged (sometimes with a format for note taking), the teacher can proceed with presenting the lecture. The use of music to establish a mood, if appropriate, or of visuals, such as pictures, posters, charts, videos, and models, will enhance the lesson. The teacher usually conducts a task

analysis and decides on the order in which chunks of information will be presented to students. This type of presentation facilitates meaning making. Often, students connect prior learnings with new learnings as a result of this approach. Although many lectures take on a traditional structure, it is possible to add vitality to lectures by varying the approach. A few examples follow.

Window Pane Lecture. The teacher begins a lesson by drawing window panes or boxes on a transparency or flip chart. The number of panes will depend on the age of the learners, as discussed in Chapter 2, and the number of content chunks. Each box is labeled as content is presented. As the lecture unfolds, the teacher draws or posts graphics, symbols, words, or other images in each window pane to illustrate the point being made. After the lecture, the teacher removes the completed window pane and asks students to re-create the images in each pane (alone or with a partner), remembering the content associated with the image. After they have re-created the images, the original is displayed so that students can check themselves for accuracy and thoroughness. Students can compare their window pane images with the original, with content and sequence in mind. Teachers then can allow time at the end for students to take notes, add content, or pose questions should they desire.

Cartoon Lecture. It has often been said that "A picture is worth a thousand words." The cartoon lecture capitalizes on this saying. Teachers locate cartoons that communicate elements of the content to be presented. Then, cartoons are displayed as key points in the lecture are given verbally. After the lecture, the cartoons are displayed and the teacher asks individuals or small groups to "rehearse" the content that goes with each cartoon. In addition to the fact that visual images enhance memory, humor also contributes to long-term memory.

Cooperative Group Lecture. Some students take poor notes or none at all. Using a group strategy can improve student note taking. Following a lecture, students can compare their notes and, as a group, write a separate set of notes that have been used collaboratively by the group. These can also be shared with absent students. It functions as a review of the content of the lecture at the same time. Experiment with different note-taking approaches—for example, mind mapping, words, outlines, or split-page note taking (pictures on the left side and words on the right). Another technique is to have students be responsible for only one component of the lecture. Following a lecture, each student shares his or her notes with another member of the group. It can be emphasized that, during the time students do not have to take notes, they can practice listening skills. A third example of this strategy is to have students prepare a set of note cards for the group to use at a later date for review purposes.

Student Lecture. Teachers can assign a topic for groups of students to research. Each group prepares a transparency listing what they consider to be the 10 most important facts they learned. (The list can be shortened to five facts if time is restricted.) Each group shares their list with the class. Another option is to have student groups prepare

an outline of the topic to present to the class. Alternatively, the teacher could have student groups brainstorm, on flip chart paper, all they know about a topic before the lecture and then, after the lecture, have class members discuss the new knowledge and insights they now have.

Key Words Lecture. Sometimes teachers don't feel comfortable drawing, so another lecture approach engages students with key words. As teachers deliver a lecture, they write key words on a flip chart in window panes. Usually, no more than seven to nine words (remember those memory spaces) are used on a page. After the lecture, the teacher asks the learners to review by associating content that is connected to a particular word in a given space or window pane. Active processing is accomplished by asking students to recall the content of the key words lecture as they talk with a peer partner.

Draw and Learn Lecture. This approach engages students in drawing and labeling as a lecture unfolds. For example, students in a lesson about bones in the hand were invited to draw around their own hands. Then, as bones were introduced, the students identified their location, drew them in, and labeled them. Students compare their efforts with one another and reference the teacher's model for feedback and accuracy.

Fill-in-the-Blanks Lecture. One of a teacher's worst nightmares is to have students who say, "Been there, done that." To circumvent this nightmare, the teacher can ask students to work in small groups and list everything they know about the topic to be taught on a flip chart. Then, the class can review what has been generated. This is often done by inviting students first to take a walk around the room examining others' charts. After this, they are seated. The teacher then highlights key points by using a yellow marker to note main ideas on the student-generated charts. Any misconceptions can be corrected during this time as well. The teacher's lecture then fills in the blanks with missing information or concepts the group needs to complete the mental picture of the lecture content. After the lecture, students are invited to form pairs and "process" what they have learned by summarizing it for their pair partners. The next step is to invite students to generate new questions they would like to pursue.

Processing Time During Lectures. As the lecture variations imply, it is important to intersperse content with active processing time for students. Mary Budd Rowe (1987) suggests that a "10 and 2" rule be considered; that is, teachers give information for about 10 minutes and then allow students processing time for 2 to 3 minutes so that discussion and questions can emerge. At this point, questions can be answered and concepts clarified before misconceptions develop and are remembered. Students may use a variety of strategies to process the content and concepts introduced or reviewed in the lecture, such as pair partners, collaborative corners, or some of the other approaches addressed in Chapter 8, on active learning. Often, students are invited to apply the information or concepts from the lecture to a real-world situation or a creative task that would facilitate deep understanding and long-term retention.

Simulations

Simulations mimic real-world situations and are important learning approaches that give students a context and vehicle to make sense of new concepts and information. The process has four steps:

1. The teacher presents the topic and concepts to be explored, as well as a brief overview of what a simulation is.
2. The teacher gets students involved in the simulation by giving the procedures, rules, roles, scoring, or goals of the simulation.
3. Students actually work through the simulation, with the teacher as monitor and facilitator giving feedback and stopping periodically to evaluate and reflect on the process.
4. The teacher debriefs, and students apply learnings from the simulation.

Examples might include a courtroom scene to explore an academic controversy or an understanding of the law of supply and demand through a warehouse inventory simulation. In one parenting class, students were given 10-pound bags of flour that were to be their "little bundles of joy." Students working in pairs (parents) gave the flour sack facial features and dressed it as a baby. They were told that they must look after the "baby" for a week and record their interactions, the care given, and related feelings associated with caring for the child. Students also had to provide baby-sitters, and the infants were to be fed, bathed, and played with appropriately. After the week, students shared their journals and reflected on the commitment and patience needed to provide for these helpless babies. This simulation was instrumental in showing students firsthand the responsibilities involved in caring for an infant that reading from a textbook couldn't possibility convey.

Summary

Teaching in extended periods of instructional time provides both opportunities and challenges for the professional in the classroom. The opportunity is to foster deep understanding of skills, concepts, and habits of mind, such as critical thinking and creative thinking. The challenge, of course, is to maintain student interest, attention, and enthusiasm. As teachers focus on helping diverse learners be successful in attaining the skills and competencies they need for their future, they realize the need for an increased instructional repertoire. Learning new strategies and then selecting the appropriate one in relation to the learning standards that have been targeted is developed through practice and reflection. Having a repertoire of approaches from which to draw, such as the models discussed in this chapter, will help address this challenge successfully.

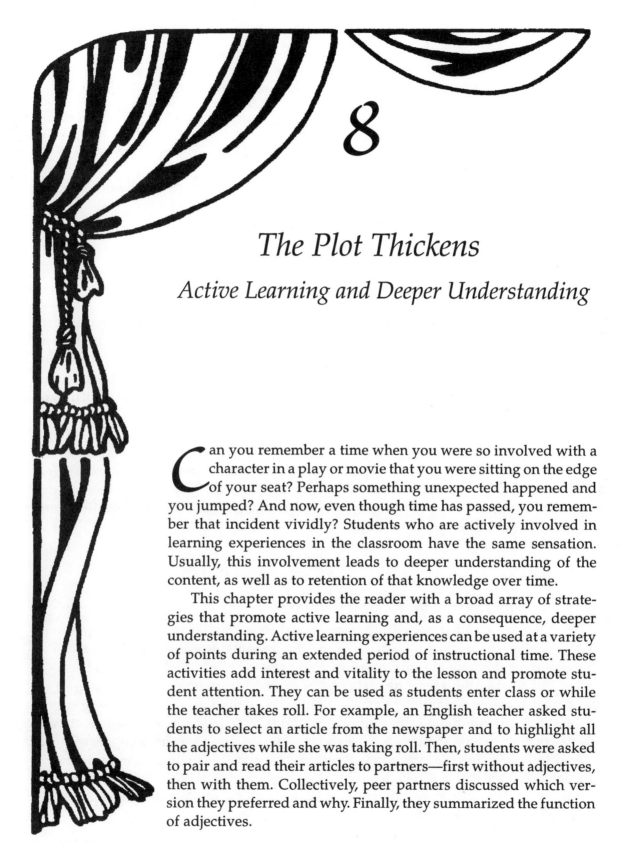

8

The Plot Thickens

Active Learning and Deeper Understanding

Can you remember a time when you were so involved with a character in a play or movie that you were sitting on the edge of your seat? Perhaps something unexpected happened and you jumped? And now, even though time has passed, you remember that incident vividly? Students who are actively involved in learning experiences in the classroom have the same sensation. Usually, this involvement leads to deeper understanding of the content, as well as to retention of that knowledge over time.

This chapter provides the reader with a broad array of strategies that promote active learning and, as a consequence, deeper understanding. Active learning experiences can be used at a variety of points during an extended period of instructional time. These activities add interest and vitality to the lesson and promote student attention. They can be used as students enter class or while the teacher takes roll. For example, an English teacher asked students to select an article from the newspaper and to highlight all the adjectives while she was taking roll. Then, students were asked to pair and read their articles to partners—first without adjectives, then with them. Collectively, peer partners discussed which version they preferred and why. Finally, they summarized the function of adjectives.

Active learning experiences can also be used during instruction. For example, one teacher handed transparencies and transparency pens to each group of learners. Students were asked to summarize with graphics, pictures, or words that portion of the lesson just delivered. Following this, individual group members presented their transparencies to the class.

Active learning experiences can also be used after content has been taught. For instance, in one classroom a teacher used a carousel brainstorming activity to determine what students were taking away from a lesson. *Carousel brainstorming* works in the following way:

1. The teacher posts flip chart paper in four to six places on a wall. (Consider putting up double sheets so that the marking pens don't bleed through the paper.)
2. The teacher numbers the pages 1 through 4, 5, or 6.
3. The teacher hangs different-colored pens by each paper.
4. The teacher writes a topic on each sheet of paper. For example, after a unit on Japan, one topic might be culture; another, key historical events; another, foods; and so on.
5. Class members number off, 1 through 4, 5, or 6, depending on the number of charts hung on the wall.
6. Students go to the chart that matches the number they have been assigned.
7. At the chart, students brainstorm what they recall that relates to the topic on their chart.
8. After a few minutes, students rotate to the next chart, taking their pens with them. Thus, individuals in front of Chart 1 would move as a group to Chart 2; those in front of Chart 2 to Chart 3; and so on.
9. At the new chart, students review what has been written on it already and then add on with their colored marker.
10. After each group has spent time at every chart, as evidenced by the multicolored writing, students take their notebooks with them as they walk around the room. As they walk, they examine the written contributions on each chart and take notes about that which they wish to remember.

As review activities, active learning experiences may be something like *shaping up a review.* With this strategy, students are asked to form groups of four. Each group is told to draw a square, a circle, and a triangle on a sheet of paper. On the square, they are to reflect on things they said, did, saw, or heard in the previous lesson that "squared" or fit with their beliefs. On the circle, they are to write questions "still going around in their heads" about the lesson content. On the triangle, they are to write three points they want to remember about the lesson. Groups may be asked to share with other groups what they have written on their shapes. The teacher collects the circle questions and addresses these in class. Sometimes these student-generated questions

show up on exams with a circle next to them to remind students that this student-generated question was addressed in class.

Another review technique that engages students in active learning is to have them create a rap, song, or poem to remind them of what they have learned. Because the brain is a pattern-seeking organ and likes rhyme and rhythm, this approach often makes content more memorable. At other times, a teacher may request students to summarize their learnings on index cards. These cards are their "tickets" out of the classroom door!

Active learning experiences can be devised as a part of homework. One teacher used a cooperative strategy called *divide and conquer.* For this strategy, students were assigned an integrated science and technology project for homework. They were asked to form groups of four and, within the groups, to count off from 1 to 4. The topic of study was the rain forest. Student 1 was to use the Internet and other sources to learn all she or he could about inhabitants of the rain forest. Student 2 was to research predators. Student 3 was to research products of the rain forest. Student 4 was to research the future of the rain forest. After they completed this homework, each group met around a piece of flip chart paper. They divided the paper into four sections. Each student filled in a section with the information she or he had researched. Then, students cut apart their sections. Students who had researched the same topic—for example, rain forest inhabitants—met across groups. They shared information they had gathered and added to their individual sections. After this was done, they returned to their original foursomes, discussed their individual contributions, and taped their sections back together. Finally, the completed flip charts were posted on the classroom walls, and students walked around and examined one another's work.

The active learning examples discussed so far often include physical movement. Medical professionals often comment that the tailbones of students who are of middle school and high school age are frequently still developing. This is one reason why, at times, these students have difficulty sitting or have been described by teachers as "wiggly"! Movement is a natural part of how students learn. Their curiosity and innate desire to discover makes them active learners by nature. More passive, older adolescents will remark that movement "perks them up" or "gets the oxygen going." Hence, including active learning experiences that involve movement is an important consideration in lesson design. Movement can also diminish stress and vitalize, in that it provides a refreshing change of pace for the learner, as well as increases oxygen levels in the brain.

Decisions about which active learning strategies to include in which part of a lesson are, of course, up to the teacher. Many teachers have referred to this part of decision making as the "orchestration of strategies," pointing out that it is important to consider a balance of passive-receptive, active and reflective strategies, as well as the *primacy-recency effect* (the mind remembers best what comes first, and next best what comes last), which suggests that a lesson optimally will have several "firsts and lasts" within an extended period of instructional time. Putting these ideas together, one teacher first had students in her French class listen to directions for a task in which they were to design clothing advertisements (passive-receptive). Second, they helped the teacher

construct a rubric to be used in grading. Then, students created advertisements by using construction paper, glitter, markers, and, of course, applied French phrases (active learning). After the advertisements were posted, the students walked around the classroom gallery and voted for their favorite creations (active learning). Finally, students returned to their seats and responded to three reflective questions in French in their journals: (a) What characteristics of the creation you voted for made it special? (b) What attributes did all creations appear to have in common? (c) What did you learn as a consequence of this activity? (reflective involvement).

Some teachers orchestrate learning in their classrooms by setting up activity centers, each with a different focus related to a common theme and each requiring the student to perform a different kind of activity. One social studies teacher set up six centers or stations. Station 1 engaged students in pairs, working at a computer. Their task was to examine the topography of a country, taking careful notes and using a note-taking guide. Station 2 engaged students in applying their learnings from Station 1 and creating a map. Station 3 involved students in reading short stories and examining artifacts and pictures to learn about the people of the country, demographics, and the culture. Station 4 provided a video-viewing experience with a graphic organizer video analysis assignment. At Station 5, students created a Venn diagram in which they compared the country and its people they studied with their own country and its people. Station 6 invited students to act out a simulation in which they role-played the family life that was typical of the people they had studied. At the end of the station activities, students wrote in their learning logs about what they had learned and which activities had been their favorites.

In one high school, the choir, band, and physical education teachers worked together. They engaged students in planning a production, including creating a script and designing choreography to accompany the music. This multi-class-period unit culminated in a "show choir" performing for the entire student body at an important assembly.

The following list of active learning strategies provides a menu of options from which to select when designing lessons for extended periods of instructional time.

Think Pair Share. Students are asked to think about an issue. Following this, they pair with a colleague and share their collective thoughts.

Write Pair Share. Students respond in writing to a reflective question. Then they pair with another student and share what they have each written.

Write a Commercial. This task requires students to summarize what they have learned in class by writing a television or radio commercial for it.

Dramatization. Students dress up and dramatize a situation they have studied in order to glean key understandings.

1-2-4 Activity. Each student first does a task alone, such as reading one of several quotes. Then, each student pairs with someone else, and the two discuss their interpre-

tations of the quote as they read. As a pair, they then meet with another pair of students and, as a foursome, discuss their collective reactions, reflections, and interpretations of their readings.

Reciprocal Teaching. After a section of content has been presented, students form groups of two by counting off by As and Bs. Each A reviews or teaches B the first part of what was presented by the teacher, providing explanations or sketches to enhance the dialogue. Each B summarizes for A the second portion of what was read. Then, collectively, the two fill in any "blanks" that either one had omitted. This strategy is also referred to as *each one teach one.*

Walk-About Review. The teacher constructs a worksheet (see Figure 8.1) that has prompts to respond to and places where students can write their comments. Students walk around the room and gather data from their colleagues, who sign this form and write about key points, insights, or implications regarding a lesson.

Figure 8.1. Sample Worksheet for Walk-About Review

Key Points:			
	Name:	Name:	Name:
Insights:			
	Name:	Name:	Name:
Implications:			
	Name:	Name:	Name:

Talk Walk. This strategy engages students in taking a walk, guided by the teacher, with a specific focus in mind. A math teacher, for example, asked students to create a formula to depict the relationship between the height of the flagpole and the shadow it cast on the blacktop. Another teacher took her students on an "induction outing" during which they gathered data about the neighborhood that surrounded the school. After they returned to class, they wrote about their findings.

Book of Problems/Stories/Art/Musical Compositions. After students have completed a unit of study, they can create class books of individual contributions representing culminating works. For instance, a math teacher had students make math problems about objects in the environment surrounding the school. Here's one problem contributed by a student: "Look at the tree at the corner of Seventh Street and Vine. Identify what types of angles its branches form." An art teacher had each student select a favorite charcoal sketch, and students created a class volume entitled *Masterpieces in Black, White, and Gray.* A music teacher had each of the students select a favorite score they had composed, and the class published this as a volume titled *Shake, Rattle, and*

We're on a Roll! One language arts class published a collection of short stories and poems entitled *Reflections.*

Clock Partners. Each student is given a handout with the face of a clock. Next to each hour are lines. Students invite 12 colleagues to become "clock partners" by signing on a line. If Sharon signs Betsy's 2:00 line, Betsy will be Sharon's 2:00 partner, for example. When a teacher wants students to dialogue about what they have just studied, she might say, "Get out your clock appointments and meet with the 2:00 person."

Baseball Teammates. Similar to the clock partner strategy, each class member gets a sheet of paper with a baseball diamond drawn on it, and students sign one another's first, second, third and home plate spots. Later, the teacher uses these sheets as a tool to inspire partner dialogue.

Experiments. As the name suggests, students either respond to teacher-designed experiments or create experiments they conduct or have their classmates complete. One science teacher asked students to predict the order of how eight different liquids (shampoo, mouthwash, baby oil, cranberry juice, hand lotion, motor oil, syrup, and liquid laundry detergent) would layer in a test tube. A math teacher created color wheels with a spinner and gave students problems about probability; for example, out of 10 spins, how many times will the spinner point to red? Students had to create a bar graph to depict their results.

Investigations. The teacher presents students with data that require them to read, analyze, inquire, research and summarize.

Create a Model. As the name implies, students are invited to construct models to depict their understandings of concepts. For instance, one teacher had students build DNA models.

Crossword Puzzles. Puzzles provide a gamelike way to review content and vocabulary. Several software programs create crossword puzzles specific to a desired content area and related vocabulary.

Graphic Organizers. These are tools that enable students to visually depict information about content, relationships, or events. They can range from simple to complex. For example, a *T chart* can be used to represent strengths or weaknesses of an argument given in the course of a debate. A *Y chart* can be used to describe what an individual demonstrating perseverance might look like, sound like, or feel like. Graphic organizers can visually display *sequence.* For example, | | | | | | might be used to chronicle a series of events leading to the Civil War. Or, a *descriptive pattern* could be used to organize facts or characteristics associated with a particular person, place, event, or thing. In this case, one might draw a circle with spokes that had circles at each end in which to note details.

Cause and effect patterns may be represented visually with a rectangle and supporting details in rectangles beneath the generalization. *Problems and their solutions* might be illustrated by an oval in which the problem is described and, under the oval, an array of possible solutions is presented, each in an oval connected to the problem oval.

Dice Toss. Each small group of students is given a die and a blank sheet of paper. Following a teaching episode, students are invited to toss their die. If it lands on one spot, students must *describe* what they have just learned. Two spots means they must *compare* what they have just learned with something else. Three spots invites students to *associate* the new learning with past experiences. Four spots indicates students must *analyze* what they have learned. Five spots suggests it's now time to *apply* the learning to a real-world situation. Six spots indicates the learners must *argue for or against something.* On the paper, students record their responses to the toss of the die.

Sitters and Movers. This strategy requires two rows of chairs to be set up, each facing the other. In a classroom, a teacher with a class of 30 students might have three groups of 10 chairs. Within each group, five chairs would be facing another five. One row of five in each group is labeled "sitters"; one row is labeled "movers." All students make up questions (and are knowledgeable about the answers) for content they have learned. In Round 1, the movers ask their questions of the sitters facing them. They listen to, prompt, and verify sitters' responses. Then, the movers rotate one seat in line so that the person in the first chair is now in the fifth and so on. After all five movers have rotated through the five chairs, they become the sitters and the former sitters become the movers and ask their questions. This strategy builds physical movement into review.

Learning Journals. Learning journals or learning logs provide a central place for students to record summaries of lessons, insights, or results of experiments or investigations. They are usually ongoing, used throughout a semester, or in some cases an entire year. Some brain researchers believe that writing activities can actually foster new neural connections! Learning journal forms can include K-W-L, writing prompts, prediction-observation-conclusion, poems, reflections, haiku, notes, illustrations, graphic organizers, songs, raps, pictures, and words. Often, the teacher comments on students' writings in these logs. At other times, students may exchange journals and share reactions to one another's thoughts.

Relays. These provide opportunities for students to line up in several lines, perhaps six lines of 5 for a class of 30 students, to conduct a particular task. In physical education, it may be practice dribbling a basketball. In mathematics, perhaps it's a problem on the chalkboard. In language arts, it may be constructing a cumulative sentence. In social studies, it may be creating a list of events leading up to World War II.

Song, Rap, Rhyme. Students can internalize learnings by constructing songs, raps, or rhymes to remember key concepts.

Listening Posts. Topics are posted around the room as "listening posts." Students go to the topic area of their choice. (If more than five students are at a post, the "overflow" must make a second choice.) Students at a post discuss the topic and, on butcher paper, summarize their discussion. Each listening post group is responsible for a 1-minute report out.

Standing Diagram. This strategy provides a visual representation of class responses. Perhaps the teacher makes a statement. Students who agree stand; those who disagree remain seated. Each group must explain their position.

Wallpaper Task. Paper is posted around the room. Markers (purchase the brands that don't bleed through the paper) are placed by each sheet of paper. Students group themselves around the papers (usually three or four students in a group) and create a sheet of wallpaper that summarizes key learnings.

Role Play. This technique allows students to practice skills in realistic situations and to get feedback on their performance. At first, when students are unfamiliar with role playing, the teacher may provide a script so that students experience the language intended to be appropriate (e.g., when students are practicing social skills, such as encouraging). In time, students may create their own scripts. Students who are observing the role playing are taught what it looks like and sounds like to be a good audience member. They are instructed in how to offer nonjudgmental, descriptive feedback. Scenarios are described before the role playing begins so that those who are role playing, as well as those in the audience, understand "the content" of the situations. After the role play, all learners debrief insights, understandings, and reflections that have evolved as a result of the activity.

Debates. In this strategy, the teacher or a student states an issue. Students choose to argue for or against it. One teacher brought in an article from a local newspaper and said, "The headline of this article reads 'In Some Homes the Toilet Seat Is a Cleaner Place to Eat Than the Kitchen Counter!' " Students on the two sides conducted research to substantiate their positions and prepared oral arguments. Then, they conducted the debate. After the debate, the class analyzed the strengths of each side's arguments and celebrated specific aspects of the performances of both sides.

Collect and Classify. This strategy requires students to collect artifacts or information and to classify the items or data by a given or constructed system of classification. Groups of students report out regarding the categories they have identified.

Log and Predict. This technique is often used to collect and log information and to make predictions as a consequence of studying the information. For instance, in one class, students logged details about weather and then made weather predictions.

Cartoon Commentaries. Cartoons are presented to students. After examining these, students write an explanation of why the cartoon is humorous. In another version of

this activity, students are provided with cartoon pictures that have empty speech balloons. Students write their own text within the balloons. One social studies teacher required students to bring in political cartoons and explain why they were intended to be funny.

Virtual Field Trips. With many schools now having access to technology, students in several classrooms have had access to virtual field trips—experiences that take them to places thousands of miles away. Virtual experiments are also available, such as dissecting a frog, in which the student uses the computer's mouse to conduct a dissection and gets feedback about her or his approach.

Many times, the lesson itself provides for active learning, such as the teacher who asked students to redesign the school parking lot to accommodate two additional cars, given a list of specifications. Students had to create a blueprint to show their work. An English teacher asked students, in pairs, to draw one slip of paper from each of four boxes labeled "character," "setting," "problem," and "solution." Each pair had to create a story based on the character, setting, problem, or solution they drew. For example, one pair drew "father," "outer space," "lost," and "compass." After stories were written, they were critiqued by other partner pairs, strengthened, and illustrated. Finally, a class book was created.

Summary

In summary, as one reflects on the many active learning experiences possible to provide students, an awareness emerges of how some strategies address the auditory learner (e.g., see Harmin, 1993, 1994), and others the visual or kinesthetic learner. It is also possible to think about the approaches from the perspective of multiple intelligences. The strategies presented herein addressed verbal-linguistic, logical-mathematical, visual-spatial, bodily-kinesthetic, musical-rhythmic, interpersonal, intrapersonal, and naturalist learners. Still another way of examining active learning is with the lens that focuses on the thinking required to perform the task. Many educators refer to this framework as *Bloom's taxonomy.* Some activities dealt with knowledge acquisition, others with comprehension, application, analysis, synthesis, or evaluation. All these strategies for active learning have in common the opportunity for students to examine, revisit, practice, and rehearse content.

Although it is impossible to individualize for every learner over the course of an extended period of instructional time, when activities are varied, selected with levels of thinking, processing channels, and multiple intelligences in mind, more learners can be reached. In the process, enthusiasm for content is generated, energy is created, and deeper understanding is fostered as a result of active engagement.

Technical Staging

Using Technology to Enhance Learning

Classroom technology is neither the play nor the cast of characters. Technology provides the stage for the performance, the costumes, the lighting, and the sound that can give life and relevancy to the performance. Technology is a tool that, when used effectively, can increase student motivation, engage students in active participation, increase student responsibility for their own learning, and increase student performance.

Today's graduates will be entering a technological workplace that will require them to think. Society is experiencing rapid technological changes while educational institutions are having difficulty keeping up. The potential of technology to enhance learning in many ways has yet to be tapped. Some schools that use block schedules have found that the extended class periods provide an increased opportunity to integrate technology into the curriculum. The longer preparation time affords teachers the time to prepare interactive lecture outlines by using presentation software, to plan to implement project-based learning, and to increase their personal use of technology as a management tool. Students benefit by having longer periods of time to work on individual or group projects. For these reasons, this chapter addresses the questions: What is technology? Why use technology in the classroom? How can a teacher effectively implement technology in the classroom? and What new responsibilities does technology place on the classroom teacher?

Technology Defined

Technology is the practical application of knowledge in a particular area (*Merriam-Webster's Collegiate Dictionary*, 1998, p. 1210). For the purpose of education, technology could be defined as a mechanical or electrical device that may be used in the learning process, educational administration, curriculum development, and staff development. Technology is not a finite tool; it is constantly evolving. Teachers' first use of technology may have been a stylus that evolved to the quill pen, to the fountain pen, and to the ballpoint pen. Teachers' first experience with electrical technology could have been a record player, which later was accompanied by filmstrips. Films and 35-mm slides shown by using a projector followed this. Television brought about the video cassette recorder, and teachers began using videotapes during instruction; this has now become integrated with the use of multimedia technology. Some examples of current technologies that may be seen in classrooms include overhead projectors, computer-delivered instruction, computerized tutorials, electronic mail, the Internet, videoconferencing, videos, databases and spreadsheets, electronic portfolios, and multimedia presentations by students.

Reasons for Using Technology in the Classroom

As technology advances, the need for teachers to make the best use of these new tools requires a paradigm shift from the traditional methods of instruction to a student-centered approach. As schools moved from traditional schedules to block schedules, some teachers found that reforming instruction was inevitable. Research shows a relationship between educational reform and using a range of instructional technologies (Means, 1994). Samples of educational reform features are heterogeneous grouping, interactive modes of instruction, student exploration, collaborative work, the teacher's role as a facilitator, authentic and multidisciplinary tasks, and performance-based assessment. Implementing technology can help make the transformation from the traditional classroom to one that uses a constructivist model. In this context, students take charge of their own learning and learn to think critically while they work in collaboration. Many of these reform features are discussed throughout this book.

Technology provides many new opportunities for students. Means (1994) states, "Reformers argue that all students should have the opportunity to practice *advance skills* within the context of tasks that are personally meaningful and challenging to students" (p. 6). Means continues by saying, "The fact that the tasks will be more complex suggests that longer blocks of time will be required to work on them, again conflicting with the notion of fixed, short periods of time for distinct subject areas" (p. 6).

Block schedules provide longer time periods for teachers to collaborate on planning interdisciplinary activities that integrate technology. When students engage in complex tasks using technology, their role changes from passive learner to active learner. After

block schedule implementation, some teachers found that using technology affected students in many ways. Students were observed spending more time on task, their motivation toward learning increased, they showed more pride in their work, and their computer skills increased, as did overall student performance. Teachers found that they were no longer the center of attention but adopted a new role as facilitator, in which they would move from group to group, suggesting ways to increase the students' search for knowledge, guiding students to new resources, checking timelines, and monitoring student progress.

Technology can have a positive impact on teachers in many ways. The ultimate benefactor of this is the student. Some teachers increased their use of technology in both classroom instruction and classroom management. Also, teachers are creating lessons by using current information, as well as by increasing communication between school and home. Increase of teacher collaboration within schools is one of many benefits of technology integration. The following list of reasons to use technology is derived from those teachers who have successfully integrated technology. The list is written with the student perspective in mind. Technology

- Develops higher level thinking by using technology software designed to teach problem-solving skills
- Increases student responsibilities by requiring them to take charge of their own learning through direct exploration and expression
- Engages students in meaningful authentic tasks
- Promotes student learning
- Creates more opportunities for students to develop multiple intelligences: bodily-kinesthetic, verbal-linguistic, interpersonal, intrapersonal, musical, visual-spatial, logical-mathematical, and naturalistic
- Increases student motivation; students demonstrate more perserverance in solving problems
- Increases collaboration among students as a consequence of cooperate work and peer tutoring
- Increases student self-esteem fostered by student success
- Provides more opportunities to display student work
- Increases students' computer skills and prepares students for the real world
- Increases student use of outside resources
- Provides students with a medium to integrate subject areas
- Exposes students to another learning method when teachers facilitate, rather than direct, instruction
- Increases student achievement when it is implemented appropriately

Those teachers who integrate technology into the curriculum will reap the rewards of their efforts for themselves and their students.

Integrating Technology Into the Curriculum

Technology is a component of education that requires considerable planning. For those teachers who are just beginning to use technology, the North Central Regional Educational Laboratory (NCREL) has available on-line a teacher's guide designed to help classroom teachers integrate technology into daily practices (McNabb, 1999). The teacher's guide, *Technology Connections for School Improvement*, can be downloaded at Web site *http://www.ncrel.org*.

Classroom teachers need to address many considerations as they plan for technology integration. Like any good tool, its use is only as good as the user. Effective teachers are organized and develop quality lesson plans that align with curriculum content standards. Technology use must be planned in alignment with both school improvement plans and content standards. Technology planning also requires the teacher to ask—and answer—the following questions:

- Does the plan take into account any district "acceptable use guidelines"?
- What equipment is available and how often?
- How proficient am I in using technology?
- To what extent are my students proficient in using technology?
- How much time do students need to complete the activity being planned?
- How do I know that the technology chosen is effective and of good quality?

Answering these types of questions can be mind-boggling to teachers just beginning to use technology. The vast amount of products and information available can be overwhelming. Teachers need to be selective in the beginning. They need to work with the technology with which they are comfortable. Figure 9.1 lists examples of technologies used by students and teachers.

Figure 9.1. Examples of Educational Technologies for Student and Teacher Use

Type	Uses	Description	Student use?	Teacher use?
Videodisc Laser disc Instructional television	Tutorial information Reinforcement Enrichment Video recording and editing equipment	Provides information in a visual format. Uses narrative that includes graphics and demonstrations.	Yes	Yes
MICROCOMPUTERS				
Computer-assisted technology	Tutorial Drill and practice Reinforcement	Requires students to answer questions and solve problems.	Yes	No
Software applications	Word processing Spreadsheets and databases Desktop publishing	Is a general-purpose technology for composition, data storage, retrieval, and analysis.		
Internet	Exploration Multimedia projects Displaying student work Posting Web pages Professional development Research Communication	Is an international network of information networks connecting millions of users around the world.	Yes	Yes
Satellites and cable systems	Distance learning	Provides interactive transmission of televised instruction from distant locations.	Yes	Yes

Often, integrating technology increases responsibilities for the teachers to manage their own staff development. Many school districts have "acceptable use guidelines" that teachers and students must follow. Some school districts employ technology personnel who are responsible for installation of software, copyrights, and licensure of software. At times, this responsibility is bestowed on the classroom teacher. Teachers can use software inventory sheets (see sample in Figure 9.2; a blank blackline master for this inventory is in Robbins & Herndon, 1998) as an effective means to document details of software installed on a classroom computer. Listed next are tips from teachers who have integrated technology:

Figure 9.2. Sample Software Inventory

Title	Description	Media type	Application	License
Screen Doors ABC	Version 1.5. operating system came installed on computer	CD-ROM of program	Runs the computer	1234-OEM-9876 For one computer
Clarence Words	Version 8.3 came installed on computer	CD-ROM of program	Word processing program	CW99-8.5-XYZ9876 For one computer
Graph, Paint and Draw	Version 4.0 purchased by district	CD-ROM of program	Creates graphs, organization charts, limited free-form painting	GPD-88775 For up to 3 PCs
State Maps	Version 1.0 Personal copy	Floppy disk	Simple program with state outline maps only	M1357 For one PC
Grading Matrix	No version listed 8/31/99 Provided by district	Floppy disk	For end-of-term grades and parental reports	Created by district for all school-related use

- *Survey students to determine their computer skills.* Students come to the classroom with varying degrees of computer experience. Survey results are helpful in determining the type of activity to assign students so that they can apply computer skills in meaningful ways. The survey may include questions like "Do you have access to a computer after school?" or "Do you know how to save a document onto a diskette?" or "Have you ever used the Internet?" The questions should be framed around the skills students need to complete the activities planned.
- *Use survey results to assign project groups.* By building groups with prior knowledge of their computer skills, the opportunity for peer tutoring naturally augments the group learning process.
- *Use survey results to assign "tech buddies."* Pairing students who are more technologically advanced with those who are less experienced can be very effective.
- *Start simply.* Use only the technologies with which you are most comfortable. Integrate them with a lesson that has been successful in the past.
- *Identify which technology skill students will need to complete the assignments.* An example is basic word processing and insertion of a graphic or picture.
- *Evaluate carefully each lesson in which technology is used.* Document what worked well and what did not. Think of any revisions that could be made for future use.
- *Draw diagrams showing how to connect equipment correctly.* Laminate them. These can be very useful when equipment has to be moved.

- *Collaborate with other teachers whenever possible.* Block schedules often create more common planning times for those teachers who teach the same courses. Teachers can take advantage of this and use the time to plan projects that authentically use technology.
- *Back up all work.* If the computer fails for any reason, stored information may be lost. Back up or copy any data or projects you do not want to re-create from scratch. Some school districts let teachers back up their work onto a server. If this is not an option, use diskettes or an external hard drive.

At times, teachers find it necessary to incorporate teaching computer skills directly into the curriculum. By letting the curriculum drive the technology, some teachers will use content to teach the computer skills they believe are necessary. An example of how this process works is a single-page individual project on a topic related to weather. The skills identified would be word processing and inserting a picture, object, or clip art. The teacher has these skills, and tech buddies can assist students who have yet to develop this skill. For this one-page individual project, each student is assigned a topic related to weather, such as clouds, hurricanes, tornadoes, hydrologic cycle, fronts, and air masses. Students research their topics with references available in the classroom. Each student uses the computer to write a paragraph discussing his or her assigned topic. The teacher may give specific directions—for example, to use a specific font and size for the paragraphs; to give their work titles, which have to be centered, boldfaced, and in a larger size font than the main body of text; to insert an object such as a graph, clip art, or picture that relates to the assigned topics. Students later would share their one pagers as preparation for a test. Teachers can use a computer interfaced with a television monitor to demonstrate easily to all students the processes required of this activity.

Presentation Software and Visual Aids

Both teacher and students can use presentation software and visual aids. Using presentation software as a delivery system can be very effective in the classroom setting. Many good user-friendly, easy-to-use products are available. Some teachers using a block schedule create mini-lectures with built-in questions that allow students to reflect on their learning. A well-planned presentation can assist teachers with pacing, which is more crucial when teaching in schedules that have extended periods of time.

Students today watch a great deal of television. Showing key points of a lecture on a television monitor connected to a computer will more likely hold students' attention. Many products on the market now enable the computer screen to be projected onto a white screen. For example, a liquid crystal display (LCD) panel can be placed on the surface of an overhead projector and connected to a computer; the result is the image displayed onto a white screen. Some teachers have found that, while using these technologies, students were more attentive, increased their amount of note taking, and

entered class discussion more freely than while using the traditional chalkboard or overhead.

Good presentations need careful planning and should not distract from the content by incorrect use of visuals and effects. Students will soon lose focus if they cannot see or understand the visuals. As teachers create their presentations, they should take into account the physical aspects of the classroom. For example, they should be aware of the lighting, the size of the room, and the distance the students would be seated from the screen. The following are tips for creating readable visuals:

- Do not overcrowd visuals.
- Show the major points only; avoid excessive text.
- Try to use six lines per visual and six words per line.
- Make sure effects and transitions are consistent; too many changes will distract students from the content of the presentation.
- Keep backgrounds simple; if using dark backgrounds, use light-colored text, such as white or yellow.
- Avoid certain color combinations: Red and green together has a tendency to vibrate; blue on black can appear fuzzy.
- Use color consistently; try to match the same concept with the same color.
- Resist the temptation to use bright colors; red, green, or orange may be used for emphasis to highlight points by circling or underlining.
- Choose fonts that are easy to read, such as Helvetica, Arial, and Times Roman.
- Avoid using all capitals; this makes the text difficult to read.
- Use sound sparingly so as not to distract from the presentation itself.
- Use clip art, pictures, and graphs in place of text to make a point.

Once a presentation is prepared, it can be saved onto the hard drive of the computer. Remember to back up all your work by also saving onto a diskette, removable hard drive, tape drive, or server if available.

Presentation software can be used in many ways in the classroom. Delivery of instruction is the most common application; however, teachers have found other creative ways of applying these technologies. One way to enhance presentations is to show students actively working. This can be done by using a digital camera for taking pictures that can be incorporated into the presentation. A regular camera could also be used, but the turnaround time increases because the film has to be developed and the pictures have to be scanned into the computer. Here are a few examples of topics of presentation prepared by teachers:

- Audiovisual biography introducing yourself
- Introduction of classroom policies and procedures
- Overview of extracurricular activities offered by the school district
- Overview of the course and course expectations

- At parent-teacher conferences, a video of students working in class
- Field trips

Students often use presentation software for group projects. Projects using technology motivate students. However, students need to be taught the skills necessary for creating good presentations. Some teachers have found that taking the time to stress the importance of presentation design helps students stay focused on the problems they are trying to solve and not on the "bells and whistles" that may be included in the software. Students also need to be taught how to plan a project and create action plans and timelines. When using project-based learning and technology, it becomes essential that assessments match the targets that have been set for the students. Some teachers develop rubrics using indicators that are student generated. Students who are shown examples of bad presentations, average presentations, and good presentations will have a better understanding of what is expected from them. The rubric shown in Figure 9.3 can be used in assessing student oral presentations.

The Internet

Each day, more and more users are logging on to the Internet. The *Internet* is a large group of computers worldwide that are interconnected. This organizational structure gave rise to the name World Wide Web (WWW or Web).

An individual user connects his or her computer to the Internet with either a dial-up modem to an internet service provider (ISP) or a local area network (LAN) administered by a school district. Most school districts have adopted written acceptable-use policies that specify who may use the district's Internet connection, time limits, and what content may be viewed or downloaded to a local computer or server. These standards must be carefully read and followed; violations have resulted in teacher terminations or student suspensions or loss of Internet privileges, depending on the severity of the violations.

Each user must have software for an Internet browser that provides a graphical interface to view the Web's content. The two most commonly used are Netscape Navigator and Microsoft's Internet Explorer. One or both of these systems usually come preinstalled on every computer or may be furnished by the ISP.

Each Web site has a specific address that identifies which computer server holds the information for it. The address for each site is displayed in the address or location bar near the top of the browser frame. A Web site can be reached directly by typing the address into the browser and striking the ENTER key.

Browsers have become more user friendly. Browsers can save the list of Web sites the user wishes to revisit. In Netscape, the user can "bookmark" a site and it will be saved with other bookmarks. In Internet Explorer, the user adds the site to his or her list of favorites. The bookmarking feature also provides a tool to document the research performed by either a student or a teacher by using a separate bookmark or favorites file for a project.

Figure 9.3. **Rubric for Student Presentations**

Criteria	1	2	3	4
Content Facts	• Content was not addressed. • Content was irrelevant. • Information presented was opinion/not fact.	• Content was addressed adequately. • Some content was irrelevant. • Fact and opinion were difficult to distinguish.	• Content was addressed. • Most facts presented were relevant. • Fact and opinion were sometimes mixed.	• Content was clearly addressed. • Fact was clearly distinguished from opinion. • Fact and opinion were clearly distinguished.
Volume Eye Contact Participation	• Presentation could not be heard. • No eye contact was made. • More than two group members did not speak.	• Volume was erratic and difficult to understand. • Some eye contact was made. • One group member did not speak.	• Volume was appropriate for part of the presentation. • Intermittent eye contact was made. • All group members spoke but not equally.	• Volume was appropriate throughout the presentation. • Good eye contact was made. • All group members spoke equally.
Media Aid	• No media aids were presented.	• Media aid used distracted from content. • Media aid was illegible.	• Media aid helped the presentation but contained one distracting element. • Media aid was difficult to read in some places.	• Media aid used enhanced the presentation and kept one's attention. • Media aid was legible.
Organization	• No organization was evident. • Flow was not logical. • Confusing.	• Presentation was off track in places. • Gaps existed. • Some of the presentation was logical and organized.	• Organization was good. • A clear plan was demonstrated. • Most of the presentation was logical and organized.	• Presentation was well organized. • A clear and complete plan was demonstrated. • All of the presentation was logical and organized.
Conclusions	• No conclusions were reported. • Presenter/Group could not answer questions.	• Some conclusions were reported and supported by data. • Presenter/Group was able to answer some questions.	• Most conclusions reported were supported by data. • Presenter/Group was able to answer most questions.	• All conclusions reported were supported by data. • Presenter/Group was able to answer all relevant questions.

It is impossible for teachers to know the address for every Web site they wish to visit. Software programs known as *search engines*, however, are designed to locate Web sites. Examples of search engines are Alta Vista, Lycos, Infoseek, Web Crawler, and Excite. Teachers can experiment with several search engines to find the ones that are easiest to use and that return the desired results.

Most search engines rely on Boolean logic to locate search topics. *Boolean logic* uses words such as AND, OR, and NOT to refine a search. Using key words will increase the likelihood that the search engine will locate the information requested. For example, a search for Virginia schools would return sites that have either *Virginia* or *schools* in the subject matter. If a query asked for both Virginia and schools, the search engine would return Web sites dealing only with schools in Virginia.

Using the Internet in schools has numerous benefits. Figure 9.4 is a listing of benefits to both teachers and students. Teachers who require students to use the Internet for class projects have found that if students are allowed to use the Internet without first having an understanding of its operation, much time can be wasted. Some students will spend a great deal of time searching for information that can be accessed from a book in a matter of seconds. Establishing student goals prior to Internet use encourages students to stay on task when searching for information.

Many times, it may be necessary for students to leave the classroom to use computers. Monitoring for student progress can be difficult in such a situation. The Internet worksheet (Figure 9.5) is a tool designed for student use but enables the teacher to evaluate the process employed by the students in using the Internet. If students use a computer supervised by another individual, some teachers have required those students to have the lab supervisor sign the worksheet to verify student work. Some teachers have also evaluated the Web sites listed by students. This sheet also enables teachers to identify students in need of further assistance.

Figure 9.4. Benefits of Using the Internet

BENEFITS OF USING THE INTERNET

For the <u>Student</u>

- ◆ Medium for publishing student work
- ◆ Communicate with people around the world
- ◆ Access to real-world current data
- ◆ Enhances peer collaboration
- ◆ Direct access to the best sources of information
- ◆ Motivates students
- ◆ Enhances higher-order thinking
- ◆ Experience success in learning to do research
- ◆ Develops multiple intelligence
- ◆ Prepares students for the real world
- ◆ Actively engages students
- ◆ Increases self-esteem

For the <u>Teacher</u>

- ◆ Supports project-based learning
- ◆ Supports curriculum
- ◆ Communicate with other teachers
- ◆ Find instructional materials for the classroom
- ◆ Research best practices
- ◆ Adds a variety of instructional strategies
- ◆ Provides opportunities for professional development
- ◆ Locate and retrieve timely information for the classroom
- ◆ Access multimedia sources
- ◆ Provides direct access to professional organizations
- ◆ Changes role from teacher to coach/facilitator
- ◆ Communicate with parents

Figure 9.5. Internet Worksheet

Name: _____ Period: _____ Date: _____

Research Topic:

Prior to logging on to the Internet, list two other resources that you researched and write a complete bibliography in the space provided.

Resources: 1. _____

2. _____

Internet search:

Log-on time: _____ **Log-off time:** _____

Search engines used:

1. _____

2. _____

3. _____

Web sites from where information was located. Write down the URL address.

1. _____

2. _____

3. _____

4. _____

Are the **Web sites** above bookmarked? Yes_____ No_____

Discuss any problems encountered while using the Internet.

Media play a major role in advertising Web sites. Teachers, as they browse educational resources, often will come across a description of a Web site that interests them. The immediate reaction is to write the Web site address on a piece of paper, which can very easily become lost. The Web site directory shown in Figure 9.6 is a means of recording Web sites for future or frequent use. Teachers have written Web addresses on sticky notes and placed them on the Web site directory to be recorded at a later time. Web sites from the student Internet Worksheet (Figure 9.5) that were found to be very resourceful could also can be recorded in this directory. This document can be very useful if Web sites the teacher previously bookmarked are no longer accessible.

Figure 9.6. Web Site Directory

Block scheduling:	Favorites:
http://carei.coled.umn.edu	
http://www.classroom.net	
http://www.aasa.org	
http://web.lwc.edu/staff/fmoore/BL/index.htm	
http://carei.coled.umn.edu/blockscheduling/schools/schools.htm	
http://www.beau.lib.la.us	
http://forum.swarthmore.edu/mathed/block.schedules.html	
Study skills:	**Education:**
http://www.nj.com/education/instructor/study1.html	http://ericir.syr.edu
http://www.studyweb.com	http://www.gsh.org
http://www.unc.edu/depts/unc_caps/TenTraps.html	http://www.thechalkboard.com
http://www.siu.edu/staffair/studyskls.htm	http://www.aaas.org
	http://www.classroom.net
	http://ncrel.org
News/Weather:	**Reference:**
http://www.cnn.com	http://www.superlibrary.com
http://www.weather.com	http://www.loc.gov
http://www.usatoday.com	http://prairieschooner.com
http://weatherunderground.com	**Shareware:**
http://www.almanac.com	http://www.shareware.com
	http://www.jumbo.com

Classroom Management

Those teachers who were in classrooms before computers often wonder how they managed. They well remember the sound made by typewriter keys in the teacher's lounge after school each day. Now, teachers use computers in several ways. The most common application is word processing. Teachers type assignments, tests, lesson plans, memos, and letters to parents. Many companies have developed software designed to make the teacher's job easier. Some types of software available can be used for grading, developing curriculum that aligns with standards and benchmarks, designing assessment, creating electronic portfolios, developing rubrics, and creating graphic organizers. Choosing and selecting software can be a tremendous task. Many schools have formed committees to evaluate and choose software for their teachers to use.

Implementation of block schedules in schools has resulted in some teachers actively engaging students in a variety of tasks that require multiple ways to assess student achievement. Teachers who have used electronic portfolios say it is a way to record, organize, and manage efficiently the collective work of students. Teachers have created products that exhibit student progress and achievements in more than one area. Teachers can scan student work to be stored for later retrieval. Some teachers have involved students in the process of selecting work to be stored.

Using Videotapes in the Classroom

Using videotapes in the classroom can enrich the curriculum. When used effectively, these resources can stimulate student thinking. Selecting media that align with the curriculum can be time-consuming. Effective teachers preview the material to establish the relevancy of the content and its connections to the content standards. Videos are shown for the purpose of learning. Many suppliers of these materials will allow teachers to obtain videos on approval.

Teachers also like to record programs from television. Prior to recording, teachers need to be familiar with copyright laws and fair use. Fair use guidelines specify under what conditions copyrighted materials may be used legally. To qualify as fair use, broadcast programs may be videotaped and used by teachers for a period not to exceed 45 calendar days. Following this time period, all such tapes must be erased. This rule has some exceptions: Some broadcast stations have sought copyright agreements to make programming easier for educators to use. Broadcast stations often post the guidelines to follow on their Web sites. The stations also make available curriculum materials free of charge that have been developed for specific programs. Keeping an inventory of all videos recorded is a way to keep track of which videotapes need to be erased and the date by which they should be erased (see sample inventory in Figure 9.7; a blackline master of this inventory is in Robbins & Herndon, 1998).

Figure 9.7. Sample Video Inventory

Title	Description	Length	Applicable unit	Date produced/ Date recorded
Weather concepts	Explains classification of clouds and how they are formed. Good fundamentals.	60 min	Meteorology	6/27/99 Can keep for 1 year
Earthquakes	Covers the earth's crust, faults, and relationship to plate tectonic theory. Strong visuals.	60 min	Plate tectonics	8/31/99 Unlimited use
Strip mining	Discusses human use of natural resources and mining regulations.	45 min	Rocks and minerals	9/15/99 Erase by 10/30/99

Videotapes are another way to deliver instruction. They can be used to reinforce, enrich, or review information. Some teachers use videos to introduce new topics. Planning for ways to use videos that make a lesson a meaningful experience for students can challenge teachers. Two methods of using these technologies are described here. First, research shows that questions interspersed throughout a textbook, rather than at the end of a chapter, increase student comprehension; this same research-based practice can apply to showing a video to students as part of the learning process. While showing a video, the teacher can stop the film frequently to ask questions and hold class discussion. This practice will keep students engaged and increase their understanding of concepts portrayed in video. Second, students can use a worksheet such as that shown in Figure 9.8 to record the major concepts illustrated in the film/video. Figure 9.8 also includes, at the bottom of the page, criteria for students to evaluate the film/video.

Figure 9.8. Film/Video Evaluation Sheet

Name: _____ Period: _____ Date: _____

Discuss five major facts/concepts discussed in this film that relate to what we are learning in class.

Films/Videos are shown in class for educational purposes.

Evaluate this film/video, using the following criteria:
- How informative was the film/video?
- Did it hold your interest? Why?
- Was it relevant to what we are learning in class?
- Did the production/graphics/design help you understand the content?

Rate this film, using the following criteria:
1. Does not meet expectations   2. Meets expectations   3. Exceeds expectations

My rating: _____ Explain your rationale for the rating you gave.

Videos can help students learn to think critically by involving them in the evaluation process. Students need to understand the operational definition of a quality video. This can be accomplished by having students brainstorm indicators of a quality video from which they can learn. Using these indicators, a simple rubric can be developed for student use. Students will watch videos from a whole new perspective. It is important that students become aware that quality videos enable them to learn and remember key concepts.

Summary

Unlike a play, in which the curtain eventually must fall and the characters bow before leaving the stage, technology will continue to evolve. Teachers will continue to learn new ways of integrating technology. Students will find themselves constantly being challenged as they continue to learn a technology that is preparing them for the world of work. As more schools adopt block scheduling, there will be an increase in the availability of technology to students. Researchers will continue to study the effects of technology on learning as educators anxiously wait in the wings for the results. The stage from which our play was performed will expand as the world becomes more accessible as a consequence of technology.

10

Bringing the Curtain Down

Closing the Lesson and Homework Techniques

One challenge for the playwright is to devise a script that will sustain audience interest and attention until the end of the play—perhaps a surprise ending or a sudden twist of fate for one of the players. The playwright might also contemplate what, after the play, audience members will carry away as memories.

In the classroom, the teacher faces a similar dilemma: how to sustain student interest and attention until the end of an extended period of instructional time. Beyond this is the additional challenge of how to inspire students to do homework to extend the potential impact of the initial classroom experience. The *Handbook of Research on Improving Student Achievement* (Cawelti, 1995) suggests that "students learn more when they complete homework that is graded, commented upon and discussed by their teachers" (p. 12). In addition, David Sousa (1998) suggests that the brain remembers best what comes first, and next best what comes last. Hence, if one wants to ensure students' enduring understanding of concepts, skills, and practices (taught in class) over time, it is crucial to plan carefully the final moments of an instructional period and to structure experiences that will extend and enhance the quality of classroom learnings.

Planning Review Strategies for Long-Term Retention

Most teachers find that a key to promoting students' ability to remember what they have learned over time rests in how many opportunities students have to rehearse, revisit, or practice what has been taught. One teacher remarked, "I ask myself, 'What evidence will I need to see in order to assure myself that students have learned?' I tell my students, 'I will judge how well I've taught by what you are able to demonstrate for me!' "

Teachers use many strategies to generate student "output" to accomplish this goal. For instance, as one teacher taught about the bones, muscles, ligaments, arteries, and nerves in the hand, she had students draw these in on a blank picture of a hand. To "see" what students learned, she had them put aside their notes, *draw around their own hands,* and fill in the blanks. A math teacher gave groups of students colored streamers. He asked the groups to compute the mean and mode of the heights of their group members. Near the end of the period, he asked students to articulate what they had done to complete the task and then generate a *"person on the street" definition* of the terms. An industrial technology teacher had each student select something she or he had done in class and write a one-page summary of the steps to the process; the summaries were displayed on the shop wall.

Another teacher periodically schedules a *"talk show" lecture* to help students revisit content. The class selects two individuals to "host" the show. These individuals, along with class members, make up questions designed to get the teacher, during a "talk show interview," to respond with the key points of a lesson. On the day of the talk show, the hosts are invited to choose their costumes from a box of dress-up clothes the teacher has acquired. Three stools are placed in the center of the room: one for the teacher, two for the student hosts. The hosts interview the teacher. And as on any talk show, audience members can ask questions as well. Students are invited to write down the lesson points the teacher addresses during the interview. The goal, of course, is to maximize the number of teacher responses that student-devised questions generate. At the end of the talk show, students compare their lists of key points they heard during the show. This adds interest, fun, and challenge to the class period. Students look forward to this event.

A social studies teacher hands each student a colored 3 × 5 card. Students have 10 minutes to write on their cards as much as they want about the lesson they've just experienced. They are able to use their cards during the exam. The teacher reflected, "Although some may perceive this as cheating, I think it is a kind way of inviting students to revisit content and highlight key points." Another teacher hands out strips of sticky dots and allows 12 minutes for students to look through their notes and highlight, with the sticky dots, key points they wish to remember.

A physical education teacher regularly schedules a *"Go for the Gold Round"* at the end of her classes, in which students have a final chance to do their best at demonstrating a skill they have been working on. After this, students shower, dress, and meet in a central location. In this setting, the teacher gives class members feedback

about their performances and reteaches and models any points or movements that need improvement.

An art teacher and a music teacher both use a strategy called *"freeze frame,"* wherein students are asked to stop what they are doing and analyze the piece they are currently working on. Students discuss their efforts and any difficult aspects of their performances, and the teacher collaborates in problem solving.

Another teacher sometimes surprises students with a *"You're on Candid Camera"* message. She pulls three names out of a hat. Those students must stand, and the teacher draws out of another hat a question related to the content they have studied. Standing students may select a sitting colleague with whom to conference and then respond to the question.

A science teacher plays a game with her students called *"I Am. Who Has?"* The teacher creates playing cards and distributes these, one to a student. A student timekeeper is appointed. Student 1 might read from her or his playing card, "I am a substance that provides energy for photosynthesis to take place." The student who has the name of this substance on her or his card responds. In this case, the student responded, "You are sunshine." Then, the student might read a prompt from a card that says, "I am a pigment found in the chloroplasts of plant cells." And the student who has the name of this substance on her or his card responds, "You are chlorophyll." The game continues until each class member has had a turn to respond. The timekeeper keeps time to see how quickly the class can move through the questions. Each class posts its time, and other classes try to beat it. A technology teacher uses this game to review computer terms and functions.

Following is a menu of options from which students may select when devising plans for vibrant class endings or for review.

Jeopardy or Wheel of Fortune. These two games, based on the familiar television games, provide an exciting medium for students to review key learnings from a lesson. Students in one classroom constructed a giant Wheel of Fortune in industrial technology class. Periodically, for different lessons, the teacher posted questions at each colored section of the wheel. Students formed teams. They spun the wheel and had to answer the question indicated by the arrow.

Questions in a Jar. Students develop questions based on the content, skills, and processes they have learned. They print the question on one side of a slip of paper and the answer on the other side. These are deposited into a jar. The class forms teams. A person from each team draws a question for her or his team. If the team answers the question correctly, they get 2 points. If not, the other team can answer the question for 1 point.

Fill in the Blanks. The teacher distributes to each student sheets of paper with several statements that have blank spaces within them. Students have 5 minutes of silence to fill in the blanks. Then, an answer key is displayed, and students correct their

work and write notes to themselves about which blanks they missed. A variation is to reproduce a familiar graphic and ask students to label the parts.

Twenty Questions. Students form pairs. Each student writes 10 questions on a card, along with 10 correct answers to the questions. Student pairs take turns asking one another their collective 20 questions, prompting their partners to help them identify the correct answer and celebrating them when they do.

Question Quadrant. A transparency is divided into four sections. The teacher or a student writes a topic in each quadrant. Students take turns brainstorming all they can recall about that topic.

Paper Pass. Each student develops two review questions and writes these on separate 5 × 8 cards. They autograph their cards and then pass their cards to one another as music is played in the background. They may sit or stand to do this. When the music stops, each class member must answer the question on the card in her or his hand. Then, the card is returned to its author, who provides verbal or written feedback to the student who has answered the question.

Analyze That Tune! An English teacher developed this game to help students review the elements of a short story. He plays a pop song that tells a story and asks students to analyze the elements of the story in graphic form, including setting, rising action, climax, falling action, and denouement.

Event Cards. The teacher prepares event cards made from 5 × 8 cards with yarn attached to each of the top corners so that the cards can be worn around the neck. Each student is given a card. Without speaking to one another, students must line up in order of the way the events around their necks occurred. After this task is completed, each student must share one fact about the event she or he is wearing.

Additional review strategies such as *shaping up a review, listening posts, wallpaper task, relays, advertisements, ticket out the door, learning journals,* and *carousel brainstorming* are described in Chapter 8.

Planning Long-Range Assignments Using Products

Sometimes longer range, collective student learnings are assessed by asking students to create products from which to summarize their understandings. A geometry teacher gave each class member a list of 100 possible topics in which applied geometry was an element. Topics were as diverse as art, dance, bridge construction, music, cars, boats—almost anything imaginable! This list contained at least one topic of interest for every student. Each student had to select a topic and then (a) write a paper, (b) create a poster, and (c) prepare an oral presentation. Rubrics were constructed collaboratively by

students and the teacher so that students clearly understood the expectations for the assignments. The three assignments were due at staggered points in time. The papers were due in 2 weeks, the posters in 3 weeks, and the oral presentation in 4 weeks. Students and teacher each graded every product. This assignment not only promoted long-term learning but also required students to apply what they had learned to a real-world context. In the process, geometry took on new meaning. The following list of possible products would invite students to review and apply what they have learned. These products also allow teachers to assess how well students have learned and what was most significant to them.

- Make a game
- Write a book
- Create a slide show
- Develop a Power Point presentation
- Make a mural
- Draw a set of blueprints
- Write a computer program
- Make a piece of art
- Keep a diary
- Write an imaginary autobiography of a historical figure
- Write an opinion article
- Plan a journey
- Create a topographical map
- Write a script and tape a conversation
- Prepare a television program
- Develop and use a questionnaire
- Create a newspaper
- Make a political cartoon
- Develop a poem
- Design and construct a model
- Present a mock trial
- Conduct a debate
- Create a recipe
- Develop a display
- Create a dance
- Make a wall hanging
- Give a demonstration
- Conduct an interview and summarize the results
- Formulate a scientific theory
- Write a song
- Be a mentor
- Make a time line
- Do something to make our world better
- Make a video presentation
- Draw a graph
- Develop a new product
- Create a new leisure-time sport
- Develop a collection of study prints
- Design a simulation
- Compile a portfolio
- Teach a lesson
- Write and illustrate a children's story
- Design and make a costume
- Grow a plant and graph its growth
- Write a biography
- Create a news report for television
- Do a pantomime
- Write a new law
- Create a bulletin board display

Although this list is not exhaustive, it will provide a springboard for other ideas. Again, as with the active learning activities in Chapter 8, the teacher must select the types of tasks while considering learning styles, processing channels, multiple intelligences, and levels of thinking desired, given the instructional context (e.g., students, time, setting) in which these will be played out.

Extending Learning Time Through Homework

One way to extend and enhance learning time, in addition to the products discussed above, is through homework.

> A synthesis of more than a dozen studies of the effects of homework in various subjects showed the assignment and completion of homework yields positive effects on academic achievement. The effects are almost tripled when teachers take the time to grade the work, make corrections and specific comments on improvements that can be made, and discuss problems and remedies with individual students and the whole class. (Cawelti, 1995, p. 12)

To be effective, homework should be

- Explained and modeled effectively in class
- Stated explicitly with defined expectations for both students and parents
- Assigned for "perfect practice" of previously taught content (Homework should *not* be assigned if content is unfamiliar; errors practiced are difficult to undo.)
- Monitored by parents (Homework partnerships provide leverage points for developing positive home-school relationships.)
- Related directly to the in-class lesson
- Appropriate to the student's level of achievement

Some schools have embellished their homework programs and policies by creating homework hotlines, after-school homework assistance centers, study groups, and study buddy programs.

Realistically, teachers often find that, because of the sheer volume, it is impossible to examine and offer specific feedback on every paper. If feedback is not provided, however, homework can be an idle exercise. Many teachers therefore have created a variety of ways to address this dilemma so that homework is meaningful and extends learnings. Here are a few strategies used in classrooms operating on a block schedule:

Classtime Correction. The teacher puts numbers into a hat. Selected students draw numbers from the hat. Numbered problems that correspond with the numbers drawn are explained to the class in detail. For the other problems, answers are provided, and

the class can ask questions about them. Another version of this is for the teacher to post homework problems on the chalkboard, overhead, or television screen and to ask students to respond. A French teacher, to develop student language fluency and understanding, asked students to address "What's the category?" and posted words such as the following:

1. mére, pere, frére, soeur, grand-pére _____
2. pain, fromage, sucre, jambon, poulet _____

This assignment was a derivative of what students did for homework, and the teacher asked them to apply it in a different context.

Answer Keys. Although this is not an optimal activity, some teachers provide students with answer keys to correct their work. Students have to analyze the nature of the mistakes they made in written form and hand papers in to the teacher.

Odd/Even Numbers and Letters of the Alphabet. Some teachers use a scanning system in which, on certain days, only odd-numbered problems are checked and, on others, only even. Students don't know which will be checked. Some teachers call for homework from students whose last names begin with certain letters, as well as from any students who wish feedback from the teacher.

Student Helpers. At some schools, college students help teachers grade papers.

Study Buddies. In some classrooms, students pair up and compare homework while the teacher monitors.

Homework in a Capsule. Homework problems are put into 35-mm film canisters. Students are handed the canisters, pop them open, and, using their homework answers or relying on their memories, answer the problems.

Inside/Outside Circles. Students form two circles, one inside the other, with each circle facing the other. Students compare answers on two homework problems with the person whom they are facing. Those inside the circle rotate by one so that every third problem is discussed with a different partner.

Peer Editing Groups. Several writing classes use a peer editing system wherein students who are familiar with scoring rubrics for writing samples analyze each other's writings and provide nonjudgmental but specific feedback.

Teacher-Student Collaboratives. Lucky Moore, a teacher from a Department of Defense School in Germany, began the year by asking students in his English class to bring in what they considered to be superb examples of writing. In class, they analyzed key

attributes of the samples and created an agreed-on rubric to assess writing. Lucky put a sample paper on the overhead projector; students scored the paper, using the rubric. They compared scores, and he discussed the concept of interrater reliability. Then he said, "This semester, before I grade your papers, I want three scores on it—one from you, based on the rubric; one from a friend, based on the rubric; and one from your parents, who are also expected to use the rubric." This meant that students had to explain the rubric to both friends and parents or caregivers to enable them to grade a student's work. "The results have been amazing," reflected Lucky. "The quality of work has gone up, and I haven't received any complaints from students or parents about grades!" Knowing where the target is and having strategies to reach it have empowered Lucky's class to achieve at high levels.

Matrix Work. Graphic organizers can enhance student understanding. One teacher uses these to help students process content they have learned as a consequence of classroom experiences and homework. The matrix shown in Figure 10.1 is an example used as an opening activity to "connect" one class session with another, as well as to review homework. Students fill in the cells of the matrix to illustrate their understandings of the attributes of each of the shapes, as well as the qualities that distinguish the shapes from one another.

Figure 10.1. Sample Matrix for a Math Graphic

Organizer	Edges	Vertices	Faces
Sphere			
Cube			
Rectangular prism			
Cylinder			
Square-based pyramid			
Cone			

Getting Assignments Back

Many teachers have expressed concern about whether students will complete and return assignments, especially if the school is on a schedule in which classes meet every other day. Here are some suggestions for enhancing return rates:

- Assign homework in class. Model what is expected and provide time for students to start work; monitor them for accuracy. If students have started and experience success, they are more likely to finish.

- Assign or have students choose study buddies so that each student has someone else in class to call.
- When working with groups, some teachers have used "callers" to remind colleagues in their groups to return homework.
- Use student self-monitoring devices, such as a chart that is colored in for homework completed.
- Provide class awards when every student returns homework.

Summary

It is a natural human phenomenon to experience a state of entropy, or "running out of steam," a bit more than halfway through an extended period of instructional time. Having a repertoire of strategies to review content, close a class session, and assign and check homework will contribute greatly to the goal of creating a classroom in which students remain positively engaged throughout a block.

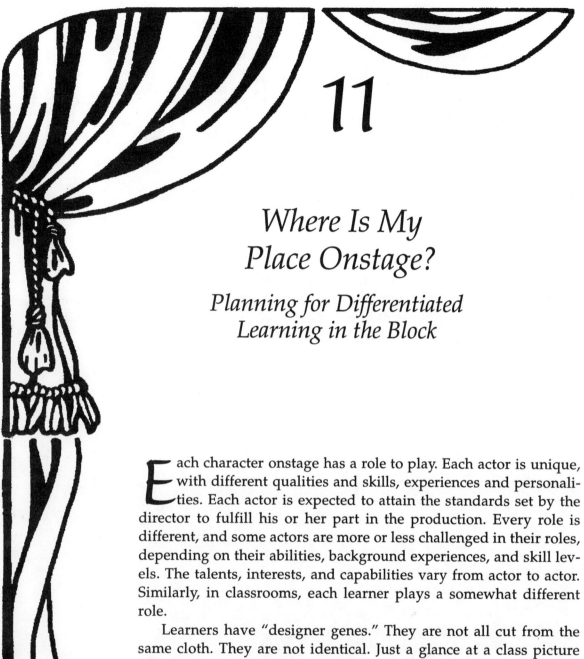

11

Where Is My Place Onstage?

Planning for Differentiated Learning in the Block

Each character onstage has a role to play. Each actor is unique, with different qualities and skills, experiences and personalities. Each actor is expected to attain the standards set by the director to fulfill his or her part in the production. Every role is different, and some actors are more or less challenged in their roles, depending on their abilities, background experiences, and skill levels. The talents, interests, and capabilities vary from actor to actor. Similarly, in classrooms, each learner plays a somewhat different role.

Learners have "designer genes." They are not all cut from the same cloth. They are not identical. Just a glance at a class picture illustrates this. Students are tall and short, some rounder than others, with various colors of skin and hair, freckles or curls. They also have had illnesses and accidents, abnormalities in prenatal or postnatal growth, birth trauma or defects, or emotional or psychological trauma and may have mild or significant learning disorders. Others have many gifts and talents that necessitate more challenging materials, tasks, and assessments so that they might reach their potential. And then there is a whole range in between. Although teachers can easily identify the physical differences, they sometimes fail to recog-

nize the reality that learners' brains differ too. Even though students' brain functioning is not visible, it is now common knowledge that information processing and dendritic growth are not identical in every brain. Thus, one style of learning doesn't accommodate all these diverse learners. In fact, learners may need very specific modifications to deal with their specific individual profiles. This adds yet another dimension to the planning process as teachers modify learning experiences and assessments to enable these diverse learners to attain the standards set for them within extended periods of instructional time. Learners do have, however, some common traits that make them more alike than dissimilar. Figure 11.1 lists some of the similar and different characteristics of most children, all children, and special needs children.

Figure 11.1. Children in the Classroom Are More Alike Than Different.

Most children
- Are able to articulate their needs
- Fit in with groups
- Know their strengths
- Have all senses functioning
- Apply their knowledge
- Make decisions about how and what they will learn

All children
- Have unique styles
- Have multiple intelligences
- Have unique interests
- Need self-confidence
- Are curious
- Need skills for life
- Need to belong
- Need to have a sense of control
- Like to be accepted by others
- Need to have security (peers and adults)
- Enjoy hands-on learning and play

Special needs children may
- Need advocates
- Require patience and acceptance
- Require flexibility in programs
- Require assistance and task analysis for success
- Require time adjustments
- Require assistive devices and special furniture
- Require additional support personnel (paraprofessional) and acceptance
- Require an individualized educational plan (IEP)

SOURCE: Adapted from a model by Goodman (1994).

Figure 11.2. Shaping Up Program Modification

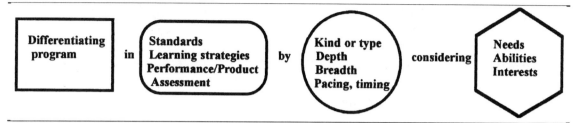

SOURCE: Modified from a model developed by the Ministry of Education, Ontario (1979, 1985).

Modifying the Program

To identify students' needs and to plan programs to meet those needs, teachers should first:

1. Identify the standards and competencies that are to be reached.
2. Explore the needs of the particular student.
3. Peruse the variety of options in these four areas: *content standards, learning strategies,* possible *products or performances,* and *assessment* practices.

When planning the curriculum for these learners, whether it be content standards, learning strategies, products, or assessments, modifications should be made.

In each of these four areas, modifications may be made by weighing the *kind or type* of standards, learning strategies, products, or assessments (See Figure 11.2). The standards themselves may need to be adjusted to suit the learner and provide challenge just beyond his or her skill level. Frequent success should be possible so that the learner is more likely to rise to the challenge to obtain a state of flow without "downshifting" from undue stress. The teacher can also modify the *depth* of the content covered or the specificity of the learning experience, product, or assessment required. Another aspect that can be modified is the *breadth* of content covered, instructional practices used, variety of products created, or assessment strategies used. The fourth consideration may be the *pacing or timing* given to the content and the instructional experience, as well as flexibility in the development of the product. The time allowed for assessment and completion of the assignment may also be varied.

Knowing the Learner

The teacher, through observation, conferencing, data collected from parents, and information garnered from other faculty members, will first develop a profile of the student. The blackline master shown in Figure 11.3 may be a helpful organizer for collecting

and organizing data. Sticky notes may be used during the day to jot down information that may be transferred to student files at the end of the day or week. In this way, teachers can collect firsthand information by observing the student as he or she functions throughout the classroom period. Observations may include, but are not limited to, physical, emotional, social, and cognitive abilities or needs. In addition to serving as an organizer, Figure 11.3 may be helpful in planning a modified program for a particular student.

Figure 11.3. Individual Student Program Modification

Student _____ Subject/Topic _____

Student profile: Challenges and needs

Consider the options outlined in Figures 11.4 through 11.9 that may be helpful for this student.

Regular program   Modifications

Standards	Kind or type	Depth	Breadth	Timing/Pacing
Learning strategy	Kind or type	Depth	Breadth	Timing/Pacing
Product or performance task	Kind or type	Depth	Breadth	Timing/Pacing
Assessment	Kind or type	Depth	Breadth	Timing/Pacing

Instructional Support in the Block

Using additional personnel in classrooms can also meet the individual needs of learners. Many students with behavioral problems may find the extended instructional time in the block difficult to handle. Giving careful consideration to timing and pacing will help. Having an instructional assistant work one on one with a student will help retain focus and attention. Some teachers include these students in the initial input period of the lesson and then have support staff work with the students during the time when they are applying the learning. This may be done in the classroom, or they may withdraw from the room for a short period to change the scenery and limit the distractions in the regular classroom.

Over the years, teachers have worked together and shared ideas to vary instructional approaches to meet students' learning needs. Brainstorming and experimenting have produced the teacher suggestions shown in Figures 11.4 through 11.9 (blackline masters). Instructional assistants and regular classroom teachers need options that may be used to meet the needs of individual learners.

The lists in Figures 11.4 through 11.7 give options a teacher might select to meet the needs of learners who may be challenged in reading, writing, mathematics, or managing time. Strategies to encourage all students and to help them remember are listed in Figures 11.8 and 11.9.

Figure 11.4. Students Challenged by Reading

	This approach may be helpful to:
	[Student's name] when . . .
Give students an advance organizer and set the context.	
Review concepts and vocabulary.	_____
Discuss questions before reading.	_____
Let students work with a partner or in a cooperative group for peer support.	_____
Give extra time and less scope.	_____
Show students how to make an outline or précis.	_____
Provide less complicated readings.	_____
Use audiotapes, videos, films.	_____
Provide an outline of the main ideas.	_____
Teach students how to skim and find the main points.	_____
Highlight/Underline important facts.	_____
Predict outcomes: What will happen next?	_____
Teach students the RAD strategy:	_____
Read a paragraph.	
Ask yourself what you have read.	
Describe it in your own words.	
Adjust quantity for students so that the task doesn't seem beyond their reach.	_____
Provide a substitute reading that is not as difficult but that includes the same ideas and concepts.	_____
Provide taped readings so that students can follow along in the text.	_____

Figure 11.5. Students Challenged by Writing

This approach may be helpful to:

Provide a detailed outline of expectations. _____

Teach the use of graphic organizers such as webs, story boards, sequence charts, or comic strips. _____

Use a word processing program to expedite the process of writing and to reduce the stress of handwriting. _____

Use word processing on the computer to facilitate "easy editing" with spell and grammar checkers. _____

Use a tape recorder, video recorder, or other medium as a substitute for writing. _____

Teach students how to develop an outline. _____

Teach students to use a "dot jot" process of recording information: jot down ideas next to dots, one idea per dot. _____

Try to reduce the amount of writing by using cloze-type activities (students fill in key words or concepts left blank in the text) instead of having students do extensive note taking. _____

"Buddy up" students with partners to write and edit. _____

Individualize the task (one-on-one conferencing). _____

Allow additional time for the process. _____

Invite a student to tell a story and a "buddy" to write it. _____

Have students record on large flip chart paper. _____

Figure 11.6. Students Challenged by Mathematics

This approach may be helpful to:

Provide manipulatives and models. _____

Teach students to make representations for illustrating their problem solving. _____

Require that students keep math logs or journals to note strategies for problem solving. _____

Give opportunities to share solutions to increase all students' repertoires of strategies. _____

Allow more time to work through solutions. _____

Pair up students to talk through problems. _____

Have students restate problems in their own words. _____

Review previously learned concepts to deepen understanding. _____

Relate problems to real-world situations. _____

Use flash cards and games to increase retention. _____

Figure 11.7. Students Challenged by Time Management

	This approach may be helpful to:
Help students identify a task and analyze the steps in sequence.	_____
Use charts to identify steps and time needed.	_____
Teach directly how to access information effectively, skills such as:	
Research skills	_____
Use of CD-ROMs	
Use of video discs	
Use peer coaching, in which other students coach, prompt, and support.	_____
Promote cooperative group learning.	_____
Use graphic organizers to organize thinking and record information.	_____
Help establish self-monitoring and reflection on the process.	_____
Encourage goal setting.	_____
Keep logs and journals that provide a record of tasks completed and reflections and goal setting.	_____
Provide students with timers.	_____
Have students record their "time on task" and compare progress.	_____
Teach students strategies to organize materials.	_____

Figure 11.8. Encouraging All Learners

	This approach may be helpful to:
Make sure the classroom is "brain compatible" and nurturing.	_____
Address as many learning styles and multiple intelligences as possible.	_____
Model inclusion of all students.	_____
Use classroom management that promotes collaborative decision making and problem solving.	_____
Teach cooperative skills to help students value and support each other.	_____
Help students understand objectives, purpose, and the relevance of learning to real life.	_____
Outlaw put-downs in the classroom.	_____
Balance challenge and skill to foster a can-do attitude.	_____
Honor diversity by talking about how differences can be an advantage; reinforce the variety of ways people learn through acknowledgment and celebration.	_____
Help each student celebrate him- or herself for good deeds and academic progress.	_____
Provide a safe environment where risk taking and experimentation are valued.	_____

Figure 11.9. Helping Students Remember . . .

	This approach may be helpful to:
Use memory pegs or mnemonics (acronyms) as "brain hooks."	_____
Use concrete material such as charts.	_____
Teach computer use, spell check, or grammar check.	_____
Break complex ideas into "manageable munchies."	_____
Chunk ideas together to develop concepts that will hold memory in a neural network.	_____
Use visual spatial intelligence, mind maps, and concept webs.	_____
Use music or rap to retain facts.	_____
Give opportunities to use information.	_____
Use computer support, such as programs for graphic organizers and webbing, that facilitate these processes without hand drawing.	_____
Provide frequent opportunities to rehearse.	_____
Encourage students to make stories to retain specific facts.	_____
Offer rhymes to help students remember.	_____

For generating creative solutions to challenging situations, teachers could employ the strategy of *SCAMPER*. This strategy, developed by Bob Eberle (1982), uses a series of options to develop creative and innovative ways of solving problems or dealing with unique situations.

The options are as follows. The acronym of SCAMPER is used to help students remember each suggestion:

S ubstitute	What else could we use instead?
C ombine	What can we add or cluster or put together?
A dapt	What can we adjust, do differently, or change to suit the situation?
M odify	How can we alter or change the form or quality? Can we magnify or minimize the form?
P ut to other uses	What else could we use this for?
E liminate	What can we remove or omit?
R everse	Could we reverse the process or turn things around?

This strategy can be useful as a catalyst for teachers to make modifications for their students with special needs so that they can learn successfully. Here is an example of how to use it to modify a program for special needs students:

S ubstitute	What learning strategy, materials, assignment, or assessment can we use for this student, considering his or her particular needs?

C ombine	What items can be chunked or grouped together for better understanding?
A dapt	How can timing and pacing be adjusted to suit the students' needs? Reconsider the task analysis to better suit the learner.
M odify	How can form or quantity be altered? Can content be magnified or minimized to accommodate the learner?
P ut to other uses	Could audiotapes, computers, videotapes, or other technology be used to augment the learning process?
E liminate	What can be removed that would make the process more streamlined? What is unnecessary or confusing?
R everse	How can the order be changed to suit the learner? Would the inductive approach work better than the "stand and deliver" approach?

Unfortunately, there is no magic formula to finding the key that will unlock the process or strategy to accommodate the needs of every learner. It is a quest that teachers undertake with each learner to find the method that will best engage and facilitate learning for that particular student.

One classroom teacher had a student named Sam. Sam was very rambunctious and lacked the ability to focus for any length of time. He also had a low tolerance for failure and would become extremely frustrated if he was not successful with his work. The teacher tried many strategies and techniques to modify Sam's instructional activities. She was careful to chunk the activities and information in amounts she was confident that Sam could handle without babying him. The teacher conducted a task analysis in which the components of a particular skill were identified and their appropriate sequence noted. With the task analysis thoughtfully constructed, Sam was more able to follow the sequence of learning activities, and his anxiety level was not as high as it would have been, if he had been presented with every component. This helped prevent him from seeing the task as overwhelming. She also had the help of parent and grandparent volunteers, one of whom had bonded very well with Sam. The teacher was very conscious of the timing and pacing of lessons as well as the importance of varying activities to keep the classroom lively at times and reflective when appropriate. Sam needed clear directions, and the teacher would often audiotape the directions so that Sam could review them and not become frustrated. Reading was not always easy for him. Pairing Sam with a partner to work on tasks also worked well because he liked to talk and ask questions as he worked. The grandparent volunteer was most helpful in helping Sam keep on task and in providing the encouragement he needed to be persistent. They would often work together when it came to the hands-on part of the lesson. A corner of the classroom with a small partition gave Sam and his mentor a quiet place to work, away from the "maddening crowd." They would sometimes go to the Resource Center for a change of scenery and to decrease distractions. Sam and his mentor kept a log and journal where they were sure to record his successes and the strategies that enabled them.

The following list of ABC's may be helpful as a guide or checklist to enhance programs so that they might meet the needs of diverse learners in classrooms. Consider the following suggestions or ideas as you work with diverse learners:

A   Accept diversity, show appreciation, and honor all learners.

B   Build alliances and foster supportive learning communities where all students feel included and respected.

C   Construct concepts by using content in a context that is relevant to students.

D   Design open-ended questions and challenges to explore that will intrigue a variety of learners.

E   Ensure appropriate challenge for individual learners by becoming familiar with their level of skill and their particular interests.

F   Facilitate choice for learners to lower their anxiety and appeal to their unique abilities, strengths, and multiple intelligences and facilitate "flow."

G   Give information by using a variety of instructional approaches and engage the learner by capturing as many senses as possible.

H   Honor collaboration and explore social skills by using cooperative structures.

I   Individual and whole class coaching facilitates the development of trust.

J   Justify group composition by considering student needs and a sociogram of class members.

K   Know how to help students transfer their classroom learning to apply it in the real world and ensure that they see meaning and relevancy in their learning.

L   Lots of variety used in assessment strategies will let students show what they know.

M   Measure and note individual student growth; celebrate progress.

N   Never assume that students understand; ask them to show what they know.

O   One size doesn't fit all; there are many roads to understanding.

P   Plan alternatives for learners so that you have a backup strategy.

Q   Questions help us know the child.

R   Revisit techniques and strategies that have worked in the past.

S   Select strategies that relate to the outcomes and that will enhance learning.

T   Taking stock periodically will help reframe challenging situations.

U   Using others for information and support helps teachers work smarter.

V   Visuals are helpful tools for learning for many learners; explore how they can be used effectively.

W   Working with others develops social skills and acceptance.

X   Xpect setbacks and challenges but be optimistic; reviewing situations and noting what worked in the past can be helpful.

Y   "Yes!" said with feeling can make a world of difference in attitude and energy.

Z   Zillions of great teachers have used thoughtful adaptations to promote learning for special learners; use the resources of colleagues to maximize strategies.

Summary

Many examples are given throughout the book to provide a smorgasbord of instructional and assessment strategies for teachers to consider in accommodating a variety of learners. Learning can take place in many ways and places, structured as individual, partner, or small- or large-group activities or learning-center-based approaches. Assessment can be tailored to include choice and creativity by considering the multiple intelligences, projects, and performances. Considering the uniqueness of each learner stretches a teacher's thinking. The teacher can then select the most appropriate mode for instruction and assessment to facilitate experiences that will help diverse students in the classroom, whether challenged or gifted, construct meaning, develop understanding, and succeed.

Stage Management

Classroom Management Strategies

All the world's a stage,
And all the men and women merely players:
They have their exits and their entrances;
And one man in his time plays many parts . . .
As You Like It, Act II, Scene 7

One could say that all classrooms are a stage, that all students are merely players having their exits and entrances, and that, in time, each plays many parts. Extended blocks of time create more opportunities for student "exits and entrances." Students choosing to exit are those who choose not to engage actively in the learning process and who may perceive that they are not connected to school. They may be preoccupied with problems at home. Students choosing to enter are those who are eager to learn and who enjoy school. School bells sound as each act of the play ends and a new act begins. Creating a quality learning environment in which all students are onstage requires the teacher to be an effective leader, coach, mentor, manager, and facilitator. This chapter offers many suggestions on how to manage a classroom effectively in an extended block so that when they are put into practice, one can create an environment in which all students can learn. The strategies and processes presented can be used to establish and maintain well-managed classrooms. In particular, those cited have been used by teachers in schools using a block schedule.

When one thinks of the teacher as a choreographer of the classroom and its players, the list of tasks to be completed is, at times, daunting. Here are but a few, organized by category.

Setting the Stage

In addition to informal learning experiences acquired by students in the "real world," the classroom is the center stage for learning. The teacher is responsible for organizing a well-managed classroom that maximizes learning, minimizes behavioral problems, and creates a positive and safe environment (e.g., see Duke, 1982). Effective teachers understand the importance that room arrangement has on the learning environment. Each school year, teachers prepare their classrooms prior to the students' arrival. Many teachers ask themselves each year, How can I arrange the room better? The following strategy allows a teacher to be able to visualize what the room would look like if changes were made; it's the same technique used by interior decorators:

1. Measure the size of the room, desks, and any other pieces of furniture.
2. Draw the shape of the room to scale on graph paper.
3. Using the same scale as you used in Step 2, draw the shape of each piece of furniture. You may want to use colored paper, making the color of the teacher's desk different from that of the students' desks. Cut out the shapes (remember to cut out the required number of student desks).
4. Place the shapes on the graph paper the way you would like to arrange the room. Move the shapes until you obtain the desired room arrangement.
5. Arrange the furniture in the room according to the design on the graph paper.

This process may appear to be time-consuming, but it can be well worth the effort. The teacher can save time by not having to move furniture around trying to discover an arrangement that may work. The graph paper and shapes can be stored in an envelope and reused in the future. When arranging the furniture in the classroom, certain considerations need to be taken into account:

- All students must be able to see and hear instruction.
- Traffic areas must be free of congestion.
- Students should have easy access to materials.
- Teacher materials and student materials should be located in separate areas.
- The teacher's desk and file cabinets should be arranged so as not to allow easy access to students. The teacher's work area should be an office within the classroom.

- The arrangement should accommodate for students working in cooperative groups.
- The needs of learners with special needs (wheelchairs, crutches, and so on) should also be considered when designing furniture placement.

Collaborative Classrooms

The success of a play is not the sole responsibility of the director, but rather is a collaborative effort of the cast, makeup artists, costume designers, stage managers, and all others involved in the production. An effective classroom is the result of the collaboration between teacher and students. Students need to feel ownership of the daily routines and procedures that make a classroom become a great place for learning to take place. Research has shown a direct correlation between student achievement and the establishment of routines and procedures during the first 3 weeks of school. If students understand what is expected of them, they are are more inclined to act appropriately. Involving students in the establishment of routines and procedures will reduce the number of discipline problems during the school year. One effective way to generate input from students is for the teacher to ask students, "What would a classroom in which all students can learn look like, sound like, and feel like?" Once this information has been gathered (see Figure 12.1, a blackline master), round-robin brainstorming may be used to devise any routines, procedures, and rules that will need to be in place to create the kind of classroom the students described.

Time Management

Time management means simply the effective use of time. For classroom teachers, time is a precious resource that cannot be wasted (Webster & Bailey, 1991). In Chapter 21 of *The First Days of School: How to Be an Effective Teacher,* Wong and Wong (1991) state, "To increase student learning and achievement, increase the amount of time the student is working" (p. 197). The Wongs describe four kinds of time at school: allocated time, instructional time, engaged time, and academic learning time. Figure 12.2 shows these times and how they are distributed.

Figure 12.1. What Would a Classroom in Which All Students Can Learn Look Like, Sound Like, and Feel Like?

What Would a Classroom in Which All Students Can Learn, Look Like, Sound Like, and Feel Like?

Looks Like	Sounds Like	Feels Like

Robbins, P., Gregory, G., & Herndon, L. E. *Thinking Inside the Block Schedule: Strategies for Teaching in Extended Periods of Time.* Copyright Corwin Press, Inc.

Figure 12.2. Types of Time at School

Types of time	Description	Distribution (%)
Allocated time	Time during which teacher instruction and student learning can take place. (Available time)	100
Instructional time	Time during which teacher is instructing.	90
Engaged time	Time during which students are involved or engaged in a task.	75
Academic learning time	Time students spend on academic tasks that will be assessed, experiencing medium and high success rates.	35

The percentages in Figure 12.2 add up to more than 100 because the teacher and students may be working simultaneously. According to the Wongs, the typical teacher consumes 90% of the allocated time at center stage, talking and working. Engaged time is about 75% of allocated time. During engaged time, students are focused; the teacher monitors, assisting students as needed. Academic learning time is the time students spend engaged in relevant curricular/instructional tasks that will ultimately be assessed and in which they experience medium and high success rates. This is the time in which student competencies would be demonstrated.

Many block schedules have 90-minute classes; such a long time period challenges the teacher to keep students on task. The goal of an effective teacher is to optimize engaged time and academic learning time. "For learning to take place, it is the student, not the teacher, who must be working" (Wong & Wong, 1991, p. 205). Good classroom managers are organized, plan well ahead, use research-based practices, teach in a variety of ways, have all materials ready, and foster student involvement in classroom activities. To prevent wasting any allocated time, the teacher can do the following:

- Always start on time. Modeling timeliness encourages students to be ready for instruction and reduces tardiness. Starting on time also shows respect for those students who are on time and ready to begin class.
- Plan and organize instructional lessons prior to meeting with students.
- Vary the instructional activities.
- Have all materials and resources available.
- Provide for some activities that foster opportunities for movement.
- Collaboratively establish classroom procedures and rules with students at the beginning of the school year.

- Build in time for students to reflect on their work.

- Have music playing during passing time. Stop the music when class is ready to begin; this provides an auditory signal to students and helps create routines.

- Use the Student Responsibility Form and the Student Assignment Sheet (Figures 12.3 and 12.4, respectively, are filled-in samples of these sheets; blank blackline masters of these figures are in Robbins & Herndon, 1998). These forms are for students to use in monitoring their attendance, time on task, coming to class prepared with materials, and completion of assignments. (Details on how to use these forms are discussed in the "Student Responsibility" section of this chapter.)

- Engage students in an activity as soon possible. Have an assignment posted on the board or overhead that students can begin immediately. This can be in the form of an essential question related to the day's curriculum or a question related to the assignment of the previous class period.

- Use sponge activities. (These activities sop up time and provide review or build readiness for a lesson about to occur.)

- Use the last 5 to 10 minutes of class time for students to reflect on the day's lesson. These reflections are often recorded in a learning journal or log.

- Allocate time near the end of class to assign homework. Providing time for students to begin homework allows the teacher the opportunity to check for student understanding and decreases error rates. Students are also more likely to complete homework because they have a good start on it.

- Use Ready/Working signs when students are in cooperative groups. These signs serve as a visual aid during seatwork to inform teachers which groups are still working on an assignment and which groups have completed an assignment. Students place the Working side of the sign facing the teacher as they work. On completion of the task, students turn the sign so that the Ready sign is facing the teacher. Often, teachers have to interrupt students as they work to ask how they are progressing. The sign technique allows teachers to glance around the room and immediately see which groups are still working and which groups have completed the assignment. An added benefit of using these signs experienced by some teachers is that students stay on task because of the visible reminder that they should be working.

Figure 12.3. Sample Student Responsibility Form

Student Name: Jennifer Jones   Class: Biology

Attendance/Tardiness

Week	Mon.	Tues.	Wed.	Thu.	Fri.
1 8/23	P	P	P	P	P
2 8/30	P	P	P	P	P
3 9/6	P	P	P	A	P
4					
5					
6					
7					
8					
9					
10					

Materials

Week	Mon.	Tues.	Wed.	Thu.	Fri.
1 8/23	4	4	4	4	4
2 8/30	3	3	3	4	4
3 9/6	4	4	4	A	4
4					
5					
6					
7					
8					
9					
10					

Task/Participation

Week	Mon.	Tues.	Wed.	Thu.	Fri.
1 8/23	3	3	3	3	3
2 8/30	4	4	4	4	4
3 9/6	4	4	4	A	4
4					
5					
6					
7					
8					
9					
10					

Assignments

Week	Mon.	Tues.	Wed.	Thu.	Fri.
1 8/23	4	4	4	4	4
2 8/30	4	4	4	4	4
3 9/6	4	4	2	A	4
4					
5					
6					
7					
8					
9					
10					

Comments	**Times for detentions/Extra help**
Looks like you had trouble staying on task the first week of school but have corrected the situation. Well done! If you need help with the work missed on 9/9, let me know. Keep up the good work, Mrs. Einstein	

Figure 12.4. Sample Student Assignment Sheet

Name: Jennifer Jones

Name of assignment	Date assigned	Due date	On time	Late	Late date	Points earned/ Points possible	A	B	C	D	F
Chapter 6 questions	9/8	9/9				10/10					
Video-DNA replication	9/11	9/11				10/10					
Quiz-DNA replication	9/12	9/12				13/15					
Group presentation-DNA	9/15	9/15				22/25					
Reflective journal	9/6	10/15			10/16	30/35					

To make the signs from the blackline master in Figure 12.5, fold the paper in half and then in half again. Overlap the top portion and the bottom portion. Staple at both ends to hold the paper together. This will form a pyramid shape that easily sits on a desk. Signs can be copied onto colored paper and laminated to increase their durability.

- Minimize open-ended discussions that are not related to the lesson objective.
- Avoid assigning busy work to fill time.
- Do not give students the opportunity to waste instructional time at the beginning and end of class time. Begin or end with an enticing activity or task. These activities provide an opportunity to review previously taught content or engage students in extended practice of key skills.
- Avoid having to repeat directions. Stating and emphasizing ahead of time that directions will be given only once encourages active listening and can increase note taking. Having directions on the chalkboard or overhead is also a useful strategy. Check for student understanding of directions. Invite a student to model appropriately the desired behaviors.
- Avoid handing out papers during instructional time. Some alternative methods are listed below:
  - ❖ Clip papers onto the Student Responsibility Cards for students to pick up as they enter the room. Copying the Student Responsibility Form on one side of card stock and the Student Assignment Sheet on the reverse side makes these cards especially useful. These cards can also be color-coded for each class.
  - ❖ Have returned papers on the students' desks before students enter the room.
  - ❖ Recruit a student who arrives early to assist in handing out papers.
  - ❖ Have in place student in-boxes and out-boxes. Students can pick up their own papers.

Figure 12.5. Sample Ready/Working Sign

Ready

Working

- Teachers who are organized run well-managed classrooms. Good organization is a time saver in itself. Teachers need to organize for themselves and for their students. Time spent organizing oneself and students at the beginning of the year can make the school year less stressful and more productive. A good place to begin is to recognize and eliminate time wasters. Here are some major time wasters:

  ❖ Lack of organization
  ❖ Lack of objectives
  ❖ Lack of priorities
  ❖ Lack of daily lesson plans
  ❖ Lack of self-discipline, indecision, and procrastination
  ❖ Lack of clear communication
  ❖ Leaving tasks unfinished
  ❖ Cluttered desk
  ❖ Students not understanding assignments
  ❖ Disruptive behavior in classrooms
  ❖ Poorly planned meetings
  ❖ Poor health habits, little exercise, and no rest
  ❖ Lack of energy due to poor nutrition
  ❖ Not using support personnel
  ❖ Trying to be perfect
  ❖ Inability to say no

Managing paper work often can be an overwhelming task. Some teachers have found themselves unprepared for the increase in paperwork that can arise in a block schedule. Employing techniques to reduce the amount of paperwork becomes essential to making effective use of teacher planning time. Color-coding folders, student cards, and student assignments is useful, especially for teachers teaching several subjects or blocks. If using white paper for student assignments, use colored paper clips to differentiate between classes or place papers into colored folders. Students often like to choose the color for their particular class.

Decisions about which papers the teacher will grade must be made ahead of instruction. Because of the increase of material covered in one day in a block schedule,

the timeliness of student feedback is a crucial concern. Research has shown that the sooner a student receives feedback regarding progress, the greater the increase in learning. One solution is to make keys of assignments and then have students correct their work themselves. This works well if using cooperative groups; the groups can correct their work together and discuss any mistakes made and ways to improve their performance. Not all student work needs to be graded; however, it should be corrected. Some teachers explain to students which work is practice and which is for assessment. Short application quizzes can be given to assess student learning on practice work, thus eliminating the need for the teacher to grade and record every worksheet.

Effective use of planning time can reduce the amount of paperwork teachers take home. Some teachers establish routines to increase productivity. Examples follow:

- Set one planning period aside each week to communicate with parents and students. Call parents of students doing well in school, as well as parents of those who are not. Contacting parents during the first few weeks of school prevents losing planning time in the future because of parental issues. It also enhances home-school relationships and fosters parental understanding of instructional/curricular goals.

- Use one planning period each week for making telephone calls, previewing videos, going through mail, and ordering supplies and materials.

- Clean off the desk each night and write on the chalkboard the next day's activities.

- Establish times that students can come in for extra help or advice. This may be two afternoons and two mornings each week. Some teachers have found that more students come in for help when the teachers set a schedule that stays the same throughout the school year. For example, the teacher can post in the classroom a sign like the one shown in Figure 12.6.

- Select one day and call it "My Day." Make sure everyone understands that this is your uninterrupted time before and after school. Student and faculty members will soon learn that this is the time you want to work with no interruptions.

- Plan on staying late one night each week. This may eliminate the need to take work home on the weekends.

- Frequently document necessary information regarding a lesson's successes and failures, student behaviors, and materials needed.

Figure 12.6. Sample Sign Advertising Teacher Availability for Extra Help

Mrs. Einstein is available before and after school on Tuesdays and Thursdays for those students who would like extra help, have questions, or would like to work on projects or need advice on school matters.

Student Responsibility

One expectation of teachers teaching in extended periods of instructional time is to increase student responsibility. This is essential as they help prepare students to become adult members of society, as well as contribute to teacher sanity! One way to help students increase responsibility for their own learning is to have them monitor their on-time performance, time on task, bringing materials to class, and completion of assignments. Prior to meeting with students, teachers should make copies of the Student Responsibility Form (sample shown in Figure 12.3; blank blackline master is in Robbins & Herndon, 1998) and the Student Assignment Sheet (sample shown in Figure 12.4 on page 152; a blackline master is in Robbins & Herndon, 1998) onto card stock. Some teachers color-code for individual classes. Every student is given a student card at the beginning of the semester. At this time, the teacher can explain the concept of the card to the class. This task provides an opportunity for the teacher to discuss with students the importance of good attendance, of bringing materials to class, of time on task, and of turning in assignments.

Some teachers involve students in the entire process by collaboratively establishing a simple rubric that can be used to record information on the cards. Having students brainstorm the indicators to establish the criteria from which rubrics can be developed establishes student ownership. Individual rubrics are created for each area: attendance, bringing materials to class, class participation/time on task, and assignment completion (see Figure 12.7).

As students enter the classroom each day, they pull their cards from an in-box where they are stored and then complete the attendance and materials sections as the teacher takes roll. Following roll or at the end of the class period, the teacher can clip all makeup work to the cards of absent students and place them back in the in-box. When students who have been absent return to class, they will find all their makeup work on the cards; this eliminates the students' need to request makeup work. At the end of the period, students complete the card sections for participation and assignments and return the cards to the in-box as they leave the classroom.

These cards can be used in several ways. They will only be effective, however, if the criteria are clearly defined for and with the students. For example, students need to know what "being on task" means and what the teacher's expectations are. The cards can also be a very useful tool for the teacher in determining how much time to allot for assignments. For example, if the majority of students marked their cards with a 2 in the assignments box, more time is needed for them to complete the assignment.

Figure 12.7. Student Responsibility Card: Sample Rubrics

SUGGESTIONS FOR USE

- **Attendance/Tardiness:** Students can mark these according to the teacher's instruction—for example, P—present, A—absent, T—tardy.

- **Materials:**
  1. Student has not brought any materials to class.
  2. Student has writing materials only.
  3. Student has writing materials and notebook.
  4. Student has writing materials

- **Task/Participation:**
  1. Student is on task 0–25% of the time.
  2. Student is on task 26–50% of the time.
  3. Student is on task 51–75% of the time.
  4. Student is on task 76–100% of the time.

- **Assignments:**
  1. Assignment 0–25% completed.
  2. Assignment 26–50% completed.
  3. Assignment 51–75% completed.
  4. Assignment 76–100% completed.

Having students keep track of all their work also increases responsibility. Using the Student Assignment Sheet can also be a time saver because students will not need to ask the teacher constantly whether they have completed all their work. Many teachers post a completed sample assignment chart for each block so that students can reference it should they have questions about assignments they have recorded on their individual sheets. Assignment sheets can be copied onto the back of the Student Responsibility Form as previously discussed. Students can keep track of when assignments were given, when they are due, whether they were submitted on time or late, and the points or grades earned. These sheets can be useful to share with parents at conferences, should any questions arise concerning assignment time frames. Copies of these forms can be sent home to parents at the beginning of the year so that they understand classroom expectations.

The cards also allow the teacher to identify early in the semester any students who have a tendency to turn in late work or lose assignments and any who are generally

disorganized. The information provided on the cards can help students improve their organizational skills and become more responsible toward their work.

Communication

Good communication between teacher and students creates a caring environment in which all students can learn. The student responsibility cards previously discussed can be used as an avenue to increase written communication between teacher and student. Some students find it easier or more comfortable to write to a teacher versus speaking to a teacher in front of colleagues. The sample communication slips shown in Figure 12.8 can easily be attached to the student responsibility cards with a paper clip (a blackline master of these slips is in Robbins & Herndon, 1998). The slips can be cut out and placed in a small box along with a pen and paper clips and be located where students can easily access them. Students can communicate with the teacher by writing messages on the slips and attaching them to their student responsibility cards, which they place in the in-box as they leave the classroom. The teacher can remove the cards from the in-box, retrieve any messages written by students, and respond to students by attaching written responses to the cards, which are returned to the in-box. The next time students come to class, they pick up their cards and read the teacher's responses. Some teachers keep a box of communication slips on their desks for easy access. Some teacher uses for the communication slips are: giving positive feedback, encouraging good behavior, building student self-esteem, asking for student input on classroom matters, arranging for conferences with students, and reminding students of any school-related items.

Effective communication with parents and guardians can directly affect students' perceptions of the teacher. More often than not, relationships with parents are established when teachers are experiencing problems with students or have concerns regarding students' work or lack of work. Many teachers have found it easier to establish relationships with parents before concerns or issues arise than after. Communicating with parents during the first 3 weeks of school to discuss expectations and to answer any questions parents may have establishes a trusting relationship for the remainder of the school year. To reap the benefits of this relationship, teachers should communicate with parents throughout the school year to discuss student progress, and to obtain data about parents' perceptions.

Some teachers have found it useful to have a place for recording notes about telephone conversations, conferences, or parental requests. Such documentation can be valuable during conferences involving parents and the principal, counselor, or student adviser. The Teacher-Parent Communication Record, a sample of which is displayed in Figure 12.9, is one way to maintain such documentation (a blackline master of this sheet is in Robbins & Herndon, 1998).

Figure 12.8. Sample Communication Slips

Daily Reminder:

You still need to turn in your reflective journal to me.

Mrs.Einstein

Awesome!
The model you made of DNA was great. It reflected a great deal of hard work.

Mrs.Einstein

Please see me . . .

How you've improved! Great job! Keep it up! Coming in for that extra help paid off! Glad you did that as your recent work has reflected more effort.

Mrs.Einstein

News Flash ! ! !

You got my attention because . . .

Figure 12.9. Sample Teacher-Parent Communication Record

Student name	Parent name	Date	Notes/Parental requests/ Teacher recommendations
Jennifer Jones	Mrs. E. Jones	6/17	Discussed the fact that Jennifer is working hard and that her journal was turned in late.
Andre Smith	Mrs. Myers	6/17	Related information regarding Andre making up work missed during his absence due to illness.
Pat Stiles	Mr. & Mrs. L. Stiles	6/17	Called to say Pat is a joy to have in class and works well with other students.
John Redfield	Mr. & Mrs. Redfield	6/17	Called to discuss John's missing assignments and to suggest that he come in for extra help after school.

Student Absences

Students need to be in the classroom for learning to take place. Sometimes when students are absent from school, the implications in a block schedule can result in more makeup work than in a traditional schedule. For those students who miss just 1 day, attaching any makeup assignments to the Student Responsibility Cards can instantly provide the student with makeup work. But what does a teacher do when students are absent for several days? Some teachers send work home whenever possible and keep in contact with the parents. Some teachers use a We Miss You Form (see sample in Figure 12.10) as a cover sheet that can be clipped to students' makeup work. After the students return, the teacher can arrange a time to assist them in catching up with their classmates.

Figure 12.10. Sample "We Miss You" Form

We Miss You!

We are sorry that you have not been able to join us for class. Here are some of the assignments you have missed. Hope to see you soon.

Assignments/Instructions:

Today (6/9) we began class with the question, "How will your knowledge of DNA replication affect you in your future role as an adult and maybe a parent?" Students recorded their responses in their reflective journals.

Next, we discussed the process of DNA protein synthesis. I have attached carbon-copied notes to this sheet. Reading pages 48-52 in your text will be useful.

The class then broke into groups to work on projects. Your group is investigating gene therapy and its application in medicine. They went to the computer lab to do further research on this project. When you return, you can check with your group to see how they progressed.

We spent the last 10 minutes of class discussing the homework assignment that I have attached to this sheet. On the worksheet, you are to label the diagram showing protein synthesis and answer the questions.

Other: Just a quick reminder that I will be collecting reflective journals next Thursday.

I hope you get well soon. Call me if you have any questions.

Mrs. Einstein

One useful strategy that helps students who have missed school is to make copies of notes that may have been taken by other students in class. A quick way to do this is to give sheets of carbon paper and plain paper to a student who has legible handwriting. Once the student has taken notes, the carbon copy can be put into a three-ring binder for absent students to use on their return. Teachers can also have students do this when giving assignments and oral directions. The three-ring binder then becomes a classroom log. The teacher can put into the binder a copy of any assignments handed to students; in this way, absent students can double-check that they received all their makeup work. Another technique is to have a daily log posted on the wall or a clipboard. The log should contain a listing of what was done in class that day. If a laptop

computer is available, students can take notes for absent class members. Some teachers audiotape classes; other teachers have assigned study buddies to help colleagues who have been absent. Some schools have instituted a homework hotline.

At times, parents pull students out of school for family vacations. In this situation, students or parents may or may not discuss this ahead of time with the teacher. If any assignments would be difficult for the students to make up, some teachers have assigned alternative assignments that students can do while on vacation. Examples of alternative assignments are listed below:

Foreign language. Have the student write in a journal, using the foreign language being learned, including all the details of the events and places seen while on vacation.

English. Have the student write an essay describing the places visited and then have the student discuss how these places compare with the town or city in which she or he lives.

Science. Have the student record and describe all the wildlife (both plants and animals), climate, and terrain seen. Using this information, the student can put together a travel brochure advertising the places visited.

Social Studies. Have the student draw a map showing how to get to the final destination. The student could keep a travel log recording all the historical buildings and landmarks seen or construct a time line depicting any historical events that may have taken place in the area.

Substitute Teachers

Sometimes during the school year, the regular classroom teacher has to be gone. Teachers who know ahead of time that they will be gone can leave all lesson plans and materials for the substitutes. Some teachers overplan in this situation to ensure that the substitute has plenty of meaningful, engaging activities for students. Leaving busy work can often make the day more challenging for the substitute.

At other times during the school year, the regular classroom teacher may become ill unexpectedly. For those teachers who are effective managers and plan ahead, a sudden absence caused by illness or other emergency is not always a major problem for the substitute teacher. The following suggestions may help the classroom teacher prepare the substitute teacher to manage the day in such a way that it does not disrupt the learning process.

- Complete a Helpful Hints for the Substitute Teacher Form (see sample in Figure 12.11; a blackline master is in Robbins & Herndon, 1998). This will help the substitute teacher locate all necessary materials, identify responsible students who may assist them, and identify which other teachers they might ask for help.

Figure 12.11. Sample Helpful Hints for the Substitute Teacher Form

Classroom teacher's name: Mrs. Einstein   Room 202

You will find the following essential items in the places indicated:

Item	Location
Grade book	In "The Teacher's Day-Planner"—middle drawer of teacher's desk.
Seating chart	In "The Teacher's Day-Planner"—middle drawer of teacher's desk.
Attendance sheets	Left-hand drawer of teacher's desk.
Teaching materials	The materials currently being used will be on the top shelf of the bookcase.
Lesson plans	In "The Teacher's Day-Planner"—middle drawer of teacher's desk.
Emergency lesson plans	In a file folder located at the front of the first drawer of the filing cabinet.
Hall passes	Left-hand drawer of teacher's desk.
Referrals	Left-hand drawer of teacher's desk.

My schedule is as follows:

Period 1—Biology
Period 2—Biology
Period 3—Preparation time
Period 4—Environmental Science

Dependable students in my classes:

Period 1—James Murray
Period 2—Andre Smith
Period 3—Preparation time
Period 4—Tina Martinez

Teachers who can help:

Mrs. Stiley and Mr. Percival

Special procedures:

Jennifer Jones will need a pass to go to the nurse at 10 a.m.

- Make sure all necessary materials are located where the substitute can easily find them.
- Leave a map of the school and lunch information on your desk. This is especially useful for those substitutes who may be in your building for the first time.
- Always leave a telephone number where you can be reached.
- Write little notes of explanation on sticky notes and attach them to the assignments to be given.
- Leave any necessary answer keys. Some substitutes will check papers during planning time whenever they can. This is a big help for the regular classroom teacher.
- Teachers who know ahead of time that they will be gone should inform students of the upcoming absence and explain what they will be doing. This shows respect for the students and can model trust. It also provides another context to work on student responsibility.
- Some teachers who use project-based learning have the class use the time they are absent for research and for working on projects.
- Always have on hand emergency lesson plans that can be used by a substitute teacher.
- Let substitute teachers know they are appreciated. A little thank-you note can say so much!

Summary

A well-choreographed play in which the actors have rehearsed, collaborated, and performed to their highest expectations results in an exciting performance that gets rave reviews. One might say that a well-managed classroom in which students have rehearsed, collaborated, and performed to their highest expectations results in an exciting environment in which all students achieve and performances receive high grades. Effective classroom management results in more time for effective teaching, greater student learning, and increased student responsibility.

13

Critics' Choice

Understanding and Assessment

Every play has critics who give reviews of the play, the playwright, the scenery, the plot, and the actors, based on their personal opinions, preferences, and likes and dislikes. In their critiques, they recommend or condemn the performance on the basis of their individual, personal reactions. What may be revered by one critic may be discredited by another. In classrooms, teachers and students cannot rely on personal opinions to assess the performances and achievement of learners. One opinion at one point in time is also not valid. Students need continuous feedback during the learning process so that they have an indication of how they are doing based on clear criteria and indicators. This is the *assessment* process—from the Latin *assessus*, "to sit beside." Periodically, students are graded at particular intervals on the basis of the quality and/or quantity of their work and how close they are to the standard. This is *evaluation*, placing a value on the growth.

The assessment process informs the learner and the teacher. The brain naturally seeks feedback. Feedback informs students about their progress. As students receive

the data, they can analyze and reflect on the information so that their progress can act as a motivator and they can set goals in areas that still have room for improvement. Feedback or assessment data can also inform the teacher about what is working, how students are doing, and what in the program needs to be changed. The information points to the next steps for the learner. Assessment data also inform the school, parents, and community.

When educators clearly identify and share standards with criteria and indicators that describe success, they enable students to internalize the "target" and thus make it more likely that the students will succeed. Richard Stiggins, founder of the Assessment Training Institute, reminds us that most students can hit any target that is clear and holds still long enough.

Extended time periods have more time for building in and facilitating teacher, peer, and self-assessments that let students know how they are progressing in relationship to the standards. The learning cycle (see Figure 4.2 in Chapter 4) keeps the learning process moving forward. *Relaxed alertness* is a term used to describe the condition of appropriate challenge in a safe environment.

With continuous feedback, support, time, choice, and an enriched environment, learners can continue to improve and to master standards. As teachers strive to enable learners to reach standards and expectations that are meaningful and worthwhile, they need to begin with the end in mind, as noted Chapter 4, on curriculum.

Understanding

Educators have long tried to get students to understand concepts and acquire knowledge. The definitions of *understand* in *Merriam-Webster's Collegiate Dictionary* (1998) include "to grasp the meaning of," "to have thorough or technical acquaintance with or expertness in the practice of," and "to be thoroughly familiar with . . ." (pp. 1288-1289). Here are some realities of acquiring understanding:

- It is not superficial, but conscious.
- It is not shallow, but deep.
- It is not instantaneous, but developmental.

People exemplify their understanding through the ability to explain, apply, empathize, interpret, define a perspective, and thus create an awareness of self-knowledge. In planning curriculum, teachers need to consider various learning experiences and assessment tools that will enable their students to develop understanding that endures. The planning model shown in Figure 13.1 is a series of thoughtful questions for teachers to consider when planning by beginning with standards in mind.

Figure 13.1. Planning Model for the Learning Cycle

Questions to consider: How will we know?

What will students know and be able to do? (skills)

_____

_____

_____

What attitudes or behaviors will be developed?

_____

_____

_____

Describe criteria and indicators for success.

_____

_____

_____

Rubrics and targets may be used at this point to show students the expectations.

What assessment tools will be used to collect data?

_____

_____

_____

What learning strategies will enable students to develop these competencies? (Remember, one size doesn't fit all.)

- _____
- _____
- _____
- _____
- _____

How will feedback be built into the process?

_____

_____

_____

How will metacognition and goal setting be addressed?

_____

_____

_____

Assessment

Extended periods of instructional time can provide students with an opportunity to explore content in depth with the goal of long-lasting understanding (Wiggins & McTighe, 1998). Larger blocks of time help us move from misconceptions to reality:

Misconceptions . . .	Reality . . .
One assessment is enough.	Many assessment tools validate data.
Personal judgment alone is enough.	Clear criteria and indicators are needed.
Teachers do assessments to students.	Students are partners in the assessment process.

To collect data on student growth and achievement, teachers can use any of the many assessment tools now available. Some assessment tools and strategies are shown in Figure 13.2.

Figure 13.2. Assessment Tools and Strategies

Products and Projects
- Dioramas
- Maps
- Research
- Video production
- Portfolios
- Models

Pen-and-Pencil Tests
- Matching
- Multiple choice
- Fill in the blanks
- Essay

Performances
- Speeches
- Presentations
- Demonstration
- Music/dances
- Exhibitions

Checklists
- Individual/peer
- Group
- Teacher
- Multiple intelligences

Observation
- Video
- Group members
- Teacher

Logs
- Factual information
- Data for reaction
- Time management

Journals
- Personal reflection
- Goal setting
- Metacognition

Brain-Compatible Assessments

The currently available cognitive research about how humans learn questions, as well as informs, educational practice in terms of assessment. The acronym *BRAIN* can help teachers focus on issues concerning assessment:

B   uilding safe environments where students feel confident and encouraged to practice and take risks in the learning process.

R   elevant and meaningful tasks are necessary to engage learners.

A   dequate time to practice, understand, and apply new learnings and receive ongoing feedback is necessary to continue to set goals and move forward.

I   ntelligence is unique to each individual. Each person learns and demonstrates understanding in unique ways.

N   egotiation or transfer to long-term memory takes time and conscious planning, including reflection and metacognition.

Let's take a closer look at each component of brain-compatible assessments.

B   Brains need a safe, risk-free environment in which to flourish.

A state of relaxed alertness is required in which learners are challenged by tasks just beyond their skill level (so that they must stretch) in a safe, nurturing, supportive environment. The environment should be enriched with manipulatives and other resources that facilitate the growth of dendrites (neural connections). Clear criteria and a variety of ways to demonstrate competencies must be provided so that students can approach learning with confidence and optimism. Developing rubrics and clear targets with students helps them internalize the expectations and clearly enhances the understanding of the learning tasks.

Clear Expectations. Athletes who compete are accustomed to being scored on a rubric. The criteria and indicators for the task are well defined and shared prior to the performance. Armed with this knowledge and comfortable that no "gotchas" will crop up toward the end, students are more able to tackle the challenge and confidently achieve the goal.

Figure 13.3 is an example of a scoring rubric that may be used for sharing expectations of a quality performance with students prior to the task of designing an oral presentation. In this case, the rubric acts as a clear target. It may be developed by the teacher or in collaboration with students. Students are often able to articulate criteria for a quality performance. Having generated the rubric, they have internalized the expectations and proceed more enlightened toward a quality presentation. The rubric is valuable not only for understanding the target but also as a coaching tool that students can use for peer feedback as they practice their presentations. Finally, it can serve as an evaluation when students are ready to give their practiced and polished delivery. If a grade is required, the teacher may weight each criterion to arrive at a final

grade. For example, the organization and coherency score may be multiplied by 3, whereas the eye contact may only be weighted by 1. In Figure 13.3, the Visual Aids section is not filled in. What do you think the indicators should be at each level?

Figure 13.3. Rubric for a Speech or Oral Presentation

Purposes:

Use during the design and practice phase to give peer feedback or to self-assess.

Use as a grading or evaluation device.

Use up front as a clear target.

| Criteria | Indicators | | | |
	1	2	3	4
Originality	Only the facts are presented.	Moments of creativity but mostly facts are presented.	Unique and creative ideas were presented.	Sparkling, creative elements of surprise and intrigue were presented.
Organization	Need to work at clarifying the message.	Topic is clear and somewhat engaging.	Focused topic engages the audience.	Topic is motivating, clear, and expands on ideas.
Coherency and flow	Need to connect ideas to have a flow.	Most ideas linked, some flawed, but pauses are distracting.	Flow from idea to idea. Linked well. Connected.	Extremely clear with purpose, and logical flow.
Voice	Monotone and lacks expression.	Some expression and volume control.	Easily heard, appropriate, and varied expression.	Clear, varied volume with creative expression.
Eye Contact	Mostly read from notes.	Occasionally glanced at audience.	Familiar with presentation and confident to make eye contact.	Obviously knowledgeable and used eye contact to engage the audience.
Visual aids				

R Relevant and meaningful tasks and assessments engage the learner.

Real-world applications engage the learner. Real-world applications, useful information, and skills applied in a meaningful context are more likely to capture and focus student attention, which in turn has the potential to facilitate learning. Authentic assessments include projects and products, performances and exhibitions, in which

standards are embedded in real-world situations. These assessments are engaging and bring relevance to learning. They also provide an opportunity for elaborative rehearsal so that new information and concepts can be more deeply explored and thus, from the experience, new connections are fostered in the brain and the information is retained in long-term memory. Such assessments also appeal to particular interests and preferences. Wiggins (1992) describes authentic assessment: "One must please a real audience, make a design work, or achieve an aesthetic effect that causes pride or dismay in the result" (p. 27). Authentic assessments generally tap into higher levels of thinking and problem-solving abilities. They connect to the real world in their application and are assessed by using judgment based on criteria. These more authentic tasks involve new roles for teachers and students as they plan and learn together. Authentic assessments include projects and products, dioramas, maps, research, video production, models, portfolios, speeches, presentations, demonstrations, music/dance performances, and exhibitions.

In these more authentic assessments, teachers should consider the following:

- Standards are selected and embedded in the tasks.
- Data collection tools are designed to track progress.
- Students learn processes to gather, analyze, manage, and synthesize information.
- A variety of levels of thinking (Bloom's or others) are tapped.
- Time management and persistence strategies are built in.
- Opportunities to work collaboratively and/or independently are considered.
- Some choice is allowed to accommodate individual interests and preferences.

When designing authentic tasks, students need guidance in planning and managing the process. Figure 13.4 is an example of an organizer that students can use to plan an exhibition.

Figure 13.4. Organizer for Planning an Exhibition

Planning an exhibition (could be used for project, product, or performance)

Topic: _____   Expectations: _____

Essential questions:

_____

_____

_____

Secondary questions:

_____

_____

_____

Preliminary brainstorm:

What do I know or think I know?	What do I want or need to know?	Where? How? When will I get it?

Planning guide:

Steps:	Time frame:	Findings:

Medium for sharing:	Resources:

SOURCE: Adapted from Ogle (1986) and Stephen, Gallagher, & Workman (1993).

Robbins, P., Gregory, G., & Herndon, L. E. *Thinking Inside the Block Schedule: Strategies for Teaching in Extended Periods of Time.* Copyright Corwin Press, Inc.

A Adequate time is needed to practice, reassess, try again,
and ultimately master concepts and skills as needed.

It takes time to rehearse and/or elaborate to produce long-term retention, whether it be declarative or procedural. The brain naturally seeks feedback. All people soon lose interest in a game or other task if they do not see progress from their efforts. Feedback is necessary to encourage continued effort and to adjust behavior and plans. It has been said that a person cannot "fatten a pig by weighing it." All those who have acquired expert or mastery levels have received continuous feedback and coaching from a variety of sources, whether from others or through self-reflection.

Observation. Often, class periods go by in a blur. With short periods, teachers get little chance to interact and observe students as they problem-solve and work together. If teachers believe that all learners need feedback, then building in time to give it is important. Longer class periods allow application time during which teachers can work with individual students on enrichment or remedial tasks. Using sticky notes, teachers can jot down observations that they make during the period and transfer them to student files. Teachers can also use checklists and observation forms. It is unrealistic, however, to think that one teacher can give adequate feedback to all students in the class, each period. That is why it is so important for teachers to help students develop observation and feedback skills that they can use with others or themselves.

Using a matrix with students' names across the top and skills listed down one side is a way teachers can track frequency of student use of particular skills. Teachers can easily observe student skills such as listening attentively, taking turns, using polite voices, and sharing tasks. They can also observe student skill development in areas such as computer use, coordination in physical activities, and organizational procedures.

Names				
Listening attentively				
Taking turns				
Using polite voices				
Sharing tasks				

Cautions in Observation. Be sure that

- Skills are carefully identified.
- Expectations are clear.
- The observation is not too complex; observe one or two behaviors and only one or two students at a time.
- Feedback is non-evaluative—only the facts are given, not a judgment; judgments should be made by the individual or group, as a response to the feedback, through self-reflection and dialogue.
- Rubrics used as a tool for giving feedback are clear and understandable; the following is an example of an observation chart for data gathering.

Often students are not aware of what a behavior, skill, or competency looks and sounds like. The following chart may be used to have students describe attributes of a particular skill.

Skill: _____   Description: Fill in the Looks like and
                                                  Sounds like columns.

Looks like	Sounds like

Observer: Check off as many behaviors as you saw or heard as you observed the group work together. Note the names of group members who used those behaviors.

I Intelligence is unique to each individual.

People acquire knowledge, develop competencies, and display or demonstrate understanding in different ways, depending on their unique, individual ways of "knowing." Therefore, teachers should consider the multiple intelligences in designing learning activities and assessment strategies. Figure 13.5, a blackline master, provides ample options for using multiple intelligences in learning and assessment. Make two copies of the blackline master and cut out the middle circle. Attach this with a paper

Figure 13.5. Multiple Intelligences Learning and Assessment

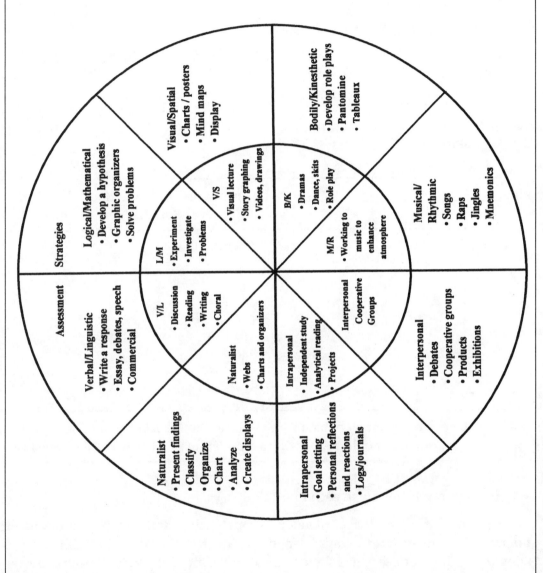

Robbins, P., Gregory, G., & Herndon, L. E. *Thinking Inside the Block Schedule: Strategies for Teaching in Extended Periods of Time.* Copyright Corwin Press,

fastener to the full sheet over the larger circle to provide a flexible wheel in the center. Turning the wheel allows one to access and select from many learning and assessment approaches to reach targeted standards.

Contracts. To further personalize instructional and assessment tasks and capitalize on students' multiple intelligences, teachers may design contracts to facilitate individualized approaches to learning. The authentic tasks mentioned previously are excellent vehicles to honor students' diverse multiple intelligences profiles and to create options in a contract. Contracts give students choice in the learning process and ownership for designing their own learning. This is highly motivating and tends to generate commitment from students. It allows for creativity, an emotional hook, and elaboration of content for long-term retention.

Teachers have been using forms of contracts for many years. It was one way of dealing with students accomplishing behavioral objectives in an individualized program (Berte, 1975; Knowles, 1986; Tomlinson, 1997, 1999; Winebrenner, 1992). A *contract* is a brain-compatible tool used to set goals for student learning. Students vary in interests and abilities, and often a contract can help the learner

- Have realistic expectations
- Stretch him- or herself
- Outline basics required
- Self-empower
- Deal with multiple intelligences
- Capitalize on strengths
- Ensure success
- Manage time effectively and efficiently

In a contract, a basic *core set* of expectations based on standards for all learners is clearly delineated at the onset of the unit. To do this, a teacher must

- Outline clearly the content and skills involved in the unit
- Develop criteria for success
- Design the assessment process
- Identify timelines
- Share grading guidelines with students
- Delineate clear expectations

A contract may include optional topics and activities, such as the following:

- Research or inquiry questions to further extend learning
- Activities for multiple intelligences
  - ❖ Presentation in an area of interest

- ❖ Exhibition
- ❖ Project
- ❖ Debate/Academic controversy
- ❖ Community outreach/Interview
- ❖ Song or rap
- ❖ Narrative or short story
- ❖ Skit or dramatization
- ❖ Role play or talk show

A contract is clearly mapped out for the student or group of students. Timelines and the core expectations are outlined for all, with opportunities to increase success through time management and planning. Opportunity is provided for negotiation and development of *flow*—that state in which the learner has a sense of control, challenge and skill levels are matched, feedback is ongoing, the learner is unconscious of time, and intrinsic motivation is present (Csikszentmihalyi, 1991). Contracts and the negotiation of choice in assessment lessen the chances of students "downshifting," emotionally hijacking, or developing a sense of helplessness and anxiety. Figure 13.6 is an example of a contract. A sample of a blank contract form is provided in Figure 13.7.

Figure 13.6. World War II Contract

To help you improve your understanding of the causes and reactions to World War II, you may complete the core activities and then choose any optional activities that, when included, will total at least 40 points.

Fill in the contract and hand it in by _____.

Core activities that everyone will do: points
  1. Read the chapter in the text and view the documentary video.
     Fill in the questionnaire. (10)   _____
  2. Using the computer program, create a time line of events that
     led to U.S. involvement in the war. (5)   _____
  3. Select one key political leader and chronicle his or her
     involvement with the war. Present your findings. (10)   _____

Optional selections:
  4. Create a photo essay depicting the events that led to U.S.
     involvement in the war. (10)   _____
  5. Draw a story map or mind map illustrating the contributing
     factors. (10)   _____
  6. Write a letter to a political leader of the time and share your
     views on why you think the United States should or should
     not be involved in the war. (5)   _____

7. Compare the music that was popular during three major
   conflicts in American history aùnd that describe the sentiment
   of the populace. (5)   _____

8. Using a Venn diagram, compare and contrast the causes of
   World War I with World War II. (10)   _____

Additional ideas here: _____

-    _____
-    _____
-    _____

Total points   _____

Signed by student _____

Signed by teacher _____

Figure 13.7. Sample Contract Form

A teacher may use this form in thinking through the development of a contract that may be given to students so that each learner can have some choice in his or her learning.

Contract for _____

Decide on the time frame for the contract.

Expectations desired:

_____

_____

_____

_____

Decide on the core activities that everyone will participate in to develop the knowledge, skills, and attitudes desired.

1. _____
2. _____
3. _____
4. _____

Consider options for students to apply or enhance their learning and thus be motivated through opportunities from a variety of areas, including choices in the multiple intelligences.

Prepare a poster or collage, write a speech, prepare a skit or role play, write a song or rap, produce a video, write a reaction paper, prepare a newspaper, build a model, make a diorama, investigate a question, integrate computer use, and so on (other ideas you can think of that would appeal to your students and that are based on standards).

_____

_____

_____

_____

Options:

1. _____

2. _____

3. _____

4. _____

N   Negotiate long-term retention.

Varied learning experiences will provide students with memorable moments. Pat Wolfe, an educational consultant noted for her insights into the implications for brain research on classroom practice (Wolfe & Sorgen, 1990), reminds teachers that real learning takes place when long-term memory is altered. The more vivid the experience, the more vivid the memory. Also, location of the learning experience, emotions associated with the learning, and contexts in which the learning occurred all contribute greatly to developing memories. Dialogue, reflection, and metacognition help solidify learnings and facilitate transfer. The use of logs and journals, metacognitive strategies, and portfolio reflections all contribute to moving learning to long-term memory. Reflection and metacognition are crucial steps in negotiating long-term retention.

Metacognition, the thinking about one's thinking, is a key to being able to access previously used strategies and information and to use it in new situations. Whether teachers give students the opportunity during the lesson (e.g., 10 min of lecture and 2 min of reflection and partner talk) or at the conclusion of the lesson to reflect on process, content, or how the new information or skill can be used in the real life of the learner, time is needed during the learning process. Strategies such as PNI (Plus, Negative, Interesting; deBono, 1976, 1985) are useful in helping students focus on specific aspects of the material.

PNI.

P   lus
    These are the things that are important . . .
    This is the upside of . . .
    This explains . . .

Now I know . . .
Now I can . . .

N egative
The downside of this is . . .
I'm concerned about . . .
What worries me is . . .
I'd like to explore . . . further because . . .

I nteresting
That is an interesting idea . . .
I never thought of things in that way . . .
This is a different way of looking at . . .

If students have viewed a video, read an article, or experienced any learning or presentation, PNI may be used to reflect and project individual or group ideas.

De Bono (1985) also created the activity *six thinking hats;* students wear the hats metaphorically, or in primary grades, students may wear actual hats as they react to new information or experiences. Individual students may choose a colored hat, or small groups may process using a specific hat. In a small group, each member may wear a different hat to ensure that all aspects of the topic are explained:

- The *white hat* views the material or topic to gather data. It is a rationale and neutral viewpoint (pure as the driven snow).
- The *gray hat* views from the downside and selects the cautions, flaws, errors, risks, and negative aspects, somewhat like playing the devil's advocate (dark side).
- The *green hat* views the situation with an eye to the creative possibilities (lush green growth). What are the opportunities and connections and new approaches?
- The *red hat* views the information and explores the feelings and emotions involved. What intuitives or gut feelings surface?
- The *yellow hat* views the situation with a "sunny outlook." What are all the positive things associated with this topic? How is this optimistic and beneficial?
- The *blue hat* is the reflective chapeau. Those who wear it define and summarize and draw conclusions from the material.

In extended time blocks, teachers and students have time to reflect and discuss issues beyond just recall for the test. Time to relate, connect, and reflect is valuable in the learning process so that new information and skills are discussed and internalized through metacognitive strategies.

Logs and Journals. These reflective tools have long been used in language arts classrooms to connect learning and clarify thoughts the individual learner has related to a character or idea. The activity further enhances writing skills. In recent times, other

subject disciplines have realized the power of logs and journals in the assessment process. Entries may be written, audiotaped, videotaped, put onto a disk, or illustrated with graphic organizers or other visual representations according to individual student interests and preferences. The power of logs and journals is in the reflection and goal setting completed by the individual or group. Often, sentence stems are given to help generate idea flow:

- What really interested me was . . .
- It makes me wonder . . .
- It was puzzling to me . . .
- I enjoyed . . .
- I was not comfortable with . . .
- I'm confused about . . .
- I want to know more about . . .
- The next step for me is . . .
- Other issues I would like to pursue . . .
- I continue to wonder about . . .

PNI or six thinking hats may also serve as a springboard for journal writing. Students can use PNI to reflect in their journals, or they can choose a particular hat (or the teacher can assign one) and wear it as they reflect. For those students who find it difficult to focus, this may be a guide as well as a creative way to deal with metacognition. Logs generally capture information and facts and track events. Journals are more reflective in relationship to the facts or events. These two activities can be done simultaneously as a time management and reflective piece with individual or small groups while working on a cooperative task.

Log entry		Journal reflections and next steps	
Date	Process	Reactions	Tomorrow I will:

Any of these sentence stems or tools may be used to exit pass or ticket out (Marshall & Burz, 1997). *Exit passes* are completed by individual students at the end of the period

to feed back reactions and reflections to the teacher. Students respond to a question or jot down two things they learned and one question they still have. This is valuable information given in a safe venue for the teacher to respond to at the beginning of the next class. Feedback from students is valuable for teachers; they can use it to help them in planning the next steps in response to students and their needs.

Portfolio Reflection. When a teacher decides to keep student portfolios, the initial decisions made are how to manage and store them, what to include, and how to assess or evaluate them. Teachers who have used portfolios as assessment tools realize, however, that the power of the portfolio is in the reflection time.

Students can use graphic organizers to facilitate reflection. They can also use a Venn diagram to compare one piece of work previously done with a more recent example. A sequence chart can track processes for students so that they can replicate them in other situations. A mind map in which students can draw symbols and representations of things that were significant in the learning can be used. The strategies in Figure 13.8 may be useful for reflections.

Figure 13.8. Strategies to Facilitate Reflection

Strategies:

  3   2   1

3	Ideas I got, or things I learned, or tips for others
2	Connections or unexpected learnings
1	Thing I'm confused about, or a step I can take

Reflection Stems:

I learned from this project . . .

I want to focus on next . . .

I included this because . . .

I would change . . . if I did this again.

I now know that . . .

This _____ made sense to me because _____

The next time I try a _____, I will _____ .

If we expect our children to make the transition to the highest level of intelligence, their environment and their role models must view "down time" or quiet time as positive experience and a welcome respite from the world's increasing deluge of sensory stimulation. (Burns, 1991, p. 73)

Summary

In longer periods or blocks, students and teachers have more time to slow down and not just cover the content, but come to understand it deeply. They share ongoing feedback, which can propel the learner into the next phase of the learning process. More time allows students and teachers to build a relationship. Relationships provide valuable connections that are often lacking in some students' lives. Relationships also influence students' perceptions of content.

Because learners have different interests and strengths and thus prefer a variety of ways to learn as well as to demonstrate their achievement, longer periods of time enable teachers and students to dialogue and set goals through reflection and metacognition. Assessment is not "teach, test, and hope for the best" in a frantic time frame, but rather should be conceived as an ongoing process of practice, feedback, and goal setting. Unlike the theater that just judges and awards symbols such as stars or thumbs up based on an individual critic's personal judgment or preference, classrooms should provide fertile ground for student growth and continuous improvement. In safe environments with a variety of engaging tasks and constructive, thoughtful feedback, students can take risks and practice and develop competencies they can take with them for life.

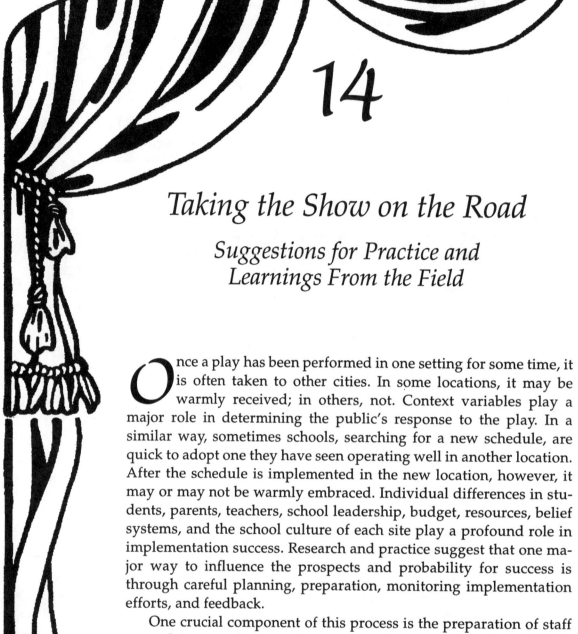

14

Taking the Show on the Road

Suggestions for Practice and Learnings From the Field

Once a play has been performed in one setting for some time, it is often taken to other cities. In some locations, it may be warmly received; in others, not. Context variables play a major role in determining the public's response to the play. In a similar way, sometimes schools, searching for a new schedule, are quick to adopt one they have seen operating well in another location. After the schedule is implemented in the new location, however, it may or may not be warmly embraced. Individual differences in students, parents, teachers, school leadership, budget, resources, belief systems, and the school culture of each site play a profound role in implementation success. Research and practice suggest that one major way to influence the prospects and probability for success is through careful planning, preparation, monitoring implementation efforts, and feedback.

One crucial component of this process is the preparation of staff to teach in extended periods of instructional time. When lessons are engaging, meaningful, and relevant, students and parents are pleased. Teachers feel good about students' responses, attention, and learning. Time flies! In contrast, when teachers simply take lessons from two traditional 45-minute periods and "glue them together" in a 90-minute block, the results can be disastrous!

The paragraphs that follow offer some final reflections from practitioners "in the block," as well as research findings that can inform practice. Although thinking "inside the block" is indeed a different

way of operating, many teachers have observed that some guidelines for success are also generalized to a traditional setting.

Research Findings

Of the many sites that have gone to the block, very few have returned to a traditional schedule. Although very few large-scale studies have been undertaken, individual school evaluation reports and dissertations have examined grade point average, honor roll achievement, numbers of failures and dropout rates, discipline referrals, and students' performance on standardized tests:

> Consistent evidence shows that students' grades improve and the number of students on the honor roll increases . . . Studies show declining failure rates in 4/4 schools and a greater likelihood that students labeled "at risk" will remain in school, especially in the 4/4 schedule, probably because students may repeat several classes but still graduate with their class . . . The number of discipline referrals to the office is reduced, typically between 25 and 50 percent . . . [I]n-school suspensions decline, teacher and student attendance improves slightly and . . . the number of class tardies is reduced. (Rettig & Canady, 1999, p. 15)

Although there has been considerable controversy regarding "hard data" on student achievement, many individual schools have reported improved test scores on state exams, SAT, and ACT scores. Student achievement on Advanced Placement tests has also increased. Many schools report that students earn more credits on the block.

Lessons Learned

When a school is making the decision to go to a block schedule, it is essential that

- All stakeholders be involved
- "Needs" and "wants" be generated and a study be done on how the specific schedules would address them
- Careful study take place involving readings, visitations, research analysis, and interviews
- Planning engage all stakeholders after a schedule is selected
- Implementation efforts be carefully monitored and modifications made based on feedback
- Celebrations of accomplishments be organized to build momentum for the implementation process

- All stakeholders realize that change is difficult and involves loss of "the familiar"
- Support be provided to enable those serving students to learn new behaviors to enhance classroom success

To enhance the process of transitioning to the block, the following are essential for those involved in the planning efforts:

- Recognize that some faculty members may be fearful about being "out of control" in an extended period of instructional time. Provide opportunities to *air concerns and problem-solve.*
- Realize that some faculty members may feel vulnerable. Seek ways to *lessen their perception of vulnerability.*
- Provide training to enable teachers and other staff to *build a repertoire of strategies* for serving students; this helps staff feel less vulnerable and more in control.
- Help staff see the *relevance* of the block to their discipline area, especially with respect to deepening students' knowledge base and experiences.
- Invite staff to see how it might be *feasible* to teach lessons in their subject areas within an extended period of instructional time.
- Continue to *involve all stakeholders* in decision making, evaluation efforts, data analysis, and replanning.
- Continue to *build trust* between leadership personnel engaged in transition planning efforts and the faculty.

Recommendations for Practice

Research-based practices for improving student achievement can inform block scheduling efforts and maximize success. *The Handbook of Research on Improving Student Achievement* (Cawelti, 1995) suggests that schools do the following:

- *Encourage parents to stimulate their children's intellectual development.* Environment plays a key role in brain development and intelligence. Verbal interaction with children, for example, has a direct impact on language and vocabulary development. Furthermore, spending time with a child, cultivating interests, engaging in hobbies, exploring, and even talking about articles in the newspaper, communicates "I care about you. You're important." In the block, interaction might be inspired by project-based learning assignments. This strengthens the bridge between home and school as well.
- *Require and grade homework.* Appropriate homework can extend class time, develop fluency with respect to concepts or operations, and teach vital skills for the workplace, such as perseverance. Feedback on homework can extend learning and give students valuable information about the relationships of their efforts and intended instructional goals.

- *Focus students on educational goals.* Providing information to students about intended curriculum "targets" enhances their progress toward those ends. It also offers a sense of meaning; this influences attention in extended periods of instructional time.

- *Incorporate direct teaching that exhibits key features and systematic steps.* Providing students with an understanding of an instructional context and identifying the staircase of skills leading to a particular desired end clarifies and enhances their learning experiences.

- *Use advance organizers that show students relationships between past learning and current learning.* This approach strengthens memory of content and processes. When students construct graphic tools and connect prior and current learnings, understanding is deepened. This is especially crucial for long-term memory of content if a student has a subject such as math in the fall semester and not in the spring.

- *Teach students multiple learning strategies and promote metacognition by providing modeling, guided practice, and application.* Extended periods of instructional time lend themselves to multiple learning strategies—many not possible during a traditional schedule. Metacognition deepens learners' experiences; this is often accomplished through cumulative learning journals in which students reflect on classroom experiences and record their insights.

- *Use mastery learning techniques for teaching subject matter.* Mastery learning is based on how the mind processes information. Using "brain-compatible" approaches enhances learning and promotes long-term memory.

- *Incorporate cooperative learning.* Teachers who have had successful experiences teaching in a block schedule report that cooperative learning is a key strategy. It fosters positive classroom climate, as well as academic achievement. When students spend extended periods of instructional time together, they need a specific structure for relating to one another, problem solving, resolving conflicts, and enhancing relationships. In addition, cooperative experiences provide valuable learnings about the skills necessary for teamwork and communication in the workplace.

The National Council of Teachers of Mathematics, National Science Teachers Association, American Association for the Advancement of Science, and National Commission on Social Studies offer several recommendations that can be accommodated within extended periods of instructional time:

- MORE experiential, inductive, hands-on learning
- MORE active learning in the classroom, with all the attendant noise and movement of students doing, talking, and collaborating
- MORE deep study of a small number of topics so that students internalize the field's method of inquiry

- MORE responsibility transferred to students for their work: goal setting, record keeping, monitoring, evaluation
- MORE choice for students: for example, picking their own books, writing topics, team partners, and research partners
- MORE enacting and modeling of the principles of democracy in school
- MORE attention to affective needs and the varying cognitive styles of individual students
- MORE cooperative, collaborative activity; developing the classroom as an inter-dependent community
- MORE reliance on teachers' descriptive evolution of student growth, including qualitative/anecdotal observations.

What Practitioners Tell Us[1]

When asked, "What skills do students need in 80- to 100-minute classes?" teachers reported the following list:

- Organizing time, materials, information
- Responsibility for own learning
- Self-direction
- Understanding directions
- Skillful listening
- Cooperative learning
- Using resources to find information or to problem-solve
- Problem solving
- Asking questions
- Taking notes
- Setting goals
- Studying and test taking
- Using notes
- Achieving goals
- Reading for meaning
- Observing
- Reading textbooks
- Finding main idea
- Memory strategies
- Interpreting and creating tables (Davenport & Tobin, 1997)

These skill areas served as a basis for the thinking behind Chapters 1 through 13 in this book.

Teachers have also commented about the advice they would give to those teaching in the block:

- Don't lecture for more than 15 minutes without processing time. Students won't remember.
- Change activities within the 80- to 100-minute period at least four times. Relate one activity to the next so that students don't loose a sense of continuity.
- Provide frequent opportunities for movement built into academic activities; for example, use standing diagrams, stand pair share, or carousel brainstorming.
- Increase student responsibility and accountability. Invite students to measure and monitor their success on charts.
- Make homework meaningful to maximize return.
- Use learning journals to promote long-term memory of content.
- Design extension projects to deepen knowledge for students who finish early.
- Seize opportunities to integrate the curriculum; it helps reinforce content and skills.
- Teach less but more in depth.
- When planning for instruction, first identify standards, benchmarks, or exam outcomes and then work backward. Decide what is most important for students to know and be able to do. You cannot cover everything. Practice selective abandonment.
- Plan transitional activities (2-5 min), such as brain teasers, to energize.
- Use cooperative learning.
- Post grades frequently so that students can track their progress. Grades can go up or down quickly.
- Use daily agendas and outcomes.
- Post time allocations for activities.
- Talk with other teachers; it's a great way to maximize your strategies and your attitude.
- Use simulations, case studies, problem-based learning, role play, community service learning, inquiry, and research to make standards and benchmarks relevant to students' lives.
- Recognize that meaningful assignments will keep students on task for longer periods of time.
- Overplan.
- Spiral lessons.
- Use authentic assessment.
- Recognize that there is no recipe. Use your ingenuity.

- Remember that you have spent many years perfecting the old system. It will take just as long to develop in the new system.

Many teachers have admitted to worrying about student absences. Strategies they have recommended for working with student absences follow:

- Keep a daily file folder of assignments so that students have a central location in which to identify work missed.
- Create a separate corner in the room where assignments are posted and copies of handouts can be found.
- Link students with study buddies. If one is absent, another can fill the other in.
- Identify a student on a rotating basis to take notes on a laptop computer. Print out these notes and make them available to the class. If a laptop is not available, have students take turns note taking and photocopy them.
- Audiotape discussions or instruction. Ask specific students to share class notes.
- Identify a student assistant "to fill students in" when they return from an absence.
- Develop a homework hotline.
- Create a Help Wanted form. Students can fill this in and make an appointment to meet with the teacher about missed instructional time.

Checklists for Teaching in
Extended Periods of Instructional Time

The following checklists have been developed as "ticklers" for planning assessment, instruction, curriculum, and classroom environment. These questions represent aspects of planning linked to the implementation success:

Assessment
- ❑ How will I assess?
- ❑ Are the standards I am assessing and the criteria clear?
- ❑ Does the assessment reflect instruction?
- ❑ How will I use assessment results for planning?
- ❑ Will the feedback to students be substantive, specific, constructive, and timely?

Curriculum
- ❑ What content will I teach?
- ❑ In what order?
- ❑ In what "chunks?"

❑ To what standards does this relate?

❑ What resources can be used (e.g., texts, CD-ROM, Internet, videos)?

❑ What prerequisite knowledge is required?

Instruction

❑ How will I gain students' attention?

❑ How will I relate today's topics to students' lives and a larger context?

❑ In what way will I share the lesson outcomes?

❑ How will I get students to recall previous knowledge that relates to this topic?

❑ How will I present the content of the lesson?

❑ What questioning strategies will I use?

❑ How will I keep the pace moving?

❑ Have I considered multiple intelligences and visual, auditory, and kinesthetic learners? receptive/expressive language?

❑ How will I actively involve students?

❑ How will I group students?

❑ How will I check for understanding?

❑ How will I monitor and adjust instruction?

❑ How will I provide for perfect practice?

❑ How will I ask students to summarize their learnings?

❑ How will I ask students to demonstrate authentically what they know and can do?

❑ How might homework reinforce learnings?

❑ How will I revisit this lesson's key points/skills to promote long-term retention?

Classroom Environment

❑ How can I create an environment characterized by "high challenge and low threat"?

❑ How can I create a climate of high expectations?

❑ How can I promote positive relationships between and among my students and myself?

❑ How can I help students develop social and emotional skills, including
  ❑ self-awareness?
  ❑ managing emotions?
  ❑ motivating oneself/delaying gratification?
  ❑ empathy?
  ❑ handling relationships? (Goleman, 1995)

❑ How can I support students in developing responsibility for
  ❑ attendance?
  ❑ coming to class with necessary materials?
  ❑ class participation?
  ❑ completing assignments?
  ❑ monitoring their progress?
❑ How can I manage time well with respect to
  ❑ pacing?
  ❑ transitions?
  ❑ beginning and ending class?
  ❑ handling distribution/collection of materials/supplies?
❑ How can I create and maintain a sense of learning community and pride among students?

Final Reflections

No doubt about it. Change is difficult, even if it is desirable. As educators strive to create meaningful learning environments within a block schedule for both adults and students in the school, there will be times of feeling overwhelmed, wanting to go back to more familiar ways, or perhaps even frustration. It is crucial to remember that collaboration, careful planning, problem solving, resource seeking, sharing, and a spirit of hope and optimism are powerful ingredients for facilitating this change process.

As the final curtain of this book draws near, let's reflect on why we all entered the teaching profession . . . because we wanted to make a difference for students. Imagine the power of influence that could be generated within a school when all the stakeholders, committed to making a difference, work together to provide meaningful learning experiences within extended periods of instructional time. A vision of this reality can help those within the schoolhouse and the surrounding community hold on to their convictions about what working within the block should be like. This vision and those convictions can steer the school through rough seas and keep it on course—a course guided by the needs of students, needs that can be satisfied when exposed to a challenging educational experience in a climate nurtured by caring adults.

Note

1. Special thanks to the Northeast Foundation for Children, Greenfield, Massachusetts 01301.

References

Armstrong, T. (1998). *Awakening genius.* Alexandria, VA: Association for Supervision and Curriculum Development.

Aronson, E. (1978). *The Jigsaw classroom.* Beverly Hills, CA: Sage.

Ausubel, D. P. (1960). The use of advance organizers in the learning and retention of meaningful verbal material. *Journal of Educational Psychology, 51,* 267-272.

Bellanca, J., & Fogarty, R. (1991). *Blueprints for thinking in the cooperative classroom.* Arlington Heights, IL: Skylight.

Bennett, B., Bennett-Rolheiser, C., & Stevhan, L. (1990). *Cooperative learning: Where heart meets mind.* Toronto, Ontario: Educational Connections.

Berte, N. (1975). *Individualizing education by learning contracts.* San Francisco: Jossey-Bass.

Brooks, J., & Brooks, M. (1993). *In search of understanding: The case for constructivist classrooms.* Alexandria, VA: Association for Supervision and Curriculum Development.

Bruner, J., Goodnow, J., & Austin, G. (1967). *A study of thinking.* New York: Science Editions.

Burns, E. (1991). *Our children, our future.* Dallas, TX: Marco Polo.

Caine R., & Caine, G. (1990). *Making connections.* Alexandria, VA: Association for Supervision and Curriculum Development.

Caine, R., & Caine, G. (1997). *Education on the edge of possibility.* Alexandria, VA: Association for Supervision and Curriculum Development.

Cantelon, T. (1991a). *The first 4 weeks of cooperative learning, activites, and materials.* Portland, OR: Prestige.

Cantelon, T. (1991b). *Structuring the classroom successfully for cooperative team learning.* Portland, OR: Prestige.

Cawelti, G. (Ed.). (1995). *Handbook of research on improving student achievement.* Arlington, VA: Educational Research Service.

Clarke, J., Wideman, R., & Eadie, S. (1990). *Together we learn.* Scarborough, Ontario: Prentice Hall.

Covey, S. (1989). *Seven habits of highly effective people.* New York: Simon & Schuster.

Csikszentmihalyi, M. (1991). *Flow: The psychology of optimal experience.* New York: HarperCollins.

Davenport, E., & Tobin, K. (1997). *HM network, HM learning and study skills group.* Newton, MA: NASSP.

deBono, E. (1976). *Teaching thinking.* New York: Penguin.

deBono, E. (1985). *Six thinking hats.* Boston: Little, Brown.

Diamond, M., & Hopson, J. (1998). *Magic trees of the mind.* New York: E. P. Dutton.

Doyle, M., & Strauss, D. (1976). *How to make meetings work.* New York: Playboy Press.

Duke, D. L. (Ed.) (1982). *Helping teachers manage classrooms.* Alexandria, VA: Association for Supervision and Curriculum Development.

Eberle, B. (1982). *Games for imagination development.* Buffalo, NY: D.O.K.

Elias, M., Tobias, S., & Friedlander, B. (1999). *Emotionally intelligent parenting.* New York: Harmony.

Fitzgerald, R. (1996, September). Brain-compatible teaching in a block schedule. *School Administrator,* pp. 18-21.

Fogarty, R. (1995). *Best practices for the learner-centered classroom: A collection of articles.* Arlington Heights, IL: Skylight.

Gardner, H. (1995, November). Reflections on multiple intelligences: Myths and messages. *Phi Delta Kappan,* pp. 200-209.

Gibbs, J. (1995). *Tribes: A new way of learning and being together.* Sausalito, CA: Center Source Systems.

Glasser, W. (1969). *Schools without failure.* New York: Harper & Row.

Goleman, D. (1995). *Emotional intelligence: Why it can matter more than IQ.* New York: Bantam.

Goleman, D. (1998). *Working with emotional intelligence.* New York: Bantam.

Goodman, G. (1994). *Inclusive classrooms from A to Z: A handbook for educators.* Columbus, OH: Teachers' Publishing Group.

Gordon, W. (1961). *Synectics.* New York: Harper & Row.

Harmin, M. (1993). *Strategies to inspire active listening.* Edwardsville, IL: Inspiring Strategy Institute.

Harmin, M. (1994). *Inspiring active learning.* Alexandria, VA: Association for Supervision and Curriculum Development.

Henderson, N., & Milstein, M. (1996). *Resiliency in schools: Making it happen for students and educators.* Thousand Oaks, CA: Corwin.

Hill, S., & Hancock, S. (1993). *Reading and writing communities.* Armadale, Australia: Eleanor Curtin.

Hord, S. M., Rutherford, W. L., Huling-Austin, L., & Hall, G. E. (1987). *Taking charge of change.* Alexandria, VA: Association for Supervision and Curriculum Development.

Johnson, D. W., Johnson, R. T., & Holubec, E. J. (1984). *Circles of learning.* Alexandria, VA: Association for Supervision and Curriculum Development.

Johnson, D. W., Johnson, R. T., & Holubec, E. J. (1988). *Cooperation in the classroom.* Edina, MN: Interaction Books.

Joyce, B., & Weil, M. (1986). *Models of teaching.* Upper Saddle River, NJ: Prentice Hall.

Kagan, S. (1992). *Cooperative learning.* San Clemente, CA: Kagan Cooperative.

Knowles, M. (1986). *Using learning contracts.* San Francisco: Jossey-Bass.

Kotulak, R. (1996). *Inside the brain: Revolutionary discoveries of how the mind works.* Kansas City, MO: Andres & McMeely.

Lyman, F., & McTighe, J. (1988, April). Cueing thinking in the classroom: The promise of theory-embedded tools. *Educational Leadership,* p. 7.

McNabb, M. L. (1999). *Technology connections for school improvement: Teacher's guide.* Oak Brook, IL: North Central Regional Educational Laboratory.

Means, B. (Ed.) (1994). *Technology and education reform: The reality behind the promise.* San Francisco: Jossey-Bass.

Merriam-Webster's collegiate dictionary (10th ed.). (1998). Springfield, MA: Merriam-Webster.

Miller, G. (1956). The magical number seven, plus or minus two: Some limits on our capacity for processing information. *Psychological Review*, pp. 81-97.

Miller, J. (1990). *Holistic learning: A teacher's guide to integrated curriculum*. Niagara, Ontario: OISE Press.

Ministry of Education, Ontario. (1985). *Programming for the gifted*. Toronto: Queen's Printer for Ontario.

Ogle, D. (1986). K-W-L: A teaching model that develops active reading of expository text. *Reading Teacher*, pp. 564-574.

Parnel, D. (1995). *Why do I have to learn this? Teaching the way people learn best*. Waco, TX: CORD Communications.

Pascal-Leon, J. (1980). Compounds, confounds, and models in developmental information processing: A reply to Trabasso and Foellinger. *Journal of Experimental Child Psychology*, pp. 18-40.

Perkins, D. N. (1986). *Knowledge as design*. Mahwah, NJ: Lawrence Erlbaum.

Pilon, G. (1988). *Workshop way*. New Orleans: Workshop Way.

Rettig, M., & Canady, R. (1999, March). The effects of block scheduling. *School Administrator*, p. 18.

Robbins, P., & Herndon, L. E. (1998). *Thinking inside the block: The teacher's day-planner*. Thousand Oaks, CA: Corwin.

Rowe, M. B. (1987, Spring). Wait time: Slowing down may be a way of speeding up. *Educator*, p. 43.

Russell, D., & Hunter, M. (1976). *Planning for effective instruction: Lesson design*. Los Angeles: Seeds Elementary School.

Secretary's Commission on Achieving Necessary Skills (SCANS). (1991, June). *What work requires of schools* (SCANS report for America 2000). Washington, DC: U.S. Department of Labor.

Skinner, B. F. (1953). Science and human behavior. New York: Macmillan.

Sousa, D. (1998). *Learning manual for how the brain learns*. Thousand Oaks, CA: Corwin.

Stephen, W., Gallagher, S., & Workman, D. (1993). Problem-based learning for the traditional and the interdisciplinary classrooms. *Journal for Gifted Education*, pp. 338-357.

Sylwester, R. (1995). *A celebration of neurons: An educator's guide to the brain*. Alexandria, VA: Association for Supervision and Curriculum Development.

Taba, H. (1967). *Teacher's handbook for elementary social studies*. Reading, MA: Addison-Wesley.

Tomlinson, C. A. (1997). *Differentiating instruction: Facilitator's guide*. Alexandria, VA: Association for Supervision and Curriculum Development.

Tomlinson, C. A. (1999). *The differentiated classroom: Responding to the needs of all learners*. Alexandria, VA: Association for Supervision and Curriculum Development.

Webster, D., & Bailey, D. (1991). *Classroom time management: Book 1. Organizing self and others*. Rochester, MN: Webley.

Wiggins, G. (1992). Creating tests worth taking. *Educational Leadership, 49*, 26-33.

Wiggins, G., & McTighe, J. (1998). *Understanding by design*. Alexandria, VA: Association for Supervision and Curriculum Development.

Winebrenner, S. (1992). *Teaching gifted kids in the regular classroom*. Minneapolis, MN: Free Spirit.

Wolfe, P., & Sorgen, M. (1990). *Mind, memory, and learning: Implications for the classroom*. Napa, CA: Author.

Wong, H. K., & Wong, R. T. (1991). *The first days of school: How to be an effective teacher*. Sunnyvale, CA: Harry K. Wong Publications.

Index

CORWIN
PRESS

The Corwin Press logo—a raven striding across an open book—represents the happy union of courage and learning. We are a professional-level publisher of books and journals for K-12 educators, and we are committed to creating and providing resources that embody these qualities. Corwin's motto is "Success for All Learners."